FORENSIC PATHOLOGY

PUBLISHED AND FORTHCOMING TITLES IN THE *ADVANCED FORENSIC SCIENCE SERIES*

Published

Forensic Fingerprints
Firearm and Toolmark Examination and Identification
Forensic Biology
Forensic Chemistry
Professional Issues in Forensic Science
Materials Analysis in Forensic Science

Forthcoming

Forensic Anthropology
Forensic Engineering
Behavioral Analysis
Digital and Documents
Forensic Toxicology and Drugs

FORENSIC PATHOLOGY

Advanced Forensic Science Series

MAX M. HOUCK, PhD, FRSC

Managing Director, Forensic & Intelligence Services, LLC, St. Petersburg, FL, USA

Amsterdam • Boston • Heidelberg • London • New York • Oxford
Paris • San Diego • San Francisco • Singapore • Sydney • Tokyo

Academic Press is an imprint of Elsevier

Academic Press is an imprint of Elsevier
125 London Wall, London EC2Y 5AS, United Kingdom
525 B Street, Suite 1800, San Diego, CA 92101-4495, United States
50 Hampshire Street, 5th Floor, Cambridge, MA 02139, United States
The Boulevard, Langford Lane, Kidlington, Oxford OX5 1GB, United Kingdom

Library of Congress Cataloging-in-Publication Data
A catalog record for this book is available from the Library of Congress

British Library Cataloguing-in-Publication Data
A catalogue record for this book is available from the British Library

ISBN: 978-0-12-802261-0
ISSN : 2352-6238

For information on all Academic Press publications
visit our website at http://www.elsevier.com/

Working together
to grow libraries in
developing countries

www.elsevier.com • www.bookaid.org

Publisher: Sara Tenney
Acquisition Editor: Elizabeth Brown
Editorial Project Manager: Joslyn Chaiprasert-Paguio
Production Project Manager: Lisa Jones
Designer: Matthew Limbert

Typeset by TNQ Books and Journals

CONTENTS

Senior Editor: Biography   xi

List of Contributors   ·   xiii

Foreword   xv

Preface   xvii

SECTION 1 OVERVIEW   1

Principles of Forensic Science   1
F Crispino, MM Houck

Forensic Classification of Evidence   7
MM Houck

Interpretation/The Comparative Method   13
MM Houck

Clinical Forensic Medicine—Overview   19
S Pollak, P Saukko

Forensic Pathology—Principles and Overview   25
T Kanchan, K Krishan

History of Forensic Sciences   29
J Hebrard, F Daoust

Key Terms   33

Review Questions   33

Discussion Questions   33

Additional Readings   34

SECTION 2 POSTMORTEM INTERVAL   35

Postmortem Interval   35
DH Ubelaker

Early and Late Postmortem Changes   41
B Madea, G Kernbach-Wighton

Estimation of the Time Since Death   55
B Madea

Vital Reactions and Wound Healing   67
P Betz

Key Terms   71

Review Questions   71

Discussion Questions   72

Additional Readings   72

SECTION 3 AUTOPSY   73

External Postmortem Examination   73
B Madea, G Kernbach-Wighton

Autopsy   83
P Saukko, S Pollak

Histopathology   89
P Saukko, S Pollak

Postmortem Imaging   97
H Vogel

Key Terms   112

Review Questions   113

Discussion Questions   113

Additional Readings   113

SECTION 4 TRAUMA   115

Blunt Injury   115
S Pollak, P Saukko

Burns and Scalds   127
M Bohnert

Asphyctic Deaths—Overview and Pathophysiology   133
CM Milroy

Strangulation   139
A Thierauf, S Pollak

Traumatic and Postural Asphyxia, Physical Restraint   149
PH Schmidt, M Kettner

Immersion Deaths   157
B Ludes

Sharp Trauma   163
U Schmidt

Systemic Response to Trauma   173
T Ishikawa, H Maeda

Gunshot Wounds   181
S Pollak, P Saukko

Domestic Violence   197
U Klopfstein, M-C Hofner

Child Abuse   205
WA Karst, HGT Nijs, RAC Bilo

Defense Wounds   211
U Schmidt

Self-Inflicted Injury   217
P Saukko, S Pollak

Torture   225
H Vogel

Traffic Injuries and Deaths   237
M Graw, J Adamec

Key Terms   244

Review Questions   245

Discussion Questions   245

Additional Readings   245

SECTION 5 CAUSES OF DEATH   **247**

Sudden Natural Death   247
A Thierauf, S Pollak

Sudden Infant Death Syndrome (SIDS)   259
T Bajanowski, M Vennemann

Hyperthermia and Hypothermia   267
T Ishikawa, H Maeda

Electrocution and Lightning Strike   275
S Pollak, P Saukko

Deaths Associated with Medical Procedures 285
G Lau, M Wang

Neonaticide 299
NEI Langlois, RW Byard, C Winskog

Key Terms 303

Review Questions 303

Discussion Questions 303

Additional Readings 304

SECTION 6 IDENTIFICATION 305

Identification 305
C Cattaneo, D Gibelli

Forensic Age Estimation 315
A Schmeling

Personal Identification in Forensic Anthropology 321
CV Hurst, A Soler, TW Fenton

Identification of the Living 331
P Gabriel, W Huckenbeck

The National Missing and Unidentified Persons System (NamUs) 343
MM Houck

Disaster Victim Identification 345
WH Goodwin, T Simmons

Airplane Crashes and Other Mass Disasters 353
O Peschel, W Eisenmenger

Key Terms 358

Review Questions 358

Discussion Questions 359

Additional Readings 359

SECTION 7 PROFESSIONAL ISSUES 361

Crime Scene to Court 361
K Ramsey, E Burton

Expert Witness Qualifications and Testimony 367
C Henderson, KW Lenz

Health and Safety 371
N Scudder, B Saw

Deaths in Custody   379
S Heide

Suicide   385
M Große Perdekamp, S Pollak, A Thierauf

National Association of Medical Examiners (NAME)   397
MM Houck

Key Terms   398

Review Questions   398

Discussion Questions   399

Acknowledgment   399

Additional Readings   399

Index   *401*

SENIOR EDITOR: BIOGRAPHY

Max M. Houck is an internationally recognized forensic expert with research interests in anthropology, trace evidence, education, and the fundamentals of forensic science, both as a science and as an enterprise. He has worked in the private sector, the public sector (at the regional and federal levels), and in academia. Dr. Houck has published in a wide variety of areas in the field, in books, book chapters, and peer-reviewed journals. His casework includes the Branch Davidian Investigation, the September 11 attacks on the Pentagon, the D.B. Cooper case, the US Embassy bombings in Africa, and the West Memphis Three case. He served for 6 years as the Chair of the Forensic Science Educational Program Accreditation Commission (FEPAC). Dr. Houck is a founding coeditor of the journal Forensic Science Policy and Management, with Jay Siegel; he has also coauthored a major textbook with Siegel, *Fundamentals of Forensic Science*. In 2012, Dr. Houck was in the top 1% of connected professionals on LinkedIn. Dr. Houck is currently the Managing Director of Forensic & Intelligence Services, LLC, St. Petersburg, FL.

LIST OF CONTRIBUTORS

J Adamec
Institute of Legal Medicine, Munich, Germany

T Bajanowski
University of Duisburg-Essen, Essen, Germany

P Betz
University of Erlangen-Nuremberg, Erlangen, Germany

RAC Bilo
Netherlands Forensic Institute, The Hague, The Netherlands

M Bohnert
University of Würzburg, Würzburg, Germany

E Burton
Greater Manchester Police Forensic Services Branch, Manchester, United Kingdom

RW Byard
Forensic Science SA, Adelaide, SA, Australia

C Cattaneo
Università degli Studi di Milano, Milano, Italy

F Crispino
Université du Québec à Trois-Rivières, Trois-Rivières, QC, Canada

F Daoust
Institut de recherche criminelle de la gendarmerie nationale, Paris, France

W Eisenmenger

TW Fenton
Michigan State University, East Lansing, MI, USA

P Gabriel
University Clinic Düsseldorf, Düsseldorf, Germany

D Gibelli
Università degli Studi di Milano, Milano, Italy

WH Goodwin
University of Central Lancashire, Preston, UK

M Graw
Institute of Legal Medicine, Munich, Germany

M Große Perdekamp
University of Freiburg, Freiburg, Germany

J Hebrard
Forensic and Criminal Intelligence Agency of the French Gendarmerie, Paris, France

S Heide
University of Halle-Wittenberg, Halle, Germany

C Henderson
Stetson University College of Law, Gulfport, FL, USA

M-C Hofner
University Center of Legal Medicine, Lausanne, Switzerland

MM Houck
Consolidated Forensic Laboratory, Washington, DC, USA

W Huckenbeck
University Clinic Düsseldorf, Düsseldorf, Germany

CV Hurst
Michigan State University, East Lansing, MI, USA

T Ishikawa
Osaka City University Medical School, Osaka, Japan

T Kanchan
Kasturba Medical College (affiliated to Manipal University), Mangalore, Karnataka, India

WA Karst
Netherlands Forensic Institute, The Hague, The Netherlands

G Kernbach-Wighton
University of Bonn, Bonn, Germany

M Kettner
Saarland University Medical School, Homburg/Saar, Germany

U Klopfstein
Bern University of Applied Sciences, Bern, Switzerland

K Krishan
Panjab University, Chandigarh, India

NEI Langlois
Forensic Science SA, Adelaide, SA, Australia

G Lau
Health Sciences Authority, Singapore, Republic of Singapore

KW Lenz
Saint Petersburg, FL, USA

B Ludes
Institut de Médecine Légale, Strasbourg, France

B Madea
University of Bonn, Bonn, Germany

H Maeda
Osaka City University Medical School, Osaka, Japan

CM Milroy
University of Ottawa, Ottawa, ON, Canada

HGT Nijs
Netherlands Forensic Institute, The Hague, The Netherlands

O Peschel
Institut für Rechtsmedizin, München, Germany

S Pollak
University of Freiburg, Freiburg, Germany

S Pollak
Universitätsklinikum Freiburg, Freiburg, Germany

K Ramsey
Greater Manchester Police Forensic Services Branch, Manchester, United Kingdom

P Saukko
University of Turku, Turku, Finland

B Saw
Australian Federal Police, Canberra, ACT, Australia

A Schmeling
Institute of Legal Medicine, Münster, Germany

PH Schmidt
Saarland University Medical School, Homburg/Saar, Germany

U Schmidt
Freiburg University Medical Center, Freiburg, Germany

N Scudder
Australian Federal Police, Canberra, ACT, Australia

T Simmons
University of Central Lancashire, Preston, UK

A Soler
Pima County Office of the Medical Examiner, Tucson, AZ, USA

A Thierauf
University of Freiburg, Freiburg, Germany

DH Ubelaker
Smithsonian Institution, NMNH, Washington, DC, USA

M Vennemann
University of Münster, Münster, Germany

H Vogel
University Hospital Eppendorf, Hamburg, Germany

M Wang
Health Sciences Authority, Singapore, Republic of Singapore

C Winskog
University of Adelaide, Adelaide, SA, Australia

FOREWORD

"The best thing for being sad", replied Merlin, beginning to puff and blow, "is to learn something. That's the only thing that never fails. You may grow old and trembling in your anatomies, you may lie awake at night listening to the disorder of your veins, you may miss your only love, you may see the world about you devastated by evil lunatics, or know your honor trampled in the sewers of baser minds. There is only one thing for it then — to learn. Learn why the world wags and what wags it. That is the only thing which the mind can never exhaust, never alienate, never be tortured by, never fear or distrust, and never dream of regretting. Learning is the only thing for you. Look what a lot of things there are to learn". — T.H. White, *The Once and Future King*

Forensic science has much to learn. The breadth of the discipline alone should render any reasonably learned person dizzy with expectations; insects, explosives, liver functions, DNA, firearms, textiles, adhesives, skeletons, and so on the list goes on forever. That is because anything, truly *anything*, can become evidence, from a single fiber to an entire ocean liner. Forensic science does not lack for specialized knowledge (some might stay too specialized), but what it is wanting is knowledge that is comprehensive, integrated, and foundational. Introductions to forensic science abound, and many highly specialized texts are also available, but a gap exists between the two: a bridge from novice to practitioner. As the 2009 NRC report noted:

Forensic science examiners need to understand the principles, practices, and contexts of scientific methodology, as well as the distinctive features of their specialty. Ideally, training should move beyond apprentice-like transmittal of practices to education based on scientifically valid principles. NRC (2009, pp. 26—27).

The *Advanced Forensic Science Series* seeks to fill that gap. It is a unique source, combining entries from the world's leading specialists who contributed to the second edition of the award-winning *Encyclopedia of Forensic Sciences* and organizing them by topic into a series of volumes that are philosophically grounded yet professionally specialized. The series is composed of 12 volumes that cover the breadth of forensic science:

1. Professional Issues
2. Biology
3. Chemistry
4. Fingerprints
5. Firearms
6. Materials Analysis
7. Pathology

8. Anthropology
9. Engineering
10. Behavioral
11. Digital and Documents
12. Toxicology and Drugs

Each volume contains sections common to all forensic sciences, such as professionalism, ethics, health and safety, and court testimony, and sections relevant to the topics in that particular subdiscipline. Pedagogy is included, providing review questions, discussion questions, the latest references in additional readings, and key words. Thus, each volume is suitable as a technical reference, an advanced textbook, or a training adjunct.

The *Advanced Forensic Science Series* provides expert information, useful teaching tools, and a ready source for instruction, research, and practice. I hope, like learning, it is the only thing for you.

M.M. Houck, PhD, FRSC
Series Editor

Reference

National Research Council, 2009. Strengthening Forensic Science in the U.S.: A Path Forward. National Academies of Science, Washington, DC.

PREFACE

All of us know we must die, but as much as we fear it, we want to know about it. Some of us want to know in order to prepare ourselves; others to discover some way, if not to avoid it, then at least to choose the time and place. Most of us want to know only just enough to experience it imaginatively and then live to tell the tale, like Lazarus returned to the light. — Michael Lesy, *The Forbidden Zone*. 1987. Farrah Straus & Giroux: New York.

Mortui vivos docent. — Latin, "The dead teach the living."

Tell anyone you are a forensic scientist and they will ask, "Oh, do you cut up dead bodies?". The assumption that all forensic science revolves around autopsies probably stems from the human fascination and repulsion with death and the prominence of medical examiners in stories and media. Death is a mystery and murder is an untimely puzzle that society demands be solved. Combine our mortality, a clinical approach to dismemberment, the secrets of how human bodies work and stop working, forensic science, and the social taboo of homicide…well, that is pretty much catnip for our species. Stories, movies, and television have all amplified our morbid fascination with forensic pathology and made us more familiar with things that, honestly, the average person would rather *not* be familiar with. As interesting as it is, most people simply could not endure conducting an autopsy and many cannot even watch. Being able, or becoming able, to do so is an important step to becoming a forensic pathologist. If a student is remotely interested in studying forensic pathology, viewing an autopsy is a good preliminary step; better to find out now rather than after years of schooling.

Pathology, the science of the causes and effects of diseases and trauma, requires an undergraduate degree, medical school, and at least a year of training (residency). Becoming a *forensic* pathology requires additional schooling in morbid anatomy, forensic science, and a residency in a morgue. While a regular pathologist can perform a hospital autopsy, for example, on a patient who has died from a long-term disease, a forensic pathologist is required for a medicolegal autopsy, one involving potentially criminal activity. The additional training in trauma and morbid anatomy is crucial to an accurate forensic "diagnosis." For example, in one study (Collins and Lantz, 1994), trauma surgeons misinterpreted both the number and the sites of the entrance and exit wounds in up to half of fatal gunshot wounds.

Knowledge about forensic pathology (although not called that) is centuries old but was not adopted as a codified field of study or a true profession in the West until the mid-1800s. Rudolf Virchow (1821−1902), a famous doctor who added microscopic examinations of diseased body tissues to the gross visual exam in his 1858 *Cellular Pathology,* signals the beginning of the modern autopsy process. The first medical examiner's office in the United States was instituted in Baltimore in 1890; in 1915, the New York City abolished the coroner system and established a medical examiner's office headed by Milton Helpern. In 1939, Maryland established the first state-wide medical examiner system in the United States and, in doing so, set the position of medical examiner apart from the political system, that is, the coroner, in the state.

The difference between a medical examiner and a coroner is the central issue surrounding death investigations in the United States. Only about half the US population is served by a medical examiner, a forensic pathologist with a medical degree, while the other half is served by a coroner, an appointed or elected position requiring no medical education or training at all (Hanzlick and Combs, 1998). If trauma surgeons—medical doctors with advanced nonforensic training—can misinterpret GSWs, why would it be expected that a coroner with no medical training at all could do better? Having a medical degree does not guarantee an ethical professional but at least a demonstrably competent one. As with many forensic sciences, politics pushes reason and science aside, while the populace suffers.

The rate at which autopsies are being conducted has dropped since the end of World War II, which is a shame. Autopsies are a quality check on the work of medical professionals and feedback is a necessary component of a quality system. Given that medical errors are the third leading cause of death, one would hope that autopsies would be on the rise again. Even with cultural or religious objections to cutting open a body, noninvasive autopsies, such as Virtopsy, can reveal sufficient information for cause and manner of death to be certified (Thali et al., 2003). Autopsies improve the quality of life by helping to solve criminal cases, improve public health, and to identify trends and diseases like no other forensic method can. Forensic pathologists are a vital link to the health, well-being, and safety of society.

References

Collins, K.A., Lantz, P.E., 1994. Interpretation of fatal, multiple, and exiting gunshot wounds by trauma specialists. Journal of Forensic Science 39 (1), 94–99.

Hanzlick, R., Combs, D., 1998. Medical examiner and coroner systems: history and trends. JAMA 279 (11), 870–874.

Thali, M.J., Yen, K., Schweitzer, W., Vock, P., Boesch, C., Ozdoba, C., Schroth, G., Ith, M., Sonnenschein, M., Doernhoefer, T., Scheurer, E., 2003. Virtopsy, a new imaging horizon in forensic pathology: virtual autopsy by postmortem multislice computed tomography (MSCT) and magnetic resonance imaging (MRI)-a feasibility study. Journal of Forensic Sciences 48 (2), 386–403.

Section 1. Overview

Forensic pathologists are like any other forensic scientist in many ways. They identify/classify things and compare them with known examples to confirm or refute hypotheses. The difference is their area of study and examination: the human body. In this sense, they learn what other medical doctors learn: how the body's systems work. Pathologists learn how these systems fail through natural causes, such as disease or accidental trauma. A forensic pathologist learns how the body's systems are forced to fail through unnatural means, such as gunshots and stabbings. Despite their apparently limited scope of education, forensic pathologists need to know a good bit about all the forensic sciences, as well as the natural and medical sciences. It can take 10 years or so to become a forensic pathologist. Although they are paid well by other forensic professionals' standards, they are typically paid far less than other medical doctors. The length of schooling, the nature of the work, and the relatively low pay means that only the truly dedicated enter and excel in this demanding profession.

Principles of Forensic Science

F Crispino, Université du Québec à Trois-Rivières, Trois-Rivières, QC, Canada
MM Houck, Consolidated Forensic Laboratory, Washington, DC, USA

Glossary

Abduction Syllogism in which one premise is certain whereas the other one is only probable, generally presented as the best explanation to the former. Hence, abduction is a type of reasoning in which we know the law and the effect, and we attempt to infer the cause.

Deduction Process of reasoning which moves from the general to the specific, and in which a conclusion follows necessarily from the stated premises. Hence, deduction is a type of reasoning in which, knowing the cause and the law, we infer the effect.

Forensic intelligence Understanding on how traces can be collected from the scene, processed, and interpreted within an holistic intelligence-led policing strategy.

Heuristic Process of reasoning by rules that are only loosely defined, generally by trial and error.

Holistic Emphasizing the importance of the whole and the interdependence of its parts.

Induction Process of deriving general principles from particular facts or instances, i.e., of reasoning that moves from the specific to the general. Hence, induction is a type of reasoning in which, knowing the cause and the effect (or a series of causes and effects), we attempt to infer the law by which the effects follow the cause.

Linkage blindness Organizational or investigative failure to recognize a common pattern shared on different cases.

Science The intellectual and practical activity encompassing the systematic study of the structure and behavior of the physical and natural world through observation and experiment. It is also defined as a systematically organized body of knowledge on a particular subject.

Given that it identifies and collects objects at crime scenes and then treats them as evidence, forensic science could appear at first glance to be only a pragmatic set of various disciplines, with practitioners adapting and developing tools and technologies to help the triers of fact (juries or judges) interpret information gained from the people, places, and things involved in a crime. The view could be—and has been—held that forensic science has no philosophic or fundamental unity and is merely the application of knowledge generated by other sciences. Indeed, many working forensic scientists regard themselves mainly as chemists, biologists, scientists, or technicians and rarely as practitioners of a homogeneous body of knowledge with common fundamental principles.

Even the 2009 National Academy of Sciences National Research Council Report failed to recognize such a concept, certainly blurred by a semantic gap in the terminology itself of field practitioners, who confuse words such as "forensic science(s)," "criminalistic(s)," "criminology," "technical police," "scientific police," and so on, and generally restrict the scientific debate on analytical techniques and methods. An independent definition of forensic science, apart from its legal aspects, would support its scientific status and return the expert to his domain as scientist and interpreter of his analyses and results to assist the lay person.

What Is Forensic Science?

In its broadest sense, forensic science describes the utility of the sciences as they pertain to legal matters, to include many disciplines, such as chemistry, biology, pathology, anthropology, toxicology, and engineering, among others. ("Forensic" comes from the Latin root *forum*, the central place of the city where disputes and debates were made public to be solved, hence, defining the law of the city. Forensic generally means of or applied to the law.) The word "criminalistics" was adopted to describe the discipline directed toward the "recognition, identification, individualization, and evaluation of physical evidence by application of the natural sciences to law-science matters." ("Kriminalistik" was coined in the late nineteenth century by Hans Gross, a researcher in criminal law and procedure to define his methodology of classifying investigative, tactical, and evidential information to be learned by magistrates at law schools to solve crimes and help convict criminals.) In the scheme as it currently stands, criminalistics is part of forensic science; the word is a regionalism and is not universally applied as defined. Difficulties in differentiating the concepts certainly invited the definition of criminalistics as the "science of individualization," isolating this specific epistemologically problematic core from the other scientific disciplines. Individualization, the concept of determining the sole source of an item, enthroned a linear process—identification or classification on to individualization—losing sight of the holistic, variable contribution of all types of evidence. Assessing the circumstances surrounding a crime, where the challenge is to integrate and organize the data in order to reconstruct a case or propose alternative propositions for events under examination, requires multiple types of evidence, some of which may be quite nuanced in their interpretation. This is also

true in the use of so-called forensic intelligence, which feeds investigative, police, or security needs, where one of the main reasons for failures is linkage blindness. Nevertheless, it seems that the essence of the forensic daily practice is hardly captured within the present definitions of both terms.

Forensic science reconstructs—in the broadest sense—past criminal events through the analysis of the physical remnants of those activities (evidence); the results of those analyses and their expert interpretation establish relationships between people, places, and objects relevant to those events. It produces these results and interpretations through logical inferences, induction, abduction, and deduction, all of which frame the hypothetico-deductive method; investigative heuristics also play a role. Translating scientific information into legal information is a particular domain of forensic science; other sciences must (or at least should) communicate their findings to the public, but forensic science is often required by law to communicate their findings to public courts. Indeed, as the Daubert Hearing stated, "[s]cientific conclusions are subject to perpetual revision as law must resolve disputes finally and quickly." This doubly difficult requirement of communicating to the public and to the law necessitates that forensic scientists should be better communicators of their work and their results. Scientific inferences are not necessarily legal proofs, and the forensic scientist must recognize that legal decisions based, in part, on their scientific work may not accord with their expert knowledge. Moreover, scientists must think in probabilities to explain evidence given possible causes, while jurists must deal in terms of belief beyond reasonable doubt. As Inman and Rudin state: "Because we [the scientists] provide results and information to parties who lack the expertise to independently understand their meaning and implications, it is up to us to furnish an accurate and complete interpretation of our results. If we do not do this, our conclusions are at best incomplete, at worst potentially misleading."

The Trace as the Basic Unit of Forensic Science

The basic unit of forensic science is the trace, the physical remnant of the past criminal activity. Traces are, by their very nature, semiotic: they represent something more than merely themselves; they are signifiers or signs for the items or events that are its source. A fiber is not the sweater it came from, a fingerprint is not the fingertip, soot in the trachea is not the victim choking from a fire, blood droplets are not the violence against the victim, but they all point to their origin (source and activity) to a greater or lesser degree of specificity. Thus, the trace is a type of proxy data, that is, an indicator of a related phenomenon but not the phenomenon itself. Traces come from the natural and manufactured items that surround us in our daily lives. Traces are, in essence, the raw material available at a crime scene which becomes forensic intelligence or knowledge. Everyday items and their traces become evidence through their involvement in criminal activities; the activities add meaning to their existing status as goods in the world; a fireplace poker is transformed into "the murder weapon" by its use as such. The meaning added should also take into account the context of the case, the circumstances under which the criminal activities occurred, boarding the trier of fact mandate.

Traces become evidence when they are recognized, accepted as relevant (if blurred) to the past event under investigation, and collected for forensic purposes. Confusing trace, sign, and evidence can obscure the very process of trace "discovery," which lies at the root of its interpretation. Evidence begins with detection by observation, which is possible because of the available knowledge of the investigator or scientist; unrecognized traces go undiscovered and do not become evidence. When the investigator's or scientist's senses are extended through instrumental sensitivity, either at the scene or in the laboratory, the amount of potential evidence considerably increased. Microscopes, alternate light sources, instrumental sensitivity, and detection limits create increases in the number of traces that can be recognized and collected. More evidence, and more evidence types, inevitably led to increases in the complexity not only of the search for traces but also to their interpretation. Feeding back into this system is the awareness of new (micro)traces that changed the search methods at scenes and in laboratories, with yet more evidence being potentially available.

Traces are ancillary to their originating process; they are a by-product of the source activity, an accidental vestige of their criminal creation. To be useful in the determination of associations, traces whose ultimate sources are unknown must be compared to samples from a known source. Comparison is the very heart of the forensic science process; the method is essentially a diagnostic one, beginning with Georges Cuvier, and is employed by many science practitioners, including medical professionals. (Including, interestingly, Arthur Conan Doyle, a medical doctor and author, whose Sherlock Holmes character references Cuvier's method in *The Five Orange Pips*.) Questioned traces, or items, may have a provenance (a known location at the time of their discovery) but this is not their originating source; a few examples may help:

Trace (questioned)	Source (known)
Fiber on victim	Sweater
Gunshot residue	Ammunition discharge
Blood droplet	Body
Tool marks in door jamb	Pry bar used to open door
Shoeprint in soil	Shoe from suspect
Fingerprint on glass	Finger from suspect

The collection of properly representative known samples is crucial to accurate forensic analyses and comparisons. Known samples can be selected through a variety of legitimate schemes, including random, portion, and judgment, and must be selected with great care. Thus, traces are accidental, and known samples are intentional.

Some of the consequences of what has been discussed so far induce the capacities and limitations of a forensic investigation based on trace analysis. A micro- to nanolevel existence allows forensic scientists to plan physical and chemical characteristics in their identifications and comparisons with other similar data. This allows forensic science to be as methodologically flexible as its objects of study require. Because time is asymmetric and each criminal action is unique, the forensic investigation and analysis in any one case is wedded, to a certain degree, to that case with no ambition to issue general laws about that event ("In all instances of John Davis being physically assaulted with a baseball bat..."). Inferences must be drawn with explicit uncertainty statements; the inferences should be revised when new data affect the traces' relevancy. Therefore, the search for traces is a recursive heuristic process taking into account the environment of the case at hand, appealing to the imagination, expertise, and competency of the investigator or scientist to propose explicative hypotheses.

Two Native Principles

With this framework, two principles can be thought of as the main native principles that support and frame philosophically forensic science. In this context, principles are understood as universal theoretical statements settled at the beginning of a deduction, which cannot be deduced from any other statement in the considered system, and give coherence to the area of study. They provide the grounds from which other truths can be derived and define a paradigm, that is, a general epistemological viewpoint, a new concept to see the natural world, issued from an empiricist corroborated tradition, accepted by the community of practitioners in the field. Ultimately, this paradigm can even pilot the perception itself.

Although similar but nonequivalent versions are used in other disciplines, Locard's exchange principle exists as the central tenant of forensic science. The principle that bears his name was never uttered as such by Locard, but its universal statement of "every contact leaves a trace" stands as a universally accepted short-hand phrasing. Locard's principle embraces all forms of contact, from biological to chemical to physical and even digital traces, and extends the usual perception of forensic science beyond dealing only with physical vestiges.

One of its corollaries is that trace deposition is continual and not reversible. Increases in the number of contacts, the types of evidence involved, and cross-transfers (A–B and B–A) also increase the complexity of determining the relevance of traces in short duration and temporally close actions.

Even the potentially fallacious rubric of "absence of evidence is not evidence of absence" leads to extended discussions on the very nature of proof, or provable, that aims to be definitive, notwithstanding the explanations for the practical aspects of the concept (lack of sensitivity, obscuring of the relevant traces, human weakness, actual absence, etc.). Applying Locard's principle needs to address three levels. First is the physical level, which deals with ease of transfer, retention, persistence, and affinity of materials, which could better support the exchange of traces from one source to another. Second is the situational or contextual level, which is the knowledge of circumstances and environments surrounding criminal events and sets the matrix for detection, identification, and proximate significance of any evidence. Third is the intelligence level, which covers the knowledge about criminal behavior in single events or series, specific problems related to current trends in criminal behavior, and communication between relevant entities (police, scientists, attorneys, etc.); these components help the investigator in the field to focus on more meaningful traces that might otherwise go undetected.

The second, and more debated, principle is Kirk's individuality principle; again, Kirk did not state this as such beyond saying that criminalistics is the science of individualization. In its strongest form, it posits that each object in the universe can be placed demonstratively into a set with one and only one member: itself. It therefore asserts the universal statement, "every object in our universe is unique." Philosophers such as Wittgenstein have argued that without defined rules or limits, terms such as "the same" or "different" are essentially meaningless. There is little question that all things are unique—two identical things can still be numerically differentiated—but the core question is, can they be distinguished at the resolution of detection applied? Simply saying "all things are unique" is not useful forensically. For example, each fingerprint left by the same finger is unique, but to be useful, each print must also be able to be traced back to its source finger. Uniqueness is therefore necessary to claim individualization, but not sufficient. Thus, it is the degree of association that matters, how similar, how different these two things being compared are. Referring to Cole, "What distinguishes … objects is not 'uniqueness'; it is their diagnosticity: our ability to assign traces of these objects to their correct source with a certain degree of specificity under certain parameters of detection and under certain rules governing such assignments," or as Osterburg stated, "to approach [individualization] as closely as the present state of science allows." Statistics, typically, is required to accurately communicate levels of comparison that are reproducible. In fact, Kirk noted that individualization was not absolute. ("On the witness stand, the criminalist must be willing to admit that *absolute identity is impossible to establish.* …The inept or biased witness may readily testify to an identity,

or to a type of identity, that does not actually exist. This can come about because of his confusion as to the nature of identity, his inability to evaluate the results of his observations, or because his general technical deficiencies preclude meaningful results" (Kirk, 1953; emphasis added).)

Nonnative Principles

Numerous guiding principles from other sciences apply centrally to forensic science, several of which come from geology, a cognate historical science to forensic science. That these principles come not from forensic science but from other sciences should not imply that they are somehow less important than Locard's or Kirk's notions. The first, and in many ways the most important, of the external principles is that of Uniformitarianism. The principle, proposed by James Hutton, popularized by Charles Lyell, and coined by William Whewell, states that natural phenomena do not change in scope, intensity, or effect with time. Paraphrased as "the present is the key to the past," the principle implies that a volcano that erupts today acts in the same way as volcanoes did 200 or 200 million years ago and, thus, allows geologists to interpret proxy data from past events through current effects. Likewise, in forensic science, bullets test fired in the laboratory today do not change in scope, intensity, or effect from bullets fired during the commission of a crime 2 days, 2 weeks, or 2 years previously. The same is true of any analysis in forensic science that requires a replication or reconstruction of processes in play during the crime's commission. Uniformitarianism offers a level of objectivity to historical sciences by posing hypotheses or relationships generally and then developing tests with respect to particular cases.

Three additional principles from geology hold as applicable to forensic science. They are as follows:

- *Superposition*: In a physical distribution, older materials are below younger materials unless a subsequent action alters this arrangement.
- *Lateral continuity*: Disassociated but similar layers can be assumed to be from the same depositional period.
- *Chronology*: It refers to the notion of absolute dates in a quantitative mode (such as "10:12 a.m." or "1670–1702") and relative dates in a relational mode (i.e., older or younger).

These three principles are attributed to Nicolaus Steno but were also formalized and applied by William Smith. A forensic example of applying the principle of superposition would be the packing of different soils in a tire tread, the most recent being the outermost. A good case of lateral continuity would be the cross-transfer of fibers in an assault, given that the chances of independent transfer and persistence prior to the time of the incident would be improbable. An example of absolute chronology in forensic science would be the simple example of a purchase receipt from a retail store with a time/date stamp on it. Examples of relative chronology abound but could range from the *terminus post quem* of a product no longer made to something hotter or colder than it should be.

See also: **Foundations:** Forensic Intelligence; History of Forensic Sciences; Overview and Meaning of Identification/Individualization; Semiotics, Heuristics, and Inferences Used by Forensic Scientists; Statistical Interpretation of Evidence: Bayesian Analysis; The Frequentist Approach to Forensic Evidence Interpretation; **Foundations/Fundamentals:** Measurement Uncertainty; **Pattern Evidence/Fingerprints (Dactyloscopy):** Friction Ridge Print Examination – Interpretation and the Comparative Method.

Further Reading

Cole, S.A., 2009. Forensics without uniqueness, conclusions without individualization: the new epistemology of forensic identification. Law, Probability and Risk 8, 233–255.

Crispino, F., 2006. Le principe de Locard est-il scientifique? Ou analyse de la scientificité des principes fondamentaux de la criminalistique. Editions Universitaires Européennes No. 523, Sarrebrücken, Germany, ISBN 978-613-1-50482-2 (2010).

Crispino, F., 2008. Nature and place of crime scene management within forensic sciences. Science and Justice 48 (1), 24–28.

Dulong, R., 2004. La rationalité spécifique de la police technique. Revue internationale de criminologie et de police technique 3 (4), 259–270.

Egger, S.A., 1984. A working definition of serial murder and the reduction of linkage blindness. Journal of Police Science and Administration 12, 348–355.

Giamalas, D.M., 2000. Criminalistics. In: Siegel, J.A., Saukko, P.J., Knupfer, G.C. (Eds.), Encyclopedia of Forensic Sciences. Academic Press, London, pp. 471–477.

Good, G. (Ed.), 1998. Sciences of the Earth, vol. 1. Garland Publishing, New York.

Houck, M.M., 2010. An Investigation into the Foundational Principles of Forensic Science (Ph.D. thesis). Curtin University of Technology, Perth.

Inman, N., Rudin, K., 2001. Principles and Practice of Criminalistics: The Profession of Forensic Science. CRC Press, Boca Raton, FL, pp. 269–270.

Kirk, P.L., 1953. Crime Investigation: Physical Evidence and the Police Laboratory. Interscience, New York, p. 10.

Kirk, P.L., 1963. The ontogeny of criminalistics. Journal of Criminal Law, Criminology and Police Science 54, 235–238.

Kuhn, T., 1970. La structure des révolutions scientifiques. Flammarion, Paris.

Kwan, Q.Y., 1976. Inference of Identity of Source (Ph.D. thesis). Berkeley University, Berkeley.

Mann, M., 2002. The value of multiple proxies. Science 297, 1481–1482.

Masterman, M., 1970. The nature of a paradigm. In: Lakatos, I., Musgrave, A. (Eds.), Criticism and the Growth of Experimental Knowledge. Cambridge University Press, Cambridge, pp. 59–86.

Moriarty, J.C., Saks, M.J., 2006. Forensic Science: Grand Goals, Tragic Flaws, and Judicial Gatekeeping. Research Paper No. 06–19. University of Akron Legal Studies.

National Research Council Committee, 2009. Identifying the Needs of the Forensic Science Community, Strengthening Forensic Science in the United States: A Path Forward. National Academy of Sciences Report. National Academy Press, Washington, DC.

Osterburg, J.W., 1968. What problems must criminalistics solve. Journal of Criminal Law, Criminology and Police Science 59 (3), 431.

Schuliar, Y., 2009. La coordination scientifique dans les investigations criminelles. Proposition d'organisation, aspects éthiques ou de la nécessité d'un nouveau métier (Ph.D. thesis). Université Paris Descartes, Paris. Université de Lausanne, Lausanne.

Sober, E., 2009. Absence of evidence and evidence of absence: evidential transitivity in connection with fossils, fishing, fine-tuning, and firing squads. Philosophical Studies 143, 63–90.

Stephens, C., 2011. A Bayesian approach to absent evidence reasoning. Informal Logic 31 (1), 56–65.

US Supreme Court No. 92–102, 1993. William Daubert, et al., Petitioners v Merrell Dow Pharmaceuticals, Inc.. Certiorari to the US Court of Appeals for the Ninth Circuit. Argued 30 March 1993. Decided 28 June 1993.

Wittgenstein, L., 1922. Tractacus Logico-Philosophicus. Gallimard Tel 311, Paris.

Relevant Websites

http://www.all-about-forensic-science.com—All-About-Forensic-Science.com, Definition of Forensic Science.
http://www.forensic-evidence.com—Forensic-Evidence.com.
http://library.thinkquest.org—Oracle ThinkQuest – What Is Forensics?

Forensic Classification of Evidence

MM Houck, Consolidated Forensic Laboratory, Washington, DC, USA

Glossary

Set Any group of real or imagined objects.
Taxon (pl. taxa) A group of one or more organisms grouped and ranked according to a set of qualitative and quantitative characteristics; a type of set.

Taxonomy The science of identifying and naming species with the intent of arranging them into a classification.

Introduction

Evidence is accidental: items are transformed into evidence by their involvement in a crime regardless of their source or mode of production. By becoming evidence, their normal meaning is enhanced and expanded. Evidence is initially categorized much as the real world; that is, based on the taxonomy created by manufacturers. Forensic science adds to this classification to further enhance or clarify the meaning of evidence relevant to the goals and procedures of the discipline.

Methods of Classification

Set Theory

Any collection of objects, real or imagined, is a set; set theory is the branch of mathematics that studies these collections. Basic set theory involves categorization and organization of the objects, sometimes using diagrams, and involves elementary operations such as set union and set intersection. Advanced topics, including cardinality, are standard in undergraduate mathematics courses. All classification schemes are based on set theory, to a greater or lesser degree.

The notion of "set" is undefined; the objects described as constituting a set create the definition. The objects in a set are called the members or elements of that set. Objects belong to a set; sets consist of their members. The members of a set may be real or imagined; they do not need to be present to be a member of that set. Membership criteria for a set should be definite and accountable. The set, "All people in this room are over 5′5″ tall," is a well-defined, if currently unknown, set—the height of the people in the room would have to be measured to accurately populate the set. If the definition is vague, then that collection may not be considered a set. For example, is "q" the

same as "Q"? If the set is "The 26 letters of the English alphabet," then they are the same member; if the set is, "The 52 upper-case and lower-case letters of the English alphabet," then they are two separate members.

Sets may be finite or infinite; a set with only one member is called a single or a singleton set. Two sets are identical if and only if they have exactly the same members. The cardinality of a set is the number of members within it, written |A| for set A. A set X is a subset of set Y if and only if every member of X is also a member of Y; for example, the set of all Philips head screwdrivers is a subset of the set of all screwdrivers. Forensic scientists would term this a "subclass" but that is a terminological and not a conceptual difference. Two more concepts are required for the remainder of our discussion. The union of X and Y is a set whose members are only the members of X, Y, or both. Thus, if X were (1, 2, 3) and Y were (2, 3, 4), then the union of X and Y, written $X \cup Y$, would contain (1, 2, 3, 4). Finally, the intersection of two sets contains only the members of both X and Y. In the previous example, the intersection of X and Y would be (2, 3), written $X \cap Y$.

Taxonomy

Natural items, such as animals, plants, or minerals, often occur as evidence. These items are classified according to schemes used in other sciences such as biology, botany, or geology. It is incumbent on the forensic scientist to be knowledgeable about the classification of naturally occurring items.

In biology, taxonomy, the practice and science of classification, refers to a formalized system for ordering and grouping things, typically living things using the Linnaean method. The taxa (the units of a taxonomic system; singular "taxon") are sufficiently fixed so as to provide a structure for classifying living things. Taxa are arranged typically in a hierarchical structure to show their relatedness (a phylogeny). In such a hierarchical relationship, the subtype has by definition the same constraints as the supertype plus one or more additional constraints. For example, "macaque" is a subtype of "monkey," so any macaque is also a monkey, but not every monkey is a macaque, and an animal needs to satisfy more constraints to be a macaque than to be a monkey. In the Linnaean method of classification, the scientific name of each species is formed by the combination of two words, the genus name ("generic" name), which is always capitalized, and a second word identifying the species within that genus. Species names (genus species) are either italicized or underlined, for example, *Homo sapiens* (humans), *Sus scrofa* (pigs), *Canis familiaris* (domesticated dogs), and *Rattus rattus* (rats).

The term "systematics" is sometimes used synonymously with "taxonomy" and may be confused with "scientific classification." However, taxonomy is properly the describing, identifying, classifying, and naming of organisms, while "classification" is focused on placing organisms within groups that show their relationships to other organisms. Systematics alone deals specifically with relationships through time, requiring recognition of the fossil record when dealing with the systematics of organisms. Systematics uses taxonomy as a primary tool in understanding organisms, as nothing about the organism's relationships with other living things can be understood without it first being properly studied and described in sufficient detail to identify and classify it correctly.

In geology, rocks are generally classified based on their chemical and mineral composition, the process by which they were formed, and by the texture of their particles. Rocks are classified as igneous (formed by cooled molten magma), sedimentary (formed by deposition and compaction of materials), or metamorphic (formed through intense changes in pressure and temperature). These three classes of rocks are further subdivided into many other sets; often, the categories' definitions are not rigid and the qualities of a rock may grade it from one class to another. The terminology of rocks and minerals, rather than describing a state, describes identifiable points along a gradient.

Manufacturing

Manufactured evidence is initially categorized by the in-house or market-specific system created by one or more manufacturers. Manufacturers of economic goods create their classifications through product identity or analytical methods. Set methods of production ensure a quality product fit for purpose and sale; the classification is based on the markets involved, the orientation of the company production methods, and the supply chain. Explicit rules exist on categories recognized by manufacturers and consumers, as either models or brands.

Materials flow downstream, from raw material sources through to a manufacturing level. Raw materials are transformed into intermediate products, also referred to as components or parts. These are assembled on the next level to form products. The products are shipped to distribution centers and from there on to retailers and customers.

Forensic Approaches to Classification

The supply network of raw materials, intermediate steps, production methods, intended consumer end use, and actual end use all contribute to the characteristics available for forensic taxonomic classification. While the forensic taxonomies are unique to that discipline, they are based on the production taxonomies used in manufacturing. These characteristics form the basis for statements of significance, that is, the relative abundance or rarity of any one particular item in a criminal context. Some objects are common but have a short-entrance horizon (e.g., iPods), but are essentially identical at the outset while others are common with long-entrance horizons (denim blue jeans), but have a high variance (regular, stone washed, acid washed, etc.). It is in the best interest of forensic scientists to understand the fundamental manufacturing processes of the items that routinely become evidence. This understanding can form the basis for statistical significance statements in courts and may provide the foundations for a more quantitative approach to testimony.

Forensic analytical methods create augmented taxonomies because the discipline uses different sets of methods and forensic scientists have different goals. Their taxonomies are based on manufactured traits, but also aftermarket qualities, and intended end use, but also "as used." The "as used" traits are those imparted to the item after purchase through either normal or criminal use. Forensic science has developed a set of rules through which the taxonomies are explicated. For example, forensic scientists are interested in the size, shape, and distribution of delustrants, microscopic grains of rutile titanium dioxide incorporated into a fiber to reduce its luster. The manufacturer has included delustrant in the fiber at a certain rate and percentage with no concern for shape or distribution (but size may be relevant). The forensic science taxonomy is based on manufacturing taxonomy but is extended by incidental characteristics that help us distinguish otherwise similar objects.

Natural, manufacturing, and forensic classifications lead to evidentiary significance because they break the world down into intelligible classes of objects related to criminal acts. Forensic science has developed an enhanced appreciation for discernment between otherwise similar objects but has yet to explicate these hierarchies to their benefit.

Class Level Information

Identification is the examination of the chemical and physical properties of an object and using them to categorize it as a member of a set. What the object is made of, its color, mass, size, and many other characteristics are used to identify an object and help refine that object's identity. Analyzing a white powder and concluding that it is cocaine is an example of identification; determining that a small translucent chip is bottle glass or yellow fibrous material and determining that they are dog hairs are also examples of identification. Most identifications are inherently hierarchical, such as classification systems themselves: in the last example, the fibrous nature of the objects restricts the following possible categories:

- Hairs
- Animal hairs
- Guard hairs
- Dog hairs
- German shepherd hairs

As the process of identification of evidence becomes more specific, it permits the analyst to classify the evidence into successively smaller classes of objects. It may not be necessary to classify the evidence beyond dog hairs if human hairs are being looked for. Multiple items can be classified differently, depending on what questions are asked. For example, the objects in **Figure 1** could be classified into "fruit" and "non-fruit," "sports related" and "nonsports related," or "organic" and "inorganic."

Sharing a class identity may indicate two objects that come from a common source. Because forensic science reveals and describes the relationships among people, places, and things

involved in criminal activities, this commonality of relationship may be critical to a successful investigation. Commonality can show interactions, limitations in points of origin, and increased significance of relationships. What is meant by a "common source" depends on the material in question, the mode of production, and the specificity of the examinations used to classify the object. For example, the "common source" for an automotive paint chip could be the following:

- the manufacturer (to distinguish it from other similar paints),
- the factory (to determine where it was made),
- the batch or lot of production (to distinguish it from other batches at the same factory),
- all the vehicles painted with that color paint, or
- the vehicle painted with that color paint involved in the crime in question.

All of these options, and they are not exhaustive, could be the goal in an investigation of determining whether two objects had a "common source."

Uniqueness and Individualization

If an object can be classified into a set with only one member (itself), it can be said to be unique. An individualized object is associated with one, and only one, source: it is unique. Uniqueness is based on two assumptions. The first assumption is that all things are unique in space and, thus, their properties are nonoverlapping. The assumption of uniqueness of space is considered axiomatic and, therefore, an inherently non-provable proposition for numerous reasons. The population

Figure 1 A range of objects may be classified in a variety of ways, depending on the question being asked. For example, given the objects in this figure, the sets would differ if the question was, "What is edible?" rather than, "What is sporting equipment?".

size of "all things that might be evidence" is simply too large to account. In addition, conclusive evidence is not readily available in typical forensic investigations. Because of this, as Schum notes, statistics are required:

> Such evidence, if it existed, would make necessary a particular hypothesis or possible conclusion being entertained. In lieu of such perfection, we often make use of masses of inconclusive evidence having additional properties: The evidence is incomplete on matters relevant to our conclusions, and it comes to us from sources (including our own observations) that are, for various reasons, not completely credible. Thus, inferences from such evidence can only be probabilistic in nature (Schum, 1994, p. 2).

A statistical analysis is therefore warranted when uncertainty, of either accounting or veracity, exists. If an absolutely certain answer to a problem could be reached, statistical methods would not be required. Most evidence exists at the class level, and although each item involved in a crime is considered unique, it still belongs to a larger class. In reality, the majority of forensic science works at a class level of resolution. Indeed, even DNA, the argued "gold standard" of forensic science, operates with classes and statistics.

It has been argued that the concept of uniqueness is necessary but not sufficient to support claims of individualization. If it is accepted that uniqueness is axiomatic, then

> What matters is whether we have analytical tools necessary to discern the characteristics that *distinguish* one object from all others or, in the forensic context, distinguish *traces* made by each object from traces

made by every other object… Every object is presumably unique at the scale of manufacture. The question is whether objects are distinguishable at the scale of detection. Since all objects in the universe are in some respects "the same" and in other respects "different" from all other objects in the universe, according to Wittgenstein, what really matters is not uniqueness but rather what rules we articulate by which we will make determinations of "sameness" and "difference" (Cole, 2009, pp. 242–243).

Although things may be numerically unique at the point of *production*, this does not help to distinguish between otherwise similar objects at the point of *detection* or *interpretation*. This is where forensic science adds value to the investigative and legal processes.

Relationships and Context

The relationships between the people, places, and things involved in crimes are central to deciding what items to examine and how to interpret the results. For example, if a sexual assault occurs and the perpetrator and victim are strangers, more evidence may be relevant than if they live together or are sexual partners. Strangers are not expected to have ever met previously and, therefore, would have not transferred evidence before the crime. People who live together would have some opportunities to transfer certain types of evidence (e.g., head hairs and carpet fibers from the living room) but not others (semen or vaginal secretions). Spouses or sexual partners, being the most intimate relationship of the

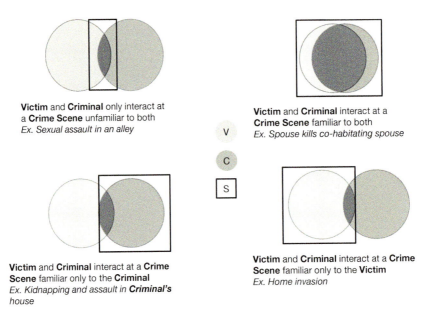

Victim and Criminal only interact at a Crime Scene unfamiliar to both
Ex. Sexual assault in an alley

Victim and Criminal interact at a Crime Scene familiar to both
Ex. Spouse kills co-habitating spouse

Victim and Criminal interact at a Crime Scene familiar only to the Criminal
Ex. Kidnapping and assault in Criminal's house

Victim and Criminal interact at a Crime Scene familiar only to the Victim
Ex. Home invasion

V
C
S

Figure 2 The relationships between suspect, victim, and scene influence what evidence is collected, and what its significance is.

three examples, would share a good deal of more information (**Figure 2**).

Stranger-on-stranger crimes beg the question of coincidental associations, that is, two things that previously have never been in contact with each other have items on them, which are analytically indistinguishable at a certain class level. Attorneys in cross-examination may ask, "Yes, but could not [insert evidence type here] really have come from anywhere? Are not [generic class level evidence] very common?" It has been proven for a wide variety of evidence that coincidental matches are extremely rare. The enormous variety of mass-produced goods, consumer choices, economic factors, biological and natural diversity, and other traits create a nearly infinite combination of comparable characteristics for the items involved in any one situation.

See also: **Foundations:** Evidence/Classification; Statistical Interpretation of Evidence: Bayesian Analysis; The Frequentist Approach to Forensic Evidence Interpretation.

Further Reading

Cole, S., 2009. Forensics without uniqueness, conclusion without individualization: the new epistemology of forensic identification. Law, Probability, and Risk 8 (3), 233–255.

Devlin, K., 1993. The Joy of Sets. Springer, Berlin.

Haq, T., Roche, G., Parker, B., 1978. Theoretical field concepts in forensic science. 1. Application to recognition and retrieval of physical evidence. Journal of Forensic Sciences 23 (1), 212–217.

Houck, M.M., 2006. Production Taxonomies as the Foundation of Forensic Significance. European Academy of Forensic Sciences, Helsinki, Finland.

Johnson, P., 1972. A History of Set Theory. Weber & Schmidt, New York.

Kwan, Q.Y., 1977. Inference of Identity of Source (Ph.D. thesis). University of California.

Schum, D.A., 1994. Evidential Foundations of Probabilistic Reasoning. John Wiley & Sons, New York.

Thornton, J., 1986. Ensembles of class characteristics in physical evidence examination. Journal of Forensic Sciences 31 (2), 501–503.

Underhill, P., 2000. Why We Buy: The Science of Shopping. Simon & Schuster, New York.

Interpretation/The Comparative Method

MM Houck, Consolidated Forensic Laboratory, Washington, DC, USA

Glossary

Alignable differences Differences that are connected to the hierarchical system of relatedness of two or more things.
Analogous trait A characteristic that is similar between two things that is not present in the last common ancestor or precedent of the group under comparison.
Analogy A cognitive process that transfers information or meaning from one subject (the analog or source) to another subject (the target).

Diagnosticity The degree to which traits classify an object.
Homologous trait A characteristic shared by a common ancestor or precedent.
Nonalignable differences Differences with no correspondence at all between the source and the target.

Introduction

Analogy, and its more specific relative comparison, is a central component of human cognition. Analogy is the process behind identification of places, objects, and people and plays a significant role in many human mental operations, such as problem solving, decisions, perception, memory, and communication. Some researchers, including Hofstadter, have even argued that cognition is analogy. Likewise, the cognitive process of analogy and the method of comparison lie at the heart of the forensic sciences. The ability to compare is predicated on some sort of classification (more properly, a taxonomy) that results in classes, groups, or sets.

Aristotle is considered the first to approach comparison as a way to arrange the world. His attempt to codify the process raised, however, an intractable problem that would only be addressed later: the classification of living things. Comparison, by itself, is a minimal technique, at best. A classification system—a taxonomy—is a prerequisite to a fuller comparative methodology. Comparative anatomy, one of the earliest formal applications of the method, goes beyond mere representation (mere comparison, that is) to explain the nature and properties of each animal.

The French naturalist Pierre Belon (1517–1564) compared the skeletal structures of birds to humans in his book *L'Histoire de la Nature des Oiseaux* (*History of the Nature of Birds*, 1555; **Figure 1**), and, along with the Flemish naturalist Andreas Vesalius (1514–1564), was one of the first naturalists to explicitly apply the comparative method in biology. Georges Cuvier (1769–1832) was the first to use comparative anatomy and taxonomy as a tool, not an end in itself, in his studies of animals and fossils. Cuvier was frustrated that biological phenomena could not be reconfigured into experimental conditions that would allow controlled testing, a difficulty common to many sciences (e.g., see Diamond). The intimate integration of a living organism's physiology with its anatomy created obstacles in teasing out and relating function to structure: once an organism was dead and prepared for dissection, its function had ceased, thus confounding the relationship of form to function. Cuvier considered that careful examinations and the interrelating of structures between specimens might also prove to be useful in revealing principles of observation and comparison. Perhaps the original scientist-as-detective, Cuvier, used scattered, fractured bits of information to reconstruct the prehistory of the Earth and its animals. In a 1798 paper, Cuvier wrote on his realization of the form and function of bones as it relates to the overall identifiable anatomy of an animal, leading to the recognition of the creature from which the bone originated:

> This assertion will not seem at all astonishing if one recalls that in the living state all the bones are assembled in a kind of framework; that the place occupied by each is easy to recognize; and that by the number and position of their articulating facets one can judge the number and direction of the bones that were attached to them. This is because the number, direction, and shape of the bones that compose each part of an animal's body are always in a necessary relation to all the other parts, in such a way that—up to a point—one can infer the whole from any one of them, and vice versa (Rudwick, 1998, p. 36).

This has been called "Cuvier's Principle of Correlation of Parts" and is a central tenet in biology and paleontology. It is

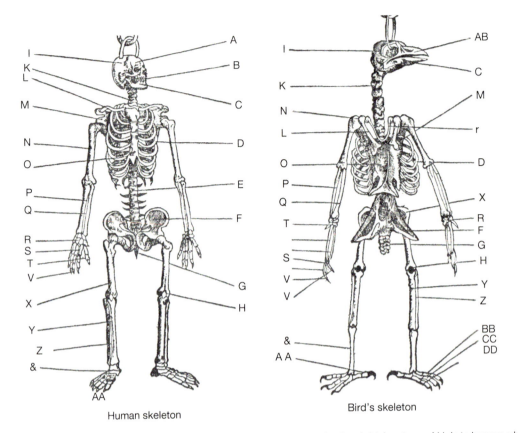

Human skeleton

Bird's skeleton

Figure 1   A drawing from Pierre Belon's 1555 book, *History of the Nature of Birds*, comparing the skeletal anatomy of birds to humans which is one of the first books using the science of comparative anatomy. Wikimedia Commons, open source.

important to note that Cuvier claimed to be able to *identify* an animal taxonomically from a single bone, but not completely *reconstruct* it, as the above quote might imply. The reconstruction would only be possible with a sufficient number of bones representing the animal in question. The comparative method has been a successful cornerstone of science ever since, with new or emerging sciences, such as ecology, moving from the purely observational or descriptive approach to that of comparison through experimental or analytical methods.

A short discussion of terms in biology will help clarify concepts used in biological comparisons. The concept of homology, the same structure under every variety of form found in different animals, is the organizing foundation for comparative anatomy. Animals share homologous traits because they also share a common ancestor with the same or related trait. By contrast, analogous traits are similarities found in organisms that were not present in the last common ancestor of the group under comparison; that is, the traits evolved separately. The canonical example of the difference between homologous and analogous traits is the wings of birds and bats: they are homologous as forearms but analogous as wings;

the latter structures evolved their functions separately. A homologous trait is termed a homolog. In biology, evolution and natural selection formed the system within which these relationships developed and were maintained, homogenized, or differentiated.

In manufacturing, other external and internal constraints form the basis for homologous and analogous traits through design, function, form, and costs. Design follows from the product's intended end use, aesthetic concerns, and cost limitations. The function and form of an object tend to correlate and variances in design cluster around necessary and sufficient criteria. In **Figure 2**, for example, although the hammer heads, opposite sides, handles, materials, weight, shape, and components all vary, they are nonetheless identifiable as hammers. If **Figure 2** were finches, as Darwin studied in the Galapagos in his historic voyage with the *Beagle*, the base process of taxonomy would be the same but the criteria and foundations—the history and causes—would obviously vary because of the vastly different processes that produce hammers and finches.

Broadly speaking, the supply chains and distribution networks of material goods are like the phylogenetic trees

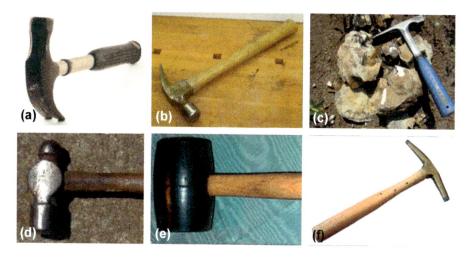

Figure 2 Hammers. All of the objects (a–f) are recognizable as hammers even though their components vary. (a) claw hammer; (b) framing hammer; (c) geological hammer; (d) ball-peen hammer; (e) rubber mallet; and (f) upholstery hammer. Wikimedia Commons, open source.

based on evolutionary descent. Regardless of whether the items are biological or manufactured, the independence of traits should not be assumed. Comparative studies that do not control for historical relationships through phylogeny or supply chains may imply spurious relationships (coincidences). Forensic science is unique in its use of the comparative method to reconstruct past criminal events and sourcing of evidence, either biological or manufactured (in essence, reverse engineering to a level of distribution or manufacturing resolution).

Analogy and Comparison within a Forensic Process

Analogy is a cognitive process that transfers information or meaning from one subject (the analog or *source*) to another subject (the *target*); it thus implies at least two things: situations or events. The source is considered to be the more complete and more complex of the two, and the target is thus less informative and incomplete in some way. The incompleteness may be due to any of several factors, alone or combined, such as damage, fracture, deterioration, or size. The elements or traits—including their relationships, such as evolutionary or supply chains—between the source and the target are mapped or aligned in a comparison. The mapping is done from what is usually the more familiar area of experience and more complete repository of information, the source, to the typically more problematic target.

Salience of the elements or traits is of prime importance: there are an innumerable number of arbitrary differences in either elements or relations that could be considered but are not useful given the question at hand ("Are both items smaller than the Empire State Building? Are they redder than a fire truck?"). Ultimately, analogy is a process to communicate that the two comparators (the source and the target) have *some* relationship in common despite any arbitrary differences. Some notion of possible or hypothetical connection must exist for the comparison to be made. As a forensic example, consider trace debris removed from the clothing of a suspect and the body of a victim: although there may be no physical evidence (hairs, fibers, glass, soil, etc.) in common, the suspect's clothing and the victim's body have, at least prima facie, a common *relationship* (the victim is the victim and the suspect is a person of interest in the crime) until proven otherwise. Thus, common relations, not common objects, are essential to analogy and comparison.

The comparison process as a method makes several assumptions. First, the space in which the comparators are mapped is assumed to be Euclidean. Second, the method embeds the comparators in a "space of minimum dimensionality" (Tversky) based on all observed salient similarities. Each object, a, is detailed and described by a set of elements or traits, A. Any observed similarities between a and another object b, denoted as $s(a, b)$, are expressed as a function of the salient traits they are determined to have in common. The comparison and any observed familiarity can be expressed as a function of three arguments (**Figure 3**):

- $A \cap B$, the features shared by a and b
- $A - B$, the features of a that are not shared by b
- $B - A$, the features of b that are not shared by a

Psychological studies show that people tend to pay more attention to the target (the comparator with less information) than to the source. In forensic science, this means that analysts

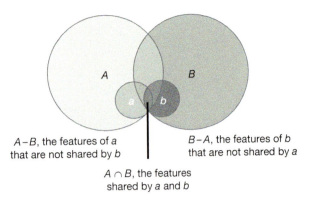

A−B, the features of a
that are not shared by b

B−A, the features of b
that are not shared by a

A ∩ B, the features
shared by a and b

Figure 3   A comparison of observed familiarities can be expressed as a function of three arguments, visualized here.

would pay more attention to the samples from the crime scene or actors than to the known samples collected. This is true even though the known has more salience, because arguably it has more information and a documented provenance than the questioned sample. For example, a toy ship is quite similar to a real ship because most of the main features of the real ship are expressed in the toy (otherwise it might not be recognized as a simulacrum of its referent). A real ship, however, is not as similar to the toy ship because many of the features of a real ship are not expressed in the toy (due to function, scale, or safety, among other factors). The reason for paying more attention to the target is, first and foremost, to determine if there is sufficiency of salient information in the target for the comparative process to occur (see Vanderkolk for a discussion on this).

The main determinant of feature salience for comparative purposes is the degree to which they classify an object, that is, their diagnosticity. A feature that serves as the basis to reassign an object from one class to another class with fewer members is more salient than one that does not. Salience is hierarchical and is based on how many members of a class share that feature; the goal is thus to place an object, by successive comparative features, into classes with increasingly fewer members. Salience of a feature, therefore, should increase inversely with the number of members of a class into which it places an object; $A \cap B$ increases and may be thought of as an expression of diagnosticity. A comparative process that does not maximize diagnosticity or exploit features that do so will have low forensic utility.

The Comparative Method within Forensic Science

The comparative method involves the aligning of the relational structures between one or more targets (items of questioned source; Qs) and one or more sources (items of known provenance or source; Ks). This alignment, to work as a method, has three constraints or requirements:

- The alignment has to be *structurally consistent*, that is, it has to observe a one-to-one correspondence between the comparators in an argumentative structure that is the same between the comparisons (*parallel connectivity*). One point of comparison can be aligned with at most one other point of comparison in the target or source. Similarly, matching relationships must have matching arguments to support them (the reason for the proposed relationship cannot be based on an unrelated argument).
- The comparison has to involve *common relations* but does not have to involve common object descriptions. All the evidence that came from the crime scene, for example, need not have originated from only one source.
- Finally, comparisons are not made merely between the objects at hand but also include all of the higher order "constraining relations" that they may share (*systematicity*). In biology, this would relate to the evolutionary and genetic connections; for manufactured materials, this would be the design factors and the supply chain of raw materials and intermediate processes that lead to a finished consumer good. The deeper the relational history, the more higher order classes that two objects share, the stronger the relationship they share, and, therefore, the greater is the chance of a shared origin. This obviates the significance of coincidental matches between otherwise similar but unrelated objects: a series of coincidences between two objects are not a salient relationship, no matter how many of them exist. Type I and type II errors stem from these coincidences.

A comparison results in a type of cross-mapping of analogous traits or phenomena that have differential relational roles in two situations (e.g., victim's clothing and crime scene). A systematic mapping between source and target is a natural method for differentiating potentially ambiguous relationships. This relates to the classification of the target and source, the identification of traits or features each has that place them in one or more sets (classes) of items. The cross-mapping is of these traits within a class. Once a source has been aligned to a target, *candidate inferences*, based on the source, can be projected onto the target, such as a shared source or history. A handgun with blood on it, for example, can be compared to a bullet removed from a victim (through test firings of similar ammunition) and determined to have been the source (to some degree of certainty) of the bullet while the blood can be tested through DNA typing with the victim's known sample and be shown to have the victim as its source (again, to some degree of certainty); the fact that the victim's blood is on the handgun indicates a shared history of occurrence (lateral contemporaneity).

Comparison is selective. The requirement of systematicity is predicated on the idea that classes or sets are flexible and hierarchical. Higher order connections predict lower order relations, and commonalities that are not a part of the aligned system of relationships are considered inconsequential: a blue shoe and a blue car have little in common other than the stated color category; likewise, the fact that the source shoe and the target print might have the same kind of outsole design recedes in importance to the fact than none of the individual traits on the sole appears in the print. Differences that are connected to the hierarchical system of relatedness are called *alignable differences*; those differences with no correspondence at all between the source and the target are called *nonalignable differences*. Alignable differences are more meaningful and salient than nonalignable ones because they exist within the same relationship system making them more relevant to each other. The strange conclusion this observation leads to is that there should be more meaningful differences for comparators that are very similar (*toy train–real train*) than for ones that are less similar (*toy train–toy ship*) because the more similar comparators will have or be derived within more common systems of relationships and will have more alignable differences. As an example, consider all the possible differences for the pair *automobile–truck* and for the pair *duck–baseball*. More alignable differences could be found for the first pair than the second: after a few differences ("You don't play sports with a duck. You don't hunt baseballs."), the list seems pointless because the two are not aligned. The details that could be elicited by comparing *automobile* with *truck*, however, could go on for some time, depending on the level of detail desired. Most sets of comparators in the world are dissimilar (which is why forensic comparisons tend to be stronger in exclusion than inclusion) and this "nonconsideration" heuristic makes sense given humans' cognitive load: "intuitively, it is when a pair of items is similar that their differences are likely to be important"

(Genter and Markman). Psychological experiments support this statement, and it seems to be an integral part of human cognition. Related to this idea is Wittgenstein's proposal 5.5303 in his work *Tractatus logico-philosophicus*: "Roughly speaking, to say of two things that they are identical is nonsense, and to say of one thing that it is identical with itself is to say nothing at all." This points to the need for a statistical evaluation of the *strength* of a comparison, either inclusive or exclusive.

See also: **Foundations:** Forensic Intelligence; Overview and Meaning of Identification/Individualization; Semiotics, Heuristics, and Inferences Used by Forensic Scientists.

Further Reading

Diamond, J., Robinson, J.A. (Eds.), 2010. Natural Experiments of History. Cambridge University Press, Cambridge, MA.

Gentner, D., Markman, A.B., 1997. Structure mapping in analogy and similarity. American Psychologist 52 (1), 45–56.

Hofstadter, D., 2001. Analogy as the core of cognition. In: Gentner, D., Holyoak, K., Kokinov, B. (Eds.), The Analogical Mind: Perspectives from Cognitive Science. MIT Press/Bradford Book, Cambridge, MA, pp. 499–538.

Markman, A.B., Genter, D., 2000. Structure mapping in the comparison process. American Journal of Psychology 113 (4), 501–538.

Pellegrin, P., 1986. Aristotle's Classification of Living Things. University of California Press, Berkeley, CA.

Rudwick, M., 1997. Georges Cuvier, Fossil Bones, and Geological Catastrophes. University of Chicago Press, Chicago.

Tversky, A., 1977. Features of similarity. Psychological Review 84, 327–352.

Vanderkolk, J., 2009. Forensic Comparative Science. Academic Press, New York.

Wittgenstein, L., 1922. Tractatus Logico-Philosophicus. Routledge, London. Translated by C. K. Ogden (1922), prepared with assistance from G. E. Moore, F. P. Ramsey, and Wittgenstein.

Clinical Forensic Medicine—Overview

S Pollak, University of Freiburg, Freiburg, Germany
P Saukko, University of Turku, Turku, Finland

Glossary

Expert witness An expert witness is a person, who by virtue of education, training, skill, or experience, is believed to have expertise and specialized knowledge in a particular field so that others (including authorities such as courts) can rely upon the expert's opinion about an evidence or fact issue.

Fact witness A fact witness is a person with knowledge about what happened in a particular case, who testifies in the case about what happened by reciting facts and/or events.

Introduction

In the wider sense, clinical forensic medicine means the application of clinical knowledge and skills to living individuals corresponding to the special needs of the respective legal, judicial, and police systems. The organization of clinical forensic work differs considerably from place to place, partly depending on the legal situation (e.g., the so-called adversary system of criminal procedure in the Anglo-Saxon tradition on the one hand and the "inquisitorial system" in Continental Europe on the other). It is therefore impossible to deal with any regional peculiarities, and this chapter is necessarily confined to a general view of the main fields of work usually done by forensic medical examiners, sometimes also called "forensic physicians," "forensic medical officers," "police surgeons," or "clinical forensic practitioners." **Table 1** shows typical reasons for their attendance although the focal points of demand may vary to a large extent.

From the topics listed in **Table 1**, it becomes obvious that clinical forensic medicine comprises a large spectrum of duties which are usually handled by doctors of several disciplines involving the medicolegal interface: legal medicine (as a "stand-alone" subject in the undergraduate curriculum at medical schools of Continental Europe), forensic pathology, psychiatry, emergency medicine, pediatrics, gynecology, public health, and others.

Due to global migration, the need for forensic age estimation in living persons without valid identification documents has greatly increased. According to current recommendations issued by the *Study Group on Forensic Age Diagnostics*, age determination in living adolescents and young adults should be based on the results of a physical examination, an X-ray of the hand, and a dental examination.

Some aspects of clinical forensic medicine are dealt with in dedicated chapters and will not be discussed here.

Clinical Examination of Living Victims

Victims of an alleged crime or suspected perpetrators often have to be examined with regard to the presence of injuries. The observations and the medical report on the wounds are likely to play an important part in any subsequent legal proceedings. Therefore, the physical examination and the documentation of the relevant results must be performed in an adequate and accurate manner. Descriptions and conclusions should be phrased in terms which are also intelligible to lay persons. If scientific language is inevitable, an explanation must be given.

It is impossible to prescribe a standardized format to suit every case, as the circumstances differ so much. Apart from the actual examination procedures, it has to be decided if samples need to be taken (e.g., blood for alcohol or drugs, genital swabs, urine, hair samples, and so on). In most cases, photography is helpful and desirable, especially in complex and patterned injuries. Sometimes even the absence of visible injuries might be important, for example, in false allegations. For detailed recording of small marks such as tiny petechiae, a magnifying glass or an operation microscope is necessary. Whenever possible, the whole body from head to toe including the genitalia should be minutely inspected in a good light. In order to prevent any reproaches, it is recommended that a chaperone should be present whenever a male physician investigates a female patient.

Each medical report should contain some basic information on the victim, that is, size, stature, body weight, etc. All

Table 1   Categories of clinical forensic work

1. Examination of living victims:
   a. Bodily injury due to criminal assault
   b. Rape or other sexual crimes in adults
   c. Physical and sexual child abuse
   d. Spouse abuse and other kinds of domestic violence
   e. Abuse of elderly persons
   f. Torture
2. Examination of suspected perpetrators
3. Examination of self-inflicted injuries
4. Medical investigation in traffic accidents:
   a. Examination of pedestrians
   b. Determination of driver versus passenger
5. Examination for fitness to drive:
   a. Assessment of impairment to drive due to alcohol and/or drugs
   b. Specimen taking (blood samples)
6. Assessment of the effect of drink and/or drugs on responsibility
7. Mental health assessment
8. Assessment of fitness to be detained and interrogated
9. Assessment of physical ability required for work
10. Reports, statements, expertise:
    a. Written and photographic documentation of medical findings
    b. Interpretation of wounds and other medical evidence
       – Conclusions as to the causation of injuries (e.g., which type of weapon has been used)
       – Assessment of the severity of bodily harm and its dangerousness
       – Identification of offensive and defensive injuries
       – Medicolegal reconstruction of the circumstances and the course of events
11. Presentation of medical evidence in court:
    a. Witness as to fact
    b. Professional witness
    c. Expert witness
12. Medical care of detainees:
    a. Short-term custody (police)
    b. Long-term custody (prison)
13. Health care of police officers
14. Determination of age

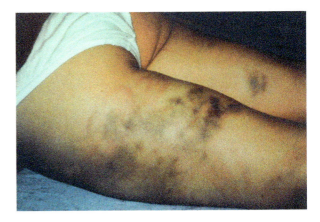

Figure 1   Bruise on the left thigh of a young woman from multiple blows with a looped extension cord.

corners, of concomitant bruises, and of all other features which may help to distinguish between lacerations, incised wounds, and other kinds of penetrating injuries. The condition of the wounds must also be assessed with regard to surgical treatment, infection, and signs of repair.

Similarly, other types of external injuries such as abrasions and bruises have to be reported with reference to their location, size, shape, and appearance. Sometimes characteristic details may be imprinted. In fresh abrasions, the skin tags sometimes indicate the direction of the blunt force. Bruising mostly concerns the subcutaneous layer, often in combination with intradermal extravasations (**Figure 1**); the latter are patterned if the skin has been pressed and squeezed into grooves (e.g., by the impact of a rubber sole). Parallel "tram-line" bruises derive from the impact of a stick or rod, which is of special importance in suspected physical child abuse (**Figure 2**). Nevertheless, it should be emphasized that most

remarkable findings must be recorded and their location defined in relation to easily identifiable marks or fixed body parts (e.g., the middle line and the distance from the sole in upright position). The size and shape of each wound should be detailed by precise measurement using a ruler or a tape measure. If there are a multitude of wounds, it might be advantageous to group them according to their kind and severity or to their location within anatomical regions. Body diagrams or sketches can be helpful.

The margins of each wound require close inspection and accurate description: whether they are lacerated or incised, whether they are shelved or excoriated, whether there is bridging or embedment of foreign material (e.g., soil, glass, paint). In addition, the examiner has to take note of the wound

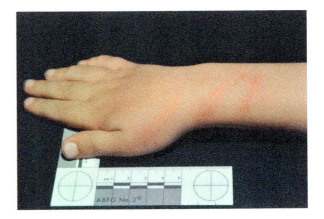

Figure 2   "Tram-line" bruises on the right hand and forearm from beating with a cane in a case of physical child abuse.

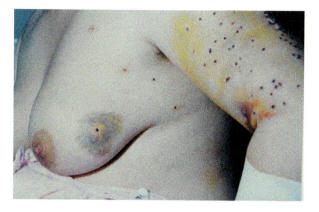

Figure 3 Surviving victim with numerous pellet injuries of the left upper arm and breast from a distant twelve-bore shotgun discharge without penetration of the thoracic wall.

bruises do not have any characteristic shape. Immediately after contusion, the skin need not show any changes of color; in cases of suspected blunt trauma, it is recommended to wait 1 or 2 days and to examine the victim a second time when extravasation has extended enough to become visible. It is well known that color changes occur within a few days so that the initially bluish-red bruise becomes greenish-yellow (**Figure 3**).

Some major points of external victim examination are specified in **Table 2**.

Injuries of Surviving Victims and of Assailants Following Attempted Manual or Ligature Strangulation

One of the common tasks of police surgeons and forensic medical experts is to examine persons who are supposed to or claim to have been strangled by hand or by ligature: for instance, in sex-related offenses such as rape, in attempted homicide, and due to maltreatment in cases of domestic violence.

In manual strangulation, the pressure on the neck is exerted externally by the hand(s) or the forearm resulting in occlusion of the blood vessels and the air passages of the neck. Most victims exhibit typical skin marks from the assailant's throttling grip: discoid or confluent bruises from finger pads,

Table 2 Important external findings in physically injured victims of criminal assaults

Body region	Findings	Kind of traumatization
Head	Excoriation	Blunt trauma to the soft tissues (e.g., kicks, blows from fists, flat hands or weapons, striking of the head against hard surfaces)
	Bruising	
	Laceration of the scalp or face	
	Bleeding from the ear	Closed blows to the ear, fracture of the base of the skull
	Bleeding from the nose	Contusion or fracture of the nose, fracture of the base of the skull, severe strangulation
	Petechiae in the eyelids, conjunctivae and facial skin	Manual strangulation, ligature strangulation, traumatic asphyxia
	Bruising or laceration of the lips, loose or damaged teeth	Blow to the mouth
Neck	Discoid bruises, fingernail marks, scratches	Attempted manual strangulation
	Ligature mark	Attempted ligature strangulation
	Intradermal bruising from folds of cloth	Neck holds or locks
	Incised wounds	Sharp force (cuts, slashes, stabs)
Trunk	Abrasions, contusions	Blunt trauma
	Tram-line bruising	Impact of a rod or similar object
	Patterned abrasion or intradermal bruising	Impact of an object with a profile surface (e.g., rubber sole)
	Bite marks (two opposing bruises/abrasions) from the dental arches	Bites (child abuse, sexual assault)
	Brush abrasion ("grazes")	Tangential contact with a rough surface (caused by dragging)
	Penetrating wounds:	
	● Incised wounds	Sharp force (stabs)
	● Shot wounds	Projectile trauma
Limbs	Fingertip bruises (especially on the medial aspect of the upper arm)	Gripping or prodding
	Stab wounds and cuts (defense injuries)	Knife attacks
	Bruises and abrasions on the back of the hand and on the outer sides of the forearms (defense injuries)	Attack from blunt instruments, fists, or feet
	Circumferential contusions of the wrists or ankles	Restraining by handcuffs, tying of hands or feet

abrasions from fingernails (crescent shaped or scratches), and erythematous markings (**Figure 4**). Nevertheless, there are some victims who do not show any external evidence although there really has been a serious strangulation: this may be true when the palm or forearm was placed over the neck and when a soft object, such as a garment or a pillow, was interposed during pressure. Prolonged gripping of the neck with concomitant occlusion of the cervical veins leads to congestion and petechial hemorrhages of the conjunctivae and on the facial skin, especially the eyelids (**Figure 5**). Radiographs of the neck may reveal fractures of the hyoid bone and/ or the thyroid cartilage; the incidence of such fractures is correlated with the extent of ossification mainly depending on the age and sex of the strangled person. Surviving victims mostly complain of pain on swallowing, on speaking, and on neck movement. Other possible symptoms following attempted strangulation are unconsciousness and sphincter incontinence.

In ligature strangulation, the pressure on the neck is effected by a constricting object (telephone cord, nylons, stockings, belt, towel, scarf) tightened around the neck by a force other than body weight. The appearance of the skin mark is influenced by the nature of the ligature (width, roughness, surface pattern), the force and duration of the strangulation, and the interaction

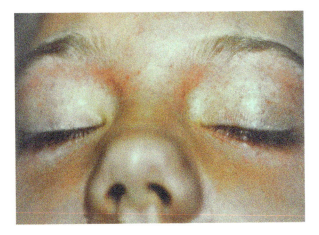

Figure 5   Petechial hemorrhages on the skin of the eyelids.

with a resisting victim (displacement of the noose in attempts to remove it). The ligature mark usually encircles the neck horizontally (**Figure 6**); in typical cases, the skin reveals a transverse streaklike reddening caused by local erythema often associated with (partial) loss of the epidermis (**Figure 7**). Congestion and petechial hemorrhages above the ligature are usually more impressive than in victims of manual strangulation. On the other hand, damage to the hyoid or to the laryngeal cartilages is less common.

Suspected assailants may present examination findings indicative of possibly having been the offender in an attempted strangulation. The most frequent injuries seen in throttlers are nail marks inflicted by the opposing victim. Nail marks have been classified morphologically into three types: impression marks, claws, and scratches. The majority of the skin lesions are

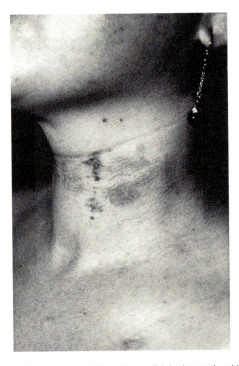

Figure 4   Neck of a rape victim with roundish bruises and scabbed abrasions from survived manual strangulation.

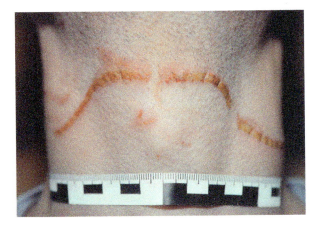

Figure 6   Sharply defined ligature mark encircling the neck; the victim had been strangled with a shoe-lace 3 days before examination.

(a)   **(b)**

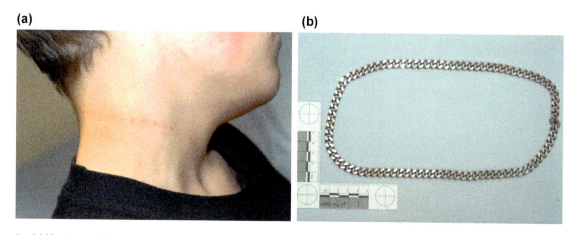

Figure 7   (a) Ligature mark from a solid-link chain tightened around the neck by twisting it in the nuchal region. The victim was a 13-year-old inmate of a supervised home. In the course of an argument, he was strangled by a 15-year-old fellow occupant until he became unconscious. Note the pattern of intracutaneous bruising reflecting the links of the chain (b).

located on the dorsal aspects of the forearms and hands; other classical sites are the face, neck, shoulders, and anterior chest wall. Another typical kind of injury, especially seen in rapists, is bite marks on the hands. If a struggle takes place, the assailant may sustain nonspecific blunt trauma from blows or from wrestling with the victim.

Medical Hazards in Police Custody

Even in countries with a high standard of health care of detainees, some deaths do occur in police cells and in prisons. A large number of custodial deaths are due to natural causes, mainly from cardiovascular diseases, which account for the great majority of sudden and unexpected deaths. Another category of fatalities concerns suicides, mostly committed by hanging. In prisoners with suicidal tendencies, it is therefore recommended to remove any objects that could be used for strangulation such as belts, ties, stockings, and bootlaces. In spite of all precautions of the custodians, some detainees manage to find devices suitable for strangulation such as strips of bedding material or clothing.

Wrist cutting is another self-injurious behavior frequently seen in police custody, either as (attempted) suicide or as self-harm without intention to die. Incised wounds may be inflicted with any sharp-edged instrument such as a piece of glass or sheet metal from a tin. Risk factors associated with self-injurious behavior include the custodial setting itself (especially in isolation cells), being under the influence of alcohol and drugs at the time of incarceration, the availability of means for self-destructive behavior, and many others.

A detainee who is suspected of being drunk and/or drugged at the time of committal needs particularly close observation. If

the prisoner has consumed a large quantity of ethanol or (illegal) drugs just before arrest, he or she may be conscious and responsive at first, but may become comatose later and die from acute alcohol or drug poisoning while he or she is erroneously thought to be sleeping off the drunkenness. This is not only true for ethanol ingestion but also for narcotic drugs (mostly heroin, methadone, and codeine). The victims do not necessarily die from the depressive effects upon the brain (especially the respiratory center); in a high percentage, a secondary aspiration of vomit is found as the immediate cause of death.

Alcohol is an important causal factor in aggression and violent resistance frequently leading to the arrest of the suspect. Physical overpowering of an offender involves the risk of inflicting injuries. In other cases, the person concerned may have sustained injuries due to falls or assaults before the police officers could intervene. It has to be stressed that even a fatal blunt trauma is not always associated with externally visible signs such as bruises, abrasions, or lacerations. The authors had to give opinions on several custody deaths due to blunt head injuries without any wound or palpable swelling; the (deep) bruise on the site of impact became visible only when the inner aspect of the scalp was inspected during autopsy.

Severe and ultimately fatal head injuries need not be associated with unconsciousness in the early posttraumatic period. In persons developing an epidural or subdural hematoma, the symptoms due to the elevated intracranial pressure may set in only after a "lucid interval" of several hours so that they are falsely thought to be uninjured. From this, it follows that cases of suspected cranial trauma require close observation and the possibility of rapid transfer to a hospital.

Torture

According to the 1975 Tokyo Declaration of the World Medical Association, torture is defined as the deliberate, systematic, or wanton infliction of physical or mental suffering by one or more persons acting alone or on the orders of any authority, to force another person to yield information, to make a confession, or for any other reason.

Torture has to be criticized as a particularly reprehensible offense against human rights; nevertheless, it does exist in numerous countries throughout the world. Within the scope of this overview, only a few medicolegal remarks on the physical manifestations of torture can be made. Unfortunately, often there is a long delay before medical examination so that conclusions as to the causation may be difficult because of the unspecificity of most scars.

Beating is probably the most common form of torture. Apart from kicks and blows from fists and flat hands, a great variety of weapons and instruments are used to inflict pain (e.g., rifle butts, clubs, and whips). When the body is struck by a rod or a similar object, each impact causes a double line of parallel bruises. Patterned abrasion or intradermal bruising may reflect characteristic details of the weapon's surface. Series of skin marks arranged in approximately the same orientation point to an unchanged position of the attacker in relation to the helpless (held or tied) victim. Heavy blows to the face are typically followed by periorbital hematomas ("black eyes"), extensive bruises and excoriation of the other facial regions, laceration of the lips and displacement of incisors, and fractures of superficial bones (nasal bone, zygomatic bone, jaws). The other main targets of beating and whipping are the back, the buttocks, the legs and the soles of the feet, the abdomen, the breasts and the genitals, which are also pinched and squeezed. Physical abuse other than blunt traumatization can only be mentioned briefly: cutting, piercing and stabbing, hair pulling, burning with cigarettes, repeated dipping of the victim's head under water, applying electric current, suspension, and sexual abuse.

See also: **Behavioral:** Forensic Psychiatry; **Forensic Medicine/Causes of Death:** Blunt Injury; Burns and Scalds; Sharp Trauma; Strangulation; **Forensic Medicine/Clinical:** Child Abuse; Defense Wounds; Self-Inflicted Injury; Traffic Injuries and Deaths.

Further Reading

Evans, V., 2005. Care in prison custody, United Kingdom. In: Payne-James, J., Byard, R.W., Corey, T.S., Henderson, C. (Eds.), Encyclopedia of Forensic and Legal Medicine, vol. 2. Elsevier, Oxford, pp. 164–169.

Gudjonsson, G.H., 2005. Fitness to be interviewed. In: Payne-James, J., Byard, R.W., Corey, T.S., Henderson, C. (Eds.), Encyclopedia of Forensic and Legal Medicine, vol. 2. Elsevier, Oxford, pp. 169–174.

Heide, S., Stiller, D., Lessig, R., Lautenschläger, C., Birkholz, M., Früchtnicht, W., 2012. Medical examination of fitness for police custody in two large German towns. International Journal of Legal Medicine 126, 27–35.

Madea, B., Saukko, P. (Eds.), 2008. Forensic Medicine in Europe. Schmidt-Römhild, Lübeck.

McLay, W.D.S. (Ed.), 2009. Clinical Forensic Medicine, third ed. Cambridge University Press, Cambridge.

Nathason, M., 2000. The physically and emotionally abused child. In: Mason, J.K., Purdue, B.N. (Eds.), The Pathology of Trauma, third ed. Arnold, London, pp. 155–175.

Payne-James, J., 2003. Assault and injury in the living. In: Payne-James, J., Busuttil, A., Smock, W. (Eds.), Forensic Medicine: Clinical and Pathological Aspects. Greenwich Medical Media, London, pp. 543–563.

Payne-James, J., Robinson, S., 2005. Care in police custody, United Kingdom. In: Payne-James, J., Byard, R.W., Carey, T.S., Henderson, C. (Eds.), Encyclopedia of Forensic and Legal Medicine, vol. 2. Elsevier, Oxford, pp. 158–164.

Pollak, S., 2004. Clinical forensic medicine and its main fields of activity from the foundation of the German Society of Legal Medicine until today. Forensic Science International 144, 269–283.

Pollak, S., Saukko, P., 2003. Atlas of Forensic Medicine, CD-ROM. Elsevier, Amsterdam (Chapter 19).

Purdue, B.N., 2000. Cutting and piercing wounds. In: Mason, J.K., Purdue, B.N. (Eds.), The Pathology of Trauma, third ed. Arnold, London, pp. 123–140.

Robinson, S., 2000. The examination of the adult victim of assault. In: Mason, J.K., Purdue, B.N. (Eds.), The Pathology of Trauma, third ed. Arnold, London, pp. 141–154.

Saukko, P., Knight, B., 2004. Knight's Forensic Pathology, third ed. Arnold, London. pp. 136–173, 235–244, 301–311.

Schmeling, A., Reisinger, W., Geserick, G., Olze, A., 2008. Forensic age estimation of live adolescents and young adults. In: Tsokos, M. (Ed.), Forensic Pathology Reviews, vol. 5, pp. 269–288.

Stark, M.M. (Ed.), 2011. Clinical Forensic Medicine: A Physician's Guide, third ed. Humana Press, Totowa, NJ.

Vanezis, P., 2000. Deaths in custody. In: Mason, J.K., Purdue, B.N. (Eds.), The Pathology of Trauma, third ed. Arnold, London, pp. 103–122.

Forensic Pathology—Principles and Overview

T Kanchan, Kasturba Medical College (affiliated to Manipal University), Mangalore, Karnataka, India
K Krishan, Panjab University, Chandigarh, India

Introduction

The word *forensics* is derived from the Latin word *forensis* meaning "public." The word "forensic," however, essentially implies "of or used in courts of law." The word "pathology" is derived from the Greek words *pathos* meaning "disease" and *logos* meaning "the study of." Forensic pathology as a speciality thus deals with both the legal and pathologic aspects of a case. Various designations are employed for specialists practicing forensic pathology in different parts of the world: forensic pathologists, medicolegal consultants, autopsy surgeons, police surgeons, medical jurists, forensic medicine experts, and so on. In this article, for the sake of uniformity, the term forensic pathologists is used for the experts practicing forensic pathology. A forensic pathologist is a pathologist who has studied the various forms of natural and nonnatural processes that lead to the death of an individual.

A key role of most forensic pathologists is the examination of a dead body, frequently known as an autopsy. "Autopsy" is derived from the Greek words *auto* meaning "self" and *opsy* meaning "to look at." Thus, autopsy means "to look at one's self" or sometimes "seeing with one's own eyes." This is not very accurate when referring to a deceased person. A better word is "necropsy," which comes from the Greek words *necros* meaning "death" and *opsy* meaning "to look at." "Postmortem examination" is another frequently used alternative term for the examination of a dead body. All in all, autopsy/necropsy/postmortem examination may be referred to as a medicolegal examination of the dead.

Role of the Forensic Pathologist

Forensic pathology deals mostly with the pathology of intentional (homicidal and suicidal) and unintentional (accidental) trauma or injury, in cases where bodily damage may be the major finding and in deaths from natural causes in cases when the cause of death cannot be certified by a physician. In addition, deaths from occupational exposure to hazardous materials and industrial deaths may be of medicolegal significance. The primary role of the forensic pathologist is to determine the cause of death based on a detailed and complete autopsy and to confirm if the cause of death is in accordance with the manner of death as proposed by the investigating agencies enquiring into sudden, suspicious, and nonnatural deaths.

In cases involving mechanical trauma/injuries, the forensic pathologist deals mostly with the examination of the deceased or injured person to determine the nature and cause of the injuries/death. The role of the forensic pathologist is vital in cases of alleged medical negligence, sexual assault, domestic violence, and torture. In criminal investigations, in addition to the examination of the victim, the forensic pathologist may be involved in the examination of the accused/suspect, the scene of the crime/death, and the collection of evidentiary material. Thus, a forensic pathologist plays a key role in criminal cases as well as in civil cases mostly involving insurance and other claims. Besides, a forensic pathologist has to attend courts of law as an expert witness, provide valuable opinion on the cases, and thus, help in the administration of justice.

Medicolegal Systems and Investigation of Deaths

The Medical Examiner and Coroner systems exist in the United States for medicolegal investigation of sudden, suspicious, and nonnatural deaths. In Australia and England and Wales, the authority to investigate death lies with a coroner, while in Scotland, the Procurator Fiscal system is responsible for the medicolegal duties. Other countries in Europe follow procedures and systems that are different from both Coroner and Medical Examiner systems. In most of the European and Asian nations, the forensic medical expert examinations are conducted based on the decision of investigating and interrogating agencies, the prosecutor, or the court.

Aims of Medicolegal Autopsy

The autopsy involves the standardized dissection of a dead body primarily to determine the cause and manner of death. Other aims of a medicolegal autopsy are to estimate the time since death, establish the identity of the deceased, and collect essential evidences surrounding the death. A medicolegal autopsy thus answers the basic questions of "why," "how," "when," and "who" with regard to sudden, suspicious, and nonnatural deaths.

Cause of Death

If a person dies under suspicious or nonnatural circumstances, the investigating authority orders an autopsy to determine the cause of death. The cause of death is the injury or disease that produces a physiological derangement in the body, resulting in the death of an individual.

The cause of death is divided into the primary and secondary causes of death. The primary cause of death includes the immediate and antecedent causes responsible for the fatal outcome, while the secondary cause of death includes the conditions that are not related to the primary cause of death but contribute substantially to the death of an individual. Format frequently followed for documenting the cause of death is depicted in **Table 1**.

For example, in a case of a fatal fall from the stairs, an elderly male suffering from senile dementia sustained head injuries. The autopsy revealed extradural hematoma in the right temporoparietal region. The cause of death can be mentioned as:

- Part I
  - Extradural hematoma: due to (or as a consequence of)
  - Blunt force trauma to the head: due to (or as a consequence of)
  - Fall from stairs
- Part II: Senile dementia

Manner of Death

The manner of death explains the circumstances associated with the death and the way in which the cause of death came about. Broadly, the manner of death can be natural or nonnatural. Nonnatural manner of death can be further classified as homicidal, suicidal, or accidental depending on the

Table 1   Format frequently followed for documenting the cause of death

Cause of death	Approximate interval between onset and death
Part I. Diseases, injuries, or complications that caused the death. Do not enter the mode of dying, such as cardiac or respiratory arrest, shock, or heart failure	
Immediate cause	1. Due to (or as a consequence of)
Antecedent cause	2. Due to (or as a consequence of)
	3. Due to (or as a consequence of)
Morbid conditions, if any, giving rise to the above cause, stating underlying conditions last	
Part II. Other significant conditions contributing to death but not resulting in the underlying cause given in Part I	

intent of the act leading to the death of an individual. Commenting on the manner of death may be a complex task. In cases where it is difficult to reach a definitive conclusion as to the manner of death, it is of utmost importance that a systematic death scene investigation, a meticulous postmortem examination, and an intelligent interpretation of the findings are carried out before a final comment on the manner of death is made.

Medicolegal Autopsy

The autopsy is a standardized procedure that comprises of a detailed external and internal examination and collection of evidentiary material. It should be kept in mind that the identity of the body is confirmed before starting the autopsy. The identity of the deceased is usually established by the near relatives of the deceased and the investigating officers. In cases of unidentified bodies, photographs are taken and identification marks are noted on the body. Examination of any congenital or acquired abnormality may help in establishing the identity of the deceased. In cases where the visual identification is difficult as in cases of dismembered, mutilated, and charred remains, dental examination and DNA profiling are often used to confirm the identity of the unknown person.

External Examination

The external examination of a body besides a detailed examination of the entire body also includes a description of the clothing of the deceased and photographs of the body. Any trauma observed on the body is noted in detail with measurements, and the same is correlated with the damage to the clothing, if any. Clothing is then removed from the dead body with utmost care, and trace evidence on the clothing or the body is preserved for further analysis at the forensic science laboratory.

After removal of clothes, the age, sex, general physique (height and weight), and state of nutrition are noted. Examination of the eyeballs and external body orifices is essential. Postmortem changes in the body are appreciated as they primarily give an insight into the time since death. Postmortem changes frequently observed on external examination that help in estimating the time of death include algor mortis, livor mortis, rigor mortis, degree of decomposition, and insect activity. In cases of mechanical violence and traumatic deaths, a detailed description of the external injuries is vital. All recent and old injuries should be photographed and described in detail with regard to their size and location on the body.

Internal Examination

The internal examination follows a detailed external examination. Internal examination starts with the dissection of the dead body and naked-eye inspection of underlying tissues and organs. The prime object of internal examination is to examine the contents of the head, neck, thorax, and abdomen for injuries/pathology.

The forensic pathologist examines the thoracoabdominal cavity usually following one of the following techniques:

- *Virchow method*: In the Virchow method, each organ is removed one by one and examined in detail.
- *Rokitansky method*: In the Rokitansky method, in situ dissection and removal of organs are carried out.
- *Ghon method*: The Ghon method is characterized by en bloc removal of organs.
- *Letulle method*: The Letulle method is characterized by en masse removal of cervical, thoracic, abdominal, and pelvic organs and their subsequent dissection into organ blocks.

Whenever required, the internal examination is followed by microscopic, biochemical, immunologic, and toxicological investigations.

Importance of Additional Investigations

Histology, postmortem biochemistry, and evaluation of postmortem parameters of metabolic dysfunctions, immunohistochemistry, postmortem toxicology, X-rays, and modern methods of imaging such as computed tomography (CT), postmortem CT angiography, and magnetic resonance imaging (MRI) are important additional investigations frequently used in modern autopsy work.

In cases of sudden unexpected deaths, the gross autopsy findings may be inconclusive, and histopathological evaluation may play a crucial role in defining the cause of death. Postmortem biochemical examinations of vitreous humor, blood, urine, and cerebrospinal fluid are other important and useful investigations in forensic autopsies that help in determining the cause of death. Biochemical markers of inflammation and infection, hormonal disturbances, alcohol intake and abuse, cardiac function status, and ischemia are reported. Postmortem analysis of glycated hemoglobin, C-reactive protein, interleukin, cholesterol, triglycerides, total bilirubin, total proteins, albumin, and troponine 1 in blood and sodium, potassium, chloride, and glucose in vitreous helps in determining the cause of death. Besides, determining the cause of death, postmortem chemistry helps in understanding the pathophysiological mechanisms involved in the death process.

Vitality and wound age estimation are the central issue in investigation of injuries and traumatic deaths. Morphological methods such as routine histology and enzyme histochemical methods are routinely employed for vitality and wound age estimation. Immunohistochemistry is the modern investigation of choice in this regard. Besides, biochemical methods are employed in evaluation of vitality.

Radiological investigations including X-rays, CT, MRI, and angiography are useful in determination of identity and evaluation of injury and death. Role of radiological techniques in analysis of gunshot wounds and osseous injuries is well known. With radiological advancement, use of modern imaging techniques is being considered an alternative to traditional autopsies in determining the cause of death. Radiological investigations can help in analysis of complex trauma pattern and fractures, and finding the location of foreign bodies and metal fragments. These are advantageous in detection of pneumothorax. Postmortem angiography can be used in evaluation of cardiovascular and hemodynamic conditions.

Evidentiary Material Collected at Autopsy

Blood samples are usually collected for chemical, toxicologic, and serologic investigations. Blood is preferably taken from peripheral veins from the groin or the neck.

In cases of suspected poisoning, the stomach and its contents, a piece of liver with gall bladder, and both kidneys are subjected to chemical and toxicologic analysis.

In addition, specific viscera and body fluids should be preserved depending on the nature of poison allegedly consumed.

In cases of alleged sexual assault, swabs are collected from genitalia for examination of body fluids along with pubic hair combings to identify any foreign materials.

In cases of gunshot wounds, the clothing and the recovered bullets are preserved and sent for forensic analysis.

In cases of unidentified bodies, fingerprints are taken and matched with the reference databases.

In decomposed, mutilated, and dismembered remains, the teeth are subjected to a forensic dental examination and DNA analysis.

Attendance of a Forensic Pathologist at the Scene of Crime/Death

The death scene should ideally be examined by a team comprising of investigating police officers, forensic scientists, and forensic pathologists. The help of forensic anthropologists may be sought in the examination of skeletal remains, that of entomologists in the examination of insects, and that of odontologists for dental examination. The inclusion of forensic pathologist in the death scene investigation team is important in examining the deceased at the scene and in reconstruction of events. Wound pattern analysis is an essential component in reconstruction of events. Wound pattern analysis and its correlation with the observations made at the scene of death can be vital in reconstruction of events. In cases of suspicious deaths, the forensic pathologists visiting the scene of death can provide vital information on the manner and circumstances of death. Moreover, the scene of death is possibly the best place to make an estimate of the time since death. Forensic pathologist at the scene of death can ensure that the vital evidence is not lost and that the same is collected appropriately. The attendance of a forensic pathologist at the scene of crime/death varies from case to case and in different setups. Scene examination that is often not considered an integral component of autopsy can thus have serious implications.

Conclusion

Forensic pathologists are required to work in close association with other specialities of the forensic sciences. Forensic pathologists play a significant role in cases of suspicious and nonsuspicious deaths. In cases of sudden death, they establish the exact cause of death, while in criminal cases, their opinion is vital to the delivery of justice. The information obtained from investigating accidental deaths and suicides can be vital to designing preventive strategies. In view of the importance of forensic pathology as a speciality, its development is essential in modern society. Association of forensic medicine and pathology with issues of public health, occupational health, and community health needs to be addressed and emphasized on.

See also: **Forensic Medicine/Pathology:** Autopsy; Early and Late Postmortem Changes; Estimation of the Time Since Death; External Postmortem Examination; Histopathology; Postmortem Imaging.

Further Reading

Coe, J.I., 1993. Postmortem chemistry update. Emphasis on forensic application. American Journal of Forensic Medicine and Pathology 14, 91–117.

DiMaio, V.J., DiMaio, D., 2001. Forensic Pathology, second ed. CRC Press LLC, Boca Raton, FL.

Dolinak, D., Matshes, E., Lew, E., 2005. Forensic Pathology – Principles and Practice. Elsevier/Academic Press, Burlington, MA.

Kanchan, T., Lobo, F.D., Menezes, R.G., Shetty, B.S.K., 2012. Histopathological investigation in forensic autopsies. In: Vultagione, J.M., Forester, K.N. (Eds.), Pathology: New Research. Nova Science Publishers, Inc., New York.

Palmiere, C., Mangin, P., 2012a. Postmortem chemistry update part I. International Journal of Legal Medicine 126, 187–198.

Palmiere, C., Mangin, P., 2012b. Postmortem chemistry update part II. International Journal of Legal Medicine 216, 199–215.

Saukko, P.J., Knight, B., 2004. Knight's Forensic Pathology, third ed. Arnold, London.

Spitz, W.U., Fisher, R.S., 2006. Spitz and Fisher's Medicolegal Investigation of Death: Guidelines for the Application of Pathology to Crime Investigation, fourth ed. Charles C Thomas, Springfield, IL.

Williams, D.J., 1996. Forensic Pathology. Elsevier Health Sciences, New York.

History of Forensic Sciences

J Hebrard, Forensic and Criminal Intelligence Agency of the French Gendarmerie, Paris, France
F Daoust, Institut de recherche criminelle de la gendarmerie nationale, Paris, France

This chapter is a revision of the previous edition article by D. Wielbo, volume 3, pp. 1070–1075, © 2000, Elsevier Ltd.

Glossary

DNA Deoxyribonucleic acid: restriction fragment length polymorphism.

Forensic science is the application of sciences pertaining to the law. It requires the complementary interaction of a wide range of scientific specialties and disciplines. The term "criminalistics" is often used interchangeably with the term forensic science. According to the American Board of Criminalistics, it is defined as the profession and scientific discipline directed to the recognition, identification, individualization, and evaluation of physical evidence by application of the physical and natural sciences to law–science matters. The history of forensic science—i.e., applying "scientific" principles to legal questions—has a long and intriguing history.

One of the oldest known reference to a specific forensic case-solving method dates back to the Chinese Quin dynasty (721–707 BC). The account of this case was found in a bamboo tablet, which was, in turn, found in a tomb. The tablet's contents refer to "examination of tangible proof regarding serious offenses." However, before such a legal and scientific basis was used to solve cases, evidence was assessed and retained in immaterial, esoteric, magical, or spiritual ways, which varied from one society to another. Even institutional evidence has long been under the influence of religions and beliefs. Evidence was often drawn from God's judgment: through certain tests, a person suspected of a crime was found guilty or innocent. For instance, the judicial duel and the cross ordeal made it possible to decide between two opposed parties, by assuming that God had given his support to the winner of the test. Whenever only one person was suspected of a crime, other ordeals determined, through various physical tests, whether that person was guilty or innocent according to the success or failure of the test. Evidence through God's judgment is found throughout history, in Hammurabi's code of laws in Mesopotamia, in ancient Egypt, or in Europe with the Francs and the Burgondes.

Despite its godly origin, this method of obtaining evidence turned out to be limited, and societies turned to confession and testimony in order to prove offenses. This type of evidence, however, which requires that the culprit acknowledge his or her offense, is deemed so important that it is implemented through complex, detailed, and formal procedures.

At the same time, experts were increasingly consulted to enlighten certain aspects of a case. Thus, "barbers—physicians" were required to give their opinions on the circumstances of someone's demise: for example, to establish whether the decedent could have been poisoned or if the decedent's body bore suspicious traces. Weapons manufacturers were sometimes used in a similar way. As early as the sixteenth century, a guild of handwriting experts was created in France to provide courts with their analysis regarding forgery issues. Even if confession and testimony were the outcome of crime investigation and remained at the heart of criminal proceedings, technical and scientific expertise was introduced in the trial out of necessity. In the eighteenth century, the United States of America started resorting to experts "with a specific training and background" that jury members could not have.

Thus, there was a progressive rise of the technical and scientific field on the legal scene; however, this expertise was used to support evidence obtained through confession, not to replace it. Moreover, each technical and scientific discipline followed its own path with no regard to others, thus building up walls, which still exist in many countries, such as the one between forensic pathology and forensic sciences.

During the second half of the nineteenth century, under the influence of a group of forensic pathologists and scientists, a new set of ideas and common views about forensic science and the law were introduced. Young industrial societies were not satisfied with confession anymore: science had to break into the investigation process and the criminal trial in order to reinforce the judicial system. These pioneers spread forensic sciences thanks to a criminological approach and the issue of crime repetition (also known as recidivism).

Because legal systems then in force were already harsher toward second offenders than first ones, identifying second offenders was a major issue. Alphonse Bertillon was hired in the 1870s by the Paris police department as a book-keeper to write down criminal facts, names, and a brief description of the arrested suspects. He quickly realized that the same people were frequently arrested by the police department under different names. Using his father's work as an anthropologist (Dr Louis Adolphe Bertillon was a professor at the Paris School of Anthropology), Alphonse Bertillon noticed the wide range of body measurements among individuals. He then created a system of measurements and photographs in order to identify second offenders. This system was tested within the Paris police department from 1882 onward and officially set up in 1888, almost 10 years after it was created. Afterward, criminal anthropometry was implemented all over the world and Bertillon's method had its hour of glory.

Bertillon also introduced criminal photography on crime scenes, which drastically changed the way crime scenes were dealt with. The crime scene was no longer ephemeral, it was engraved on photographs, thanks to which traces left on the crime scene could be tracked, recorded, and used. According to Bertillon, one should only rely on physical clues. Many works were carried out, starting in Europe, and contributed to building modern forensic sciences.

In Austria, Hans Gross, an Austrian judge, imposed training in forensic sciences upon lawyers, and, in particular, upon examining magistrates ("juges d'instruction") as early as 1893. His work was particularly advanced in its design and displays. His training provided judges with an overall view of forensic sciences, from scientific investigations to forensic analyses. Gross always took as a starting point the reconstruction of the crime scene. He was the one to introduce the word "criminalistics."

In Italy, from 1876 Cesare Lombroso led the way for a whole research movement. Doctor Salavatore Ottolenghi covered a wider scientific range (forensic pathology, identification, anthropology, fingerprints, and a large part of psychology). In 1896, he set up a class of "polizia scientifica" and in 1902, he created a "scuola di polizia" (a police academy).

Lombroso's work was questioned by the Lyon school of thought, which included Alexandre Lacassagne, a forensic pathologist, and its student Edmond Locard. They denied any scientific value to stereotyped interpretations (such as considering any person with a tattoo on their skin as a potential offender) and more generally rejected the born criminal theory. While Bertillon had not yet started his job within the Paris police department, Professor Alexandre Lacassagne combined modern forensic pathology to forensic sciences thanks to the range of his research work. Head of the "Criminal Anthropology Journal" from 1895 to 1914, he displayed his influence and his will to gather all fields of new knowledge. Doctor Edmond Locard was the greatest example of the necessary

combination of forensic pathology and forensic sciences. In 1910, he founded his own laboratory in the attic of Lyon's law court and named it "Anthropological and criminal expertise unit." He is recognized for the inception of the Locard exchange principle, "Every contact leaves a trace," the basic tenet of forensic sciences.

In Switzerland, Rodolphe Archibald Reiss took on an international standing thanks to his dynamism and his ability to combine emerging forensic knowledge and his research work that he implemented on crime scenes and in the laboratory. Founder of the Forensic Science College at Lausanne University, he directed the college and taught classes. Having a PhD in chemistry, he became one of the major references in the forensic field. He paid tribute to Bertillon's work (he worked with him for a few months, in particular, on criminal photography, criminal anthropometry, and on the "spoken portrait"), and befriended Locard. Reiss became an authority in forensic science through his great capacity for work; his curiosity; and his research in chemistry, photography, and any science or technique that could be useful for criminal investigation. Reiss, who had been born in Germany, rapidly appeared as an international model to follow, and was able to acquire Swiss citizenship. In 1909, Reiss founded the college at Lausanne University. He left Switzerland in 1914 to carry out a mission for the Serbian authorities to keep track of war crimes committed by the Austrian–Hungarian army on the civilian population in Serbia. He remained in Serbia until his death in 1929.

In the United States, forensic sciences quickly became central to criminal proceedings, in part because the adversarial judicial system encouraged parties to make use of forensic sciences. In the latter part of the 1920s, Los Angeles Chief of Police August Vollmer, of the Los Angeles County Sheriff's department, developed the first United States Police crime laboratory. The FBI crime laboratory was subsequently established in 1932. Edward Oscar Heinrich (1881–1953) founded the first private laboratory at Berkeley University. He was then followed by scientist Paul Kirk, who defined forensic sciences as individualization sciences, and foreshadowed current issues in forensic sciences through his work. Kirk set up in 1937 the first academic criminalistics program in the United States at the University of California.

During those early years, which were blooming with new concepts, it is worth noting that new identification methods and fields came in and out of the area of forensic sciences, thus upsetting barely established bases. For instance, criminal anthropometry, which had recently been adopted by a large number of foreign police departments, was challenged by the new field of fingerprints. Fingerprints provided methods that were useful in two fields: the fight against recidivism and traces at crime scenes. In 1823, the Czech physiologist Jan Major Purkinje described papillary drawings and claimed they were individualized. From 1858, after having observed Bengali workers authenticating deeds with fingerprints as a substitute for their signatures, Sir Williams Herschel tested this method to identify persons. In 1880, doctor Henry Faulds published an article that suggested collecting fingerprints to identify offenders. As far back as 1891, in Argentina, Juan Vucetich created a classification system using fingerprints. That system was still used in South America and in some European countries (including Switzerland) until the coming of the computer age. In 1892, Vucetich was the first one to identify a criminal; thanks to fingerprints comparison. In Europe, Sir Francis Galton set the principle that fingerprints were permanent throughout life in his book *Fingerprints* in 1892. He also created a classification system which was improved by Edward Richard Henry, head of London police department.

After the explosion of ideas by the great forerunners at the end of the nineteenth century and at the beginning of the twentieth century, their heirs and students (such as Bayle in Paris, Mezger in Germany, Sodermann in Sweden, Bischoff in Switzerland, and so on), gathered, coordinated, completed, and developed their masters' fields of research and initiatives in forensic sciences. Through systematization of scientific methods and through academic teaching, they made forensic sciences a part of criminal proceedings for good.

Thereafter, some countries stopped allowing new research in forensic science to be used in judicial proceedings, believing the field to be mature. Great Britain and France were affected by this attitude in the 1970s and 1980s. This shortcoming was highlighted by some criminal cases where confession of the culprit was systematically sought, therefore making criminal proceedings stagnate and casting aside scientific progress. It led to dropping the scientific movement which had favored the creation and development of forensic sciences. At the end of the 1980s, the realization of this setback enabled those countries to go back to an international scientific and legal standard, according to which physical evidence is collected and processed before being used as evidence in a court of law. Since the 1990s, confession is no longer the greatest kind of criminal evidence. Forensic sciences have become the scientific benchmark that legal systems cannot do without and that stands next to, if not ahead of, other kinds of criminal evidence in priority.

At the end of the twentieth and beginning of the twenty-first centuries, information technologies joined the area of forensic sciences. Criminalistics already included fingerprints, ballistics, toxicology, arson and explosives investigations, documents and handwriting analyses, microanalysis, traffic accidentology, anthropology, entomology, and so on. The field continued to expand as new forensic fields of identification, such as DNA technology, new tools that managed evidence, such as automated fingerprint identification system, and new means of criminality, such as cybercrime, became available.

Evolving from classical serology, DNA profiling could be considered the modern-day technique revolutionizing personal identification in forensic science. In the mid-1980s, Sir Alex Jeffreys developed the techniques allowing the profile analysis of DNA. After publishing his achievements in Nature in 1985, Jeffreys was subsequently called upon to apply his techniques to solve the first crime in 1986. In combination with the British Home Office Forensic Science Service, his DNA profiling techniques were used to identify Colin Pitchfork as the murderer of Dawn Ashworth and Lynda Mann in Leicestershire, England. Cetus Corporation furthered the developments of DNA profiling and molecular biology techniques in personal identification during the rest of the 1980s with the development of the polymerase chain reaction (PCR). With PCR technology applied to short tandem repeats (STRs), it became possible to generate DNA profiles from tiny stains, minute amount of DNA, or fragmented DNA where longer variable number tandem repeats (VNTRs) failed to give any informative data.

Although STR analysis together with PCR amplification enabled forensic laboratories to increase sensitivity of the method and, therefore, to obtain complete DNA profiles from low DNA templates, the problem of DNA degradation of numerous crime scene samples, leading to inconclusive results, had to be solved. During 1996, the FBI DNA Analysis Unit began using mitochondrial DNA. In 2003, STR primers were redesigned to generate shorter amplicons. This approach, named "mini-STR," significantly improved the success rate for poor-quality samples. Nowadays 9-plex mini-STR amplification kits are on the market, and mini-STRs are implemented in various standard 15-plex STR amplification kits. These types of analyses can be applied to compromised biological samples and samples with low quantity of nuclear DNA such as hair, old bones, or teeth, allowing the examination of evidence that may not have been suitable for comparison before the development of these techniques.

While it is admitted that DNA profiling is a powerful tool for human identity testing, it is also very limited since a profile itself—in the absence of reference—provides no information to investigators with regard to the identity of the suspect. This is the reason why, in the middle of the 1990s, national DNA databases were created, first in Europe and in the United States, and later throughout the world. These DNA databases are very useful for linking serial crimes and unsolved cases with repeat offenders. In 2005, the Prüm treaty was signed up by seven European countries. This European formal decision was made to facilitate and encourage automatic exchange of DNA profiles between Member states in order to fight better against cross-border crimes. More recently, forensic scientists started to use DNA databases as an intelligence tool with the aim of finding relatives of unidentified offenders. Questions now arise on the forensic coding part of DNA, which could give phenotypes of offenders. Although this may raise some ethical and social issues, clearly DNA databases have revolutionized forensic science.

Digital evidence covers a wide range of media: optical, magnetic, and electronic, as well as several kinds of heterogeneous data types (audio, video, desktop applications, and proprietary format), which can make a sum of very different short stories out of the whole history of digital evidence. More globally, one common story could be the research for data information in digital evidence. Beginning in the 1970s, when the viruses were discovered on Arpanet, researchers studied these programs' functionalities and tried to discover their authors. This was not necessarily very difficult because, in most of the cases, the authors identified themselves in their program or claimed authorship for fame. Although it was first easy to analyze digital information, this work quickly became complicated with the expansion and availability of the Internet, personal computers, multiple versions of operating systems, and the explosion of data storage capacity. Fortunately, at the same time, analysis tools enabling tasks automation—such as Encase, FTK, and XWays Forensics—were developing at a similar rate. These programs retrieve information and quickly analyze huge amounts of diverse information. Today, digital evidence encompasses Internet browsing history, contents of e-mail, instant messaging records, deleted data, encrypted data, and so forth. Digital evidence can be found on personal computers, mobile phones, global positioning system devices, smart (chip-based) cards, embedded systems, identity cards, and so forth.

Throughout the world, there are now significant pressures on all forensic laboratories to implement quality management systems, and the concept of crime laboratory accreditation has gained wide acceptance in the forensic community. Accreditation is a process through which an organization becomes formally recognized to perform specific services. The laboratory seeking accreditation has to establish a structure with aims/goals, a management system, and technical facilities. All of this information is then documented in a laboratory internal quality manual. To date, there are two main accrediting bodies through which forensic laboratories are accredited around the world: The American Society of Crime Laboratory Directors/Laboratory Accreditation Board Legacy program, and the International Organization for Standardization/International Electrotechnical Commission standard 17025, which was designed for laboratories that perform testing and calibration. These national institutions are independent and duly authorized. The accreditation process is composed of three stages: the organization prepares for accreditation, then obtains it, and finally maintains it. Although the exact process varies based on the accrediting body, each organization seeking accreditation must undergo a thorough assessment conducted by a team of experts. During this assessment, the laboratory procedures and facilities are reviewed and checked against written protocols to determine compliance and noncompliance. Crime laboratory accreditation presents several advantages and drawbacks, and is an important part of creating and maintaining a comprehensive quality system. In Europe, ENFSI (European Network

of Forensic Sciences) created in 1992 encourages laboratories to comply with best practice and international standards for quality and competence assurance.

Forensic science continues to be supplemented by new fields and new tools, and is still proving its vitality and relevance. After laying down the great principles, consolidating scientific methods, and undertaking constant research to develop new techniques and new capabilities, researchers in forensic science have proved that the field is still growing and maturing. Since 1993, the US Daubert decision has laid down the principle where, before admitting expert testimony, judges have to ensure that the testimony will be reliable, that the expert has sufficient scientific knowledge, and that the expert's methods were appropriately applied to the facts at hand. Interpretation of evidence is now more questioned and appreciated by both scientists and lawyers. As a consequence, a new perspective promoting discussion on the reliability of scientific examination has developed. Far from questioning the sciences on which the examinations are based, the Bayesian probabilistic approach must help both sides in a criminal trial to better understand the value of the evidence presented by the opposing side. Paradoxically and ironically, this current evaluation phase relies on the brilliant demonstration carried out by the scientists Henri Poincare, Gaston Darboux, and Paul Appell during the appeal hearing held in the Dreyfus case. From 1963, Paul L. Kirk has pointed out the weaknesses of evidence resulting from clues and has suggested solutions to assess the validity of evidence using the implementation of strong statistical bases to assess the evidence reliability.

Although these developments could be said to call forensic science into question, these developments are actually the beneficial result of the evolution of forensic science: they secure the chain of evidence from the crime scene to the trial. The current priorities for forensic science are the application of quality assurance standards in the chain of custody, from sampling procedures to examinations; the need to supervise laboratories, the knowledge of experts and crime scene investigators; and an understanding of how hypotheses should be formulated from the facts of the case.

Forensic science developed from a very pragmatic point of view. First, there was a need to identify persistent offenders. Second, there was a need to apply technical procedures to criminal investigations and implement the lessons learned. Third, protocols and scientific methods were applied to the chain of custody, from sampling procedures through examinations. Presently, a control phase has been implemented to ensure that results are accurate. By measuring uncertainty and using a fundamental scientific review approach, to give maturity to forensic science turn out to be the next perspective that could also participate to a better understanding of the science on its own. This will give forensic science a fair role in trials in compliance with the Justice principles including equality of opportunity.

See also: **Chemistry/Trace/Forensic Geosciences:** Crime Scene Considerations; **Documents:** Handwriting; **Pattern Evidence/ Fingerprints (Dactyloscopy):** Identification and Classification.

Further Reading

Bell, S., 2008. Crime and Circumstance: Investigating the History of Forensic Science. Praeger Publishers, Westport.

Daubert vs Merrel Dow Pharmaceuticals, no 92–102 du 28 juin 1993, rendu par la Cour Suprême des Etats-Unis.

Jeffreys, A.J., Wilson, V., Thein, S.L., 1985. Individual specific fingerprints of human DNA. Nature 316, 76–79.

Kirk, P., 1974. Crime Investigation. Kriege Science against Crime London Aldus, Malabar, FL.

Kirk, P.L., 1963. The ontology of criminalistics. The Journal of Criminal Law, Criminology and Police Science 54, 236–241.

Lee, H.C., Palmbach, T., Miller, M., 2001. Henry Lee's Crime Scene Handbook. Academic Press, San Diego.

Locard E., n.d. Traité de criminalistique, vol. I à vii. Joannès Desvigne et fils Editeurs, Lyon.

National Academy of Sciences, 2009. Strengthening Forensic Science in the United States: A Path Forward. The National Academies Press, Washington, DC.

Saferstein, R., 2006. Criminalistics: An Introduction to Forensic Science (College Edition), ninth ed. Prentice Hall, NJ.

Tilstone, W.J., Savage, K.A., Clark, L.A., 2010. Forensic Science: An Encyclopedia of History, Methods, and Techniques. ABC-CLIO, Santa Barbara.

Key Terms

Analogy, Autopsy, Cause of death, Classification, Clinical examination, Clinical forensic medicine, Comparison, Crime, Crime scene investigation, Criminalistics, DNA, Documentation of medical findings, Epistemology, Evidence, Forensic, Forensic medical examiner, Forensic medicine, Forensic pathology, Forensic radiology, Forensic science, Histopathology, History, Immunohistochemistry, Information technology, Interpretation, Kirk, Locard, Manner of death, Method, Paradigm, Pioneers, Police custody, Postmortem chemistry, Reconstruction of events, Science, Set, Strangulation, Taxon, Taxonomy, Torture, Traffic medicine, Vitality and wound age assessment.

Review Questions

1. If the "basic unit of forensic science is the trace," how do general unknowns fit within this conceptual framework? What would they be a "physical remnant" of?
2. What are the three levels that Locard's principle needs to address?
3. Besides Locard's principle, what else do Crispino and Houck consider to be a "native" forensic principle?
4. What are the nonnative principles that forensic sciences uses? Give an example of each one in action.
5. What is the difference between uniqueness and individualization?
6. List at least five reasons why a clinical forensic practitioner would be required for testimony.
7. Do forensic pathologists only work on the dead? Give an example to support your answer.
8. List basic and specific information a forensic pathologist would record when examining a victim.
9. What are some of the medical hazards related to being in police custody?
10. What is probably the most common form of torture?
11. What does the word "autopsy" mean?
12. What is the primary role of a forensic pathologist?
13. How do death investigations differ by country? Are they all conducted by medical examiners?
14. What is the difference between cause and manner of death?
15. How is cause of death worded?
16. Who was Alphonse Bertillon? Why is he important to forensic science?
17. What are some of the first types of forensic evidence in history?
18. Who was Cesare Lombroso?
19. Why did Lacassagne and Locard refute Lombroso's work?
20. Who was the first person to suggest collecting fingerprints to identify offenders?

Discussion Questions

1. Why is the difference between cause and manner of death important? Which one is more medical and which is more legal in nature? Why?

2. What is the difference between a medical examiner and a coroner in the US? Why is this distinction important for death investigations?
3. When would a forensic pathologist be called to examine a living person? What could they do?
4. Why did societies turn from "divine judgment" to other forms of evidence? What kinds of evidence did they use instead?
5. Why did forensic science develop from a pragmatic point of view? How did that shape the profession?

Additional Readings

Drake, S.A., Giardino, E., Giardino, A., Nolte, K., 2016. Leadership decisions influencing medicolegal death investigation: "We wear a lot of hats." Forensic Science Policy & Management: An International Journal 7 (3–4), 51–57.

Gall, J.A., 2015. DNA and the minimum requirements for DNA contamination from a clinical forensic perspective. Pathology-Journal of the RCPA 47, S21–S22.

Levy, B., 2015. The need for informatics to support forensic pathology and death investigation. Journal of Pathology Informatics 6.

Mangin, P., Bonbled, F., Väli, M., Luna, A., Bajanowski, T., Hougen, H.P., Ludes, B., Ferrara, D., Cusack, D., Keller, E., Vieira, N., 2015. European council of legal medicine (ECLM) accreditation of forensic pathology services in Europe. International Journal of Legal Medicine 129 (2), 395–403.

Section 2. Postmortem Interval

Forensic pathology, such as other forensic sciences, is obsessively concerned with timelines and history. Knowing when a person died can often rule out various hypotheses or affirm alibis. The process of decomposition is basically entropic in nature; that is, a complex system falls apart into simpler and simpler components. Clues as to where in that devolving process a body is are sometimes faint, brief, and obscured. Establishing a postmortem interval—as opposed to a time since death—is a less precise but more accurate method. Biochemistry and the chemistry of decomposition are being researched more and perhaps will move forensic science from the morphology of death to the chemistry of dissolution.

Postmortem Interval

DH Ubelaker, Smithsonian Institution, NMNH, Washington, DC, USA

Glossary

Arthropods Invertebrate organisms of the phylum Arthropoda (includes insects, crustaceans, arachnids, and myriapods).
Barnacle Marine crustaceans.

Entomology The scientific study of insects.
Sphagnum A type of moss.

Estimation of the postmortem interval of relatively recently deceased individuals in early stages of postmortem change generally falls within the discipline of forensic pathology. Such estimations depend on observations of the condition of the soft tissues of the cadaver but often are supplemented with information from the context of the recovery site, as well as what is known regarding the deceased individual's activities during life. Accuracy is strongly correlated with time since death. As the postmortem period increases, the time range and difficulty of estimation increase as well.

In the immediate postmortem period, body temperature (algor mortis), the extent of body muscular relaxation, body stiffening (rigor mortis), skin discoloration (livor mortis), and the stages of decomposition all provide valuable clues. The early stages of decomposition include both autolysis (breakdown of tissues by digestive enzymes) and putrefaction (impact of bacterial activity). However, research and casework experience have revealed that many factors can influence these processes and complicate interpretation. Such factors include climatic conditions, clothing, body temperature at time of death, postmortem environmental context, and antemortem conditions of the individual (body size, muscular development, pathological conditions, and age at death).

With advanced decomposition and/or alteration of human remains by thermal events or fragmentation, the need for anthropological perspective becomes enhanced. This perspective relies extensively on observations of the conditions of both soft and hard tissues but is supplemented by expertise in entomology, botany, and other fields.

Entomology

Forensic entomology plays an especially important role in assessing the early stages of decomposition. Although this represents a field distinct from forensic anthropology, anthropologists frequently are involved in the recovery of entomological evidence and/or recognize the need for evaluation by entomologists. Although many different kinds of arthropods can be involved in human decomposition, the two most important groups are flies (Diptera) and beetles (Coleoptera). The flies are attracted to moist tissue and thus are early arrivals to remains. The fly larvae are responsible for considerable reduction of soft tissue. In the chain of arthropod succession, beetles generally arrive later, being attracted by more desiccated tissue. Other arthropods may also arrive to consume feeding insects. A forensic entomologist may collect adults, eggs, and larvae; identify the type of arthropod present; and use that information to assess time since death.

Blow flies (a large family of flies including the secondary screwworm fly (*Cochliomyia macellaria*), the Arctic blow fly (*Protophormia terraenovae*), green bottle fly (*Lucilia* sp.), blue bottle fly (*Calliphora vomitoria*), and bronze bottle fly (*Lucilia cuprina*)) are of particular entomological interest. Adult flies deposit large numbers of eggs that rapidly hatch. The larvae (maggots) molt into multiple instars before the formation of the puparia and the emergence of the adult. The timing of each of these growth stages has been researched, enabling this information to be used to estimate time since death. Interpretation also considers temperature and other relative information.

Botany

A variety of botanical evidence also can provide useful information if properly recovered and documented. Roots from plants growing nearby can penetrate human remains and their immediate surroundings. If properly sampled, identified, and assessed, roots can reveal a minimum time since death. In such studies, the association with the remains must be clearly established. Leaves, branches, and a variety of other plant materials also can prove useful depending upon the circumstances of the case.

Other Animal and Cultural Indicators

Anthropological assessment of postmortem interval can also be aided through many other biological materials that might be associated with human remains. Examples can include barnacle formation in marine environments and the presence of the nests of flying insects. Evaluation by the appropriate specialist may reveal the minimum time required for the evidence to have been associated with the remains.

Observations of cultural practices also may provide vital clues. Patterns of dental alteration, skull deformation, or even trephination (surgical-type alterations in crania) may suggest an ancient origin of human remains. Extreme dental wear (attrition) suggesting a very rapid rate of wear was common in ancient times but rare among modern populations. Certain types of surgical practices and orthopedic devices also can be dated, linking remains to particular periods of the past.

Tissue Morphology

Traditionally, forensic anthropologists have evaluated time since death utilizing observations on the extent of preservation of soft and hard tissues. However, casework and experimental research have revealed the complex taphonomic factors that affect soft-tissue decomposition and hard-tissue alteration, complicating this assessment. Primary influencing factors include temperature, environmental pH, amount of moisture, and oxygen availability. Other related factors include age and constitution of the individual, body treatment after death, extent and type of injury to the individual, extent of exposure to scavenging animals, protection by clothing or other materials, climate, seasonality, burial type, burial depth, and local vegetation patterns.

The timing and pattern of postmortem change demonstrate regional variation and even differences in microenvironments within regions. Dry environments can induce rapid bloating followed by extensive mummification. In contrast, a body exposed above ground in a tropical environment can be reduced to a skeleton within 2 weeks. The decomposition process can be influenced by mechanical injury as well as extensive freezing and thawing.

Although the exceptions are impressive and extensively influenced by the factors discussed above, a general sequence of postmortem alteration has been noted in temperate climates. This sequence begins with fresh remains with no discoloration and then proceeds through early decomposition and advanced decomposition and culminates in skeletonization. In their research, Megyesi et al. noted that the manifestation of these stages varies in different areas of the body. Their research indicates that, for the head and neck, early decomposition begins with a pink–white appearance with some skin slippage and hair loss. The process then proceeds to include gray to green discoloration with some retained fresh-appearing flesh. This is followed by desiccation of the nose, ears, and lips with brownish discoloration at the margins. Later, fluid is purged from the eyes, ears, nose, and mouth with some bloating of the neck and face. This stage culminates in brown to black flesh discoloration.

Advanced decomposition in the head and neck begins with a caving in of the tissues of the eyes and throat. This stage is followed by some moisture retention but less than 50% bone exposure. The remaining soft tissue then becomes desiccated.

The skeletonized stage begins with bone exposure progressing to more than 50% of the area with the presence of greasy material and some decomposing tissue. Desiccated tissue is then recognized followed by dryness of the bones themselves but with some grease retention. The final stage is represented by dry bones.

For the trunk, Megyesi et al. recognize a slightly different sequence. The early decomposition process begins with a pink–white appearance with some marbling and skin slippage. This proceeds to a gray/green discoloration with some retained fresh-appearing flesh. Bloating then occurs with green discoloration and fluid loss. A postbloating phase then involves gas release and black discoloration.

Advanced decomposition of the trunk begins with caving in of the abdominal cavity and general sagging of flesh areas followed by moist-tissue retention but less than 50% bone exposure. The remaining tissue then becomes desiccated.

The final skeletonization stage of the trunk is marked by retention of some body fluids and grease. Retained desiccated tissue then covers less than 50% of the area. This is followed by largely dry bones but with some grease retention. The final stage is dry bones.

For the limbs, Megyesi et al. note that early decomposition begins with a pink–white appearance with some skin slippage of the hands and/or feet. A gray/green discoloration then occurs with some marbling and fresh flesh retention. Desiccation of the fingers, toes, and other areas is then noted with some brown discoloration. The skin then takes on a leathery appearance with brown/black discoloration.

Advanced decomposition in the limbs begins with the presence of some moist tissue and less than 50% bone exposure. The tissue then becomes desiccated.

The skeletonization phase begins with more than 50% bone exposure with retention of some body fluids. The bones then become largely dry but with some grease retention. The final stage is dry bone.

Megyesi et al. produced not only the above detailed description of the general sequence of skeletonization of human remains, but also a method to estimate the postmortem interval. Their approach considers not only the stage of decomposition/skeletonization of the remains but also a calculation of degree days in recognition of the key role of temperature in the rate of decomposition.

In 2011, Vass proposed a more complex approach to estimate the postmortem interval. Based largely on research conducted at the University of Tennessee, Vass differentiates processes involved in remains recovered from surface context versus those from the subsurface. The Vass approach also considers temperature, but in addition, moisture and oxygen partial pressure.

Mummification

Mummification represents a variant of the postmortem process usually involving extreme desiccation. Although mummification can occur within dry microenvironments in most locations, it is most commonly associated with arid regions of the world. Since mummified/desiccated tissue is extremely resistant to further alteration as long as low humidity is maintained, its presence can complicate estimates of postmortem interval. In dry regions of the world, naturally mummified remains have

been dated to hundreds of years ago. Mummification can also result from thermal factors, chemical factors, anaerobiasis (anaerobic conditions), excarnation (defleshing), and other conditions.

Preservation by cooling represents the primary thermal factor resulting in mummification. While cool temperatures can slow the decomposition process, freezing of course prolongs preservation as long as low temperatures are maintained. Maintenance of low temperature, either accidentally, naturally, or purposefully, can complicate interpretations of postmortem interval. High temperatures also can promote rapid desiccation and mummification.

Chemical factors can include the presence of heavy metals and chelation. Mercury, copper, and arsenic have all been implicated in unusual soft-tissue preservation. Prolonged soft-tissue preservation in the vicinity of copper artifacts represents a well-known phenomenon in remains from both archeological and forensic contexts. Arsenic also represents a well-known preservative of soft tissue and historically has been used by embalmers. Chelation refers to chemical agents that combine with other materials, reducing their availability to the bacteria of decomposition. Peat bogs are well-known sources of chelating agents that facilitate long-term preservation of soft tissues. The sphagnum in peat bogs also can generate a tanning process.

Other factors that can contribute to the mummification process and long-term preservation include certain resins and spice, lime, lye, salt, and even bat guano. In ancient times, encasement of remains in plasterlike material succeeded in producing long-term preservation of soft tissue.

Adipocere

Adipocere represents a special form of mummification variously referred to as corpse wax or grave wax. Although definitions vary considerably, most recognize its tenacious nature that it can present a waxy, greasy, or crumbly appearance and can vary in consistency from soft to hard and in coloration from gray to white. It represents a form of arrested decomposition of soft tissue involving saponification of fat/adipose tissue that can preserve aspects of original morphology. The term is derived from the Latin words "adeps" (fat) and "cere" (wax), and its use can be traced back to as early as 1789 in France. Chemical analysis has detected the saturated fatty acids of palmitic, myristic, stearic, and 10-hydroxy stearic acid. Unsaturated fatty acids present include oleic, palmitoleic, and linoleic.

Although formation is usually associated with prolonged exposure of human remains to damp environments, adipocere can form in dry environments, water submersion, and cold sea water. Although adipocere most commonly forms in individuals with high body fat and in body areas with an elevated fat component, formation can occur in individuals of all ages, both sexes, and in both embalmed and unembalmed remains. Moisture presence is an important factor, but it can originate from the environment of the remains or from the body itself. Burial in soils that retain moisture can promote adipocere formation but a variety of soils may be involved. The presence of clothing that can retain moisture favors formation. Adipocere formation can be slowed or prevented if the body is protected by plastic. Although climatic conditions of the general environment are important, factors in the microenvironment of the remains are most critical. Factors favorable to adipocere formation include mildly alkaline pH, warm temperature, anaerobic conditions, and moisture. Cold temperature, lime, and aerobic conditions are limiting factors. Clearly, many factors other than postmortem interval are involved in adipocere formation.

Although early indications of adipocere formation have been detected only a few hours after death, clearly visible expressions usually require weeks. Formation of morphologically apparent adipocere has been reported between 5 weeks and 3 months.

Once formed, adipocere can remain extremely resistant to alteration as long as appropriate environmental conditions are maintained. Adipocere can be retained in remains dating back hundreds of years. However, if environmental conditions are altered, adipocere may degrade. Conditions favorable to the degradation of formed adipocere include air exposure, increased environmental moisture, fungal growth, and the presence of gram-positive bacteria. Clearly, adipocere formation complicates estimation of the postmortem interval.

Chemical Approaches

A variety of chemical approaches have been attempted to estimate the postmortem interval. Those involving analysis of bone include carbonate analysis, fluorescence, specific gravity, superconductivity, nitrogen content, quantification of amino acids, analysis of neurotransmitters and decomposition by-products, benzidine testing of bone surfaces, luminal testing, odor analysis, and X-ray diffraction studies of bone crystalline structure. Although these approaches have shown some promise, lack of definition of influencing taphonomic factors has limited their application.

In 1992, Vass et al. reported research on volatile fatty acids resulting from soft-tissue decomposition that could be detected from soil associated with human remains. Experimental research revealed that patterns of volatile fatty acids could be detected in associated soils during soft-tissue decomposition and of specific anions and cations in the skeletal phase. In consideration of degree days, this information offered useful perspective on time since death.

Some research attention also has focused on immunological approaches to evaluating time since death, the fat content

of bone, and histological techniques. Immunological approaches document the effect of time since death on properties of bone protein, but existing approaches are limited by soil contamination and other factors. Research has documented the decrease in bone fat content over time, especially within histological structures, but measures lack the precision necessary to reliably determine postmortem interval.

Radiocarbon Analysis

In the traditional application, radiocarbon dating provides a widely used approach to estimating the antiquity of relatively ancient remains. Used primarily for remains found in archeological contexts, radiocarbon analysis can provide absolute dating for remains likely of considerable antiquity. This approach recognizes that the isotope carbon-14 is mildly radioactive and decays at a predictable rate. The half-life of carbon-14 is about 5730 years. The extent of degradation is measured from the standard present in 1950. After about 50 000–60 000 years, most decay has taken place and the amount of carbon-14 is too small to accurately measure. Thus, while radiocarbon dating (using isotopic degradation) has proven useful for analysis of relatively ancient remains, it generally is not applicable to modern forensic cases, other than to document when cases thought perhaps to be of modern origin are actually of great antiquity.

In recent years, radiocarbon isotope analysis (distinct from radiocarbon dating as described above) has emerged as a very useful approach to evaluating the postmortem interval in modern remains. Atmospheric testing of thermonuclear devices during the 1950s and early 1960s unleashed large amounts of radiocarbon (carbon-14) into the atmosphere. The quantity increased sharply until 1963, when, following cessation of testing, atmospheric levels began a gradual descent. However, in 2011, the atmospheric levels remain above those documented prior to the bomb-pulse period. Through the food chain, these modern elevated levels of radiocarbon have been incorporated into the tissues of all living organisms, including humans. For this reason, elevated levels of radiocarbon represent an isotopic marker of the modern period and can distinguish tissues formed during this period from those that formed earlier. Using this knowledge in regard to recovered human remains, samples can be collected and analyzed for radiocarbon content. If elevated levels are detected, the analysis clearly indicates that the individual was alive during the bomb-curve period. Since the bomb-curve period corresponds generally to the period of forensic interest in human remains, the technique has emerged as a key contributor to postmortem interval evaluation.

Analysis basically reveals average values within the samples submitted and must consider the nature of the tissue analyzed. Dental enamel forms during the preadult years and does not remodel. Thus, even in mature adults, the radiocarbon content of dental enamel reflects dietary radiocarbon levels at the age when the dental crown formed. Bone does remodel but at different rates depending on the type of bone tissue. Cancellous bone, especially that associated with blood-forming tissue (e.g., bodies of vertebrae), remodels more rapidly than compact bone (such as that found in the outer layer of long bone diaphyses). Most soft tissues of the body, especially internal organs, remodel at much faster rates. Thus, analysis of the different tissues presents varying radiocarbon values that document different life stages of an individual. Interpretation of these values with recognition of their formation times allows proper placement on the bomb curve (older ascending portion, apex, or more recent descending portion). This information, considered with the estimated age at death of the individual, may reveal important aspects of the postmortem interval, the approximate date of death, and even the approximate birth date.

See also: **Anthropology/Odontology:** Animal Effects on Bones; Forensic Taphonomy; **Forensic Medicine/Pathology:** Early and Late Postmortem Changes; Estimation of the Time Since Death.

Further Reading

Aufderheide, A.C., 2003. The Scientific Study of Mummies. Cambridge University Press, Cambridge, UK.

Coyle, H.M. (Ed.), 2005. Forensic Botany: Principles and Applications to Criminal Casework. CRC Press, Boca Raton, FL.

Forbes, S., Nugent, K., 2009. Dating of anthropological skeletal remains of forensic interest. In: Blau, S., Ubelaker, D.H. (Eds.), Handbook of Forensic Anthropology and Archaeology. Left Coast Press, Walnut Creek, CA, pp. 164–173.

Haglund, W.D., Sorg, M.H. (Eds.), 2006. Forensic Taphonomy: The Postmortem Fate of Human Remains. CRC Press, Boca Raton, FL.

Haskell, N.H., Williams, R.E. (Eds.), 2008. Entomology and Death: A Procedural Guide, second ed. Forensic Entomology Partners, Clemson, SC.

Megyesi, M.S., Nawrocki, S.P., Haskell, N.H., 2005. Using accumulated degree-days to estimate the postmortem interval from decomposed human remains. Journal of Forensic Sciences 50, 618–626.

Ubelaker, D.H., 2001. Artificial radiocarbon as an indicator of recent origin of organic remains in forensic cases. Journal of Forensic Sciences 46, 1285–1287.

Ubelaker, D.H., Buchholz, B.A., 2006. Complexities in the use of the bomb-curve radiocarbon to determine time since death of human skeletal remains. Forensic Science Communications 8 (2), 1–9.

Ubelaker, D.H., Buchholz, B.A., Stewart, J.E.B., 2006. Analysis of artificial radiocarbon in different skeletal and dental tissue types to evaluate date of death. Journal of Forensic Sciences 51, 484–488.

Ubelaker, D.H., Zarenko, K., 2011. Adipocere: what is known after over two centuries of research. Forensic Science International 208 (1–3), 167–172.

Vass, A.A., 2011. The elusive universal post-mortem interval formula. Forensic Science International 204, 34–40.

Vass, A.A., Barshick, S., Sega, G., et al., 2002. Decomposition chemistry of human remains: a new methodology for determining the postmortem interval. Journal of Forensic Sciences 47, 542–553.

Vass, A.A., Bass, W.W., Wolt, J.D., Foss, J.E., Ammons, J.T., 1992. Time since death determinations of human cadavers using soil solution. Journal of Forensic Sciences 37, 1236–1253.

Vass, A.A., Smith, R.R., Thompson, C.V., Burnett, M.N., Dulgerian, N., Eckenrode, B.A., 2008. Odor analysis of decomposing buried human remains. Journal of Forensic Sciences 53, 384–391.

Early and Late Postmortem Changes

B Madea, University of Bonn, Bonn, Germany
G Kernbach-Wighton, University of Bonn, Bonn, Germany

Introduction

Dying and death are continuous final biological processes that have been undefined for a long time. In his work on contemporary Roman law, the well-respected nineteenth-century jurist Friedrich Carl von Savigny wrote that death represents such an elementary and natural event that has no need for closer definitions of its elements. It was not until the introduction of machines to take over circulatory or respiratory functions that the need for a legal definition of death arose, such as would protect a physician from judicial prosecution (e.g., turning off of life-support systems). Today, the accepted criteria for death are irreversible cessation of respiratory or circulatory functions, or determination of brain death following serious primary or secondary brain damage, where, in the case of brain death, functioning of the cerebrum, cerebellum, and medulla oblongata has ceased.

Supravitality

Irreversible circulatory or respiratory arrest is the main criterion for death, followed by early postmortem changes, lividity, and rigor mortis. However, metabolism of tissues does not cease immediately after death but continues for some hours. Supravitality is the survival of tissues under global ischemia. Supravital reactions are reactions of tissue on excitation which are much like those during life. The supravital period is specific for each tissue, depending on specific metabolisms (enzymes, substrates) and local temperature. The main energy-producing metabolic processes in the early postmortem period are the creatine kinase reaction and anaerobic glycolysis. Studies on global ischemia in various organs focus mainly on organ preservation and organ transplantation. The latency period is defined as an undisturbed time interval characterized by continuing aerobic energy production. The survival period is the interval to the point following which every aspect of life ceases. During the survival period, there may be spontaneous activity of organs (e.g., instantaneous but decreasing myocardial contractility), and also reagibility (e.g., response of muscles

to stimulation). The resuscitation period is defined as the duration of global ischemia after which the ability to recover expires. The resuscitation period mainly comprises the interval when complete recovery of morphological, functional, and biochemical parameters in the postischemic period is still possible. Some supravital reactions are of great practical importance in forensic medicine as they can easily be examined at the scene of crime and provide immediate results on the time elapsed since death: these are mechanical and electrical excitability of skeletal muscles and the pharmacological excitability of the iris.

Mechanical Excitability of the Muscle

The mechanical excitability of skeletal muscle is examined by rigorously hitting a muscle with the back of a knife or a chisel, for example, the biceps brachii muscle, in a perpendicular direction; other muscles can be examined as well but reference figures for estimating the time since death are available for the biceps brachii muscle only.

Electrical Excitability of the Skeletal Muscle

In the early postmortem interval, excitation causes strong contraction of muscles including those distant from the electrodes, while with increasing postmortem interval, contraction will become weaker and muscular response will be confined to the excitation location, a reaction pattern intensely involving more or less all muscles. Finally, only fascicular twitching or movement of the electrodes will be visible. The most extensive investigations have been carried out on orbicularis oculi muscles as its movements are easy to identify. For the orbicularis oculi muscle, needle electrodes are inserted in 15–20 mm distance into the nasal part of the upper eyelid at 5–7 mm depth. The muscular response is graded into six stages (**Figure 1**). In the very early postmortem stage (degree VI), the whole ipsilateral muscle will contract, whereas in degree V, only the upper and lower

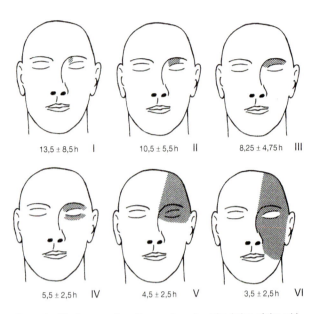

13,5 ± 8,5 h   I   10,5 ± 5,5 h   II   8,25 ± 4,75 h   III

5,5 ± 2,5 h   IV   4,5 ± 2,5 h   V   3,5 ± 2,5 h   VI

Figure 1 Six degrees of positive reaction after stimulation of the orbicularis occuli muscle (see also **Table 1**).

eyelid and forehead will respond. With increasing postmortem interval, reactions will be confined to the excitation location.

For stimulation, a small square wave generator producing constant current rectangular impulses of 300 mA at 10 ms duration is used at a repetition rate of 50 ms (producer and supplier: Peschke J, http://home.t-online.de/home/j-peschke/rztg1.htm).

Pharmacological Excitability of the Iris

Compared to skeletal muscles, the smooth iris muscle is irritable by electrical and pharmacological stimulation for a much longer period of time. In some cases, excitability by subconjunctival injection of noradrenaline or acetylcholine may persist up to 46 hpm.

Postmortem Lividity

After irreversible circulatory arrest, postmortem lividity develops as the earliest postmortem change. Following circulatory arrest, hydrostatic pressure becomes the leading force within the parallelogram of forces comprising blood pressure, structural barriers, tissue turgor, and pressure from underlying surfaces. Hypostasis means the movement of body fluids according to gravity. All compartments are involved in hypostasis, not only intravascular but transcellular fluids as well. Influenced by gravity, blood moves to the lowest parts within

the vascular system; in a supine position, it flows to the back, buttocks, thighs, calves, and back of the neck. Irregular facial pink patches, especially over the cheeks in the agonal period, are caused by local stasis. Postmortem cutaneous lividity is a consequence of movement of blood into capillaries of the corium. It may appear 20–30 min postmortem, still as pink patches in the early stages becoming gradually confluent with increasing postmortem time. Due to consumption of oxygen, the color changes from pink to dark pink or bluish.

In areas of intense hypostasis, cutaneous petechial hemorrhages due to capillary ruptures, called vibices, may develop. It is not only the development of lividity or of color that is of diagnostic and criminalistic relevance, but also its distribution, as well as the phenomena of fixation (disappearance after turning the body) and disappearance (blanching) on blunt/thumb pressure.

In case of carbon monoxide poisoning and cyanide toxicity, the color of hypostasis is typically cherry pinkish, while methemoglobin intoxication is brownish. Due to lack of dissociation of oxygen from hemoglobin, a bright pink color may be seen in hypothermia as well. In a body transferred from a cold environment into normal room temperature, typical zonal segmentation of hypostasis may be seen with a dark bluish color in the rewarmed areas.

Of predominant criminalistic significance are the phenomena of disappearance on pressure and disappearance of lividity after turning the body. In the early stages, lividity will completely disappear on soft thumb pressure, but with ongoing postmortem interval, the pressure also has to increase. Later, lividity will disappear only incompletely on pressure, and finally it will not disappear at all.

If the body is turned in the early postmortem interval, some or all of the hypostasis may move to different areas. In a comparatively later postmortem interval, only some of the hypostasis will migrate down to new areas, and only slight blanching will be noted in the original region.

With increasing postmortem time, disappearance of lividity on thumb pressure and relocation after shifting decreases and then ceases completely.

The best statistical data available for the different criteria of lividity were summarized by Mallach, who calculated mean values, standard deviations, and 95% limits of confidence based on textbook reports (**Table 1**). As better data are still missing, these data are still undisputed. However, it should be kept in mind that these data do not represent absolute thresholds. Investigations based on quantitative measurements of livor mortis have not yet gained practical importance.

Rigor Mortis

The second postmortem change and sign of death, developing in normal ambient temperature about 3–4 h postmortem after primary flaccidity, is rigor mortis, which was misinterpreted as

Table 1   Time course of different criteria of lividity. Statistical calculations by Mallach based on textbook reports. The statistical calculations are not based on cross-sectional or longitudinal studies but on empiric knowledge quoted in textbooks

	$\bar{x}$	s	2s		Range of scatter		Number of quotations
			Lower limit	Upper limit	Lower limit	Upper limit	
Development	¾	½	–	2	¼	3	17
Confluence	2(½)	1	¾	4(¼)	1	4	5
Greatest distension and intensity	9(½)	4(½)	½	18(¼)	3	16	7
Displacement							
1. Complete on thumb pressure	5(½)	6	–	17(½)	1	20	5
2. Incomplete on sharp pressure (forceps)	17	10(½)	–	37(½)	10	36	4
Displacement after turning the body							
1. Complete	3(¾)	1	2	5(½)	2	6	11
2. Incomplete	11	4(½)	2(¼)	20	4	24	11
3. Only little pallor	18(½)	8	2(½)	34(½)	10	30	7

$\bar{x}$, mean value; s, standard deviation.

the sign of death until the nineteenth century, although Shakespeare (Romeo and Juliet, Act. IV, Scene 1) described all elements of rigor mortis very well:

> Each part, deprived of supple government, shall, stiff and stark and cold, appear like death.

With irreversible circulatory arrest, all muscles will become completely flaccid due to loss of tone. In the early postmortem interval, adenosine triphosphate (ATP), the biochemical source of energy, can be resynthesized via the creatine kinase reaction and anaerobic glycolysis. Once the ATP level has fallen below 85% of the initial value, actin and myosin filaments form a complex which is not split so that the muscle remains inextensible. Development and state of rigor mortis are proven subjectively by bending a joint: either the muscles are flaccid or during development of rigor mortis some resistance may be noted. If rigor is fully developed, even a strong examiner cannot flex or stretch a joint.

Rigor must not be mixed up with cold stiffening. When rigor is present, hypostasis must be present as well, whereas in cases of cold stiffening (body core temperature 30–33 °C), hypostasis is absent.

The development and state of rigor should be examined in several joints (mandibular joint, finger, knee, elbow) to assess whether it is still in progress or has already reached its maximum.

Rigor mortis does not commence in all muscles simultaneously. Nysten's rule (1881) that rigor starts in the mandibular joint, muscles of the trunk, then in the lower, and lastly in the upper extremities applies to most cases with dying in a supine position. However, in cases with glycogen depletion during agony in the lower extremities, rigor will commence there.

Dissolution of rigor mortis is due to protein degradation (increase of ammonia, NH_3).

As in different fibers of a muscle, rigor does not start simultaneously but successively; this phenomenon can be used for a rough estimation of the time since death as well. If some of the fibers have already become stiff, this stiffness can be broken by bending a joint; rigor may now develop in other, not yet stiffened fibers. Depending on the time when stiffness has been broken, rigor may develop again on a higher or lower level unless it was already fully developed (**Figure 2**). This phenomenon of reestablishment of rigor mortis may be seen up to 6–8 h postmortem, and in very low ambient temperatures up to 12 h postmortem.

Secondary flaccidity of muscles may become apparent in normal ambient temperature after 2 days. In low ambient temperatures, fully developed rigor mortis may linger for 2 weeks and longer.

Cadaveric rigidity, cataleptic spasm, and instantaneous rigor are names for a phenomenon that is always mentioned in textbooks but nonexistent in practice. Not a single case reported in the literature withstands criticism.

Rigor mortis can be found not only in skeletal muscles but also in smooth muscles, for example, the skin. Rigidity of the smooth musculi arrectores pilorum can be seen as goose pimples (cutis anserina).

Development, duration, and dissolution of rigor mortis depend on the amount of glycogen in the muscle at the moment of death, ambient temperature, and other factors.

Therefore, rigor may develop very fast in persons who die close to exhaustion due to physical exertion or from electrocution. All of the criteria of rigor mortis mentioned earlier (e.g., development, reestablishment, full development, duration, resolution) are time dependent. This was already evident from one of the rare studies from the nineteenth century on rigor

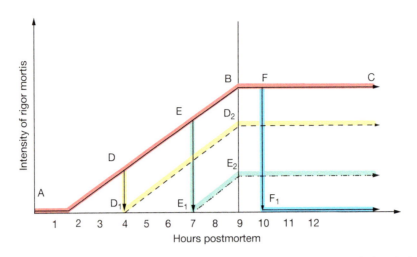

Figure 2   Reestablishment of rigor mortis after breaking. The later rigor during development of rigor mortis is broken, the lower will be the level after reestablishment. If rigor is broken after it has already been fully developed (F), it will not be reestablished at all.

mortis. Niderkorn, who determined the time necessary for the completion of rigor mortis in 113 bodies, found it fully established after 4–7 h in 76 corpses (67%). In two cases, rigidity was complete within 2 h postmortem, and in two others, within 13 h postmortem.

However, interindividual variability from endogenous and exogenous factors covers a wide range. Longitudinal studies on large random samples are missing; however, a number of animal experiments taking into account various factors influencing the time course of rigor mortis have been published. Devices for objective measurement of rigor mortis have been developed but have not yet gained practical importance.

The best available data despite all justifiable criticism originate again from Mallach, based on the compilation of literature (1811–1969) with statistical analyses (**Table 2**). These figures again cannot claim to be absolute limit values.

Table 2   Time course of different criteria of rigor mortis according to the calculations by Mallach based on textbook reports

Rigor state	Average hours postmortem and standard deviation	Range of scatter in hours (2s)		Number of quotations
		Lower limit	Upper limit	
Beginning	3 ± 2	–	7	26
Maximum	8 ± 1	6	10	28
Duration	57 ± 14	29	85	27
Complete resolution	76 ± 32	12	140	27

Like lividity, rigor mortis can give only a rough estimate, and no high accuracy can be expected. It never should be examined isolated.

Algor Mortis, Postmortem Body Cooling

If the ambient temperature is lower than the body core temperature (normally 37.2 °C), the body temperature will decrease postmortem. The postmortem drop of the body temperature results from four factors: convection, conduction, radiation, and evaporation, the first two being the leading causes.

Postmortem heat production is low as anaerobic glycolysis ceases within a few hours postmortem. Convective heat transport within the body stops with circulatory arrest. Heat exchange is then mainly based on conduction. The conductive heat transport within the body is mainly due to temperature differences of neighboring tissue layers. As the heat conductivity of body tissues is rather low, conductive heat transport within the body proceeds slowly.

The rate of cooling depends on various conditions and varies with several factors:

● ambient conditions (temperature, wind, rain, humidity)
● weight of the body, mass/surface area ratio
● posture of the body (extended or thighs flexed on the abdomen)
● clothing/covering

In case of temperature differences between body center and surface or body surface and surrounding temperature, heat transport basically takes place radially, from the axial center of

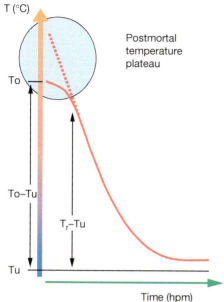

T (°C)

Postmortal
temperature
plateau

To

To–Tu

T_r–Tu

Tu

Time (hpm)

Figure 3 Sigmoid shape of the cooling curve, which is best described by Marshall and Hoare's two-exponential term. The quotient ($T_r − T_a$/$T_0 − T_a$) is a good measure of the progress of cooling. If this quotient Q is <0.3, only a minimum interval of the time since death should be given. T_0, rectal temperature at death ($T = 0$); T_r, rectal temperature at any time, and T_a, ambient temperature.

the body to the surroundings. Postmortem cooling of core temperatures (e.g., rectal temperature) is best represented by a sigmoid curve comprising three phases (**Figure 3**):

- initial phase, the so-called temperature plateau or lag period during which the body temperature remains relatively constant
- intermediate phase, with a rapid drop of the body temperature
- terminal phase, in which the drop slows down continuously as the core temperature approaches that of the environment

The postmortem temperature plateau is mainly determined by physical preconditions as it is due to the fact that central axial temperatures cannot begin to decrease until a heat gradient is set up between the core of the body and its surface. This delay is variable and may last for some hours.

Its duration depends on the same influencing factors as the exponential cooling curve following the plateau (radius, radial position of measuring site, cooling conditions). The shorter the temperature plateau, the steeper the curve drops away.

The postmortem temperature plateau causes a sigmoid shape of the cooling curves at any site of measurement far from the surface. It is a combined effect of the postmortem

temperature plateau followed by single exponential cooling according to Newton's law.

Different temperature probe sites were used (surface skin temperature, axilla, liver, rectum, brain temperatures); for practical purposes, only central core temperature. Authors in the nineteenth century, using rectal temperatures, described a lag time, the postmortem temperature plateau, before exponential body cooling according to Newton's law commences (**Figure 3**).

A mathematical expression of rectal cooling after death was published by Marshall and Hoare, taking into account the sigmoid shape of the cooling curve. They performed experiments under "standard conditions of cooling" which were defined as "naked body with dry surfaces, lying extended on a thermally indifferent base, in still air." Their mathematical model was expressed in a two-exponential term:

$$Q = \frac{T_r - T_a}{T_0 - T_a}$$

$$A \exp(Bt) + (1 - A)\exp\frac{(AB)}{A - 1}t$$

where Q, standardized temperature; T_r, rectal temperature at any time t; T_0, rectal temperature at death ($t = 0$); T_a, ambient temperature; A, constant; B, constant; t, time of death.

The second exponential term is subtracted from Newton's exponential term taking into account that temperature plateau is from zero, increasing temperature reduction.

This mathematical expression is valid for all central axial temperatures and represents the ultimate success in modeling body cooling for the purposes of estimating the time since death.

The exponential form with the constant B expresses the exponential drop of temperature following the plateau according to Newton's law of cooling; the term with the constant A as part of the exponent describes the postmortem temperature plateau.

The experimental work which led to an identification of these constants is outlined in several original papers and two monographs, which are referred to here.

With this empirical solution of Marshall and Hoare's formula, the time since death can be computed either according to

$$Q = \frac{T_r - T_a}{37.2 - T_a} = 1.25 \exp(Bt) - 0.25 \exp(5Bt)$$

(for ambient temperatures up to 23 °C) or

$$Q = \frac{T_r - T_a}{37.2 - T_a} = 1.11 \exp(Bt) - 0.11 \exp(10Bt)$$

(for ambient temperatures over 23 °C)using computer programs developed by Henssge or using a nomogram (**Figure 4**).

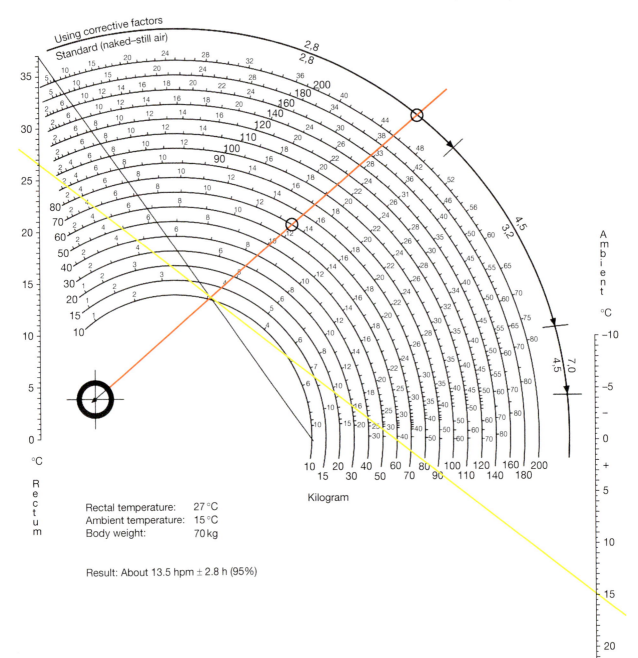

Figure 4 **Figure 4** Temperature–time of death nomogram for ambient temperatures up to 23 °C. At the scene of crime, for instance, a rectal temperature of 27 °C at an ambient temperature of 15 °C was measured. At first, the point of the scale of the measured rectal temperature and that of the ambient temperature have to be joined by a straight line (yellow) which crosses the diagonal of the nomogram at a specific point. For the second step, a second straight line has to be drawn passing through the center of the circle (lower left of the nomogram) and the intersection of the first line and the diagonal (red line). The second line crosses the semicircles for different body weights. The time since death (in this case, for 70 kg body weight) can be read off at the intersection of the semicircle of the given body weight. The intersection gives the mean time since death, and the intersection with the outer circle, the 95% limits of confidence, which may be higher if corrective factors have to be used.

The nomogram is valid for the chosen standard conditions of cooling (naked body with dry surfaces, lying extended on a thermally indifferent base, in still air). Conditions which accelerate or delay body cooling compared to standard conditions (e.g., deposition in water, wind on the one hand, clothing, covering on the other) theoretically reduce or increase the real body weight. Extensive cooling experiments under varying cooling conditions led to empiric corrective factors for the body weight (**Table 3**). With these the nomogram can also be used for nonstandard cases. The corrective factors themselves depend on the body weight in case of low and/or high body weights under higher thermic insulation conditions. Higher body weights need lower factors and, vice versa, lower weights require higher factors. The nomogram can also be used in cases of sudden changes of ambient temperatures.

From all methods developed to estimate the time since death, the nomogram method based on the double exponential term by Marshall and Hoare is by far the most successful and reliable one because

- Actual cooling conditions can be taken into consideration quantitatively.
- Data on the precision of the method are available.
- Field studies have confirmed the accuracy and reliability of the method.

Postmortem Changes

Due to their time sequence, the early signs of death in a cadaver (rigor mortis and livor mortis), along with the supravital reactions, are today instrumental in accurately determining the postmortem interval (i.e., the time elapsed since onset of death). Immediately following the early signs of decay, the later stages begin. These cannot be separated strictly chronologically. They lead not only to decomposition of the cadaver, but in some cases also to its preservation. Different exogenous and endogenous factors contribute to destruction and decomposition of a corpse. Among endogenous factors are autolysis, putrefaction, and decay, while exogenous factors include animal predation, exposure to the elements, and mechanical injury.

Onset and extent of postmortem changes are influenced by many extrinsic and intrinsic factors (**Table 4**).

Various dissimilar signs of advanced decay may appear simultaneously in a cadaver resulting from changes to the surrounding conditions. If a corpse is exposed due to its position to different environmental conditions (such as lying in a roadside ditch, half-submerged in water, half-exposed to air), varying processes of decay may occur simultaneously.

Table 3 Empiric corrective factors (c.f.) for body weights. The listed values of c.f. apply to bodies of average weight (70 kg) in an extended position on a thermally indifferent supporting base

Dry clothing/covering	Air	Corrective factor	Wet through clothing/covering wet body surface	In air	In water
		0.35	Naked		Flowing
		0.5	Naked		Still
		0.7	Naked	Moving	
		0.7	1–2 thin layers	Moving	
Naked	Moving	0.75			
1–2 thin layers	Moving	0.9	2 or more thicker layers	Moving	
Naked	Still	1.0			
1–2 thin layers	Still	1.1			
2–3 thin layers		1.2	2 thicker layers	Still	
1–2 thicker layers	Moving or still	1.2	More than 2 thicker layers	Still	
3–4 thin layers		1.3			
More thin/thicker layers	Without influence	1.4			
		–			
Thick blanket		1.8			
		–			
+		2.4			
		–			
Clothing combined		2.8			

"Thermally indifferent" supporting bases are, for example, usual floors of rooms, dry soil, lawn, asphalt. In comparison, bases which appear more thermally insulating heat than conducting should additionally be taken into account. (1) Excessively thickly upholstered bases require c.f. of 1.3 for naked bodies. In cases of clothed bodies, c.f. should be increased by 0.1 units (thickly clothed) to 0.3 units (very thickly clothed). (2) Insulating but not excessively thickly upholstered bases such as a mattress (bed) or thick carpet require c.f. of 1.1–1.2 for naked bodies. (3) Bases that accelerate cooling, for example, concrete, stony, or tiled bases on ground, require c.f. up to 0.75 for naked bodies. (4) In cases of clothed bodies lying on bases, c.f. should be reduced by 0.1 units (thicker clothes) or by 0.2 units (very thin clothes).

Table 4   Intrinsic and extrinsic factors influencing onset and extent of postmortem changes (according to Tsokos, 2005)

Acceleration of onset and extent of postmortem changes
Death occurring in a hot, moist environment/under high ambient
    temperatures
Body surface insulation by warm clothing or other covering
Considerable time interval elapsed after death until artifactual cooling of
    the body was started
Subject was overweight/had a high fat content
Subject suffered/died from underlying infection or sepsis
Subject was intoxicated (e.g., with illicit drugs such as heroin)
Subject suffered/died from open wounds (perforating/penetrating
    traumatic injuries such as stab wounds, gunshot wounds, impalement
    injuries) or during surgical procedures
Deceleration of onset and extent of postmortem changes[a]
Death occurred in a cold, dry environment/under low ambient
    temperatures
Subject was scantily dressed/naked/undressed shortly after death
Subject was stored in a cooling device shortly after death

[a] These factors decelerate the rate of postmortem changes but do not in general alter
the underlying postmortem biological processes.

Autolysis (Self-digestion)

Autolysis is defined as the destruction of an organ's structures by its own enzymes. Organs, such as the pancreas, which are already rich in enzymes in life, are thus subject to very quick self-digestion after death. Under convenient circumstances, for example, when a cadaver is stored at high temperatures, only a few hours are required to render a histological diagnosis of the organ itself impossible. Due to the effects of gastric acid, autolysis of the stomach lining occurs relatively quickly, possibly leading to complete softening. The adrenal medulla is also destroyed quite rapidly.

Putrefaction

Contrary to autolysis, putrefaction described as a "heterolytic" alkaline colliquative process on a reductive basis caused by bacteria displays typical characteristics while progressing, both visual (bloating) and olfactory (foul ammoniacal odors), due to the production of gases (hydrogen sulfide, hydrocarbons) and the release of ammonia. Body parts particularly affected by bloating from gas accumulation are all tissues with a low turgor ("liquid" pressure from within), such as eyelids, mouth, and tongue, which may become monstrously swollen. The abdomen may also become extremely swollen due to gas accumulation. Gas production is the main reason for drowned bodies soon floating at the water surface. The abdominal wall shows a greenish discoloration, resulting from production of sulf-hemoglobin as oxygen is used up by intestinal bacteria. As this process requires oxygen, the green discoloration caused by

Figure 5   Venous marbling over an arm.

sulfhemoglobin accumulation first appears over those parts of the body where the intestines lie closest to the abdominal wall, such as the lower right abdomen. Discoloration may then, however, gradually extend to the entire body surface. The spread of bacteria within the veins in subcutaneous fatty tissue and hemolysis of red blood cells causes the venous "marbling" of the skin (**Figure 5**). A further feature of putre-faction is the formation of putrefaction transudates (accu-mulations of putrefied fluids) leaking out of the dermis and causing the epidermis to detach from the dermis. Such putrefactive blisters may grow to large sizes, finally even tearing apart the epidermis, causing it to come off in shreds and exposing the dermis, which can very quickly dry out and change to brown. In addition, during putrefaction, hair and nails loosen and can then easily be pulled out. This looseness of finger- and toenails and hair found in drowned bodies is an important criterion for determining the length of time of their deposition in water. In the course of putrefaction, there is finally liquefaction of fatty tissues. Liquid fat may then leak out of the body like butter or margarine when there are skin defects, and there might be decomposition of the body's proteins (proteolysis), during which there is accumulation of biogenic amines (putrescine, cadaverine, histamine, choline, etc.) as well as cadaveric alkaloids, referred to as ptomaines (cadaveric poisoning). Even though these ptomaines have shown muscarinic atropine-like effects in tests on animals, we cannot use the term ptomaine/cadaveric poisoning to indicate that it makes the area around a putrescent corpse "toxic." Health risks from corpses, similar to those from living people, originate from infectious pathogens (tuberculosis, hepatitis, human immunodeficiency virus (HIV)), as these pathogens are able to survive the death of their host (the deceased person) (**Table 5**).

During bacterial proteolysis, certain amino acids such as delta-aminovaleric acid or gamma-aminobutyric acid can be found in brain and liver, which can be used to make a rough estimate of the time elapsed since death. Further symptoms arising from gas accumulation and gas bloating are the formation of so-called foam organs—organs permeated with gas and macroscopically detectable cavities—as well as the leaking of putrefactive fluids from mouth, nose, anus, and genitalia. In pregnant women, the pressure arising from putrefactive gas may cause the fetus to be expelled through the genitalia, a phenomenon described by the macabre term

Table 5 Morphological changes in the putrefaction phase. Aboveground exposure at 20–24 °C (68–75 °F) without insect infestation

Indication	Interval after death
Initial greenish discoloration of the abdominal skin	1–2 days
Cutaneous venous marbling	2–4 days
Beginning of filmlike slippage of the epidermis	5–6 days
Loss of pigmentation in the *stratum germinativum*	6–8 days
Putrefactive blisters and putrefactive transudates in the body cavities	8–14 days
Putrefactive emphysema in the *subcutis*	8–14 days
Bloating of abdominal cavities	8–14 days
Diffusion of all fluids, collapse of organs	Usually not until months later
Beginning of mummifying	Usually not until months later
Dehydration of soft tissues	

Please note that this table gives only rough indications for the sequence of putrefaction in cadavers exposed aboveground at a relatively narrow range of temperature. Numerous deviations are possible, depending on the body is built, the underlying surface, coverings, and terminal illness.
According to Berg, S., 2004. Todeszeitbestimmung in der spätpostmortalen Phase. In: Brinkmann, B., Madea, B. (Eds.), Handbuch Gerichtliche Medizin, Band 1. Springer, Berlin, Heidelberg, New York, pp. 191–204.

"coffin birth." While early signs of decomposition can be used for a rough estimate of the time of death, the sequence of symptoms of decay depending on previous organ disease, duration of agony, environmental conditions, especially the ambient temperature, bacterial infestation, and other factors are so variable that one cannot draw conclusions regarding the time of death (**Table 6**), but make very gross estimates only. A rule of thumb going back to the Berlin forensic physician

Johann Ludwig Casper (1796–1864)—named Casper's Law, after him—says that 1 week in air equals 2 weeks in water equals 8 weeks buried in the ground. Casper's Law thus highlights the decomposition process under different environmental conditions (air, water, earth) but does not allow precise determination of time of death.

Preservation of Decomposing Bodies

Regarding the skin, the essential signs of putrefaction are hemolysis, transudation, and accumulation of gas. It is possible to prevent signs of putrefaction for a longer period of time by special storage conditions, for which it is of utmost importance that packaging of the body or body parts is extremely airtight.

Experimental investigation of the influence of vinyl materials on postmortem alterations in rabbit and mice cadavers kept in plastic bags of different air volumes (3 l/five pints, one liter/13/4 pints, no air) at room temperature revealed a clearly delayed decomposition by storage in plastic materials. The volume of air in the bag is obviously of great importance for the progression of decay. In one particular case of a body which had been dismembered to hide evidence with the parts wrapped in plastic bags, an extremely good state of preservation after a period of 2 years allowed even positive dactyloscopic identification, despite epidermolysis (**Figure 6**). Along with the inhumation of the body parts in winter time, one factor for preservation in this case was considered to be the very airtight packing into plastic bags, together with physical covering clearly contributing to delayed decomposition processes.

Destruction of Corpses by Maggots

Maggots may contribute significantly to the destruction of a corpse (**Figure 7**). Flies may begin to lay eggs on a body even

Table 6 Criteria used in estimating the age of inhumed bones, average indications for neutral to alkaline, calcareous soil subject to weather conditions

Indication	Interval in years						
	0–5	5–10	10–20	30–50	50–100	100–1000	>1000
Odor activity	+	−	−	−	−	−	−
Impregnation of fat at the epiphyses	+	+	−	−	−	−	−
Remnants of soft tissue	+	+	(+)	−	−	−	−
Adipocere efflorescence on the surface	+	+	+	−	−	−	−
Filling of the medullary cavity	+	+	+	(+)	−	−	−
Presence of adipocere, histological	+	+	+	+	(+)		
Presence of collagen, histological	+	+	+	+	+	+	(+)
UV fluorescence	+	+	+	+	+	+	(+)
Hardness, heaviness	+	+	+	+	+	+	(+)

Reproduced from Berg, S., 2004. Todeszeitbestimmung in der spätpostmortalen Phase. In: Brinkmann, B., Madea, B. (Eds.), Handbuch Gerichtliche Medizin, Band 1. Springer, Berlin, Heidelberg, New York, pp. 191–204.

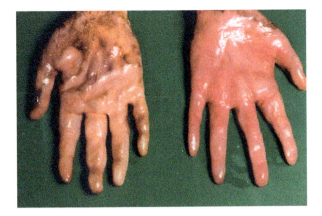

Figure 6   Body parts found in garbage bags.

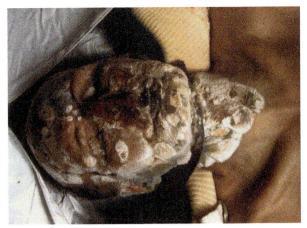

Figure 8   Mold colonizing over a cadaver.

Decomposition

Decomposition, as distinct from putrefaction, is a dry, acidic process on an oxidative basis, leading to the splitting off of acids (H_2CO_3, H_3PO_4, and H_2SO_4). Decomposition is accompanied by a rancid odor described as a musty or rotting smell. Very often colonies of mold can be found (**Figure 8**).

The Chemistry of Decomposition

While putrefaction is mainly an anaerobic bacterial reduction process, decomposition is dominated by aerobic microbiological processes, which may create pungent, rotten odors originating from the metabolic products of oxidation.

Period up to Skeletonization

The period up to skeletonization varies widely, depending on the storage conditions of the body; this has already been expressed by Casper's Law, saying that a corpse on the ground decomposes more quickly than one in water or underground, although the ratios Casper has defined are certainly also subject to numerous variations. Bodies lying on the surface of the ground are as a rule skeletonized within 1 year, and after 2 years the bones are almost completely free from soft tissues. Considerable proportions of soft part reduction during summer result from maggot infestation and animal predation. Such conditions may make a body completely skeletonized within a few weeks (**Figure 9**). If a body is stored underground, the time required for skeletonization depends essentially on the composition of the surrounding soil. Under normal conditions, with usually water-permeable, aerated soil at a depth between 1 and 2 m (3 ft 3 in. to 6 ft 6 in.), about 5–7 years are needed for

Figure 7   Development cycle of the fly: egg mass, maggots, pupae, and adult flies. Original Dr. Marco Strehler, Institute of Forensic Medicine, University of Bonn.

in the period preceding death. Depending on the ambient conditions, egg deposits can often be seen in the nostrils and in the angles of mouth and eyes. Egg deposits develop into maggots, then pupae, followed by empty pupal shells and adult flies. The development cycle lasts between 3 and 5 weeks, depending on species and temperatures. Maggots produce enzymes which can break down proteins and feed on disintegrated soft tissues. In summer, it is possible for maggots to reduce an aboveground cadaver nearly completely to a skeleton within a few weeks time. For the coroner, an additional problem is that eggs are frequently deposited in wounds to the skin while the subject is still alive, resulting in extensive destruction to the wounds with loss of evidence regarding the cause of death.

after burial, but more rarely after the third or fourth decade. Remains of clothing can be preserved for longer. With ongoing time, the originally smooth surfaces of buried bones show signs of wear. Deterioration of the bone surfaces strongly depends on the composition of the surrounding soil (**Figure 10(a)**). Bones may lie intact in graves and crypts for centuries, and several criteria allow for rough estimates of their ages (**Table 6**). Therefore, the medullary cavities of relatively recently living bones still show adipocere, whereas centuries-old bones are free of adipocere (**Figure 10(b)**). Even after soft tissues, particularly muscles and inner organs, have largely been consumed during the advanced stages of putrefaction and decomposition, there are often portions of more decay-resistant skin still present covering the bones.

Figure 9 A cadaver partially skeletonized by maggot infestation. Post-mortem interval of about 2 weeks in an apartment in summer.

complete skeletonization, although considerably longer periods have been recorded. In warmer climate, skeletonization normally happens in clearly shorter periods. Results of exhumations indicate, however, that even after burial times of 5–7 years, some bodies plus clothing were often found well preserved. In some cases, even the inner organs with the gastrointestinal tract were still intact. This is of particular importance as, among other issues, toxic substances and their routes of ingestion have to be determined. Bodies interred in crypts or sarcophagi may undergo mummification (see later). A form of interment particularly in warmer countries is the mausoleum, usually a marble-clad building with up to five aboveground rows of sealed cells. Depending on ventilation and time of interment (summer or winter), mummification or putrefaction, larval infestation, and gangrenous decay occur. The rate of decomposition is considered between that of aboveground exposure and burial in soil. Finally, special conditions apply to burials in mass graves. Even if bodies are buried together simultaneously, they may display quite different degrees of decomposition. Bodies lying at the periphery are usually extensively decomposed, while bodies at the center may still have good preservation of soft tissues (see later) with pronounced grave wax formation (see later). The bones of bodies lying aboveground are, as a rule, completely skeletonized after 1–2 years, showing no remnants of soft tissues, and no traces of cartilage or tendons. In inhumed bodies, remnants of soft tissues may still be found up to the second decade

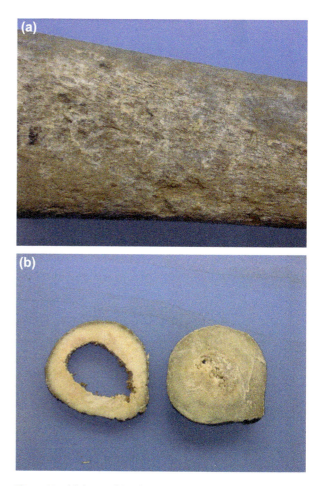

Figure 10 (a) A several-hundred-year-old bone with deterioration of the bone surface. (b) Left: Centuries-old bone (cross section) with empty medullary cavity. Right: The medullary cavity of a bone from a recently living individual, filled with adipocere.

Figure 11   Characteristic mice gnaw markings on the epidermis of the left hand.

Animal Predation

Even in the early postmortem interval, there may already be traces of animal predation, not only from rats or mice, or—in water—crabs and fish, but also from pets (dogs and cats). Mice will typically gnaw away the epidermis, leaving characteristic gnaw marks (**Figure 11**).

Extensive damage by a dog to soft tissues immediately after death can be explained by the dog's wish to obtain a reaction from its lifeless owner, first licking the face, and then, without result, behaving instinctively, biting, and mutilating.

Preservation Processes in Cadavers

While natural processes described so far (autolysis, putrefaction, and decomposition) cause dissolution and disintegration of the cadaver down to bones and tendons, special environmental conditions may preserve the body. Preservation processes include mummification and adipocere formation, which are also found in bog and permafrost corpses.

Mummification

Mummification usually takes place when the water in the body's tissues evaporates due to dryness and good ventilation. Mummification from natural processes may occur in bodies buried in churches or crypts (e.g., the lead cellar of Bremen cathedral), but it can also be seen in bodies lain at home or indoors for some time. Mummification dries the skin into a hard leathery state, dehydration sometimes causing the body to be fixed in the position it had assumed at the time of death. Furthermore, there is substantial weight loss, due to desiccation and shrinking of tissues. Rapid loss of water contributes to mummification, caused by storage in dry drafty air on a warm and dry ground. Mummification leading to leathery, hard stiffening of the skin may, under appropriate environmental conditions, begins relatively quickly (already after 2–3 days), starting at the limbs (fingers, toes, tips of the nose, and chin, ears, skin over the cheekbones). Pronounced mummification, however, as a rule, is not detectable until after several weeks.

Decomposition of the Body in the Grave—Saponification

A body buried in soil should be reduced to a skeleton after 15–20 years, at the most. It is well recognized that skeletons may remain preserved much longer (e.g., several centuries). Whether a corpse largely decomposes within this period, however, also depends mainly on properties of the soil—mineral composition and aeration—and on groundwater conditions.

Grounds where the coffins actually lie in groundwater are unsuitable for burials, or where the area of decay constantly or temporarily contains groundwater, or even areas subject to flooding used for the production of water for public use. Nevertheless, under such conditions, preservation processes such as saponification—formation of adipocere or grave wax—may occur. Saponification can be observed in bodies having lain in a completely or partially hermetic damp environment (e.g., water corpses and damp graves). During formation of adipocere, unsaturated fats (oleic acids) are converted into saturated fats (palmitic and stearic acids). Saponification begins in the skin after about 6 weeks and in muscles after 3–4 months. Entire extremities may be converted into adipocere, although this requires several months to years (**Figure 12(a)–(d)**). The term adipocere (adeps = fat, cera = wax) goes back to Fourcroy (1789) and Thouret (1792) who, during the closure of a cemetery in Paris, noticed that the bodies buried there, some in groups, had not "wasted away," but had been preserved in the same characteristic way.

Permafrost Bodies

Extensive body preservation may also occur in permanently frozen ground. Permafrost bodies were found in northern Canada, for example, in the early 1980s. The bodies were of members of the Franklin expedition in the 1840s. The cadaver found in the Hauslabjoch area of the Italian Alps ("Ötzi") is a famous frozen body from central Europe.

Bog Bodies

In bog bodies, the effects of humic acid include bone demineralization, tanning of soft tissues, and typical reddening of the hair. Due to preservation of the body surfaces, it is possible to

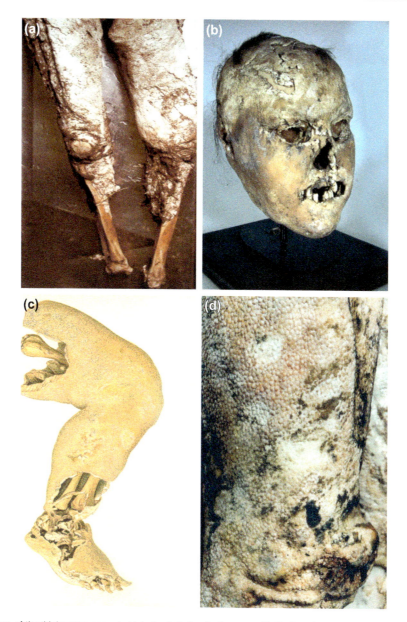

Figure 12 (a) Soft tissues of the thighs were converted into hard shells of adipocere, with the long bones hanging loosely. (b) Saponification of the head. (c) The leg of a newborn child, with saponification, after lying in flowing water for several months. The outer shape of the leg was preserved; the chalklike brittle mass, which looks like a stiff tube, contains loose bones. The muscles are missing. (d) The texture of the fat nodules in the subcutaneous fatty tissue was fixed by adipocere formation (*état mammellone*).

collect significant evidence on circumstances and cause of death. Along with the presence of tannin and humic acid, a third factor is the oxygen-poor peaty soil suppressing putrefaction processes, which thus contributes to good preservation. Along with tanning of skin and hair, some of the internal organs remain preserved, but muscle and fatty tissue usually disintegrate. The high acid content of the soil softens bones.

Bog bodies are of special value, not only archeologically, but also forensically, as evidence of injury relating to the cause of death has been saved by preservation of the body.

See also: **Forensic Medicine/Pathology:** Autopsy; Estimation of the Time Since Death; External Postmortem Examination.

Further Reading

Aufderheide, A.C., 2003. The Scientific Study of Mummies. Cambridge University Press, Cambridge.

Beattie, O., Geiger, J., 1992. Der eisige Schlaf. Das Schicksal der Franklin-Expedition. München Zürich: Piper (originally published 1987 as: Frozen in Time: The fate of the Franklin expedition by Bloomsbury Publishing Ltd., London).

Berg, S., 2004. Todeszeitbestimmung in der spätpostmortalen Phase. In: Brinkmann, B., Madea, B. (Eds.), Handbuch Gerichtliche Medizin, Bd. 1. Springer, Berlin, Heidelberg, New York, pp. 191–204.

Doberentz, E., Madea, B., 2010. Estimating the time of immersion of bodies found in water – an evaluation of a common method to estimate the minimum time interval of immersion. Revista Española de Medicina Legal 36 (2), 40–50.

Dotzauer, G., 1958. Idiomuskulärer Wulst und postmortale Blutung. Dtsch Z Gesamte Gerichtl Medical Journal 46, 761–771.

Haglund, W.D., Sorg, M.H., 1997. Forensic Taphonomy. CRC Press, Boca Raton.

Henssge, C., 1988. Death time estimation in case work. I. The rectal temperature time of death nomogram. Forensic Science International 38, 209–236.

Henssge, C., 1992. Rectal temperature time of death nomogram: dependence of corrective factors on the body weight under stronger thermic insulation conditions. Forensic Science International 54, 51–56.

Henssge, C., 2002. Temperature based methods II. In: Henssge, C., Knight, B., Krompecher, T., Madea, B., Nokes, L. (Eds.), The Estimation of the Time Since Death in the Early Postmortem Period, second ed. Edward Arnold, London.

Henssge, C., Knight, B., Krompecher, T., Madea, B., Nokes, L., 2002. The Estimation of the Time Since Death in the Early Postmortem Period, second ed. Edward Arnold, London.

Henssge, C., Madea, B., 1988. Methoden zur Bestimmung der Todeszeit an Leichen. Schmidt-Römhild-Verlag, Lübeck.

Henssge, C., Madea, B., 2004. Estimation of the time since death in the early postmortem period. Forensic Science International 144, 167–175.

Henssge, C., Madea, B., 2004. Leichenerscheinungen und Todeszeitbestimmung. In: Brinkmann, B., Madea, B. (Eds.), Handbuch Gerichtliche Medizin, Bd. I. Springer, Berlin, Heidelberg, New York, pp. 79–150.

Henssge, C., Madea, B., 2007. Estimation of time since death. Forensic Science International 165, 182–184.

Klein, A., Klein, S., 1978. Todeszeitbestimmung am menschlichen Auge (M.D. thesis). Dresden University, Dresden.

Krause, D., 2004. Späte Leichenveränderungen. In: Brinkmann, B., Madea, B. (Eds.), Handbuch Gerichtliche Medizin, Bd. 1. Springer, Berlin, Heidelberg, New York, pp. 150–170.

Krompecher, T., 2002. Rigor mortis: estimation of the time since death by the evaluation of the cadaveric rigidity. In: Henssge, C., Knight, B., Krompecher, T., Madea, B., Nokes, L. (Eds.), The Estimation of the Time Since Death in the Early Postmortem Period, second ed. Edward Arnold, London, pp. 144–160.

Madea, B., 1994. Importance of supravitality in forensic medicine. Forensic Science International 69, 221–241.

Madea, B., 2002. Muscle and tissue changes after death. In: Henssge, C., Knight, B., Krompecher, T., Madea, B., Nokes, L. (Eds.), The Estimation of the Time Since Death in the Early Postmortem Period. Edward Arnold, London, pp. 134–208.

Madea, B., 2005. Is there recent progress in the estimation of the postmortem interval by means of thanatochemistry? Forensic Science International 151, 139–149.

Madea, B., 2009a. Death: time of. In: Jamieson, A., Moenssens, A. (Eds.), Wiley Encyclopaedia of Forensic Sciences, vol. 2. John Wiley and Sons Ltd., Chichester, pp. 697–716.

Madea, B., 2009b. Time of death determination. In: Jamieson, A., Moenssens, A. (Eds.), Wiley Encyclopaedia of Forensic Sciences, vol. 5. John Wiley and Sons Ltd., Chichester, pp. 2466–2479.

Madea, B., Henssge, C., 2003. Timing of death. In: Payne-James, J., Busuttil, A., Smock, W. (Eds.), Forensic Medicine: Clinical and Pathological Aspects. Greenwich Medical Media Limited, London, pp. 91–114.

Madea, B., Preuss, J., Musshoff, F., 2010. From flourishing life to dust – the natural cycle of growth and decay. In: Wieczorek, A., Rosendahl, W. (Eds.), Mummies of the World. Prestel, Munich, Berlin, London, New York, pp. 14–29.

Mallach, H.J., 1964. Zur Frage der Todeszeitbestimmung. Berliner Medizin 18, 577–582.

Marshall, T.K., Hoare, F.E., 1962. I. Estimating the time of death. The rectal cooling after death and its mathematical expression. II. The use of the cooling formula in the study of postmortem body cooling. III. The use of the body temperature in estimating the time of death. Journal of Forest Science 7, 56–81, 189–210, 211–221.

Pounder, J., 2000. Postmortem interval. In: Siegel, J.A., Saukko, P.J., Knupfer, G.C. (Eds.), Encyclopaedia of Forensic Sciences, vol. 3. Academic Press, San Diego, pp. 1167–1172.

Spindler, K., Wilfing, H., Rastbichler-Zissernig, E., Zurnedden, D., Nothdurfter, H., 1996. Human Mummies. A Global Survey for the Status and the Techniques of Conservation. Springer, Wien, New York.

Tsokos, M., 2005. Postmortem changes and artefacts occurring during the early postmortem interval. In: Tsokos, M. (Ed.), Forensic Pathology Reviews, vol. 3. Humana Press, Totowa, pp. 183–237.

Wieczorek, A., Rosendahl, W. (Eds.), 2010. Mummies of the World. Prestel, Munich, Berlin, London, New York.

Estimation of the Time Since Death

B Madea, University of Bonn, Bonn, Germany

Introduction

Estimation of the time since death is a practical task in daily forensic casework. The main objective is to give the police a first estimation on the time since death already at the place where the body was found. Methods of estimating the time since death should be of course as precise as possible but even more important is reliability. The main principle of determining the time since death is the calculation of a measurable date along a time-dependent curve back to the start point. Characteristics of the curve (e.g., the slope) and the starting point are influenced by internal and external and antemortem and postmortem conditions. Therefore, the estimation of the time since death will never reveal a time point but an interval.

Methods of estimating the time since death are based on two different approaches:

- Which antemortem changes, either physiological or pathological, can be detected and allow, together with police investigations, a conclusion on the time since death (survival time)?

Methods such as wound age estimation and gastric emptying when time and volume of the last meal are known follow this approach.

- Which postmortem changes allow a conclusion to be made on the time since death?

Most methods which are used in practice follow this second approach.

There is a huge literature on methods proposed for estimating the time since death. However, most have never gained practical importance.

The methods proposed for estimating the time since death are completely different in nature:

- Predominantly physical processes such as body cooling and hypostasis
- Metabolic processes, for example, concentration changes of metabolites, substrates, activity of enzymes
- Autolysis (loss of selective membrane permeability, diffusion according to Fick's law with increase or decrease of analytes in various body fluids, morphological changes)
- Physicochemical processes (supravital reagibility, rigor mortis, immunological reactivity)
- Bacterial processes (putrefaction)

Furthermore, the methods for estimating the time since death are not only different in nature, but have a widely differing scientific value concerning the underlying scientific background, the mode of investigation, and the validation of the method.

The highest scientific value is of course attributed to methods with a quantitative measurement of the postmortem changes, with a mathematical description which takes into account influencing factors quantitatively. Clear data on the precision of the method are available, and these data have been proved on independent material and in field studies.

On the other hand, the lowest scientific evidence for death time estimation is acquired by methods that provide just a subjective description of the postmortem change. The progression of postmortem change is entirely dependent on ambient factors. However, these ambient factors cannot be taken into account quantitatively.

For estimating the postmortem interval (PMI) during criminal investigations, different sources are used (Pounder):

1. Evidence on the body of the deceased (postmortem changes)
2. Information from the environment in the vicinity of the body (date of the newspaper, open TV program)
3. Anamnestic factors concerning the deceased's habits (leaving the apartment, arriving at work, day-to-day activity)

For the forensic investigation of the time since death, all sources of information on the time since death should always be used, though the focus of the forensic pathologist is of course the postmortem changes.

Temperature of Corpses

From all methods of death time estimation, postmortem body cooling has been studied most extensively and some of the investigations in the following list fulfill the criteria for high-quality research:

Quantitative measurement, mathematical description, taking into account influencing factors quantitatively, declaration of precision, and proof of precision on independent material.

The cooling of bodies is mainly a physical process and the factors affecting the rate at which a body cools after death were identified long ago.

For estimation of the time since death only central core temperatures such as rectal temperature or brain temperature should be taken as a surface can cool down already during life (**Figure 1**). The Glasgow professor, Henry Rainy, was one of the first to realize that Newton's law of cooling does not describe the decrease of rectal temperature due to the postmortem temperature plateau. Rainy transferred Newton's rule of cooling to the cooling of bodies and, thus, he considered the environmental temperature. By measuring the temperature several times, he could even determine experimentally the individual steepness of temperature decrease. Furthermore, he had already identified the postmortem temperature plateau as the declination of the single-exponential model and he consequently identified the estimated time since death using Newton's law as minimum time. By multiplication with 1.5, he revealed also a maximum time.

It was not before the two-exponential model of Marshall and Hoare in 1962 that a real breakthrough could be noticed: the exponential term with exponent p stands for the postmortem temperature plateau and that with exponent Z for the Newton-part of cooling after the plateau:

$$\frac{T - T_u}{T_0 - T_u} = e^{-Zt} - e^{-pt} = \frac{P}{p - Z}e^{-Zt} - \frac{Z}{Z - p}e^{-pt}$$

where T is the deep rectal temperature (°C); T_0 is the rectal temperature at death, fixed at 37.2 °C; T_u is the ambient temperature (°C), t is the time of death (h); $Z = 0.059 - 0.00059 \ (0.8 \ AM^{-1})$ with A, body surface according to DuBois and M, body weight; $P = -0.4$.

In 1974, Brown and Marshall demonstrated that more than two-exponential terms complicated the model without leading to more precise results. With this model, Marshall could individually determine time of death by a single measurement of the rectal temperature considering body proportions and (constant) ambient temperature under standardized conditions of cooling (unclothed, not covered, standing air, stretched supine position). Surprisingly, this breakthrough in death time determination did not meet with great response. The new model was only described in a general application report and included in one textbook.

Rectal Temperature Time of Death Nomogram

A further breakthrough was achieved with the investigations by Henssge who presented a simplified method to determine the Newton cooling coefficient. He determined statistical figures for the deviation between calculated and real death times for cooling under standardized conditions. These data on the precision were at first valid for standard conditions of body cooling:

● naked body with dry surfaces
● lying extended on the back
● on a thermally indifferent base
● in still air
● in surroundings without any source of strong heat radiation
● in constant ambient temperature

Furthermore, Henssge extended the application spectrum of the double-exponential formula to different cooling conditions by using empirical body weight correction factors and published nomograms for reading the time since death instead of calculating it.

From all methods of estimating the time since death, the nomogram method by Henssge based on body cooling after death is the most intensively investigated, most precise, and reliable procedure. For the application of the nomogram method in case work, the following points have to be taken into consideration:

Inspection of the body posture, clothing, covering, sunshine on the body, windows (closes, opened: when?), radiators, floor (thermally indifferent?) on the scene of crime.

Measurement of ambient temperature (air) close to the body and at the same level (10–20 cm above the base);

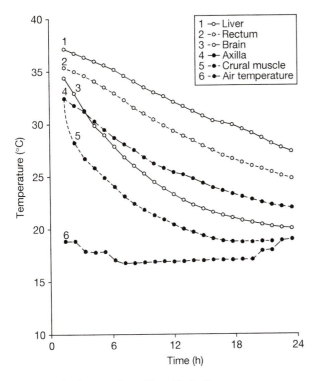

Figure 1 Cooling curve from different body sites.

Legend of figure:
1 –○– Liver
2 –◦– Rectum
3 –◇– Brain
4 –●– Axilla
5 –●– Crural muscle
6 –●– Air temperature

Axis labels: Temperature (°C) (vertical), Time (h) (horizontal)

measurement of the temperature of the underlying surface as well. Have any changes of thermic conditions been made since the body was found?

Single measurement of deep rectal temperature at the scene using an officially calibrated electronic thermometer with probes for measuring air, surface, and rectal temperature. The deep rectal temperature must at least be measured 8 cm within the anal sphincter.

Estimation of the body weight. At autopsy control to check whether the estimation was correct.

Evaluation of the corrective factor. Are there any conditions which accelerate or delay cooling compared to standard conditions? For rectal temperature, thermic conditions of the lower trunk only are relevant:

- clothing/covering
- resting or moving air
- kind of supporting base
- in cases of strong insulation conditions and very high or low body weight, the corrective factor must be adapted to the body weight
- use of the nomogram

Requirements for use:

- no strong radiation (e.g., sun, heater, cooling system)
- no strong fever or general hypothermia
- place of death must be the scene where the body was found
- no uncertain severe changes of the cooling conditions in the period between death and examination
- no high thermal conductivity of the surface beneath the body

- longer agonal period after fatal injury (time since death may be inconsistent with the time of assault)

Connect the points on the scales for rectal and ambient temperature by a straight line. This line crosses the diagonal at a particular point. Draw a second straight line going through the center of the circle below left of the nomogram and the intersection of the first line and the diagonal. The second line crosses the semicircles which represent the body weight. At the intersection of the semicircle with the body weight, the time of death can be read. The second line touches a segment of the outmost semicircle. Here the permissible variation of 95% can be seen for standard cases or cases using corrective factors.

The nomogram was at first constructed for chosen standard conditions of cooling (naked body with dry surfaces, lying extended on a thermally indifferent base in still air). Conditions with improved or delayed body cooling compared to standard conditions reduce or increase the real body weight. Extensive cooling experiments under varying cooling conditions led to empirically found corrective factors for body weight (**Table 1**). With these corrective factors, the nomogram can be used for nonstandard cases as well. Systematic examination revealed that higher correction factors (e.g., for clothes and/or blankets) have to be used for lower body weights. That means that corrective factors themselves are dependent on the body weight. Higher body weights need lower factors and, vice versa, lower weights need higher factors. Furthermore, the nomogram can also be used in cases of sudden change of ambient temperature and in cases with ranges of the ambient temperature and the corrective factor. This nomogram was developed for ambient temperatures below 23 °C. For ambient

Table 1 Empiric corrective factors for body weight

Dry clothing/covering	Air	Corrective factor	Wet through clothing/covering wet body surface	In air	In water
		0.35	Naked		Flowing
		0.5	Naked		Still
		0.7	Naked	Moving	
		0.7	1–2 thin layers	Moving	
Naked	Moving	0.75			
1–2 thin layers	Moving	0.9	2 or more thicker layers	Moving	
Naked	Still	1.0			
1–2 thin layers	Still	1.1	2 thicker layers	Still	
2–3 thin layers		1.2	More than 2 thicker layers	Still	
1–2 thicker layers	Moving	1.2			
3–4 thin layers	or	1.3			
More thin/thicker layers	Still	1.4			
	Without influence	–			
Thick blanket		1.8			
+		–			
Clothing combined		2.4			
		2.8			

temperatures above 23 °C, another nomogram was developed based on the published material of De Saram et al.

Brain Temperature Time of Death Nomogram(s1)

The two-exponential model by Marshall and Hoare was also suitable for the mathematical description of the brain temperature drop curve:

$$\frac{T_{Brain} - T_u}{37.2 - T_u} = 1.135e^{-0.127t} - 0.135e^{-1.07t}$$

According to the rectal temperature time of death nomogram, a brain temperature time of death nomogram was constructed. Up to 6.5 h postmortem, the most precise computation of time of death was achieved by the exclusive application of brain temperature, which gave a time of death within ±1.5 h (95% confidence limits). Between 6.5 and 10.5 h postmortem, the brain/rectum-combined computation of time of death balanced in the ratio of 6–4 was the most precise one, at ±2.4 h. Beyond 10.5 h postmortem, the most precise computation of time of death was achieved by exclusive application of rectal temperature, which gave a time of death within ±3.2 h.

Field Studies

Meanwhile, both a single center and a multicenter study on the accuracy of the nomogram method compared to the investigations of the police were carried out. Both studies covered a wide range of ambient temperatures, body weights, and corrective factors. The estimated period did not contradict the investigated period in any of the cases. Especially in the early stages, police investigations can be greatly supported by this method.

Cooling Dummy

More than 20 years ago, a cooling dummy which reproduces almost exactly the cooling of corpses was developed. With this dummy, cooling can be simulated in any condition, for example, even at the location where the body was found. The cooling dummy is an essential help in cases when body cooling under rare cooling conditions has to be evaluated.

Compound Method

From all methods of death time estimation, the nomogram method is the most intensively investigated, most precise, and reliable procedure. However, in the best case, a precision of ±2.8 h around the mean value (95% confidence limits) can be

achieved. Therefore, other methods of death time estimation should be used to narrow down this range further (electrical and mechanical excitability of skeletal muscles; chemical excitability of the iris; lividity and rigor mortis) (**Table 2**). But how to use the different data on various time-dependent postmortem changes?

Mean values do not represent the time frame in which a special degree of postmortem changes may be positive. For instance, the mean value of degree IV of electrical excitability of the orbicularis oculi muscle is 5.5 h; however, it may be positive between 3 and 8 h. Therefore, not the mean values but the upper and lower range should be used for death time estimation. For case work, the data of the described times of death and supravital reactions were, together with the signs of death estimation, based on the nomogram rearranged into a special chart which facilitates the choice of the subsequent helpful criteria in an actual case (**Figure 2**). In casework, the examination begins with taking rectal and ambient temperatures and choosing the appropriate corrective factor and a first estimation of the time since death using the nomogram. Concerning temperature measurements and choosing the appropriate corrective factor, see the chapter on early and late postmortem changes. Then the further criteria are examined. Especially those criteria are of interest which can narrow down the time frame by the nomogram method further. Using this chart at the scene of crime or a computer program, it is guaranteed that nothing will be forgotten and the inspection and examination of the body is efficient and complete concerning death time estimation. For instance, at the scene of crime, the nomogram method reveals a death time between 4.5 h (lower limit) and 10.5 h (upper limit) (**Figure 3**). The lower limit can be confirmed or improved only by a criterion with a higher value than 4.5 h, and the upper limit can be reduced only by a criterion with a lower value than 10.1 h. The electrical excitability of facial muscles (musculus orbicularis oculi) showed a positive reaction according to degree IV; that means time since death was below 8 h. Therefore, the upper limit of death time estimation (10.1 h) could be reduced to 8 h. In the early postmortem period especially, the combined application of the nomogram method and electrical excitability of facial muscles increases the precision of death time estimation from body cooling alone. Even if the result of the nomogram method is not improved but just confirmed, this confirms also the self-confidence of the investigator in his opinion and statement of the time since death as his estimation is based on two independent criteria. If the nomogram method must not be used, for example, in cases of hypothermia or fire in the setting where the body was found, the other methods may give reliable results on the death time estimation.

A recent field study on the compound method on 72 consecutive cases over a long-lasting PMI revealed that in 49 cases the limits of the period since death by the temperature methods were improved by the nontemperature methods. The

Table 2   Table for estimation of the time since death based on supravital reactions and postmortem changes

		Time after death (hpm)
Electrical excitability		
Musculus orbicularis oculi	VI Upper and lower eyelid + forehead + cheek	1–6
	V Upper and lower eyelid + forehead	2–7
	IV Upper and lower eyelid	3–8
	III Whole upper eyelid	3.5–13
	II 1/3 to 2/3 of the upper eyelid	5–16
	I Upper eyelid local around the puncture electrodes	5–22
Musculus orbicularis oris		3–11
Thenar muscle		Up to 12
Hypo thenar muscle		Up to 12
Pharmacological excitability of the iris		
Mydriatica	Noradrenalin/adrenalin	14–46
	Tropicamid	5–30
	Atropine/cyclopent	3–10
Miotica	Acetylcholine	14–46
Drop of body core temperature (rectal temperature)	At first temperature plateau of 2–3 h, thereafter approximately 0.5–1.5 $°C\ h^{-1}$, depending on ambient temperature, clothing, covering, body proportions, weather conditions (wind, rain)	
Drying of the cornea (open eyes)	After 45 min	
Drying of the cornea (closed eyes)	After 24 min	
Postmortem lividity		
Beginning	After 15–20 min	
Confluence	~1–2 h	
Maximum	After a few hours (~6–8)	
Complete displacement on thumb pressure	~10 h (10–20 hpm)	
Displacement after turning the body	~10 h	
Rigor mortis (jaw)	After 2–4 h	
Complete rigidity	After 6–8 h	
Beginning of resolution	After 2–3 days depending on the ambient temperature	
Reestablishment possible	Up to 8–12 hpm	
Complete resolution	After 3–4 days, in deep ambient temperatures, rigor mortis may be preserved much longer	

degree of electrical excitability was the most valuable additional method, but the classical signs of death may improve the nomogram results as well.

Further Methods

Vitreous Potassium

There is huge literature especially on chemical methods of death time estimation. Among these are many in vitro methods. Most chemical methods of death time estimation have a factor in common that they are of no value in practice. While the earlier studies were mainly carried out on blood and cerebrospinal fluid (CSF), for more than 60 years, most investigations have been performed on vitreous humor (VH). This is mainly due to the fact that VH is topographically isolated and well protected and, thus, autolytic changes proceed slower compared to blood and CSF. The most studied parameter in VH is potassium. Postmortem rise of the potassium concentration (K^+) in VH has been known for 50 years and has been recommended for the estimation of the time since death. However, the practical application has been hampered by different results concerning the accuracy of death time estimation. Optimistic results of early investigations with an accuracy of death time estimation of ±9.4 h in a time period up to 104 h postmortem could not have been confirmed by succeeding investigations.

The correlation and the strength of correlation between K^+ and the time since death depend on different factors such as cause of death, duration of agonal period, ambient temperature, etc. These factors influencing the accuracy of death time estimation can partly be taken into consideration by using internal standards (urea concentration as an indicator of an antemortem electrolyte dysregualtion). For example, in cases with electrolyte dysregulation due to impaired renal function, the precision of death time estimation by vitreous potassium is

CASE   DATE   TIME

p. m *Lividity*

Beginning	YES	☐	0	< 3 ☐	NO
Confluence	YES	☐	> 1	< 4 ☐	NO
Maximum	YES	☐	> 3	< 16 ☐	NO
Thumb pressure	NO	☐	> 1	< 20 ☐	YES

Rigor mortis

Beginning	YES	☐	> 0.5	< 7 ☐	NO
Maximum	YES	☐	> 2	< 20 ☐	NO

Electrical excitability

I Upper eyelid	NO	☐	> 5	< 22 ☐	YES
II $\frac{1}{3}$ – $\frac{2}{3}$ upper eyelid	NO	☐	> 5	< 16 ☐	YES
III Whole upper eyelid	NO	☐	> 3.5	< 13 ☐	YES
IV Plus lower eyelid	NO	☐	> 3	< 8 ☐	YES
V Plus forehead	NO	☐	> 2	< 7 ☐	YES
VI Plus cheek	NO	☐	> 1	< 6 ☐	YES
Orbicularis oris muscle	NO	☐	> 3	< 11 ☐	YES

Nomogram

1 2 3 4 5 6 7 8 9 10 11 12 13 14 15 16 17 18 19 20 21 22

Routine

Supplement

Idiomuscular contraction	NO	☐	> 1.5	< 2.5 ☐	YES	Zsako's phenomenon
Complete displacement of Livores after turning the body	NO	☐	> 2	< 6 ☐	YES	Complete displacement of livores
Re-establishment of rigor	NO	☐	> 2	< 8 ☐	YES	Re-establishment of rigor
Atropine/Cyclopent	NO	☐	> 3	< 10 ☐	YES	Atropine/Cyclopent
Incomplete displacement of Livores after turning the body	NO	☐	> 4	< 13 ☐	YES	Idiomuscular contraction
				< 24 ☐	YES	Incomplete displacement of livores after turning the body
Mydriaticum Roche	NO	☐	> 5	< 30 ☐	YES	Mydriaticum Roche
Acetylcholine	NO	☐	> 14	< 45 ☐	YES	Acetylcholine

RESULT   [>]   [<]

TIME OF DEATH   between   [   ]   and   [   ]

Figure 2   Integrating chart for casework at a scene of crime.

CASE 11/87		DATE 12.1.87		Time 10.00

p. m Lividity

Beginning	YES	☐	0	< 3	☐ NO
Confluence	YES	☐	> 1	< 4	☐ NO
Maximum	YES	☒	> 3	< 16	☐ NO
Thumb pressure	NO	☐	> 1	< 20	☒ YES

Rigor mortis

Beginning	YES	☐	> 0.5	< 7	☐ NO
Maximum	YES	☒	> 2	< 20	☐ NO

Electrical excitability

I Upper eyelid	NO	☐	> 5	< 22	☐ YES
II $\frac{1}{3}-\frac{2}{3}$ upper eyelid	NO	☐	> 5	< 16	☐ YES
III Whole upper eyelid	NO	☐	> 3.5	< 13	☐ YES
IV Plus lower eyelid	NO	☐	> 3	< 8	☒ YES
V Plus forehead	NO	☒	> 2	< 7	☐ YES
VI Plus cheek	NO	☐	> 1	< 6	☐ YES
Orbicularis oris muscle	NO	☐	> 3	< 11	☐ YES

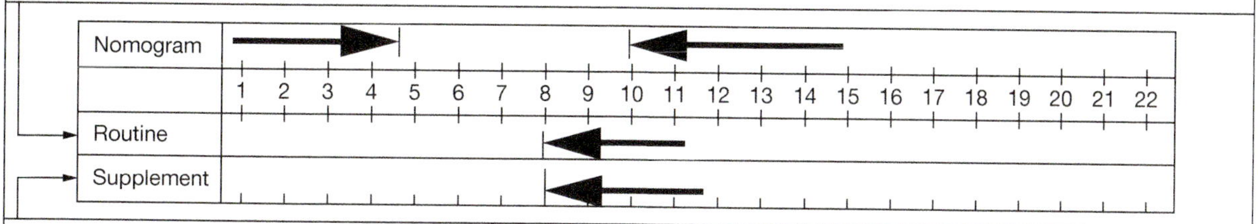

Nomogram / Routine / Supplement scale 1–22

Idiomuscular contraction	NO	☐ > 1.5	< 2.5	☐ YES	Zsako's phenomenon
Complete displacement of Livores after turning the body	NO	☐ > 2	< 6	☐ YES	Complete displacement of livores
Re-establishment of rigor	NO	☐ > 2	< 8	☒ YES	Re-establishment of rigor
Atropine/Cyclopent	NO	☒ > 3	< 10	☐ YES	Atropine/Cyclopent
Incomplete displacement of Livores after turning the body	NO	☐ > 4	< 13	☐ YES	Idiomuscular contraction
			< 24	☐ YES	Incomplete displacement of livores after turning the body
Mydriaticum Roche	NO	☐ > 5	< 30	☐ YES	Mydriaticum Roche
Acetylcholine	NO	☐ > 14	< 45	☐ YES	Acetylcholine

RESULT   > 4,5   < 8

TIME OF DEATH   between   02.00   and   05.30

Figure 3 Integrating chart for casework at a scene of crime with an example.

lower than in cases with normal renal function. However, even in the most favorable case, precision of death time estimation is ±22 h up to 5–6 days postmortem.

In most investigations on vitreous potassium, the PMI has been used as the independent and K^+ as the dependent variable in linear regression analysis between PMI and K^+. According to a recommendation of Munoz et al., however, K^+ should be used as the independent variable for regression analysis. According to the authors, this approach leads to a higher accuracy of death time estimation. This could be confirmed by own calculations.

Another statistical approach has reevaluated six large studies on the rise of vitreous K^+ using a local regression analysis (Loess procedure). Based on this reevaluation, an accuracy of death time estimation has been recommended (95% limits of confidence of ±1 h in the early PMI and ±10 h, 110 h postmortem) which has surpassed even optimistic results of earlier investigations. This recommended accuracy of death time estimation has been checked on an own random sample of 492 cases. Only 153 cases have been within the predicted PMI, while 339 lay outside with a systematic overestimation of the time since death. Furthermore, the accuracy of death time estimation cannot be confirmed. As the precision of death time estimation by vitreous potassium is low, the author knows of no case worldwide where this method has been used as evidence for the PMI. The amount of literature on vitreous potassium is reciprocal to its practical importance.

Gastric Contents and Time Since Death

Although examination of gastric contents is mentioned as a method to determine the time since death nearly in every textbook, gastric content alone allows only a rough estimation of the interval between the last meal and death. Time and size of the last meal have to be known to derive conclusions on the survival time between last food intake and death. State of digestion and the distribution of the last meal in the stomach and upper intestine have far long been proposed as a method to estimate the time since death. Even if the volume of the last meal is not known, the type of the meal (breakfast, lunch, dinner) may allow rough estimation of the daytime when death occurred. Gastric emptying has been studied and quantified in the last decades using different methods (radiologic, intubation, aspiration, radio isotopes, ultrasound, absorption kinetics of orally administered solutes, pheromagnetic traces). Liquids leave the stomach much faster than solids. While gastric emptying obviously follows an exponential function for liquids, solids show a linear emptying pattern. The following gastric emptying times are given in the literature: 1–3 h for a light small-volume meal; 3–5 h for a medium-sized meal; 5–8 h for a large meal. However, it must be kept in mind that different anatomical and functional disorders cause delayed or rapid gastric emptying. According to a review by Horowitz and Pounder, only solid components of a mixed solid and liquid meal should be considered and the weight of the stomach content should be compared with an estimated weight of the last meal and reference made to the known 50% emptying times for the solid components of meals of various sizes.

Putrefaction

Putrefaction is a bacterial process, predominantly influenced by environmental factors, mainly ambient temperature, but by underlying diseases and body proportions as well. Medical treatment with antibiotics in the terminal phase may delay putrefactive changes. Otherwise, in cases of sepsis, advanced putrefaction may be seen soon after death. Advanced stages of putrefaction may be seen within a few hours after death which, in moderate or cold climate, are not seen after weeks. Even in relatively constant ambient temperatures, the progression of putrefaction varies considerably (**Table 3**). Therefore, putrefactive changes are not a sound method for estimation of the PMI.

Recently, there seems to have been a change, since methods developed in radiology such as H magnetic resonance spectroscopy (MRS) have been applied for the identification of metabolites emerging during decomposition of brain tissue as a step toward quantitative determination of PMIs in putrefaction.

Brain decomposition resulted in reproducible concentration changes of known metabolites and the appearance of decay products that had to be characterized first.

Table 3   Progression of putrefaction of bodies in air, temperature of about 20 °C

Progression of putrefaction of bodies in air, temperature of about 20 °C	
After 1–2 days	Green discoloration of abdominal wall, softening of eyeballs.
After 3–5 days	Dark green discoloration of great parts of the abdominal wall. Some patchy green discolorations of the skin of other body regions. Bloody fluid leaking out from mouth and nostrils. Marbling.
After 8–12 days	Whole body surface dark green. Face, neck, and thoracic wall partly reddish green. Bloating of abdomen, scrotum, and face. Fingernails still fixed. Hair loose, begins to peel.
After 4–20 days	Whole body green or reddish brown. Bloating of the whole body. Blisters, partly filled with putrefactive fluid, partly burst with desiccation of the dermis. Eyes (iris, pupil, sclera) reddish brown discolored. Fingernails peeling.

The investigations on postmortem decompositions by H MRS may represent a real progress in research for the following reasons:

- A noninvasive chemical analysis in situ is possible with quantitation of analytes.
- Longitudinal studies of postmortem changes with reproducible results are possible.
- The sheep model seems to be valid for human brains as well.
- With this model, influencing factors such as temperature can be easily studied.
- The definition of analytical functions for the time courses of 10 metabolites up to 400 h postmortem was successful.
- Prediction of PMI based on the combination of five metabolites correlates very well with true time postmortem up to 250 h postmortem.
- These metabolic changes cover a PMI where no other method allows a quantitative calculation of the time since death with any acceptable degree of certainty.

Putrefaction in Water

For bodies recovered from water, quite a good and reliable method for estimating the minimum and maximum water time has been developed based on putrefactive changes which are visible at external examination or at the dissection of the body.

This is mainly due to the fact that water temperature is relatively constant over a longer period of time and during day and night, while air temperature differs not only from day to night but from one day to the other. Morphological findings which are taken into consideration for the estimation of duration of immersion in immersed bodies are listed below:

External findings

1. Rigor mortis
2. Lividity
3. Marbling
4. Bloating of face, scrotum, subcutaneous tissue
5. Discoloration of skin (green, black, reddish)
6. Loss of epidermis
7. Loss of hairs
8. Hands
   (a) washerwomen's skin
   (b) loosening of nails
   (c) peeling of skin
   (d) loss of nails
9. Feet
   (a) washerwomen's skin
   (b) loosening of nails
   (c) peeling of skin
   (d) loss of nail

Internal findings

1. Volume of transudate in pleural cavity
2. Heart without blood
3. Liquefaction of brain

The warmer the water, the sooner a definite stage of putrefaction is achieved. From the mean water temperature for each month and the stages of decomposition, the German forensic pathologist Reh developed a chart with the minimum time intervals of immersion. Considering all 16 parameters for estimating the minimum time of immersion, the chart provided in **Table 4** can be used. On the left side are the useful criteria: in the first line the months, in the second line the mean water temperature, and in the following line the minimum time interval in days.

As many criteria as possible should be used for estimating the minimum time interval since death. With more than only one or two criteria, the result will become more reliable. For estimating the minimum time interval, the mean water temperature which is nearest to the actual water temperature at the time of recovery should be used. With this chart, not only the minimum time interval of immersion can be estimated but also the maximal interval by considering those criteria which have not yet developed. If, in June, marbling, bloating, and discoloration of the body have developed, and the nails are loose but not lost, it may be concluded that the interval of immersion is over 3 days but below 8 days. Our personal experience with this chart is quite good as it is much better than the old rules of thumb because it takes the actual temperature for the progression of putrefaction into consideration.

A recent evaluation of own cases revealed that the actual water temperatures (of the river Rhine) have risen during the last 40 years. Especially in summer, reliable results can only be expected when the actual water temperature is similar to the temperatures in the table. Therefore, for higher water temperatures, the time interval of immersion may be underestimated when using the table since systematic observations on the progression of putrefaction in correlation to the elevated water temperature are missing. Therefore, the table should be adapted to the elevated water temperatures.

Immunohistochemical Detection of Insulin, Thyroglobulin, and Calcitonin

Although morphological methods on death time estimation are of no practical value in forensic practice, there seems to be some change by the application of immunohistochemistry methods. Wehner et al. studied whether a positive immunoreaction to various antigens such as insulin, thyroglobulin, or calcitonin is correlated with the time since death. The

Table 4   Chart to estimate the minimal time interval of immersion

Month	January	February	March	April	May	June	July	August	September	October	November	December
Ø Median water temperature (°C)	3.5	3.9	5.8	9.9	13.0	17.4	18.6	18.6	17.3	13.2	8.8	4.7
1. Marbling	32	25	16 (23)	9–10	4–5	2	1–2	2	3	4–5	10	17
2. Distension of tissues by gas	35	25	16 (23)	10	4–5	2–3	2	3	3–4	7	10	17
3. Discoloration of the body	35	25	16 (23)	(14)	4–5	2	2	3	3–4	7	10	17
4. Peeling of the epidermis	35	25	16 (23)	(16)	4–5	3	2	3	3–4	7	10	17
5. Hair lost	35	25	16 (23)	10–12	4–5	2–3	2–3	3	3–4	7	10	17
6. Hands: beginning of wrinkling	(1)	(1) 28–30	(12 h)			(6 h)			2 h		2 h	(1)
7. Nails become loose	Over 35	(40) 30–32	23	16	5	2–3	3	3	3–4	11	17	28
8. Peeling of skin in glove form	35	(45)	23	16	10	3	3	3–4	4	7	20	28
9. Nails lost	Over 53	45	30 (40)	21	14	8	3	4	10	Over 11	20	Over 35
10. Feet: beginning of wrinkling	(1)	(1)	(12 h)	(1)		(6 h)	0.5 h		2 h		2 h	(1)
11. Nails become loose	Over 53	40	26 (35)	17	10	5	3	4	8	12	17	28
12. Peeling of skin	Over 53	60	35	16	10	5	3	5–6	8–9	Over 11 (14)	20	28
13. Nails lost	Over 53	Over 60	53	Over 35	Over 28	Over 10	3	Over 10	Over 10	Over 11	Over 20	Over 35
14. Transudate in pleural cavity[a]	35	25 (40)	18 (35)	10	5	3–4	3	3	11	5	Over 20	
15. Heart without blood	Over 39	32–34 (40)	23	14–15	9	4	3	3	5	11	20	28
16. Brain liquefied	35	30 (40)	(23)	14–16	5	3–4	3	3	6	10	17	28

First line: months; second line: median water temperature for the month; left column: signs of putrefaction and maceration; following columns: minimal time interval in days. If, for example, in July, marbling, distension of tissues by gas, discoloration of the body, peeling of the epidermis, loosening of finger and feet nails, peeling of the skin of hands and feet, and a liquefied brain are observed, the minimum time interval of immersion would be about 2–3 days.
[a]Volume over 500 ml.

philosophy of these investigations is that with increasing PMI the tertiary structure of the antigen undergoes postmortem changes and due to protein denaturation stainings become negative.

Meanwhile, a chart was developed to give a rough estimation on the time since death by immunohistochemical methods.

See also: **Forensic Medicine/Pathology:** Autopsy; Early and Late Postmortem Changes; External Postmortem Examination.

Further Reading

De Saram, G.S.W., Webster, G., Kathirgamatamby, N., 1955. Post-mortem temperature and the time of death. The Journal of Criminal Law and Criminology 46, 562–577.

Henssge, C., 1988. Death time estimation in case work. I. The rectal temperature time of death nomogram. Forensic Science International 38, 209–236.

Henssge, C., 1992. Rectal temperature time of death nomogram: dependence of corrective factors on the body weight under stronger thermic insulation conditions. Forensic Science International 54, 51–56.

Henssge, C., 2002. Temperature based methods II. In: Henssge, C., Knight, B., Krompecher, T., Madea, B., Nokes, L. (Eds.), The Estimation of the Time since Death in the Early Post-mortem Period, second ed. Edward Arnold, London.

Henssge, C., Althaus, L., Bolt, J., et al., 2000. Experiences with a compound method for estimating the time since death. I. Rectal temperature nomogram for time since death. II. Integration of non-temperature-based methods. International Journal of Legal Medicine (6), 303–319, 320–331.

Henssge, C., Beckmann, E.R., Wischhusen, F., Brinkmann, B., 1984. A determination of time of death by measuring central brain temperature. Zeitschrift für Rechtsmedizin 93, 1–22.

Henssge, C., Knight, B., Krompecher, T., Madea, B., Nokes, L. (Eds.), 2002. The Estimation of the Time since Death in the Early Postmortem Period, second ed. Edward Arnold, London.

Henssge, C., Madea, B., 1988. Methoden zur Bestimmung der Todeszeit an Leichen. Schmidt-Römhild-Verlag, Lübeck.

Henssge, C., Madea, B., 2004a. Estimation of the time since death in the early postmortem period. Forensic Science International 144 (2–3), 167–175.

Henssge, C., Madea, B., 2004b. Frühe Leichenerscheinungen und Todeszeitbestimmung im frühpostmortalen Intervall. In: Brinkmann, B., Madea, B. (Eds.), Handbuch Rechtsmedizin, Bd. I. Springer, Berlin/Heidelberg/New York, pp. 79–150.

Horowitz, M., Maddern, G.J., Chatterton, B.E., Collins, P.J., Harding, P.E., Sherman, D.J.C., 1984. Changes in gastric emptying rates with age. Clinical Science 67, 213–218.

Horowitz, M., Pounder, D.J., 1985. Gastric emptying – forensic implications of current concepts. Medicine, Science, and the Law 25, 201–214.

Ith, M., Bigler, P., Scheurer, E., et al., 2002a. Observation and identification of metabolites emerging during postmortem decomposition of brain tissue by means of in situ ^{1}H-magnetic resonance spectroscopy. Magnetic Resonances in Medicine 48, 915–920.

Ith, M., Bigler, P., Scheurer, E., et al., 2002b. Identification of metabolites emerging during autolysis and bacterial heterolysis of decomposing brain tissue by ^{1}H-MRS in situ and in vitro. Proceedings of the International Society for Magnetic Resonance in Medicine 10, 580.

Knight, B., 2002. The use of gastric contents in estimating time since death. In: Henssge, C., Knight, B., Krompecher, T., Madea, B., Nokes, L. (Eds.), The Estimation of the Time since Death in the Early Postmortem Period, second ed. Edward Arnold, London, pp. 209–215.

Madea, B., 1992. Estimating time of death from measurement of electrical excitability of skeletal muscle. Journal of the Forensic Science Society 32, 117–129.

Madea, B., 1994. Importance of supravitality in forensic medicine. Forensic Science International 69, 221–241.

Madea, B., 2002. Gastric contents and time since death. In: Henssge, C., Knight, B., Krompecher, T., Madea, B., Nokes, L. (Eds.), The Estimation of the Time since Death in the Early Postmortem Period, second ed. Edward Arnold, London, pp. 215–225.

Madea, B., 2005. Is there recent progress in the estimation of the postmortem interval by means of thanatochemistry? Forensic Science International 151, 139–149.

Madea, B., 2009a. Death: time of. In: Jamieson, A., Moenssens, A. (Eds.), Wiley Encyclopaedia of Forensic Sciences, vol. 2. John Wiley and Sons Ltd., Chichester, pp. 697–716.

Madea, B., 2009b. Time of death determination. In: Jamieson, A., Moenssens, A. (Eds.), Wiley Encyclopaedia of Forensic Sciences, vol. 5. John Wiley and Sons Ltd., Chichester, pp. 2466–2479.

Madea, B., Henssge, C., 1990. Electrical excitability of skeletal muscle postmortem in casework. Forensic Science International 47, 207–227.

Madea, B., Henssge, C., 2002. Eye changes after death. In: Henssge, C., Knight, B., Krompecher, T., Madea, B., Nokes, L. (Eds.), The Estimation of the Time since Death in the Early Postmortem Period, second ed. Edward Arnold, London.

Madea, B., Henssge, C., 2003. Timing of death. In: Payne-James, J., Busuttil, A. (Eds.), Forensic Medicine: Clinical and Pathological Aspects. Greenwich Medical Media Limited, London, pp. 91–114.

Madea, B., Herrmann, N., Henssge, C., 1990. Precision of estimating the time since death by vitreous potassium – comparison of two different equations. Forensic Science International 46, 277–284.

Madea, B., Käferstein, H., Herrmann, N., Sticht, G., 1994. Hypoxanthine in vitreous humour and cerebrospinal fluid – a marker of postmortem interval and prolonged (vital) hypoxia? Remarks also on hypoxanthine in SIDS. Forensic Science International 65, 19–31.

Madea, B., Rödig, A., 2006. Time of death dependent criteria in vitreous humor – precision of estimating the time since death. Forensic Science International 164, 87–92.

Mallach, H.J., Mittmeyer, H.J., 1971. Totenstarre und Totenflecke. Zeitschrift für Rechtsmedizin 69, 70–78.

Musshoff, F., Klotzbach, H., Block, W., Traeber, F., Schild, H., Madea, B., 2010. Comparison of post-mortem metabolic changes in sheep brain tissue in isolated heads and whole animals using ^{1}H-MR spectroscopy – preliminary results. International Journal of Legal Medicine. http://dx.doi.org/10.1007/s00414-010-0463-3 published online 07 May 2010.

Pounder, J., 2000. Postmortem interval. In: Siegel, J.A., Saukko, P.J., Knupfer, G.C. (Eds.), Encyclopaedia of Forensic Sciences, vol. 3. Academic Press, San Diego, pp. 1167–1172.

Prokop, O., 1975. Supravitale Erscheinungen. In: Prokop, O., Göhler, W. (Eds.), Forensische Medizin. Volk und Gesundheit, Berlin, pp. 16–27.

Scheurer, E., Ith, M., Dietrich, R., et al., 2003. Statistical evaluation of ^{1}H-MR spectra of the brain in situ for quantitative determination of postmortem intervals (PMI). Proceedings of the International Society for Magnetic Resonance in Medicine 11, 569.

Scheurer, E., Ith, M., Dietrich, D., et al., 2005. Statistical evaluation of time-dependent metabolite concentrations: estimation of postmortem intervals based on in situ ^{1}H MRS of the brain. NMR in Biomedicine 18 (3), 163–172.

Tröger, H.D., Baur, C., Spann, K.W., 1987. Mageninhalt und Todeszeitbestimmung. Schmidt-Römhild, Lübeck.

Tsokos, M., 2005. Postmortem changes and artifacts occurring during the early postmortem interval. Forensic Pathology Reviews 3, 183–237.

Wehner, F., Wehner, H.D., Schieffer, M.C., Subke, J., 1999. Delimitation of the time of death by immunohistochemical detection of insulin in pancreatic b-cells. Forensic Science International 105, 161–169.

Wehner, F., Wehner, H.D., Schieffer, M.C., Subke, J., 2000. Delimitation of the time of death by immunohistochemical detection of calcitonin. Forensic Science International 122, 89–94.

Wehner, F., Wehner, H.D., Subke, J., 2001. Delimitation of the time of death by immunohistochemical detection of thyroglobulin. Forensic Science International 110, 199–206.

Relevant Websites

http://www.rechtsmedizin.uni-bonn.de—For the practical application of Henssge's nomogram, no photocopies from the nomogram of textbooks should be used since there might be photocopier/scanner distortions. The nomograms can be downloaded from the homepage of the Institute of Forensic Medicine, University of Bonn.

http://shadow.pohn.kom—Those who use an iPhone or blackberry "App" should look this website.

http://home.t-online.de—Square wave generators can be purchased online.

Vital Reactions and Wound Healing

P Betz, University of Erlangen-Nuremberg, Erlangen, Germany

Physiology of Skin Wound Healing

Wound healing is a type of inflammation and characterized by an inflammatory response and repair processes induced by the tissue damage. These reactive changes can be divided into an initial vascular phase, in cellular reactions, and proliferative changes, which were mediated by the time-dependent appearance and disappearance of a lot of different molecules detectable in the cellular and extracellular matrix. The different phases of these tissue complex reactions were recently described in detail under forensic aspects by Cecchi.

Early Vascular Phase

Immediately after severe tissue trauma, fibrin occurs in the damaged area as a result of the clotting process. However, fibrin can be induced up to approximately 6 h after death, so fibrin detection does not unambiguously provide evidence of the vitality of a wound, even though some authors assume that vital fibrin reactions can be distinguished from postmortem ones by morphological criteria.

Every relevant tissue alteration is followed by an early vascular reaction. This forensically very interesting phase starts with an activation of endothelial cells triggered by different mediator substances such as leukotrienes, prostaglandins, nitric oxide, and plasma proteases, for example. The release of these mediators leads to changes in tissue perfusion and to an enhanced vascular permeability, which enables, in particular, an interaction between the endothelium and hematogenous leukocytes. The extracellular communication is hereby related to soluble mediators such as adhesion molecules (selectins, interstitial cell adhesion molecule (ICAM)), different growth factors such as platelet-derived growth factor, transforming growth factor, vascular endothelial growth factors, epithelial growth factors, fibroblast growth factors (FGFs), and so on, vascular cell adhesion molecules (VCAMs), chemokines, and cytokines (IL-1β, IL-6, and IL-8), which were produced by several cell types.

The cascade of cytokines also regulates the induction of cell adhesion molecules and selectins on activated endothelial cells and is, therefore, involved in the migration of leukocytes out of the vascular space. In this context, ICAM-1 acts as a ligand of the leukocyte function-associated antigen (LFA-1), whereas VCAM-1 is a ligand of the very late activation antigen 4 (VLA-4).

Different selectins are responsible for the attachment of the leukocytes at the vascular endothelium. After margination, the leukocytes actively permeate the vessel wall, attracted by several chemotactic agents such as degraded proteins, complement complexes, lymphokines, leukotrienes, thromboxanes, fibrin, and fibronectin and produce for themselves mediators, for example, different interleukins or tumor necrosis factor. In addition to these cellular and extracellular localized processes, fibronectin is involved in leukocyte migration because of its chemotactic properties, but it also provides a provisional matrix for migration of the leukocytes. It is synthesized by fibroblasts, endothelial cells, macrophages, and keratinocytes and shows a high affinity to collagen subtype III. Fibronectin enhances the attachment of fibroblasts and endothelial cells and seems to be involved in angiogenesis as well as in contraction of the granulation tissue (**Figure 1**).

Cellular Reactions

On such a provisional matrix, in particular, poly-morphonuclear (PMN) cells infiltrate, followed by macrophages, chemotactic agents such as degraded proteins, complement, lymphokines, and thromboxanes are attracted to the damaged area. The PMN cells contribute to lysis of erythrocytes and phagocytosis of necrotic tissue by the release of proteinases and lysozyme, respectively. They also influence the permeability of the capillaries.

Although the migration of neutrophils and macrophages begins simultaneously, the reduced mobility of macrophages explains their later appearance in the wound area. However, neutrophils, which predominate in the early phase of the cellular reaction, rather quickly disappear from the lesion area, so that macrophages now dominate. In addition to the process of cell infiltration, changes in the stage of cell activation occur, which can be detected by quantification of RNA and DNA synthesis. The infiltrating cells also release hydrolytic enzymes, complement, and arachidonic acid derivates, and they are mainly responsible for the phagocytosis of necrotic tissue. Depending on the material incorporated, several subtypes can be identified after a few days. Lipophages show a typical foamlike cytoplasm, whereas erythrophages are characterized by the presence of incorporated erythrocytes (**Figure 2**).

Inside the macrophages, the erythrocytes and their hemoglobin are degraded. This degradation process is induced by

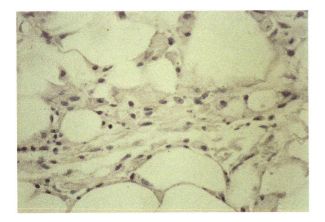

Figure 1   Lipophages in a 21-day-old lesion, hematoxylin and eosin stain, 350×.

microsomal hemoxygenase and siderin results. This pigment, which is blue, can be detected in Prussian blue-stained sections and it is easily distinguished from crystallized bilirubin, so-called hematoidin. In contrast to hemosiderin, this pigment seems to be quickly reabsorbed and it is infrequently seen during wound healing.

Macrophages can be divided into several subtypes with respect to their different phagocytic activities, and also according to the time-dependent expression of different immunohistochemically detectable antigens, for example, early- (27 E 10), intermediate- (RM 3/1), late- (25 F 9), and chronic (G 16/1)-stage inflammation markers.

Although lymphocytes are mainly involved in chronic inflammation, they also play a part in healing wounds even though this is the subject of debate. Different definitions of a positive result and difficulties in distinguishing lymphocytes

from neutrophils by routine histological methods may be the reasons for reported differences. Therefore, only relevant lymphocytic infiltrates should be regarded as a reactive change.

In the area of the lesion, leukocytes, mainly PMN, and activated monocytes release proteins such as monokines and growth factors that, in combination with other factors such as fibrin degradation products, stimulate the proliferation and activation of fibroblasts.

Proliferative Changes

Proliferation can be detected by demonstration of the nuclear antigen Ki 67, which is expressed in the G_1-, G_2-, S-, and M-phases of the cell cycle and also occurs during physiological regeneration. Under pathological conditions, for example, in wound healing, enhanced proliferative activity can be observed.

Cell proliferation in physiological or pathological conditions is closely associated with apoptosis. Apoptotic changes can be demonstrated by detection of the $p53$ tumor suppressor gene, which arrests the cell in the G_1- or G_2-phase to enable DNA reparation. If the reparation processes are unsuccessful, $p53$ initiates apoptosis and as a result, DNA fragments can be found.

Fibroblasts proliferate, and also migrate into the wound area attracted by the chemotactic properties of collagen fragments, fibronectin, complement, and lymphokines. The activation of fibroblasts is mediated by fibrin or fibrin degradation products, respectively, but also by growth factors, thrombocytes, and macrophages. Activated fibroblasts are characterized by enhanced enzyme activities detectable by enzyme histochemical techniques. Under forensic conditions, a time-dependent increase in the activity of adenosine triphosphatase, nonspecific esterase, aminopeptidase, and acid as well as alkaline phosphatase has been investigated (**Figure 3**).

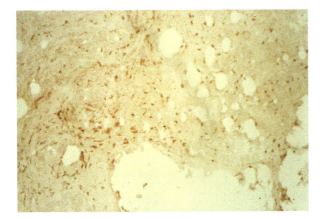

Figure 2   Nonspecific esterases in a 4-h-aged skin wound, 180×.

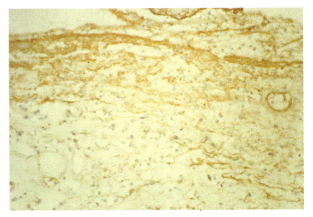

Figure 3   Fibronectin-positive networks with infiltrating granulocytes, 3-day-old skin wound, 180×.

Additionally, activated fibroblasts synthesize several extracellular matrix components such as cell adhesion molecules (e.g., tenascin), which are mainly expressed during embryogenesis, and also in malignant tumors and during wound healing. Owing to its typical structure-combining domains of epidermal growth factor, fibronectin, and fibrin, tenascin seems to be involved in cell migration and in the regulation of cell adhesion as well as acting as a mitogenic stimulus.

Some fibroblasts differentiate into myofibroblasts, which are contractile due to their actin content. They are involved in stabilizing and contracting the granulation tissue by the expression of different basement membrane components such as laminin, heparan sulfate proteoglycan, and collagen type IV.

Fibroblasts also synthesize proteins to replace necrotic tissue, in particular, different collagen subtypes. Collagens are proteins of the extracellular matrix with different molecular structures and are responsible for different biological functions. Collagen I is characterized by considerable mechanical properties, whereas collagen III seems to be involved in wound contraction. Collagen V participates in the migration of capillary and endothelial cells during angiogenesis and mediates cell–substrate adhesion by binding on heparan sulfate proteoglycan. Collagen VI mediates the attachment of interstitial structures in the connective tissue- and cell-binding activities (**Figure 4**).

At the same time, as the damaged connective tissue is being repaired, keratinocytes are stimulated and activated in order to cover the epidermal defect by migration and proliferation. Migrating keratinocytes, which also contain actin-like contractile elements, are derived from intact superficial keratinocyte layers and from adjacent skin appendages. They also use a provisional matrix of fibrin and fibronectin, which is replaced by a basement membrane after reepithelialization is complete. The basement membrane collagen types IV and VII are responsible for the mechanical stabilization of the newly built epidermis, whereas laminin and heparan sulfate proteoglycan are involved in cell–cell and cell–substrate interactions. The basement membrane components are mainly synthesized by the migrating keratinocytes, in contrast to the interstitial collagen subtypes, which are produced by fibroblasts (**Figure 5**).

Afterward, the keratinocytes differentiate: the keratinocytes can be seen by the expression of keratin subtypes or other markers such as involucrin, filaggrin, and transglutaminase.

The initial cell-rich granulation tissue characterized by numerous fibroblasts and developing blood vessels is finally transformed into a permanent scar. During this process, enhanced apoptosis is responsible for cell reduction.

Principles of Forensic Wound Age Estimation

As discussed, every phase of the healing process is characterized by the chronologic but overlapping appearance and disappearance of several reactive changes and the time-dependent detection of these features is the basis of every wound age estimation.

Even though the age of a certain lesion cannot be determined precisely due to various factors influencing the rapidity of the reparation process, such as individual age, malnutrition, malignant, or severe metabolic disorders, the postinfliction interval of a wound can be approximately estimated by different criteria and the reliability of the statement depends on the number of evaluated parameters.

The earliest appearance of such a variable established in systematic investigations determines the minimum age of a lesion with a positive reaction. If a variable regularly occurs in a specific time interval (regular appearance), that is, such a reaction can be detected in every "control" specimen investigated, a postinfliction interval of less or more than that

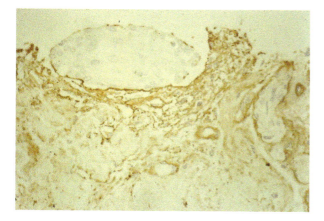

Figure 4 Collagen VI-positive networks in an 11-day-old human skin wound, 180×.

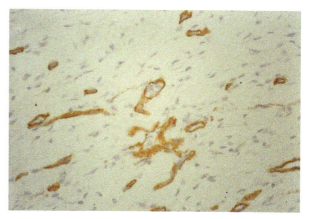

Figure 5 Collagen IV-positive basement membranes in new forming vessels, 16 days of wound age, 350×.

specific time interval is indicated. The latest appearance of a reaction can principally contribute to the estimation of advanced wound ages. However, this criterion is considerably influenced by the initial extent of the wound area and, therefore, it is of limited diagnostic value. From a practical point of view, it is almost exclusively the earliest appearance of reactive changes that is of forensic relevance since the diagnostic value of a positive finding considerably exceeds that of the negative results, which may be absent in a section of the specimen but present in other parts of the lesion.

Independent of what technique is used, one of the most important conditions for a forensically useful age estimation of wounds is a clear evidence of a positive reaction. Morphological features similar to postmortem changes are without diagnostic value.

In forensic practice, in particular, morphological features are useful for wound age estimation and they can be detected by routine histological, enzyme histochemical, or immunohistochemical techniques. Routine histological staining procedures, for example, hematoxylin and eosin staining or the Prussian blue reaction, can easily be performed but a specific and unambiguous detection of several reactive changes is not always possible. The number of variables that can be demonstrated by enzyme histochemistry is also reduced and an irregular appearance of positive findings must be taken into consideration even though the advantage can be seen in the resistance to putrefaction. Immunohistochemistry is more sensitive to autolysis, depending on the antigen investigated, but allows specific detection of numerous parameters expressed during the healing process.

Immunohistochemically detectable reactions, however, must be evaluated critically with respect to nonspecific background staining or other artifacts. Typical networklike structures distant from the wound margins and outside the bleeding zone can be regarded as positive for the immunohistochemical detection of fibronectin, tenascin, or interstitial collagens, for example. Furthermore, the collagen reaction must be associated with fibroblasts because of the presence of destroyed connective tissue fibers in the damaged area. Negative as well as

Table 1   Parameters of vitality of human skin wounds (postinflection interval <30 min)

Variable	Earliest occurrence (min)
TGF-β1, IL-8	>1 min
P-selectin	>1 min
TNF-α positive mast cells	5
BFGF, defensin 3	10
Fibronectin	10–20
IL-1β, IL-6, TNF-α	15–20
Neutrophil granulocytes	15–30

BFGF, basic fibroblast growth factor; *TGF*, transforming growth factor; *TNF*, tumor necrosis factor.

Table 2   Variables of shorter postinflection intervals in human skin wounds (30 min–24 h)

Variable	Earliest occurrence
VCAM-1	30 min
ICAM-1	50–60 min
Antitriptase- and antichymase-positive mast cells	1 h
Enhanced enzyme activity in fibroblasts	~2 h
Anti-27E10-positive macrophages	2–3 h
IL-1α-, IL-8-, MCP-1-, MIP-α-positive neutrophils	4 h
Ubiquitin-positive neutrophils	4 h
Macrophages > neutrophils	20 h

VCAM, vascular cell adhesion molecule; *ICAM*, interstitial cell adhesion molecule.

positive controls to prove the specificity of a reaction are necessary. Specimens showing relevant background staining cannot be evaluated.

The quality of the sections is also of very importance and it is only in optimally thin sections that a reliable evaluation is possible. In addition, a sufficient number of specimens per skin wound (in our opinion at least three specimens) must be investigated to confirm a negative finding. However, as aforementioned, conclusions based on positive findings are to be preferred. In addition, the histomorphological techniques have

Table 3   Variables of advanced postinflection intervals in human skin wounds (>24 h)

Variable	Earliest occurrence
Fibroblast proliferation	1.5 days
Fibroblast apoptosis	1–2 days
Myofibroblast expression of laminin heparan sulfate, proteoglycan	1.5 days
Tenascin	2 days
Migrating keratinocytes	2 days
Collagen III	2–3 days
Collagen V, VI	3 days
Lipophages, erythrophages	3 days
Siderophages, hemosiderin	3 days
Granulation tissue	3 days
p53-positive fibroblasts	3 days
Myofibroblast expression of collagen IV	4 days
Basement membrane fragments	4 days
Myofibroblast expression of α-actin	5 days
Complete reepithelialization (of surgical wounds)	5 days
Macrophage marker RM 3/1	7 days
Hematoidin, lymphocyte infiltrates	8 days
Complete basement membrane (in surgical wounds)	8 days
Macrophage marker 25 F 9	11 days
Macrophage marker G 16/1	12 days
Complete staining for keratin 5 (in surgical wounds)	13 days

recently been supplemented by biochemical methods, for example, identifying metabolites of inflammation mediators, and by proteomic and genomic technologies for detecting cell stage activation markers, which can probably contribute to a more exact forensic wound age estimation in the future. The earliest appearance of actually used parameters of vitality and forensic age estimation of human skin wounds is listed up in Tables 1–3.

See also: **Forensic Medicine/Pathology:** Early and Late Postmortem Changes; Histopathology.

Further Reading

Betz, P., 1994. Histological and enzyme histochemical parameters for the age estimation of human skin wounds. International Journal of Legal Mediane 107, 60–68.
Betz, P., 1995. Immunohistochemical parameters for the age estimation of human skin wounds. American Journal of Forensic Medicine and Pathology 16, 203–209.
Betz, P., 2003. Pathophysiology of wound healing. In: Payne-James, J., Busuttil, A., Smock, W. (Eds.), Forensic Medicine. Clinical and Pathological Aspects. Greenwich Medical Media, London, pp. 81–90.
Brinkmann, B., Madea, B., 2004. Handbuch Gerichtliche Medizin, vol. 1. Springer, Berlin, pp. 297–333.
Cecchi, R., 2010. Estimating wound age: looking into the future. International Journal of Legal Mediane 124, 523–536.
Cohnheim, J., 1867. Über Entzündung und Eiterung. Virchows Archiv [A] 40, 1–79.
Dreßler, J., Bachmann, L., Koch, R., Müller, E., 1998. Enhanced expression of selectins in human skin wounds. International Journal of Legal Medicine 112, 39–44.
Hausmann, R., Nerlich, A., Betz, P., 1998. The time-related expression of p53 protein in human skin wounds – a quantitative immunohistochemical analysis. International Journal of Legal Medicine 111, 169–172.
Laiho, K., Tenhunen, R., 1984. Hemoglobin-degrading enzymes in experimental subcutaneous hematomas. Zeitschrift für Rechtsmedizin 93, 193–198.
Pollack, S.V., 1979. Wound healing. A review: I. The biology of wound healing. Journal of Dermatology and Surgical Oncology 5, 389–393.
Raekallio, J., 1970. Enzyme Histochemistry of Wound Healing. Fischer, Stuttgart, Germany.
Raekallio, J., 1973. Estimation of the age of injuries by histochemical and biochemical methods. Zeitschrift für Rechtsmedizin 73, 83–102.

Key Terms

Adipocere, Animal predation, Autolysis, Bodies recovered from water, Body cooling, Bog bodies, Bones, Corrective factors, Death and dying, Decay, Decomposition, Desiccation, Electrical excitability of facial muscles, Enzyme histochemistry, Forensic histopathology, Gastric content and time since death, Immunohistochemistry, Mechanical and electrical excitability of skeletal muscles, Mechanical excitability, Mummification, Nomogram method, Permafrost bodies, Pharmacological excitability of the iris, Postmortem, Postmortem body cooling, Postmortem changes, Postmortem lividity, Preservation, Preservation of decomposing bodies, Putrefaction, Radiocarbon analysis, Rigor mortis, Skeleton, Supravital reactions, Supravitality, Time since death, Vital reaction, Volatile fatty acids, Wound age, Wound age estimation.

Review Questions

1. What is the "postmortem interval"? How is that different from "time of death"?
2. As the postmortem interval increases, what also increases?
3. What is autolysis? What is putrefaction?
4. What other sciences play a role in determining postmortem interval?
5. What is adipocere? What role does it play in postmortem interval?
6. What is the difference between endogenous and exogenous factors in decomposition? List three differences for each factor.
7. What was a crucial factor in creating a need for a *legal* definition of death?
8. What is postmortem lividity? What is its role in forensic pathology?
9. How can you distinguish between rigor mortis and cold stiffening?
10. What is algol mortis? What is the most reliable method to determine it?
11. What is saponification?
12. What is a "bog body"?
13. How is vitreous potassium used in estimates of time since death?
14. Can gastric contents be used to help in estimating time since death? Why or why not?
15. Does temperature affect decomposition? If so, how?
16. What is a vital reaction? Why does it matter to forensic pathology?
17. Define "wound healing."
18. What is one of the most important conditions for a forensic age estimation of a wound?
19. What is the earliest physiological response to a wound or tissue damage?
20. Which group of insects play the most significant role in decomposition?

Discussion Questions

1. How does putrefaction in water differ from putrefaction out of water? What factors change the processes?
2. Why are nontemperature methods more accurate for estimating time since death?
3. At what point does estimation of time since death become too unreliable for forensic purposes? Why?
4. If a body is indoors, what "environmental" factors could influence the rate of decomposition?
5. What role do animals (of all types) influence the rate of decomposition? How does their absence alter the rate of decomposition?

Additional Readings

Alapo, L., 2016. Humans-pigs-rabbits decomposition study to impact court cases worldwide. Tennessee Today. Online at: http://tntoday.utk.edu/2016/04/27/humanspigsrabbits-decomposition-study-impact-court-cases-worldwide/.

Damann, F.E., Williams, D.E., Layton, A.C., 2015. Potential use of bacterial community succession in decaying human bone for estimating postmortem interval. Journal of Forensic Sciences 60 (4), 844–850.

Fronczek, J., Lulf, R., Korkmaz, H.I., Witte, B.I., van de Goot, F.R., Begieneman, M.P., Krijnen, P.A., Rozendaal, L., Niessen, H.W., Reijnders, U.J., 2015. Analysis of morphological characteristics and expression levels of extracellular matrix proteins in skin wounds to determine wound age in living subjects in forensic medicine. Forensic Science International 246, 86–91.

Ishida, Y., Kimura, A., Nosaka, M., Kuninaka, Y., Shimada, E., Yamamoto, H., Nishiyama, K., Inaka, S., Takayasu, T., Eisenmenger, W., Kondo, T., 2015. Detection of endothelial progenitor cells in human skin wounds and its application for wound age determination. International Journal of Legal Medicine 129 (5), 1049–1054.

Williams, T., Soni, S., White, J., Can, G., Javan, G.T., 2015. Evaluation of DNA degradation using flow cytometry: promising tool for postmortem interval determination. The American Journal of Forensic Medicine and Pathology 36 (2), 104–110.

Section 3. Autopsy

The autopsy is a method, like any other in science. The procedures are standardized and routinized to help the pathologist and technicians (often called *dieners*, German for "servant") focus on the body and its clues, rather than worrying about what to do next. Virchow's addition of microscopic tissue examination (histopathology) brought the autopsy into the full modern notion of a medicolegal postmortem examination. As an aside, the word autopsy comes from the Greek for "to see for oneself" and could apply to any type of examination that one does; necropsy, also Greek for the examination of the dead, is more general but typically is used to describe an autopsy on an animal.

External Postmortem Examination

B Madea and G Kernbach-Wighton, University of Bonn, Bonn, Germany

Introduction

The external postmortem examination is of significance with respect to the following issues:

- death certification
- as part of the autopsy
- for identification purposes (e.g., identification of disaster victims)

The external examination of each deceased person by a physician has the greatest practical relevance because it is required for death certification.

External Examination before Death Certification

For the external postmortem examination, the physician has to fulfill a wide range of tasks concerning different legal and social aspects (**Table 1**). The terminology of death certification can be found in **Table 2**.

The first and most important purpose of the external postmortem examination is the determination of death, not only in the interest of the decedent but also as a social requirement.

Safe determination of the cause of death and underlying diseases is also essential.

Mortality statistics and resource sharing in the health-care system are both based on data on underlying diseases and causes of death. An exact definition of the manner of death is essential to guarantee legal certainty but may also have consequences in other legal areas (civil law, insurance law, or compensation law).

The legal bases for external postmortem examinations vary from country to country and even between different counties within one country. An external postmortem examination has to be carried out once a dead body is found.

- A human corpse is:
  - The body of a dead person as long as tissue continuity has not been destroyed by putrefaction.
  - The body of a dead neonate (irrespective of the body weight) if it has completely left the womb and if after leaving the womb it showed one of the three signs of life (heart beat, umbilical pulsation, and breathing).
  - A stillbirth (stillborn baby weighing ≥ 500 g).
  - The head or torso separated from a body that cannot be reassembled.
- The following are not corpses:
  - Skeletons either partial or complete.
  - Miscarriages (stillborn fetuses with a birth weight <500 g; no requirement to report the death).

The body should be examined without delay once notice of the death has been received. In many countries, any physician may certify a death, but in some counties, a physician who is related to the deceased may not be allowed to

Table 1   Functions and importance of the external postmortem examination

1. Determination of death	Social and individual interest in correct determination of death, ending of the normative protection of life, civil registers
2. Determination of the cause of death	Medical aspects, mortality statistics, epidemiology, resource sharing within the health-care system, development of public health programs, allocation of health-care resources
3. Manner of death	Legal security, detection of homicides, classification of conditions of death on requests by civil law, insurance law, or compensation law
4. Determination of time of death	Civil registers, inheritance law
5. Transmitted diseases according to the Infection Protection Act	Hygienic aspects as social interest
6. Obligations to report	● If the manner of death is unnatural/undetermined ● If the identity of the deceased is not known ● According to the Infection Protection Act

Source: According to Madea, 2006. Die ärztliche Leichenschau. Rechtsgrundlagen – Praktische Durchführung – Problemlösungen, second ed. Springer, Berlin, Heidelberg, NY.

Table 2   Terminology of death certification

Term	Definition
Cause of death statement	Included in part I and part II of the certification of death
Underlying cause of death	The reason/alteration standing at the beginning of the course of events resulting in death
Immediate cause of death	The last circumstances caused by the underlying conditions directly linked to the occurrence of death
Antecedent ("intervening" or "intermediate") cause of death	An alteration also caused by the underlying conditions, but not defined as the immediate cause of death
Mechanisms of death	Physiological or biochemical alterations resulting in death via their lethal effects, but not equivalent to the underlying cause of death
Manner of death	Death classification based on five definitions: natural, homicidal, suicidal, accidental, or undetermined taking into account the actual circumstances

Source: According to Myers et al., 1998. Improving the accuracy of death certification. Canadian Medical Association Journal 158, 1317–1323.

certify a death. Every private practice physician (in the area covered by his or her practice) and hospital physicians has the obligation to certify a death. A careful examination of the naked body is mandatory. Careless examination of a body may constitute a regulatory offense. If living people are injured as a consequence of careless medical examination of a dead body, charges may be made against the physician in charge (if, for instance, carbon monoxide poisoning is overlooked and other persons also suffer asphyxiation by carbon monoxide). Emergency doctors may complete a preliminary death certification, but the regular external examination has to be carried out by another doctor (this varies from country to country).

Cases in which the manner of death is unnatural or unexplained, or the identity of the body is unknown, have to be reported to the police. All cases that fall under the Infection Protection Act have to be reported to the local health office. All doctors who have previously treated the deceased have to provide necessary information if asked to do so.

Determination of Death/Death and Dying

Definitively establishing that death has occurred is straightforward. Cessation of vital functions can be determined with certainty by the following criteria:

● Presence of definite signs of death (livor, rigor, advanced postmortem changes).
● Failure of attempted resuscitation for approximately 30 min, confirmed by approximately 30 min of a flatline electrocardiogram (ECG) despite carrying out appropriate measures and after ruling out general hypothermia or intoxication by central depressant drugs.
● Brain death (can be determined under clinical conditions only during assisted ventilation).
● Physical trauma that is incompatible with life.
● Determination of death is uncomplicated if there are obvious postmortem changes (e.g., rigor mortis, livor mortis, putrefaction, and injuries that are incompatible with life).

Apparent Death

Determination of death might be difficult within the phase of vita minima and vita reducta with increasing devitalization before certain death signs appear because of heart and circulatory arrest. Within vita minima and vita reducta with dysregulation of functional systems and their coordination and increasing devitalization, life expressions (respiration and circulation) may be abandoned and might not be seen when examined superficially. Causes and conditions leading to vita minima and vita reducta were summarized by Prokop, a medical examiner from Berlin, who called it the "AEIOU rule" (**Table 3**).

Great care is required if there is suspicion of conditions according to the AEIOU rule, meaning intoxication with hypnotics, carbon monoxide, and alcohol; hypothermia; electrical accidents; apoplexy; brain pressure; metabolic coma; epileptic seizures; hypoxic brain damage; missing life expressions; and missing certain signs of death at the same time. In these cases, the following is essential.

Do not fill out any death certifications if there are no certain signs of death.

In case of doubt, the physician has to wait for help (emergency doctor) or admission to a hospital has to be arranged. In any case, the behavior of the physician depends on information about the anamnesis and patient's prognosis.

The so-called uncertain signs of death such as fixed pupils, wide pupils, areflexia, loss of cardiac activity, loss of respiration, and dropping core temperature are meaningless if an examination has been done improperly, especially if the reversibility/irreversibility of the condition has not been questioned (**Table 4**). For example, absence of a peripheral pulse within the centralization of the circulation, as in cases of hypothermia, does not say anything about a lack of cardiac activity. Minimum breathing excursions from abdominal respiration do not "catch one's eye" in fully clothed persons. A body surface that feels cold when the ambient temperature is low or wet clothing is worn does not give any information about the core temperature. When pupil width is estimated, possible intoxication always has to be kept in mind (the so-called ABC toxins: alcohol, amphetamine, belladonna, and cannabis).

Table 3 Complexes of causes for vita minima/vita reducta

A—alcohol, anemia, anoxemia
E—electricity, stroke of lightning
I—injury (head injury)
O—opium, anesthetics, neuropharmacological drugs
U—uremia (and other metabolic coma), hypothermia

Source: According to Prokop.

Table 4 So-called uncertain signs of death

Apparent death—vita minima—vita reducta

- Fixed pupils, dilated pupils
- Areflexia
- Missing cardiac activity
- Dropping core temperature

Are no "uncertain signs of death" because of
- Absence of peripheral pulse ≠ absence of heart activity
- Minimum breathing excursions within abdominal respiration do not "catch one's eye" in fully clothed persons
- Body surface may feel cold when the ambient temperature is low and wet clothing is worn
- Was it tested, maybe on hands?—≠ core temperature (warmth regulation in coldness—minimum blood)
- Flow
- Pupils' width? Reaction to light stimulus? ABC toxins
- Proprioceptive and polysynaptic reflexes, other reflexes than corneal reflex?

From the medical and legal points of view, failure of heart resuscitation is a reliable criterion to stop a correct but unsuccessful reanimation. Normally, one will stop cardiopulmonary resuscitation if there is no success after 30–40 min or if heart reactivation seems unlikely. This includes the following criteria:

- Absence of spontaneous electrical activity (zero voltage line in the ECG).
- Signs of electromechanical decoupling (deformed QRS complexes in the ECG but absence of palpable pulse on large vessels).
- Continuous ventricular fibrillation with frequency deceleration and a progressive decrease in amplitudes.
- These signs show definite and irreversible cardiac death if the patient is normothermic and there are no other specific conditions.
- If patients are hypothermic, if they are near-drowning victims, or in cases of intoxication, resuscitation has to be performed longer than the time specified earlier until detoxification occurs or the body warms up. Only then does the decision to stop reanimation make sense.

Centrally acting medication and general hypothermia have to be excluded. Emergency doctors have formulated the principle: "No one is dead until he or she is warm and dead." Determination of death may follow if resuscitation is unsuccessful and the core temperature is at least 32 °C or below.

Brain Death

Brain death is defined as the irreversible loss of general functions of the brain, cerebellum, and brain stem, whereas heart and circulatory functions may be maintained by controlled ventilation. Brain death is the death of a human being. The criteria for brain death are as follows:

1. Requirements
   a. acute severe primary or secondary brain damage
   b. exclusion of intoxication, neuromuscular blockade, hypothermia, circulatory shock, and metabolic and endocrine coma
2. Clinical symptoms
   a. unconsciousness/coma
   b. fixed pupils of both medium or strongly dilated pupils (no application of mydriatic drugs)
   c. absence of oculocephalic reflex
   d. absence of corneal reflex
   e. absence of pain response in the trigeminus area
   f. absence of pharyngeal reflex
   g. loss of spontaneous respiration
3. Supplementary examination
   a. zero voltage line in the electroencephalogram (EEG)
   b. termination of evoked potentials
   c. cerebral circulation arrest

Time Since Death

The procedure for ascertaining the time of death depends on the nature of the case (**Table 5**). Medical examiners use a wide range of methods, which are outlined in the article about postmortem changes and estimation of the time since death.

Table 5   Ascertaining the time of death

- Death under medical supervision
  - Document the time of observed cardiovascular arrest
- Dead body found
  - Establish upper and lower time limits by stating the following:
    - Last signs of life on…
    - Found dead on…or
    - Estimate how long the body has been dead on the basis of how far the signs of death have advanced
- Cases in which death occurred after brief agony and was observed by witnesses
  - Time of death as reported by relatives, witnesses, etc.
- Care must be taken when near relatives die more or less simultaneously (e.g., childless couple)
  - Documentation must be very detailed and correct because there may be issues related to inheritance

Determining the Cause of Death

In the confidential part of the death certificate, under the heading "Cause of death," the course of the disease is documented within a causal chain (**Figure 1**).

The immediate cause of death is given in Part Ia and the preceding causes—diseases that resulted in the immediate cause of death—in Parts Ib and Ic, with the underlying disease(s) coming last. Finally, other important diseases that contributed to death but are not linked to the underlying diseases are given in Part II. The most important epidemiologic information is derived from the underlying cause of death, which is used for mortality statistics.

The major significance of the cause of death is a statistical one: how many people die from a certain disease? This is opposed to the final cause of death, which gives information about what people are suffering from and the particular disease that caused their death.

According to Federal Statistical Office recommendations, if nothing precise is known, the entry "cause of death unknown or unascertained" is preferable to vague speculation. Under no circumstances should constituent elements of every death process, such as "cardiac arrest," "respiratory arrest," or "electromechanical decoupling," be included in any part of the cause of death cascade, from underlying disease to the immediate cause of death.

Then, in the right column, the duration (time interval) of the disease has to be recorded, taking as the starting point the estimated onset of the disease and not the time of diagnosis. The entries on time intervals also work as a plausibility check on the cause of death cascade. For adequate certification of the cause of death, knowledge of the medical history of the patient and the circumstances leading to her or his death are essential. A careful analysis of the relationship between the medical history and medical treatment may already provide important information for the cause of death certification. If the deceased is not personally known to the certifying physician, appropriate information is required from the treating physician.

A formal and correctly arranged cascade for mortality statistics leading from the direct cause of death to the underlying disease would be, for example:

- (Ia) esophageal variceal bleeding as a consequence of
- (Ib) backflow within the portal vein
- (Ic) liver cirrhosis (underlying disease)
- (II) diabetes mellitus or
- (Ia) retention pneumonia
- (Ib) obturating bronchial carcinoma

If the cause of death given in Ia is not the consequence of further complications or underlying diseases known from the patient's history, no further entries are needed, for example:

- (Ia): Cranial gunshot wound

Cause of death		Approximate interval between onset and death
I Immediate cause* Enter diseases, injuries, or complications that caused death. Sequentially list conditions leading to immediate cause; enter underlying cause last.	a) .... due to (or as a consequence of) b) .... due to (or as a consequence of) c) .... due to (or as a consequence of) d) .... underlying condition	....
II Other significant conditions contributing to death but not to the underlying cause	....	....
* This does not mean the manner of dying, e.g., cardiac arrest, respiratory arrest, etc. It means the disease, injury, or complication which caused death.		

Figure 1 International form for cause of death medical certificate.

Final indirect causes of death can be divided into the organ-related ones and those that are not organ related.

Within the prestructured entries on underlying disease and cause of death on the death certificate, according to World Health Organization guidelines, physicians should mentally review the entire history of their patient's illness. In particular, they should ask themselves whether such a final morbidity was present that would be expected to lead to the patient's death at the time given by the circumstances described. "Hard" and "soft" causes of death should be distinguished: hard causes of death are present when the underlying disease of death and immediate cause of death are closely related, appear in a close sequence in time, and there is a close causal relationship between them, for example, in a case of clinically diagnosed myocardial infarction resulting in cardiac rupture and hence pericardial tamponade. Here, the underlying disease and immediate cause of death are present within one organ system (linear type of death).

Soft diagnoses are, for example, characterized by a patient who suffers from more than one underlying disease, none of which suggests itself a priori as the cause of death, and the cause of death remains multifactorial.

In addition, one may be guided by "death types" that have been described as a "thanatological bridge" between the underlying disease and the immediate cause of death (**Figure 2**):

- *Linear type of death*: Underlying disease and immediate cause are within one organ system
- *Diverging type of death*: Organ-specific underlying cause but non-organ-specific immediate cause
- *Converging type of death*: Underlying diseases in various organ systems lead to death via a final pathogenetic phase common to all of them
- *Complex type of death*: Underlying diseases in various organ systems with more than one non-organ-specific immediate cause of death

If the cause of death remains unclear in a case of unexpected death of a healthy person, this should be noted on the death certificate. Federal Statistical Office recommendations on entering the cause of death and important terms are given in **Table 6**. When only insufficient information is available to describe the immediate cause of death, for example, because the patient did not seek medical attendance, descriptive statements should be used, such as prostate carcinoma with lung and bone metastases or found dead with a history of severe coronary atherosclerosis and recent myocardial infarction.

Finally, particular problems arise with deaths due to old age or in connection with medical procedures. "Senility" and "old age" are not causes of death. Retrospective examinations of deaths of those over 85 years and over 100 years old have shown that in each case, morphologically ascertainable

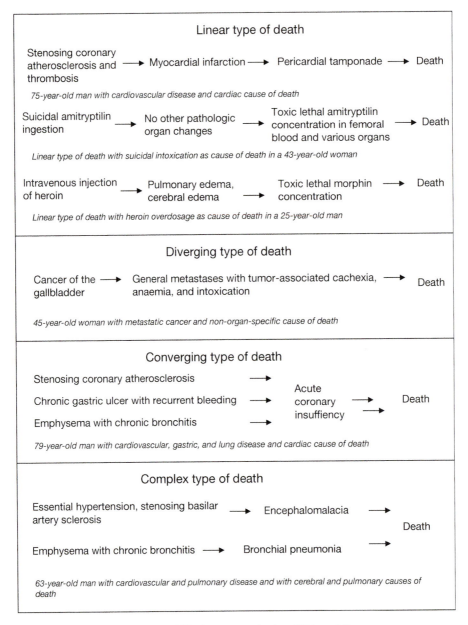

Figure 2 Types of death (according to Leis and Thieke and Nizze): case examples from Thieke and Nizze.

underlying diseases and immediate causes of death were present. If appropriate, the diagnosed diseases that contributed to the occurrence of death can be descriptively listed as a multifactorial converging type of death in order to avoid "makeshift" diagnoses.

Regarding deaths attributable to medical procedures, the first notable point is a considerable discrepancy between the deaths recorded in the federal statistics as due to

complications of medical and surgical treatment and the data derived from epidemiological research on death cases due to maltreatment.

Epidemiological research for Germany revealed that 17 500 deaths per year are suspected to be the results of medical malpractice—these figures are consistent with international data—whereas the Federal Statistical Office mentions 399 deaths only as complications of medical and surgical treatment

Table 6   Causes of death: examples and important aspects

Pneumonia	<ul><li>Primary, hypostatic, aspiration, and other underlying cause</li><li>Pathogen</li><li>If seen as a consequence of immobility or debility: the cause of the immobility or debility</li></ul>
Infection	<ul><li>Primary or secondary pathogen<ul><li>If primary, bacterial or viral</li><li>If secondary, more information about the primary infection required</li></ul></li></ul>
Urinary infection	<ul><li>Localization in the urinary tract, pathogen, and other underlying cause</li><li>If a consequence of immobility or debility, the cause of the immobility or debility</li></ul>
Renal failure	<ul><li>Acute, chronic, or terminal; underlying cause (e.g., hypertension, atherosclerosis, cardiovascular disease)</li><li>If a consequence of immobility or debility, the cause of immobility or debility</li></ul>
Hepatitis	<ul><li>Acute or chronic, alcohol related</li><li>If viral: type (A, B, C, D, or E)</li></ul>
Infarction	<ul><li>Atherosclerotic, due to thrombosis or embolism</li></ul>
Thrombosis	<ul><li>Arterial or venous—include vascular designation</li><li>Intracranial sinus—purulent, nonpurulent, venous (state which vein)</li><li>If postoperative or in an immobile patient; disease that was the reason for surgery or immobilization</li></ul>
Pulmonary embolism	<ul><li>If younger than 75 years: cause</li><li>If postoperative: disease that was the reason for surgery or immobilization</li></ul>
Leukemia	<ul><li>Acute/subacute/chronic</li><li>Lymphatic/myelogenous/monocytic</li></ul>
Alcohol/medical drugs/narcotics	<ul><li>Long-term abuse or drinking</li><li>Dependency</li></ul>
Complication of surgery	<ul><li>Disease that was the reason for surgery</li></ul>
Dementia	<ul><li>Cause (e.g., senility, Alzheimer's disease, multiple infarction)</li></ul>
Accidental death	<ul><li>Details of circumstances (e.g., bicyclist hit by a car)</li><li>Accident, suicidal, violent assault, or circumstances unknown</li><li>Accident site (e.g., in the street, at home, etc.), activity at the time of death (playing golf, going to the movies, working, etc.)</li></ul>
Tumor	<ul><li>Benign, malignant, location, metastases</li></ul>

Source: According to Federal Statistical Office recommendations. www.destatis.de.

in 2007. It clearly appears that a considerable number of unreported cases exist, raising the question of whether under relevant circumstances the attending physician should issue the death certificate or whether, irrespective of the existence or otherwise of suspicion, such cases should always be subject to an official investigation.

Consistency between Cause of Death Diagnosis on the Death Certificate and Following Autopsy

Numerous studies have been published on the validity of the clinically determined cause of death as entered on the death certificate in comparison to pathoanatomical findings. The Görlitz study (1986–1987), with a nearly 100% autopsy rate (1060 deaths out of which a postmortem was carried out in 1023), showed incongruity between certificate and autopsy findings in a total of 45% of male deaths and 48.8% of female deaths. Among hospital deaths, there were incongruities of the underlying disease in 42.9% of men and 44% of women; among deaths in care homes, the corresponding figures were 63.2% of men and 57.8% of women; for deaths occurring elsewhere (at home, in public, etc.), the results were 41.3% of men and 50.7% of women. Among iatrogenic deaths, the rate of incongruities between underlying diseases as determined clinically and found at autopsy was as high as 72%, and inconsistencies for the immediate causes of death were 45.8%.

Numerous studies have differentiated and operationalized the discrepancies between clinically determined causes of death and those determined at autopsy (major mistake, class 1; major mistake, class 2; minor mistake). According to various statistics, class 1 major mistakes, which have consequences for the treatment and survival of the patient, occur in 11–25% of all deaths, while class 2 major mistakes, which have no consequences for treatment and survival, are found in 17–40% of deaths.

According to a meta-analysis by Shojania et al., class 1 major mistakes have decreased in the past 40 years but do still occur in about 8–10% of deaths.

Manner of Death

According to cause-of-death statistics, around 4% of deaths in Germany result from unnatural causes (**Figure 3**). Around 10 000 cases per year are due to suicide, 6000 are caused by accidents at home, just under 6000 result from transport accidents, and 526 deaths result from physical assaults.

Retrospective analyses of death certificates for which the manner and cause of death have been checked at autopsy suggest that unnatural deaths are around 33–50% more frequent than reflected in the federal statistics and that it could be assumed that there are around 81 000 unnatural deaths every year. From the judicial point of view, a particular concern is the number of homicides that remain undiscovered by means of medical death certification. A multicenter study suggests that every year around 1200 homicides remain

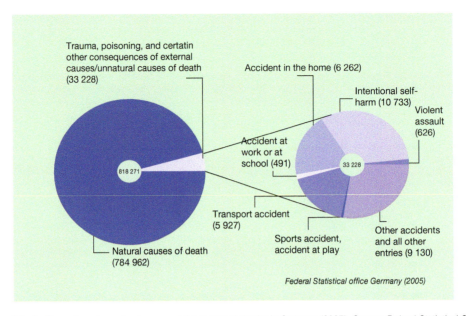

Trauma, poisoning, and certatin other consequences of external causes/unnatural causes of death (33 228)

Accident in the home (6 262)

Intentional self-harm (10 733)

Violent assault (626)

Accident at work or at school (491)

818 271

33 228

Transport accident (5 927)

Sports accident, accident at play

Other accidents and all other entries (9 130)

Natural causes of death (784 962)

Federal Statistical office Germany (2005)

Figure 3   Causes of death. Proportion of unnatural causes of death among deaths in Germany (2007). Source: Federal Statistical Office.

unidentified on death certificates in Germany. This large number of unrecorded cases was repeatedly confirmed by incidental findings of homicide or even serial murders (including those in care homes and hospitals). Six percent of hospital physicians regularly attest exclusively natural death; 30% tick the box for natural death even in cases of violence, poisoning, suicide, or following medical intervention. In assessing the manner of death, the certifying physician decides whether a death will come to the attention of the investigating authorities at all. Assessing the manner of death is thus a task requiring extreme responsibility not only from the judicial point of view (detection of homicides) but also in terms of the interests of the bereaved (e.g., compensation claims after a fatal accident). "Natural" is death from an internal cause (disease), when the deceased person has suffered from a disease that can be identified precisely and from which death was anticipated; the death occurred entirely independently of any external factors of legal significance. The prerequisite for attesting a natural death is thus the existence of an underlying disease of death known from the patient's medical history with a poor prognosis for survival.

"Unnatural," by contrast, is death attributable to an event caused, triggered, or influenced from outside, irrespective of whether due to the fault of the patient himself or herself or of a third party. Unnatural deaths, therefore, are those due to the following:

- Physical assault
- Accident (irrespective of whose fault)
- Homicide

- Poisoning
- Suicide
- Treatment errors/medical malpractice
- Fatal consequences of any of the first six points

The interval between an external event at the beginning of the causal chain that leads to death and the occurrence of that death can thus be indefinitely long (it may be years). If the cause of death cannot be ascertained when the death certificate is issued, the manner of death will therefore also remain unclear.

The attestation of natural death always assumes that a clear cause of death can be given. In this connection, it is worrying that about 50–70% of physicians certify a "natural" death for deaths following femoral neck fractures, 20% for deaths during injections, and 30–40% for intraoperative deaths.

If on the one hand unnatural deaths are considerably underrepresented in official statistics, and on the other hand both physicians in private practice and those working in emergency departments report attempts by the police to influence them to certify a death as natural although no cause of death is apparent, the death ought to be certified at least as unexplained. In an anonymous survey of randomly selected physicians from the area of the Westphalia–Lippe Medical Association, 41% of physicians in private practice and 47% of emergency room physicians reported such attempts to influence death certification. The background of these attempts is that investigating authorities have a teleologically narrowed understanding of the term "unnatural death" as meaning "death in which there is a possibility of third-party guilt."

If a natural death is certified, no further investigations are necessary. Indicators that a death may be unnatural may arise from the case history and findings: for example, sudden death without a known previous illness, "prima facie" accidents and suicides, farewell letters, etc. Findings that tend to indicate unnatural death are conjunctival hemorrhages, unusual color or livor mortis, remains of tablets in the oral area, and signs of injury.

Unsuitable criteria for indications of natural death are age, especially when no preexisting life-threatening diseases are known, and the absence of visible trauma.

Regarding deaths in hospital, especially when the patient was under medical treatment for a long enough period, the error rate should also be relatively low; problem areas here are failure to identify causal connections to trauma at the beginning of the fatal causal chain and deaths related to medical procedures. In the inpatient setting, there are occasional reports of initially unrecognized series of killings by physicians or nursing personnel.

The danger of errors and scope for deception are, without doubt, greatest when death is certified by private practice physicians at home; typical mistakes and sources of error, in order of frequency, are as follows:

- Inexperience
- General carelessness
- Careless examination of the body
- Consideration of the emotional state of relatives

Furthermore, however, there are sometimes also unfavorable external conditions, such as poor lighting, and simply not being adept at the job, and there are no flexible solutions such as calling in an appropriately qualified certifying physician. Physicians in private practice especially can find themselves being confronted with a collision of interests, such as also being the physician for the relatives of the deceased. Attesting an unexplained death puts them at risk of triggering investigations that could mean losing the relatives as patients. Compared to a physician working in private practice, the hospital physician finds himself in a more protected position (death in the medically dominated environment of a hospital rather than in the private area).

Problem Areas

Problems that may repeatedly arise within the hospital context are as follows:

- Deaths in connection with medical interventions and
- Deaths following injury from a fall or other violent events in which the causal connection with violence from another person or other external event is not identified and therefore death is wrongly certified as natural

For deaths occurring unexpectedly that are linked to medical interventions, the manner of death should always be certified as "unexplained" so that an official autopsy can be carried out to investigate the underlying and immediate causes of death objectively. This is the only basis from which an opinion can be expressed on any question of maltreatment. Certifying the manner of death as unexplained or unnatural does not signify an admission of maltreatment.

For physicians in private practice, the main problems may arise when bodies are found at home, patients die unexpectedly, and death occurs because of old age.

If the cause of death cannot be established from external examination of the body or from interviewing any doctors previously involved in treatment, this should be recorded and the manner of death certified as unexplained. With the elderly, there is always the question as to whether the case history and severity of the diagnosed disease explain the occurrence of death at this particular moment.

Whenever the cause of death cannot be established by external examination, an autopsy should be carried out, as is still usual in many countries in Europe. In Germany, the present autopsy rate is less than 5% of all deaths; the rate of hospital autopsies in particular has been dropping sharply in recent years, while judicial autopsies have remained relatively stable at 2% of deaths (compared to autopsy rates of 20–30% in England, Scotland and Wales, Sweden, and Finland).

These autopsies, which are required for valid cause of death statistics and for the national mortality registers, would, however, have to be remunerated adequately, which unfortunately they are not at present.

See also: **Forensic Medicine/Pathology:** Autopsy; Early and Late Postmortem Changes; Estimation of the Time Since Death.

Further Reading

Berzlanovic, A., Keil, W., Waldhoer, T., Sim, E., Fasching, P., Fazeny-Dörner, B., 2005. Do centenarians die healthy? An autopsy study. Journal of Gerontology 60, 862–865.

Burton, J.L., 2007. The external examination: an often neglected autopsy component. Current Diagnostic Pathology 13, 357–365.

Burton, J.L., Rutty, G.N., 2010. The Hospital Autopsy, third ed. Hodder Arnold, London.

Ferris, J.A.J., 2005. Autopsy. Adult. In: Payne-James, J., Byard, R.W., Corey, T.C., Henderson, C. (Eds.), Encyclopedia of Forensic and Legal Medicine, vol. 1. Academic Press, London, pp. 183–192.

Hanzlick, R., 1993. Death certificate. The need of further guidance. The American Journal of Forensic Medicine and Pathology 14, 249–252.

Hanzlick, R., 2007. Death Investigation – Systems and Procedures. CRC Press, Boca Raton, FL.

Interpol, 2002. Disaster Victim Identification Forms. Available from: http://www.interpol.int/Public/ICPO/FactSheets/FS02.pdf.

Junbelic, N.I., 2005. Mass disasters. Role of forensic pathologists. In: Payne-James, J., Byard, R.W., Corey, T.S., Henderson, C. (Eds.), Encyclopedia of Forensic and Legal Medicine, vol. 1. Academic Press, London, pp. 197–207.

Leis, J., 1982. Die Todesursache unter indivudal-pathologischen Gesichtspunkten. Deutsche Medizinische Wochenschrift 107, 1069–1072.

Madea, B., 2006. Die ärztliche Leichenschau Rechtsgrundlagen – Praktische Durchführung – Problemlösungen, second ed. Springer, Berlin, Heidelberg, NY.

Madea, B., Rothschild, M., 2010. The postmortem external examination. Deutsches Ärzteblatt International 107 (33), 575–588.

Magrane, B.P., Gilliland, G.F., King, D.A., 1997. Certification of death by family physicians. American Family Physician 56, 1433–1438.

Maudsley, G., Williams, E.N., 1996. Inaccuracy in death certification – where are we now? Journal of Public Health Medicine 18, 59–66.

Myers, K., Farquhar, D.R.E., 1998. Improving the accuracy of death certification. Canadian Medical Association Journal 158, 1317–1323.

Pounder, D., Jones, M., Peschel, H., 2011. How can we reduce the number of coroner autopsies? Lessons from Scotland and the Dundee initiative. Journal of the Royal Society of Medicine 104, 19–24.

Rutty, G.N., 2010. The external examination. In: Burton, J.L., Rutty, G.N. (Eds.), The Hospital Autopsy, third ed. Hodder Arnold, London, pp. 90–103.

Shojania, K., Burton, E., McDonald, K., et al., October 2002. The Autopsy as an Outcome and Performance Measure. Evidence Report/Technology Assessment Number 58 (Prepared by the University of California at San Francisco-Stanford, Evidence-Based Practice Center under Contract No. 290-97-0013). AHRQ Publication for Health Care Research and Quality.

Thieke, C., Nizze, H., 1988. Sterbenstypen: Thanatologische Brücke zwischen Grundleiden und Todesursache. Pathologe 9, 240–244.

Wagner, S., 2009. Death Scene Investigation. A Field Guide. CRC Press, Boca Raton.

Relevant Websites

http://www.rechtsmedizin.uni-bonn.de/—Causes of Death: Examples and Important Aspects Federal Statistical Office Recommendation.

www.destatis.de—Homepage of the Institute of Forensic Medicine, Bonn University.

Autopsy

P Saukko, University of Turku, Turku, Finland
S Pollak, University of Freiburg, Freiburg, Germany

Semantically, the most accurate description of the dissection of a dead body is "necropsy," though the word "autopsy" (from the ancient Greek "autopsia," "to see for oneself," from αυτος (autos, "oneself") and όψις (opsis, "eye")) is so extensively used that there is rarely ambiguity about its meaning. Another alternative, albeit, less precise is "postmortem examination." It is a detailed systematic external and internal examination of a corpse usually carried out as a hospital autopsy by a pathologist or as a medicolegal one, by one or more medicolegal experts to ascertain the immediate, underlying, and possible contributing causes of death, and in the latter type of autopsy depending on the jurisdiction, also the manner of death. However, in some parts of the world where autopsies are seldom performed, this may be limited to external examination of the body without dissection.

"Verbal autopsy" is used as a public health tool to find out the probable causes of death in populations, mainly in Africa and Asia, lacking vital registration and medical certification. Verbal autopsy is an interview carried out with family members and/or caregivers of the deceased using a structured questionnaire to find out signs and symptoms and other relevant information that can later be used to assign a probable underlying cause of death.

Short Historical Overview

Anatomical Dissection

The prerequisite for the whole idea of an autopsy or necropsy was the knowledge of human anatomy, and the history of autopsy shows three, partly overlapping, paths of development: anatomical dissection, medicolegal autopsy, and clinical or hospital autopsy. The first of them lasted almost 2000 years from the first known school of anatomy in Alexandria around 320 BC, where human dissections were carried out, till the publication of the great textbook of anatomy *De humani corporis fabrica* in 1543 by Andreas Vesalius (1514–1564), the "Father of Anatomy," marking the overthrow of traditional Galenic anatomy.

The possibility to dissect human bodies varied greatly at times. There are reports on occasional dissections that took place in the twelfth and thirteenth centuries. Probably one of the earliest known is the one ordered by the Norwegian King

Sigurd Jorsalfar in 1111. On his return from Jerusalem with his followers, they stopped in Byzantium (present Istanbul), where many of them died, and Jorsalfar ordered a dissection to find out whether the cause of death had been liver damage by too strong wine. In 1391, the University of Lérida in Spain was given permission by King John I of Aragon to dissect the body of a criminal once every 3 years.

In Vienna, the first anatomical dissection took place in 1404 and in Prague, somewhat later in 1460.

A rare and good consideration to the practice of postmortem examination in the fifteenth century is given by a collection of autopsy records, *De Abditis Nonnullis Ac Mirandis Morborum Et Sanationum Causis*—"The Hidden Causes of Disease," published in 1507 after the death of a Florentine physician Antonio Benivieni (1443–1502) by his brother, Geronimo. He had requested another Florentine physician, Giovanni Rosato, to choose and edit the cases for collection. Some medical historians have credited Benivieni as one of the founders of the science of pathology, and he was the first physician to our knowledge to ask permission of the relatives of his patients to perform necropsies in obscure cases.

Felix Platter I, the famous anatomist in Basel, was said to have performed more than 300 autopsies since 1559 (**Figure 1**).

Medicolegal Autopsy

The historical development that eventually led to the present-day "cause-of-death" investigation system and autopsy was preceded by the external examination of a dead body, the practice of which began in ancient China more than 2000 years ago. Systematic external investigation of dead bodies, particularly in violent or sudden unexpected or unwitnessed deaths, was introduced during a period called "the Warring States" (475–221 BC). The earliest known written instructions to government officials, who had the responsibility to carry out these examinations, originate from the Qin dynasty (221–207 BC). During the Song dynasty (960–1279 AD), these officials were obliged to investigate violent or suspicious deaths within 4 h under pain of punishment.

In other parts of the world, medicolegal investigation of deaths was introduced much later due to requirements of the judicial system.

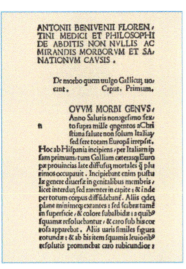

Figure 1 The opening chapter of *De Abditis Nonnullis Ac Mirandis Morborum Et Sanationum Causis*—"The Hidden Causes of Disease," published in 1507 after the death of Antonio Benivieni (1443–1502).

According to Singer, the earliest medicolegal dissections took place at the University of Bologna, Italy, between 1266 and 1275. The first known postmortem examination on the American continent was performed in Hispaniola in 1533. In France, Ambroise Paré performed the first medicolegal autopsy in 1562, and the first autopsy performed in Eastern Europe was probably the one of King Stephen Báthory of Poland in 1586.

Our knowledge of the old autopsy procedures is rather scanty. With few exceptions, detailed written autopsy records exist mainly for relatively recent times. Such exceptions are reports on the autopsy of Emperor Maximilian II from 1576 and of Markgrave Jakob III of Baden. The latter died in 1590, at the age of 28, after a sudden illness that had lasted 9 days. A medicolegal autopsy was ordered and performed by two professors of the Freiburg University Faculty of Medicine. Their report pointed at poisoning by arsenic powder.

The principles of modern medicolegal investigation were developed based on the codes of sixteenth-century Europe: the Bamberg Code (Constitutio Bambergensis) in 1507, the Caroline Code (Constitutio Criminalis Carolina) in 1532, and later, the Theresian Code (Constitutio Criminalis Theresiana) in 1769.

The Austrian decree of 1855 contain very detailed instructions in 134 paragraphs as to the performance of medicolegal autopsy, and what is worth mentioning is that it is still today, a valid legislation in Austria. Similar, although not as detailed, is the Prussian edict of 1875. Both of these instructions can be considered as the culminating point of legislation dealing with the performance of medicolegal autopsy.

Clinical Autopsy

Clinical autopsy, as we understand it today, took much longer to develop and became meaningful first after the introduction of improved autopsy techniques and new concepts of pathogenesis of diseases by Carl von Rokitansky (1804–1878) and cellular pathology by Rudolf Virchow (1821–1902) (**Figure 2**).

In the beginning of the nineteenth century, increased attention was paid to the actual autopsy technique. Prost, a French physician, insisted in 1802 that all organs of the body should be examined, and declared that 3 h was the minimum time for a postmortem examination. In 1846, Rudolf Virchow, then prosector in Berlin, insisted on regularity and method and definitive technique. The classical techniques, which are still in use today, are more or less modifications of those introduced by Rokitansky, Virchow, Ghon, and Letulle, among others.

In 1872, Francis Delafield's *A Handbook of Postmortem Examination and Morbid Anatomy* was published in New York, and German and English editions of Rudolf Virchow's book on autopsy technique were published in 1876 (**Figure 3**).

The Present Use of Autopsy

Medicolegal Autopsy

Further development of medicolegal autopsy has been characterized and greatly influenced by the judicial system adopted in any given country, the main emphasis being on the detection and investigation of criminal and other unnatural or unexpected deaths. Due to different legislation and practices, there exists great variation in medicolegal autopsy rates between the

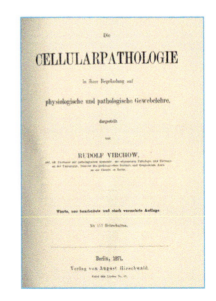

Figure 2 Title page of the fourth Edition of Virchows' *Cellular Pathology* published in 1871.

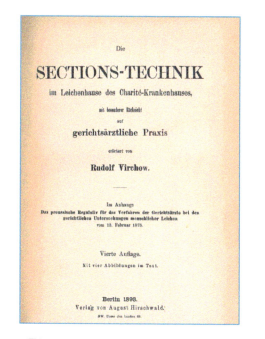

Figure 3 Title page of the fourth Edition of Virchow's book on autopsy technique in 1893.

countries. It is generally problematic to get access to this information, though some countries publish these figures regularly as background information on their mortality statistics. In England and Wales, some 230 600 (47%) deaths were reported to coroners in 2010. Of these, 44% involved a post-mortem examination resulting in a coroner's autopsy rate of 20.6% of all registered deaths. The following medicolegal autopsy rates of all deaths for 2010 were available from Statistics: Norway (3.9%), Sweden (10.3%), and Finland (23.2%).

In addition to the national measures to create guidelines and to harmonize medicolegal autopsy, there has been an increasing international interest to achieve harmonized and internationally recognized rules on the way medicolegal autopsies should be carried out. This has become imperative, especially from the point of human rights as well as due to the increasing need for international collaboration in the investigation of mass disasters such as the 2004 Indian Ocean earthquake and Tsunami and the 2010 Haiti earthquake, both of which had an estimated death toll of over 220 000. These and the loss of thousands of human lives in various armed conflicts around the world should have made it quite clear to everyone, what implications a properly functioning medicolegal system, or the lack of it, may have upon society.

In May 1989, UN Economic and Social Council adopted in its resolution 1989/65 the Principles on the Effective Prevention and Investigation of Extra-Legal, Arbitrary and Summary

Executions that had been created by cooperation with inter-governmental and nongovernmental organizations, especially the Minnesota Lawyers International Human Rights Committee. Later in 1991, the General Assembly of the United Nations endorsed the Model Autopsy Protocol of the United Nations.

European Council of Legal Medicine (ECLM) is an official body, registered according to the German law in Cologne and deals with scientific, educational, and professional matters on European level. It has delegates nominated by the national medicolegal associations from all European Union and European Economic Space member countries. Since the early 1990s, the ECLM has been active in this field as well and its document "Harmonisation of the Performance of the Medico-Legal Autopsy" was adopted by the General Assembly in London in 1995.

The Council of Europe is an intergovernmental organization which aims among others to protect human rights and pluralist democracy. It should not be confused with the European Union. The two organizations are quite distinct; however, all the 27 European Union states are also members of the Council of Europe, which currently has altogether 47 Member States. In its 43rd Ordinary Session, the Parliamentary Assembly of the Council of Europe adopted Recommendation 1159 on the harmonization of autopsy rules. Following this recommendation, a Working Party of international experts in legal medicine and law, with representation from the Interpol as well as the International Academy of Legal Medicine, was established in 1996 under the Committee of Bioethics to make a proposal for Autopsy Rules. One of the guidelines used in the work was the Autopsy Rule produced earlier by the ECLM. The Working Party finished its work in November 1998, and this new Pan-European Recommendation No. R (99)3 on the Harmonization of Medico-Legal Autopsy Rules and Its Explanatory Memorandum were adopted by the Committee of Ministers on February 2, 1999, at the 658th meeting of the Ministers' Deputies. Although the document is a "recommendation" by nature and hence strictly speaking not legally binding, it has, however, legal implications because all 47 Council of Europe member countries have agreed to implement these principles into their national legislations.

Many national authorities and professional organizations have created their own guidelines and standards, among others such as:

● The Code of practice and performance standards for forensic pathologists by the Home Office Policy Advisory Board for Forensic Pathology and The Royal College of Pathologists, UK, November 2004, with additions, such as Guidelines on Autopsy Practice Scenarios for specific types of death, January 2005, and Coronial autopsies and current practice: Accuracy of cause of death and tissue sampling, November 2007.

- Forensic Autopsy Performance Standards by the National Association of Medical Examiners, USA, October 2005.
- Swiss Principles and Rules for Medico-Legal Autopsy by the Swiss Society of Legal Medicine, April 2007.
- Guidelines on Autopsy Practice for Forensic Pathologists, Criminally Suspicious Cases and Homicides by the Ontario Forensic Pathology Service, October 2007.
- The Code of Practice and Performance Standards for Forensic Pathologists dealing with Suspicious Deaths in Scotland by Scottish Government, COPFS, and The Royal College of Pathologists, November 2007.

Accreditation

Accreditation is a procedure by which an authoritative body gives formal recognition that a body or person is competent to carry out specific tasks: this aims to increase the credibility and acceptability of the reports and certificates issued by them. It is achieved by ensuring that the infrastructure, personnel, and the methods comply with preestablished criteria. The structure, processes, policies, and goals of the body to be accredited are described in a quality manual. Standard operating procedures have to be defined to describe the specific tasks that will be carried out by the entity. Recently, several German and Swiss institutes of legal medicine have been accredited by their respective national accrediting bodies regarding medicolegal activities including autopsies.

Clinical Autopsy

Despite the invention of more sophisticated investigative and imaging techniques, clinical autopsy has been shown to have maintained its value and remain an essential factor in the quality assurance of medical care. Regardless of this, there has been a progressive decline in autopsy rates throughout the world. The mandatory 20% autopsy rate required for accreditation of postgraduate training in the United States was withdrawn in 1971, on the grounds that each institution should set its own rate but that ideally should be close to 100%.

According to the World Health Organization (WHO) statistics published in 1998, the total autopsy rates varied in Europe in 1996 between 6% (Malta) and 49% (Hungary), and in other parts of the world reported to the WHO between 4% (Japan) and 21% (Australia). A more recent compilation of similar statistics is unfortunately not available. According to the WHO:

An assessment of the quality of cause-of-death information by WHO suggested that ideal systems operate in only 29 of 115 countries that report such statistics to WHO; these systems represent less than 13% of the world's population. In the remaining countries, mortality statistics suffer from one or more of the following problems: incomplete registration of births and deaths, lay reporting of the cause of death, poor coverage, and incorrect reporting of ages.

The reasons for this decline are many and complex: over-reliance on the new diagnostic techniques, low appreciation of autopsy work, poorly performed autopsies by inexperienced trainees without proper supervision, long delay of autopsy reports, economical factors, fear of malpractice litigation, and so forth to name just a few.

The standardization and harmonization of clinical autopsy has taken place primarily at the national level. The quality of health care and quality assurance and audit have become increasingly important and have been introduced from laboratory medicine even for autopsies.

Objectives of Autopsy

An autopsy is a detailed systematic external and internal examination of a corpse carried out by a pathologist or one or more medicolegal experts to ascertain the underlying and possible contributing causes of death and, depending on the jurisdiction, also the manner of death. Before the pathologist can begin the examination, he/she must be sure that he/she has been authorized to perform the autopsy on that particular body. An assessment of possible risks that may be involved with the autopsy must be considered and necessary health and safety precautions taken. The autopsy and all related measures must be carried out in a manner consistent with medical ethics and respecting the dignity of the deceased.

An autopsy is performed to achieve one or more of the following objectives:

1. To identify the body or record characteristics that may assist in identifying the deceased
2. To determine the cause of death or, in the newborn, whether live birth occurred
3. To determine the mode of dying and time of death, where necessary and possible
4. To demonstrate all external and internal abnormalities, malformations, and diseases
5. To detect, describe, and record any external and internal injuries
6. To obtain samples for any ancillary investigations
7. To obtain photographs, videos, or, when appropriate and possible, use postmortem imaging techniques, and retain samples for evidential or teaching use
8. To provide a full written report and expert interpretation of the findings
9. To restore the body to the best possible cosmetic condition before the release

In addition to anatomical dissection, there are basically two main types of autopsy:

1. The clinical autopsy is to investigate the extent of a known disease and the effectiveness of treatment, and it is

sometimes performed also for medical audit or research purposes. Almost invariably, the consent of relatives is needed unless the deceased has given the consent antemortem.

2. The medicolegal or forensic autopsy, which is ordered by the competent legal authority (a coroner, a medical examiner, a procurator fiscal, a magistrate, a judge, or the police), to investigate sudden unexpected, suspicious, unnatural, or criminal deaths. Moreover, unidentified bodies or deaths occurring in special circumstances such as deaths in police custody or during imprisonment are often subjected to a medicolegal autopsy. In most jurisdictions, permission of the relatives is not required.

Autopsy Techniques

Both clinical and medicolegal autopsy may involve different strategies and techniques depending on the questions they are expected to answer. Autopsy technique in adults is generally somewhat different from pediatric autopsies.

The scope of medicolegal autopsy is much often broader than that of clinical autopsy and may include the investigation of the scene of death. All background information on the circumstances of death is of paramount importance for the choice of the right approach. In medicolegal autopsy, the examination of the clothing is often an essential part of the external examination, whereas in clinical autopsy, it is generally not. Both types of autopsies should consist of full external and internal examination of the body including the dissection and investigation of all three body cavities.

The external examination

- External description of the body includes the age, sex, build, height, ethnic group and weight, nutritional state, skin color, and other characteristics of the deceased such as scars or tattoos.
- Description of postmortem changes including all essential details relating to rigor mortis, hypostasis, and decomposition.
- Careful investigation and description of all body surfaces and orifices including color, length, density, and distribution of hair, color of irises and sclerae, presence or absence of petechiae, or any other abnormalities or injuries. The examination should be carried out systematically and include head, neck, trunk, upper and lower extremities, and the back.

The internal examination

Examination of the body cavities include the description of the presence of gas (pneumothorax), fluids (effusions or exudates), or foreign bodies and the measurement of their volume, appearance of the internal surfaces and anatomical boundaries, as well as location and external appearance of organs.

The classical autopsy techniques vary mainly in the order in which the organs are removed:

1. The organs may be removed one by one (Technique of R. Virchow).
2. Cervical, thoracic, abdominal, and pelvic organs can each be removed as separate blocks (Technique of A. Ghon).
3. They may be removed as one single block, which is then subsequently dissected into organ blocks (Technique of M. Letulle).
4. All organs are dissected in situ (Technique of C. Rokitansky).

All organs have to be dissected, the outer appearance as well as the cut surfaces described, and the weight of major organs recorded. The hollow organs have to be opened and their content described and measured. All relevant vessels, arteries, and veins as well as ducts have to be dissected. All abnormalities must be described by location and size.

Sampling

Histological examination of the main organs should be performed in all autopsies. The need for further ancillary investigations may depend on whether the cause of death has been established with the necessary degree of certainty and, if not, additional samples have to be taken for toxicological or other investigations. For toxicology, this may include peripheral blood, vitreous humor, cerebrospinal fluid, bile, hair samples, or other relevant tissues. When retaining tissues, one has to take into consideration the possible restrictions depending on the national legislation.

Special procedures

Sometimes special procedures and modifications of normal dissection techniques are necessary. The stage at which radiology is employed in an autopsy will vary according to the individual circumstances, and the most sophisticated techniques are available only for a very few. When available, computed tomography is the best technique for visualization of gaseous findings, such as air embolism, or when detecting gas accumulation in diving fatalities, or when locating foreign objects or skeletal trauma. Postmortem magnetic resonance imaging can be used to document soft tissue injuries in any kind of blunt trauma. Where neck trauma is suspected, the brain and the organs of the chest cavity have to be removed prior to the dissection of the neck to drain the blood from the area to avoid artifactual bleeding. Postoperative autopsies may present various problems with medicolegal implications, such as complications of anesthesia, surgical intervention, or postoperative care. However, detailed description of these special dissection procedures and techniques is beyond the scope of this presentation.

Autopsy Report

The report is an essential part of the autopsy. It should be full, detailed, and comprehensive. The medicolegal autopsy report, in particular, should be comprehensive even to the nonmedical reader. In addition to the factual, positive, and negative gross, microscopical, and analytical findings, the pathologist should conclude with a discussion on the significance of the findings. Where the findings are of uncertain nature and there are several competing causes, the pathologist should try to give an opinion as to their probability.

> *See also:* **Forensic Medicine/Pathology:** Early and Late Postmortem Changes; Estimation of the Time Since Death; External Postmortem Examination; Forensic Pathology—Principles and Overview; Histopathology; Postmortem Imaging; Vital Reactions and Wound Healing.

Further Reading

Council of Europe, 2000. Recommendation no. R (99) 3 of the Committee of Ministers to member states on the harmonization of medico-legal autopsy rules. Forensic Science International 111 (1–3), 5–58.

Jackowski, C., et al., 2005. Virtopsy: postmortem imaging of the human heart in situ using MSCT and MRI. Forensic Science International 149 (1), 11–23.

King, L.S., Meehan, M.C., 1973. A history of the autopsy: a review. American Journal of Pathology 73 (2), 514–544.

Ludwig, J. (Ed.), 2002. Handbook of Autopsy Practice, third ed. Humana, Totowa, NJ, p. 592.

Roberts, I.S., et al., 2012. Post-mortem imaging as an alternative to autopsy in the diagnosis of adult deaths: a validation study. Lancet 379 (9811), 136–142.

Saukko, P., Knight, B., 2004. Knight's Forensic Pathology, third ed. Arnold, London. 662 pp.

Saukko, P., Pollak, S., 2005. Autopsy, procedures and standards. In: Jason, P.-J. (Ed.), Encyclopedia of Forensic and Legal Medicine. Elsevier, Oxford, pp. 166–171.

Saukko, P.J., Pollak, S., 2009. Autopsy. In: Jamieson, A., Moenssens, A. (Eds.), Wiley Encyclopedia of Forensic Science. Wiley, Chichester, pp. 256–262.

Tzu, S., 1981. The washing away of wrongs. In: Sivin, N. (Ed.), Science, Medicine, and Technology in East Asia, vol. 1. The University of Michigan Center for Chinese Studies, Ann Arbor, MI.

Histopathology

P Saukko, University of Turku, Turku, Finland
S Pollak, University of Freiburg, Freiburg, Germany

Brief Historical Introduction to Histopathology

After the first observations of animal and plant tissues in the early seventeenth century by Galileo, Hooke, Malpighi, and Leeuwenhoek, among others, using a newly invented instrument, the microscope, actual microscopic anatomy took a long time to develop. The father of modern histopathology, Marie-François Xavier Bichat (1771–1802), who was the first to introduce the systematic concept of tissues as distinct entities, did not use microscopy. René Théophile Hyacinthe Laennec (1781–1826), another famous French physician, was against the use of the microscope. Factors usually mentioned as obstacles to the scientific use of the microscope at this point were that it was surrounded by secrecy, the instrument was expensive, there were technical difficulties, and it was used by outsiders and lay people as a toy, and it only gradually found acceptance by the academia. According to Majno and Joris, the turning point was the perfection of the achromatic objective by J.J. Lister in 1830. Shortly thereafter, the microscope found its way into medical schools. It also took quite a long time until the millennia-old galenic theories about the pathogenesis of diseases were discarded and replaced by the modern concepts of cellular pathology in the second half of the nineteenth century. The first handbook of human histology for physicians and students by the Swiss anatomist Albert von Koelliker, who was, according to Garrison, "the most distinguished histologist of the early period," was published in Leipzig in 1852 (**Figure 1**). von Koelliker was among the first to introduce the newer techniques of fixation, sectioning, and staining into microscopy. Probably the first official recommendation by a competent authority to use microscopy can be found in a Prussian decree on the procedure of medicolegal autopsy (1875), which recommended (§5) that the forensic doctor should have a microscope with two objective lenses and a minimum of 400-fold magnification. In his book about dissection techniques, Rudolf Virchow (1821–1902) also emphasized that, especially for medicolegal practice, certain pathological changes cannot be recognized by the naked eye but only with the help of a microscope or a magnifying glass.

Pathology/Histopathology as a Medical Specialty

Pathology exists as a medical specialty in most countries, but there are differences as to the length and contents of the training as well as the number of subspecialties. In the United States, postgraduate training takes 4 years in the form of a pathology residency, after which the candidate can apply for certification either within Anatomical Pathology or Clinical Pathology or Combined Anatomical Pathology and Clinical Pathology, which are the primary specialties recognized by the American Board of Pathology. Subspecialty certification is possible in Blood Banking/Transfusion Medicine, Chemical Pathology, Clinical Informatics, Cytopathology, Dermatopathology, Forensic Pathology, Hematology, Medical Microbiology, Molecular Genetic Pathology, Neuropathology, and Pediatric Pathology. The American Osteopathic Board of Pathology recognizes three specialty areas: Anatomic Pathology, Laboratory Medicine, and Forensic Pathology. In the United Kingdom, specialty training in Histopathology takes between 5 and 5.5 years to complete and takes place under the oversight of the Royal College of Pathologists and the General Medical Council. Within the European Union, the mutual recognition of medical specialties is regulated on the basis of the minimum period of training, which in Pathological Anatomy is currently 4 years, but varies from country to country, as seen in the case of the United Kingdom (Directive 2005/36/EC of the European Parliament and of the Council). This has significance mainly from the point of view of free movement of labor, that is, if the same specialty exists in two or more member countries, the specialist can move to practice his or her specialty in such a country without facing major bureaucratic issues.

Autopsy Histopathology

Medicolegal or forensic autopsy is performed at the behest and per the instructions of the legal authority responsible for the investigation of sudden and unexpected, suspicious, obscure, unnatural, occupational, litigious, or criminal deaths. Depending on the jurisdiction, the legal authority that decides

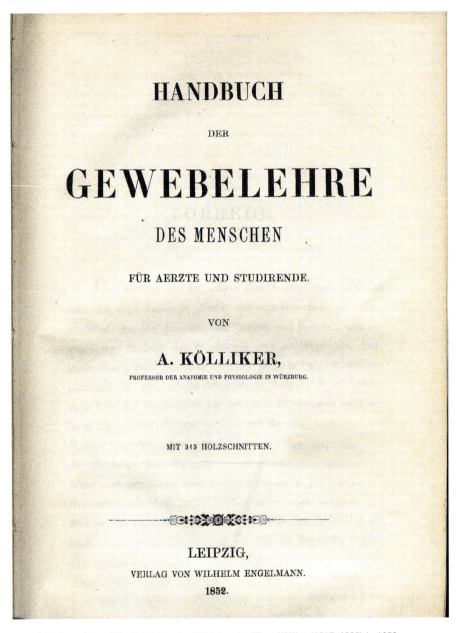

Figure 1   The title page of the first edition of the first textbook of histology by Albert Kölliker (1817–1905) in 1852.

whether medicolegal autopsy is necessary may be a coroner, a medical examiner, a procurator fiscal, a magistrate, a judge, or the police; the systems vary considerably from country to country. Consent of relatives is usually not required.

It is often said that medicolegal autopsies are carried out in public interest, referring to the general welfare of the whole population. This expression is somewhat misleading and confusing because ultimately, in most cases, it is a question of

the interest of an individual. Hence, the society or the legal authority is in a way representing the interest of the individual(s) because when the autopsy is ordered and carried out, there may be no knowledge about the person who will actually benefit or suffer from the results of the investigation.

Medicolegal autopsy often differs from hospital autopsy insofar as there may be no preliminary knowledge of the deceased or of either possible illnesses or circumstances of death, and the deceased may even be unidentified and just found dead. Therefore, the forensic pathologist ought to be prepared for every eventuality because presumed natural death may turn out to be practically anything, even a homicide. According to a survey by the Swedish National Board of Forensic Medicine (1994), approximately 8% of homicides in Sweden were detected first during medicolegal autopsy, and according to another survey by Saukko, this occurred in about 4% of homicides in Finland. In principle, due to the possibility that results of a medicolegal autopsy may be used as evidence in a court of law, appropriate quality and procedural standards should apply at every step, as if it were a criminal investigation. Such a practice is rarely applied, unless it is obvious or at least suspected from the beginning of the investigation that the death is associated with a crime.

The International Code of Medical Ethics of the World Medical Association states: "A physician shall, in all types of medical practice, be dedicated to providing competent medical service in full technical and moral independence, with compassion and respect for human dignity." This means that the forensic pathologist should be able to independently decide, for example, the extent of any ancillary investigations considered necessary. Although this is the case in some jurisdictions, there are others where there are restrictions due to the nature of the investigative procedure. The decision whether to carry out histological analysis may depend on the legal authority and not the pathologist: for example, in Germany, the public prosecutor in charge of the investigation of the medicolegal cause of the death in question decides what ancillary investigations (histology, toxicology, etc.) are necessary.

The starting point of autopsy histopathology is different from clinical histopathology insofar as the sampling usually takes place at least several hours or even days postmortem, and the tissues can be altered by autolysis and putrefaction, whereas bioptic tissues or surgical samples can be processed immediately to minimize postmortem artifacts.

Forensic Histopathology

Forensic histopathology deals with assessment of histological findings in any forensically relevant context and their significance as forensic evidence, with the ultimate goal to serve proper administration of justice. It deals with basic phenomena such as postmortem changes in cells and tissues and their differentiation from vital changes, the timing and causes of injuries whether of mechanical or physicochemical origin, as well as exclusion or confirmation of any other pathological changes and their significance as possible underlying or contributing causes of death. In addition to the disease- and cause of death-related histopathology, questions may arise as to the human origin of tissue fragments when these have been recovered while investigating clandestine burial sites or in

connection with mass disasters or whenever there is a need to establish personal identity from any tissue by applying molecular biological methods. Occasionally, the question of kinship may arise first after the death and autopsy of a putative parent. In case tissue has been retained for histology, formalin-fixed, paraffin-embedded tissue blocks can be used for DNA extraction to investigate the issue.

Quality

The earlier mentioned Prussian decree on the procedure of medicolegal autopsy (1875) and its recommendation to use microscopy imply that, even in those early days of histopathology, the necessity for high standards and quality in medicolegal investigations was fully recognized. However, it took quite some time before the idea of quality control, quality assurance, and audit found its way into medicine. Although the necessity of quality systems is now better understood, there are significant regional, national, and individual differences in the standard of practice. As Cordner has pointed out, "The major change that has occurred in the last 20 years in considering autopsy quality is that the autopsy must be reviewable." Without a full histological survey, this is not feasible. Quality also depends on the standards of specialized education, continuing professional development, and harmonization of investigative procedures, which are still far from being uniform.

Guidelines

Guidelines usually represent recommendations allowing some variation in practice. The most recent trend, particularly in the medicolegal field, seems to be moving toward accreditation that necessitates the introduction of standardized operational procedures. Accreditation procedures have usually been applied to calibration and testing laboratories, but the European Network of Forensic Science Institutes and European Cooperation for Accreditation, the European network of nationally recognized accreditation bodies located in the European geographical area, are currently working on a joint project aiming to define which standard, ISO/IEC 17020 or ISO/IEC 17025, is to be used for the different forensic fields.

Currently, many autopsy guidelines express a view on autopsy histology.

A recommendation of the Council of Europe: Rec (99) 3 of the Committee of Ministers to Member States on the harmonization of medicolegal autopsy rules, adopted by the Committee of Ministers on February 2, 1999, states in Section 6 Sampling: "the following minimum rules should be applied:

1. in all autopsies, the basic sampling scheme includes specimens from the main organs for histology."

The Royal College of Pathologists (United Kingdom) *Guidelines on Autopsy Practice*, September 2002, takes a similar position in Section 9 Autopsy histology:

> 9.2. As best practice, sampling of all major organs for histology in all autopsies is recommended.

And further emphasizing the importance of histology to the cause of death investigation:

> 9.6.2. If in advance of the autopsy, discussions with a Coroner indicates to the pathologist that retention of material that may be relevant to the investigation will not be permitted, the pathologist should decline the request to perform the autopsy.

The Code of Practice and Performance Standards for Forensic Pathologists by the Home Office Policy Advisory Board for Forensic Pathology and The Royal College of Pathologists, November 2004, and Code of Practice and Performance Standards for Forensic Pathologists dealing with Suspicious Deaths in Scotland by the Scottish Government, COPFS, and The Royal College of Pathologists, November 2007, have the same standpoint toward postmortem histology:

> A histological examination of the major organs (assuming that they are not heavily decomposed) should be made by the pathologists themselves in all suspicious deaths. Histology is of value in confirming, evaluating, and sometimes revising the course of natural disease processes that may have contributed to the cause of the death. Other samples should be taken for histological examination depending on the circumstances of the case, for example, for the purposes of aging injuries. The reasons behind any decision not to undertake a histological examination must be adequately recorded, in order that the pathologist may be in a position to defend this decision if required.

The Ontario Forensic Pathology Service: Practice Manual for Pathologists (October 2009, Version 2.0) states:

In Section 1.11, Histology and ancillary tests: "If death has occurred due to a natural condition, histology should be used to provide reviewable documentation of the lethal disease/lesion," and in Section 2.6, Histology, ancillary testing, and consultations: "Routine histology and toxicology are performed in all homicide and criminally suspicious cases, as determined by the state of the body."

Methods

Sampling

Sampling of tissues has to be carried out in a systematic manner from obvious or suspected pathological findings, or when no such pathology is seen, representative samples should be taken from all main organs. Special sampling protocols and procedures have been recommended by various authors and/or professional organizations and may apply, for instance, in sudden cardiac deaths, in pediatric cases such as sudden infant death syndrome/sudden unexpected death in infancy, or sudden death in epilepsy (SUDEP). Sites from which the samples have been taken should be appropriately recorded in the autopsy protocol to ensure topographical correlation and comparison with macroscopical findings and possible later review and quality assurance measures. In all medicolegal cases involving specimens for histology, they should be identified on receipt, matched with request forms, and receive an accession number to guarantee an unbroken chain of evidence accounting for the handling and processing of each sample from the moment of its appropriation. Specimens should be handled with care. When trimming the tissues for fixation or embedding, they should be cut with sharp instruments in order to avoid artifactual changes.

Fixation

Tissue specimens can be used as frozen fresh tissue that is cut using a cryostat or autolytic processes, and bacterial degradation can be stopped and the proteins stabilized by chemical fixation. The choice of the optimal fixation method depends on the staining methods. For routine histopathology, most tissues are fixed using buffered formaldehyde. The size and the thickness of the specimen must be in correct proportion to the chosen fixative and appropriate fixation time to avoid fixation artifacts. Special methods such as immunohistochemistry may necessitate shorter fixation times than classical histochemistry, as too long a fixation may destroy the antigenic properties of the tissue and produce false-negative results. Special procedures are often necessary for enzyme or immunohistochemical methods or to demonstrate substances that are easily inactivated, destroyed, or removed during routine fixation or tissue-processing procedures. After fixation, the tissue samples are processed either manually or using automated tissue processors, dehydrated, and embedded in paraffin wax to allow them to be cut into thin sections with a microtome (usually 4–7 μm) for light microscopy. In transmission electron microscopy, samples are usually embedded in epoxy resin and cut with an ultramicrotome into ultrathin sections that are stained using heavy metals such as lead, uranium, or tungsten.

All stages of specimen handling—embedding, cutting, and staining—and the choice of materials are important and contribute to the final result, and each of them can be a potential source of artifacts that may endanger the correct interpretation of the findings.

Staining

The tissue sections are mounted on a glass slide and can be observed in their native form, for example, to detect foreign bodies such as asbestos in the lungs, but usually they are stained using various techniques to provide better contrast by natural or synthetic dyes or by complementary enzyme or immunohistochemical staining methods, depending on the purpose. The affinity of tissues to a given stain depends on complex physicochemical interactions between the solvent, dye, and tissue. Due to their characteristic affinity to different tissue components, the dyes help to recognize morphological features of normal tissue and to differentiate them from pathological changes. Injured tissue may show an altered affinity to a given stain, for instance, increased cytoplasmic eosinophilia resulting from increased binding of eosin by cytoplasmic proteins with hematoxylin–eosin stain as seen, for example, in ischemic neurons in the brain or in myocardial injury. Many of the classical staining methods, such as hematoxylin–eosin, Mallory's phosphotungstic acid-hematoxylin, or van Gieson stain, among others, were introduced in the nineteenth century and are mainly used to visualize morphological changes in the cells and tissues; many of them are still in use today.

Special techniques are used to demonstrate specific components such as iron in cells or tissues. In Perls' Prussian or Berlin blue reaction (Max Perls, 1843–1881), the section is treated with dilute hydrochloric acid to release ferric ions from binding proteins. These ions will react with potassium ferrocyanide to produce an insoluble blue compound. Fats or lipids have to be stained using frozen sections as fixation and tissue processing usually remove them (Oil-red-O or Sudan stain).

Microorganisms, such as *Mycobacterium tuberculosis*, can be demonstrated using Ziehl–Neelsen stain or bacteria using Gram stain. Periodic acid-Schiff or PAS stain can be used to stain fungi. It also stains glycogen, mucin, mucoprotein, and glycoprotein. Viral antigens can be detected using immunohistochemistry by specific, typically monoclonal, antibodies against viral protein generated in laboratory animals. The sensitivity and specificity vary according to the type of the virus (**Figure 2**).

In "in situ hybridization," a labeled viral DNA or RNA probe is used to localize a specific DNA or RNA sequence of the virus within a tissue section.

Enzyme histochemical methods were used in the 1960s and 1970s particularly in animal experiments and also to some extent for diagnostic purposes on autopsy material. As routine fixation and subsequent tissue processing destroy or diminish the enzyme histochemical reactivity of most enzymes, cryostat sections from fresh frozen tissue have to be used. Enzyme histochemical methods are usually named after the individual enzymes, implying that the method might indicate the biochemical activity of the enzyme in question. However, the enzyme histochemical reactivity does not necessarily correlate with the actual biochemical activity of the enzyme in question, suggesting that other factors, such as the presence of auxiliary enzyme systems or other cofactors of the histochemical reaction, may be rate limiting. Therefore, these methods also need

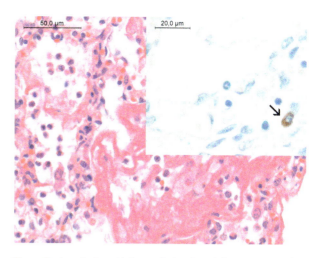

Figure 2 Localization of influenza B-virus in an inflammatory round cell (insert/red arrow) in the lung of an infant. (Antibody courtesy of Dr. Tytti Vuorinen, Department of Virology, University of Turku).

to be validated accordingly before they can be applied to diagnostics in the medicolegal context.

Some conventional histological methods, such as acid fuchsin or hematoxylin-basic fuchsin-picric acid stain, where a shift in color was claimed to indicate early myocardial ischemia, have been shown to be unreliable for such diagnostic purposes.

The advances of immunohistochemistry and the availability of a large number of new antibodies have made the use of immunohistochemical methods common even in medicolegal problems, in particular in the context of vitality and aging of wounds, head injury, and early myocardial injury. So far, the results have been difficult to assess because of diverse findings and sometimes also because of shortcomings in the experimental design and control material. It is obvious that in experienced hands with well-established and properly validated methods, immunohistochemistry can be of advantage over conventional histochemistry.

Histopathological Diagnosis

Histopathological diagnosis is the result of a complex cognitive process requiring knowledge and experience, attention, and recognition of the characteristic features necessary to identify the disease process in question. This can be achieved either by recognition of purely morphological changes in tissues or cellular structures, such as loss of structural elements such as cerebellar Purkinje cells in chronic alcoholism, deposition of abnormal proteins in tissues such as amyloid in cardiac amyloidosis, or invasive growth of tissue as in malignant tumors or infiltration and destruction of normal tissue elements by inflammatory cells as in infections caused by microorganisms, to name a few examples. Furthermore, the observed histopathological changes need to be assessed for their significance as a possible cause of death. The correctness of the results can be further influenced, in addition to the intellectual factors, by methodological issues and individual working habits such as sampling rate (a low number of samples decreases the probability of hitting focal lesions such as seen, for example, in myocarditis), the use of correct fixation and staining methods, and proper positive and negative controls when appropriate, particularly when applying immunohisto-chemical methods.

Histological Findings as Forensic Evidence

The knowledge of the significance and evidential value of histological data is essential for the administration of justice. However, there are few controlled studies on the reliability of histological diagnoses in the forensic context. In an unpub-lished survey, we assessed the frequency of myocarditis diag-noses by 20 forensic pathologists during a 10-year period in Finland, comprising over 70 000 medicolegal autopsies. When correlating the frequency of such diagnoses with the overall frequency of histology taken in postmortems by the same pathologists, there were obvious discrepancies concerning some individual pathologists showing, for example, a high and above-average frequency of myocarditis diagnoses although the overall frequency of histology sampling was significantly below average. This led to a study where all death certificates with myocarditis recorded as the underlying cause of death in Fin-land from 1970 to 1998 were collected retrospectively. All cases with cardiac autopsy samples and clinical data available ($n = 142$) were included, and the cardiac samples were reex-amined. The histopathological reanalysis showed that only 32% of the 142 subjects met the Dallas criteria for myocarditis. The most evident cause of death in the Dallas-negative subjects was ischemic heart disease (IHD) ($n = 78$, 55% of all cases), suggesting that myocarditis is overdiagnosed in routine autopsies, particularly in patients who have died suddenly or are found dead.

According to Janssen, the significance and evidential value of histological data can be approached and discussed from the following aspects: "first, according to the evidential value of the tissue data itself; second, according to its position within the framework of evaluation which results from the facts of the case that have come to light in combination with other findings." He further grades the evidential value of forensic histology results into three groups (slightly modified from Janssen, 1984):

Group 1: Comprises histological findings where identification of their cause, character, and chronological pathogenesis is

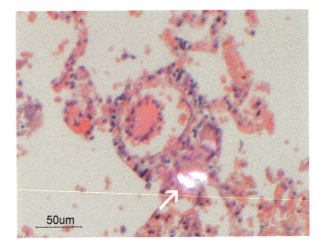

Figure 3 Microscopic view of a small foreign-body granuloma (arrow) in polarized light showing birefringent material from the use of adulter-ated drugs, within the pulmonary vessel wall of an intravenous drug addict.

definite, permitting conclusions about the etiology and causality independent of any further data, for example, in certain stages of tuberculosis and foreign-body granulomas (**Figure 3**).

Group 2: Comprises findings that have forensically verifiable significance in association with further premises. The pres-ence of additional facts is, therefore, a prerequisite for the conclusiveness of such evidence.

Janssen describes as an example, suspected homicide by means of an assault to the neck where isolated fresh hemorrhages in the deep soft parts of the victim's neck can be considered as evidence of strangulation only in combi-nation with corresponding injuries of the overlying skin and larynx and further indications of asphyxiation and vascular congestion. As such, the hemorrhages alone are not unequivocal and not of conclusive significance.

Group 3: Comprises findings that neither singly nor in combination with other facts represent evidence that excludes all other possibilities of causal explanation. Examples are acute vascular congestion, pulmonary emphysema, petechial serous hemorrhages, cerebral edema, and the majority of all parenchymal necroses. Janssen considers these findings either inappropriate or only of limited use as forensic-histological proof.

Problem Areas

In those jurisdictions where sudden, unexpected natural deaths belong to the domain of forensic pathologists, these may comprise around half of the autopsy workload. The majority of

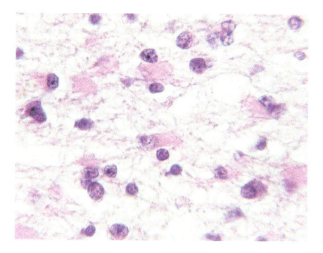

Figure 4 Malignant brain tumor (astrocytoma) detected first by microscopy in a victim of sudden unexpected death.

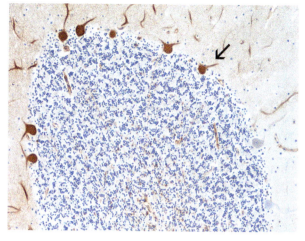

Figure 5 A 4-year-old girl was found dead in her bed. Cerebellar Purkinje cells show fibrinogen immunoreactivity (black arrow pointing at one of the seven positive cells) suggesting breakdown of the blood–brain barrier and leakage of plasma fibrinogen in probable sudden death in epilepsy (SUDEP).

these, at least in industrialized countries, are usually due to IHD, the reliable diagnosis of which is still a diagnosis per exclusion as sclerosis and stenosis of coronary arteries as such are not sufficient to diagnose sudden cardiac death. Early morphological changes of injury, as seen in light microscopy, are unspecific, and even a fresh myocardial infarction visible to the naked eye does not necessarily prove that the person died because of it (**Figure 4**).

Other problematic areas where special expertise and methodology are necessary are, for example, deaths associated with medical investigative or therapeutic procedures, head injury, SUDEP, and pediatric forensic pathology where a forensic neuropathologist or forensic pediatric pathologist should be consulted and involved at an early stage of investigation (**Figure 5**).

Special medicolegal questions such as the timing of injury necessitate solid expertise from the pathologist and properly validated methodology and should preferably be based on experimental research and proved in practical casework.

Considering the high requirements for the reliability of forensic evidence, it is essential that histological examination is an integral part of every autopsy. There are studies that have reported that histology brings new evidence in only a given percentage of cases. This may be correct but one should be aware that all such cases have been identified in hindsight and it is practically impossible to know in advance with any certainty what might be the result in the particular case now under investigation. New questions may arise afterward and may remain unanswered if histology samples have not been taken. An autopsy is not complete and reviewable without histology, and both sampling and microscopy should preferably be in the same hands and carried out by the same pathologist who performed the autopsy.

See also: **Forensic Medicine/Causes of Death:** Sudden Infant Death Syndrome (SIDS); Sudden Natural Death; **Forensic Medicine/Pathology:** Autopsy; Deaths Associated with Medical Procedures; Early and Late Postmortem Changes; Estimation of the Time Since Death; External Postmortem Examination; Forensic Pathology—Principles and Overview; Vital Reactions and Wound Healing.

Further Reading

Cordner, S., 2012. Histology in forensic practice. Forensic Science, Medicine, and Pathology 8, 71–72.

Council of Europe, 2000. Recommendation no. R (99) 3 of the Committee of Ministers to member states on the harmonization of medico-legal autopsy rules. Forensic Science International 111, 5–58.

Home Office Policy Advisory Board for Forensic Pathology and The Royal College of Pathologists, 2004. Code of Practice and Performance Standards for Forensic Pathologists. The Royal College of Pathologists, London, p. 23.

Ikegaya, H., Heino, J., Laaksonen, H., Toivonen, S., Kalimo, H., Saukko, P., 2004. Accumulation of plasma proteins in Purkinje cells as an indicator of blood–brain barrier breakdown. Forensic Science International 146, 121–124.

Janssen, W., 1984. Forensic Histopathology. Springer Verlag, Berlin.

Kytö, V., Saukko, P., Lignitz, E., et al., 2005. Diagnosis and presentation of fatal myocarditis. Human Pathology 36, 1003–1007.

Pryce, J.W., Paine, S.M., Weber, M.A., Harding, B., Jacques, T.S., Sebire, N.J., 2012. Role of routine neuropathological examination for determining cause of death in sudden unexpected deaths in infancy (SUDI). Journal of Clinical Pathology 65, 257–261.

Royal-College-of-Pathologists, 2002. Guidelines on Autopsy Practice. Royal College of Pathologists, London.

Saukko, P., Knight, B., 2004. Knight's Forensic Pathology. Arnold, London.

Saukko, P.J., Pollak, S., 2009. Histology. In: Jamieson, A., Moenssens, A. (Eds.), Wiley Encyclopedia of Forensic Science. John Wiley & Sons Ltd., Chichester, pp. 1468–1473.

Scottish Government, Crown Office Procurator Fiscal Service and the Royal College of Pathologists, 2007. Code of Practice and Performance Standards for Forensic Pathologists Dealing with Suspicious Deaths in Scotland. Scottish Government, Edinburgh, p. 27.

Weber, M.A., Pryce, J.W., Ashworth, M.T., Malone, M., Sebire, N.J., 2012. Histological examination in sudden unexpected death in infancy: evidence base for histological sampling. Journal of Clinical Pathology 65, 58–63.

Relevant Websites

http://www.rcpath.org/—The Royal College of Pathologists.
http://www.wma.net/en/10home/index.html—World Medical Association.

Postmortem Imaging

H Vogel, University Hospital Eppendorf, Hamburg, Germany

Glossary

MinIP Minimal intensity projection.
MSCT Multislice computed tomography used instead of multidetector computed tomography.

PMCT Postmortem computed tomography.
PMI Postmortem imaging.

Introduction

Compared to antemortem forensic imaging, postmortem imaging (PMI) deals with a negative selection. The approach is different: X-ray exposure matters little. Repetition is possible. PMI shall show evidence of the cause of death and not injuries for future treatment. PMI challenges the radiologist. He or she must analyze the whole body and, in most cases, he or she knows little or nothing about the deceased's preexisting diseases, if any. The radiologist has to distinguish changes due to lethal disease from those due to nonlethal disease, and lethal from nonlethal trauma. He or she has to recognize causes of death and consider postmortem changes. After death, decay gas and shifting fluids form patterns, which are absent in clinical diagnostic imaging; these must be interpreted.

PMI includes radiographs, fluoroscopy, and postmortem computed tomography (PMCT). In PMCT, multislice CT (MSCT) has advantages over single-slice CT; MSCT furnishes 3D data with higher resolution. The display of 3D images has a better quality. This has advantages when the direction of an impact has to be determined and when complicated traumata have to be demonstrated.

Postmortem Changes: Gas and Fluids

Gas refers to air or decay gas. Air in the tissues indicate injuries and has to be differentiated from decay gas. Gravity and decay displace fluids after death. Gas and fluids produce patterns, which can simulate symptoms of trauma or disease.

Gas

Chemistry allows for recognition of decay gas and its differentiation from air. This analysis is only rarely available and, if available, it is time consuming and expensive. Therefore, it is profitable to use other means of differentiation. In the vessels, air and decay gas appear on radiographs as negative filling. Air and decay gas differ from each other; they show different distributions and appear at different times. These patterns are typical and permit discrimination in most cases. In cases of doubt, PMI indicates the best localization, from where the forensic pathologist can obtain the gas for analysis by puncture.

After death, decay gas is first visible in the vessels, thereafter in the cavities (pleural, subarachnoid, and peritoneal), and last, in the parenchymal organs, the muscles, and the soft tissue. Decay gas (and air) migrates upward; therefore, it can be seen in the ventral vessels of the liver and the anterior chest wall. The differential diagnosis has to consider air embolism, and air replacing blood via a vascular opening or injury. The time until decay gas appears after death varies: in corpses without cooling, decay gas emerges earlier and in a larger quantity than in those conserved by cooling. However, late appearance does occur. These variations in time of decay gas formation make it difficult for a reliable guess about the time passed since death.

In isolated cases, decay gas filling the vessels allows for visualization of vascular pathologies, similar to postmortem pneumoangiography. Even virtual endoscopy can be performed. This is valid for pulmonary embolism, vascular stenosis, and vascular occlusion (**Figure 1(a) and (b)**).

Because air and decay gas migrate upward, it is possible to fill and analyze vessels by changing the position of the corpse. In air embolism, the superior vena cava (SVC) and its feeding veins are dilated. Similar dilation also involves the right heart and pulmonary artery. Air embolism may occur as a complication of skull and facial bone fractures. This means that upon observing air in the veins and in the right heart, one has to look for fractures passing through the jugular foramen, and with air in the arteries, fractures via the carotid canal must be looked for. On suspicion of air embolism, the analysis must pay attention to those vessels where the air could have passed. Pneumothorax due to trauma, gunshots, and sharp trauma is

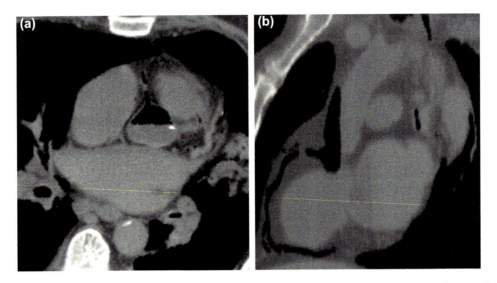

Figure 1   (a and b) Incomplete occlusion of the right coronary artery. The coronary artery is filled with gas coming from the ascending aorta. Gas peripheral of the occlusion indicates a gas passage. postmortem computed tomography. Axial (a) and sagittal (b) display.

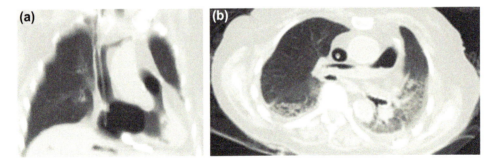

Figure 2   (a and b) Gas in the superior vena cava in the right heart and in the pulmonary artery. Central venous catheter till the right atrium. No gas in the ascending aorta. Calcifications of the pericardium. Differential diagnosis between air passage through the catheter either antemortem during cardiac massage with thorax compression (possible) or postmortem when disconnecting the catheter (possible) and postmortem decay gas (improbable). Frontal (a) and axial (b) display.

also a cause of air embolism. In clinical medicine, air embolism is known as a complication of punctures. Gas in the vessels of the heart or brain connected to a sudden death in angiography suggests an air injection. This hypothesis becomes more probable when decay gas cannot be found in other vessels, especially in those of the liver, and when the PMCT has been performed shortly after death, that is, before decay gas appears. Cardiac massage in reanimation is another cause: in cardiac massage, air can be aspirated via vascular catheters and cause air embolism. Air in the cerebral and/or cardiac vessels disappears by transport and absorption. This has to be taken into account when no air is found. This has to be expected when, after futile reanimation, hours have passed before death is declared. Shortly after death, the brain damage may be visible

in PMCT and postmortem magnetic resonance imaging (PMMRI), as would have been before death had been declared. This time window, however, is narrow.

After decay gas becomes visible in the vessels, it appears in the head (between the brain and skull), the pleural space, and the peritoneal space. In general, it appears first in the peritoneal space—a possible explanation is gas production by enterobacteria. In case of absence of peritoneal gas, this means that gas in the pleural space and in the head is probably not decay gas. In consequence, one must look for a cause of a pneumothorax or for an open skull fracture. After reanimation, a bilateral pneumothorax induces the search of air bubbles in the tissue, which indicates attempts of vascular punctures of the vena jugularis or vena axillaris. At these sites, traces of bleeding are less common.

In the tissue, decay gas appears after it has become visible in the vessels first and thereafter in the peritoneal space. This is valid for parenchyma of organs, soft tissue, and muscles. Bubbles of decay gas first become visible in the pancreas and the spleen, and thereafter in the liver, the kidney, and the lung. When these sites do not show gas, gas inclusions in the trunk wall, the soft tissue of the neck, and the extremities are likely due to trauma and not due to decay. In suspected suicide, decay gas near the wrist joint may indicate a trauma due to a self-afflicted cut.

In PMCT, gas filling of the vertebral vessels and of those of the base of the skull may mimic fractures. A correct interpretation is possible by visualizing the characteristic vascular pattern; the filling with gas of neighboring vessels is an indication. Gas filling visualizes underlying disease; gastric varices are an example.

Case Report

The corpse was dedicated to the anatomy department. It contained gas (decay gas or air) in the SVC and in the right heart (**Figure 2(a) and (b)**). No gas could be found in other vessels or in the left heart. A vascular catheter had been inserted into the right jugular vein; it passed via the SVC and ended in the right atrium.

Information about antemortem treatment and underlying diseases is lacking. The fact that the corpse is dedicated to the anatomy indicates that natural death has been attested and that reanimation was not tried. Extended calcifications of the pericardium suggest cardiac disease. Little fluid in the lung excludes pulmonary edema when death had occurred. The differential diagnosis has to be made with the cardinal symptom "gas in the SVC accompanying a central venous catheter." It concerns the following:

- Aspiration of air (resulting in air embolism), possibly in the course of cardiac massage or by faulty infusion
- Postmortem replacement of blood by air
- Decay gas postmortem

Decay gas seems improbable: Gas can only be seen in the SVC and its feeding vessels, in the right heart, and in the pulmonary artery. Gas cannot be found in other places, especially not in the hepatic vessels. Postmortem replacement of blood by air seems unlikely: The gas filling of the SVC, the right heart, and the pulmonary artery is combined with distension. In the case of postmortem replacement, these vessels would not be distended; their aspect would be that of a collapse.

Aspiration of air seems possible but is not proved: the changing pressure during cardiac massage could have sucked in air via an open catheter. However, there are no rib fractures, which are normally seen when external cardiac massage has occurred.

Fluid

Water is the main component of the extracellular and intracellular fluids; the blood; and the fluid in the cerebrospinal, pleural, peritoneal, and pericardial space. After death, gravity induces a displacement. Patterns result; they have to be recognized when performing PMI. Leveling occurs via connecting openings. The following are examples:

- Paranasal sinuses: Leveling occurs between fluid in the pharynx and the different sinuses, if the foramina are open. In general, there is no early opacity due to leveling between the pharynx and the cavities of the petrous bone, because the Eustachian tube is not open.
- Esophagus, the trachea, and the pharynx.
- Trachea and the bronchial system.

Fluid displacement also occurs in the parenchyma of organs. This is visible in the following:

- Lung: During the first hours after death, above the pulmonary septa, densities due to migrating fluid are visible; later, they are visible above the dorsal chest wall only. Layers occur due to fluid in the lung and pleural effusions. There is leveling between these layers and the free fluid in the trachea and the bronchi.
- Brain: Sulcus effacement, which starts in the occipital region. The brain volume increases; only early PMCT or PMMRI allows differentiation between antemortem cerebral edema and postmortem fluid shift.
- Other parenchymal organs (liver, pancreas, adrenal glands, and kidneys) and the digestive tract.
- Large vessels of the chest: The aorta shows an indentation, and thereafter the form of a trefoil. These changes are more marked after massive blood loss.

In the vessels, blood shows layers by sedimentation of erythrocytes. This is visible in the aortic arch. In the brain, the occipital sinuses and large veins emerge; the same happens with the middle cerebral artery.

In the aorta, the heart, and the pulmonary artery, postmortem thrombus formation is visible as an oval, well-defined structure. This structure is hyperdense in most cases. However, hypodense thrombi also occur. The differential diagnosis of postmortem thrombus formation concerns a preexisting embolus, especially in antemortem pulmonary embolism. If antemortem pulmonary embolism is suspected, the morphology of the structure in question can be visualized with injecting air in the vascular system (pneumoangiography). This injection is possible via a central venous catheter. This approach can be combined with virtual endoscopy. The surface of an antemortem embolus differs from that of a postmortem thrombus.

The large thoracic vessels and the heart change their form when the water diffuses into the tissue and into the cavities/spaces of the body. In cross-section images, the aorta changes from round/oval to trefoil and collapses, the SVC changes from round to oval, and the pulmonary artery narrows. These changes are marked after massive blood loss. If these changes of form are accompanied by increasing fluid in the lungs and pleural effusion, the radiologist should suggest postmortem changes. Massive fluid in the lungs and pleural effusions without changes of form is in favor of antemortem pulmonary edema and cardiac insufficiency. Massive change of form without increased fluid in the lungs indicates blood loss.

Gunshot

PMI localizes the bullet and its fragments, shows its path, and helps to recognize its size and type. In civil unrest cases, PMI may show deadly effects of "nonlethal weapons" such as rubber bullets and plastic bullets.

Localization is possible with radiographs and PMCT. This facilitates detection of a projectile displaced by blood flow (bullet embolism), gravity, and movements, such as in the digestive tract. Furthermore, PMCT shows injuries of organs. In decomposed bodies, a radiograph or a PMCT easily localizes a bullet. This localization indicates the possibility of a lethal shot. This is also valid if soft tissue injuries can no longer be proved in the decomposed organs.

Entry and exit of a bullet indicate the direction. In gunshot injuries to the head, the differentiation between entry and exit holes in flat bones is primarily based on the cratering effect in the direction of fire. In the skull, the rule of Puppe also allows recognizing both (**Figure 3**). This rule states that an existing fracture (due to the entry of the bullet) stops the propagation of a second fracture (due to the exit). Furthermore, Puppe's rule permits one to determine the sequence of gunshots. MSCT provides images for demonstration by 3D reconstruction.

In the trunk and extremities, bubbles and blood indicate the entrance and the exit wounds. In the head and in the trunk, fractures, fragments of bones and of the bullet (dots), blood, and injuries of organs indicate the path. Air in the vessels is due to a vascular injury. It must be differentiated from bubbles in the tissue; a display with MinIP (minimal intensity projection) helps. Dots appear at a distance of several centimeters from the bullet's path. This is typical for high-velocity gunshots and contact gunshots. The bone can deflect a bullet; a special form is the tangential shot in the skull.

Radiographs and (better) PMCTs show injuries. In general, fractures are easy to recognize. In the case of metal artifacts, the base of the skull may be a problem. A thorough analysis of a PMCT is mandatory to recognize all fractures and to determine their extents. The facial bones may be a problem too; after a shot into the mouth, PMCT shows the extension of the fractures, and vascular and cerebral injuries. 3D reconstruction permits demonstration. PMCT shows large bleedings. Their localization, quantity, and pattern reveal the source. Injuries of

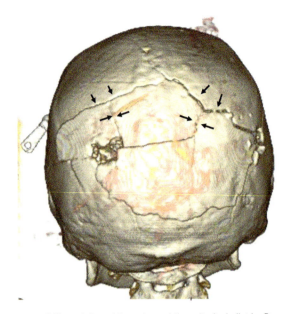

Figure 3   Differentiation of the entry and the exit of a bullet by Puppe's rule: When two fracture lines (arrows) of a solid surface intersect, it is possible to tell which one has been made first.

the heart, the lung, and large vessels may show up directly. Air in the peritoneum, the pleura, the tissue, and between the brain and skull and in the spinal canal indicates an opening to the exterior, to an air-containing organ or cavity (digestive tract, trachea, paranasal sinus, and lung). The injury itself is not

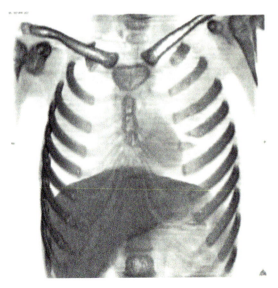

Figure 4   Transections of a rib by a stab on the left side. Child.

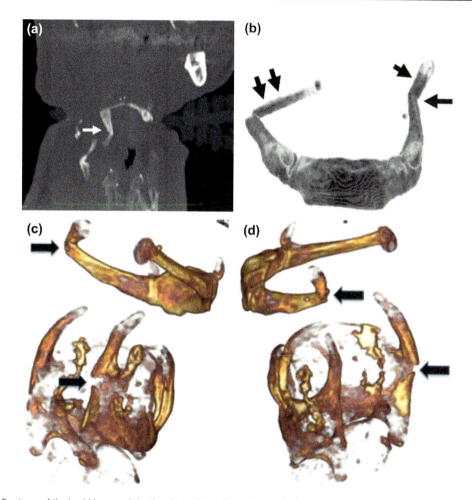

Figure 5   (a–d) Fractures of the hyoid bone and the thyroid cartilage. Strangulation. (a) Angulation of the hyoid bone (arrow). Frontal display (b) hyoid bone with bilateral fractures of the larger horn (arrows). (c and d) Fractures of the thyroid cartilage (arrow) and the hyoid bone (arrow). 3D display, oblique projection.

always visible; for example, when the lung has collapsed after a gunshot or a sharp trauma. Gunshot-induced air embolism may be the cause of death. The gas patterns allow for differentiation between decay gas and air.

Radiographs show projectiles and their characteristics. PMCT has limits due to metal artifacts. The determination of the projectile's caliber has to take magnification into account. Errors are possible. High-velocity injuries produce characteristic patterns; this is valid for disintegrating projectiles (dumdum), low velocity injuries, and coated and semicoated bullets as well.

Rubber and plastic bullets can be lethal when they enter the brain, the chest, or the abdomen. If they are detected in PMI, a detailed analysis is possible.

The integration of the 3D data of a PMCT into a 3D data set obtained at the site of a crime gives valuable information about the sequence of the actions.

Explosion

PMI shows injuries by the blast (lung lacerations and fractures), the explosive device (fragments of the weapon, nails, and shrapnel), and secondary injuries, among others, due to destroyed buildings. Suicide terrorist attacks have provoked the possibility that bone fragments of the attackers and other victims can be forced into the victim's body. They must be recognized for further investigation (DNA and infection such as

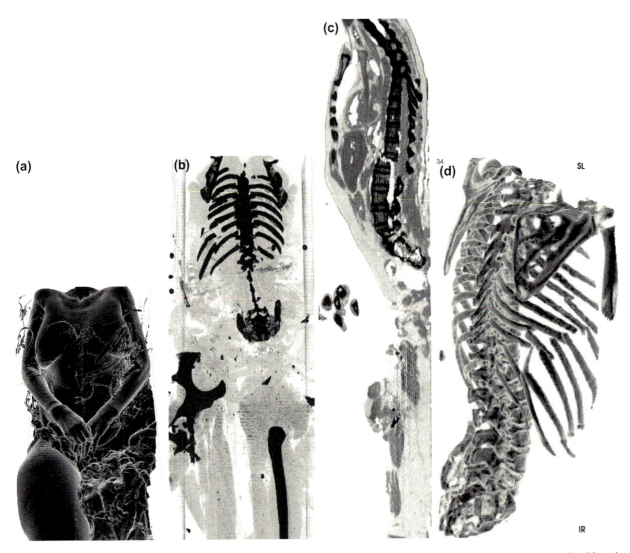

Figure 6   (a–d) Run over by a bus. (a) The 3D reconstruction (surface mode) shows the track of the bus wheel. (b and c) In the sagittal and frontal view, the damage to the body is apparent. (d) 3D display of the bones shows where the body has been hit (rib fractures, separation of pelvis and spine).

HIV). In war, PMI informs about the used weapon. This affects the military planning. The use of forbidden weapons (e.g., cluster bombs) can be proved by PMI.

Sharp Trauma

Transection of the rib cartilage and of the bone indicates the applied force (**Figure 4**). This is valid for other structures too, such as a silicon mamma prosthesis. The sharp trauma/stab creates bubbles and bleeding; it injures organs (heart, lung, vessels, and larynx). These tracks are the base for determining the direction and the depth of the trauma. Broken-off fragments of the weapon involved furnish additional information. Marking the wound with contrast substance has been proposed. Inspection gives the number and the localization of stabs more accurately than surface reconstruction. The information as to where the stabs are, supports the radiologist in his or her interpretation. The analysis of local bleeding, a pneumothorax, and air in the vessels help determine the sequence of stabs and cuts. The radiologist has to differentiate between air embolism and air replacing lost blood, and he or she must look for defense fractures of the hand.

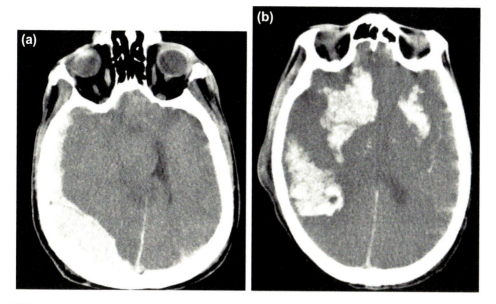

Figure 7 (a and b) Intracerebral bleeding. (a) Subdural, epidural, and subarachnoidal bleeding. Space occupying, the midline is displaced to the left. (b) Bleeding into the right and the left cerebral parenchyma and subarachnoidal bleeding.

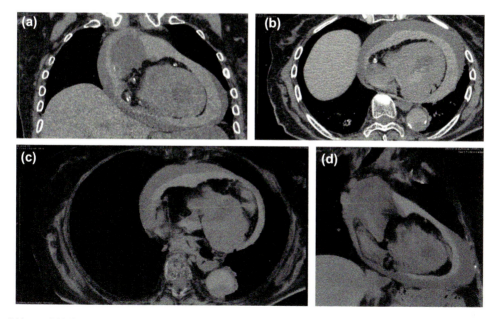

Figure 8 (a–d) Myocardial infarction with rupture into the pericardium. (a and b) Blood with layers in the pericardium. (c and d) Blood in the myocardium allows localizing the rupture.

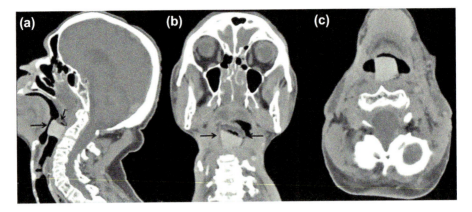

Figure 9   (a–c) Bolus death. The meat bolus (arrows) obstructs the airways in the larynx. (a) Sagittal view; (b) frontal view; and (c) axial view.

Suffocation and Strangulation

PMI visualizes the obstruction of the airways or injuries of the airways, especially the larynx. The radiologist has to look for fractures of the hyoid bone, the thyroid cartilage, and for ruptures of the membranes, which connect them (**Figure 5(a)–(d)**). 3D display of the larynx should show the bone and the cartilage; this helps analyze the intensity of the acting forces and their direction. Air in the cartilage and in the hyoid bone indicates fractures; air between the hyoid bone and thyroid cartilage indicates membrane rupture. Injuries of the airways provoke bleeding, which can block the airways. Fractures in the cervical spine indicate sudden flexions. Brain changes need to be visualized early; otherwise, they cannot be differentiated from postmortem changes.

Deceleration Trauma, Compression, Blunt Trauma, and Blows

Lethal traumata due to deceleration, compression, blunt force, and blows usually involve several organs and regions. In general, these are cases of multiple traumata. PMI has to visualize the injuries for determining the cause of death, and their patterns for differentiating accidents from inflicted trauma. 3D images of the skeleton (**Figure 6(a)–(d)**) demonstrate the mechanism to jurists and relatives. Modified images show the injuries of organs and the bleeding. The complexity of these injuries demands a thorough analysis; otherwise, important details are missed. This is valid for injuries of the larynx—it is advisable to examine the larynx with a 3D display visualizing the cartilage and the bones; furthermore, one has to search for air in the soft tissue and blood in the neighborhood so as to not overlook ruptures of membranes and ligaments.

Water-Logged Corpse, Drowning, and Aspiration

Water-logged corpses often display signs of decay. Decay gas is visible in the vessels, the cavities, and the tissue. Virtual endoscopy of the heart is possible. Obstructions of brain and heart vessels show up; the pathologist must verify them. Liquid in the paranasal sinus is not specific to drowning. It does not prove it—PMI demonstrates liquid in every third deceased person, with little connection to the cause of death. Foam in the trachea and the bronchus suggests aspiration; the aspiration becomes more probable when similar foam is found in the esophagus and in the pharynx. Aspiration is highly probable when silicates are visible in the trachea or the bronchi in water-logged bodies. However, the radiologist needs to have in mind that after death, the tonus change of the upper esophageal sphincter promotes the fluid exchange. An aspiration has probably occurred, when a tooth is found in a bronchus and is missing in the jaw. Bubbles in the soft tissue of the defect indicate the recent loss. Children aspirate nuts and toys, which do not show up on radiographs or even PMCT, unless radiopaque (toys).

Sudden Death

The term "sudden death" informs that death has occurred suddenly, that there is no knowledge of a possible preexisting disease, and that there is no hint of a crime. PMI has the aim to reveal the cause of death and to exclude a violent death. PMCT shows cerebral and cardiac causes. Within the cranial vault, the cause of death can be parenchymal, subdural, epidural, or subarachnoid bleeding (**Figure 7(a) and (b)**), extended infarction, and tumor. These lesions are space occupying; they are accompanied by swelling, incarceration,

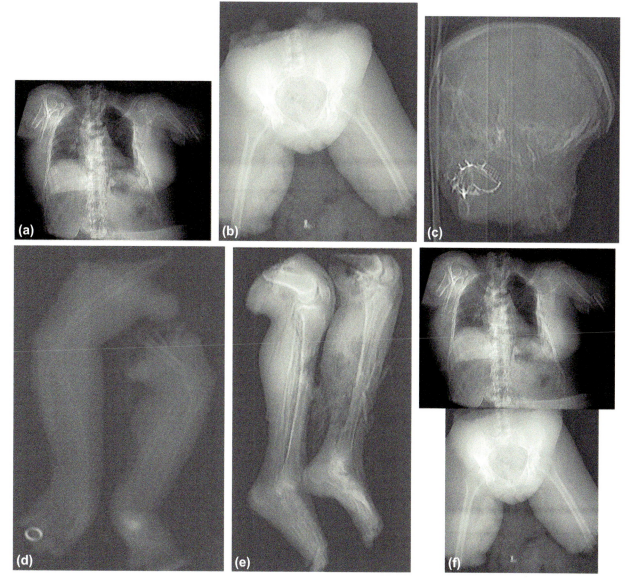

Figure 10 (a–k) Composing the body. (a–e) These parts were discovered in different places. They were partially burnt. (f) Image fusion, using radiographs, showed that the two trunk parts fitted to each other; the upper and the lower lumbar vertebral columns complemented one another. (g) 3D display of the upper and the lower cervical spine. They complement one another. (h) 3D display of the fragments of the upper-left arm complement one another. (i) 3D reconstruction of the head showed impacts (blows) to the front and to the back of the head. (j) Blood in the ventricles indicates that these impacts had occurred during lifetime. (k) 3D display of the hyoid bone showed a fracture of the right major horn of the hyoid. This fracture was not explained by the decapitation; it indicated additional violence.

and disturbed circulation of the cerebrospinal fluid. The diagnosis antemortem edema is problematic; it is only possible, when PMCT and/or PMMRI have been made shortly after death. A radiograph showing a knife in the head suggests a violent death.

Nontraumatic perforation of the myocardium with hemopericardium is a cause of natural cardiac death. Sometimes, PMCT and PMMRI visualize a trail of blood in the myocardium (**Figure 8(a)–(d)**). Another cause of a natural death is the ruptured aortic aneurysm in the chest and in the abdomen. A

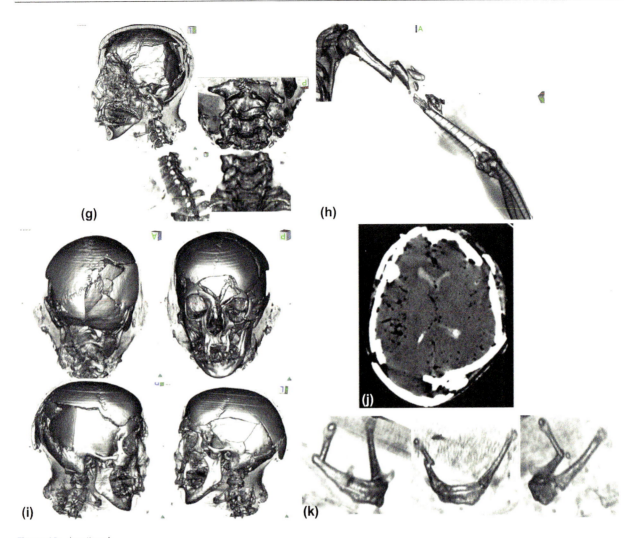

(g)

(h)

(i)

(j)

(k)

Figure 10   (*continued*).

large cardiac aneurysm suggests a cardiac cause; the same is valid in the case of calcifications of the pericardium. Such calcifications can be due to a bullet, which may have been there for decades. A bilateral pneumothorax and an air embolism are usually caused by traumata and not by natural diseases. Bolus death with obstruction of the airways is easy to see in PMCT (**Figure 9(a)–(c)**).

Pulmonary embolism is rarely detectable without applying contrast substance. The embolus has no contrast difference permitting the diagnosis. Its morphology does not show up in PMCT and PMMRI unless a contrast substance is given; air injection (pneumoangiography) fills the pulmonary artery and its branches. The embolus becomes visible; its surface can be seen in virtual endoscopy. Angiography with positive contrast substance produces equal results.

Identification

The pathologist assigns bones to humans. PMI is secondary. However, PMI allows one to differentiate between human bones and animal bones. PMI helps to detect bullets and metals, even if covered by bone. Its localization hints at violent death.

In unidentified bodies, PMI is meant to visualize details allowing the identification, i.e., traces of preceding surgery with metal implants. The X-ray morphology of the paranasal sinus and the anterior chest wall varies. This offers a chance to compare postmortem and antemortem radiographs for identification. Multislice PMCT leads to a 3D data set. This data set allows producing images similar to radiographs. These radiographs obtained with PMCT are usable for comparison.

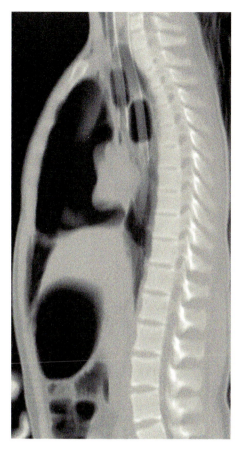

Figure 11 Two tracheal tubes. The first tube had been left in the esophagus for facilitating the second intubation.

Using a curved mode, PMCT also produces images apt for comparison with orthopantomograms.

PMI may help to determine the deceased's age. The proceeding is that of age determination in the living. Radiographs (PMCT) of the left (nondominating) hand, orthopantomograms, and radiographs of the sternoclavicular joint are part of established methods. Sex determination is also possible. In general, however, the radiologist has less experience than the pathologist determining the age and the sex of an unknown deceased.

Case Report (Figure 10(a)–(f))

Human parts were found (**Figure 10(a)–(e)**). They had been set on fire. The police asked, whether they belonged to only one or several persons. Image fusion with radiographs showed that the two trunk parts fitted to each other; the upper and the lower lumbar vertebral column complemented one another

(**Figure 10(f)**). 3D display of the upper and the lower cervical spine demonstrated the same (**Figure 10(g)**); the fragments of the upper arms also fitted to each other (**Figure 10(h)**). So the answer to the question was that the discovered parts belonged to one person only.

How death had occurred was of interest thereafter. 3D reconstruction of the head (**Figure 10(i)**) proved that there had been impacts (blows) to the front and to the back of the head. Blood in the ventricles indicated that these impacts had occurred during lifetime (**Figure 10(j)**). Gas in the cerebral vessels could have replaced the blood after decapitation. However, the analysis of the larynx, which was cut through between the hyoid bone and the thyroid cartilage, with 3D display evinced a hyoid fracture of the right major horn of the hyoid (**Figure 10(k)**). This fracture was not explained by the decapitation. It indicated additional violence.

Reanimation

Reanimation is performed after a collapse, an accident, or inflicted violence (gunshot, sharp trauma, blow). Reanimation concerns respiration (intubation or tracheotomy, ventilation by mask, or tracheal or tracheostomy tube), circulation (chest compression), and medication (vessel puncture). These different measures leave traces visible in PMI. PMCT shows these traces in detail.

Respiration

The tracheal tube can end in a bronchus, or in the esophagus; the blocking balloon can lie in the pharynx compressing the vocal cord. Two tubes can be present (**Figure 11**)—the first was left in the esophagus to facilitate the placement of the second tube.

Air bubbles and emphysema (and bleeding) indicate injuries of the pharynx, the mucosa, and the trachea. Pharynx tubes with two balloons are supposed to be more secure than simple tracheal tubes; however, detailed analysis in PMCT shows that there is not always a free airway to the trachea.

Tracheotomy may fail. In small children, the trachea is sometimes difficult to enter. In adults, the posterior wall of pharynx can be perforated; the tracheostomy tube can end outside the lumen.

Mask ventilation and ventilation via a tube in the esophagus inflate the gastrointestinal tract (meteorism). If this is visible, the intubation probably has been difficult, even if the tube is finally in the correct position. Similarly, neck emphysema (with a tracheostomy tube in correct position) points to difficulties performing the tracheostomy. In both cases, the time span prior to ventilation might have been extended significantly.

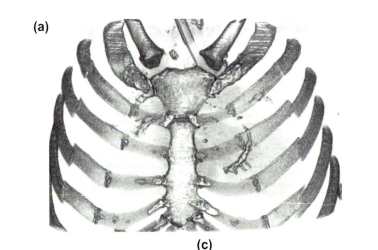

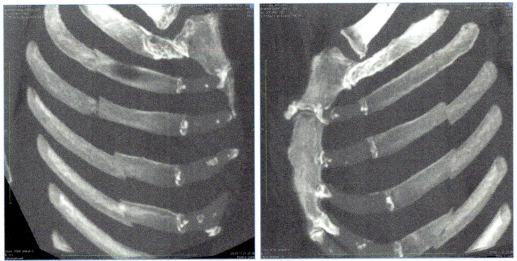

Figure 12 (a–c) Rib fractures due to chest compression in reanimation. Rib one is spared. 3D view.

Circulation

Chest compression fractures the ribs. Fractures of ribs 2–6 are typical. Rib 1 is normally spared. Ribs 7–9 can be fractured too. In general, the fractures show a characteristic pattern (**Figure 12(a)–(c)**); the fractures of the upper ribs are nearer to the sternum. The lower ribs may have a fractured cartilage, which is more difficult to detect even on PMCT. It is advisable to differentiate between fractures with complete interruption of the bone, and infractions showing an angulation only. These infractions are not necessarily instable. After chest compression in reanimation, gas is usually seen in the hepatic vessels. This gas appears with a distribution pattern, which is different from that of gas entering the vascular system by suction via an open

vascular catheter. The latter is found in the large vessels of the upper half of the body; the liver is often spared.

Medication

Vascular punctures may provoke a pneumothorax, sometimes bilateral. Bleeding may occur too. If pneumothorax and/or bleeding are/is present, the radiologist has to look for puncture traces, which are bubbles and (rarely) bleeding localized at the sites typical for punctures. A catheter outside the vessels makes interpretation easier. Always, one has to keep in mind that the preceding trauma could have provoked the pneumothorax and the bleeding. A vascular catheter in a wrong position could

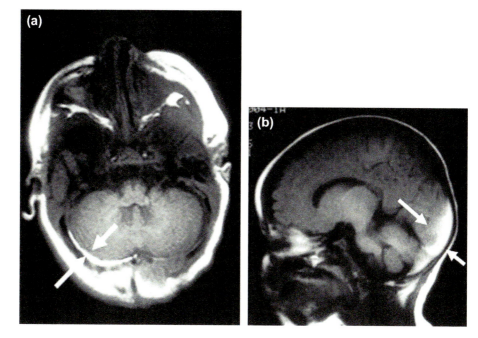

Figure 13   (a and b) Bleeding infratentorial (arrows). PMMRI.

have hindered the passage of an infusion and of injected medicaments.

PMI and especially PMCT can be a tool for quality control. They allow evaluating the performed reanimation. They furnish information that is otherwise more difficult to obtain or cannot be obtained at all. This is valid, if tubes and catheters are removed before autopsy.

Invasive Medicine and Care

After invasive actions, PMI exhibits success and failure; this concerns the position of vascular stents and aortic valves. After endoscopy, bleeding and perforation become visible. The demonstration with images facilitate the evaluation of the procedure and to avoid complications in the future. This is also valid for treating complication. In singular cases, complications become visible; this could be either due to the invasive action or the following treatment.

PMI shows a decubitus and its extent, urinary retention, the position of a urinary catheter, and the position of a gastric tube or its malposition. Such observations may raise the question, whether a poor prognosis of a patient affects attention and care.

The malposition of a catheter puts the patient at risk. Multiple vascular catheters suggest difficulties in their placement

and limited control of their position; additional edema hints at difficulties in fluid management.

After surgery, the proceedings in PMI and clinical diagnostic imaging are similar. PMI has the advantage that there is no limiting exposure dose, and therefore, repetition is possible; on the other hand, functional imaging with contrast medium is not possible, which limits the possibilities to recognize vital parts of the myocardium.

Child Abuse, Infanticide, Neonaticide, and Stillbirth

The radiologist must look for older trauma even if a lethal trauma is apparent. Fractures of different age and unfitting for the age suggest child abuse. PMI, PMCT, and PMMRI enlarge the spectrum; showing bleedings and fractures, and allow age determination (**Figure 13(a) and (b)**). However, they have limitations compared to clinical CT and MRI, which allow analyzing the perfusion of organs with contrast substances.

In shaken baby syndrome, PMCT, PMMRI, and PM-sonography usually show the intracranial bleeding. PMCT is also useful to find rib fractures, mainly infractions characterized by angulation and incomplete interruption of the corticalis. These infractions result when treating the baby.

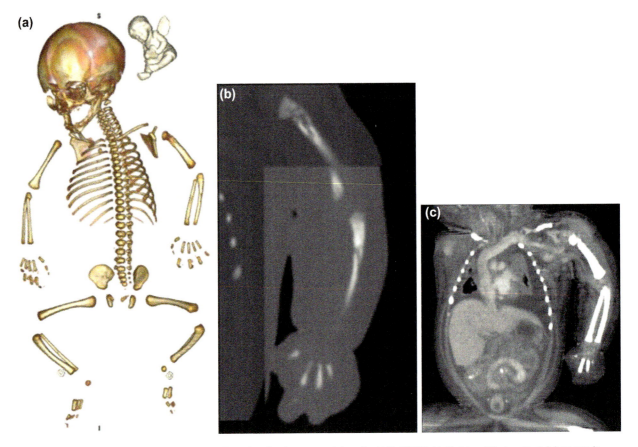

Figure 14 (a–c) Fractures of the left arm. a–v malformation. Death on second day after birth. PMCT. (a) Skeleton, 3D view: the left humerus is thicker than the right. There is a slight difference between the right and the left forearm. (b) Left arm, frontal view. The humerus and the ulna are too thick; they are fractured. (c) Frontal view. Upper chest with enlarged vessels (here veins) on the left suggesting an a–v malformation involving the bones and explaining the pathologic fractures.

The differential diagnosis of multiple fractures of different ages concerns birth trauma, osteogenesis imperfecta, congenital malformations, and anomalies. "Menke syndrome" with multiple extra suture bones is an example: a hereditary disturbance of the copper metabolism.

The death of a child may be planned or due to neglect. The cause of death may be obvious or obscure. PMCT allows visualizing details with possible connection to the death and demonstrating the findings. Examples are the projectile in the head, the bilateral hematopneumothorax due to stabs, the tracheal tube in the mouth after failed reanimation, and the foreign body in the larynx after failed tracheotomy.

A stillbirth raises the question of its cause. Malformation guides the analysis; this helps to decide about future pregnancies. PMCT visualizes malformations of the skeleton.

Sometimes, malformation of systems and organs can be seen, too (**Figure 14(a)–(c)**). Fractures raise the question of birth trauma. Furthermore, the (re)animation of the newborn can be analyzed: Pneumothorax may be due to punctures and drainages. Air can enter the vascular system postmortem, when withdrawing a catheter or antemortem by punctures. Catheter malposition indicates the difficulties of the neonatologist. Air in the lung and air in the digestive tract indicate life after birth; however, decay gas can mimic these findings. One has to keep in mind that decay produces gas; however, fluid may migrate after death into the lung and mimic airless lungs.

Dead newborns should be examined for trauma with PMCT. In the case of postmortem deformation and decay, reconstruction of the skeleton is useful. This is mandatory if violent death is a possibility.

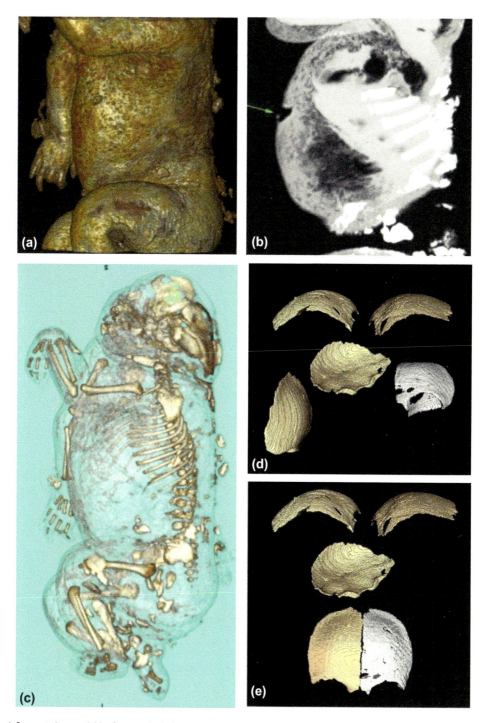

Figure 15   (a–g) Suspected neonaticide. Corpse of a baby found in a river. (a and b) Decay. Stab wound in the trunk. (c) 3D view of the skeleton. The head is deformed. (d) Digital separation of the bones of the skull. No fracture apparent. (e and f) Digital reconstruction of the skull. No fracture apparent. (g) 3D view of the skeleton. Fracture of the eighth rib on the right.

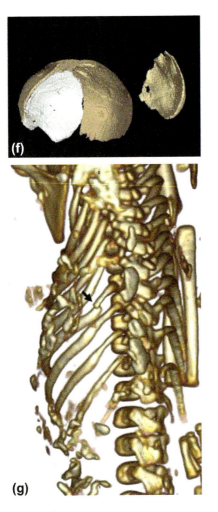

Figure 15 (*continued*).

Case Report (Figure 15(a)–(g))

The corpse of the baby was found in a river. The trunk had a stab wound (**Figure 15(a) and (b)**). The skeleton was intact; however, the head was deformed (**Figure 15(c)**). The radiologist searched fractures. Therefore, he isolated the bones of the skull for digital reconstruction (**Figure 15(d)**). No fracture evinced (**Figure 15(e) and (f)**). The analysis of the trunk showed a fracture of the eighth rib on the right (**Figure 15(g)**).

Conclusion

PMI is a tool for the pathologist. PMCT and PMMRI show a rupture of the heart and aorta, cerebral bleeding, and bilateral pneumothorax as causes of death. They may exhibit additional diseases. Radiographs and PMCT localize bullets and other foreign bodies. The visualization of tracheal and gastric tubes and vascular and urinary catheters offers possibilities for quality control. PMCT's strengths lie in its ability to reveal gas: air embolism and failed punctures. The 3D data set of PMCT and PMMRI can be reviewed repeatedly. A display in 3D helps to demonstrate findings to legal persons and relatives.

> *See also:* **Anthropology/Odontology:** Postmortem Interval; **Forensic Medicine/Causes of Death:** Strangulation; **Forensic Medicine/Clinical:** Neonaticide; **Forensic Medicine/Pathology:** Early and Late Postmortem Changes; Estimation of the Time Since Death.

Further Reading

Brogdon, B.G., Vogel, H., McDowell, J.D., 2003. A Radiological Atlas of Abuse, Torture, Terrorism, and Inflicted Trauma. CRC Press, Boca Raton, FL.

Goyen, M., 2007. Real Whole-Body MRI: Requirements, Indications, Perspectives. Mcgraw-Hill Medical, New York.

Kneubuehl, B.P., 2011. Wound Ballistics: Basics and Application. Springer, Berlin, Heidelberg.

Knieriem, U., 2012. Validierung der CT-gestützten Beurteilung von Koronararterien sowie gewebespende-relevanter Gefäßabschnitte am Beispiel der Arteria femoralis Inaug. University of Hamburg (Dissertation).

Nushida, H., Vogel, H., Püschel, K., Heinemann (Eds.), 2011. Der durchsichtige Tote – Post mortem CT und forensische Radiologie. Verlag Dr. Kovac, Hamburg.

Scharf, L.B., 2011. Virtuelle Endoskopie mit Computertomographie post mortem: Herz, Aortenklappe, Mitralklappe. Verlag Dr. Kovac, Hamburg.

Thali, M.J., Dirnhofer, R., Vock, P., 2008. The Virtopsy Approach: 3D Optical and Radiological Scanning and Reconstruction in Forensic Medicine. CRC Press, Boca Raton, FL.

Thali, M.J., Viner, M.D., Brogdon, B.G. (Eds.), 2011. Brogdon's Forensic Radiology, second ed. CRC Press, Boca Raton, FL.

Vogel, H., 2008. Violence, War, Borders. X-rays: Evidence and Threat. Shaker-Verlag, Aachen.

Vogel, B., 2011. Das traumatisierte Herz. Befunde der bildgebenden Diagnostik bei Verstorbenen und Lebenden. Südwestdeutscher Verlag für Hochschulschriften, Saarbrücken.

Key Terms

Apparent death, Aspiration, Audit, Autopsy, Autopsy guidelines, Autopsy rate, Autopsy report, Autopsy rules, Autopsy techniques, Blow, Blunt trauma, Care, Cause of death, Child abuse, Code of practice, Compression trauma, Death certification, Decay gas, Deceleration trauma, Dissection, Drowning, Evidence, Explosion, External examination, External postmortem examination,

Guideline, Gunshot, Identification, Immediate cause of death, Infanticide, Invasive Medicine, Manner of death, Medical specialty, Microscopy, Mortality statistics, Multislice CT, Necropsy, Neonaticide, Postmortem changes, Postmortem CT, Postmortem examination, Postmortem imaging, Quality control, Reanimation, Sharp trauma, Stillbirth, Strangulation, Sudden death, Suffocation, Time of death, Underlying cause of death, Vita minima, Water-logged corpse.

Review Questions

1. Why are external postmortem examinations important?
2. According to the World Health Organization, what has to be part of the death certificate?
3. What is of the utmost importance to certify cause of death? Why?
4. Are the legal bases for postmortem examinations consistent from country to country?
5. Why is the definition of a human corpse so complicated?
6. What constitutes "death"?
7. Why is it called the "AEIOU" rule?
8. What factors can lead to apparent death?
9. List at least four reasons to determine an unnatural death.
10. Name the scientists who had an influence over the standardization of the autopsy method.
11. What is histopathology?
12. What instrument is central to histopathology? Who emphasized its use and why?
13. When is histopathology necessary?
14. What has been the biggest change to autopsies in the last 20 years?
15. How are tissue samples prepared for histopathology?
16. Why are stains used in histopathology?
17. Why are histopathological examinations useful forensically?
18. How can postmortem imaging be used to assist a medicolegal investigation?
19. What types of postmortem imaging are commonly used?
20. Explain how postmortem imaging could help identify someone?

Discussion Questions

1. Why has the ability to dissect deceased humans varied through history and culture?
2. Why is standardization of the autopsy as a method important? When did it become standardized?
3. What is the difference between a medicolegal autopsy and a clinical autopsy? Why is this an important difference?
4. Discuss the sampling procedures for histopathology? Why should they be standardized? When should other samples be taken and why?
5. Computer assisted tomography scans (CAT scans) are exceptionally precise imaging tools, allowing three-dimensional imaging of a body. Virtual autopsies, where the body is not cut open, are now conducted by CAT scans in instances where the relatives do not want the body cut open, typically for religious or cultural reasons. There are other reasons to use these tools during a death investigation. What do you think they are? How can this technology be used in "normal cases"? Should there be an option to *not* cut open a body for a medicolegal autopsy based on religious beliefs? Why or why not?

Additional Readings

Ahmad, M., Rahman, F.N., 2015. Virtual autopsy: a new trend in forensic investigation. Journal of Armed Forces Medical College, Bangladesh 9 (2), 100–106.

Al-Waheeb, S., Al-Kandary, N., Aljerian, K., 2015. Forensic autopsy practice in the Middle East: comparisons with the west. Journal of Forensic and Legal Medicine 32, 4–9.

Bieri, U., Moch, H., Dehler, S., Korol, D., Rohrmann, S., 2015. Changes in autopsy rates among cancer patients and their impact on cancer statistics from a public health point of view: a longitudinal study from 1980 to 2010 with data from Cancer Registry Zurich. Virchows Archiv 466 (6), 637–643.

Bolliger, S.A., Thali, M.J., 2015. Imaging and virtual autopsy: looking back and forward. Philosophical Transactions of the Royal Society B 370 (1674), 20140253.

Lloyd, K.L., Suvarna, S.K., 2016. The cardiac pathology of non-natural (forensic) deaths. Medicine, Science and the Law 56 (2), 154.

Sogawa, N., Michiue, T., Ishikawa, T., Inamori-Kawamoto, O., Oritani, S., Maeda, H., 2015. Postmortem CT morphometry of great vessels with regard to the cause of death for investigating terminal circulatory status in forensic autopsy. International Journal of Legal Medicine 129 (3), 551–558.

Suzuki, H., Hasegawa, I., Hoshino, N., Fukunaga, T., 2015. Two forensic autopsy cases of death due to upper gastrointestinal hemorrhage: a comparison of postmortem computed tomography and autopsy findings. Legal Medicine 17 (3), 198–200.

Section 4. Trauma

Violence is a mainstay in criminal activity, and trauma is the end result of violence to a person. Trauma can also be the outcome of accidents or self-inflicted injuries, and a forensic pathologist must be able to not only see the trauma and infer what may have caused it but also determine the manner in which it was inflicted. Old, healed trauma must also be studied so that the pathologist can assess whether the wound was antemortem (before death), postmortem (after death), or perimortem (around the time of death). Again, reconstructions and a focus on timelines are central to the work of any forensic professional and pathologists are no different.

Blunt Injury

S Pollak, University of Freiburg, Freiburg, Germany
P Saukko, University of Turku, Turku, Finland

Glossary

Deceleration trauma When a body being in motion is forcibly stopped, the inner organs tend to continue the movement due to inertia so that the anatomical structures are subjected to tractive and shearing forces.

Fat embolism The term "fat embolism" indicates the presence of fat globules in the small vessels of the lungs and sometimes also in the systemic circulation, mostly as a consequence of major bone and/or soft tissue trauma.

Hematotympanum The term refers to the presence of blood in the tympanic cavity of the middle ear, often resulting from a basal skull fracture involving the petrous bone.

Lucid interval A temporary improvement after a head trauma followed by secondary deterioration (typically caused by a space-occupying intracranial hematoma).

Subarachnoid space This term describes the interval between the arachnoid membrane and the deeper pia mater (two meninges surrounding the brain and the spinal cord). The subarachnoid space normally contains the cerebrospinal fluid. In head injuries or as a consequence of a ruptured cerebral aneurysm, a hemorrhage may spread into the subarachnoid space leading to elevated intracranial pressure.

Introduction

The term "blunt trauma" can be defined as a damage to the body due to mechanical force applied either by the impact of a moving blunt object or by movement of the body against a hard surface, both mechanisms resulting in the transfer of kinetic energy high enough to produce an injury (mainly by compression, traction, torsion, and shear stresses). Blunt-force injuries occur in criminal assaults (e.g., a blow with a blunt-edged instrument, a punch, or a kick), in physical child abuse, in traffic and industrial accidents, in suicides (a jump from a height), and in accidental falls brought about by the victims themselves.

Blunt Injuries to the Integument

Abrasions

Abrasions are superficial injuries to the skin characterized by a traumatic removal, detachment, or destruction of the epidermis, mostly caused by friction. In the so-called tangential or brush abrasions, a lateral rubbing action scrapes off the superficial layers of the skin (e.g., from the body's sliding across a rough surface) and leaves a denuded corium, which is initially covered with serosanguineous fluid. In fresh grazes, the direction of impact can often be determined by the abraded epidermal shreds that remain attached to the end of the scrape. At a later time, the tissue fluid dries out and forms a brownish scab. If the lesion does not reach the dermis, it heals within several days without scarring. Infliction just before or after death results in a leathery ("parchment-like") appearance with a yellowish-brown discoloration (**Figure 1**).

Another type of abrasion is caused by a vertical impact to the skin (the so-called pressure or crushing abrasion). In such cases, the injuring object may be reflected by the shape of the skin injury so that the patterned abrasion can be regarded as an imprint of the causative object.

Contusions

Contusions or bruises are extravasations of blood within the soft tissues originating from ruptured vessels as a result of blunt trauma. In this context, only the contusions that are visible externally are considered. Textbooks usually differentiate between intradermal and subcutaneous bruises. In the first-mentioned category, the hemorrhage is located directly under the epidermis, that is, in the corium. This kind of superficial hematoma is usually sharply defined and red in color, whereas the more common bruises of the deeper subcutaneous layer have blurred edges and, at least initially, are in bluish-purple color.

Intradermal bruises may reflect the surface configuration of the impacting object (**Figure 2**). The skin that is squeezed into

grooves will show intradermal bleeding, whereas the areas exposed to the elevated parts remain pale. Especially in falls from a height, the texture of the clothing may produce a pattern of intradermal bruises corresponding to the weaving structure. Patterned extravasations of this type are also seen in tire tread marks when an individual is run over by a wheel, and in bruises from vertical stamping with ribbed soles.

Subcutaneous bruises are usually nonpatterned. Nevertheless, there may be bruising of special significance. If the body is struck by a stick, a broom handle, a pool cue, a rod, or any other elongated instrument, every blow leaves a double "tramline" bruise consisting of two parallel linear hematomas with an undamaged zone in between. Victims of blunt-force violence often sustain contusions from self-defense, typically located on the ulnar aspects of the forearms and on the back of the hands. The upper arms may show groups of roundish bruises from fingertip pressure in cases of vigorous gripping. A periorbital hematoma ("black eye") is induced either by a direct impact (e.g., a punch or a kick) or an indirect impact (due to seepage of blood from a fractured orbital roof, a fractured nasal bone, or from a neighboring scalp injury of the forehead; **Figure 3**).

In general, bruises are regarded as a sign of vitality indicating that the contusion was inflicted prior to death. During life, the blood from ruptured vessels is forced into the soft tissue by active extravasation. Nevertheless, to a limited extent, postmortem formation of contusions is possible due to passive ooze of blood. In surviving victims, a deep bruise may not become apparent on the skin until several hours or even days later because of the slow percolation of free blood from the original site to superficial tissue layers.

In a living person, the contusion undergoes a temporal series of color changes. Initially, most subcutaneous bruises appear purple-blue. As the hematoma resolves during the healing process, the hemoglobin released from the red blood cells is chemically degraded into other pigments such as

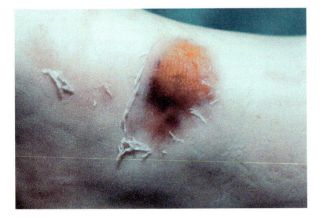

Figure 1   Tangential abrasion confined to the upper layers of the skin. The shreds of epidermis indicate the direction of impact. The central parts of the denuded corium show a parchment-like discoloration from drying.

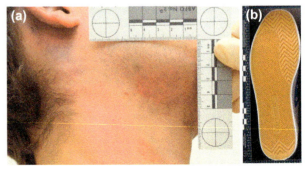

Figure 2   (a) Intradermal bruising corresponding to the ribbed sole pattern of the perpetrator's training shoes. (b) The imprint was caused by stamping actions against the face and neck of the victim lying on the ground.

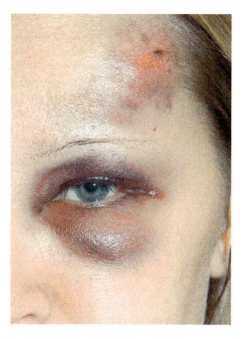

Figure 3 Periorbital hematoma of a live victim from a blow to the left frontal region. As a result of gravitational movement, the blood from the injured forehead spread to the eyelids within 1 day.

hemosiderin, biliverdin, and bilirubin. The color changes—usually over the course of several days—to green and yellow before it finally disappears (**Figure 4**). However, the rate of change is quite variable and depends on numerous factors, above all, the extent of the bruise.

The size of an intradermal or subcutaneous hematoma is not always indicative of the intensity of the force applied to the affected area. Elderly people or patients suffering from bleeding diathesis may get bruises from slight knocks or for other minor reasons. On the other hand, the absence of an externally visible injury does not necessarily mean that there was no relevant trauma. Subcutaneous bruises of surviving victims are often followed by gravity shifting of the hemorrhage leading to a secondary downward movement of the hematoma.

A special type of blunt injury to the soft tissues is frequently seen in pedestrians who have been struck or run over by motor vehicles. Both the skin and the subcutaneous layer may be avulsed from the underlying fascia or bones by shearing forces so that a blood-filled pocket is formed, typically in combination with a crush damage to the adjoining fatty tissue.

Lacerations

Lacerations are tears of the skin or of internal organs (see below). They may be caused by blows from blunt objects (such as a hammer, a whipped pistol, a rod, the toecaps of heavy footwear, or a fist); other lacerations are produced by an impact from vehicles or by a fall to the ground. Lacerations occur most commonly in body regions where the integument directly overlies a firm bony base acting as support (scalp, face, back of the hand, and shins). When the force acts on the skin, the subcutaneous tissue is squeezed between the injuring object and the bony platform so that the integument is compressed and crushed until it tears and splits sideways (**Figures 5 and 6**).

Lacerations are characterized by abraded, bruised, and crushed wound margins. The edges of the tears are typically irregular and ragged with bridging tissue strands (vessels, nerves, and fibers) running from side to side. The wound slits may be linear (especially in blows with a narrow, edged instrument), Y-shaped, or starlike. If the impacting object hits the skin at an oblique angle, one of the edges will be ripped

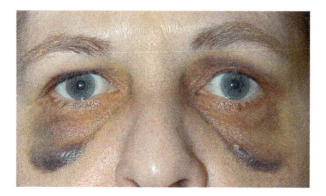

Figure 4 "Black eyes" inflicted by a single fist blow to the root of the nose (6 days before the photograph was taken). Note the yellow color on the periphery of the bruises.

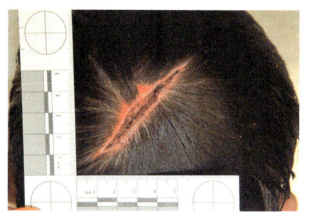

Figure 5 Occipital region of a 41-year-old man showing a slitlike laceration of the scalp surrounded by a reddish excoriation. The injury was caused by a fall on a concrete step when climbing over the balustrade of a balcony.

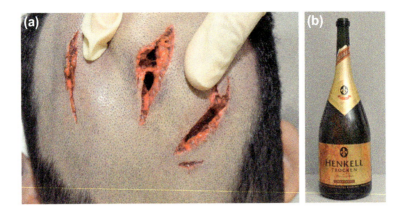

Figure 6   (a) Occipital region of a 27-year-old man, whose scalp had been shaved before autopsy, showing four lacerations from blows with an empty 3-L champagne bottle (b). Note the bridging tissue strand between the wound margins.

away resulting in unilateral undermining (undercutting and avulsion), which indicates the direction of the force. Sometimes foreign material from the causative instrument/surface is deposited in the depth of the wound slit. The abrasion surrounding the tear may correspond to the shape and dimensions of the impacting blunt-surfaced instrument or—in the case of a fall to the ground—the area of contact.

Head Injuries

The head is a common target in assaults with blunt objects; other common causes of head injuries are traffic accidents, falls from a height, and falls from a standing position. The area of impact usually reveals injuries of the scalp or the facial skin, but it has to be stressed that severe and even lethal traumatization is not necessarily associated with scalp bruising, marked swelling, excoriation, and/or laceration. There may be no externally visible signs, especially in skin areas covered with hair and in cases of a fall onto a flat surface. An impact site on the vertex suggests that the head sustained a blow, whereas, in falls from standing positions, the scalp injuries are expected at the level of the brim of the hat.

Skull Fractures

These may involve the cranial vault, the base of the skull, and the facial skeleton. Although the presence of a skull fracture indicates severe traumatization, the fracture itself rarely threatens the victim's life. There are several types of skull fractures to be distinguished.

Single or multiple *linear fractures* are caused either by a blow with an object with a broad flat surface area or by a fall on the head so that the skull is deformed (flattening/indenting at the point of impact and outward bending/bulging in the periphery). The fracture lines originate where the bone is bent outward and therefore is exposed to traction forces exceeding the limits of the bone's elasticity; from these extruded parts of the skull, the fractures extend toward the area of impact, and also in the opposite direction. For this reason, either of the ends is often in congruity with the impact injury of the scalp. Several fracture lines may radiate outward from a central point of impact (**Figure 7(b)**) where the skull is often depressed and/or shattered to pieces forming a *spider's web* or mosaic pattern consisting of circular and radiating linear fractures (**Figure 8**). The sequence of skull injuries may be determined according to Puppe's rule: a later fracture does not cross a preexisting fracture line but terminates when reaching an earlier one.

Before fusion of the cranial sutures (i.e., in children and young adults), a fracture may travel along the seam resulting in diastasis (*diastatic fractures*). If a gaping fracture runs from one side of the cranial base to the other (mostly after lateral impact or side-to-side compression), this transverse type is called a *hinge fracture* because of the independent movement of the front and rear halves of the skull base.

Longitudinal fractures of the base of the skull often occur due to a fall on the occiput; in such instances, the linear fractures typically run through the posterior fossa either ending near the foramen magnum (**Figure 9**) or extending to the floor of the middle and anterior fossa. On the other hand, longitudinal fractures of the base can also be produced by impaction of the frontal region.

Depending on its course and location, a *base fracture* may be followed by several *clinical signs:* bleeding from the ear (in fractures of the temporal bone with concomitant hematotympanom and rupture of the eardrum); bleeding from the

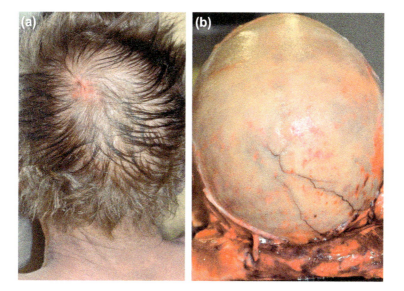

Figure 7   Fatal head trauma caused by a fall on the occiput. External examination of the scalp had only shown an inconspicuous skin abrasion and a shallow laceration (a). From this area of impact, linear fractures extended to the base of the skull (b).

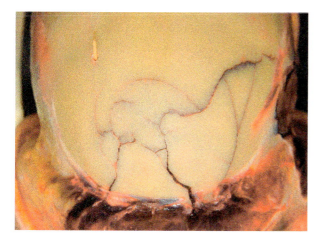

Figure 8   Frontal bone (squama) with linear fractures radiating outward from the area of impact and several additional circular fractures ("spider's web")—a 70-year-old car driver in a head-on collision.

nose and mouth (in fractures involving paranasal sinuses, which provide a communication with the nasopharynx); periorbital hematoma (from fractures of the orbital roofs); leakage of cerebrospinal fluid coming out of the nose or the ear (if the dura is injured along the fracture); and bacterial infection of the meninges (by spread from the nasal cavity, the paranasal sinuses, and the middle ear, especially when the fracture is accompanied by a tear of the dura).

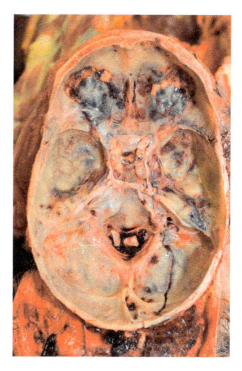

Figure 9   Base of the skull with linear fracture in the posterior fossa sustained in a fall on the occiput. Note the presence of secondary fractures in the anterior fossa floor.

Some special types of skull fractures can only be mentioned briefly. A *ring fracture* is located in the posterior fossa and encircles the foramen magnum. It occurs mostly in falls from a height onto the victim's feet or buttocks so that the cervical spine is driven into the skull. Another mechanism is seen in deceleration traumas, for instance, in head-on collisions, in passengers with fastened seat belts: Due to inertia, the nonrestrained head will continue to move forward exerting traction forces on the base of the skull.

Bone impressions and *depressed fractures* are always localized at the point of impact where the head is struck with an object having a relatively small surface area such as a hammer or a protruding corner of a piece of furniture. The outline of a clean-cut defect in the outer table may reproduce the shape and size of a sharp-edged instrument. If only limited force is applied, the depressed fracture can be restricted either to the outer or, less often, to the inner table of the skull (the latter with inward displacement of the bone fragments). A depressed fracture from a blow that struck the skullcap at an angle may be concentrically terraced. *Hole fractures* from bullets perforating a flat bone of the skull are mostly roundish and clean-cut at the site of entrance, but beveled out in a craterlike manner, at the exit site.

Blunt force applied to the occiput, mostly as a consequence of a fall on the back of the head, often causes independent fractures of the anterior cranial fossa such as cracks of the thin orbital roofs (*secondary fractures* at the site of the contrecoup; cf. **Figure 9**).

Intracranial Hemorrhages

A space-occupying bleeding into the brain membranes is followed by local displacement of the brain and raised intracranial pressure with concomitant flattening of the cerebral hemispheres. Intracranial hematomas as well as traumatic brain swelling, which often accompanies head injuries, may result in transtentorial (uncal) herniation (in cases of supratentorial mass lesion) and/or herniation of the cerebellar tonsils, which are forced into the foramen magnum leading to compression of the brain stem with secondary damage and failure of the medullary respiratory centers.

From the clinical and forensic point of view, the possible occurrence of a so-called lucid or latent interval has to be mentioned. After initial unconsciousness (due to cerebral concussion), there may be a symptomless period of several hours or even days before the victim becomes comatose again because of the increased hemorrhage and, consequently, the raised intracranial pressure.

Epidural (extradural) hemorrhages are located between the skull and the underlying dura mater, which is stripped from the bone by bleeding from a torn vessel (**Figure 10**). Epidural hematomas have a typical disk- or lens-shaped appearance. The most common site is the temporal and the adjacent parietal

Figure 10   Extradural (epidural) hemorrhage in the parietotemporal area. The hematoma is located between the inner surface of the skull and the detached dura.

region where the branches of the middle meningeal artery are easily lacerated in the course of a transecting fracture line. Since the well-adherent dura has to be avulsed from the bone, epidural hematomas more frequently originate from arterial bleeding than from venous bleeding (e.g., due to a torn dural sinus). In the great majority, an extradural hemorrhage is associated with a cranial fracture.

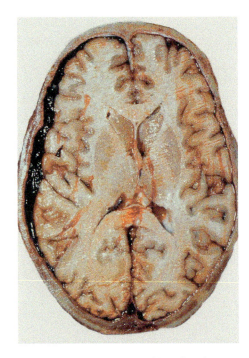

Figure 11   Acute subdural hemorrhage. The unilateral space-occupying lesion has slightly shifted the midline of the brain to the opposite side.

Subdural hematomas are intracranial bleedings located beneath the dura mater and above the arachnoid (**Figure 11**). Most often, the hemorrhage results from the tearing of over-stretched bridging veins that traverse the subdural space between the surface of the cerebral hemispheres and the superior sagittal sinus. Other possible sources of subdural bleeding are injuries to venous sinuses or to the cerebral parenchyma (such as cerebral contusions with concomitant laceration of the arachnoid). The subdural hemorrhage usually covers one cerebral hemisphere in a caplike manner from the parasagittal area via the lateral surface down to the basal fossas; on a horizontal section, it appears as a sickle-shaped accumulation of blood. In contrast to epidural hematomas, subdural hemorrhages are often not associated with skull fractures; additional damage to the brain tissue may also be absent. A high percentage of subdural bleedings are caused by acceleration or deceleration of the head, for instance, in falls when the head impacts a hard surface, and also in traffic accidents and physical child abuse (battered child and shaken baby syndrome). Apart from acute and subacute subdural hemorrhages, there are prolonged cases of hematoma formation and organization, mainly in elderly people and sometimes without a history of previous traumatization. Such chronic subdural hematomas typically consist of brown and gelatinous blood accumulations adherent to the meninges and sometimes covered with a tough membrane.

Traumatic subarachnoid bleeding may result from damage to the cortex such as brain contusion (e.g., contrecoup lesions), from penetrating injuries to the brain, and as a consequence of vessel tears within the subarachnoid space. An extensive hemorrhage on the ventral surface and around the brain stem may arise from a laceration of an artery belonging to the circle of Willis or from another great vessel (such as a torn basilar and vertebral artery).

Cerebral Injuries

"*Concussion* of the brain" is a clinical diagnosis which means a disorder of cerebral function following immediately upon a (blunt) head injury. It is usually characterized by a transient loss of consciousness (initial coma) with subsequent amnesia from the actual moment of trauma; it is often combined with retrograde amnesia and vegetative signs such as nausea and vomiting. In mere concussions, the unconsciousness lasts only for a relatively short time (<1 h) and the brain tissue does not show any evidence of structural damage. Nevertheless, even a simple cerebral concussion may be followed by the victim's death, if the head trauma is joined by interfering mechanisms (for instance, drowning or aspiration of gastric contents during unconsciousness).

Cerebral contusions are traumatic lesions of the brain frequently seen in the cortex and sometimes extending into the underlying white matter (**Figure 12**). Fresh contusion

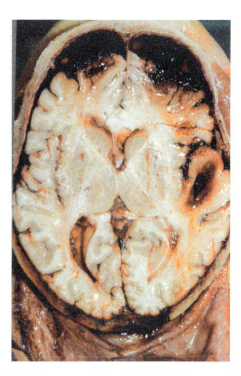

Figure 12 Contrecoup contusions of the frontal poles opposite to the point of impact (fall on the back of the head) with concomitant subarachnoid hematoma; traumatic intracerebral (subcortical) hematoma in the white matter of the right temporal lobe (in close vicinity to cerebral contusions in the overlying cortex).

Figure 13 Close-up view of a contused brain region with characteristic streaklike, densely arranged hemorrhages in the cortex (cut surface).

hemorrhages are mostly located on the crests of the gyri and composed of grouped streaklike or punctate blood extravasations (**Figure 13**). The cortical lesions are often covered with subarachnoid bleeding. In contrast to cerebral contusions, the term "laceration" means a major destruction of the anatomical context (for instance, mechanical separation of the tissue due to bone fragments or penetrating bullets). In the case of survival, the contusion hemorrhages are reabsorbed and assume a yellowish-brown appearance with softening and, finally, liquefaction of the affected areas.

Due to the injuring mechanism, most cerebral contusions occur in brain regions that are directly opposite to the point of impact. This contrecoup type of contusion is classically caused by a fall on the occiput, when the moving head is suddenly decelerated with the consequence that the inlying brain is damaged due to inertia. In falls on the back of the head, the contrecoup areas of the brain (poles and undersurfaces of the frontal and temporal lobes) are subjected to an ultrashort negative pressure ("cavitation") resulting in vessel ruptures and cortical hemorrhages (**Figure 14**). On the other hand, the so-called coup contusions arise at the area of impact due to the local deformation and compression of the brain. Even severe coup and contrecoup injuries are not necessarily associated with skull fractures. In victims with both coup and contrecoup lesions, the degree of contrecoup damage is usually marked. Fracture contusions are localized in topographical correspondence to fracture lines and/or depressed fractures.

Diffuse axonal injury (DAI) is considered a consequence of shear and tensile strains from sudden acceleration/deceleration or rotational movements of the head. Overstretching of the nerve fibers in the white matter leads to axonal injury varying from temporary dysfunction to anatomical transection, the latter being followed by microscopically visible club-shaped retraction balls on the axons. The sites of predilection include the corpus callosum, the parasagittal white matter, the superior peduncles, and the upper brain stem. In the course of the repair process, microglial cells proliferate in the areas of axon damage. In victims of substantial head injuries, especially after traffic accidents, DAI may be responsible for prolonged coma and a fatal outcome even in the absence of an intracranial mass lesion.

Cerebral edema is a frequent finding in significant head injuries. The formation of edema is due to an increase in the fluid content of the brain, predominantly in the white matter. Posttraumatic edema may be generalized (diffuse) or related to focal tissue damage (e.g., adjacent to an area of cerebral contusion or laceration). At autopsy, the weight of the brain is increased and the gyri are pale and flattened with shallow sulci in between. From the pathogenetic point of view, edema is attributed to a heightened vascular permeability which in turn may be worsened by additional hypoxia.

As with space-occupying lesions such as subdural or epidural hematomas, cerebral edema is a common cause of raised intracranial pressure. The enlarged volume of the edematous brain results in a displacement of cerebral tissue downward through the midbrain opening resulting in grooving of the unci and/or hippocampal herniation. Expansion of the subtentorial brain leads to herniation of the cerebellar tonsils which are forced into the foramen magnum. Herniation with concomitant compression of the brain stem may be followed by secondary hemorrhages (localized in the midbrain and pons) and finally by lethal dysfunction of the vital centers.

Injuries of the Chest

Nonpenetrating blunt force may damage the thoracic wall and/or the chest organs. *Rib fractures* are caused by either direct or indirect violence. In the first case, a localized force is applied and the underlying ribs are broken in the contact area; the other (indirect) type of rib fracture occurs away from the impact, mainly due to compression of the chest.

Rib fractures are frequently associated with *complications* that may be dangerous or even life threatening.

● If a victim sustains numerous fractures, the rib cage loses its rigidity so that the injured section of the chest wall will not participate in the expansion of the thorax during inspiration with the result of paradoxical respiration (*flail chest*) and concomitant hypoxia.

● Sharp, pointed ends of the rib fragments may penetrate the pleura and lacerate the lung and/or the intercostal blood

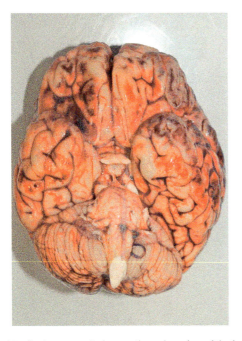

Figure 14   Contrecoup contusions on the undersurface of the frontal and temporal lobes (mostly located at the crests of the convolutions) with slight subarachnoid hemorrhage.

vessels with consecutive bleeding into the chest cavity (*hemothorax*).

- A leak in the visceral pleura permits air to enter the pleural cavity (*pneumothorax*) so that the lung collapses, if it is not fixed to the chest wall by preexisting pleural adhesions. A valvelike leakage in the pleura leads to a so-called tension pneumothorax caused by an increasing pressure of trapped air in the pleural cavity and followed by a complete collapse of the affected lung and a shift of the mediastinum to the opposite side.

- The presence of air bubbles in the subcutis or in the mediastinum (*subcutaneous/mediastinal emphysema*) may derive from injuries of the trachea, the bronchi, the thoracic wall, or the lungs by air entering the adjacent soft tissues.

Blunt-force injuries to the *lung* are mainly encountered as contusions or lacerations. A contusion is typically caused by a substantial impact on the chest with consecutive inward bending of the thoracic cage. In young victims, contusions are not necessarily accompanied by fractures of the ribs or of the sternum because of the high pliability of the juvenile thoracic cage. From the morphological point of view, a contused lung shows bruising either as a subpleural suffusion or as an intrapulmonary hemorrhage. Lacerations of the lung can result when a severe compressive or crushing force is applied to the chest so that the pulmonary tissue bursts or tears. Another possible mechanism is inward displacement of a fractured rib which impales the lung (**Figure 15**).

Blunt traumatization of the *heart* manifests as concussion, contusion, or myocardial rupture. In most cases, the force is directly applied to the anterior chest, which compresses or crushes the heart between the sternum and the vertebral column. Bruises of the cardiac wall may be localized in the subepicardial fatty tissue (sometimes in combination with posttraumatic coronary occlusion) or within the myocardium, which then appears dark red from interstitial hemorrhage. Lacerations of the heart are most often seen in the relatively thin right ventricle or in the atria; they are less common in the left ventricle, the papillary muscles, the cardiac valves, the interatrial, and the interventricular septum. The risk of cardiac rupture is especially high during diastole when the heart chambers are filled with blood and therefore easily burst when they are exposed to a sudden compressive force. Such injuries usually have a fatal outcome either from massive blood loss and hemorrhagic shock (if the pericardial sac is torn and the blood pours into a pleural cavity) or from cardiac tamponade (blood accumulation in the pericardial sac resulting in insufficient filling of the cardiac chambers and impaired forward circulation).

Traumatic aortic ruptures typically occur in vehicular accidents and in falls from a height. The most important mechanism is sudden deceleration, possibly in combination with compression and/or shearing. Traction forces tear the aorta

Figure 15 Serial rib fractures of the right hemithorax with concomitant laceration of the lung.

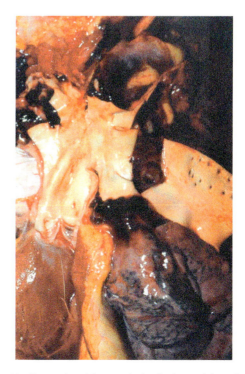

Figure 16 Transection of the aorta in the distal part of the arch (deceleration injury).

transversely at two sites of predisposition: in the descending part of its arcus (near the attachment of the ligamentum arteriosum) (**Figure 16**) or immediately above the cusps of the aortic valve. Other locations (for instance, in association with a dislocated vertebral fracture) are rather rare. The laceration of the aorta may occur as either a complete or a partial transection. In the latter case, the outer layers of the vascular wall are not damaged; the intimal tears are often multiple, semicircular, and parallel (so-called ladder-rung tears). If the trauma is survived at least for a short time, a parietal thrombosis or a posttraumatic aneurysm may follow as a secondary complication.

Abdominal Injuries

Blunt-force injuries of the abdomen are frequently seen in traffic and work accidents, in child and spouse abuse, in other criminal assaults (with kicking, stamping, and punching), as well as in suicidal falls from heights. The abdominal organs most vulnerable to blunt trauma are the solid liver and spleen on the one side and the mesentery on the other. Concomitant external signs of blunt traumatization such as contusions or abrasions are by no means obligatory. Substantial injuries to the liver, the spleen, and the mesentery have always to be regarded as life threatening and potentially fatal, especially in cases without rapid surgical treatment. The main reason is internal bleeding into the peritoneal cavity from lacerations (**Figures 17 and 18**). Ruptures of the liver and spleen can be classified as either transcapsular or subcapsular lacerations. In the first case, both capsule and parenchyma are injured so that the blood instantaneously pours into the peritoneal cavity. The second type of laceration is characterized by the initial formation of a subcapsular hematoma which expands continuously

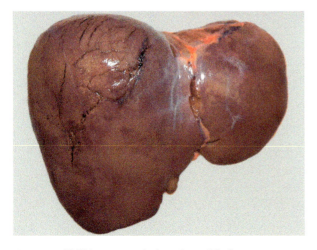

Figure 17   Multiple transcapsular lacerations of the liver.

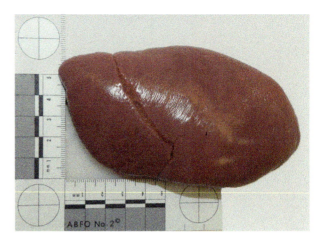

Figure 18   Laceration of the spleen.

and possibly causes a delayed rupture when the covering capsule tears due to overstretching (mostly several hours or even days after the trauma).

The stomach and the intestine are less susceptible to blunt traumatization than the parenchymatous abdominal organs. The hollow viscera are more likely to rupture, if they are filled with food or fluid. Another reason why the intestine or stomach might be prone to damage is squeezing of the organs between the indented abdominal wall and the lumbar vertebrae. Fatal outcomes from contusions or lacerations of the gastrointestinal tract are usually due to diffuse peritonitis.

Renal injuries are a relatively rare source of severe bleeding as the kidneys are located deep behind the peritoneum. Nevertheless, they can be ruptured by a heavy impact to the loin (for instance, in traffic accidents or assaults).

Although the empty urinary bladder is placed within the pelvis, when filled it moves upward and is therefore exposed to blunt traumatization of the lower abdomen. Consequently, rupture of the empty bladder is expected to be extraperitoneal and accompanied with pelvic fractures, whereas a bladder distended with urine may rupture into the peritoneal cavity.

Blunt traumatization of a pregnant uterus is a possible cause of fetal death, mostly due to separation or rupture of the placenta.

Injuries to the Extremities

Besides injuries to the skin and the subcutaneous layer (see above), other anatomical structures such as the muscles, the bones, and the joints may be involved in blunt-force trauma. Extensive crushing of the soft tissues, the formation of blood-filled cavities, comminuted fractures, and severance of large vessels are common findings in victims of automobile–

pedestrian accidents. Internal bleeding (from closed injuries) and external bleeding (from traumatic amputation, severe avulsive wounds, and compound fractures) are important factors contributing to hemorrhagic shock. Another sequel to blunt trauma is pulmonary and systemic fat embolism (caused by globules of fat, usually subsequent to fractures or damage of fatty tissues). In cases of prolonged survival, intercurrent infection and pulmonary embolism (originating from post-traumatic venous thrombosis) are dangerous and often fatal complications of an originally nonlethal injury.

See also: **Forensic Medicine/Causes of Death:** Systemic Response to Trauma; **Forensic Medicine/Clinical:** Child Abuse; Defense Wounds; **Forensic Medicine/Pathology:** Autopsy; Forensic Pathology – Principles and Overview.

Further Reading

Case, M., 2005. Head trauma: neuropathology. In: Payne-James, J., Byard, R.W., Corey, T.S., Henderson, C. (Eds.), Encyclopedia of Forensic and Legal Medicine, vol. 2. Elsevier Science, Amsterdam, pp. 472–480.

DiMaio, V.J., DiMaio, D., 2001. Forensic Pathology, second ed. CRC Press, Boca Raton, FL, pp. 92–185.

Hausmann, R., 2004. Timing of cortical contusions in human brain injury. In: Tsokos, M. (Ed.), Forensic Pathology Reviews, vol. 1. Humana Press, Totowa, NJ, pp. 53–75.

Henn, V., Lignitz, E., 2004. Kicking and trampling to death. In: Tsokos, M. (Ed.), Forensic Pathology Reviews, vol. 1. Humana Press, Totowa, NJ, pp. 31–50.

Kieser, J., Whittle, K., Wong, B., et al., 2008. Understanding craniofacial blunt force injury: a biomechanical perspective. In: Tsokos, M. (Ed.), Forensic Pathology Reviews, vol. 5. Humana Press, Totowa, NJ, pp. 39–51.

Lau, G., Teo, C.E.S., Chao, T., 2003. The pathology of trauma and death associated with fall from heights. In: Payne-James, J., Busuttil, A., Smock, W. (Eds.), Forensic Medicine: Clinical and Pathological Aspects. Greenwich Medical Media, London, pp. 321–335.

Marks, P., 2003. Head injury – fatal and nonfatal (and other neurologic causes of sudden death). In: Payne-James, J., Busuttil, A., Smock, W. (Eds.), Forensic Medicine: Clinical and Pathological Aspects. Greenwich Medical Media, London, pp. 321–335.

Marks, P., 2005. Deaths: trauma, head, and spine. In: Payne-James, J., Byard, R.W., Corey, T.S., Henderson, C. (Eds.), Encyclopedia of Forensic and Legal Medicine, vol. 2. Elsevier Science, Amsterdam, pp. 75–81.

Marks, P., 2005. Head trauma: pediatric and adult, clinical aspects. In: Payne-James, J., Byard, R.W., Corey, T.S., Henderson, C. (Eds.), Encyclopedia of Forensic and Legal Medicine, vol. 2. Elsevier Science, Amsterdam, pp. 461–472.

Oehmichen, M., Auer, R.N., König, H.G., 2006. Forensic Neuropathology and Associated Neurology. Springer, Berlin, Heidelberg, pp. 97–270.

Pollak, S., Saukko, P., 2003. Atlas of Forensic Medicine: CD-ROM. Chapter 5. Elsevier, Amsterdam.

Pollak, S., Saukko, P.J., 2009. Blunt force trauma. In: Jamieson, A., Moenssens, A. (Eds.), Wiley Encyclopedia of Forensic Science. Wiley, Chichester, pp. 396–441.

Saukko, P., Knight, B., 2004. Knight's Forensic Pathology, third ed. Arnold, London, pp. 136–221.

Spitz, W.U., 2006. Blunt force injury. In: Spitz, W.U. (Ed.), Spitz and Fisher's Medicolegal Investigation of Death, fourth ed. Thomas, Springfield, IL, pp. 460–531.

Türk, E., 2008. Fatal falls from height. In: Tsokos, M. (Ed.), Forensic Pathology Reviews, vol. 5. Humana Press, Totowa, NJ, pp. 25–38.

Burns and Scalds

M Bohnert, University of Würzburg, Würzburg, Germany

Introduction

The possible findings in burned bodies cover a broad spectrum, ranging from minor, local, and superficial burns of the skin to calcined skeletal remains without any soft tissue left and total incineration. The extent of the tissue changes depends on the temperature actually applied to the body, the time for which it is applied, the kind of transmission of the heat to the body, and other prevailing conditions. In most cases, the heat acts on the body beyond death. Consequently, the changes found are largely of postmortem origin.

The forensic investigation of deaths related to a fire is important to determine the manner and cause of death, the vitality of the findings, and the identity of the victim. In some cases, questions concerning the dynamics and the duration of the fire have also to be answered.

External Findings

Among the externally discernible changes, the various stages of skin burns, the results of tissue shrinkage, and the consumption by the fire are the dominant features. In most fire deaths, the body was exposed postmortem to temperatures of several hundred degrees Celsius for at least some minutes, often by direct contact with the flames. Although destruction may be very extensive, in most of the cases, the organs of the thorax and abdomen can usually still be assessed quite well and body fluids as well as tissue samples can be obtained for further investigations.

Burns

Skin burns are categorized into four degrees with each degree characterizing a certain depth of the skin lesion. The categories are (degree 1) superficial burns, (degree 2a) superficial partial-thickness burns associated with necrosis of the upper layers of the epidermis, (degree 2b) deep partial-thickness burns associated with necrosis of the entire thickness of the epidermis, (degree 3) full-thickness burns with necrosis involving the dermis as well, and (degree 4) charring in which the heat lesion reaches deeper soft-tissue layers. First-degree burns are characterized by a reddening of the skin. As a postmortem residue, a red margin may occasionally be observed. Second-degree burns are characterized by fluid-filled skin blisters. Second-degree burns of the palms of the hands and the soles of the feet appear as whitish discolorations of the epidermis associated with swelling, wrinkling, and vesicular detachment up to glove-like peeling. The findings resemble the so-called washerwoman's skin, as it is seen after prolonged exposure to a moist environment. The skin in third-degree burns is firm and discolored brown.

Heat changes of the hair occur at temperatures above about 150 °C. This can be used to differentiate between burns and scalds or to indicate the approximate temperature reached by the skin in smoldering fires. The hair gets frizzy and brittle and assumes a fox red or a dark brown to black color. Temperatures of about 200 °C lead to the formation of gas bubbles in the shaft. At 240 °C, the hair becomes frizzy due to the melting of the hair keratins. Above 300 °C, charring occurs.

The distribution of burn injuries is seldom evenly spread and depends on various conditions. Especially, tight-fitting clothes can protect the underlying skin from burns for a long time. In cases of suicidal self-incineration using fire accelerants, burns may be absent from the feet and lower legs if the incineration took place while the body was in an upright position. In burns caused by low heat, deep, anatomically circumscribed signs of consumption by the fire may occur. These are formed when the fire is maintained according to the wick principle: In those parts of the body where the skin has burned away, liquefied subcutaneous fatty tissue leaks out and maintains the fire.

Shrinkage of Tissue

The reasons why the tissue shrinks are the loss of fluid and the degradation of the muscles and tendons caused by the heat. Externally, it is characterized by tightening of the skin, splitting of the skin, protrusion of the tongue from the open mouth, petechial hemorrhages in the region of the neck and head, and the so-called pugilistic attitude.

The typical posture of charred bodies is called the pugilistic or boxer's attitude with the arms being abducted in the shoulder joint and flexed in the elbow joint and the legs being abducted in the hip joint and flexed in the hip and knee joint. The flexion of the joints of the extremities is due to the predominance of the flexor muscles. This may even result in dislocation, most often recognizable at the wrists.

Splitting of the skin is a frequently observed phenomenon in charred bodies. It is very rare in burns of minor severity. If it appears in such cases, prolonged exposure to the heat has to be assumed. The splits have sharp edges that can be approximated, are often linear, but occasionally also angled. In most cases, they reach the subcutaneous fatty tissue, and sometimes also the outer muscle layers. In this context, little attention is paid to the fact that the tissue exposed in the depth of the splits is usually unburned and often not even sooted. Most likely, the splits form during the cooling of the body.

Protrusion of the tongue from the open mouth is due to the heat-related shrinkage of the soft tissue of the neck. In the presence of severe burns on the neck and/or thorax, petechial hemorrhages may occasionally be found in the lids and conjunctivae. For their formation, congestion due to the shrinkage of the soft tissue of the neck by heat or heat rigidity of the thorax while the circulation is still intact is discussed. So, petechial hemorrhages in the region of the neck and head would have to be regarded as a vital sign.

Consumption by Fire

The question as to what extent the level of charring in a burned body allows one to draw conclusions regarding the duration of the fire is rarely asked. In the literature, there are few reports on this topic, most of which refer to observations made during cremations. These studies showed that the course of events follows a fixed chronological order. Thirty minutes after the fire has been in full progress, all body cavities are exposed and the distal portions of the extremities are amputated. The exposed bones show signs of calcination. After a minimum of 50 min and a maximum of 80 min, the internal organs are largely incinerated and the burned torso breaks apart. However, when applying the findings of the cremations to real fire deaths, one should take into consideration that these are usually not exposed to a constant temperature level for a long period of time; a fire develops in several stages and it will often not be possible to reconstruct the temperatures reached in these individual stages.

Internal Findings

The internal findings in fire deaths are the result of a fixation of the tissue by the heat, processes of shrinking, thermal changes of the content and distribution of tissue fluids, and a rising gas pressure in hollow spaces. After the fire has opened the body cavities, direct burns occur on the internal surfaces as well. The loss of fluid and, after exposure of the body cavities, the direct effect of the heat cause shrinking of the internal organs, which become firm, hardened, and cooked by the heat (so-called "puppet organs"). The surface of the organs becomes increasingly bosselated and is reduced to a spongelike residual

structure in the end. The tissue is meanwhile completely desiccated and disintegrates into ash at the slightest touch.

Respiratory Tract

The respiratory tract is the most important organ system for the diagnosis of vitality. Where fire fumes were inhaled, deposits of soot particles will be found. Edema, mucosal bleeding, and patchy or vesicular detachment of the mucosa in the nose, mouth, pharynx, larynx, trachea, and bronchi may be indicative of an inhalation of hot gases. Often, increased secretion of mucus is observed in the air passages. This may be interpreted as an attempt to cool the surfaces of the air passages and thus as a sign of vitality, if other causes for the secretion of mucus (bronchial asthma and catarrhal bronchitis) have been ruled out. Damage caused to the respiratory tract by dry heat is limited more to the upper portions. The inhaled hot air is sufficiently cooled down by the mucosa of the airways so that after exposure to a "normal fire," hardly any changes are found in the medium and small bronchi.

Vessels

Intensive red discoloration of the intima of the vessels can be regularly observed in fire victims. This finding is the result of hemolysis occurring at temperatures above 52 °C. Even at 48 °C, erythrocytes begin to dissolve. If the circulation is still intact, the erythrocyte fragments ("fragmentocytes") can be demonstrated microscopically in other organs also, which has to be interpreted as a sign of vitality.

Gastrointestinal Tract

The abdominal wall protects the abdominal organs from direct damage by the flames for a relatively long period of time. However, as a result of the heating of the body, the tissue fluids boil away and the pressure inside the hollow organs and the abdominal cavity builds up, which often leads to the rupture of the abdominal wall and the prolapse of intestinal loops. Consumption of the abdominal wall by the fire further promotes the rupture. In rare cases, heat-related ruptures of the gastrointestinal organs are found, before they were directly exposed to the fire.

Bones

The skeleton is damaged by the fire, but it is not consumed completely. Even if it is exposed to a fire with high temperatures over a long period of time, there will usually still be remains to allow macroscopic assessment and successful determination of the species, the body measurements, and the sex as well as to identify skeletal anomalies and the presence of possible injuries.

At temperatures above 700 °C, complete combustion of the organic substances with incineration and recrystallization of the inorganic matter occurs, which is called "calcination." The bones are grayish-white, desiccated, and disintegrate easily. The surface shows characteristic tears partly reflecting the course of the trabeculae, but often also being irregular in structure.

In charred or calcined bones, a minor mechanical strain may be enough to cause fractures. Especially in fractures localized within charred bone areas, the possibility of artifacts should be considered. But several authors have stressed expressly that injuries sustained during life can be demonstrated even on charred or calcined bones.

In the assessment, special attention must be paid to the bony skullcap. In about 33% of all fire deaths, the skullcap is partially destroyed and the interior of the skull is exposed, which makes assessment even more difficult. Isolated fractures of the external table are seen especially in cases where a defined area of the skullcap was in direct contact with the flames. Prolonged exposure to heat causes fractures of the entire thickness of the skullcap, with occasional bursting of the sutures of the skull. The tears in the skullcap caused by heat may radiate from a center, but can sometimes also be elliptic or circular in shape or resemble a spider's web fracture. In rare cases, round or oval bone fragments may burst outward. Distinction of this finding from a gunshot injury may be difficult.

Cranial Cavity and Brain

A frequent finding is the epidural heat hematoma. It is not a vital sign, but a postmortem effect due to the shift of fluid from the diploe and the venous sinuses when the skullcap is in direct contact with the flames. Accordingly, charring of the bony skull is usually found above the site of the heat hematoma. It is dry, crumbly, and of brick-red color. Occasionally, it may be surrounded by fat and in rare cases, accumulations of fat without extravasations of blood can also be found in the epidural space. Apart from that, the hematoma is sometimes found to be interspersed with brain tissue when the dura mater is torn due to shrinkage by heat.

Postmortem extravasates of blood may occur in all cavities of the skull including the ventricles of the brain. But hemorrhages can be found in the brain tissue itself as a result of the shrinkage of tissue with laceration of small blood vessels. In these cases, distinction between postmortem and vital hemorrhages can be particularly difficult.

When the skullcap is intact, the brain of fire victims is often shrunken and of a hardened consistency with filled sulci on the surface. Histologically, condensation of the vessels and widening of the Virchow–Robinson spaces have been described. Again, this finding may be explained as the result of a loss of fluid and does not prove a vital thermal damage to the tissue.

Toxicology

In fire victims, the concentrations of carbon monoxide hemoglobin (CO-Hb), methemoglobin (Met-Hb), and cyanide (CN) should be routinely determined in the corpse blood as part of the toxicological investigations. Concentrations of more than 10% CO-Hb and more than 0.2 mg l^{-1} CN in the blood suggest that fire fumes were inhaled and are to be considered as signs of vitality. A positive result for Met-Hb indicates that nitrous gases formed during the fire and were inhaled. As the sole cause of death, elevated concentrations of CO-Hb and CN have to be considered especially in victims showing only minor heat changes on the body. Blood concentrations of more than 50% CO-Hb and 2.6 mg l^{-1} CN are considered as lethal.

In deaths following flash fires, pulmonary tissue should also be kept as evidence to demonstrate the use of fire accelerants. As these substances are volatile, it is advisable to store the samples in airtight containers and to investigate them rapidly by means of headspace capillary GC-MS. A positive result for fire accelerants in the pulmonary tissue is also regarded as a sign of vitality.

Histology

Histological examination of the respiratory tract is especially valuable to demonstrate changes due to the inhalation of hot gases. However, it should be remembered in this context that certain findings, for example, nucleic elongation and palisade arrangement in the epithelium of the respiratory tract, may also be due to postmortem effects of heat on the body. On the other hand, other findings such as hyperemia and edema of the mucosa of the respiratory passages as well as interstitial and intraalveolar pulmonary edema are unspecific. Detachment of the mucosa from the epiglottis, the trachea, and the bronchi may also be due to autolysis and decomposition, although rarely in the vesicular form, characteristic of thermal effects. The histological parameters should also be assessed only in context. In our experience, the combination of pseudogoblet cells, increased secretion of mucus, and vesicular detachment of the epithelium is highly indicative of vital effects of heat on the respiratory system. Histological findings of the pulmonary tissue in cases of rapid death may be due to acute congestion, interstitial and sectional intraalveolar pulmonary edema, and acute emphysema, as well as microthrombi.

Diagnosis of Vitality

The signs of a vital exposure to the fire are summarized in **Table 1**. External signs that the body was exposed to heat when the victim was still alive may be the absence of burns and/or soot deposits in the corners of the eyes (so-called

Table 1   Signs of vitality after exposure to fire fumes versus heat

Exposure to fire fumes	Exposure to heat
Macroscopic findings	
Soot deposits in the airways	Crow's feet, incompletely singed eyelashes
Soot deposits in the esophagus	Skin blisters
Soot deposits in the stomach	Vesicular/patchy detachment of the pharyngeal mucosa or epiglottis
	Edematous swelling of the epiglottis
	Vesicular/patchy detachment of the upper esophageal mucosa
Histological findings	
Soot deposits in trachea and bronchi	Vesicular detachment of the tracheal and bronchial mucosa
	Pseudogoblet cells
	Massive secretion of mucus
	Nucleic elongation and palisade arrangement of the mucosal epithelium in trachea and bronchi
	Hyperemia and edema of the tracheal and bronchial mucosa
Toxicological findings	
CO-Hb concentration >10%	
Cyanide concentration >0.2 ng ml^{-1}	

crow's feet) and incompletely singed eyelashes, which result from squinting the eyes. However, these findings are usually discernible only if the body was not or was only slightly consumed by the fire. As this is rare in deaths due to heat exposure, the internal findings are much more important than the external findings.

The most important constellation of findings to prove that the victim was alive during a fire is the combination of a CO-Hb concentration above 10% and soot deposits in the respiratory tract, the esophagus, and the stomach. In fact, these parameters show only whether the victim was exposed to *fire fumes* while alive; they are not indicative of vital *heat* exposure. Consequences of an inhalation of hot gases may be edematous swelling and vesicular or patchy detachment of the mucosa in the pharynx, the larynx, and/or the upper section of the esophagus.

Although there is a certain relation between the vitality parameters of soot aspiration and CO-Hb, there is no reliable correlation. Deposits of soot in the airways should never lead to the premature conclusion that the victim died of intoxication by fire fumes. Soot particles may, under certain circumstances, occur in the respiratory tract also if burning was exclusively postmortem. On the other hand, the absence of soot in the respiratory tract does not allow to draw the conclusion that exposure to the fire occurred postmortem.

Signs of vitality may be partly absent in cases of undoubtedly vital burning. The significance of one vitality parameter alone is therefore limited.

Determination of the Cause of Death

The issues of vitality and cause of death are closely linked. For example, a high CO-Hb concentration in corpse blood supplies information regarding the cause of both the death and vitality. Apart from the signs of vitality, the absence of other causes of death is an essential condition for the conclusion that death was due to the fire. The diagnosis of a fire to cover up a homicide requires the presence of fatal injuries inflicted by another person *and* the absence of the classical parameters of vitality.

The presence of mechanical lesions or severe pathological findings together with (seemingly) absent vital parameters may cause diagnostic problems. While in the presence of potentially fatal injuries (e.g., polytrauma following car accidents) perimortal burning has to be discussed, differentiation between peracute death due to the effects of heat and purely postmortem burning may be very difficult. In cases of this type, the CO-Hb concentrations in the corpse blood may be below 10%, the oral, pharyngeal, and laryngeal mucosa may show no heat damage, and there may be no soot aspiration. The most likely pathophysiological mechanism is a fulminant shock. However, in some cases, the questions regarding the cause of death and the vitality cannot be answered definitely.

Scalds

Scalds are the result of the effect of moist heat, usually hot water and/or steam, while scalding by other hot liquids, especially hot oil, is a comparatively rare picture to be examined in forensic practice. As the thermal conductivity of water and steam is much higher, they produce worse injuries than dry heat even after short exposure, as from the very beginning the actual skin temperature is considerably higher with moist heat and moist heat penetrates to deeper layers of the tissue much better than dry heat.

An actual skin temperature of 44 °C is regarded as the lowest temperature needed to cause damage to the skin; at this temperature, a second-degree to third-degree scald would be reached after an exposure time of 6 h. Between 44 and 51 °C, a temperature increase of 1 °C reduces the exposure time needed for a certain degree of skin injury by half. Above 51 °C, there is no convective heat transport via the skin capillaries anymore and the heat penetrates into the deeper tissue layers.

External Findings

Typical for the effect of moist heat is a uniform injury pattern of all the affected skin areas with sharply demarcated edges. Pouring a hot liquid over the skin may produce a streak-like trickle pattern. Scalds due to immersion are characterized by a straight, horizontal burn pattern corresponding to the level of the liquid. With tight-fitting clothes, the underlying skin areas may often be spared from scalding. As the temperatures applied by moist heat are usually lower than those of dry heat (water boils at 100 °C), moist heat does not produce fourth-degree skin burns (charring), heat-related exposures of body cavities, or amputations.

Internal Findings

The internal findings are unspecific. They are consequences of the shock associated with scalding which can also be regarded as the cause of death. If hot steam is inhaled, the temperature hardly declines along the air passages, so that a direct thermal damage may occur even in the peripheral parts of the respiratory tract. For differentiation between hot steam and dry air, the so-called "pleura sign" can be used at autopsy. If hot steam was inhaled, the parietal pleura is reddened, whereas the costodiaphragmatic angles are pale. In deaths caused by the effects of dry heat, this sign is absent even if the circumstances suggest a fire with high temperatures.

See also: **Chemistry/Trace/Fire Investigation:** Physics/Thermodynamics; Thermal Degradation; **Forensic Medicine/Causes of Death:** Systemic Response to Trauma; **Forensic Medicine/Clinical:** Hyperthermia and Hypothermia; **Forensic Medicine/Pathology:** Autopsy; External Postmortem Examination; Histopathology; **Investigations:** Fire Patterns and Their Interpretation; Fire Scene Inspection Methodology; Types of Fires.

Further Reading

Bohnert, M., 2004. Morphological findings in burned bodies. In: Tsokos, M. (Ed.), Forensic Pathology Reviews, vol. 1. Humana Press, Totowa, NJ, pp. 3–27.
Bohnert, M., Rost, T., Pollak, S., 1998. The degree of destruction of human bodies in relation to the duration of the fire. Forensic Science International 95, 11–21.
Bohnert, M., Werner, C.R., Pollak, S., 2003. Problems associated with the diagnosis of vitality in burned bodies. Forensic Science International 135, 197–205.
Cox, R.A., Burke, A.S., Oliveras, G., et al., 2005. Acute bronchial obstruction in sheep: histopathology and gland cytokine expression. Experimental Lung Research 31, 819–837.
DeHaan, J.D., Campbell, S.J., Nurbakhsh, S., 1999. Combustion of animal fat and its implications for the consumption of human bodies in fires. Science and Justice 39, 27–38.
DeHaan, J.D., Nurbakhsh, S., 2001. Sustained combustion of an animal carcass and its implications for the consumption of human bodies in fires. Journal of Forensic Sciences 46, 1076–1081.
Glassman, D.N., Crow, R.M., 1996. Standardization model for describing the extent of burn injury to human remains. Journal of Forensic Sciences 41, 152–154.
Schmidt, C.W., Symes, S.A. (Eds.), 2008. The Analysis of Burned Human Remains. Academic Press, Amsterdam.

Asphyctic Deaths—Overview and Pathophysiology

CM Milroy, University of Ottawa, Ottawa, ON, Canada

Glossary

Sphygmomanometer Equipment to measure blood pressure.

Valsalva maneuver Forceful exhalation against a closed upper airway.

Introduction

Asphyxia is a very commonly used term in medicine, and particularly forensic medicine, though the characteristics that are used to diagnose asphyxia are poorly defined and often absent in cases of classic "asphyxia." The term asphyxia derives from ancient Greek and etymologically means absence of the pulse (σφυγμός—sphygmós). (Sphygmomanometer has the same origin.) However, it has come to mean deaths associated with deprivation of oxygen. While most deaths will ultimately result by starvation of oxygen to vital organs, "asphyxial" deaths are separately classified in forensic medicine. Different texts have classified asphyxial deaths into different ways, so there is a lack of uniformity in definition.

Signs of Asphyxia

Asphyxial deaths have been associated with specific pathological findings. Classically, the literature has reported five so-called signs of asphyxia as follows:

1. Congestion
2. Cyanosis
3. Fluidity of blood
4. Dilatation of the right side of the heart
5. Petechiae

None of these signs is specific and they are so commonly found in nonasphyxial deaths and absent in asphyxial deaths that they have been referred to by Lester Adelson in a memorable quote as the obsolete quintet.

Of these signs, congestion and cyanosis are almost universal findings to a greater or lesser degree in most autopsies. Fluidity of blood has long been shown to correlate with the rapidity of death rather than whether there has been deprivation of oxygen or dilation of the right side of the heart is a nonspecific and subjective finding.

Of Lester Adelson's obsolete quintet, petechiae merit some discussion as the mechanism of their causation and significance has been more debated. Petechiae are pinhead-sized hemorrhages most commonly associated with compression of the neck but may be seen in natural deaths including cardiac disease. Petechial bruising describes a separate type of appearance to a bruise. Other causes of petechiae include clotting disorders, coughing, retching, and vomiting. They may be seen in internal organs, typically in thoracic organs. Over-reliance on these findings has led to inappropriate diagnoses of deaths from asphyxia.

Petechiae have been stated to be associated with raised intravascular pressure, hypoxia, and raised carbon dioxide. Of these mechanisms, only raised intravascular pressure has any scientific evidence to support it, in the absence of a bleeding diathesis. Raised intravascular pressure accounts for why they are seen in compression of the neck, coughing, retching, and similar acts that raise venous pressure, but not, for example, in most smothering deaths or suffocation. In compression of the neck, one of the common scenarios that petechiae are seen in, they result from obstruction of the venous return with continued arterial pressure, resulting in engorgement of the vascular system and rupture of venules resulting in petechiae appearing. Although petechiae are sometimes said to arise from rupture of capillaries, it has been pointed out that these structures are too small to result in macroscopically visible hemorrhage. The most common places to observe petechiae are in the conjunctivae, in the external eyelids, on facial skin, behind the ears, and on the mucosal surface of the oral cavity. Petechiae are invariably seen on the inside of the scalp following reflection at autopsy. These subscalp petechiae are an artifact of dissection and are not diagnostic of anything. In deaths where there has been a head down postmortem position, the scalp, face, and neck can become very congested, and petechiae and confluent areas of bleeding may be seen. Artifactual bleeding may be seen in the neck, even with careful dissection after draining the blood.

Mechanisms of Asphyxia

In classifying deaths from asphyxia, rather than referring to deaths from asphyxia, a more accurate approach is one where the mechanism of the production of asphyxia is described.

The deaths that fall into the category of "asphyxia" deaths can be broadly categorized as follows:

1. Suffocation (breathing in a nonviable environment)
2. The mechanical asphyxias
   a. Smothering
   b. Plastic bag asphyxia
   c. Choking
   d. Compression of the neck
   e. Traumatic asphyxia
   f. Positional/restraint asphyxia
   g. Drowning
   h. Autoerotic sexual asphyxia
   i. The "choking game"
3. Chemical "asphyxiants"

Suffocation

The term suffocation is best reserved for cases where there has been inhalation of a vitiated atmosphere. These deaths can occur when a person enters an atmosphere where there is inadequate oxygen or where the oxygen gets used up. Typical examples include mines and silos, where there has been a reduction in environmental oxygen and a buildup of carbon dioxide. Collapse can be very rapid and coworkers may die when they enter the same atmosphere in an attempt to rescue them. Characteristically asphyxial signs are absent. One case seen by the author involved three men in the cable room of a ship where the anchor was stored. These rooms typically have low oxygen levels as the iron in the cable rusts and oxygen is used up in making iron oxide. A worker entered the room without appropriate breathing apparatus and collapsed. His two colleagues attempting to rescue him without breathing apparatus also collapsed, and all three died. Subsequent analysis of the oxygen level in the room showed it to be reduced. This illustrates that the autopsy must be interpreted with other information, as the autopsies did not disclose the cause of death.

Another scenario encountered is when people become trapped in fridges or are placed in a trunk or similar closed environment. As the oxygen is used up and carbon monoxide builds up, death will occur.

Smothering

The term smothering should be used when an external object has been used to obstruct the upper airway. This obstructs normal respiration. It is often achieved with soft material and when autopsy signs are absent. If duct tape or similar material has been used and removed, there may be adhesive material still present around the mouth, which can give a clue to the previous presence of the tape and other injuries possibly being present.

Plastic Bag Asphyxia

Plastic bag asphyxia is a specific form of obstruction of the upper airway. Asphyxial signs are typically absent. It may also be accompanied by the administration of the irrespirable gas helium, which has been recommended as a method of suicide by certain euthanasia supporters.

Choking

Choking is a term best used when there is obstruction of the internal airway by food or other obstructing material, though it has been used for external compression of the neck. The "choking game" is described below. It is commonly encountered in intoxicated people or in patients with neurological disorders that prevent adequate swallowing. Occasionally, cases are encountered where material is forced into the mouth and airway, either by an assailant or by self-infliction. Such acts may be encountered in psychiatrically disordered patients and people determined to commit suicide, such as by stuffing a sock or tissue paper into the throat.

Compression of the Neck

Compression of the neck is a broad category of actions that results in obstruction of the vasculature and airway. These deaths are classified and described in the sections below.

Hanging

There is a compression of the neck by suspension by a ligature. Hanging can be separated into short-drop and long-drop suspension. The latter, most typified by judicial execution, is meant to result in fracture of the neck rather than compression of the vasculature and airway, which occurs in "short-drop" suspension. Long-drop hangings may be seen in suicides, such as hangings off bridges and similar structures. If the drop is of sufficient length, decapitation may occur.

Hanging may be achieved even though a significant part of the victim's body is on the ground, as there is sufficient weight even in the head to achieve vascular compression. There is characteristically a parchmented ligature mark, but where there is a broad ligature, such as a sheet, the ligature mark can be subtle or absent. In compression with full suspension, petechiae are typically absent and the face appears pale. In these cases, there is complete compression of the carotid arteries with no blood flowing above the level of the compressing force. In contrast, in partial suspension, petechiae and congestion above the level of the ligature are more commonly encountered.

Hanging is typically suicidal but may occur by accident or rarely be homicidal. With homicidal hanging, either the victim is incapacitated or there is a significant disparity in strength between assailant(s) and victim. Rarely homicidal hanging has been reported through subterfuge. Internal findings may be absent in hanging or include bruising of the strap muscles and fracturing of the hyoid bone and laryngeal cartilages.

Ligature Strangulation

There is a compression of the neck without suspension. Petechiae more commonly occur with ligature strangulation than hanging as the compressive force is typically slower, allowing congestion of vessels to occur. External signs of the ligature may be subtle where the ligature is broad. This is commonly homicidal but may occur in suicides or by accident. Where a low suspension hanging has occurred, differentiating ligature strangulation may be extremely difficult, where the person has been cut down and the ligature removed. Where a stick or similar object is placed under the ligature and twisted to constrict the ligature, the mechanism is referred to a Spanish windlass. Garroting is a special form of ligature strangulation where the intention is to fracture the neck. It was used as a form of judicial execution.

Manual Strangulation

This is also called throttling and occurs when the hands (hence manual) are used to compress the neck. External marks of violence can be quite subtle, but usually finger pressure bruises and abrasions from fingernails are seen. The abrasions may be from the victim's own fingernails, where they have attempted to remove the assailants compressing hands. Internally, there is typically bruising in the strap muscles. Damage to the hyoid bone and laryngeal cartilages is more common in manual strangulation, but depends on age, with younger people having elastic cartilage. Fractures are invariably present in people over 50 years of age.

Palmar Strangulation

Polson describes a method of neck compression where the accused denied gripping the neck but stated that he had placed one palm on the mouth and another on the front of the neck, so that pressure is over the larynx. The victim, a 52-year-old woman, had fractures of both superior horns and bruising in the neck. Polson was able to reproduce the fractures on cadavers.

Neck Holds

There are two basic neck holds, "choke" holds and the carotid sleeper. With the carotid sleeper, when correctly applied, the neck is held in the crook of the arm and then the arm is compressed so that the carotid arteries are obstructed. When used in law enforcement hold and martial arts, once the person has become unconscious, the hold is released. If the hold is continued then death will result from a lack of blood supply to the brain. The airway is supposed to be maintained with this hold. The term mugging was originally applied to this hold, though it has become a term used for any street robbery. This is in contrast to the "choke" hold or bar hold, where either the forearm or a similar shaped object such as a police truncheon is placed across the neck and then forced onto the neck. This causes compression of the airway with collapse of the trachea rather than just obstruction of the carotid arteries.

Traumatic (Crush) Asphyxia

Traumatic asphyxia, also known as crush asphyxia, occurs when there is pressure placed on the chest so that normal respiration cannot occur. Traumatic asphyxia may occur when there is crushing in a crowd, as has happened in a number of sports stadia disasters, such as in Hillsborough, Sheffield, UK, in 1989 in which 96 people lost their lives. Ninety four died on the day and only fourteen of the victims arrived in hospital.

Individual cases of traumatic asphyxia may be encountered in such scenarios as vehicular collisions, collapse of trenches, and industrial equipment incidents.

At autopsy, there is typically prominent congestion of the upper half of the body with prominent petechiae. Other injuries indicating the site of compression may be present. These deaths often have the most florid congestion and petechiae of all the asphyxial death.

Burking

Burking is a special type of asphyxial death derived from the activities of the early nineteenth century body snatchers Burke and Hare. Burke and Hare killed 16 victims and sold the bodies for anatomical dissection. Hare turned King's evidence (state immunity) and gave a description of the method of killing. He stated that Burke "got stridelegs on the top of the woman on the floor, and she cried out a little, and he kept in her breath… He pressed down her head with his breast… He put one hand under the nose and the other under the chin, under her mouth…" External injury was absent. It is noteworthy that Christison stated one of the victims—"presented the signs of asphyxia—vague enough in general and in this instance particularly so, because the murderers left no external local marks…" illustrating the problem of identifying many deaths classified as asphyxia.

Positional and Restraint Asphyxia

The term positional asphyxia has been used in two main ways in forensic medicine. First, it has been used in people who manage to get themselves into a position where they then cannot properly breathe. This may be because they are intoxicated or are otherwise incapacitated, such as from a head injury, and so cannot extricate themselves from the position.

The second usage has been in deaths associated with restraint. In these often controversial cases, it has been argued that these deaths are not from the restraint/position the person has been placed in, but the underlying condition that caused the person to become involved in the struggle. These people are typically intoxicated with cocaine or have an underlying major psychiatric disorder and die following a struggle with law enforcement or health-care personnel. Research on healthy volunteers has shown that placing someone on their back and compressing the back with a weight is equivalent to a person placing their knee on the back, and it does not significantly alter their clinical respiratory function. It is thus argued that the position these people are placed in does not cause their death. One hypothesis made is that these people are dying of restraint asphyxia. One proposed mechanism of death has been catecholamine excess causing cardiac arrhythmia, possibly combined with a degree of deoxygenation during the struggle. Another evolving possibility is that these are vulnerable people with associated underlying disorders such as cardiac conduction and long QT syndrome. Whether these deaths are true, asphyxia deaths remains disputed. The science of these deaths is evolving and many of these deaths are likely multifactorial.

Drowning

Drowning can be considered a form of an asphyxial death, though it is separated because of the special circumstances. However, in wet drowning, there is obstruction of normal respiration by liquid in the airway. Dry drowning, where there is no evidence of fluid present in the airway, has been proposed to be due to a reflex cardiac arrest or possibly by laryngeal spasm.

Autoerotic Sexual Asphyxia

It is well recognized that some deaths involve sexual activity and restriction of oxygen supply. The victims are almost exclusively male. The mechanisms of production of asphyxia encompass those described above but with the intention of producing temporary asphyxia for sexual pleasure and not death. They are commonly hangings, but other mechanisms may occur, including the use of plastic bags and combined with drug or volatile substance use. Bizarre mechanisms are occasionally encountered and knowledge of the possibility of self-inflicted injury may enlighten the investigation. Sexual asphyxia produced by couples may also occur.

The Choking Game

As well as autoerotic asphyxia, induced asphyxia for nonsexual pleasure may be seen and is known as the "choking game." This is most commonly seen in adolescents. The mechanism of production of asphyxia most often involves compression of the neck or compression of the chest. Subjects may also hyperventilate and then perform the Valsalva maneuver.

Chemical Asphyxiants

There are two main chemical asphyxiants encountered in forensic medicine, such as carbon monoxide poisoning and cyanide. These two substances may be encountered together in fires or as separate poisons. Their mechanism of depriving cells of oxygen is different. Carbon monoxide combines with hemoglobin to produce carboxyhemoglobin and prevents oxygen reaching cells. In comparison, cyanide stops cellular metabolism by interfering with cytochrome c oxidase. Both are associated with lividity being redder than normal. This is because of the formation of carboxyhemoglobin in carbon monoxide, which imparts a cherry red appearance to blood. With cyanide, there is a failure to use up oxygen, so blood remains oxygenated. While cyanide and hemoglobin combine to form a compound in vivo, which has a red color, little is produced in fatal cyanide poisoning. A similar reddening of the skin can be seen in bodies that have been refrigerated and where no chemical asphyxiant has been administered. Hydrogen sulfide is another chemical asphyxiant, which may be encountered. It has the unusual feature of turning the brain green. It has been used in suicides by combining polysulfide-containing fungicides with a strong acid.

Conclusions

Deaths from deprivation of oxygen are one of the main mechanisms of death in forensic medicine. There are no specific findings of asphyxia at autopsy. While terminology may vary slightly, as long as the proposed mechanism of production of the deprivation is explained, then confusion should be eliminated.

See also: **Forensic Medicine/Causes of Death:** Immersion Deaths; Strangulation.

Further Reading

Adelson, L., 1974. The Pathology of Homicide: A Vade Mecum for Pathologist, Prosecutor and Defense Counsel. Charles C Thomas, Springfield.

DiMaio, V.J., DiMaio, D., 2001. Forensic Pathology. CRC, Boca Raton.

Ely, S.F., Hirsch, C.S., 2000. Asphyxial deaths and petechiae: a review. Journal of Forensic Science 45, 1148–1150.

Linkletter, M., Gordon, K., Dooley, J., 2010. The choking game and YouTube: a dangerous combination. Clinical Pediatrics 49, 274–279.

Milroy, C.M., Parai, J.L., 2011. Images in forensic pathology. Hydrogen sulphide discolouration of the brain. Forensic Medicine, Science and Pathology 7, 225–226.

Pollanen, M.S., Perera, S.D., Clutterbuck, D.J., 2009. Hemorrhagic lividity of the neck: controlled induction of postmortem hypostatic hemorrhages. American Journal of Forensic Medicine and Pathology 30, 322–326.

Polson, C.J., Gee, D.J., Knight, B., 1985. The Essentials of Forensic Medicine, fourth ed. Pergamon, Oxford.

Saukko, P., Knight, B., 2004. Knight's Forensic Pathology, third ed. Arnold, London.

Sauvageau, A., Boghossian, E., 2010. Classification of asphyxia: the need for standardization. Journal of Forensic Science 55, 1259–1267.

Spitz, W.S., Spitz, D.J. (Eds.), 2006. Spitz and Fisher's Medico-Legal Investigation of Death, fourth ed. Charles C Thomas, Springfield.

Strangulation

A Thierauf and S Pollak, University of Freiburg, Freiburg, Germany

Glossary

Asphyxia A condition of severely deficient supply of oxygen to the body, resulting in hypoxia and hypercapnia.
Hypercapnia A condition where there is too much carbon dioxide in the blood.
Hypoxia A pathological condition in which the body is deprived of an adequate oxygen supply.

Petechiae Punctiform bleeding caused by an acute rise in venous pressure.
Strangulation External pressure applied to the neck, mostly by using hands or a ligature.

The term "strangulation" refers to asphyxia as a result of external pressure on the neck. There are three principal forms of strangulation: hanging, strangulation by ligature, and manual strangulation. All of them deprive the body of oxygen and typically impair the blood supply to the brain.

The neck contains the anatomical structures ensuring the transport of respiratory gases and blood: larynx and trachea, the arterial blood vessels (which transport oxygen-rich blood to the head and especially the brain), and the large cervical veins (through which oxygen-poor blood flows back to the heart). Compression of the cervical soft tissues can occlude the respiratory tract and/or the blood vessels. The pathophysiological consequences depend on the localization, kind, duration, and intensity of the pressure. In the following, the impairing mechanisms of strangulation, its subclassifications, and the respective morphological findings are discussed.

Airway Occlusion

Ventilation can be interrupted in different ways: First, direct pressure on the airways can reduce their width, making the passage of air more difficult. If the pressure forces displace the cervical soft tissue upward and backward, this causes occlusion ("tamponade") of the upper respiratory tract, as the root of the tongue is pressed against the palate and the posterior wall of the pharynx. The force needed for airway occlusion is higher than that required for the occlusion of blood vessels.

Compression of the Cervical Arteries

The brain is supplied with oxygen-rich blood via the carotid and the vertebral arteries. The latter are well protected in the depth of dorsal neck structures as they run along the spine; they enter the cranial cavity through the foramen magnum of the occipital bone. The carotid arteries are localized on either side of the larynx and surrounded by soft tissue. Occlusion of the carotid arteries requires a slightly higher pressure than occlusion of the thin-walled jugular veins.

The duration of the neck compression is also of crucial importance. When the carotid arteries are occluded, the victim becomes unconscious within seconds, while after isolated interruption of the airways, consciousness and the ability to act may be retained for more than a minute under certain circumstances. For a limited period of time, the impairment of brain functions is still reversible. If total occlusion of the blood and oxygen supply continues, irreversible damage with a fatal outcome is to be expected within 3–5 min.

Occlusion of the Neck Veins

Comparatively low pressure forces are required to impair the blood flow in the cervical veins. From the head, blood is transported back to the trunk via the paired jugular and the vertebral veins. The former run between the cervical muscles and are wrapped by soft tissue, the latter are well protected in the depth and descend along the spine.

Although there are many connections between the cervical veins, sudden occlusion, as it occurs in strangulation, is poorly tolerated and compensated. If the arterial blood flow continues, the acute interruption of the venous blood flow leads to vascular congestion in the head with consecutive cyanosis, soft-tissue swelling, and petechial hemorrhages (**Figure 1**).

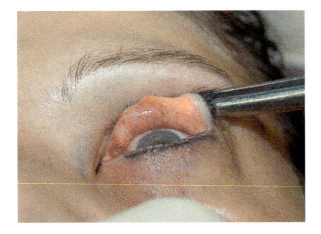

Figure 1   Petechial hemorrhages in the conjunctiva of the left upper eyelid.

Petechiae are punctiform extravasations of blood; they are a classic symptom of venous congestion and occur preferably in the conjunctivae of the eyes, the oral mucosa, and the skin behind the ears, although they can generally be found anywhere above the level of compression. At autopsy, they can also be detected on inner surfaces such as the root of the tongue and the epiglottis, the perimysium of the temporal muscles, and the periosteum of the skullcap. Massive congestion can even be associated with bleeding from the mouth, nose, or ears.

Autopsy Findings

The mechanism actually responsible for death, namely, hypoxia cannot be detected at autopsy, because after death the oxygen is used up in all body tissues. However, the pressure force itself may cause local damage: Bruising of subcutaneous and muscle tissue as well as fractures of the laryngeal cartilages and the hyoid bone occur as direct consequences of pressure and tension forces. Cyanosis, petechiae, and sometimes also blood extravasations from the mouth, nose, or ears are morphological correlates of blood congestion in the head region.

Apart from the local injuries on the neck and possible signs of congestion, further asphyxia-related, but unspecific, findings may be seen: blood congestion of the internal organs (whereas the spleen appears rather anemic), pulmonary edema (which is often hemorrhagic), overinflation of the lungs, a liquid state of the blood, and subpleural pulmonary hemorrhages ("Tardieu spots").

Reflex Mechanisms

The question whether reflex mechanisms play a part in strangulation-related death is controversially discussed. Just

above the bifurcation of the common carotid artery, the so-called glomus caroticum is located, which monitors intravasal pressure by means of baroreceptors and controls blood pressure and heart rate via feedback systems. The impulses are sent to the brain and from there via the vagus nerve to the target organ, the heart. The vagus nerve belongs to the parasympathetic part of the autonomic nervous system and can cause a drop in the heart rate, a decrease of the cardiac output, and, in extreme cases, even a cardiac arrest.

The feedback systems are activated not only by an elevated intravascular pressure but also by external compression. According to the more recent literature, it seems questionable whether strangulation really causes reflexogenic cardiac arrest, especially in healthy victims. On the other hand, in the presence of preexisting vascular pathology, pressure exerted on the carotid sinus may actually trigger an excessive and potentially lethal reflex response.

Hanging

In many countries, hanging is the most common method of suicide. Homicide by hanging is very rare. Occasionally, suicidal hanging is simulated to cover up a previous homicide.

Accidents by hanging occur in both children and adults: in infants and toddlers, especially by becoming entangled in rods and strings, whereas older children may strangle themselves in playgrounds, for example, when a bicycle helmet gets caught in a jungle gym. Adult persons in nursing care (often suffering from dementia) may accidentally strangulate themselves with belt restraints. Most accidents, however, occur in connection with autoerotic practices.

Mechanism

Hanging involves compression of the cervical soft tissues by a noose running around the neck and fixed above it. Thus, the causative force results from the gravitational drag of the body's weight. In most cases, the compression force is sufficient to interrupt the blood supply to the brain with consecutive hypoxia. In addition, the air passages are often blocked.

The rapid loss of consciousness accompanied by muscular atony limits the chance of self-rescue. Survived attempts at hanging are rare; they are observed if the ligature breaks or some other person rescues the victim at an early stage.

Shortly after becoming unconscious, most victims develop spasms which may cause injuries mainly on the extremities. In the agonal phase, saliva may flow from the mouth in a vertical trickle pattern. Sometimes, sperm or stool is discharged. The heartbeat can survive the irreversible brain damage by several minutes.

Methods of Hanging

Not only cords and ropes but also belts, cables, straps, wires, clothes, strips of bed sheets, and shoelaces are objects frequently used as ligatures. For correctly interpreting a case, it is indispensable to know the type and appearance of the noose and the hanging device.

The noose need not encircle the neck completely; isolated pressure on the front of the neck is sufficient for effective strangulation. Apart from nooses with slipknots, open nooses are used. The knot can be movable or not, close to the neck or away from it. The point of suspension is not always located on the back of the neck, but also on its front or side.

For death by hanging, it is not necessary that the body be completely suspended. The gravitational pull of a partly supported body usually also effects a neck compression sufficient to cause death.

Hanging Mark

The skin of the neck usually shows a hanging mark or furrow reflecting the course of the noose and the respective device (**Figure 2(a)–(d)**). Sometimes the hanging mark can be very discreet or even absent altogether, if the ligature used was wide and soft, the force exerted by the noose was small (in partly supported bodies), or if the body was suspended for a short time only.

In most cases, the noose runs upward ("ascending") toward the point of suspension. The furrow is usually deepest and most

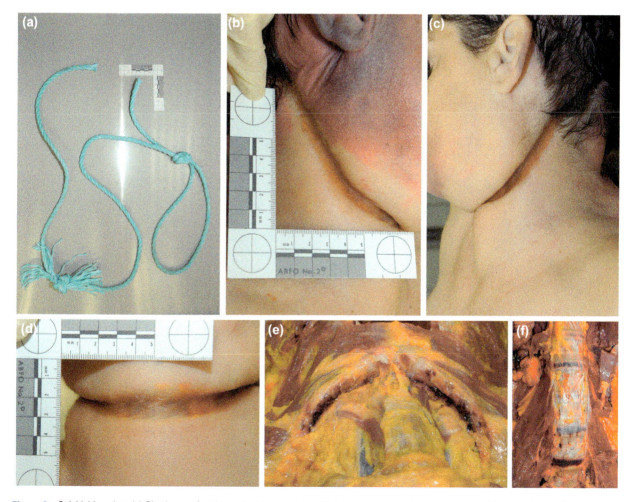

Figure 2 Suicidal hanging. (a) Plastic rope forming a single-turn noose with a fixed (unmovable) knot. (b and c) Right and left side of the neck showing a steeply ascending hanging mark. (d) Frontal aspect of the neck with a deep, parched furrow. (e) Anterior neck after removal of the skin and the sternocleidomastoid muscles: The cranial aspects of the collar bones show blood extravasation at the sites where the muscles had been attached. (f) Anterior aspects of the lumbar spine with Simon's hemorrhages at the level of the intervertebral disks.

distinct opposite the knot and becomes more shallow toward the highest point of the noose. After removal of the hanging device, a superficial abrasion of the skin is often discernible, which tends to parch, resulting in a brownish discoloration with time. If the noose consists of several turns or if the hanging device has a relief-like surface, linear or patterned elevations ("ridges") with intracutaneous bleeding and/or fluid-filled blisters may be seen between the impressed parts of the hanging mark. Sometimes soft textiles such as a scarf or a handkerchief are interposed between the noose and the neck as a cushion.

The appearance of the hanging mark depends on the nature of the ligature, the exerted tension, the duration of suspension, and the possible presence of any interposed material such as head hair, clothing, or jewelry. From a criminalistic point of view, it is essential to distinguish between suicidal, accidental, and homicidal hanging, as well as postmortem suspension. It must be pointed out, however, that the local findings caused by the noose are not suitable to prove vital hanging.

Further External Findings

Depending on the position of the suspended body, hypostasis is localized in the deepest body regions, most often the lower extremities, hands, and forearms. The course of the noose and the drag acting on the ligature decide whether only the venous vessels of the neck are occluded or whether both veins and arteries are affected. The tip of the tongue is often wedged between the front teeth and parched brown.

Blood congestion in the head may be completely absent (in the majority of cases), but may also be very pronounced. If the body is freely suspended and the knot is located on the back of the neck or in the occipital region, the decisive pathomechanism will be the interrupted blood perfusion of the brain; then, no congestion of the head is observed, as the blood flow through the arteries is stopped by the tightening noose. In highly atypical hanging situations (e.g., with the body sitting, kneeling, or lying) and/or when the point of suspension is on the side or front of the neck, sometimes only the thin-walled veins, but not the arteries of the neck, are occluded so that blood congestion can develop above the level of strangulation.

Autopsy Findings

The hanging mark is typically not bruised, as the pressure of the noose prevents blood from leaking from the affected vessels. On the other hand, blood extravasations are often seen at the origin of the straight neck muscles (**Figure 2(e)**). This is due to the strain exercised by the drag of the suspended body.

Pressure exerted on the anterior neck region displaces the hyoid bone and the larynx against the bony support of the spine. As long as these structures are still deformable, as in young persons, injury need not necessarily occur. With advanced ossification (in older and especially in male individuals), the probability increases that hanging will cause fracture of the superior horns of the thyroid cartilage and/or the greater horns of the hyoid bone. The laminae of the thyroid cartilage and the cricoid cartilage are rarely affected. Although fractures of the larynx and the hyoid bone are indicative of a deformation due to pressure, they are not life threatening per se.

In rare cases, victims of hanging show transverse intimal tears in the common carotid arteries due to overstretching. In survivors, such intimal tears may cause secondary complications, for example, thrombosis or dissection of the vascular wall. A common finding—especially if the body was (almost) completely suspended—is found along the lower thoracic and lumbar spine, namely, streaky blood extravasations on the frontal aspects of the intervertebral disks ("Simon's hemorrhages," **Figure 2(f)**).

Bony lesions of the upper spine are rare and were most frequently described in the context of "judicial hangings." Fracture dislocation with transection of the cord will occur only if the body falls from a sufficient height before the noose around the neck tightens. Dislocation is typically seen between the second and third cervical vertebra. If the length of drop is several meters, complete decapitation may occur (**Figure 3(a) and (b)**).

Strangulation by Ligature

Strangulation by ligature is most often encountered as a homicidal or suicidal act. In homicides, it is not uncommon that ligature strangulation is combined with other forms of violence. In suicides by ligature strangulation, knots and/or ligatures with multiple turns prevent subsequent loosening of the noose.

Fatal accidents are rare, the more so as moderate compression of the neck does not lead to immediate unconsciousness. Under unfortunate circumstances, clothes worn around the neck such as a scarf or a tie may get caught in machinery. Accidental self-strangulation is also seen in autoerotic practices. Survived ligature strangulations occur in attempted homicides, rape, and other criminal offenses.

Mechanism

In homicidal ligature strangulation, compression of the cervical soft tissues is mostly affected such that the assailant pulls apart the crossed ends of the noose with his hands. Powerful tightening of a collar or scarf may have the same effect. Contrary to the hanging noose, the constricting object is typically not fixed to a structure away from the body. The circular pressure exercised on the cervical soft tissues mostly leads to a combination of asphyxia, venous blood congestion, and more or less pronounced obstruction of arterial blood supply. This combination is characterized by congestion of the head with soft-tissue swelling, cyanosis, petechial hemorrhages, and sometimes bleeding from the mouth, nose, or ears.

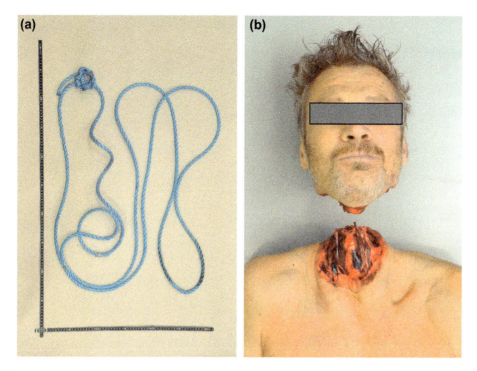

Figure 3 Decapitation from suicidal hanging (rope fixed to balcony railing). (a) Hanging device (plastic rope). (b) Head severed from the body at the level of the hanging mark.

Ligature Mark

The typical strangulation mark encircles the neck almost horizontally and is usually not as deep as the furrow seen in hangings (**Figure 4(a)–(c)**). When there was a dynamic fight between the assailant and the victim, even a ligature with only one circular turn may produce a highly variable ligature mark imitating multiple loops and showing an ascending or descending course. The individual findings depend on the nature of the ligature (width, roughness, and surface pattern) and the strength of the assailant in relation to the victim. The ligature mark may present only as a circular streak without hypostasis (**Figure 5(a)–(c)**). After at least partial abrasion, the unprotected corium tends to parch and assumes a brownish leathery appearance. The presence of congestion signs above the strangulation level suggests a vital traumatization (**Figure 6(a) and (b)**).

Autopsy Findings

Concomitant findings are blood extravasations in the subcutaneous fatty tissue and the cervical muscles, fractures of the larynx and/or the hyoid bone, as well as signs of congestion at the root of the tongue. The hemorrhages may be caused either directly by the pressure of the ligature or indirectly by blood

congestion. Whether laryngeal/hyoid fractures occur is not only dependent on the intensity of the cervical compression, but also on the degree of ossification of the primarily cartilaginous structures.

Manual Strangulation

Virtually, all manual strangulations with fatal outcomes are homicides. Recently, accidental deaths have also been observed in young persons trying to get a "kick" out of the hypoxia resulting from manual compression of the neck.

Mechanism

Manual strangulation involves compression of the neck by using either one or both hands or by exercising pressure with another part of the body such as the forearm or knee. This can trigger different pathomechanisms: Prolonged compression of the larynx impairs the exchange of gases and causes asphyxia. Compression of the lateral parts of the neck may occlude the great cervical vessels. Dependent on whether strangulation is carried out with one or both hands, the assailant is rarely able to completely interrupt the arterial blood flow to the head. If the venous blood flow is mainly obstructed and the arterial

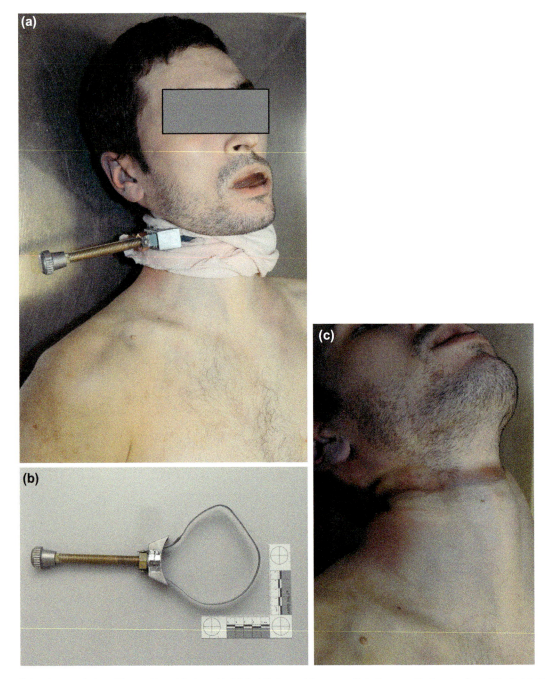

Figure 4   Suicidal strangulation with a cushioned ligature. (a) Original findings at the scene. Note the cyanotic discoloration of the facial skin in comparison with the pale skin below the level of strangulation and the protruding tongue. (b) Strangling device after removal from the neck. (c) Parched ligature mark horizontally encircling the neck.

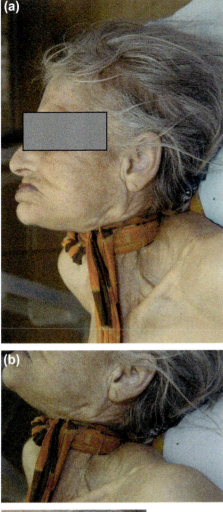

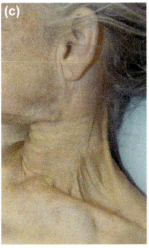

blood supply continues at least to some extent, a congestion syndrome will develop. Consequently, asphyxia and venous congestion are the main pathophysiological mechanisms. As in strangulation by ligature, the typical findings are congestion of the head with (at least temporary) cyanosis, petechial hemorrhages, and sometimes bleeding from the mouth, nose, or ears.

Skin Marks from Manual Strangulation

Local skin lesions from the throttling grip of the assailant are the most important external finding (**Figure 7**). Intra- and subcutaneous hematomas, skin abrasions, and erythematous markings may be present on the anterior and lateral neck, in the mandibular region and the nape. Typical findings are round, oval, or confluent bruises caused by the pressure of the fingertips as well as scratch-like and crescent-shaped abrasions from the fingernails. External findings on the neck may be insignificant or even completely absent, if the pressure was exercised over a large area or a soft object such as a cushion or scarf were interposed.

Autopsy Findings

By dissecting the cervical soft tissues layer by layer, blood extravasations can be identified in the subcutaneous fatty tissue, under the perimysium of the muscles and below the fibrous capsule of the thyroid gland as a consequence of direct pressure. Fractures of the hyoid bone, the thyroid cartilage, and the cricoid cartilage with concomitant hematomas in the surrounding connective tissue are common, but by no means obligatory. Especially in children and young women, the laryngeal structures are cartilaginous and highly deformable, so that fractures do not necessarily occur.

In the marginal and apical portions of the tongue, one often finds hemorrhages caused by squeezing of the tissue between the teeth of the upper and lower jaws. In addition, subepithelial congestion hemorrhages may be discernible at the root of the tongue. A high percentage of victims show not only local findings on the neck, but also concomitant injuries on other parts of the body. These are mostly due to blunt traumatization, for example, hematomas caused by blows to the face or defense injuries on the upper extremities. By defending themselves, the victims often cause injuries on the assailant's body (scratch-like excoriations from fingernails, bite marks, etc.).

Figure 5 Suicidal self-strangulation with a scarf. (a) Ligature fastened with a simple knot on the front of the neck. (b) Close-up view of the ligature on the left side of the neck. (c) Findings after removal of the ligature with shallow impression of the skin, but without any parching.

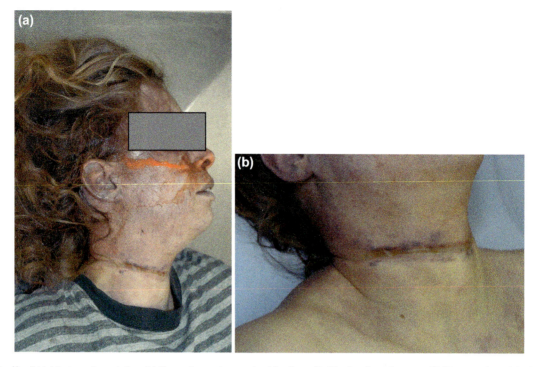

Figure 6   Homicidal ligature strangulation. (a) Congestion and cyanosis of the face with bleeding from the nose. (b) Close-up view of the horizontal ligature mark with partial discoloration from parching.

Victims surviving acts of manual strangulation may show mere reddening of the cervical skin as a sign of mechanical irritation or "classical" grip marks such as hematomas and abrasions. Petechial hemorrhages in the conjunctivae tend to merge and then resemble an extensive hyposphagma.

Petechial hemorrhages in the facial skin and conjunctivae are actually one of the typical consequences of strangulation, both

manual and by ligature, but they are not specific, as they may also have other causes (expulsive labor, fits of coughing, etc.).

Clinical symptoms after survived strangulation include dysphagia, local tenderness to pressure, pain on moving the neck, and dysphonia (hoarseness). Swelling and space-occupying hemorrhages in the cervical soft tissues may cause delayed life-threatening respiratory obstruction. Prolonged strangulation is often associated with loss of consciousness and involuntary discharge of urine and/or feces.

> *See also:* **Forensic Medicine/Causes of Death:** Asphyctic Deaths—Overview and Pathophysiology; Traumatic and Postural Asphyxia, Physical Restraint; **Forensic Medicine/Clinical:** Clinical Forensic Medicine—Overview; **Forensic Medicine/Pathology:** External Postmortem Examination.

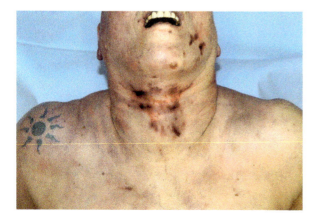

Figure 7   Homicide by manual strangulation. Multiple grip marks (excoriations and/or hematomas) on the front of the neck and at the level of the lower jaw.

Further Reading

Betz, P., Eisenmenger, W., 1996. Frequency of throat-skeleton fractures in hanging. American Journal of Forensic Medicine and Pathology 17, 191–193.

Brinkmann, B., Bone, H.-G., Booke, M., Du Chesne, A., Maxeiner, H., Ersticken, 2004. In: Brinkmann, B., Madea, B. (Eds.), Handbuch gerichtliche Medizin, vol. 1. Springer-Verlag, Berlin, Heidelberg, pp. 699–796.

Brinkmann, B., Püschel, K., 1990. Ersticken. Springer-Verlag, Heidelberg, Berlin.

Di Maio, D., Di Maio, V.J.M., 2001. Forensic Pathology, second ed. CRC Press, Boca Raton, FL.

Eisenmenger, W., Gilg, T., 2003. Asphyxia. In: Payne-James, J., Busuttil, A., Smock, W. (Eds.), Forensic Medicine: Clinical and Pathological Aspects. Greenwich Medical Media Ltd., London, pp. 259–273.

Oesterhelweg, L., Thali, M.J., 2009. Strangulation. In: Thali, M.J., Dirnhofer, R., Vock, P. (Eds.), The Virtopsy Approach. CRC Press, Boca Raton, FL, pp. 334–338.

Pollak, S., Saukko, P., 2003. Atlas of Forensic Medicine. CD-ROM. Elsevier, Amsterdam (Chapter 8).

Pollanen, M.S., 2001. Subtle fatal manual neck compression. Medicine, Science and the Law 41, 135–140.

Pollanen, M.S., 2009. Asphyxia. In: Jamieson, A., Moenssens, A. (Eds.), Wiley Encyclopedia of Forensic Science, vol. 1. Wiley, Chichester, pp. 224–234.

Purdue, B.N., 2000. Asphyxial and related deaths. In: Mason, J.K., Purdue, B.N. (Eds.), The Pathology of Trauma, third ed. Arnold, London, pp. 230–252.

Saukko, P., Knight, B., 2004. Fatal pressure on the neck. In: Saukko, P., Knight, B. (Eds.), Knight's Forensic Medicine, third ed. Arnold, London, pp. 368–394.

Spitz, W.U., 2006. Asphyxia. In: Spitz, W.U., Spitz, D.J. (Eds.), Spitz and Fisher's Medicolegal Investigation of Death: Guidelines for the Application of Pathology to Crime Investigation, fourth ed. Charles C. Thomas, Springfield, IL, pp. 444–497.

Traumatic and Postural Asphyxia, Physical Restraint

PH Schmidt and M Kettner, Saarland University Medical School, Homburg/Saar, Germany

During physiological breathing, inspiratory and expiratory movements assure a constant exchange of ambient and intrapulmonary air, thus satisfying the organism's oxygen requirements. Breathing movements depend on the coordinated action of the respiratory muscles, which are under the control of the brain stem respiratory center. Breathing in a neutral body position without physical stress is mainly dependent on contractions of the diaphragm (abdominal or negative-pressure breathing) and/or contractions of the external intercostal muscles (costal breathing). These contractions generate negative intrathoracic pressure, allowing the lungs to expand. Expiration is accomplished by relaxation of the inspiratory muscles and elastic recoil of the lungs.

During deep inspiration and expiration, the involvement and coordination of respiratory muscles are more complex. The external intercostals, scalenes, minor and major pectoralis, sternocleidomastoid, and serratus anterior muscles pull the ribs up and out, and the diaphragm contracts, thereby pushing the contents of the abdomen toward the pelvis. During forced expiration, the internal intercostal muscles pull the ribs down and in, and the abdominal muscles contract, pushing the abdominal contents toward the diaphragm. Recruitment of the involved muscles is always dependent on their capability to contract, which, among other things, is determined by body posture.

Deaths attributed to traumatic asphyxia, positional or postural asphyxia, and physical restraint share a common mechanism, which is the mechanically induced inability to recruit respiratory muscles (and thus allow chest cage excursions) that is caused by either mechanical compression of the chest or a particular position of the body. These deaths can thus be subsumed under the term mechanical asphyxia. To differentiate between these three subdiagnoses, the exact circumstances of death must be included in all forensic considerations. However, the unequivocal determination of the cause of death as traumatic asphyxia, positional/postural asphyxia, or physical restraint may not always be possible because of the fluid transition between these entities, for example, death associated with wedging. In some cases, the chain of events includes elements of more than one subdiagnosis, and, in other cases, a specific mechanism cannot be categorized as traumatic-, positional-, or restraint associated. Furthermore, clear classification of a specific case may be impossible because of a combination of additional cofactors

leading to death. Therefore, it has to be stressed that the diagnosis of these entities is mainly a diagnosis of exclusion, with the constant need to improve the diagnostic tools being used.

Traumatic Asphyxia

Traumatic asphyxia was first described by Ollivier d'Angers in 1837, when he noticed the relatively uniform morphological features of decedents who had been trampled by crowds on the Field of Mars in Paris on Bastille Day of the same year. Over 60 years later, the morphological signs seen by d'Angers were integrated into Perthes' concept of pressure congestion, which provided the first explanation for the distinct discoloration and pattern of petechial bleeding (**Table 1**). It showed that the absence of venous valves in the inflow region of the superior vena cava allowed for the reflux of venous blood associated with chest compression into the neck and head region.

In cases of traumatic asphyxia, the restriction of respiratory movements and chest wall excursions is caused by external compression of the chest or upper abdominal region, for example, by a heavy object, matter burying the victim (landslide), or by being trampled by a crowd of people. From a pathophysiological perspective, massive compression of the chest or upper abdomen inhibits the inspiratory movements that provide not only oxygen to the organism but also the negative intrathoracic pressure needed to transport blood to the right heart. In addition, it causes reflow of blood to the neck and head region, which leads to cessation of cerebral blood flow, thus resulting in loss of consciousness and, ultimately, death.

Traumatic asphyxia may occur in accidental as well as homicidal settings. Accidental traumatic asphyxia is a frequent occurrence in severe automobile accidents, when occupants have been wedged between parts of the vehicle. It also appears as riot crushes in mass disasters, such as during the 2006 Hajj in Saudi Arabia, the soccer game riots in Bradford (UK); and Brussels (Belgium) in 1985, Hillsborough (UK) in 1989. It occurs during construction accidents, for example, when workers are wedged between a wall and sliding soil or are trapped under heavy machinery. Children are especially at risk of being trapped under heavy objects, such as unbolted cupboards. In all these cases, the considerable weight disparity between the compressing object or force and the compressed

Table 1   External findings in traumatic asphyxia

External findings in cases of traumatic asphyxia (Perthes pressure congestion, Ollivier syndrome)

- *Masque ecchymotique*: discoloration of the face, neck, and upper parts of the body (depending on the location and degree of congestion)
- Discoloration absent at pressure points (clothing trapped between object and skin, object contact areas)
- Facial and neck edema
- Mucocutaneous petechiae, subconjunctival ecchymoses
- In cases surviving traumatic asphyxia: nonxanthochromic disappearance of face and neck discoloration

Table 2   Internal and microscopic findings in traumatic asphyxia

Internal and microscopic findings in cases of traumatic asphyxia

- Internal petechiae and ecchymoses (e.g., pharyngeal, nasal, laryngeal, epiglottic, tracheal, subpleural, and subepicardial)
- Pulmonary congestion with subsequent edema
- Cerebral edema and petechiae
- Fractures (e.g., ribs, clavicles, and sternum)
- Lacerations of abdominal organs (e.g., spleen)
- Retinal hemorrhages (Purtscher syndrome)
- Tympanic hemorrhages
- Pulmonary microembolism (fat and bone marrow)
- Hypoxic changes in internal organs (e.g., vacuolization and swelling of hepatocytes)

person has been reported to be an important predictor of outcome, along with the duration of compression.

Crushing a person with a heavy object has also been described as a means of homicide. Other homicidal settings for traumatic asphyxia include compression of a victim's chest by the aggressor's use of thighs and knees ("leg scissors"), possibly leading to "jack-knife" injuries or in the case of a child "accordion" compression of the thorax.

Typical but rather nonspecific external findings in cases of traumatic asphyxia include significant purplish-red discoloration, edema, mucocutaneous bleeding, including petechiae and subconjunctival ecchymoses of the head and neck, and ecchymoses on upper body parts, which occur depending on the degree of compression and the body level where compression is applied, and that spare pressure points. In some cases, petechial bleeding may also be seen in the lower limbs, such as in the popliteal fossa. In cases surviving traumatic asphyxia, the discolorations resolve without a xanthochromic stage, whereas concomitant ecchymoses from other causes show xanthochromia before resolving. Neurological and other sequelae may include loss of consciousness, obnubilation, convulsions, agitation, disorientation, atonic motor paresis, transient hearing loss caused by tympanic hemorrhage, and vision disorders caused by retinal hemorrhage and edema (Purtscher retinopathy).

In addition to the external findings, autopsy may reveal internal petechiae and ecchymoses, and congested internal organs, including pulmonary and cerebral congestion. Moreover, lacerations of internal organs such as the spleen and liver, and fractures may be seen. Microscopic examination has found hypoxic changes attributable to asphyxia in various organs including vacuolization and swelling of hepatocytes, renal tubular epithelial cells, and cardiomyocytes. In addition, bone marrow and fat microemboli from bone fractures may be seen in the lung (**Table 2**).

Traumatic asphyxia may be established as the cause of death in the presence of the typical findings as described, and in the absence of other fatal injuries or competing natural causes of death. Toxicological analysis of autopsy specimens must be performed to exclude intoxication or incapacitation caused by alcohol or drug intake.

Postural or Positional Asphyxia

Postural or positional asphyxia have been defined as a fatal condition resulting from unusual orientation of the body, either induced or voluntary, that mechanically interferes with pulmonary ventilation by obstruction of the airways and interference with chest wall excursions. It is further characterized by the inability of the individual to extricate himself or herself from the position, which may have a variety of causes, including intoxication (alcohol and drugs), neurological impairment, physical impairment, physical restraint, loss of consciousness, or a combination.

In positional asphyxia, death is attributed to impairment of ventilatory function caused by a body position that results in either compression or occlusion of the airways at different levels or the inability to perform inspiratory and expiratory movements. Pathophysiologically, the underlying mechanism can be determined from the circumstances surrounding death. The diagnosis of death due to postural/positional asphyxia therefore strongly depends on information regarding the exact position of the body upon discovery of the decedent and the autoptical and toxicological exclusion of other natural or unnatural causes of death (**Table 3**).

Positional asphyxia has been reported as the cause of death in a wide spectrum of death scenarios and subsequent autoptical findings. Cases of hyperextension of the trunk and neck region, for example, falls down stairs that result in a head hyperextension against an adjacent wall (**Figures 1 and 2**), or the body in a knee–chest position with rotated head and hyperextended neck, have been categorized as positional asphyxia. Cases of hyperflexion of the neck and the abdominal region, for example, recreational suspension or being trapped in bathtubs or tire piles ("jack-knife position"), have also been categorized as positional asphyxia. Whereas death may be

Table 3 Diagnostic criteria for positional asphyxia in cases of accidental asphyxial death

Diagnostic criteria for positional asphyxia

- Discovery in a position precluding normal breathing, or interfering with pulmonary ventilation
- Evidence that the decedent placed himself/herself in the position inadvertently, that is, without deliberate action of another person
- Reasonable explanation that the decedent could not extricate himself/herself from the fatal position
- Exclusion of other unnatural causes of death (e.g., intoxication) with a reasonable degree of certainty
- Cardiovascular or respiratory or other potentially life-threatening disease: if present, unrelated to the terminal episode or, alternatively, feasible as predisposing to positional asphyxia

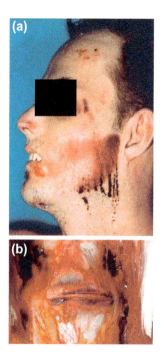

Figure 2 Postmortem findings: abrasions of the left cheek and parallel perpendicular scratch marks consistent with the scene (a). Simon's sign seen at the front of the lumbar intervertebral disk at level L2/3 (b). Images courtesy of Dr. S. Padosch.

Figure 1 Positional asphyxia: side view (a) and top view (b) of a 23-year-old individual in a prone position, who fell down the staircase under the influence of alcohol (blood alcohol concentration 2.60 g l^{-1}; urine alcohol concentration 3.26 g l^{-1}). Body position with maximum hyperextension of the cervical and lumbar spine. Position of upper and lower limbs does not indicate unsuccessful self-extrication attempts. Images courtesy of Dr. S. Padosch.

attributed to compression or occlusion of the airways in cases of hyperextension of the neck with or without a rotatory component, in neck and abdominal hyperflexion, incapacitation of respiratory muscles is the major pathophysiological mechanism. Both scenarios have been well documented in many cases, which frequently show an additional aggravation by the consumption of alcohol found in a large number of positional asphyxia decedents.

Alcohol has been shown to decrease total peripheral vascular resistance, arterial blood pressure, heart rate, and myocardial contractility. Furthermore, the occurrence of supraventricular and ventricular tachyarrhythmias and an increased endogenous catecholamine response have been observed. In addition, alcohol may exert a central depressant effect on the respiratory center in the brain stem, thus fatally aggravating the mechanical impairment of ventilation.

Cases of reverse suspension (head-down position) have been described associated not only with sports accidents in particular (alpinists, speleologists, and parachutists), but also with accidents resulting from certain sexual activities. In all these cases, hydrostatic pressure increases in the upper body, which does not have compensatory mechanisms such as the venous valves of the lower body. Increased hydrostatic pressure results in the pooling of blood in parts of the upper body and diminished flow of venous blood to the right heart, with subsequent hypovolemic shock. In crucifixions, death may be attributed to a combination of dehydration, hypovolemic shock, and mechanical or positional asphyxia, since both chest cage and intercostals are fixed in an extreme inspiratory position during the process of raising up the crucified individual.

In addition to the pathophysiological considerations underlying the mechanical components of positional asphyxia, additional impairment must be considered. Not only preexisting organic diseases, but also physical stress, panic-induced catecholamine release, and consequent arrhythmias of a heart already sensitized by an elevated level of exercise and hypoxia may contribute to the occurrence of death. According to the concept of death caused by exposure to abnormal stress ("critical stress"), death occurs if the capacity of the organism is exceeded. If the organism is already impaired by other independent factors, the primary stress level is elevated to a secondary stress level, and an additional lower level of stress will exceed the critical capacity causing the death of the individual. With reference to positional asphyxia, the level of primary stress may be markedly elevated by preexisting medical conditions, alcohol, or drugs, and positional asphyxia becomes the ultimate insult that exceeds the limit of critical capacity (**Figure 3**).

As with traumatic asphyxia, the relatively nonspecific external findings of positional asphyxia include petechial bleeding (skin and conjunctivae) in addition to cephalic congestion and swelling, which have been found in up to 50% of positional asphyxia cases. Subject to the position of the body upon discovery and the underlying mechanism leading to this position, external examination of the decedent may yield varying patterns of scratches, hematomas, and abrasions, and a distinct distribution pattern of postmortem hypostasis, which corresponds to the scene of discovery.

Findings on internal examination may include congestion of the base of the tongue, the epiglottis, and the trachea. Congestion and edema of the brain and the lungs (with the mean combined lung weight amounting to more than 1000 g) are observed. Hemorrhagic infiltration of chest and neck muscles indicates rupture of muscle fascia, which is caused by strained respiratory movements attempting to compensate for constriction imposed by body position. During the convulsive phase, hemorrhaging may occur, which may be located in the muscles of the axillae and upper back, and in the major pectoralis muscles, as well as in the periosteum of the clavicle at the junction with the sternocleidomastoid muscle. In cases associated with abdominal suspension, bruising of the chest wall and diaphragm, peripancreatic hemorrhage, and rupture of the spleen may be seen. In addition, there may be underlying organic diseases that are not inherently lethal, but may lead to collapse into a lethal position, from which the victim is incapable of extricating himself/herself because of weakness, paralysis, or loss of consciousness. In cases of suspected positional asphyxia, toxicological analysis of autopsy specimens is mandatory for determining the reasons for incapacitation of the decedent, and for excluding agents of intoxication, which may be responsible for the occurrence of death.

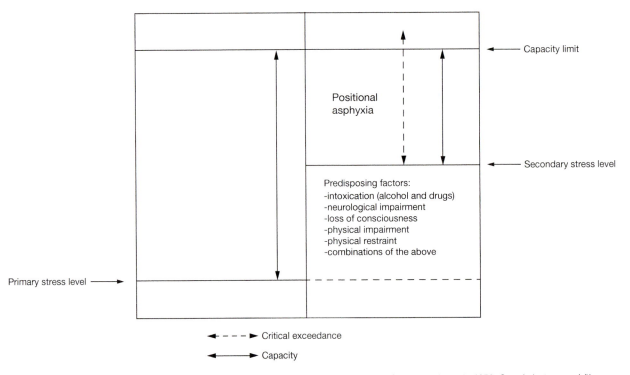

Figure 3   Stress levels and critical capacity exceedance in positional asphyxia. Adapted from Schoenmackers, J., 1950. Grenzbelastung und überraschender Tod. Medizinische Klinik 45, 790–795; Padosch, S.A., Schmidt, P.H., Kröner, L.U., Madea, B., 2005. Death due to positional asphyxia under severe alcoholisation: pathophysiologic and forensic considerations. Forensic Science International 149, 67–73; Byard, R.W., Wick, R., Gilbert, J.D., 2008. Conditions and circumstances predisposing to death from positional asphyxia in adults. Journal of Forensic and Legal Medicine 15, 415–419.

In summary, fatalities caused by positional asphyxia are characterized by the scarcity and nonspecificity of morphological findings. Positional asphyxia must be identified as the major factor in the cause of death, although other factors may have been involved and contributed to the occurrence of death at a certain time, but by themselves could not be responsible for death. Autopsy results serve either to confirm conclusions drawn from thorough assessment of the scene or to identify injuries or other evidence that implicates the involvement of another person or persons. Furthermore, the autopsy serves to diagnose probable risk factors and exclude other natural or unnatural causes of death.

Restraint Asphyxia

As the term "positional asphyxia" implies passive or accidental entrapment of the decedent, the term "restraint asphyxia" was proposed to identify the sudden deaths of individuals in a restrained prone position. This has included many cases that were hogtied (restraint of a person with wrists and ankles behind the back and bound together by means of a cord or hobbling device). When this method has been employed by law enforcement authorities to incapacitate a suspect, additional weight (normally, body weight) was usually placed on the chest of the suspect. In other cases of restraint asphyxia, acutely psychotic patients or other patients in mental health clinics who were involved in altercations, died after being subdued by techniques such as the "therapeutic basket hold."

Although the classical scenario leading to restraint asphyxia is well known to forensic experts, a comprehensive explanation for all deaths does not exist. However, many of the situations leading to death associated with restraint asphyxia share similarities. They are usually highly charged, with the individual behaving irrationally (in some cases, referred to as excited delirium, caused by psychiatric disease and/or substance abuse), which leads to severe physical exertion on the part of others, who restrain the individual in a hogtied prone position. Furthermore, these decedents are preponderantly male and overweight, with a mean age of 30 years.

Clinically, the restrained person becomes quiet and develops cardiac arrest after a period of vigorous struggle. Hyperthermia seems to be present in most cases. Initial evidence supporting the adverse effects of the prone restraint position on ventilation and circulation was provided by a study of healthy subjects who were placed in the hogtied position after attaining a maximum heart rate of 120 beats per minute on a stationary cross-country ski track. The subjects in the restraint position exhibited a prolonged recovery time for both heart rate and peripheral oxygen saturation. The results of this study were not thought to be valid, because the method for determining oxygen saturation was believed to be inaccurate (no direct measure of ventilatory function and findings inconsistent with results from exercise physiology). Therefore, in a successive study, healthy volunteers underwent pulmonary function testing (PFT) in a sitting, supine, prone, and body restraint position. In a second series of experiments, they were exposed to a 4-min exercise period followed by a 15-min period either sitting or in the restraint position. Serial arterial blood gas measurement, electrocardiography, pulse oximetry monitoring, and PFT (forced vital capacity, mean forced expiratory volume, and maximal voluntary ventilation), found a progressive decrease in pulmonary function associated with body position (sitting to supine to prone to restraint), and exercise did not result in additional impairment. However, it is difficult to generalize the findings of these experiments to the relevant forensic conditions seen in restraint asphyxia, because of significant differences between the study and the usual cases of restraint asphyxia. The study volunteers were healthy, tested negative for alcohol and drugs, and had not experienced struggle or psychological stress.

In cases of restraint asphyxia, excited delirium was frequently induced by psychoactive stimulative drugs, especially cocaine. Cocaine causes extreme sympathetic activation by blocking the presynaptic uptake of catecholamines, dopamine, and serotonin, which leads to increased myocardial contractility, blood pressure, and heart rate. Coronary artery vasoconstriction, microvascular resistance, and enhanced thrombogenecity of blood also exacerbate the physical condition of the cocaine user. Sympathetic stimulation is further increased by verbal and physical interaction with the people attempting to control the individual manifesting delirium. Excited delirium is characterized by constant, purposeless, and often violent activity, coupled with incoherent or meaningless speech, hallucinations, and paranoid delusions and can predispose to sudden death by causing neurally mediated cardiac arrest. Recently, a hypothesis was proposed that some cases of unexpected death in custody might be attributed to a clinical syndrome called stress cardiomyopathy, and the findings have been compared to the findings in takotsubo cardiomyopathy.

In conclusion, the mechanism of death in restraint asphyxia may be a fatal cardiac dysrhythmia or respiratory arrest induced by an imbalance of increased cardiac oxygen demand and decreased oxygen delivery caused by the interaction of several factors. Psychiatric or drug-induced agitated delirium coupled with police confrontation generates catecholamine-mediated stress of the cardiovascular system. The hyperactivity associated with excited delirium, struggle with the police, and ventilatory work to overcome the restraint increase the demands for oxygen delivery. Finally, the hogtied position may inhibit movements of the chest wall and diaphragm, thus impairing ventilation in a situation of high oxygen demand.

External examination of cases of restraint asphyxia yields typical, nonspecific signs, including petechial bleeding (skin and conjunctivae) and a pattern of injury that may include hematoma, characteristic abrasions of the wrists and ankles, and lacerations caused by the previous struggle to restrain the decedent. Autoptically, preexisting medical conditions contributing to the occurrence of death may be found, but which are not sufficient to be monocausal causes of death. Furthermore, varying degrees of internal organ injuries caused by the applied physical force may be found. Toxicological analysis is a prerequisite in cases of suspected physical restraint and may explain the observed state of excited delirium, clarify the dosages and intake of prescribed drugs, or characterize an intoxication-related fatality.

Other Mechanical Asphyxia Cases

There are some cases in which either mechanical asphyxia is the sole cause of death but cannot be solely attributed to a traumatic event, certain body position, or application of restraint techniques, or mechanical asphyxia may not be the sole cause of death but may play a crucial role, for example, in a setting of homicide.

Mechanical Asphyxia During Institutional Restraint

Mechanical asphyxias during institutional restraint occur usually in bedridden or otherwise incapacitated patients of nursing homes and hospitals. A scenario, which is usually categorized as death due to positional asphyxia, is an entrapment of a patient between bed rails and mattress. Subject to the body position, it may also be categorized as strangulation. In praxi, it is frequently not diagnosed, since medical staff may modify body position of the decedent during resuscitation efforts. In other cases, posey restraints, vests, or jackets used to restrain a patient in a highly charged situation may not have been used correctly. Fixation may be too loose, therefore allowing the body to slip through the posey restraint leading to a hanging position, which can be categorized as positional asphyxia or hanging subject to the body and head position. In addition, the restraint may not be fixed correctly to the bed. While the patient moves, he or she may slip off the mattress attaining a suspended position.

Incaprettamento

In "incaprettamento," a ritualized form of ligature strangulation associated with the Italian mafia, the decedent is usually found in a prone position with wrists and ankles tied together with additional ligature of the neck, which is connected to the lower extremities. This scenario is either arranged postmortem or used to let the victim strangulate himself or herself, once the legs are lowered due to physical exhaustion. Scenarios similar to the abovementioned may also be seen in autoerotic asphyxia deaths.

Burking

The term "burking" originates from the type of serial murders committed in Edinburgh, Scotland, in 1827 and 1828 by William Burke and William Hare, who sold the cadavers of their victims to a local anatomist. "Burking" refers to a method of killing that combines mechanical chest compression caused by sitting on the chest of the victim, with the simultaneous smothering of the victim by covering the nose and mouth and pushing up the lower jaw.

Constrictor Snakes

Deaths due to constrictor snakes, for example, pythonidae, are rare occurrences. In the few reports of authenticated fatal constrictor snake attacks, mechanical asphyxia due to chest compression was assumed as the cause of death. Upon discovery, the snake may display a characteristic silhouette and be unable to move or has died of asphyxiation during ingestion of the victim.

See also: **Forensic Medicine/Causes of Death:** Asphyctic Deaths—Overview and Pathophysiology; Strangulation; **Forensic Medicine/Clinical:** Deaths in Custody; Traffic Injuries and Deaths.

Further Reading

Bell, M.D., Rao, V.J., Wetli, C.V., Rodriguez, R.N., 1992. Positional asphyxiation in adults. American Journal of Forensic Medicine and Pathology 13, 101–107.

Byard, R.W., Wick, R., Gilbert, J.D., 2008. Conditions and circumstances predisposing to death from positional asphyxia in adults. Journal of Forensic and Legal Medicine 15, 415–419.

Chan, T.C., Vilke, G.M., Neuman, T., 1998. Reexamination of custody restraint position and positional asphyxia. American Journal of Forensic Medicine and Pathology 19, 201–205.

DiMaio, V.J., DiMaio, D., 2001. Forensic Pathology, second ed. CRC Press, Boca Raton, FL.

Madea, B., 2007. Praxis Rechtsmedizin, second ed. Springer, Heidelberg.

Mason, J.K., Purdue, B.N., 2000. The Pathology of Trauma, third ed. Arnold, London.

Ohtabachi, M., Cevik, C., Bagdure, S., Nugent, K., 2010. Excited delirium, restraints, and unexpected death. American Journal of Forensic Medicine and Pathology 31, 107–112.

Padosch, S.A., Schmidt, P.H., Kröner, L.U., Madea, B., 2005. Death due to positional asphyxia under severe alcoholisation: pathophysiologic and forensic considerations. Forensic Science International 149, 67–73.

Reay, D.T., Howard, J.D., Fligner, C.L., Ward, R.J., 1988. Effects of positional restraint on oxygen saturation and heart rate following exercise. American Journal of Forensic Medicine and Pathology 9, 16–18.

Saukko, P., Knight, B., 2000. Knight's Forensic Pathology, third ed. Arnold, London.

Sauvageau, A., Boghossian, E., 2010. Classification of asphyxia: the need for standardization. Journal of Forensic Sciences 55, 1259–1267.

Shkrum, M.J., Ramsay, D.A., 2007. Forensic Pathology of Trauma: Common Problems for the Pathologist. Humana Press, Totowa, NJ.

Spitz, W.U., 2006. Spitz and Fisher's Medicolegal Investigation of Death: Guidelines for the Application of Pathology to Crime Investigation. Charles C. Thomas, Springfield.

Immersion Deaths

B Ludes, Institut de Médecine Légale, Strasbourg, France

Introduction

The determination of the diagnosis of death by immersion is one of the most difficult tasks in forensic medicine. The death of a victim found in water is not necessarily related to drowning and the autopsy examination as well as complementary laboratory investigations must be performed to assess this diagnosis. These investigations comprise biochemical and histological analyses and the diatom test.

Immersion deaths can be considered as death by drowning defined as death due to submersion in a liquid. The fundamental mechanism of death in acute drowning is reversible cerebral anoxia, and the consequence of drowning is hypoxemia.

Physiopathology

A series of phases have been described in the death by drowning, consisting of breath holding, involuntary inspiration, gasping for air, loss of consciousness, and death. The cerebral hypoxia leads to irreversible brain damage and death occurs. The irreversibility of the cerebral lesions depends on several factors such as the individual's age, previous health, breath-holding tolerance, and the temperature of the water. Consciousness is usually lost within 3 min of submersion. One of the questions is also to estimate the volume of water that has been inhaled. This volume ranges from a relatively small to a very large one. Large quantities of water can pass, after inhalation, through the alveolar–capillary interface and enter the circulation. A review of the literature showed that no evidence exists, that large volumes of inhaled water can increase blood volume, which can cause significant electrolyte imbalances or hemolysis or acute cardiac failure. The determining factor is the alteration of the pulmonary surfactant, which induces the collapse of the alveoli, leading to intrapulmonary shunting of blood via atelectatic pulmonary tissue and hypoxia due to a lack of pulmonary oxygen perfusion.

Another mechanism of hypoxia consists of a vagal reflex that may be induced by inhalation of water. This reflex increases peripheral airway resistance with pulmonary vasoconstriction, development of pulmonary hypertension, decreased lung compliance, and a reduction in ventilation–perfusion ratios. A kind of vasovagal stimulation by intense stimulation of cutaneous nerve endings or stimulation of nerve endings in the mucosa of the eardrum, pharynx, or larynx by sudden immersion of cold water can lead to a reflex cardiac arrest. The inhalation of a small quantity of cold water may also induce a laryngeal spasm, which could lead to lethal hypoxemia by airway closure, but this mechanism is not favored by Knight because of the long time during which the larynx must be kept closed and thus prevent entry of water. It is clear that neither autopsy findings nor biological tests give any evidence of drowning in those cases. Approximately 10% of the drowned humans die during laryngospasm or breath holding without actually aspirating fluid.

The hydrostatic pressure of water on a person induces a significant increase in the work of breathing and the cardiovascular response is an increase in heart rate and cardiac output, which can induce cardiac arrhythmia particularly in a person with cardiovascular disease. Following prolonged immersion in cold water, hypothermia will be observed when the deep body temperature drops below 35 °C. Death by ventricular fibrillation and finally by asystole may occur due to very low body temperature.

Autopsy Findings

The autopsy must identify all pathologic lesions as well as evidence of drowning. The major sign of immersion is skin maceration, which begins within minutes in warm water and becomes visible after a longer time interval in cold water immersion. The skin becomes wrinkled, pale, and sodden like a "washerwoman's skin." First, these changes can be seen at the fingertips, palms, and the back of the hands, and, later, the soles. After a period, the thick keratin of the hands and feet becomes detached and peels off in a "glove and stocking" fashion—the nails and hair become loosened after a few days—but no changes may be observed if the body is in the water for only a few hours.

Other immersion signs such as *cutis anserina*, postmortem distribution of hypostasis, and the presence of mud, silt, or sand on or in the body have been described but have no diagnostic value even if the external material (sand, mud, etc.) is found situated deep in the respiratory passage and in the stomach. In fact, if the body has been rolled by waves, the presence of this material is not an evidence of aspiration.

The signs of drowning depend on the delay of body recovery from the water and on the development of putrefaction phenomena, which alter the positive signs of drowning. In freshly drowned bodies, large amounts of froth can be present around the nostrils and mouth as well as in the upper and lower airways. This fluid is not a specific sign of drowning because it is similar in appearance to the edema of left ventricular failure, but, in cases of drowning, the volume of froth is generally greater than in the other cases.

Lung weights are usually higher in drowning cases but a normal weight is possible in some drowning cases and in "dry-drowning" deaths caused by vasovagal reflex. In drowning cases, the lungs may be overinflated, filling the thoracic cavity, with the indentations of the ribs at their lateral parts, and being generally waterlogged, referred to as *emphysema aquosum*, but the absence of these signs does not exclude true drowning. The surfaces of the lungs are pale and crepitant. The fluid is trapped in the lower airways and blocks the passive collapse of the bronchi that normally occurs after death and the lungs do not collapse. Subpleural blebs of emphysema may also be observed at the surface of the lungs. It is important to emphasize that no pathognomonic findings have been detected in other organs during autopsy, in cases related to drowning.

Postmortem injuries to the face, the back of the hands, knees, and toes from dragging along the bottom may be present. Evidence of animal activities may also be found on bodies that have spent a long time in the water. Accidental or suicidal injuries inflicted on a person before his or her falling or entering into the water can also be seen. Differentiation between ante- and postmortem injuries is a very difficult task because of the lack of the usual criteria of antemortem infliction, namely in perimortally sustained injuries.

Histology

The histologic analyses of the diagnosis of death by drowning must focus on the state of alveolar expansion, identification or exclusion of previous disorders, and detection of signs linked with hypoxia.

These investigations must be performed on all the organs and not only on the lungs to make the difference between a death by drowning and other causes of death in water.

There are no specific findings in drowning cases but some aspects linked with water aspiration will be highlighted. It must be taken in to account that putrefaction will often complicate the histologic examination. The changes in the lungs induced by the water aspiration are heterogeneously distributed and multiple sections must be examined to assess the diagnostic. Several staining techniques must be used such as hematoxylin and eosin (H and E), and stains for elastic fibers (orcein) and reticulin fibers (Gordon–Sweet). The most important histologic findings in the lungs are interstitial congestion, edema, alveolar macrophages, alveolar hemorrhage, and alveolar wall disruption called *emphysema aquosum*. *Emphysema aquosum* is morphologically characterized by empty and dilated alveoli explained by a wash-out effect of the water which may remove the macrophages from the alveoli. Another important histologic feature is the acute dilatation of the alveoli with extension, elongation, and thinning of the septa leading to a compression of the alveolar capillaries. In other closed organs (brain, heart, liver), the histologic changes are not specific and are only indicative of hypoxia and are evident in acute congestion, localized perivascular extravasation, and swelling of the capillary endothelia. The examination of the heart to eliminate a disease being involved in the death is of particular interest.

The Biochemical Markers

Most of the current biological and thanatochemical markers of drowning are actually not accepted by the forensic community because they do not provide any reliable evidence of drowning.

The bases of these tests are the physical and biochemical modifications that occur in the arterial blood compared to the venous blood; in freshwater drowning, such modifications may be due to the marked hemodilution by inhalation of large volumes of water, which pass through the alveolar–capillary interface and enter the circulation, and in saltwater drowning, they may be due to the hemoconcentration caused by electrolyte shifts. It is important to remember that the cardiac hemodilution methods are limited by the lack of specificity and the lack of sensitivity caused by putrefaction.

The literature has reported on chemical changes in plasma not providing reliable evidence of drowning. It has been assumed that electrolyte shifts may be observed with blood volume changes such as hemoconcentration in saltwater drowning or hemodilution in freshwater.

Today, it is no longer accepted that differences in sodium, chloride, and potassium concentrations between the blood within the right and the left ventricles could be considered as a sign of drowning. In fact, such electrolyte concentration changes have been described in many other causes of death.

Strontium levels in blood have been particularly studied and have a diagnostic value in drowning in seawater. The strontium concentration must be higher in the drowning water than in living individuals.

In cases of seawater drowning, serum level of strontium is confirmed as the best parameter for diagnosis. In cases of freshwater drowning, this marker depends on the concentration of strontium in the water, which must be higher than the concentration in the serum of the victims. Several authors have proposed the detection of genes encoding small-subunit ribosomal RNA (16s rDNA) for plankton detection in tissues, allowing the diagnosis of drowning by this method. In fact, the qualitative or quantitative identification of various planktons could be employed for the determination of drowning. As most of the 16s rDNA sequences are relatively conserved, they contain a few variable regions. Sequence comparison of the variable regions of 16s rDNA can provide sufficient information to allow the discrimination of both, close and distant phylogenetic relationships. The interest of this method is the independence on the morphologic characteristics.

Two pairs of specific primers were designed according to the sequence information of a picoplankton in Lake Biwa, Japan, and used to amplify the segments of 16s rDNA. Other authors designed a set of phylum-special primers for selective amplification of the 16s rDNA segment of cyanobacteria and diatoms from a variety of natural settings and were able to identify different strains using denaturing gradient gel electrophoresis methods.

Detection of chlorophyll-related genes of *Euglena gracilis* and *Skeletorema costatum* was also proposed by several authors to identify plankton by molecular biology methods, but all these technologies give only qualitative results in demonstrating the presence of these algae in victim's tissues. The quantitative approach, provided by the concentration of diatoms in the tissues that can be achieved by the diatom test is not possible by methods using molecular biology, which are not able to evaluate the site of drowning.

The Diatom Test

Diatoms belong to the bacillariophycae, which are a class of microscopic unicellular algae involving more than 15 000 species living either in freshwater or in seawater or brackish water. The cell structure of these algae is unique and consists of a frustule that is made up of two valves filling together to enclose the cytoplasmic contents. This frustule is made of a hard silicaceous skeleton, highly complex in shape, and extremely resistant to putrefaction, enzymatic or acid digestion, and to fire destruction. The classification of diatoms is based on the structure of their siliceous valves showing different symmetry, dividing diatoms into two main groups—centric diatoms and elongated or pennate diatoms.

The use of this test to assess the diagnosis of drowning is very controversial because such algae have been found at autopsy in nondrowned victims and there is the possibility of a false positive. Other authors have stated that under defined conditions, the diatom analysis is able to discriminate between drowning and nondrowning cases.

Following the figure of 20 diatoms per microscope slide set for lung findings allows for a sufficient concentration for the exclusion of sources of error. Our group proposed the following criteria for a positive test based on qualitative and quantitative diatom identification.

Analysis may be considered positive if 20 diatoms are identified per 100 μl of a pellet sediment extracted from a 2-g lung sample (**Figures 1 and 2**). For other closed organs (**Figures 3–7**), such as brain, liver, kidney, and bone marrow, more than five complete diatoms per 100 μl of a pellet sediment extracted from a 2-g tissue sample with the exclusion of fragments are required for confirmation of water inhalation. It is very important to point out that in our experience, if diatoms were present in the organs, they were also present in the lungs, and when none were present in the lungs, none were found in other organs. About false-positive results, no diatoms were found in tissue samples from the control subjects.

Qualitative analysis allows for identification of the type of diatom and for comparison with those extracted from the water samples (**Figures 8–10**) taken at the site where the victim was found. In our experience and also as considered by other authors, false-positive cases can be excluded by the comparison of quantitative analysis, identification, and comparison between species found in the water and those in the tissue samples.

The water samples are collected according to a strict protocol. Two samples of 100 ml of water, each containing diatoms sampled by scraping stones found in adjacent water, are collected in clean containers at the site where the body was found or where the immersion is believed to have occurred. All reagents and glass containers must be assessed for the presence of contamination by diatoms, and diatom-free water used to prepare reagents. Contamination from exogenous diatoms can occur during autopsy itself by contact with algae attached to the clothes and skin of the victim. So, the method of sampling needs strict protocols to avoid contamination by diatoms at the steps of the analysis.

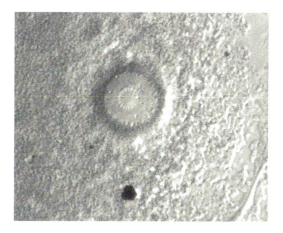

Figure 1 *Navicula protracta* (24 × 7 μm), lung sample.

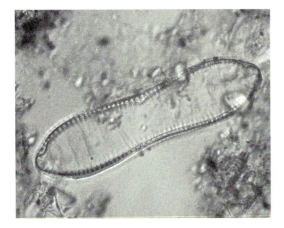

Figure 2 *Navicula radiosa* (65 × 10 μm), lung sample.

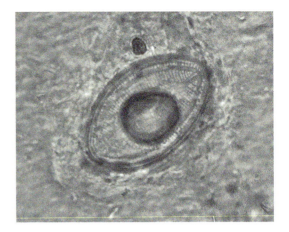

Figure 5 *Cocconeis placentula* (24 × 9 μm), brain sample.

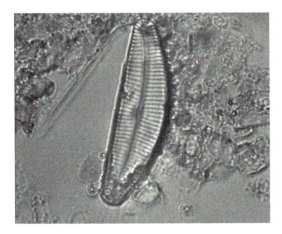

Figure 3 *Cyclotella stelligera* (diameter 20 μm), liver sample.

Figure 6 *Cocconeis placenta* (34 × 22 μm), brain sample.

Figure 4 *Cymbella helvetica* (40 × 10 μm), kidney sample.

Figure 7 *Nitzschia recta* (55 × 5 μm), bone marrow sample.

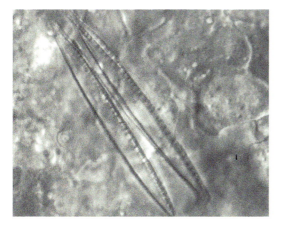

Figure 8 *Cymatopleura solea* (70 × 17 μm), water sample.

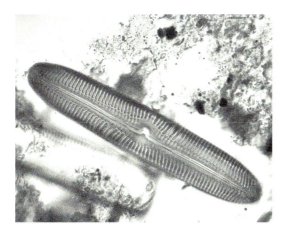

Figure 9 *Pinnularia viridis* (120 × 22 μm), water sample.

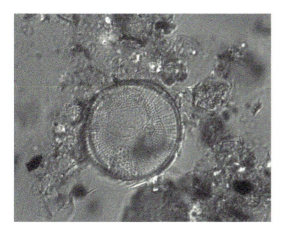

Figure 10 *Stephanodiscus neostraea* (diameter 25 μm), water sample.

This test cannot be used reliably to establish the diagnosis of drowning when the immersion water contains few or no diatoms, which is the case in bathtub drowning or in winter when drowning occurs in iced water.

Due to the seasonal variations of the concentrations of diatoms, which are present all the year round in rivers and lakes, a water-monitoring program was set up to monitor the diatom populations in the main rivers in our area. This monitoring showed that the diatom profiles of each river appear to be specific if one considers the five most frequent species in a given month. In a given river, the same diatom profiles could be determined but the relative abundance of each diatom varies along the course of the river. A particular algae profile can be linked to a pollution source and can be so far a marker of a particular site of drowning.

The qualitative analysis of the diatoms reflects the ecologic properties of the environment in which the death had taken place. The site of drowning may be determined by comparison of water samples with the lung samples. In fact, the lungs can show the diatom profile of the inhaled water, but, due to their size, the diatoms found in the other organs are less than 50–60 μm in diameter, leading to the possibility of their passing the alveoli–capillary barrier even after destruction of the alveoli by the water.

The possibility of indicating whether drowning occurred in freshwater, brackish water, or in the sea was also described.

The quantitative analysis criterion is crucial for the interpretation of the results, but more essential is the qualitative comparison between the diatom microflora in the immersion water and the diatoms found in the tissues.

With respect to these two criteria, the diatom test avoids false-positive results due to contamination of exogenous origin or from the laboratory.

Conclusion

The diagnosis of drowning is one of the most difficult tasks in forensic medicine; if it is a fresh body, some autopsy findings can give an indication of death by drowning, but they are not specific enough; these findings are absent in putrefied bodies. Therefore, lung microscopic observations and biological or diatom tests were developed. The microscopic studies may provide some reliable results in fresh lung samples, sometimes with a lack of specificity, and the biological tests are still controversial according to the literature. The determination of strontium levels in blood and in water samples is proposed in seawater drowning or in freshwater drowning; the diatom test may be the most reliable analysis to assess the diagnosis of drowning in both fresh and decomposed bodies. The diagnosis of drowning can be proposed only after considering the totality of the investigations: the external examinations and autopsy, histologic analyses, microscopic observations, biochemical analyses, diatom tests, and a special glance at the circumstances of the death and the procedure of body recovery.

See also: **Forensic Medicine/Clinical:** Suicide; **Methods:** Gas Chromatography; Mass Spectrometry; **Toxicology:** Postmortem Specimens; **Toxicology/Alcohol:** Alcohol: Postmortem; **Toxicology/Drugs of Abuse:** Postmortem Blood.

Further Reading

Abe, S., Suto, M., Nakamura, H., et al., 2003. A novel PCR method for identifying plankton in cases of death by drowning. Medicine, Science, and the Law 43, 23–30.

Auer, A., Möttönen, M., 1988. Diatoms and drowning. Zeitschrift für Rechtsmedizin 101, 87–98.

Bray, M., 1985. Chemical estimation of fresh water immersion intervals. American Journal of Forensic Medicine and Pathology 61, 133–139.

Coutselinis, A., Boukis, D., 1976. The estimation of magnesium concentration in cerebrospinal fluid as a method of drowning diagnosis in seawater. Forensic Science 7, 109–111.

Davis, J., 1986. Bodies found in the water: an investigative approach. American Journal of Forensic Medicine and Pathology 7, 281–287.

De Rijk, P., Neefs, J.M., Ven de Peer, Y., De Wachter, R., 1992. Compilation of small ribosomal subunit RNA sequences. Nucleic Acid Research 20, 2075–2089.

DiMaio, D.J., DiMaio, V.J.M., 1989. Drowning. In: DiMaio, D.J., DiMaio, V.J.M. (Eds.), Forensic Pathology. Elsevier, Amsterdam, pp. 357–365.

Foged, N., 1983. Diatoms and drowning-once more. Forensic Science International 21, 153–159.

Fornes, P., Pepin, G., Heudes, D., Lecomte, D., 1988. Diagnosis of drowning by computer-assisted histomorphometry of lungs with blood strontium determination. Journal of Forensic Sciences 43 (3), 772–776.

Gylseth, B., Mowe, G., 1979. Diatoms in the lung tissue. Lancer 29, 1375.

He, F., Huang, D., Liu, L., Shu, X., Yin, H., 2008. Lix: a novel PCR-DGGE-based method for identification plankton 165 rDNA for the diagnosis of drowning. Forensic Science International 176, 152–156.

Hendey, N.I., 1973. The diagnosis value of diatoms in the cases of drowning. Medicine, Science, and the Law 13 (1), 23–34.

Hendey, N.I., 1980. Lester to the editor, diatoms and browning. A review. Medicine, Science, and the Law 20 (4), 289.

Jeanmonod, R., Staub, C.H., Mermillod, B., 1992. The reliability of cardiac haemo-dilution as a diagnostic test of drowning. Forensic Science International 52, 171–180.

Kane, M., Fukunaga, T., Maeda, H., Nishi, K., 1996. The detection of picoplankton 16S rDNA in case of drowning. International Journal of Legal Medicine 108, 323–326.

Kane, M., Fukunaga, T., Maeda, H., Nishi, K., 2000. Phylogenetic analysis of pico-plankton in Lake Biwa and application to legal medicine. Electrophoresis 21, 351–354.

Karkola, K., Neittaanmaki, H., 1981. Diagnosis of drowning by investigation of left heart blood. Forensic Science International 18, 149–153.

Knight, B., 1991. Immersion deaths. In: Knight, B. (Ed.), Forensic Pathology. Arnold E., London, pp. 360–374.

Ludes, B., Coste, M., North, N., Doray, S., Tracqui, A., Kintz, P., 1999. Diatom analysis in victim's tissues as an indicator of the site of drowning. International Journal of Legal Medicine 112, 163–166.

Ludes, B., Coste, M., Tracqui, A., Mangin, P., 1996. Continuous river monitoring of the diatoms in die diagnosis of drowning. Journal of Forensic Sciences 41 (3), 425–428.

Ludes, B., Fornes, P., 2003. Drowning. In: Payne-James, J., Busuttil, A., Smock, W. (Eds.), Forensic Medicine: Clinical and Pathological Aspects. Greenwich Medical Media, London, pp. 247–257.

Ludes, B., Quantin, S., Coste, M., Mangin, P., 1994. Application of a simple enzymatic digestion method for diatom detection in the diagnosis of drowning in putrefied corpses by diatom analysis. International Journal of Medicine 107, 37–41.

Modell, J.H., Davis, J.H., 1969. Electrolyte changes in human drowning victims. Anesthesiology 30, 414–417.

Moritz, A.R., 1944. Chemicals methods for the determination of death by drowning. Physiological Reviews 24, 70–88.

Neidhart, D.A., Greedyke, R.I.V.I., 1967. The significance of diatom demonstration in the diagnosis of death by drowning. American Journal of Clinical Pathology 48 (4), 377–382.

Nübel, U., Garcia-Pichel, F., Muyzer, G., 1997. PCR primers to amplify 16S rRNA genes from cyanobacteria. Applied and Environmental Microbiology 63, 3327–3332.

Ornato, J.P., 1986. The resuscitation of near-drowning victims. Journal of the American Medical Association 256, 75–77.

Peabody, A.J., 1977. Diatom in forensic science. Journal of Forensic Science Society 17, 81–87.

Piette, M.H.A., De Letter, E.A., 2006. Drowning: still a difficult autopsy diagnosis. Forensic Science International 163, 1–9.

Piette, M., Timperman, J., 1989. Serum strontium estimation as a medico-legal diagnostic indicator of drowning. Medicine, Science, and the Law 29, 162–171.

Pollanen, M.S., 1997. The diagnosis value of the diatom test for drowning. II. Validity: analysis of diatoms in bone marrow and drowning medium. Journal of Forensic Sciences 42 (2), 286–290.

Pollanen, M.S., 1998. Forensic Diatomology and Drowning. Elsevier, Amsterdam.

Pollanen, M.S., Cheug, C., Chiasson, D.A., 1997. The diagnosis value of the diatom test for drowning. I. Utility: a retrospective analysis of 771 cases of drowning in Ontario, Canada. Journal of Forensic Sciences 42 (2), 281–285.

Pounder, D.J., 2005. Drowning. In: Payne-James, J., Byard, R.W., Corey, T.S., Henderson, C. (Eds.), Encyclopedia of Forensic and Legal Medicine. Elsevier Academic Press, Amsterdam, pp. 227–232.

Schellmann, B., Sperl, W., 1979. Nachweis im Knochenmark (Femur) Nichter-trunkener. Zeitschrift für Rechtsmedizin 83, 319–324.

Schneider, V., 1980. Detection of diatoms in the bone marrow of non-drowning victims. Zeitschrift für Rechtsmedizin 85 (4), 315–317.

Schneider, V., 1990. Zur Diatomeen Assoziations Methode: Alt-bekannte 'neu' entdeckt? Z Kriminalistik 44, 461.

Schneider, V., Kolb, K.H., 1969. Liber den nachweis von radioaktiv marlcierten Dia-tomeen in den Organen in den Organen. Beitrage zur Gerichd Medizin 25, 158–164.

Suto, M., Abe, S., Nakamura, H., et al., 2003. Phytoplankton gene detection in drowned rabbits. Legal Medicine 5, S142–S144.

Sharp Trauma

U Schmidt, Freiburg University Medical Center, Freiburg, Germany

Glossary

Epigastrium The part of the upper abdomen immediately over the stomach.

Fibrin Insoluble protein formed from fibrinogen during the clotting of blood; deposition of fibrin is also a response of different tissues to inflammation or injury.

Zygomatic bone The bone that forms the prominent part of the cheek and the outer side of the eye socket.

Introduction

Sharp-force injuries are the second most common cause of injury following trauma by blunt force. They are caused by sharp-pointed or keen-edged instruments, resulting in incised wounds, that is, cuts or slashes, stab wounds, or chop wounds, depending on the implement used and the manner of infliction.

Upon examination of sharp-force injuries, the forensic expert will be asked to differentiate between suicidal, homicidal, and accidental origins. Diagnostic findings, which are essential to make this distinction, include the following:

- kind of injury sustained by the victim (incised, stab, or chop wound);
- pattern of injuries, that is, their number and anatomical localization;
- characteristics of the instrument or weapon used;
- sequelae (e.g., from lesions to vessels and inner organs) or cause of death; and
- findings at the scene such as blood traces or bloodstain patterns.

Additional questions often raised in court are related to the level of force that had to be applied by the perpetrator, the chronological sequence of injuries inflicted to the victim, and the victim's capability of acting after traumatization.

Epidemiology

Partly owing to a restricted access to firearms, sharp force is the most frequent method of homicide in many European countries. Here, it accounts for about one-third of all killings, mostly by stabbing with knives. In the United States, killing by sharp force is second to gunfire. 80–90% of the perpetrators are male and aged between 20 and 40 years, which roughly corresponds to the general data contained in criminal statistics on homicides independent of how they were committed.

As regards the number of victims of sharp-force homicides, both sexes are almost evenly affected. As an exception, several studies from Scandinavian countries stated a considerably lower share of female victims (30% on average). Regarding bodily harm, male victims as well as male perpetrators are overrepresented, which is also in line with the circumstances generally known for acts of violence. As in other kinds of assault, a high percentage of offenders as well as victims are under the influence of alcohol and/or drugs of abuse.

Most frequently, sharp-force fatalities occur at the victim's home. This is especially the case when male perpetrators kill female victims, since homicides by sharp force often result from domestic conflicts between life partners. On the other hand, knife attacks involving a male perpetrator and a male victim often take place in the public space, as they frequently arise from personal disputes between (intoxicated) opponents.

According to the literature, sharp force accounts for 10–15.4% of attempted, but only for 2–3.1% of completed, suicides. Fatal injuries result more often from stabs to the chest (precordial region and epigastrium) and stabs/cuts to the neck than from cutting the wrists. The latter is frequently found in attempted suicides.

Accidental sharp-force fatalities are very rare. They account for ~2% of all sharp-force fatalities and for 0.3% of accidental deaths, respectively. In these cases, death is usually caused by exsanguination.

Self-inflicted injuries by sharp force are frequent in patients suffering from personality disorders, especially borderline personality, the majority of them being female adolescents. Apart from individuals with mental disorders, self-inflicted wounds are also seen in fictitious assaults and alleged sexual offenses. The wound morphology and the arrangement of the mostly superficial skin lesions often allow for a diagnosis on the spot.

Diagnosis is more difficult in cases of self-mutilation aiming at insurance fraud. Typical examples are chop wounds to the nondominant hand and fingers resulting in amputation of one or two digits, most often the thumb with the index finger ranking second.

Wound Morphology and Biomechanics

Blunt- and sharp-force injuries show some fundamental morphological differences allowing diagnostic differentiation. Contrary to injuries caused by blunt force, sharp-force injuries have cleanly severed wound edges, usually without concomitant abrasions or contusions. Tissue bridges between the wound edges, which are due to the unequal tear resistance of different types of tissues, are also absent in sharp-trauma injuries.

Incised Wounds: Cuts and Slashes

Cut wounds occur when a sharp-edged instrument moves in a direction tangential to the body surface. A cut formally describes an incision of the skin and the underlying soft tissue, whereas a slash implies cutting with a violent sweeping movement. Depending on its position in relation to the cleavage lines of the skin, the wound may gape more or less in a spindle-shaped way with the greatest depth in the middle decreasing toward the wound ends (**Figure 1**).

This is to be expected especially if the cut is localized on a curved part of the body surface, for example, in a longitudinal cut wound across the zygomatic bone or a transverse cut on the upper arm or calf. Both wound ends are pointed often forming a superficial "tail" or shallow incision. If the cutting edge is moved in an acute angle to the body surface, one of the wound edges is oblique, while the opposite one shows undermining. Sometimes, even a flap-like ablation of soft tissue can result. If cuts are located above bony structures (e.g., the skull), concomitant cut-like transection of the periosteum is occasionally seen (**Figure 2**). The only conclusion to be drawn from a cut wound is generally that it was caused by a sharp-edged instrument. The wound morphology alone usually does not provide hints as to characteristic features of the causative weapon/implement.

Stab Wounds

A stab wound is caused by a pointed object thrust into the body. In stabs to the trunk, the abdominal and/or thoracic cavities may be affected.

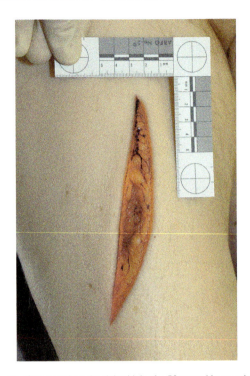

Figure 1 Cut wound on the right thigh of a 56-year-old man who was killed by sharp force and gunfire: clean-cut wound margins without any concomitant abrasions or hematomas. The wound shows its greatest depth in the middle decreasing toward the wound ends.

Under certain circumstances, some features of the stabbing instrument are reflected by the wound morphology. For example, a stab wound from a single-edged blade may show one sharply pointed end—corresponding to the cutting edge of the blade—and one rounded end on the side of the knife's back (**Figure 3**). As in incised wounds, the wound margins can be beveled or undermined when the blade enters the body at an oblique angle.

According to the dynamics of knife attacks, there is considerable relative movement between the assailant and the victim, and an irregular wound configuration is often found. When the knife has plunged into the body, turning of the victim or twisting of the blade before withdrawal causes L-, Y-, or V-shaped wounds (**Figure 4**).

Atypically shaped wounds can also result from stabs through skin folds or creases. "Incised stab wounds" result from a combination of cutting and stabbing movements. The wound may start as a cut, which terminates as a stab wound; on the other hand, some stab wounds turn into an incised wound as the knife is withdrawn at a shallow angle (**Figure 5**). Incised stab wounds are frequently found in victims of knife attacks.

Conclusions drawn from a stab wound on the properties of the stabbing instrument are subject to some uncertainties.

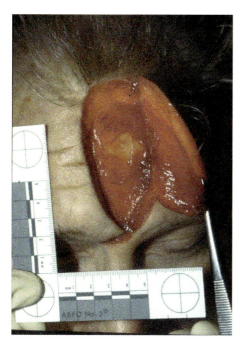

Figure 2 Cut wound on the forehead of a 59-year-old man who was killed by sharp force. The tangential movement of the knife led to flap-like ablation of the scalp. Also, the frontal bone's periosteum was severed.

Owing to the elasticity of the skin, the width of the blade can only be roughly estimated even in the case of an orthogonal penetration without any additional cutting. Stab wounds associated with a hematoma or an imprint abrasion ("hilt

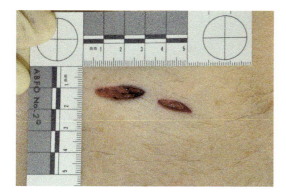

Figure 3 Two stab wounds to the chest in a man killed by stabbing. As both wounds were inflicted with a single-edged foldable pocketknife, each of them shows a pointed wound end on the right side, and a more rounded end on the left side. The differing lengths of the skin wounds result from a differing depth of penetration and are related to the variable width of the tapered blade.

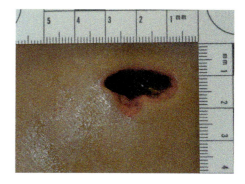

Figure 4 Abdominal stab wound in a young man who was involved in a fight between drunken opponents. The L-shape indicates that the blade was twisted in the body before withdrawal.

mark") indicate that the blade was vigorously pushed in up to its end. The construction parts of the knife contacting the body surface may then be reflected by a patterned hilt mark (**Figure 6**). In this case, the length of the blade can be roughly estimated from the depth of the wound track, provided its end is clearly defined.

A vigorous stab up to the hilt can indent the soft tissues so that the depth of the wound track may exceed the length of the causative knife blade.

Where stable bony structures such as the spine are hit by a stab, the stabbing instrument may bend and occasionally parts of it (e.g., the tip) may break off and lodge in the wound track or quite often within the injured bone. Such fitting pieces found during autopsy help to identify the causative implement. When a knife is drawn over a bone or cartilage tangentially, the wound may reflect a serrated blade. The same applies to tangential movements across the skin in a transverse direction to the blade, which may produce parallel abrasions on the skin. Stab wounds perforating parenchymatous organs or muscles

Figure 5 Incised stab wound on the neck of a 40-year-old man who was killed with a Swiss Army knife. Dissection of the wound track showed complete transection of the right common carotid artery and partial transection of the right internal jugular vein.

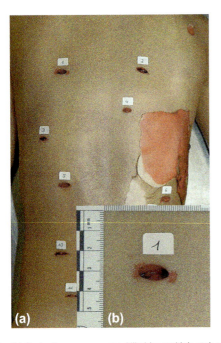

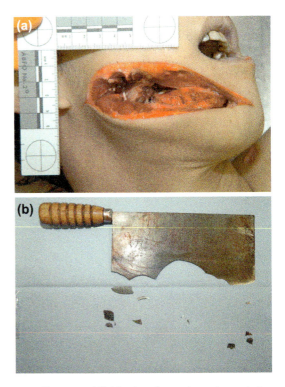

Figure 6   (a) Back of a young woman killed by multiple stab wounds (numbering does not refer to chronological sequence). The perpetrator tried to cover up the crime by arson, which led to superficial burns on the right side of the victim's body. The weapon involved was a single-edged butterfly knife. (b) Stab wound showing square skin abrasions on its ends. These "hilt marks" resulted from the knife's handle contacting the body surface when the knife was vigorously plunged into the body. Both wound ends are rounded due to the penetration of the ungrinded part of the blade ("ricasso," near the handle) into the body.

Figure 7   Young man killed by sharp force using a chopper knife. (a) Chop wound on the right mandible, which is also cleaved. (b) Several pieces of the chopper knife's thin-edged blade broke off during the attack and were recovered from several wounds upon autopsy.

occasionally show parallel lines reflecting the teeth of a serrated blade.

Stabbing instruments do not necessarily have to be edged, and there is a variety of pointed implements that are used to inflict stab wounds, for example, ice picks, forks, pens, scissors, and screwdrivers. When originating from such an implement, wound margins are often abraded. Wounds may show characteristic features, such as the flat Z-shaped injuries resulting from a closed pair of scissors or the four-point-star-shaped wounds caused by a Phillips screwdriver.

Chop Wounds

Chop wounds are caused by rather heavy objects with a sharp edge (e.g., axes, hatchets, cutlasses, and chopper knives) and/or very long blades (e.g., swords, sabers, and machetes). These objects sometimes cause injuries showing both sharp- and blunt-force elements, for example, additional fractures of the skullcap in blows to the head. Usually, heavy cutting weapons cause smooth-edged soft-tissue transections, although the wound margins may be abraded or contused when the penetrating object is wedge shaped as, for example, an axe. Of diagnostic significance is a smooth-edged skin and soft-tissue lesion combined with a notch-like injury of the underlying bone; this constellation indicates a sharp-force injury and suggests that a heavy cutting weapon was used (**Figure 7**).

Injuries from Glass

Whenever broken bottles or pieces of glass are used for cutting or stabbing, the wound margins can show concomitant skin abrasions, notches, or hematomas (**Figure 8**). In 1929, Canuto described shallow epidermal transections on the wound ends which result from the keen breaking edges of the glass shards—so-called "Canuto's ends." Due to the three dimensionality of glass shards entering the body, two parallel epidermal transections can be found in many of these wounds (cf. **Figure 8(c)**). Another morphological feature is the displacement of body hair into the wound track that has also

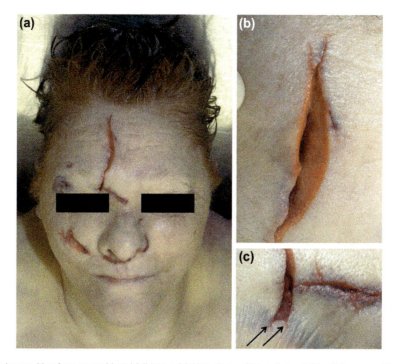

Figure 8 (a) Several injuries resulting from an accidental fall into a drinking glass, which splintered. The victim was a 64-year-old drunken woman. Fatal bleeding was conditioned by a preexisting coagulopathy due to liver cirrhosis. (b) The wounds show characteristics of a sharp-force injury, as well as concomitant abrasions, cuts, and hematomas (forehead). (c) Shallow epidermal cuts on the edges of an almost square wound end caused by a keen-edged glass shard (root of the nose/right eye).

been attributed to the thickness of the glass shards' fracture surface. If stab-like injuries occur, splinters of glass may be found within the wound track as well, which facilitates the correct diagnosis. Valuable hints can often be derived from the findings at the scene, for example, broken glasses or bottles.

If an intact drinking glass is thrown against an individual, the glass may splinter as it hits the head, and resulting glass fragments or splinters can be found on the victim's clothing or hair. In addition, the glass fragments can cause superficial lesions of undraped skin in the head and neck regions. However, experiments show that these wounds hardly exceed a few millimeters in depth; deep, penetrating wounds of the neck are not to be expected. They can occur, however, when a drinking glass or bottle is broken before throwing it. This relates especially to vigorously thrown glass shards with spike-like protrusions. Systematic studies on the injuring potential of thrown (household) knives are still lacking.

The Physics and Dynamics of Stabbing

Numerous studies have been conducted to assess the thresholds of different physical parameters, which have to be passed to effect a stab wound on a victim's body. Many of these studies are based on specific questions related to the reconstruction of injuries, for example, whether it is possible to sustain a (fatal) stab wound by merely "running or falling" into a knife. Already in the nineteenth century, reports were published in the literature stating that it cannot be entirely ruled out that at least stabs penetrating only the soft tissue are of accidental origin. For example, this may happen if the hand holding the knife is fixed in front of the trunk and no evasive movement is possible. The force or energy necessary for penetration not only depends on the stabbing impulse and velocity or the resistance of the different perforated structures (clothing, skin, soft tissue, internal organs, and bone), but also depends on the properties of the stabbing instrument used, especially the shape of the tip.

How far a stabbing object is able to penetrate essentially depends on the (elastic) resistance of the clothing and the skin, the presence of bony structures along the wound track, and also the reach of the arm holding the knife. Test stabs conducted by various authors showed that a mean force of 57–77 N was necessary to overcome the elastic resistance of uncovered skin. Additional layers of clothing increase these values by 62–112 N with tight-fitting clothes requiring a lower amount of force than loose-fitting clothes. Up to 200 N was necessary to perforate

Figure 9 Examples of common blade tip geometries. From left: Boning knife with straight back and curved cutting edge ('back-point' blade); butterfly knife with slightly curved back ("drop-point" blade); foldable knife with concavely curved back at the tip ("clip-point" blade); slightly tapered foldable knife with the point lying on the blade's longitudinal centerline ("spear-point" blade); bread knife with a curved back and a straight, serrated cutting edge ("sheepsfoot" blade).

pigskin. The impact velocity measured ranged between 1–2 and 7 m s^{-1} for stabs subjectively regarded as weak or vigorous by the test persons.

Additional aspects to be considered are the weight of the knife used, the geometry of the blade tip, and the angle of the blade's point (**Figure 9**): stabbing with a "sheepsfoot" blade showing a straight cutting edge and curving back as in many bread knives will require higher penetrating forces than stabbing with a symmetrically pointed "spear-point" blade or "needle-point" blade. The latter one is highly tapered, often twin-edged, showing a long and narrow point. It is commonly referred to as a "stiletto" or a "dagger." Household knives often show "back-point" blades ("straight-spine" blades) with a flat back and curved cutting edge or "drop-point" blades with a convexly formed back. "Clip-point" blades with a concavely formed back at the tip are often seen in bowie, survival, and hunting knives as well as in pocket and other foldable knives. The smaller the angle of the blade's point, the lower are the forces required to induce a penetrating injury.

Depending on the structure of the bone, different amounts of force are necessary for perforation. Generally, one can assume that a submaximal stabbing impulse is sufficient to perforate thin bones such as the shoulder blade, the bones forming the eye sockets (especially the frontal and the zygomatic bone), and the temporal squama, as well as the ribs. Perforation of the temporal squama requires a force of about 250 N, parietal bone of about 500 N. However, in stabs effected with an elevated arm moving downwards ("overarm stabbing"), impact loading on the knife often approaches 1000 N; usual impact velocities range between 6 and 10 m s^{-1}.

An essential problem of the biomechanical investigation of stabbing processes is that there is still no validated model adequately simulating the mechanical properties of the skin of living human individuals.

Sequelae and Causes of Death

The predominant cause of death after sharp-force trauma is exsanguination. The pathological and anatomical diagnoses are made on the basis of sparse, inconspicuous hypostasis, pale internal organs with their characteristic color, a flaccid spleen with a wrinkled capsule, and the presence of striped subendocardial hemorrhages in the outflow channel of the left ventricle (the so-called exsanguinating hemorrhage).

Internal exsanguination is generally associated with a large accumulation of blood in the affected body cavities. The blood volume of an adult accounts for about 6–8% of his body weight. A loss of one-third of the blood volume is regarded as life threatening and of two-third as usually fatal. Other relevant factors are the speed of the blood loss, which depends on the type and the caliber of the severed vessel(s), and the localization of the injury. For example, if blood rapidly flows from a major arterial vessel into a preformed cavity, considerably smaller blood loss can already lead to death. In stab wounds of the abdominal region, the soft-tissue layers sometimes move in opposite directions after removal of the stabbing instrument so that no major external bleeding is seen. In spite of perforation of the abdominal wall and involvement of internal organs, the victim may retain the capability of acting until the clinical signs of blood volume deficiency become manifest, which may take several hours.

Cumulative surveys of the injuries found in criminal assaults and homicides with sharp-force trauma show that most injuries are localized on the chest and neck. This is attributed to the fact that a great number of offenses start with the victim and perpetrator initially facing each other in an upright position and that most stabs are effected with an elevated arm moving downwards. Consequently, lesions of the thoracic organs account for a large percentage of the potential sequelae and deaths. Stabs to the thorax may perforate the thoracic cavities and result in a pneumo- or hematothorax. A bilateral pneumothorax can be fatal because it restricts respiration. If the lungs are affected and blood seeps into the respiratory tract, blood aspiration is an important proof of vitality, but massive aspiration of blood can also be fatal in itself.

Stabs to the heart can cause cardiac tamponade. If 150–200 ml blood accumulates in the pericardial sac, blood influx during the diastole is so severely impaired that cardiac arrest results from the compression of the heart. Smaller ventricular lesions may cause successively increasing tamponades with volumes up to several 100 ml. Even then, the victim may retain the ability to act for some time.

If large veins in the proximity of the heart, for example, on the neck, are affected, a negative pressure in these vessels can cause air embolism. Especially in stab and cut wounds of the cervical region, one always has to check at autopsy whether the right cardiac ventricle contains air. Gas volumes of 70–150 ml are considered sufficient for fatal air embolism.

Injuries involving the central nervous system may occur, though they are rare. They include stabs to the cerebral skull (temporal squama and orbita) with direct damage to the brain or intracranial bleeding.

Homicide, Suicide, and Accident

Fatal sharp-force injuries are mainly found in homicides. In the literature, the relation of homicides versus suicides ranges between 4:1 and 5:2. As stated above, accidents with a lethal outcome are very rare. Several cases of fatal bleeding due to incision of major vessels, for example, by architectural glass, have been reported, and—despite its rarity—a "break, enter, and die syndrome" has been termed for such fatalities occurring during illegal break-ins. Thorough information about the situation at the scene is therefore indispensable to elucidate the course of an accident.

Various criteria have been tested for their significance and sensitivity as to diagnosing a homicide by sharp force and differentiating it from a suicidal act. Although the sensitivity of discriminating morphological criteria is not very high, some of them are satisfactorily specific. These are tentative or hesitation injuries in suicides and defense injuries in homicides. Tentative or hesitation injuries are mostly shallow cuts or minute stab wounds, which do not necessarily completely perforate the skin, and which can often be found adjacent to perforating injuries (**Figure 10**). Baring the injured area prior to cutting or stabbing suggests a suicidal act. It is important to realize that the reverse conclusion is not valid. As an example, less than half of the victims injured or killed by sharp force show defense injuries. So, the absence of defense injuries by no means excludes a homicidal act or an assault.

Relevant information can be derived from the pattern of injuries found on a victim's body. In suicides, injuries tend to be grouped in circumscribed body regions. They are preferably located in anatomical regions suggesting a fatal outcome. These include the precordial region; the epigastric angle where the apex beat—the cardiac impulse—can be felt; and regions where the pulse may be palpated, especially the wrists (radial artery) and neck (carotid artery), and also the cubital region (brachial artery), the hollow knee (popliteal artery), near the ankle joint (posterior tibial artery), and even the temporal region (temporal artery—**Figure 11**). Injuries to the trunk are predominantly localized on the front of the body. The suicide's

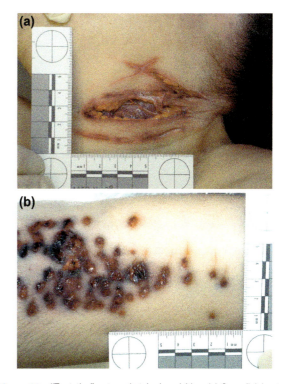

Figure 10 "Tentative" cuts and stabs in suicides. (a) Superficial cuts on the left side of a 53-year-old woman's neck, who used a scalpel to kill herself. Cause of death was exsanguination due to subtotal transection of the right internal jugular vein. (b) Multiple superficial stabs without any injury of great blood vessels in the left cubital region of a 39-year-old man.

handedness and the accessibility or reachability of the injured areas also have to be taken into account: Thus, right-handers tend to inflict wrist cuts predominantly on their left arm. If the suicide retains the ability to act for some time, the victim may be able to clean or remove the object used.

Some additional criteria are considered to be predictive of either homicide or suicide: bone and/or cartilage wounds are more frequently seen in homicides than in suicides; the longitudinal axes of stab wounds to the chest tend to be horizontal in suicides resulting from the blade being inserted through an intercostal space; and multiple sharp-force damage to the clothing corresponding to the victim's injuries is more often seen in homicides, whereas the large majority of suicides bares the target region before cutting or stabbing. However, suicides stabbing the precordial region without baring their chests are no unusual finding; in these cases, associations with psychiatric disorders or acute intoxication with alcohol or drugs of abuse has been stated.

Another feature that is rarely mentioned is the observation of suicides showing extensive blood traces on their palms,

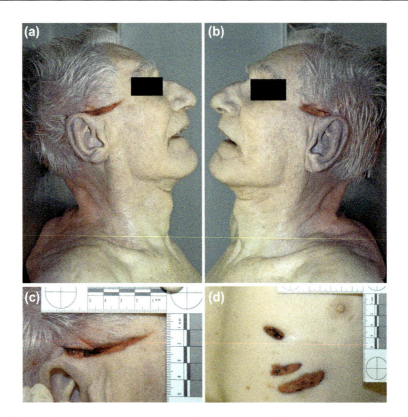

Figure 11 Suicide of an 86-year-old man by stabs to the chest. (a–c) Cuts in the left and right temporal regions. (d) Three stab wounds on the left side of the thorax with associated tentative injuries. Cause of death was a penetrating injury to the heart with pericardial tamponade and injury of the left lung with hematothorax.

which is usually not the case in victims of homicides unless they sustained defense injuries on their hands.

Last but not least, the findings at the scene and—if present—biological trace evidence have to be considered. Although there are some criteria helping to correctly diagnose a homicide, suicide, or accident, the decision has to be made for each individual case considering as much information as possible.

Capability of Acting

For the reconstruction of an event, it is often necessary to assess whether the victim was still able to act after sustaining a stab or cut wound. In this respect, the capability of performing complex and targeted actions requiring full consciousness has to be distinguished from instinctive actions such as flight or defense reflexes. The decisive criterion of incapacitation is usually the onset of unconsciousness.

Immediate incapacitation after sustaining a stab or cut wound is relatively rare. This has been reported after injuries to

the brainstem, for example, by a stab to the nape or through the posterior wall of the pharynx, after severance of both carotid arteries or after (almost complete) transection of the thoracic aorta with a sudden, significant fall in blood pressure. Lesions of the cerebrum or cerebellum by a penetrating pointed object need not necessarily lead to incapacitation. Essential factors for the rapid onset of unconsciousness are not only the size and anatomical localization of the affected brain area, but also whether major vessels are involved (especially the arteria cerebri media in stabs to the temporal region) associated with intracranial bleeding and possible blunt traumatization of the skull.

After stabs and cuts to the cervical region, it is by no means impossible that the capability of acting is retained for several minutes. This depends on whether the relatively well-protected major arteries and veins of the neck are affected at all, whether the vessel has been completely severed and whether the blood can freely escape from the injured vessel. After suicidal cuts to the neck, considerable damage to the larynx and trachea but only minor vascular damage is quite often observed, which can also result in a prolonged ability to act. In some cases, the unsuccessful attempt to commit suicide by cuts to the neck may prompt the individual to inflict injuries to other body regions or to apply a second suicide method (e.g., jump from a height; complex suicide).

Even stabs to the heart are usually not associated with immediate incapacitation. Especially with short lesions of the left ventricle, the ability to act is often retained for several minutes. After 2- to 3-mm-long perforations of the endocardium, the ability to act was reported to continue for several hours due to slow loss of blood. Occasionally, histomorphological signs of wound healing such as deposition of fibrin and granulocytic infiltration along the track of the stab injury can be demonstrated.

Pulmonary or abdominal injuries normally do not result in immediate incapacitation.

> *See also:* **Forensic Medicine/Causes of Death:** Blunt Injury; Systemic Response to Trauma; **Forensic Medicine/Clinical:** Defense Wounds; Self-Inflicted Injury; Suicide.

Further Reading

Bohnert, M., Hüttemann, H., Schmidt, U., 2006. Homicides by sharp force. In: Tsokos, M. (Ed.), Forensic Pathology Reviews, vol. 4. Humana Press, Totowa, NJ, pp. 65–89.

Buris, L., 1993. Forensic Medicine. Springer, Budapest, pp. 55–64.

Eisenmenger, W., 2004. Spitze, scharfe und halbscharfe Gewalt. In: Brinkmann, B., Madea, B. (Eds.), Handbuch gerichtliche Medizin. Springer, Berlin, Heidelberg, New York, pp. 571–591 (in German).

Gilchrist, M.D., Keenan, S., Curtis, M., Cassidy, M., Byrne, G., Destrade, M., 2008. Measuring knife stab penetration into skin simulant using a novel biaxial tension device. Forensic Science International 177, 52–65.

Jansen, E., Buster, M.C., Zuur, A.L., Das, C., 2009. Fatality of suicide attempts in Amsterdam 1996–2005. Crisis 30, 180–185.

Karger, B., Niemeyer, J., Brinkmann, B., 1999. Physical activity following fatal injury from sharp pointed weapons. International Journal of Legal Medicine 112, 188–191.

Lew, E., Matshes, E., 2005. Sharp force injuries. In: Dolniak, D., Matshes, E.W., Lew, E.O. (Eds.), Forensic Pathology – Principles and Practice. Elsevier Academic Press, Oxford, pp. 143–162.

Payne-James, J., Vanezis, P., 2005. Sharp and cutting-edge wounds. In: Byard, R.W., Corey, T.S., Henderson, C. (Eds.), Encyclopedia of Forensic and Legal Medicine, vol. 3. Elsevier Academic Press, Oxford, pp. 119–129.

Pollak, S., Saukko, P.J., 2003. Atlas of Forensic Medicine. CD-ROM, Chapter 6 (sharp trauma). Elsevier, Amsterdam.

Pollak, S., Saukko, P.J., 2008. Wounds, sharp injury. In: Jamieson, A., Moenssens, A. (Eds.), Wiley Encyclopedia of Forensic Science. John Wiley & Sons Ltd., Chichester, pp. 2646–2660.

Prokop, O., 1975. Einwirkung von scharfer Gewalt. In: Prokop, O., Göhler, W. (Eds.), Forensische Medizin, third ed. VEB Volk & Gesundheit, Berlin, pp. 166–179 (in German).

Schmidt, U., 2010. Sharp force injuries in 'clinical' forensic medicine. Forensic Science International 195, 1–5.

Spitz, W.U., 2006. Sharp force injury. In: Spitz, W.U. (Ed.), Spitz and Fisher's Medicolegal Investigation of Death, fourth ed. Thomas, Springfield, IL, pp. 252–309.

Vanezis, P., 2003. Sharp force trauma. In: Payne-James, J., Busuttil, A., Smock, W. (Eds.), Forensic Medicine: Clinical and Pathological Aspects. Greenwich Medical Media, London, pp. 307–319.

Systemic Response to Trauma

T Ishikawa and H Maeda, Osaka City University Medical School, Osaka, Japan

Glossary

Acute kidney injury (AKI) Clinical syndrome involving a rapid loss of kidney function from various causes, including hypovolemia, nephrotoxic substances, and obstruction of the urinary tract, often occurring as part of multiple organ dysfunction syndrome; earlier terminology was acute renal failure.

Acute lung injury (ALI) A diffuse heterogeneous lung injury characterized by hypoxemia, noncardiogenic pulmonary edema, low-lung compliance, and widespread capillary leakage; a less severe form of acute respiratory distress syndrome.

Acute respiratory distress syndrome (ARDS) A clinical syndrome with diagnostic criteria, presenting with severe dyspnea of acute onset, hypoxemia, and bilateral infiltrates consistent with pulmonary edema on a chest radiograph, without evidence of a cardiac cause (left atrial hypertension), arising from diffuse lung injury, either directly as the immediate result of an insult or indirectly as the consequence secondary to a remote insult.

Bacterial translocation The invasion or permeation of bacteria or bacterial products through the intestinal mucosal lining into either the lymphatics or the visceral circulation due to an impaired mucosal barrier, leading to toxemia followed by immune response activation.

Burn shock A specific form of shock arising from severe injury by heat, involving a unique combination of hypovolemic and distributive shock, accompanied by cardiogenic shock; the main feature is severe hypovolemia and massive edema resulting from rapid loss of plasma into the interstitium in the burn region.

Cardiogenic shock A form of shock resulting from cardiac pump failure due to serious heart disease or trauma, for example, myocardial infarction and cardiac contusion.

Compartment syndrome A condition involving edema or bleeding in the skeletal muscle compartment covered by the fascia, resulting in elevated pressure in the confined anatomic space and subsequent compression of muscles, blood vessels, and nerves.

Crush syndrome A condition involving release of the limbs or trunk and pelvis after a prolonged period of compression, leading to rhabdomyolysis and subsequent renal failure.

Cytokine storm Uncontrolled immune response, caused by disruption of the homeostasis of the inflammatory process as a result of the overwhelming production of cytokines.

Cytokines Hormone-like, low-molecular-weight proteins, which are secreted by various cells, including macrophages, lymphocytes, mast cells, endothelial cells, and fibroblasts, and regulate the intensity and duration of the immune response, and mediate cell-to-cell interaction, including interleukin, interferon, lymphokine, and chemokine.

Disseminated intravascular coagulation (DIC) A hemorrhagic clinical syndrome, characterized by widespread intravascular clotting and consequent systemic bleeding, as the result of disturbed balance between coagulation and fibrinolysis in the systemic circulation. Widespread intravascular clotting compromises tissue perfusion, leading to multiple organ dysfunction.

Distributive shock A form of shock due to inappropriate pooling of peripheral blood in dilated venous beds and decreased blood perfusion of other organs.

Hemorrhagic shock A form of hypovolemic shock, involving reduced circulatory blood volume due to massive hemorrhage.

Hypovolemic shock A form of shock due to reduced circulatory blood volume, subclassified into hemorrhagic and nonhemorrhagic forms. The heart cannot pump enough blood to the body because of marked loss of circulating blood volume.

Inflammatory mediator A spectrum of substances released from cells that regulates or causes inflammatory processes: chemokines, usually composed of 8–10 kDa of polypeptide cytokines that are chemokinetic and chemotactic, stimulating leukocyte movement and attraction.

Local vitality Local vital reaction or biological reactivity at the sites of insult.

Multiple organ dysfunction syndrome (MODS) A clinical condition defined as the presence of altered organ function, usually involving two or more organ systems, in an acutely ill patient such that homeostasis cannot be maintained without intervention, describing the process as a continuum of physiological derangement (dysfunction) that changes over time, instead of earlier terminology such as multiple organ failure and multisystem organ failure.

Neurogenic shock Systemic neural paralysis, for example, spinal cord injury above the upper thoracic level, presents with a form of distributive shock due to inappropriate pooling of peripheral blood in denervated venous beds and decreased blood perfusion of other organs.

Obstructive shock A form of shock caused by obstruction of blood flow, for example, hemopericardium from cardiac or aortic rupture compresses the heart (cardiac tamponade) and diminishes cardiac output, accompanied by increased central venous pressure and decreased pulmonary arterial pressure, thus causing obstructive shock.

Oxidant The substance that is reduced and therefore oxidizes other components, for example, superoxide, nitric acid, and peroxidized lipids.

Sepsis Systemic inflammatory response syndrome as the result of a confirmed infectious process; this is different from "bacteremia," which merely implies the presence of viable bacteria in the blood.

Shock A complex syndrome resulting in inadequate tissue perfusion and cellular oxygenation, which may be caused by either systemic hypotension or disturbed blood distribution.

Stress response Stress due to various physical and mental insults, which induces local responses in cells at the sites of insult as well as systemic responses, involving neurogenic reactions and humoral responses in the hypothalamic–pituitary–adrenal axis.

Stress ulcer Gastric or duodenal ulcer in patients with extensive superficial burns (Curling ulcer), intracranial lesions (Cushing ulcer), or severe bodily injury.

Systemic inflammatory response syndrome (SIRS) A clinical concept that implies a systemic inflammatory process arising from a variety of severe insults, including infection and noninfectious causes. The systemic response is termed "sepsis" when it is the result of a confirmed infectious process.

Traumatic shock A conventional term indicating shock arising from traumas in a broad sense but is of practical benefit to explain complex systemic dysfunction following multiple traumas, where the pathophysiology cannot be attributed to a specific category of shock.

Introduction

Traumas cause various systemic responses apart from local damage at the sites of insult, leading to death, in three phases: (1) immediate responses or deterioration characteristic of the respective trauma, (2) responses secondary to trauma in the early phase, and (3) delayed complications, sequela, or debilitation. The second-phase responses include trauma-induced shock, and further serious conditions, including systemic inflammatory response syndrome (SIRS) and sepsis, multiple organ dysfunction syndrome (MODS), and related morbidity involving coagulopathy and characteristic organ damage. These are mostly related to death in hospital and are primarily clinical concepts with definitions in the context of intensive care to prevent death and predict prognosis; however, relevant evaluation is needed in postmortem investigation, using pathology, biochemistry, and molecular pathology.

Systemic Responses Immediately Caused by Traumas

Pathophysiology and Clinical Manifestation

Severe traumas can immediately cause rapid deterioration of the whole body function, involving systemic ischemia due to blood loss from injury to major vessels or viscera, general hypoxia due to mechanical asphyxiation, functional derangement due to intoxication and thermal hazards (hyperthermia and hypothermia), possible neurogenic shock due to massive blunt force, or extreme heat or cold, and other dysfunctions, for example, due to electrocution and barotraumas. Such extreme traumas may result in cardiopulmonary arrest and death before clinical intervention (prehospital death), or may be untreatable in hospital; the death is unpreventable. In the latter cases, systemic dysfunctions due to traumas present with the relevant clinical symptoms and signs of diagnostic significance.

Postmortem Findings

At autopsy, the pathology of traumas may be usually apparent; however, the morphology is otherwise mostly unspecific, showing classic signs of acute death, as well as anemia in hemorrhagic death or congestion and/or edema in other deaths; therefore, the assessment of local vitality in response to an insult and systemic responses is important to establish a causal relationship between the trauma and death. In these cases, postmortem biochemistry can detect extreme stress responses to fatal insults, as demonstrated by catecholamine and serotonin measurements in blood, body fluids and/or urine, and life-threatening organ damage using tissue-specific biomarkers, which are partly characteristic of respective traumas. Ubiquitin immunohistochemistry of the midbrain is a possible indicator of neuronal stress response.

Shock: A Systemic Response to Traumas in Acute Phase

General Aspect

Shock involves complex clinical conditions in critically ill patients and can be defined as a complex syndrome resulting in inadequate tissue perfusion and cellular oxygenation, which may be caused by either systemic hypotension or disturbed blood distribution. Hypoperfusion leads to tissue hypoxia and further pathophysiology, causing multiple organ damage and dysfunction, and death ultimately, depending on the severity and duration; tissue hypoxia induces complex physiological changes, involving reperfusion injury, leading to local vasoconstriction, thrombosis, impaired perfusion, release of oxidants, and direct damage to cells, followed by activation of neutrophils and release of cytokines. This complex syndrome can clinically be categorized into (1) hypovolemic, (2) obstructive, (3) cardiogenic, and (4) distributive shock. Hypovolemic shock is subclassified into hemorrhagic and nonhemorrhagic forms, and includes "traumatic shock" and "burn shock" from practical aspects with reference to the respective etiologies. In forensic casework, assessment of postmortem findings related to the individual characteristics of shock with regard to trauma is needed to establish the cause and process of death.

Hemorrhagic Shock

Pathophysiology and clinical manifestation

After injury to vessels or viscera, reduced circulatory blood volume (hypovolemia) due to hemorrhage first induces compensatory sympathetic cardiovascular responses, involving vasoconstriction to divert blood from the skin, skeletal muscles, and other viscera and to enhance venous return, followed by neurohumoral reactions 10–60 min later, involving activation of the renin–angiotensin system and release of vasopression to promote vasoconstriction as well as sodium and water retention. Clinical manifestations substantially differ depending on bleeding velocity; tachycardia alone may be apparent before the sudden appearance of hypotension in gradual blood loss up to 30% (about 1500 ml in adults). In parallel, tissue hypoxia due to hypoperfusion initiates the inflammatory process, thus causing multiple organ damage and dysfunction, and ultimately death.

Postmortem findings

All viscera are mostly anemic in acute death, often without involvement of the brain and/or renal medulla, suggesting disturbed blood distribution in the death process; hematological or biochemical changes are usually not evident. Subacute fatalities show anemic and edematous viscera with a decreased blood erythrocyte count, hypoproteinemia in biochemistry with possible elevation of serum erythropoitin, and the increased permeability of microvascular endothelia, damage to extracellular matrix and endothelial tight junctions, and inflammatory responses in molecular pathology of the lung.

Traumatic Shock

Pathophysiology and clinical manifestation

"Traumatic shock" is a conventional term indicating shock arising from traumas in a broad sense but is of practical benefit to explain complex systemic dysfunction following multiple traumas, where the pathophysiology cannot be attributed to a specific category of shock. Traumas involving multiple viscera cause complex systemic dysfunction resulting from the combined effect of impaired cardiovascular, respiratory, and/or central nervous systems, mainly including hypovolemia due to hemorrhage and plasma extravasation into the interstitial component (third spacing) in most cases, possibly accompanied by cardiac pump failure because of cardiac contusion, hemopericardium, tension pneumothorax or air embolism, respiratory distress due to chest injury, and/or vasodilatation due to autonomic dysfunction caused by brain or cervical-upper thoracic spinal cord injury, as well as sepsis in the later phase. In addition, release of the limbs or trunk and pelvis after a prolonged period of compression causes rhabdomyolysis and subsequent renal failure (crush syndrome), and advanced skeletal muscle edema results in similar renal failure (compartment syndrome), presenting with a shocklike status.

The main pathophysiology results from tissue hypoxia due to hypoperfusion, which initiates the inflammatory process, leading to multiple organ damage and dysfunction, as in hemorrhagic shock; however, primary organ injuries aggravate systemic deterioration more seriously.

Postmortem findings

"Traumatic shock" due to multiple trauma, defined in a narrow sense, presents with general findings similar to those of subacute death from hemorrhagic shock, without any isolated trauma that can explain fatal hemorrhage or other forms of fatal shock. Hematological and biochemical findings are similar to those of hemorrhagic shock, but involve inflammatory responses.

Burn Shock

Pathophysiology and clinical manifestation

"Burn shock" is a specific form arising from severe injury by heat. The severity generally depends on the depth and extent of the burn; mortality is high when more than 20–30% of the body surface area is involved, especially in children and elderly people, and increases by complication of inhalation injury involving airway burns. Burn shock is a unique combination of hypovolemic and distributive shock, accompanied by cardiogenic shock. Burns initially causes capillary leakage syndrome as below, resulting in severe hypovolemia and massive edema (increased interstitial fluid). The shock is easily aggravated by infection, leading to SIRS and sepsis. Cardiac output is reduced as the combined result of hypovolemia, increased ventricular afterload, and decreased contractility, possibly affected by circulating mediators and impaired calcium transport in the myocardium.

In the burn region, damage to the microvasculature causes rapid loss of plasma into the interstitium. The circulation ceases within minutes to hours, and the capillaries are packed with erythrocytes and microthrombi, aggravating the inflammatory process. Edema in the burn region becomes maximal after 24 h. The cellular damage is potentially reversible, but the injury to the microcirculation is progressive over 48 h (shock phase), involving inflammatory processes with the release of vasoactive substances; the inflammatory response in the zone of stasis is responsible for burn edema and shock in this period. The systemic microcirculation immediately loses vessel wall integrity, allowing the escape of plasma proteins into the interstitium, thus resulting in precipitous decrease of intravascular colloid osmotic pressure and subsequent loss of fluid from the circulatory system; the change in fluid distribution in each compartment is marked with increased intracellular and interstitial volumes at the expense of plasma and blood volume. These cause hypovolemia with hemoconcentration, massive edema, decreased urine output, and cardiovascular dysfunction. Consequently, the combined effect of systemic microvascular damage, massive edema with impaired lymphatic drainage, and reduced cardiac output impair tissue perfusion and oxygen delivery.

Postmortem findings

In prolonged death after critical care, edema is evident in the whole body, especially in the burn region, and whole viscera are markedly edematous. Postmortem biochemistry demonstrates the terminal features of burn shock, including hypoproteinemia, elevated blood urea nitrogen and creatinine due to renal failure, hypocalcemia due to skeletal muscle damage, elevated serum C-reactive protein (CRP) and neopterin as signs of an advanced inflammatory process, and elevated serum erythropoietin, suggesting prolonged tissue hypoxia. In earlier death, hemolysis with erythrocyte fragmentation is detected as a sign of deep burns. In molecular pathology, endogenous inflammatory mediators involved in the pathogenesis of burn shock include interleukins, histamine, serotonin, oxidants, and eicosanoids. Severe burns trigger circulating mediators, for example, tumor necrosis factor (TNF)-α, interleukins, and interferon-γ, ultimately resulting in SIRS and MODS.

Other Shock Specific to Isolated Trauma

Apart from hypovolemic shock arising from massive hemorrhage or tissue damage, isolated single traumas result in specific forms of shock, characteristic of the respective visceral injuries. For instance, cardiac contusion involving pump failure causes cardiogenic shock, resulting in hypoperfusion and subsequent multiple organ dysfunction; the typical hemodynamic profile of left-sided heart failure includes decreased cardiac output accompanied by elevated pulmonary arterial and pulmonary capillary wedge pressures (left atrial hypertension) and systemic hypotension, while right-sided heart failure involves elevated right ventricular diastolic pressure with decreased pulmonary arterial pressure. Cardiac or aortic rupture may cause hemopericardium, which compresses the heart (cardiac tamponade) and diminishes cardiac output, accompanied by jugular venous distention with increased central venous pressure and decreased pulmonary arterial pressure, thus causing obstructive shock. Venous air embolism and tension pneumothorax, involving disturbed venous return, may also diminish pulmonary arterial blood flow. Neurogenic shock in spinal cord injury above the upper thoracic level presents with a form of distributive shock due to inappropriate pooling of peripheral blood in denervated venous beds and decreased blood perfusion of other organs. In postmortem investigations, these fatal outcomes should be assessed with reference to individual traumas by comprehensive analysis of autopsy findings.

Advanced Systemic Responses to Traumas in Early Phase

General Aspect

In the early phase after trauma, the respective local and systemic tissue damage due to the insult and subsequent general hypoxia resulting from hypoperfusion (shock) activates systemic inflammatory processes, leading to further deterioration of the general condition; the pathophysiology includes SIRS and sepsis, and MODS in the context of clinical management, combined with coagulopathy and damage to life-supporting organs, ultimately resulting in death. Characteristic pathologies include disseminated intravascular coagulation (DIC); acute respiratory distress syndrome (ARDS); and acute kidney injury (AKI); and the brain, liver, and gastrointestinal tract are also frequently involved.

Systemic Inflammatory Response Syndrome and Sepsis

Concept and definition

SIRS is a clinical concept that implies a systemic inflammatory process arising from a variety of severe insults, including infection and noninfectious causes. The systemic response is termed "sepsis" when it is the result of a confirmed infectious process; however, this is different from "bacteremia," which merely implies the presence of viable bacteria in the blood. The clinical diagnostic criteria to define SIRS consist of two or more coexisting conditions: (1) fever or hypothermia (body temperature >38 or $<36\,^{\circ}C$), (2) tachycardia (heart rate >90 beats min^{-1}), (3) tachypnea (respiratory rate >20 breaths min^{-1}) or low $PaCO_2$ (<32 mm Hg), and (4) an abnormal leukocyte count ($>12\,000$/cu mm or <4000/cu mm, or $>10\%$ immature, band forms); however, postmortem investigation can demonstrate relevant morphological and biochemical findings.

Pathophysiology and clinical manifestation

The pathophysiology of SIRS consists of common elements, independent of the initiating insult, with partial differences. The process may be divided into three stages: (1) initiation of the inflammatory process at the primary injury site, involving the production of cytokines to promote repair, (2) release of some local cytokines into the systemic circulation to activate remote tissue-protective and repair-promoting systems, including the hypothalamic–pituitary–adrenal axis, and to recruit macrophages and platelets, under the control of suppression of proinflammatory mediators and the release of endogenous antagonists, and (3) disruption of the homeostasis of the inflammatory process as the result of overwhelming production of cytokines, leading to a "cytokine storm" (uncontrolled immune response). Bacterial infection is a major factor that exaggerates the final stage of SIRS; bacterial endotoxins and exotoxins are potent initiators of the inflammatory cascade. Consequently, the initiation of numerous humoral cascades and the reticular endothelial system activates coagulation and complement cascades, causing coagulopathy and vascular endothelial damage involving microvascular thrombosis, vasodilatation, and increased vascular permeability, leading to loss of circulatory integrity and end organ dysfunction ultimately.

The molecular basis of SIRS involves complex multisystem interactions mediated by various cells, including macrophages, monocytes, mast cells, platelets, and endothelial cells. The TNF-α and interleukin (IL)-1 are first released within 1 h of an insult and activate further inflammatory cascades modulated by transcription factors such as nuclear factor (NF)-κB, which is activated by various stimuli, including TNF-α and IL-1, as well as bacterial toxins, oxidants, and other physical and chemical stressors. IL-6, IL-8, and interferon γ are the primary proinflammatory mediators induced by NF-κB. IL-6 stimulates the release of acute phase reactants, including CRP and procalcitonin; measurements of CRP, IL-6, IL-8, and procalcitonin are included in routine diagnostic laboratory analyses.

Among the clinical criteria of SIRS, the respiratory rate is the most sensitive marker of the severity of illness, and hypotension is indicative of a serious condition involving sepsis and/or severe dehydration; however, careful consideration is needed for patients of extreme age (infants and the elderly), who may not present with typical manifestations.

Postmortem findings

It is apparently not possible to evaluate the physical parameters mentioned in clinical criteria at autopsy; however, macromorphology of the edematous viscera represents organ dysfunction in protracted death under deteriorating vitality after trauma; MODS is mostly involved in the terminal death process. The histology demonstrates the overall inflammatory cell infiltration involving activated neutrophils and macrophages in life-supporting organs (heart, lung, liver, kidney, and brain), indicating systemic inflammation in response to trauma, and bacterial colonies in sepsis. Postmortem microbiology detects the responsible bacteria in the blood, which coincide with the histology. Biochemical markers of inflammation and immune disorder, including serum CRP and neopterin, are useful to demonstrate advanced inflammatory responses with reference to clinical findings. A spectrum of cytokines is a possible marker in postmortem biochemistry and molecular pathology. In addition, MODS as the terminal status can be assessed by biochemistry, as described below.

Multiple Organ Dysfunction Syndrome

Concept and definition

MODS is clinically defined as the presence of altered organ function in an acutely ill patient such that homeostasis cannot be maintained without intervention. It usually involves two or more organ systems; respiratory distress is most common, followed by hepatic damage, gastrointestinal bleeding, and renal dysfunction. This term was introduced to describe the process as a continuum of physiological derangement (dysfunction) that changes over time, and earlier terminologies such as multiple organ failure and multisystem organ failure are no longer used clinically.

Pathophysiology and clinical manifestation

MODS is classified into two forms with a continuum, including (1) the direct result immediately arising from an insult in the relatively early phase (primary MODS) and

(2) the consequence of advanced SIRS following an insult (secondary MODS). Primary MODS develops after several specific traumas, which can cause severe systemic tissue ischemia, hypoxia, or inflammation, for example, asphyxiation, pulmonary contusion, crush syndrome, and hyperthermia. Secondary MODS usually appears after an interval following an insult and represents the end stage of SIRS, commonly involving sepsis; the onset and progression of systemic inflammatory response are more evident than in primary MODS.

Theoretical pathogenesis involves (1) bacterial translocation in the intestine because of increased permeability and altered immune function of mucosae, resulting from hypoperfusion and subsequent ischemia, enhanced by hepatic dysfunction, leading to toxemia followed by immune response activation (gut hypothesis), (2) contribution of endotoxin following Gram-negative bacterial infection, leading to macrophage activation (endotoxin-macrophage hypothesis), (3) hypoxia-induced tissue damage due to protracted hypoperfusion, accompanied by microvascular thrombosis (tissue hypoxia-microvascular hypothesis), (4) contribution of a second insult in the presence of an innate immune system primed by injury (two-event theory), and (5) combined effect of these mechanisms (integrated hypothesis).

The clinical course is stratified into four stages (sepsis-related organ failure assessment scoring system; the European Society of Intensive Care Medicine), scoring the physiological measures of dysfunction in six organ systems (respiration, coagulation, liver, cardiovascular, central nervous system, and renal): (1) increased volume requirements and mild respiratory alkalosis, accompanied by oliguria, hyperglycemia, and increased insulin requirements, (2) tachypnea, hypocapnea, and hypoxemia with moderate liver dysfunction and possible hematological abnormalities, (3) shock with azotemia and acid–base disturbances with significant coagulation abnormalities, and (4) vasopressor dependence with oliguria or anuria, followed by ischemic colitis and lactic acidosis. ARDS and AKI are frequent complications.

Postmortem findings

Macropathology of MODS includes general edema, overall cloudy swelling of viscera with multiple hemorrhages, congested lungs with pleural effusion, brain softening, and multiple hemorrhages or erosions of gastrointestinal mucosae. The histology demonstrates hyaline membranes of the lungs with complication of pneumonia; focal necrosis in the heart, liver, kidney, and spleen; and microvascular thrombosis with accumulation of neutrophils and platelets. Centrilobular necrosis of the liver represents profound hypoperfusion.

Immunohistochemistry demonstrates abnormal pulmonary surfactant distribution in lungs, representing the stage and severity of ARDS, increased thrombomodulin expression in vascular endothelia, suggesting dysfunctional coagulation, activated neutrophils and macrophages involved in SIRS, and brain and myocardial injury.

Postmortem biochemistry demonstrates advanced hypoproteinemia, hypoalbuminemia, and hypocholesteremia representing a serious general condition. Tissue-specific serum biomarkers to detect organ damage or dysfunction include pulmonary surfactants, myocardial markers, bilirubin, and cholinesterase as indicators of liver function, nonprotein nitrogen for renal dysfunction, and erythropoietin as an indicator of prolonged hypoxia. Serum CRP and neopterin are useful markers of SIRS as a major cause of MODS.

Disseminated Intravascular Coagulation

Pathophysiology and clinical manifestation

DIC is a clinical syndrome, which is a relatively common coagulopathy, characterized by widespread intravascular clotting and consequent systemic bleeding as the result of disturbed balance between coagulation and fibrinolysis in the systemic circulation by pathological processes. The pathogenesis involves (1) abnormal clotting sequence involving consumption of platelets and coagulation factors, triggered by tissue injury or intravascular disorders; (2) uncontrolled thrombin formation overwhelming the inhibitor system, accompanied by acceleration of the coagulation process; (3) subsequent fibrin deposition in small- and mid-sized vessels of multiple organs; (4) abnormal fibrinolysis by plasmin with impaired physiological anticoagulant mechanisms involving thrombin formation; (5) release of fibrin degradation products, affecting platelet function and inhibiting fibrin polymerization; and (6) decreased coagulation inhibition level. Widespread intravascular clotting compromises tissue perfusion, especially in lungs, kidney, liver, and brain, leading to multiple organ dysfunction. In these processes, several proinflammatory cytokines such as TNF-α and IL-6 play key roles in mediating coagulation disorders by the expression and release of tissue factor (a transmembrane glycoprotein) in endothelial cells and monocytes, with a close relationship to SIRS. The expression of tissue factor also depends on P-selectin in the venules, which is induced by soft-tissue injury. DIC develops either as the immediate direct result of intravascular disorders such as amniotic fluid embolism, fat embolism, acute hemolytic transfusion reaction, and snake or insect envenomation, leading to SIRS, or as part of SIRS arising from other insults, in accordance with the severity of the originating insult; however, hypoxia or ischemia alone can change coagulation and fibrinolysis through multiple pathways.

The consequence is life threatening; DIC is most often encountered in the critical care setting. Clinical manifestations are varied, depending on the severity of impaired hemostasis and underlying conditions. The most common findings are bleeding ranging from oozing at venipuncture sites, petechiae, and ecchymoses on the skin to severe bleeding in the gastrointestinal tract, lungs, and brain. The diagnosis is based on clinical signs of bleeding tendency and laboratory findings, including thrombocytopenia, erythrocyte fragmentation, prolonged coagulation time, and fibrin degradation products (D-dimer).

Postmortem findings

Macropathology typically presents with multiple petechiae and ecchymoses, and oozing at sites of clinical intervention on the skin, gastrointestinal bleeding, and overall multiple hemorrhages in the viscera, especially the lung and brain. The histology demonstrates the morphological presentation of "DIC" as detected by multisite fibrin thrombi in capillaries and mid-sized vessels with multiple hemorrhages overall in the brain, heart, lungs, kidney, adrenal, spleen, and liver, accompanied by the findings of systemic inflammation in cases of the terminal stage of SIRS.

Acute Lung Injury and Acute Respiratory Distress Syndrome

Pathophysiology and clinical manifestation

ARDS and a less severe form of acute lung injury are clinical syndromes with diagnostic criteria, presenting with severe dyspnea of acute onset, hypoxemia, and bilateral infiltrates consistent with pulmonary edema on a chest radiograph, without evidence of a cardiac cause (left atrial hypertension). These arise from diffuse lung injury, either directly as the immediate result of an insult (e.g., pulmonary contusion, aspiration, near drowning, and toxic/irritant gas inhalation) or indirectly as the consequence secondary to a remote insult (e.g., head trauma, multiple bone fractures, and burn).

The development of ARDS is marked by three phases with characteristic clinical and pathological features. (1) Exudative phase: In the first week following an insult, alveolar injury causes the leakage of protein-rich edema fluid in the interstitial and alveolar spaces, accompanied by activation of proinflammatory mediators such as TNF-α and IL-1, inducing leukocyte infiltration and hyaline membrane formation involving aggregation of condensed plasma proteins with cellular debris and dysfunctional pulmonary surfactants, as well as microvascular injury with microthrombi and hemorrhages and fibrocellular proliferation. Edema fluid predominantly accumulates in the dependent portions of lungs, which diminishes aeration, causing atelectasis, leading to severe hypoxemia and hypercapnea. Consequently, dyspnea develops rapidly with bilateral diffuse pulmonary infiltrates; however, mechanical ventilation can aggravate the alveolar injury. (2) Proliferative phase: During the second to third week, when not

recovered, progressive lung injury develops, involving early changes of pulmonary fibrosis. Organization of alveolar exudates with lymphocyte-predominant inflammatory cell infiltration, accompanied by proliferation of type II alveolar cells. (3) Fibrotic phase: After 3–4 weeks, when the clinical course is protracted, pulmonary fibrosis develops; extensive alveolar and interstitial fibrosis disrupts lung structures, leading to emphysema-like changes with vascular occlusion, resulting in pulmonary hypertension.

Postmortem findings

The macro- and micropathology described above are detected in accordance with each phase. Immunohistochemistry and biochemistry are useful to demonstrate the inflammatory process, and alveolar injury involving dysfunction of pulmonary surfactants.

Miscellaneous

Apart from SIRS and MODS, there are several specific forms of organ damage and dysfunction caused by remote responses to trauma, which may contribute to the death process. These include fat embolism following bone fracture or soft-tissue injury; renal dysfunction due to rhabdomyolysis, typically in crush syndrome; and gastrointestinal "stress ulcers," especially after head injury (Cushing ulcer) and burn (Curling ulcer), and neurogenic pulmonary edema after head trauma.

Delayed Complications

Severe trauma may leave survivors with physical and mental aftereffects, leading to physical and mental disability: sequela or debilitation. In particular, severe head injury may result in seriously ill conditions affecting various organs and physical functions, including immunodeficiency, leading to opportunistic infections or shortening of life. Otherwise, immobility and inadequate water intake can cause pulmonary embolism as a cause of sudden death. Posttraumatic stress disorder as a psychological aftereffect may partly be attributed to dysfunction of the central nervous system in response to exposure to an extreme traumatic event.

See also: **Biology/DNA:** Forensic Laboratory Efficiency & Funding; **Forensic Medicine/Causes of Death:** Blunt Injury; Burns and Scalds; Immersion Deaths; Sharp Trauma; Strangulation; **Forensic Medicine/Pathology:** Autopsy; Forensic Pathology—Principles and Overview; Histopathology; Postmortem Imaging; Vital Reactions and Wound Healing.

Further Reading

Fauci, A.S., Braunwald, E., Kasper, D.L., Hauser, S.L., et al. (Eds.), 2008, Harrison's Principles of Internal Medicine, seventeenth ed., vol. 2. McGraw Hill, New York, pp. 1673–1713.

Irwin, R.S., Rippe, J.M. (Eds.), 2008. Irwin and Rippe's Intensive Care Medicine, sixth ed. Lippincott-Raven, Philadelphia, pp. 1831–1952.

Maeda, H., Zhu, B.L., Ishikawa, T., Michiue, T., 2010. Forensic molecular pathology of violent deaths. Forensic Science International 203, 83–92.

Maeda, H., Ishikawa, T., Michiue, T., 2011. Forensic biochemistry for functional investigation of death: concept and practical application. Legal Medicine (Tokyo) 13, 55–67.

Marx, J.A., Hockberger, R.S., Walls, R.M., Adams, J.G., et al., 2010. In: Rosen's Emergency Medicine, Concepts and Clinical Practice, seventh ed., vol. 2. Elsevier, Philadelphia, pp. 1848–1853.

Gunshot Wounds

S Pollak, University of Freiburg, Freiburg, Germany
P Saukko, University of Turku, Turku, Finland

Parts of this article were published in the form of a book chapter in Wiley *Encyclopedia of Forensic Science* (A. Jamieson and A. Moenssens (eds)), volume 3, pp. 1380–1401, 2009. Reuse was kindly permitted by John Wiley & Sons Ltd.

Glossary

Bullet embolism Weak bullets or pellets may enter a blood vessel on one side without being able to perforate the opposite side so that they remain inside the vessel where they are transported along arteries or veins until they lodge in a more distal part of the systemic or pulmonary circulation (in body parts away from the wound channel).

Kinetic energy The kinetic energy of a moving object is equal to the mass multiplied by the square of the speed, multiplied by the constant 1/2. In SI units, the kinetic energy is measured in joules.

Simulant In the context of wound ballistics, simulants are materials that react to bullets in a manner similar to homogenous tissue as regards density, elasticity, capacity to absorb energy, etc. Therefore, they are suited for reproducible wound ballistic experiments. The most common simulants of soft tissues are gelatine and glycerine soap.

Introduction

Firearm injuries are regarded as a special form of blunt trauma. The damage to the organism is caused by the impact of a single projectile (or a multitude of pellets) propelled from a barrel by high-pressure combustion gases and striking the body at a high velocity. Gunshot wounds, in a broader sense, are also lesions caused by blank-cartridge weapons as well as injuries due to livestock stunners, stud guns used in the construction industry, and similar devices.

Wound Ballistics

Exterior ballistics deals with the behavior of the projectile after leaving the barrel (trajectory, velocity, etc.), while terminal ballistics covers the interaction between the projectile and the target. If the target is a human or animal body, one speaks of wound ballistics.

Fundamentals of the Wounding Capacity

The wounding capacity of a projectile is partly due to the direct destruction of anatomical structures along the bullet track by crushing, punching, and tearing. Another type of lesion is caused by changes in the pressure and displacement of tissue (with stretching and shearing) around the permanent wound channel. The extent of mechanical damage depends on the amount of kinetic energy (Ek) released in the tissue.

When a projectile penetrates the tissue, it is displaced laterally (radially)—that is, at right angles to the bullet path—thus forming a temporary wound cavity, whose diameter can be considerably larger than the bullet. The radially displaced tissue then moves back in the opposite direction toward the geometric bullet path.

The process just described is especially marked with high-energy projectiles, such as those fired from military and hunting rifles. In fluid-filled organs (e.g., heart, urinary bladder) or in the skull, the radial expansion may lead to a hydrodynamic effect with bursting of the encasing structures. Cases in which the brain is completely flung out of the cranial cavity are referred to as exenteration shots. Even a shot with a smaller transfer of Ek may cause indirect lesions away from the wound track, for example, skull fractures, cerebral contusions, and stretch mark-like tears of the facial skin.

The "permanent" wound channel represents the destructive passage of the bullet itself. The path is filled with blood and is surrounded by a more or less wide zone in which the tissue was temporarily stretched, thus suffering structural damage ("zone of extravasation").

By firing test shots at "simulants" such as gelatin or glycerin soap, the transfer of Ek in biological soft tissue can be visualized, as the density of these materials is similar to that of muscle. In contrast to elastic gelatin, soap shows an almost plastic deformation. The bullet path and the volume of the cavitation remaining after the firing of the shot are proportionate to the energy transferred.

A stable bullet with a low deformation potential (full-jacketed projectile, as used in military ammunition) produces a "narrow channel" in the simulant at first, which then opens into the larger temporary cavity as the projectile moves in a sideways position (when tumbling) and imparts more energy to the surrounding tissue. An expanding deformation of the projectile also increases the effect of the radial displacement and thus the volume of cavitation. In deformation projectiles (e.g., semijacketed hollow-point bullets as used in civilian hunting ammunition), the cavity starts forming immediately after penetration. A fragmentation of the projectile results in a multitude of wound tracks.

When projectiles of identical design, head configuration, and mass are fired, the transfer of energy in a dense medium and thus the extent of the temporary cavity essentially depend on the velocity of the bullet.

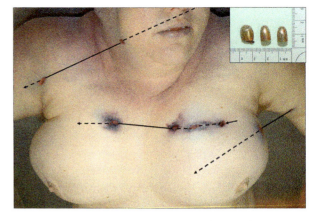

Figure 1   Forty-three-year-old homicide victim killed by three gunshots. The shots were fired from a 7.65-mm caliber pistol. Each of the bullets entered more than one body part (reentry shots). The full-jacketed bullets recovered at autopsy are shown in the right upper corner.

Wound Track

In gunshot injuries, the bullet may remain lodged in the body, or perforate it completely (through-and-through shot), or hit only the surface tangentially (graze wounds). In the first-mentioned type of gunshot wound, there is an entrance, but no exit wound. Rather often, projectiles traveling at a low velocity remain lodged under the tough and resilient skin on the side of the body opposite to the entrance wound, where their final position can be recognized by a hematoma and/or a palpable resistance. A radiological examination is advisable in any case to determine and document the localization of bullets and bullet fragments retained in the body.

For the determination of the angle of fire (in relation to the horizontal, sagittal, and frontal planes of the body), it is imperative that the length of the wound track and the localization of the entry and exit wounds or, in shots with the projectile retained inside the body, the final position (height from the plantar plane and the lateral distance from the median plane) of the bullet are exactly measured and recorded.

In most cases, the wound track in the body is linear. A full-jacketed rifle bullet, however, may produce a curved bullet path if its length in the body is longer than 20–30 cm. The deviation from the straight line begins when the projectile first moves into a lateral position, that is, in the region of the first cavitation, as the pressure gradient along the projectile becomes asymmetrical, thus creating a force component lateral to the direction of the movement.

Nonlinear bullet paths are often caused by internal ricochet. Inside the cranial cavity, such ricochets are seen in 10–25% of the cases and occur if the projectile is deflected from the internal table of the skull with a low residual energy. Bullets either ricochet back into the brain at an acute angle or pass along the inner surface of the skull producing a curved wound track in the underlying brain.

The latter type of ricochet occurs not only on the concave side of the cranium but also on other inner surfaces (e.g., ribs) if a concave boundary surface continuously changes the direction of the bullet.

In a perforating shot, the projectile produces an exit wound as it leaves the body. Bullets with a low residual energy are sometimes no longer capable of perforating the clothing covering the exit wound. After having passed through one part of the body (e.g., the upper arm), the bullet may reenter another part (e.g., the thorax; **Figure 1**).

Graze shots produce groovelike lesions on the body surface, occasionally accompanied by short tears along the wound edges. If a projectile strikes the body with low residual energy, but does not penetrate, the affected skin may show an excoriation and/or a hematoma.

Intermediate Targets, Deflection of the Projectile

For the interpretation of a gunshot wound, it may be essential to know if the projectile struck the human body primarily or if it interacted with an intermediate object. For example, if the bullet first passes through an intermediate target, such as a door, the typical "ring of dirt" on the site where it entered the clothing or the body is missing, because the grayish-black depositions adhering to the bullet surface were already wiped off at the primary target.

When a bullet passes through the dense medium of an intermediate target, it loses its gyroscopic stability, resulting in a rotation around a lateral axis. If such a bullet then hits the body in an oblique or sideways position, the entrance wound is elongated and there is a higher loss of energy in the initial section of the wound track. Analogous effects may be seen when the bullet was already deformed at the primary target.

If a projectile is deflected by an intermediary target instead of penetrating it, one speaks of a ricochet. A change of direction may happen, for example, if the bullet strikes stone, concrete, or asphalt. In such cases, the bullet often shows a flattened, mirror-like surface. The deformation and/or fragmentation of the ricochet bullet may cause an atypical entrance wound with no or an incomplete ring of dirt. Owing to the loss of velocity and the instability of the ricocheting projectile, its depth of penetration is less than in primary hits after an undisturbed trajectory.

Lethal Gunshot Injuries

According to statistical investigations, about 20% of gunshot injuries are primarily lethal, that is, the victims die before receiving medical care.

Generally, fatal consequences of a gunshot wound have also to be expected if weapons are used, which lay people would not consider very dangerous (e.g., air guns, blank-cartridge weapons, and 0.22 caliber rimfire rifles). For example, bullets fired from conventional air guns (with a common barrel diameter of 0.22 or 0.177 in., that is, 5.6 and 4.5 mm, respectively) may perforate the thin temporal squama or penetrate into the cranium via the orbital cavity. The gas jet of blank-cartridge guns has repeatedly caused penetrating skin lesions, bone fractures, and lethal injuries of vessels or organs, when fired from a very short distance. Of course, projectiles with a low energy fired from 0.22 caliber rimfire weapons may also produce fatal injuries if major organs or great vessels are hit along the bullet track.

In gunshot injuries with a fatal outcome, the direct lethal effect may be due to various causes. A special case is the gunshot-related "exenteration" of the brain from the skull. When the shot strikes the nape of the neck or the occipital region, it may directly destroy vital centers of the brain stem. More often, it is not the cerebral lesion as such, but the subsequent increase in the intracranial pressure (due to intracerebral, subarachnoidal, and subdural bleeding, sometimes associated with cerebral edema) that is responsible for the lethal outcome.

Gunshot fractures of the bony skull base are often followed by a hemorrhage into the nasopharynx; if the victim is unconscious, fatal aspiration of blood will result. Gunshot-related lacerations of the venous sinuses may act as entrance sites for air bubbles, possibly leading to death from venous air embolism.

Injuries to the heart, great vessels, or parenchymatous organs cause massive internal bleeding with consecutive hemorrhagic shock. Gunshots to the lung with traumatic pneumothorax are an acute threat because of the impaired respiration—especially if both sides are involved. Inflammatory complications are potential causes of delayed death.

Ability to Act

It is often wrongly believed that a gunshot to the head or the trunk always incapacitates the victim immediately. This opinion is disproved by a multitude of well-documented cases in which gunshot victims performed surprisingly differentiated actions even after severe traumatization of vital organs.

If a victim becomes unable to act, this is usually due to functional impairment of the central nervous system caused either directly by tissue lesions or indirectly by insufficient oxygen supply. Immediate incapacitation is to be expected if the bullet destroyed parts of the brain essential for physical activity—with exenteration of the entire organ in extreme cases. Targets of immediate incapacitation are the upper cervical spinal cord, the brain stem, the cerebellum, the basal ganglia, the motor areas of the cerebral cortex, and the large motor nerve tracts. The bullet need not necessarily pass through these cerebral regions directly, as the gunshot-related pressure and shearing forces can also damage nerve structures and impair functions away from the bullet path.

Cerebral hypoxia with consecutive unconsciousness following gunshots to the chest is mostly due to massive loss of blood. However, even if the bullet strikes the heart, the aorta, or other large arteries, blood circulation will hardly cease immediately and even then the oxygen reserves left in the brain may be sufficient for simple and short actions. Consequently, rapid, but not immediate, incapacitation is to be expected after gunshot injuries of the heart, the aorta, and the pulmonary artery. On the other hand, victims will go down immediately if struck in the spinal cord.

The pathophysiological considerations just described have significant implications for the assessment of suicides in which several shots were fired. Continued ability to act after a cerebral gunshot injury is observed especially if low-energy ammunition was used and/or the bullet track did not involve the abovementioned structures of immediate incapacitation (upper cerebral spinal cord, brain stem, motor cortex areas, and large motor pathways). In most suicides with more than one shot to the head, only the frontal lobe(s) or one of the temporal lobes of the brain is involved. Multiple gunshots to the cardiac region are seen more often than multiple suicidal shots to the cerebral cranium.

Stopping Power

The term "stopping power" is used to characterize the potential biological effect of a projectile, in particular, its capacity to prevent a person from moving or attacking. Actually, the idea conveyed by movies and TV films that the impact of a bullet stops or even knocks down the affected person is not true in real situations. Bullets do not have the potential to throw people off their feet. Otherwise, the person who shoots the gun would be knocked over, as action and reaction are equal and opposite.

In fact, the effectiveness of the projectile depends on the amount of energy transferred to the body, leading to local displacement and destruction of tissue. In this context, the shape of the bullet is essential for its effectiveness: If the bullet head is blunt, deceleration and energy transfer are larger. However, in real cases, the effect of a bullet not only results from its effectiveness but also to a large extent from the point of impact, that is, from the affected region and the relevant anatomical structures.

Embolism of Projectiles

The rarely seen transport of bullets or shot pellets within the vascular system is called embolization. Most of the embolized projectiles are of smaller caliber and low velocity, which is sufficient only to penetrate the artery or vein, but not to exit the vessel again, so that the foreign body, which is now localized inside the vessel, may be moved to a region of the body away from the bullet path, where it can be easily visualized by radiography.

Bullet and pellet embolization is mostly seen in the arterial system (entry via the heart or the aorta and transport, e.g., to the leg arteries). In rare cases, a projectile may enter a vein and travel from there to the (right) ventricle or to the branches of the pulmonary artery.

Delayed Effects

In survived gunshot injuries with retained bullets or pellets, the question arises as to whether this may cause chronic lead poisoning. Generally, the risk is assessed as being very low. Most cases reported in the literature refer to patients with projectiles lodged in the joints or bones. The latency period until an intoxication becomes manifest ranges from a few months to several decades.

Criminalistic Aspects

The purpose of clinical examination or autopsy of persons with gunshot injuries is to answer the following questions:

- Do the findings confirm the assumption of a gunshot injury?
- Number of hits?
- Did a striking projectile pass through the body or is it lodged in the body or did it produce a graze wound?

- What was the direction and angle of fire (trajectory)?
- Are there any clues as to the type of weapon and ammunition used?
- From what distance was the shot fired (contact shot, close-range shot, distant shot)?
- Do the wound characteristics in connection with the traces at the scene suggest self-infliction or involvement of another party?
- Did the gunshot injury result in immediate incapacitation?

Entrance and Exit Wounds

In order to determine the direction of fire, it is imperative that entrance and exit wounds are interpreted correctly.

Characteristics of Entrance Wounds

Typical features of an entrance wound in the skin are as follows:

- punched-out hole (i.e., a central tissue substance defect that cannot be closed by approximation of its edges);
- marginal zone without epidermis (abrasion ring); and
- grayish-black ring of dirt (provided that the projectile did not pass through another target first).

When the shot was fired either with the muzzle in contact or at close/intermediate range, the respective signs can be regarded as further evidence of a bullet entry wound (**Figure 2(a)**).

Entrance Hole

The central entrance defect is roundish (if the projectile strikes at a right angle, **Figure 2(d)**) or oval (if it strikes at an oblique angle, **Figure 2(e)**). The diameter is usually smaller than that of the bullet.

The discrepancy between the caliber of the projectile and the diameter of the permanent entrance hole can be explained by the elastic behavior of the skin: On impact of the bullet head, the edges of the defect temporarily move centrifugally due to the radial forces causing a reversible widening of the bullet entrance hole. When the deformation forces cease, the elastic skin resumes its former shape so that the permanent entrance defect may be much smaller than the diameter of the bullet (this discrepancy is particularly marked on the palms of the hands and soles of the feet). The size of the skin wound, therefore, does not allow one to draw accurate conclusions as to the caliber of the projectile.

The reason for the skin defect remaining at the entrance site is essentially that the projectile transports tissue particles into the depth of the wound track. Moreover, at the moment of impact, small skin particles are flung back against the direction of fire.

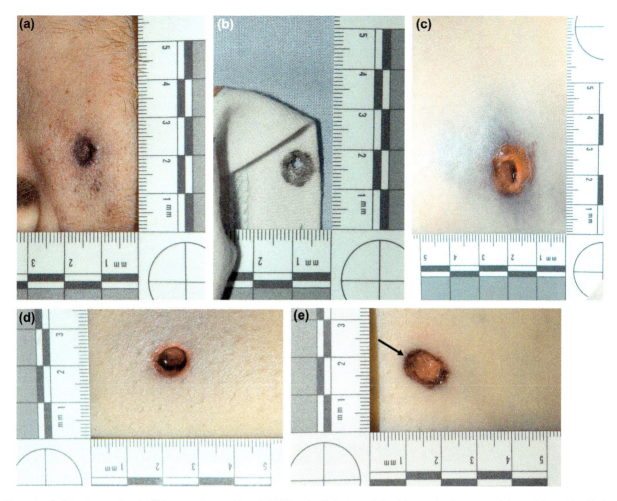

Figure 2 Bullet entrance sites. (a) Entry wound caused by a 0.22 LR projectile in front of the right ear showing a central tissue defect with a black ring of dirt covering the underlying abrasion collar. On the surrounding skin a zone of faint soot soiling and stippling can be seen (close-range shot). (b) Bullet hole in the uppermost layer of the clothing with a pronounced bullet wipe-off. (c) Bullet entrance wound in the chest (originally covered by clothing) with a wide abrasion ring but without a ring of dirt (round nosed bullet, caliber 7.65 mm). (d) Entrance wound with punched-out skin defect and a remarkably narrow abrasion ring (9 × 19 mm police deployment cartridge QD PEP). (e) Angled shot (direction indicated by arrow).

Abrasion Collar (Abrasion Ring/Margin/Rim)

The central entrance hole is usually surrounded by a circumferential loss of epidermis (and its natural pigmentation), forming a moist, reddish margin when fresh and later assuming a brownish color due to the drying of the unprotected corium (**Figure 2(c) and (e)**).

With the help of high-speed photography, Sellier was able to prove already in 1967 that the epidermis-free margin of the entrance wound is not caused by any major indenting with consecutive overstretching and local friction. When the bullet head strikes the skin, backspatter of marginal tissue particles is induced by the pressure exerted on the entrance site. The former idea that the bullet head indents the skin before penetration,

thus causing marginal abrasion, is not correct. It also does not result from the bullet being hot nor from its rotating movement.

In the peripheral parts of the abrasion collar, the epidermis is often torn and detached like wallpaper, so that parching can progress beyond the epidermis-free zone after prolonged exposure to air. When the bullet strikes at an oblique angle, the abrasion ring is elliptic and eccentric, being wider on the side from which the shot was fired. A unilateral widening of the abrasion collar thus gives an indication of the direction in which the bullet was traveling.

If the skin of the entrance region is under water, no abrasion ring is formed. The same is true for shots to the palms and soles. Entrance wounds from high-velocity centerfire rifles may lack a typical abrasion collar but show small splits radiating from the edges (the so-called microtears).

Bullet Wipe-Off ("Ring of Dirt," "Grease Ring")

The criminalistic importance of the bullet wipe is due to the fact that—at least on the primary target—this finding is a reliable sign of a bullet entrance.

The term bullet wipe refers to the mechanism of formation: when the projectile hits a skin region not covered by clothing, sooty remnants and other residues deposited on the bullet's head are transferred to the wound margin, so that a grayish-blackish ring (partly) overlies the abrasion collar (**Figure 2(a)**). More often, this ring of dirt is seen on the uppermost textile layer (**Figure 2(b)**), but not (or only vaguely) on the margin of the entrance wound. In oblique gunshots, the bullet wipe is eccentrically enlarged on the side from which the shot was fired. The bullet wipe is not a sign of a close-range or a contact shot, as it also occurs in distant shots.

Exit Wounds

The exit wound presents as a slit-like or stellate severance of tissue (**Figure 3**). In typical cases, there is—in contrast to the entry wound—no real hole, that is, no tissue defect. This means

that the wound usually can be closed by bringing the edges into apposition. An exit wound produced by a bullet passing sideways through the skin may be slit-like and, therefore, mistaken for a stab wound.

Often, though not always, the size of the exit wound is larger than that of the entry wound. In practice, the uncritical application of this unreliable "rule" often leads to misinterpretations. Thus, contact shots fired to the head may show stellate entrance wounds with long radial tears; in such cases, the exit wound may be much smaller (**Figure 4**). In cases of splinter injuries (e.g., by fragments of explosive weapons), the entry wound is always larger than the corresponding exit. The differentiation between entrance and exit should never be made on the basis of simply comparing the wound dimensions.

The size of the exit wound mainly depends on the diameter of the temporary cavity at the site where the bullet leaves the body. In some cases, bone splinters carried along may also contribute to a larger exit hole. Many projectiles leave the body deformed and/or tumbling, which may also influence the shape of the exit wound.

It goes without saying that exit wounds cannot have a bullet wipe. Occasionally, the margins of the exit wound are abraded (shored) when a firm object (e.g., tight-fitting clothes, floor, wall, or back of a chair) is pressed against the body at the site of the exiting projectile (**Figure 3(c)**). Under such circumstances, the skin around the exit is abraded by the supporting surface.

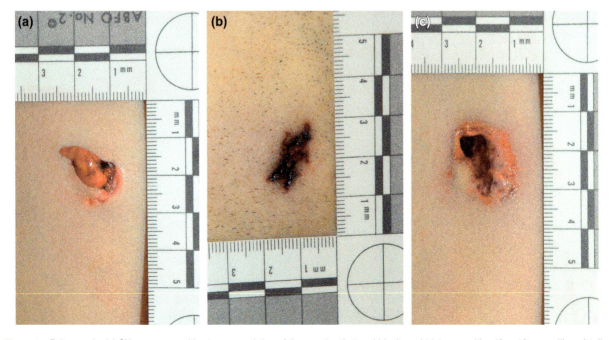

Figure 3   Exit wounds. (a) Skin severance without any excoriation of the margins that could be brought into apposition (9 × 19 mm caliber pistol). (b) Stellate exit wound of the cheek (caliber .30-06 hunting rifle). (c) Shared exit wound on the back (9 × 19 mm caliber pistol). At the moment of discharge, the exit region was in contact with the ground.

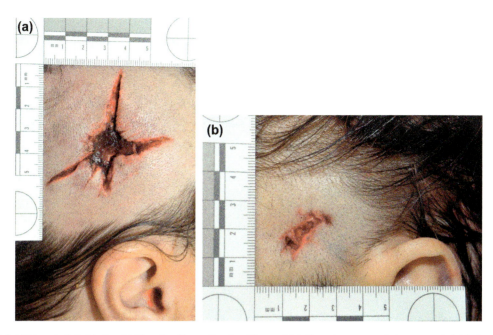

Figure 4 (a) Suicidal contact shot to the right temple with a caliber 9 × 19 mm pistol. The entrance wound shows a central defect and radial lacerations of different length. (b) Irregularly shaped exit wound close to the left ear. The maximum diameter of the exit wound is smaller than the larger splits at the entry site.

In contrast to the "original" abrasion ring around the entry wound, in "shored" or "supported" exits, the area of abrasion is not concentric, but irregular or lopsided and often disproportionately large.

Classification of Entrance Wounds in Relation to the Range from Muzzle to Target

To understand the different features of gunshot entry wounds, it is necessary to be familiar with the major processes occurring when a firearm is discharged. As the trigger is pulled, the firing pin is released and strikes the primer in the base of the cartridge case. The detonating primer ignites the propellant. The subsequent burning (deflagration) of the gunpowder generates a large amount of expanding gas, which is under high pressure and propels the projectile down the barrel. The gas is composed of carbon monoxide, carbon dioxide, oxides of nitrogen, and other compounds. A small percentage of the powder grains remains unburned or only partly burned.

Already before the projectile leaves the barrel, a cloud of gunsmoke exits the muzzle. The term gunsmoke refers to the grayish-black combustion products of the powder that has not fully converted to gases. Essentially, gunsmoke consists of carbon in the form of soot.

Apart from the combustion gases and the finely dispersed soot, there are always unburned and partly burned powder grains expelled along with the projectile. The cloud of powder soot rapidly decelerates so that smoke soiling is to be expected only relatively close to the muzzle. The larger powder grains (having a diameter of at least several tenths of a millimeter) can also reach more distant targets.

The diameter of the spread and the density of soot and/or powder particles on a target are not only dependent on the range of fire but also on the cartridge type and the weapon (length of the barrel). Consequently, the range of discharge can only be evaluated by firing test shots with the respective weapon and ammunition.

In handguns, macroscopically visible traces of gunsmoke are to be expected up to a range of several centimeters. Depending on the weapon and ammunition, gunpowder grains may reach targets several decimeters away (in rifles also more than 1 m). The use of silencers strongly reduces the deposition of soot and powder particles, thus creating the false impression of a larger range of fire.

When a gun is discharged, two different light phenomena can be observed: first, the flame—a short, mostly dark red jet of fire caused by the not yet completely finished combustion of the powder particles; second, the muzzle flash—a glaring fire ball some distance away from the barrel end caused by the reaction of the incompletely oxidized combustion gases with the oxygen in the air.

With nitro powder, the extremely short impact of the muzzle flame is usually not sufficient to cause substantial burns on the clothing or skin. Sometimes, frizzing may be seen on the hair near the entry wound. Thermal damage is possible in shots with nitro ammunition fired from a very short distance (near contact), if textiles made of thermolabile synthetic fibers melt on the underlying skin. If black powder ammunition is used, close-range shots may cause impressively large burns.

In forensic medicine, three ranges of fire are distinguished according to morphological criteria:

- contact range
- short/close and medium/intermediate range
- long/distant range

Contact Shots

The term "contact shot" means that the muzzle was held against the body surface at the time of discharge. In contact shots, soot-containing combustion gases are propelled into the depth of the entry wound. They expand beneath the skin and blacken the initial section of the wound track (pocket-like undermining, "powder cavity" containing soot and gunpowder particles). As the combustion gases have a high content of carbon monoxide (up to 50%), the surrounding tissue often assumes a bright cherry-red color (cf. **Figure 7(b)**). In tight (hard) contact shots, nearly all the combustion products enter the wound (**Figure 5**),

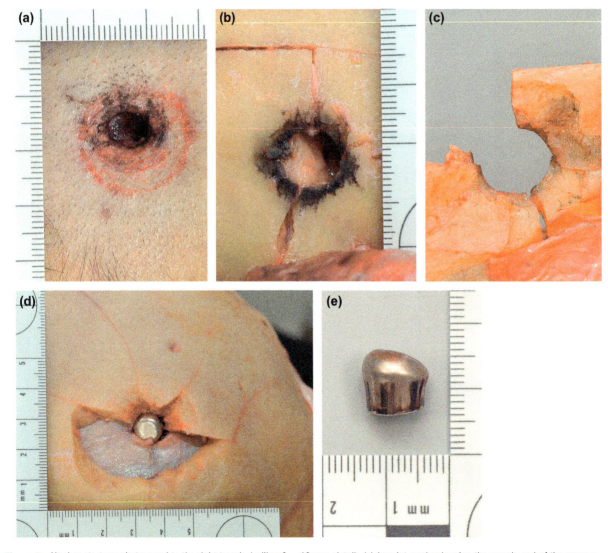

Figure 5   Hard-contact gunshot wound to the right temple (caliber 9 × 19 mm pistol). (a) Imprint mark mirroring the muzzle end of the weapon. (b) Entrance hole in the underlying skull surrounded by intense blackening from powder soot. (c) Inner surface of the skull showing a cone-shaped widening of the hole. (d) Final position of the flattened projectile (e) on the left side of the skullcap.

whereas in loose, angled, or incomplete contacts, some soot may escape between the muzzle and skin so that the adjacent surface is blackened (**Figures 6 and 7**).

The entrance region is bloated by the inrushing powder gases and balloons backward against the muzzle end of the weapon, which is imprinted on the skin causing a "muzzle abrasion" ("barrel marking," "muzzle contusion"). Mechanically, the muzzle imprint is mostly a patterned pressure abrasion with a tendency toward parching after exposure to air or—less frequently—an intradermal bruise (**Figure 5(a)**). Apart from the barrel end (or its contours), other constructional parts situated near the muzzle, such as the front sight and/or the recoil spring guide may also be imprinted.

The muzzle contusion allows one to draw the following significant conclusions:

- The weapon was in contact with the skin at the instant of discharge.
- The configuration of the imprint mark corresponds with the constructional elements being in line with the muzzle or just behind. Therefore, the imprint mark can characterize the type of weapon used (e.g., revolver or pistol) or even a specific make or model.
- The imprint configuration may provide information as to the way in which the weapon was held at the moment of discharge. For example, an imprint of the front sight below the bullet entrance means that the weapon had been held upside down (i.e., with the handle pointing upward).

If the entrance wound is above a bony support (e.g., in the frontal and temporal regions), the subcutaneous expansion of the penetrating combustion gases may cause radial skin tears due to overstretching, resulting in a stellate wound of entrance (cf. **Figure 4**). This additional sign of a contact shot is facultative: Shots fired with low-energy ammunition such as 0.22 LR or 6.35 mm do not necessarily cause stellate lacerations even at sites having a bony support. Away from the entrance wound, stretch mark-like tears of the facial skin may occur, especially in shots to the forehead and the submental region.

Close- and Intermediate-Range Shots

In close-/intermediate-range shots, GSR (gunshot residues: soot and/or powder particles) are deposited around the entry wound. Usually, a distinction is made between close-range shots and medium (intermediate)-range shots.

Close-range shots are defined by the presence of a zone of powder soot soiling surrounding the bullet entrance (often associated with additional powder tattooing; **Figures 2(a) and 8**). The grayish-black soot leads to skin or textile discoloration of a cloudy structure, whose intensity decreases with growing firing distance. Shots fired at an oblique angle result in an asymmetrical soot pattern with unilateral extension on the side of the shooter or away from it (depending on the angle at which the shot was fired and the range of fire). Interfering objects, such as clothing or body parts (hand), may partially

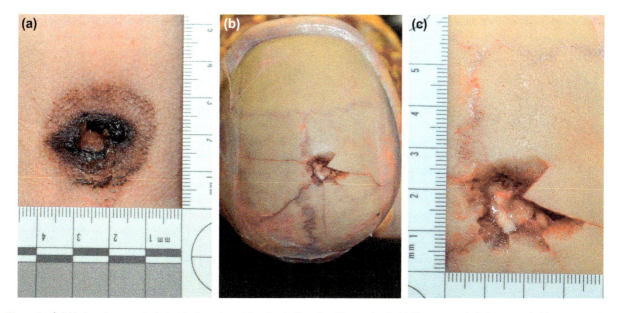

Figure 6 Suicide by a loose-contact shot to the submental region (caliber 9 × 19 mm pistol). (a) The entrance hole is surrounded by a concentric zone of intense powder soot blackening. (b) Exit site in the parietal region showing "outward beveling" of the bone defect and radial fractures extending from the gunshot hole. (c) Close-up view of the exit in bone.

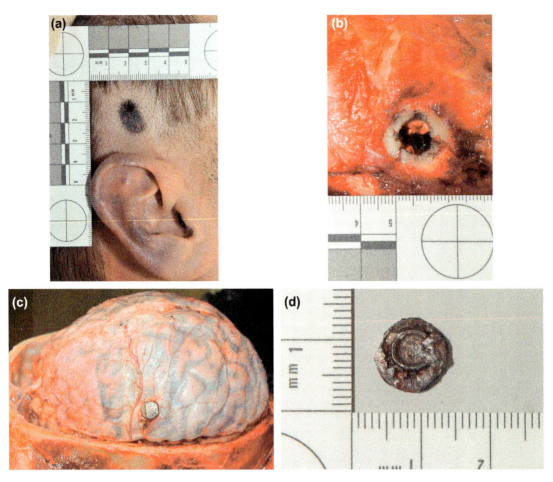

Figure 7 Angled contact shot to the right temple, 0.22-caliber rimfire rifle, suicide. (a) Entrance wound with eccentric soot blackening of the margins. (b) Entrance hole in skull surrounded by faint soot staining. The muscle tissue adhering to the bone has a cherry-red color due to the formation of carboxyhemoglobin and -myoglobin. (c) Left side of the cranial vault after removal of the skullcap; the mushroomed lead bullet (d) was lodged between dura and bone.

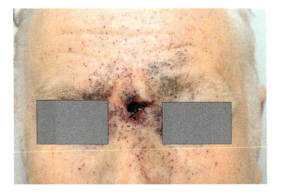

Figure 8 Homicidal close-range shot with a black powder gun (caliber 0.44 muzzle loading percussion pistol) showing soot soiling, pronounced stippling and singeing of the eyebrows.

filter out the gunsmoke. Flash suppressors, which are often used in military rifles, have lateral smoke outlets, which may produce a flower-like pattern of soot with several radial petals corresponding to the number of slits. In revolvers, there is a gap between the cylinder and the barrel, which allows the combustion gases to emerge sideward. The soot and the powder grains escaping from the gap may produce a characteristic linear or L-shaped mark if the skin or a fabric is in close proximity at the time of discharge.

The term medium-range shot is used if no zone of powder soot blackening is discernible around the entry wound any more, but there are unburned or partially burned gunpowder grains deposited on, or forced into, the skin or clothing. The penetrating capacity of the powder grains depends on the propellant (flake or ball powder, grain size), the weapon, the range of fire, and the surface properties of the target. At short shooting distances, grains may be driven through thin textiles and cause stippling on the underlying skin.

On the skin, the powder particles cause either superficial epidermal lesions (with subsequent drying) or—if deposited beneath the epithelium—petechial dermal hemorrhages. According to some authors, the term tattooing should be used to describe forceful in-driving, whereas the term stippling means the mere presence of impact markings.

The distribution pattern of powder tattooing/stippling varies according to the angle of fire: only perpendicular shots produce a radially symmetrical picture; in most other cases, the affected skin area is elliptic in shape. The entry wound may be localized outside the tattooing if the powder grains were partly filtered out by clothing or other primary targets. Pseudo-tattoo marks can be due to the fragments of an intermediate target, such as the window of a car. In such cases, fragments of glass may produce irregular stippling lesions on the person seated behind the perforated window.

Distant-Range Shots

In forensic usage, the term distant shot means that the weapon was discharged from such a distance that no soot and no powder grains could reach the body surface (skin or clothing in covered body regions). The minimum range for this type of gunshot wounds varies not only depending on the weapon and ammunition but also on the sensibility of the investigation method used.

The special methods of determining the range of fire cannot be discussed here. For securing and adequately preserving any GSR that may be present on the clothing or in the vicinity of entry wounds, close cooperation with the responsible experts is necessary. In any case, the relevant findings should be documented by photographs and also by X-rays, whenever possible.

Shotgun Injuries

Shotguns are hunting or sporting weapons intended to be fired from the shoulder. They are either single or double barreled, the barrels in the latter ones being arranged either side by side or "up and under." A so-called pump gun has a pipe magazine under the barrel, which can take up several cartridges. Usual shotgun shells with birdshot or buckshot contain a multitude of pellets, which first travel together for a short distance and then separate more and more. The increasing dispersal of the shot improves the hunter's chance of striking a moving target, such as a hare or a flying duck. The criminal use of shotguns on humans is common, and improvisations, such as sawn-off barrels, facilitate the handling and hiding of the weapon. Shortening the barrel results in an increased spread of the pellets in mid-range and distant-range shotgun discharges. Shot

pellets are made from lead, which is easily deformed when striking dense tissue (**Figure 9(d)**).

A shotgun contact wound is produced when the muzzle is placed tightly against the body surface. The entrance wound roughly corresponds to the gauge and is of circular shape in most body regions, but stellate over the bone (due to the expansion of the inrushing gases with consecutive backward ballooning of the skin). Sometimes, there is a clear imprint abrasion mark, for example, from the front sight or—in double-barreled weapons—from the nonfiring muzzle. The wound edges may be blackened, but most of the soot enters the body and is deposited in the depth of the wound. The surrounding muscle is often colored cherry-red due to carbon monoxide. An intraoral discharge or a contact wound to the head (forehead, temple, or under the jaw) leads to massive destruction of the skull (bursting of the head or shooting off of the face) and is occasionally associated with evisceration of the brain.

Even in cases with extreme splitting of the face and the scalp, careful approximation of the wound edges helps in finding the entrance site. Loose-contact discharge allows the escape of sooty combustion gases, staining the skin around the entrance hole. Intermediate-range shots are characterized by the presence of stippling/tattooing from unburned propellant (up to 1 m, depending on the type of powder). In close-distance discharges, additional smoke soiling is seen.

The injury pattern of shot ammunition is mainly influenced by the distance between the muzzle and the target: As the range increases, the initially circular entrance hole shows scalloping of the wound edge (nibbling or crenation); from a distance of approximately 2 m, peripheral pellets produce satellite-like holes outside the central entry defect (**Figure 9**). Ranges of several meters are characterized by a sieve-like wound pattern. If shots are fired from short distances, wads or plastic cups may either penetrate the body together with the shot or cause excoriations of characteristic shape on the victim's skin ("wad abrasion").

Shotgun slugs are large, single lead projectiles destined for smooth-bore shotguns and also for those having a choke at the end of the barrel. The hitting accuracy of shotgun slugs is considerably lower than that of rifle projectiles; as a consequence, they should not be used for distances beyond 35–50 m in hunting. Some shotgun slugs are designed according to the arrow principle (heavy front part and light rear part).

Internal Findings

The gunshot lesions of the inner organs can be discussed only briefly here. Special mention should be made, however, of bullet holes in the flat bones of the skull (cf. **Figures 5(b,d), 6(b,c), and 7(b)**). On the entrance side, the bone defect in the outer table is sharp edged and its minimum diameter roughly

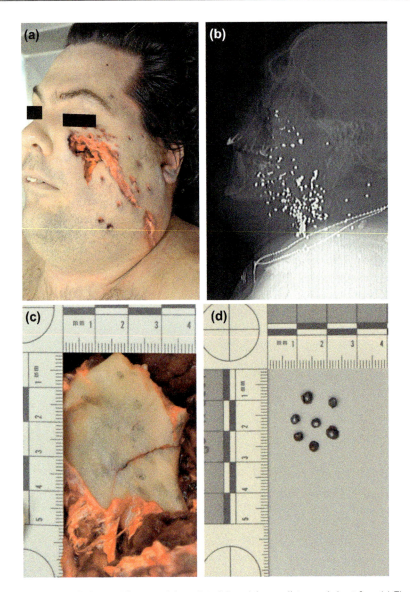

Figure 9 Homicide committed with a 16-G shotgun (diameter of the pellets 3.5 mm) from a distance of about 2 m. (a) The medial margin of the entrance wound is crenated whereas the lateral side is lacerated and surrounded by satellite holes from peripheral pellets and grazing pellet wounds. (b) Radiological documentation of the shot pattern. (c) Left ramus of the fragmented mandible with grayish lead debris from ricocheting pellets (d).

corresponds to the caliber of the projectile, whereas the inner table is beveled out in a cone-like manner. This characteristic widening on the exit side allows one to determine the direction of fire even in an isolated bone. For gunshot exit holes of the skull, the opposite is true: The outer table shows a crater-like defect (outward beveling). Projectiles striking at an acute angle produce keyhole-shaped entrance defects in flat bones with partial cratering of the outer table at the side away from the shooter. So the manner in which the bone breaks may

indicate the inclination of the bullet path. Beveling is not restricted to the skullcap, as it is also seen in other flat bones, such as the sternum, the pelvis, and the ribs.

In contact shots to the cerebral cranium (e.g., the frontal, temporal, parietal, and occipital regions), soot deposits are found not only under the skin, but also around the bone defect (cf. **Figures 5(b) and 7(b)**) and on the underside of the lifted-off periosteum, often even on the outer surface of the dura mater.

In many cases, radial fractures extend from gunshot holes of the skull (cf. **Figures 5(b) and 6(b,c)**). According to Puppe's rule, a secondary fracture line will cease when it meets a pre-existing fracture line, which may help one to determine the sequence of shots.

In soft tissue, the wound track collapses and/or is filled with blood. Postmortem probing of the bullet path involves the risk of causing artifacts and should therefore be avoided. Parenchymatous organs, such as the liver, the kidneys, and the spleen, may show large stellate wounds at the sites of entry and exit.

Whole projectiles or bullet fragments removed from the body by surgical intervention or during autopsy must be preserved for further laboratory investigation, including ballistic comparison. A recovered projectile provides information regarding the caliber, twist direction, number and width of lands and grooves as well as of the individual characteristics imparted by the inner surface of the barrel.

Blank firing pistols and revolvers are detailed facsimiles of real handguns. The blank cartridges destined for these weapons contain gunpowder, but no projectile. If the muzzle is held in close proximity to the body surface or even in contact with it, the gas jet from the blank gun is capable of penetrating the skin and causing potentially fatal injuries.

Forensic Examination and Documentation

In all firearm fatalities, careful documentation is of utmost importance. This includes taking photographs and close-up views of each wound using a scale. The clothing must be preserved, as the uppermost layer may exhibit the bullet wipe around entrance holes and depositions of soot and/or powder particles in close- and medium-range shots, respectively.

Whenever possible, X-rays should be taken before autopsy in two planes (anteroposterior as well as lateral views). They are not only useful for permanent and objective documentation but also helpful in exactly locating and characterizing all bullets and any metal fragments, including separated jackets. Radiographs are also a valuable tool to find projectiles lodged in body regions, which are hardly accessible during autopsy (e.g., within the vertebral column). In addition, X-rays provide evidence that a bullet might have been deflected or embolized.

All wounds have to be described exactly with regard to their location using fixed landmarks, such as the base of the heels, the midline, the height above the buttocks, and the distance from the top of the head. The documentation should also mention the size and shape of each wound, the features of the wound margins and their surroundings, the presence or absence of GSR such as soot or stippling on the clothing and/or skin, the total length of the wound tracks, and, of course, the injuries to the internal organs.

It is important to recover any bullets or major parts thereof from the body of the victim. Subsequent laboratory investigations may help in identifying the bullet type and assigning the fired bullet to a specific weapon.

Manner of Death

To classify a gunshot wound as suicidal, homicidal, or accidental, a synoptic evaluation of the scene and the circumstances of the case; the evidence obtained from the injuries, the victim's clothing; and the laboratory investigations concerning the weapon, ammunition, and the range of fire has to be made. Easy access to weapons due to permissive legislation is associated with increased rates of firearm homicide and suicide.

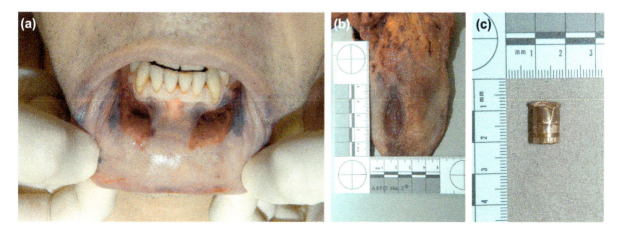

Figure 10   Intraoral shot from a 9 × 19 mm caliber pistol (suicide). (a) Symmetrical tears on the inner surface of the lower lip. (b) Dorsum of the tongue with soot deposition (near the apex) and tangential wound from the projectile (c).

From the medicolegal point of view, the question has to be answered whether the entry wound is localized in a region typical for suicides: temple (cf. **Figures 4, 5, and 7**), mouth (**Figure 10**), cardiac region, forehead, and submental region (cf. **Figure 6(a)**). In almost all cases of suicide, the muzzle is held against the body or inserted into the oral cavity. In shots to the chest, the skin is seldom bared before. In more than 20% of the suicides committed with pistols or revolvers, the weapon is found clutched in the firing hand.

The examination of hands to detect GSR, especially lead, antimony, and barium originating from the primer, can be mentioned only briefly here. These residues escape mainly from the cylinder–barrel gap (in revolvers) or from the ejection port (in automatic pistols) and come to rest on the skin and/or clothing, where they can be collected for subsequent chemical analysis. The presence of GSR is detected by flameless atomic absorption spectroscopy or by scanning electron microscope–energy dispersive X-ray spectrometry.

Sometimes, clues suggesting suicide are found even on examination with the naked eye (**Figure 11**), for example, spray of blood or tissue deposits on the firing hand ("backspatter" from the entry wound), traces of soot on thumb and index finger (if the muzzle end was held against the entrance site with one hand), or injuries from the edges of the recoiling slide. Direct and prolonged contact of the skin with the steel parts of the weapon in a moist environment promotes the formation of brownish rust stains. This phenomenon is found especially in suicides, although it is no proof that the shot was self-inflicted.

Injuries Caused by Explosives

In peacetime, injuries and fatalities owing to the detonation of explosives (letter or parcel bombs) are seen mainly in connection with politically motivated or terrorist attacks against persons, vehicles, and buildings. Accidents are mostly due to natural gas ignitions, chemical explosions, or improper handling of explosives, fireworks, etc. In countries without terrorist activities, suicides by explosives are rare and usually

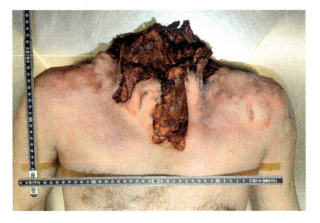

Figure 12 Occupation-related suicide of a blaster who had placed the explosive charge next to the back of his neck resulting in decapitation with concomitant soot soiling.

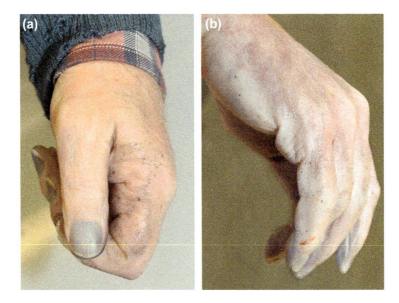

Figure 11 (a) Left hand used by a suicide to steady the barrel of a pistol: soot depositions on the radial aspect of the index finger. (b) Ulnar aspect of the right hand which had fired a pistol. The skin is spattered with a spray of blood.

restricted to persons with a pertinent professional experience (**Figure 12**).

The injury pattern is typically characterized by a complex combination of different lesions. Mechanical tissue destruction up to traumatic amputation and evisceration is caused by blunt force (exploding device and other objects impacting the body, pressure wave), often associated with penetrating injuries from splinters, burning, and soot blackening of the skin. The internal examination may reveal organ and vascular damage, skeletal fractures, ruptured tympanic membranes, and acute pulmonary emphysema. A complete body X-ray examination should be performed whenever possible.

See also: **Pattern Evidence:** Shotgun Ammunition on a Target; **Pattern Evidence/Firearms:** Humane Killing Tools; Laboratory Analysis; Range; Residues.

Further Reading

Besant-Matthews, P.E., 2000. Examinations and interpretation of rifled firearm injuries. In: Mason, J.K., Purdue, B.N. (Eds.), The Pathology of Trauma, third ed. Arnold, London, pp. 47–60.

Bolliger, S.A., Kneubuehl, B.P., Thali, M.J., 2009. Gunshot. In: Thali, M.J., Dirnhofer, R., Vock, P. (Eds.), The Virtopsy Approach. CRC Press, Boca Raton, FL, pp. 318–331.

Cassidy, M., 2000. Smooth-bore firearm injuries. In: Mason, J.K., Purdue, B.N. (Eds.), The Pathology of Trauma. Arnold, London, pp. 61–74.

Crane, J., 2005. Explosive injury. In: Payne-James, J., Byard, R.W., Corey, T.S., Henderson, C. (Eds.), Encyclopedia of Forensic and Legal Medicine, vol. 3. Elsevier, Oxford, pp. 98–100.

Dana, S.E., DiMaio, V.J.M., 2003. Gunshot trauma. In: Payne-James, J., Busuttil, A., Smock, W. (Eds.), Forensic Medicine: Clinical and Pathological Aspects. Greenwich Medical Media, London, pp. 149–168.

DiMaio, V.J.M., 1999. Gunshot Wounds: Practical Aspects of Firearms, Ballistics, and Forensic Techniques, second ed. CRC Press, Boca Raton, FL.

Dodd, M.J., 2006. Terminal Ballistics: A Text and Atlas of Gunshot Wounds. CRC Press, Boca Raton, FL.

Grosse Perdekamp, M., Vennemann, B., Mattern, D., Serr, A., Pollak, S., 2005. Tissue defect at the gunshot entrance wound: what happens to the skin? International Journal of Legal Medicine 119 (4), 217–222.

Karger, B., 2008. Forensic ballistics. In: Tsokos, M. (Ed.), Forensic Pathology Reviews, vol. 5. Humana Press, Totowa, NJ, pp. 139–172.

Kirk, G.M., 2005. Firearm injuries. In: Payne-James, J., Byard, R.W., Corey, T.S., Henderson, C. (Eds.), Encyclopedia of Forensic and Legal Medicine, vol. 3. Elsevier, Oxford, pp. 110–118.

Lew, E., Dolinak, D., Matshes, E., 2005. Firearm injuries. In: Dolinak, D., Matshes, E.W., Lew, E.O. (Eds.), Forensic Pathology; Principles and Practice. Elsevier Academic Press, Burlington, MA, pp. 163–200.

Naidoo, S.R., 2005. Ballistic trauma, overview and statistics. In: Payne-James, J., Byard, R.W., Corey, T.S., Henderson, C. (Eds.), Encyclopedia of Forensic and Legal Medicine, vol. 1. Elsevier, Oxford, pp. 271–283.

Pollak, S., Rothschild, M.A., 2004. Gunshot injuries as a topic of medicolegal research in the German-speaking countries from the beginning of the 20th century up to the present time. Forensic Science International 144 (2–3), 201–210.

Pollak, S., Saukko, P., 2003. Injuries Due to Guns and Explosives. Atlas of Forensic Medicine (CD-ROM). Elsevier, Amsterdam (Chapter 7).

Saukko, P., Knight, B., 2004. Knight's Forensic Pathology, third ed. Arnold, London, pp. 245–280.

Sellier, K., 1969. Bullet entry studies of the skin. Beiträge zur Gerichtlichen Medizin 25, 265–270.

Sellier, K.G., Kneubuehl, B.P., 1994. Wound Ballistics and the Scientific Background. Elsevier, Amsterdam.

Smock, W.S., 2000. Evaluation of gunshot wounds. In: Siegel, J.A., Saukko, P.J., Knupfer, G.C. (Eds.), Encyclopedia of Forensic Sciences, vol. 1. Academic Press, London, pp. 378–384.

Spitz, W.U., 2006a. Injury by gunfire. In: Spitz, W.U. (Ed.), Spitz and Fisher's Medicolegal Investigation of Death, fourth ed. Thomas, Springfield, IL, pp. 607–746.

Spitz, W.U., 2006b. Medicolegal considerations of bomb explosions. In: Spitz, W.U. (Ed.), Spitz and Fisher's Medicolegal Investigation of Death, fourth ed. Thomas, Springfield, IL, pp. 777–782.

Domestic Violence

U Klopfstein, Bern University of Applied Sciences, Bern, Switzerland
M-C Hofner, University Center of Legal Medicine, Lausanne, Switzerland

Glossary

DV Domestic violence.

ED Emergency department.

Introduction

Domestic violence (DV), including intimate partner violence, is a worldwide phenomenon and a major public health issue. The mortality and morbidity caused by DV as well as its burden of disease are high. DV appears worldwide, affecting individuals in every community, regardless of age, economic status, race, religion, nationality, or educational background. In 1980, the Duluth Minnesota Domestic Abuse Intervention Project became a model for further interventions in many states and countries worldwide. Today, in all continents, ambitious efforts are being made by politicians, lawyers, social workers, and community leaders, and increasingly by medical specialists and forensic experts to combat this kind of violence, mostly against women. The WHO published in 2002 a comprehensive world report on violence and health as well as several studies on violence against women and organized an international network for prevention of violence. During the last few decades, first Canada and the United States, followed by Australia and many states in Europe, introduced new laws, hoping that DV would no longer be hidden in the privacy of the family, but would come out as a public affair. One example is "The Violence Against Women Act" (www.womenshealth.gov/violence/legislation/), which supports communities in their effort to help protect victims and to educate perpetrators.

The US Department of Justice, for example, declaimed that "between 1993 and 2008, there was a 53% drop in the number of nonfatal, violent acts committed by intimate partners," maybe as a result of all these efforts.

Because of the increased interest related to law enforcement for DV, the importance of an optimal evidence-based criminal prosecution was raised in parallel. Experts in the forensic field have to coordinate their efforts to improve their knowledge of the characteristics and the diagnosis of DV, evidence collection, and the documentation of important signs of physical or sexual violence.

This chapter helps to improve this knowledge and provide a summary of the issue of DV for science and practice.

Definition

In the worldwide literature, DV is equated with violence against women. The United Nations defines violence against women as "any act of gender-based violence that results in, or is likely to result in, physical, sexual or mental harm or suffering to women, including threats of such acts, coercion or arbitrary deprivation of liberty, whether occurring in public or in private life."

DV concerns not only women as victims but also men and children, and the perpetrators could be any member of the family. So the definition of DV must be expanded to include "a pattern of abusive behavior in any relationship that is used by one partner to gain or maintain power and control over another intimate partner or member of the domestic unit. DV can be physical, sexual, emotional, economic, or psychological actions, threat of actions or negligence that influence another person. This includes any behavior that intimidates, manipulates, humiliates, isolates, deprives, frightens, terrorizes, coerces, threatens, blames, hurts, injures, or wounds someone."

An important reason for maintaining the circle of violence is the perpetrator's ambition to keep his power and control over the victim. The Duluth Model of power and control suggests a patriarchal system as the basis for maintaining violence in families and partnerships. This model does not include male victims of DV, and men's organizations created an alternative model for female perpetrators (see www.batteredmen.com/duluwomn.htm).

Epidemiology

The WHO demonstrated in their multicountry study that:

- Between 15% and 71% of women reported physical or sexual violence by a husband or partner.
- Between 24% and 40% of women said that their first sexual experience was not consensual.
- Between 4% and 12% of women reported being physically abused during pregnancy.

The "End Violence Against Women (EVAW) Coalition," United Kingdom, declaims on its Web site that DV is under-reported even when the phenomenon "accounts for 16% of all violent crime and will affect one in four women in their life-time." Identical data are reported in countries with a low average income and in peaceful and wealthy countries such as Switzerland.

The home office statistical bulletin 2007 of the United Kingdom describes that DV had the highest rate of repeated victimization. More than one-third of the victims have been

victimized more than once. Most often (in 87% of cases), males count as perpetrators. It is a crime very often reported; the authors of the bulletin estimate that every minute one case of DV is reported to the police in the United Kingdom. The crime scene is almost always the home, but only a minority of cases is registered as serious. Nevertheless, DV can end fatally; the WHO reports that every year, 5000 women are killed by family members. In England and Wales, on an average two women are murdered every week by a partner. So DV, even though it is seldom a serious crime in the common sense of the law, is not a harmless phenomenon.

Data about male victims vary in the literature and it is discussed as a controversial topic. The fact is that male victims show significantly less severe injuries than female victims. For example, bone fractures and skull fractures are rarely seen in male victims in contrast to females. Houry et al. examined the differences between female and male victims and perpetrators using the "Women's Experience with Battering Scale" on a Level 1 trauma center in 2008. The authors found a DV victimization prevalence of 22%. Generally, they found similar rates of victimization and perpetration in men and women. Some authors guess that the women who batter their partners do it often as a reaction to their own victimization experiences and that male victims suffer less from a loss of power and control in a violent partnership. This may explain why women show more symptoms of psychological stress, psychosomatic disorders, and depression after violent experiences. If a male victim of a physical assault by women is examined, the mechanism of self-defense for the female perpetrator has to be discussed. This is why it is always very important to examine both partners physically after an incident of DV to prove typical self-defense injuries (**Figures 2 and 4**).

Kimmel described the differences between female and male violence very systematically in his 2002 publication. The fact is that about 90% of the aggressive acts are performed by males,

Figure 1   The circle of violence.

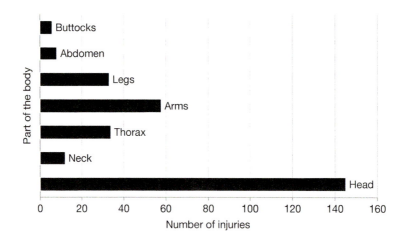

Figure 2   Injuries on different parts of the body. Copyright Swiss Medical Weekly, 2010; 140, w1347.

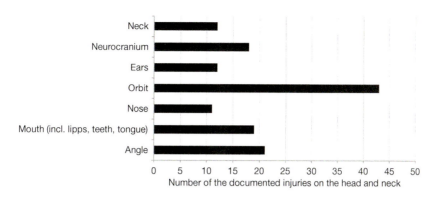

Figure 3   Localization of the injuries in the region of the head and neck. Copyright Swiss Medical Weekly, 2010; 140, w1347.

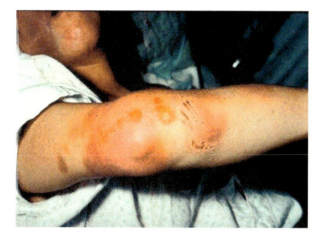

Figure 4   Bruises on the forearm as a typical sign of self-defense. Copyright University of forensic medicine at the University of Berne.

and the damages are much more serious when a man is the perpetrator.

Even so, for practice and science it is most important to also think about male victims of DV and to include them in prevention and screening programs (see later).

Risk Factors for DV

The highest risk factor worldwide is being a woman. Abramsky et al. analyzed the data collected by the WHO multicountry study on women's health and DV to identify risk and protective factors. The most important are the following:

- History of abuse. There is a very strong correlation between experiences of DV in childhood and DV in the partnership.
- Younger age of the women.
- Attitudes to support the husbands' beating.
- One partner having alcohol-related problems. Generally, alcohol and drug abuse. Already in 1999, Kyriacou had

shown an increased risk for injuries in case of alcohol and drug abuse by men.
- Involvement of one partner in nonpartner violence; this means violence in a public area.

Characteristics of DV

Here it should be discussed why it is worth including a special chapter on DV in an encyclopedia of forensic sciences. In combating this harmful and expensive phenomenon and performing investigations in cases of DV, specialized knowledge is essential because of the following reasons (**Table 1**).

This table shows the very complex nature of DV. Interventions always require an interdisciplinary approach.

DV is seldom an isolated incident. Because of its typical pattern, also called the circle of violence, there is often a spiral-like escalating repetition of the violence.

Kyriacou et al. described the dynamics of the violent relationship as an imbalance of power, and the coercive control of one partner as a trigger of the escalation.

Phases of the circle of violence

Typically, the incidents of violence follow a well-defined dynamic. The circle may turn like a wheel with a certain regularity or like a spiral with an aggravating violence as a term of an exacerbating situation (**Figure 1**).

In times of harmony, the couple live in love and peace. But often, caught in the circle of violence, these periods become shorter and shorter. Only help from outside could break this turning wheel.

Criminal prosecution and punishment in a criminal sense may not be enough to break the circle. Education programs for the perpetrators as well as support for the victims are very important for a couple to learn how to live without violence.

All investigators in cases of DV and other professionals should understand the dynamics of this circle. Indeed, each professional may see the victim and the perpetrator at different

Table 1   Differences between domestic violence (DV) and other interpersonal violence

DV	Public (urban) violence
Victims are more often women than men	Victims are more often men than women
The perpetrator is more likely to be unique, a man well known to the victim	Perpetrator could be unique or multiple, of either gender, and often unknown to the victim
Repeated incidents	One or limited incidents
Rarely a singular incident	
The place of incident is almost always the home	The place of incident is almost always a public place
Significant induced comorbidity such as psychosomatic disorders, unspecific pain syndrome, higher level of suicide, depression, substance abuse, gynecological problem, etc.	Limited "collateral damage," such as post traumatic demoralization syndrome (PTDS)
Injuries often declared as "accidental" and not as inflicted	Injuries are clearly declared as inflicted
Diagnosis of DV must be actively performed by the examiner	There is almost no doubt about the diagnosis of a nonaccidental injury
In most countries, relevant criminal prosecution with complete forensic documentation and evidence collection follows even when the injuries are superficial, such as bruising, hematomas, etc., and the incident is not reported as a serious crime	Criminal prosecution and complete evidence collection in most countries only in cases with serious injuries or with a special criminal interest
Children are often involved. They must be protected from former incidents and fatal outcomes	Normally no children involved
Combination of several forms of violence such as sexual, psychological, and physical violence	Delimitable forms of different violence
Risk assessment is important to prevent repeated violence, violence against children, retaliation by the perpetrator, and fatal outcomes	Risk assessment is important to prevent revenge process

moments, thereby sometimes holding contradictory opinions of the situation. Considering the different phases of the circle allows for a better collaboration between the police, the justice system, social workers, and medical officers, all professionally involved at different steps of the circle. Moreover, it is a very important instrument for risk assessment. When it is clear that the wheel is turning faster and faster, and when the violence is getting heavier, then a fatal outcome must be considered and corresponding procedures must be induced, such as an

interdisciplinary, high professional-level risk assessment. Most homicides by partners are committed close to the separation or divorce of the couple. At such times, the assessment of risk is very important to avoid such fatal outcomes.

Diagnosis of DV

Screening

A retrospective assessment of medical reports in Switzerland by Klopfstein et al. showed an average proportion of 0.4% documented female patients affected by DV. This figure is far below the proportions to be expected from more recent data. In her literature review, Olive notes a minimal prevalence of 6% of female emergency department (ED) patients; other studies report a prevalence of between 6% and 30% of female ED patients. In a prospective analysis, Dearwater et al. found 2.2% of an ED's injured female patients to be victims of DV. Studies on the prevalence of DV among the population worldwide report that every 4th to 5th woman could be affected by DV. According to this data, it is hypothesized that in the absence of screening, most of the victims of DV remain unidentified in medical settings.

Obviously, many medical doctors fear to ask about DV. That is why, first in the Unites States, and then in Europe, Australia and Canada, guidelines have been developed to screen for DV, for example, from "The Family Violence Prevention Fund San Francisco." Also, The American Academy of Family Physicians, the American College of Physicians, the American Medical Association, and the American College of Obstetricians and Gynecologists recommend screening for DV. The Department of Health in England recommends that health professionals consider "routine enquiry" of some or all women patients for a history of DV. In Australia, the "Queensland DV Initiative Screening Tool" has been established by the Queensland Government. If there is no evidence for general screening benefits, a "routine enquiry" and "case finding" are largely recommended by medical instances, including by WHO. However, in any kind of procedure, it is very important to educate the involved professionals. They must be prepared for positive signs of DV and able to act appropriately and in an interdisciplinary manner.

Setting up regular screening leads to a higher prevalence of DV in a medical setting.

Pattern of Injuries After DV

1. The typical injuries caused by DV result from blunt violence, mostly subsequent to fist blows, less commonly from kicks. Not very often, the victims present lesions from weapons such as knives or gunshot wounds. Most often, it is the head that is affected, especially the facial region (**Figures 3 and 5**). Victims of assault-related injuries often displayed blunt violence

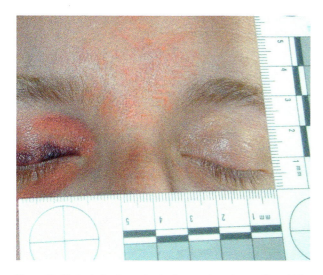

Figure 5 Marks in the form of subcutaneous hematomas after a kick with a shoe. The marks show the sole of the shoe. Copyright University of Forensic Medicine at the University of Berne.

injuries, and showed 13 times more head injuries than unintentional injury victims. There is a well-reported accumulation of head injuries in nonaccidental incidents.

It remains doubtful whether the localization and type of injuries alone can be considered as predictors or indicators of assault-related injuries, the predictive value being too faint. Localizations of injuries in relationship to the injured person's age could indeed lead to a significant predictive assertion. Allen et al. classified the body in different areas and found out that central areas such as the head, neck, and chest more often displayed wounds resulting from assault-related injuries. The limbs are more often accidentally injured.

From the forensic medical perspective, arm injuries deserve particular attention as probable defense injuries (**Figure 4**) above. To identify a self-defense injury may help to distinguish between the victim and perpetrator.

Special attention must be paid because of the danger to life. The character of an injury such as a kick in the face (**Figure 5**) or the use of weapons may allow one to draw conclusions regarding the intention of the perpetrator, such as impulsiveness or a feeling of disrespect for the victim. For example, when the body is full of contusions, it is a sign of uncontrolled and impulsive violence, which at some time could lead to a fatal outcome.

Aspects for the Criminal Prosecution

Criminal prosecution of DV is possible only when the behavior of the perpetrator is defined as criminal under state law. For example, when physical violence is used or there are threats of

such violence and it is clear that the potential aggressor can carry out the threats, the abuse is an assault. Emotional or financial abuse will not be prosecuted because it usually does not rise to the level of an otherwise defined crime (**Table 2**).

Partner violence does not often lead to severe injuries in the penal sense of the term such as injuries linked with a danger to life, a mutilation, or a disfigurement or lasting impairment. Even in 1999, Kyriacou et al. had shown in a case control study that the victims showed mostly contusions and abrasions, and only in 10% of cases were there fractures and dislocations.

Collateral harm such as psychosomatic disorders and other stress-related damage or a potentially dangerous situation that threatens to escalate is not usually considered in a penal prosecution. That is why in most countries, DV is a crime of misdemeanor with a corresponding penal outcome.

Nevertheless, it is very important to proceed with a complete forensic investigation in cases of DV, so as to not miss hidden proofs of physical force and violence (**Figure 6**).

Strangulation is a special situation. It is often seen in violence against women. Most of the victims studied were strangled by an intimate partner manually. More than one-third of the victims described a history of DV. It is considered a danger to life if petechial hemorrhages can be proven in the facial skin, including the conjunctiva of the eye and other mucous membranes as a result of compression of the neck and obstruction of the venous return with continued arterial pressure and engorgement of the vascular system. To detect internal injuries as significant signs of a relevant strangulation, Yen et al. noted an increased accuracy with magnetic resonance imaging of the neck after strangulation. Classification of the forensic estimation of the danger to life is more objective with the

Table 2 Misdemeanor of crime under US Federal State Law (original text)

A "misdemeanor crime of domestic violence" means an offense that: is a misdemeanor under Federal or State law;

has, as an element, the use or attempted use of physical force, or the threatened use of a deadly weapon; and

was committed by a current or former spouse, parent, or guardian of the victim, by a person with whom the victim shares a child in common, by a person who is cohabiting with or has cohabited with the victim as a spouse, parent, or guardian, or by a person similarly situated to a spouse, parent, or guardian of the victim.

However, a person is not considered to have been convicted of a misdemeanor crime of domestic violence unless:

the person was represented by counsel in the case, or knowingly and intelligently waived the right of counsel in the case; and

in the case of a prosecution for which a person was entitled to a jury trial in the jurisdiction in which the case was tried, either

the case was tried by a jury, or

the person knowingly and intelligently waived the right to have the case tried by a jury, by a guilty plea or otherwise.

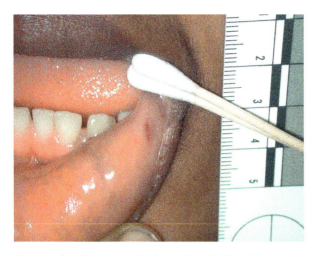

Figure 6 Small laceration on the inner side of the lips as the sign of a hit against the mouth. The teeth are like a skewback for the smooth mucosa of the lips. Copyright University of Forensic Medicine at the University of Berne.

radiology approach. Not only are the legal consequences important, but a strangulation in cases of DV is also considered as an important predictor of a higher risk for a fatal attack and a coincidence of sexual violence.

Documentation

In all cases of DV, a complete and standardized medical report should be prepared for medicolegal purposes. Often, victims first avoid a criminal prosecution, but for future investigations it is important to have a detailed documentation from the beginning of the incident. It also protects the views and interests of the victims and improves the outcome of a criminal prosecution.

Standardized forensic medicine documentation is important for the purpose of legal equality and to ensure quality service to victims of violence who receive medical certificates.

Criminal investigation of victims of violence includes clarification of the following questions:

1. Has an offense been committed? Are there self-inflicted injuries, accidental injuries, or nonaccidental injuries?
2. What is the extent of the injuries? Are they superficial injuries, severe lesions, only in parts of the body or overall?
3. What is the age of the injuries? What was the time of the incident?
4. What is the cause of the injuries? Was there a presumption of a weapon being used?

In court proceedings, an expert should be able to provide answers to the above-mentioned questions without having examined the victim himself and only by studying the medical documents.

That is why a complete forensic documentation should include the following information:

1. Personal data
2. History, for example, information on the exact and complete circumstances of the offense, as related by the victim. Statements from the victim about threats, especially death threats or threats with an instrument, coercion, prohibition from making or receiving phone calls or leaving home, etc. are important to ask for and to be related with the victim's word. In addition, it may be important to ask for, and relate to, identical circumstances in the past.
3. Injuries:
   a. Type (bloodshot, laceration, etc.)
   b. Localization
   c. Extent, size, dimension
   d. Age of the injury
   e. Shape
      i. The "type of injury" category can be considered complete when a diagnosis is stated in the report (e.g., bruise, cut, scratch) or when the wound morphology, that is, the wound's edges, base, and surrounding area, allows a wound diagnosis to be established.
      ii. Description of wound localization is considered sufficient when the injured part of the body can be located.
      iii. Indications of size are met when the unit of measurement is given (usually centimeter).
      iv. The wound's age is considered defined if it is evaluated in the report (recent, old, etc.) or if the wound's description allows a conclusion to be drawn.
      v. The shape is considered given with a bidimensional description of an injury or with concrete indications of the shape.

To obtain the highest quality of forensic documentation, photos and sketches must show the following: localization, color, extent, and shape of the lesions.

Clinical forensic radiology may become very important for an objective and long-lasting documentation.

As mentioned earlier, even very small and inconspicuous lesions could be very important to differentiate the aggressor from the victim (**Figure 6**). In this figure, there is the mark of a hit against the mouth in the form of a small scratch on the inner side of the lip. So the region behind the ears should always be inspected to not miss possible hematomas after a hit on the head (**Figure 7**).

Sexual Violence and DV

Sexual violence concerns more women than men worldwide and is often a part of DV. For the perpetrator, rape is a means to

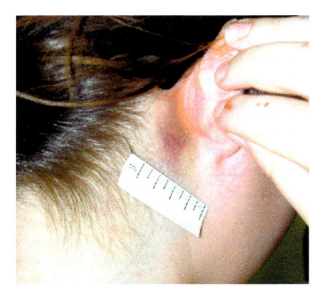

Figure 7 Hematoma behind the ear as a typical nonaccidental injury. Copyright University of Forensic Medicine at the University of Berne.

get control over the wife or partner. In every investigation, it is a very important matter to consider, because for women it is not easy to talk openly about it. In screening programs, the investigators noted great shame in the victims when they had to answer questions on this issue. In forensic investigations, the documentation of even very inconspicuous lesions is very important to prove coercion. In every investigation, the victim should be treated with respect and understanding to avoid a secondary victimization.

Children and DV

Normal, healthy development in children requires a secure environment. In families with repeated outbreaks of violence, the children are under enormous and constant stress. It is considered that every form of violence inside a family means psychological maltreatment of the child. The prevalence of children affected by DV is high and its negative impacts are well known. It is estimated that about 30–60% of the children in families with DV are exposed to child maltreatment. After a screening for DV in a pediatric primary care clinic, it was found that a high rate of psychological violence could have been shown when children experienced DV. A total of 12% of the families screened positive. Other studies pointed out that exposure to DV leads to significantly higher levels of behavior problems such as internalizing behavior with a higher level of suicidality or aggressive behavior. Maltreatment of pets by children can be correlated with inner familial violence.

There is a strong relationship between child abuse and child experience with DV and a higher lifetime risk for DV. To break the harmful circle of violence, children must be supported and empowered to lead a life without violence. To take them out of the family can cause feelings of helplessness, especially when the children know that their mother is still in danger.

The assistance of children with experience of DV requires high professionalism and experienced child health-care specialists who can help victims of child abuse and neglected as well as traumatized children.

Conclusions

DV is a very complex field and requires an interdisciplinary approach. There are important differences between DV and public violence. These differences have to be considered when planning preventions, political measures, criminal prosecutions, and interventions in a medical and social setting.

Complete medical reports should be prepared even when there is no criminal prosecution initiated by the victim, because he or she is not yet ready to leave the violent relationship. The victim may initiate criminal prosecution later. In this prospective criminal action, documentation of former incidents will be of great interest and support to the victim. But criminal proceeding alone cannot resolve the problems in a violent partnership and family. Psychological and social interventions provided by specialists are required to break the vicious circle.

See also: **Forensic Medicine/Causes of Death:** Strangulation; **Forensic Medicine/Clinical:** Child Abuse; Defense Wounds; Self-Inflicted Injury; Sexual Violence; **Management/Quality in Forensic Science:** Principles of Quality Assurance; Risk Management.

Further Reading

Abramsky, T., Watts, C.H., Garcia-Moreno, C., et al., 2011. What factors are associated with recent intimate partner violence? Findings from the WHO multi-country study on women's health and domestic violence. BMC Public Health 16 (11), 109.
Allen, T., Noval, S.A., Bench, L.L., 2007. Patterns of injuries: accident or abuse. Violence Against Women 13 (8), 802–816.
Dearwater, StR., et al., 1998. Prevalence of intimate partner abuse in women treated at community hospital emergency departments. Journal of the American Medical Association 280, 433–438.
Dubowitz, H., Prescott, L., Feigelmann, S., Lane, W., Kim, J., 2008. Screening for intimate partner violence in a pediatric primary care clinic. Pediatrics 121 (1), e85–e91.
Hofner, M.C., Burquier, R., Huissoud, T., Romain, N., Graz, B., Mangin, P., 2009. Characteristics of victims of violence admitted to a specialized medico-legal unit in Switzerland. Journal of Forensic and Legal Medicine 16 (5), 269–272.
Houry, D., Rhodes, K.V., Kemball, R.S., et al., 2008. Differences in female and male victims and perpetrators of partner violence with respect to WEB scores. Journal of Interpersonal Violence 23 (8), 1041–1055.

Kimmel, M.S., 2002. 'Gender symmetry' in domestic violence: a substantive and methodological research review. Special Issue: Women's Use of Violence in Intimate Relationships Violence Against Women 8 (11).

Klopfstein, U., Kamber, J., Zimmermann, H., 2010. On the way to light the dark: a retrospective inquiry into the registered cases of domestic violence towards women over a six year period with a semi-quantitative analysis of the corresponding forensic documentation. Swiss Medical Weekly 140, w13047.

Kyriacou, D.N., 1999. Risk factors for injury to women from domestic violence. New England Journal of Medicine 341 (25), 1892–1898.

Olive, P., 2005. Care for emergency department patients who have experienced domestic violence: a review of the evidence base. Journal of Clinical Nursing 16 (9), 1736–1748.

Pearson, C., Hester, M., Harvin, N., 2007. Making an Impact, Children and Domestic Violence, second ed. Jessica Kingsley Publisher, London and Philadelphia.

Plattner, T., Bolliger, S., Zollinger, U., 2005. Forensic assessment of survived strangulation. Forensic Science International 153 (2–3), 202–207.

Shields, L.B., Corey, T.S., Weakley-Jones, B., Stewart, D., 2010. Living victims of strangulation: a 10-year review of cases in a metropolitan community. American Journal of Forensic Medicine and Pathology 31 (4), 320–325.

Wilbur, L., et al., 2001. Survey results of women who have been strangled while in an abusive relationship. Journal of Emergency Medicine 21 (3), 297–302.

Yen, K., et al., 2007. Clinical forensic radiology in strangulation victims: forensic expertise based on magnetic resonance imaging (MRI) findings. International Journal of Legal Medicine 121 (2), 115–123.

Relevant Websites

http://www.acog.org/departments—The American College of Obstetricians and Gynecologists: Health care for Women.

http://www.atf.gov/firearms/faq/misdemeanor-domestic-violence.html#description—Bureau of Alcohol, Tobacco, Firearms and Explosives.

http://www.batteredmen.com/duluwomn.htm—Website Batteredmen.

http://www.breakthecycle.org/html%20files/I_4a_startstatis.htm—Break the Cycle (2006 Startling Statistics).

http://www.coe.int/t/dg2/equality/DOMESTICVIOLENCECAMPAIGN/—Campaign to Combat Violence Against Women, Including Domestic Violence. Council of Europe (2006–2008).

http://www.dvrc-or.org/domestic/violence/resources/C72/—The Circle of Violence.

http://ec.europa.eu/public_opinion/archives/ebs/ebs_344_en.pdf—Domestic Violence Against Women, Report from the European Commission 2010.

http://en.wikipedia.org/wiki/Duluth_model; http://www.womenshealth.gov/violence/legislation/—The Duluth Model.

http://www.endviolenceagainstwomen.org.uk/pages/domestic_violence.html—End Violence Against Women (EVAW) Coalition, UK.

http://www.endviolenceagainstwomen.org.uk/pages/domestic_violence.html—The Family Violence Prevention Fund San Francisco.

http://www.health.qld.gov.au/violence/domestic/dvpubs/DVIForm.PDF—Domestic Violence in Australia.

http://news.bbc.co.uk/2/shared/bsp/hi/pdfs/17_07_07_crime.pdf—The Home Office Statistical Bulletin 2007.

http://new.vawnet.org/Assoc_Files_VAWnet/screpol.pdf—Screening of Domestic Violence.

http://www.ovw.usdoj.gov/domviolence.htm—US Department of Justice.

http://www.unicef-irc.org/publications/pdf/digest6e.pdf—Overview of Domestic Violence against Women and Girls, UNICEF 2000.

http://www.who.int/gender/violence/who_multicountry_study/en/—WHO-Websites.

http://www.who.int/mediacentre/factsheets/fs239/en/—The WHO Factsheets About Domestic Violence.

http://www.womenshealth.gov/violence/legislation/—Laws on Violence Against Women.

Child Abuse

WA Karst, HGT Nijs, and RAC Bilo, Netherlands Forensic Institute, The Hague, The Netherlands

This article is a revision of the previous edition article by R.E.I. Roberts and J.V. Evans, volume 1, pp. 368–374, © 2000, Elsevier Ltd.

Introduction

Child abuse is the physical, sexual, or emotional mistreatment, or neglect of a child. These broadly defined categories may overlap. In the United States, the Center for Disease Control and Prevention and the Department of Children and Families define child maltreatment as any act or series of acts of commission or omission by a parent or other caregiver that results in harm, potential for harm, or threat of harm to a child. Abuse can occur in a child's home, or in the organizations, schools, or communities a child interacts with.

Role of the Physician or Child Care Professional

Everyone involved in the care of children has a responsibility to recognize the possibility of abuse and/or to maintain the child's welfare. Assessment and investigation of suspected abuse is a multidisciplinary task, involving welfare agencies, health professionals, and the criminal and civil justice systems. For the medical part, preferably a child abuse physician is consulted in suspected cases.

The physician evaluating children who may have been abused is faced with many challenges. In addition to providing the diagnosis and treatment, the physician must also ensure the child's safety, assist in the collection of possible evidence, and report any suspected abuse to the state child protective services agency (depending on legislation).

Physical Abuse

Nonaccidental injury may range in its presentation from no discernable injury at all to a few bruises and scratches to a severely or fatally injured child. Several general "red flags" in initial presentation with regard to child abuse are given in **Table 1**. Training and support in the recognition of these "red flags" is important to any health-care professional.

Differential Diagnosis

It is important to exclude other possible explanations for the medical findings.

The differential diagnosis can be approached first in broad terms: make a distinction between a medical condition and trauma. Subsequently, in case of trauma, make a distinction between an accidental trauma and a nonaccidental (inflicted) trauma.

Take a full medical history and always complete a thorough examination ("head-to-toe" below 5 or 10 years of age). Beware of clustered or patterned (sometimes "tell tale") injuries. Decide whether (non)accidental injury, carelessness, neglect, or perhaps traditional cultural practice offers the most satisfactory explanation for the clinical findings.

The developmental stage of the child must be considered. A baby is not independently mobile, and a clear explanation is required for any bruise or injury (and a clotting disorder should be ruled out). However, accidents beyond imagination do occur.

"Those who cruise" (mobile children), are at risk by definition in acquiring injuries, especially in the front or over bony parts of the body. Some more specific "red flags," common patterns of injury in child abuse cases, are listed in **Table 2**.

Common skin conditions mimicking child abuse should be carefully considered such as the Mongolian spot, juvenile striae or stretch marks, marks from coin rubbing (or other traditional practices), and dermatological conditions (e.g., erythema annulare, lichen sclerosis, impetigo, herpes zoster).

Aging bruises is possible to some extent. If yellow is present, the age of the bruise is at least 18 h (but not vice versa in the absence of yellow). Bruises may appear after only several days, may migrate depending on gravity, and usually may remain visible for 1–2 weeks. Other injuries cannot be aged more than in terms of "recent" or "old" (yet, this distinction may be important from a forensic point of view).

Human bite marks characteristically show an oval or circular mark of two opposing U-shaped arches (in contrast with V-shaped arches from cats and dogs), including superficial puncture wounds and drag marks, and (petechial) hemorrhages. In addition, bites may be confused with skin conditions such as ringworm, erythema annulare, and pityriasis rosea. One must consider taking DNA swabs in a fresh bite and consulting a forensic odontologist.

In case of any suspicion of child abuse, a skeletal survey should be performed, especially in the young (below 5 years).

Table 1   General "red flags" in initial presentation

(Unaccounted) Delay in seeking medical care
Other person than caretaker presents the child
Absent, inadequate, or changing explanation
Injuries of (clearly) different ages
History of previous injury
Failure to thrive
Parent shows little, or excessive, concern
Frozen watchfulness of the child

Approved international protocols are available at American College of Radiology of Royal College of Paediatrics and Child Health. X-rays or other images should be reread by a (pediatric) radiologist with specific expertise.

Abusive head trauma (AHT) is the major cause of death after physical abuse, mostly in the first year of life. AHT occurs as a result of acceleration–deceleration trauma as in vigorous shaking (formerly known as "shaken baby syndrome"), direct impact as in punching the head or throwing the child's head against a wall, or a combination of both. AHT is associated with retinal hemorrhages, encephalopathy, skin bruising, subdural fluid (blood) collection, (posterior) rib fractures, and so on in various combinations and in various degrees. AHT may be present without any visible injury and with nonspecific clinical findings (breathing or drinking difficulties, vomiting). Therefore, the diagnosis of AHT is often not considered or missed initially. In many cases, not a single event has occurred but a series of events.

Accidental or birth-related skull fractures are typically single, narrow, hairline fractures, involving usually one bone (the parietal). The location of the fracture may not be the location of the impact because of pliability of the skull of the very young.

Nonaccidental skull fractures are typically multiple, complex, and branched. Skull fractures cannot be dated radiologically because of absence of callus formation (the margins of the fracture "fade away" in months).

Table 2   "Red flags," common patterns of injury

Any bruising on a baby
Clustered or patterned bruises or injuries (finger tip, grip, or pinch marks)
"Tramline bruising" or bruises carrying an imprint
Bruises not over bony parts
Finger marks/hand redness and weals ("slap mark")
Bilateral black eyes
Torn upper frenulum
Bite marks
Cigarette burns
Scalds and burns
Fractures

Rib fractures are usually without clinical signs (occult) and detected only on X-ray or CT-scan. They are seen most commonly in infants and young children. In infants without bone disease, the extreme pliability of the ribs implies that such fractures only occur after the application of considerable force when compressing the sternum toward the vertebral column (such as in an acceleration–deceleration trauma).

A negative X-ray should be repeated after 2 weeks. The presence of callus formation then indicates the presence of rib fractures, apparently former occult. Rib fractures, and long bones in general, may be dated radiologically to some extent (e.g., subperiostal bone formation about 1 week, callous formation about 2 weeks).

Epiphyseal and metaphyseal fractures are injuries typical of nonaccidental injury. Pulling and twisting forces applied to the limbs, for example, during vigorous shaking, lead to shearing forces resulting in "classical metaphyseal lesions."

Several different types of fracture of different ages and in different sites may indicate multiple traumas clearly separated in time. Fractures may occur without any skin sign (such as a hematoma).

Burns and scalds are also commonly seen in physical abuse. Again, the explanation given in relation to the injury pattern is important to ascertain. Accidental scalds usually occur in a "spill"-like fashion, typically leading to a scald affecting the upper trunk and/or upper limbs or face. The scald may show an irregular edge, variable depth (with less depth in the periphery), flowlike pattern, and "sparing effects" due to skin folds or clothing.

Nonaccidental scalds from hot water usually affect the trunk or lower limbs with or without involvement of the buttocks and/or perineum. Characteristically, there is a clear demarcation line (in a stocking manner for feet, or glovelike manner for hands). Nonaccidental scalds may be accompanied by other signs of child abuse such as fractures (often clinically occult). Therefore, a skeletal survey should be performed as a part of the medical work-up.

Nonaccidental cigarette burns typically form a circular or oval punched-out lesion 0.6–1.0 cm across, which heals with scarring because it involves the full thickness of the skin.

Severe other forms of scalding or burning may occur (e.g., caustic burns or deliberately contacting hot objects such as a steaming iron).

Again, also consider a differential diagnosis as several skin conditions may mimic burns (impetigo (bullosa), photodermatitis, hereditary skin conditions, and hypersensitivity).

Sexual Abuse

Child sexual abuse is defined as the involvement of a child in sexual activity that he or she does not fully comprehend, is unable to give informed consent to, or for which the child is not developmentally prepared, or else that violates the laws or social taboos of society.

Children can be sexually abused by both adults and children.

The prevalence of child sexual abuse is difficult to determine, because it is unclear that how often sexual abuse remains undetected. The worldwide prevalence is estimated at 20% among girls and 8% among boys. Studies using the law enforcement as well as victim self-report data found that more than 90% of the perpetrators of sexual offenses against minors were male. Strangers are the offenders in approximately 10% of child sexual abuse cases.

Child sexual abuse can sometimes result in physical harm, such as bleeding from lacerations or sexually transmitted diseases. Psychological harm is a far more common effect, however. Common psychological effects are depression, post-traumatic stress disorder, anxiety, poor self-esteem, and behavior problems including substance abuse and self-destructive behavior.

The Medical Examination

Clinicians should be aware of the importance of adequately obtaining the medical history in suspected child sexual abuse. It depends on local circumstances and legislation whether the history taking can be done without limitations. Often children's statements are more important for legal outcome than the medical findings.

It is important that a clinician who examines the genitals of a minor is familiar with the evidence regarding the interpretation of findings. The incorrect interpretation of findings can result in far-reaching consequences, not only if a finding is incorrectly related to sexual abuse, but also if a relevant finding is not being recognized. If a clinician does not know how to interpret a specific finding, a consultation from an experienced colleague is needed before any statements are made. High-quality photo documentation, preferably using video-colposcopy, is strongly recommended because of the possible important role in consultation or for forensic purposes.

If acute sexual abuse is suspected (less than a few days ago), the child should be examined as soon as possible because of the rapidly diminishing chance to collect forensic samples and the rapid healing of lesions in the anogenital region. The likelihood of positive DNA sampling is highest within hours after the event and falls rapidly. Obvious genital injuries can heal within a few days, and even deep lacerations heal without scarring. Prophylaxis for sexually transmitted infections and emergency contraception also require a rapid assessment. In acute cases, the child must not be allowed to wash and all clothing and other relevant items must be retained unwashed till the examination (**Tables 3 and 4**).

Only clinicians with the ability to communicate comfortably with children about sensitive issues should perform the

Table 3 Guidance on persistence of spermatozoa and other cellular material on skin, hair, and in body orifices following some sexual acts

Sexual act	Persistence of semen or other cellular material
Ejaculation on skin/hair	Up to 2 days
Penis in mouth	Up to 2 days
Vaginal intercourse prepubertal	Up to 3 days
Vaginal intercourse postpubertal	Up to 7 days
Anal intercourse	Up to 3 days

From Royal College of Paediatrics and Child, 2008. Health Forensic Samples and Their Collection. The Physical Signs of Child Sexual Abuse. An Evidence-Based Review and Guidance for Best Practice. Royal College of Paediatrics and Child Health, London, pp. 137–139.

examination. It should be respected if children withdraw consent for any part of the examination. The child should be allowed to choose who they wish to be present. If a parent or carer is unavailable or if an adolescent prefers to be examined without parent or carer, a chaperone should be present during the physical examination.

The physical examination should be performed from head to toe. The anogenital examination should be performed in supine frog-leg position with hips flexed and the soles of the feet touching. Young children might be examined on a carer's lap. It is recommended to examine prepubertal girls in prone knee–chest position as well. One should not use a speculum in prepubertal girls. In pubertal girls, a sterile Foley catheter could be used for demonstrating injuries in folds. The slightly inflated Foley catheter could be withdrawn from the vagina until the balloon rests against the internal aspect of the hymen. Using

Table 4 Implications of commonly encountered sexually transmitted (ST) or sexually associated (SA) infections for diagnosis and reporting of sexual abuse among infants and prepubertal children

ST/SA confirmed	Evidence for sexual abuse
Gonorrhea[a]	Diagnostic
Syphilis[a]	Diagnostic
Human immunodeficiency virus[b]	Diagnostic
Chlamydia trachomatis[a]	Diagnostic
Trichomonas vaginalis	Highly suspicious
Condylomata acuminata (anogenital warts)[a]	Suspicious
Genital herpes[a]	Suspicious
Bacterial vaginosis	Inconclusive

[a]If not likely to be perinatally acquired and rare nonsexual, transmission is excluded.
[b]If not likely to be acquired perinatally or through transfusion.
Kellogg, N., American Academy of Pediatrics Committee on Child Abuse and Neglect, 2005. The evaluation of child abuse in children. Pediatrics 116 (2), 506–512.

toluidine dye on the perineum and posterior fourchette might detect minor tissue injuries. However, minor tissue injury to these regions is a nonspecific finding for trauma and can be caused by other irritative and infectious conditions.

The Interpretation of Medical Findings

Genital Findings in Girls

Knowledge of normal variants of the genital area and the changes that take place in its appearance with age is indispensable (**Figure 1**). Common normal findings include redness of the labia and perineum, periurethral or vestibular bands, and congenital variants in the appearance of the hymen, including crescentic and annular. Urethral prolapse, lichen sclerosis, and failure of the midline fusion are conditions that are known to be mistaken for abuse sometimes.

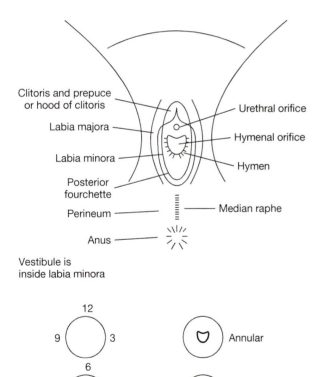

Vestibule is inside labia minora

Figure 1   The prepubertal vulva.

The interpretation of medical findings starts with using appropriate and descriptive terms. Acute hymenal disruptions should be described as lacerations. Nonacute partial hymenal injury should be described as notches, and nonacute disruptions complete to the base of the hymen should be described as transections. Hymenal injuries heal rapidly and except for extensive injuries, can leave no residua (e.g., scars).

Accidental trauma could result in injury to the fourchette posterior or vestibule and bruising of the labia. The hymen will only be damaged if there is a penetrative component to the injury. Bumps, mounds, and tags of the hymen are common and are not the result of trauma.

When hymenal transections in the posterior portion of the hymen, hymenal lacerations, or extensive bruising on the hymen are found, penetrative injury should be strongly suspected. Superficial notches in the posterior hymen have been reported in abused and nonabused prepubertal girls. Deep notches in the posterior half of the hymen have only been reported in prepubertal girls with a history of vaginal penetration. In pubertal girls, posterior deep notches have been reported more often in girls with a history of vaginal penetration than in girls without vaginal penetration.

In earlier days, the hymenal width and the size of the hymenal orifice were considered important in the evaluation of child sexual abuse. It has been suggested that larger hymenal openings or narrowed hymenal rims imply that penetration has taken place. The fact is that larger hymenal openings and narrowed hymenal rims are nondiscriminatory for sexual abuse.

Genital Findings in Boys

Medical findings in sexually abused boys are less common than in sexually abused girls, and are not well reported in the medical literature. Genital injuries in sexually abused boys occur predominantly to the penis. Testicular or scrotal injuries are more frequently associated with accidental injury than sexual abuse. Acute lacerations or bruising of the penis are strongly suspicious for sexual abuse.

Anal Findings in Girls and Boys

Reflex anal dilatation, perianal venous congestion, and skin tags are seen in both sexually abused and nonsexually abused children. Reflex anal dilatation, which is a dynamic response of the opening of the anus due to relaxation of the internal and external sphincter muscles with minimal buttock traction, should be distinguished from anal laxity or reduced anal tone. Anal laxity has been described in sexually abused children, but there are no studies of anal laxity in children selected for nonabuse. Anal dilatation, which is not immediate and does not have an anterior–posterior diameter of 2 cm or more, is nonspecific. Chronic constipation, sedation, anesthesia, and neuromuscular conditions are more common causes for an immediate anal dilatation to a diameter of 2 cm or more than sexual abuse.

Perianal lacerations extending deep to the external anal sphincter are indicative of blunt force penetrating trauma. Lacerations or extensive bruising of perianal tissues are the result of acute trauma. Perianal lacerations should be distinguished from anal fissures, which are usually the result from constipation, and from the linea pectinata or dentata, which is normal anatomy and which could be commonly seen when examining a child.

Recording the Findings in Possible Child Abuse Cases

Findings should be recorded in writing and in images to enable discussion among professionals, peer reviews, education, and court procedures. Visual information should be photographed. Legal verification is required stating the identity of the child and the circumstances under which the photographs were taken.

In taking photographs, follow forensic standards in a standardized order to enable recognition of the affected body part and adequate (focused) close-ups at 90° to the surface with a measuring scale correctly applied.

Interpretation of Findings

The health professional should keep an open mind and assess any evidence objectively, considering all possible alternative explanations—whether in the course of court or otherwise ("fact finding").

Beware of the risk of overinterpretation, especially in cases of suspected sexual abuse (e.g., normal anatomy such as periurethral bands or a cribiform hymen has been interpreted as scars in a context of earlier sexual abuse). Also, underinterpretation is possible, especially in cases of AHT because of minor or nonspecific clinical signs.

See also: **Forensic Medicine/Causes of Death:** Burns and Scalds; **Forensic Medicine/Clinical:** Defense Wounds; Domestic Violence; Sexual Violence; Torture.

Further Reading

Adams, J.A., 2011. Medical evaluation of suspected child sexual abuse: 2011 update. Journal of Child Sexual Abuse 20 (5), 588–605.

Bilo, R.A.C., Robben, S.G.F., Van Rijn, R.R., 2010. Forensic Aspects of Pediatric Fractures. Differentiating Accidental Trauma from Child Abuse. Springer, Heidelberg.

Bilo, R.A.C., Oranje, A.P., Shwayder, T., Hobbs, C.J., 2012. Cutaneous Manifestations of Child Abuse and Their Differential Diagnosis – Blunt Force Trauma. Springer, Heidelberg.

Christian, C.W., Block, R., 2009. Abuse head trauma in infants and children. Policy statement, American Academy of Pediatrics. Pediatrics 123, 1409–1411.

Finkel, M.A., Giardino, A.P., 2009. Medical Evaluation of Child Sexual Abuse. A Practical Guide, third ed. American Academy of Pediatrics, Elk Grove Village, IL.

Jenny, C., 2011. Child Abuse and Neglect. Diagnosis, Treatment, and Evidence. Elsevier Saunders, St. Louis, MI.

Royal College of Paediatrics and Child Health, 2008. The Physical Signs of Child Sexual Abuse. An Evidence-Based Review and Guidance for Best Practice. Royal College of Paediatrics and Child Health, London.

United Nations, 2009. UNTS Volume Number 1577. Convention on the Rights of the Child.

Defense Wounds

U Schmidt, Freiburg University Medical Center, Freiburg, Germany

This article is a revision of the previous edition article by S. Pollak and P.J. Saukko, volume 1, pp. 374–378, © 2000, Elsevier Ltd.

Glossary

Blank cartridge pistol A pistol with a cartridge containing gunpowder but no bullet, usually used for training, as a signal or for purposes of self-defense.

Laceration A wound/tear of skin and soft tissue resulting from blunt (but not sharp) force.

Introduction

The presence of defense wounds is justly considered an important sign that an individual has been the victim of an assault. Another aspect of medicolegal significance concerns the physical activity of the victim: defense wounds indicate that the attacked person was—at least initially—conscious and able to use his limbs for protection resulting in injuries to the forearms or hands or—in rare cases—to the legs. When sustaining defense wounds, the victim must have been aware of the assault (anticipating the blow or thrust) and fit for the natural reaction of protecting himself.

Defense Wounds from Knife Attacks

Such injuries are seen when the victim attempts to ward off a knife either by seizing it or by raising forearms and hands to protect other body regions (head, neck, and chest).

Traditionally, a distinction is made in the literature between "active" and "passive" defense wounds. According to this distinction, "active" defense wounds occur when the victim grasps the knife with the hand with the injury then being located on the palmar side of the hand. The "passive" wound type is sustained when the victim raises their hands or arms to protect the attacked body region; in this case, the injuries will primarily be located on the extensor side.

There are only a small number of papers available with detailed statements as to the frequency and distribution of defense wounds. The frequency of such wounds indicated for victims killed by sharp force usually ranges between 30% and 50%, and almost half of the victims (46%) who have survived a knife attack also show defense wounds. In victims primarily fit for reaction, the probability of the presence of defense wounds increases with the number of hits placed on the body.

If, in spite of multiple stabs, no defense injuries are found, it has to be considered that the victim may have been unable to react or impaired in his ability to defend himself already before the use of sharp force: for example, in knife attacks on a sleeping person, in unexpected assaults, and in victims made unconscious before the attack. The absence of defense wounds is also observed when the victim was held or tied. The same also largely applies to those cases where severe traumatization of a different type (e.g., by blunt force) occurred before the use of sharp force. Moreover, it is to be expected that in cases of very high blood alcohol concentrations or under the influence of drugs, the ability to defend oneself adequately against an assault is reduced.

A study of a large number of cases with regard to the localization of defense wounds found about the same number of injuries on the flexor and the extensor side, often combined in the same victim. It seems justified to express doubts as to the stereotyped distinction between active and passive defense wounds. First, the various possible ways of stabbing with a knife must be taken into consideration. Different ways of moving the knife (in downward or upward direction) may produce defense wounds on either the extensor or flexor side of the arm. An injury on the extensor side of the limbs may also occur if the victim tries to seize the knife and the blade comes into contact with the back of the hand or the extensor side of the forearm.

In an attempt to grasp the knife, the fingers of the victim may close around the blade, which cuts across the flexures of the phalanges as the knife is withdrawn (**Figure 1**). In this case, several fingers may be injured by a single impact of the cutting edge sometimes even completely severing the flexor tendons. Another typical location is the web between the thumb and the index finger. Incised wounds of the hands are often "shelved" so that one margin forms a flap of skin (**Figure 2**). Hand injuries are frequently located at the transition from the flexor

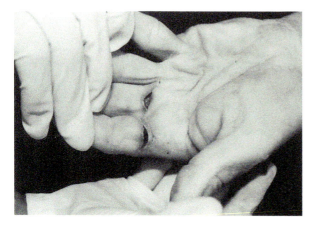

Figure 1   Two cuts on the palmar surface of the left hand caused by the cutting edge of a machete when the victim attempted to clutch the weapon.

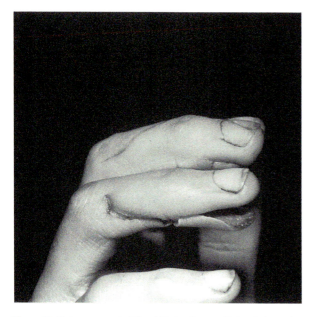

Figure 2   Defense wound of the right ring finger with beveled margin forming a skin flap.

to the extensor side of the fingers. Such wounds are typically encountered if the victim tries to protect himself by holding his hand against the knife with spread fingers.

It should be mentioned that in killed victims, more than two-thirds of all defense wounds are found on the left arm or left hand. This phenomenon has mostly been attributed to the fact that many offenses start with the victim and the assailant being in an upright face-to-face position. In this case, the left

arm of the victim will be nearest to the mostly right-handed perpetrator and thus will be injured more easily. This explanation is also supported by the fact that in killed victims, the left side of the body or trunk is more frequently affected by sharp force injuries. It has also been stated that the victim may unconsciously ward off an attack with the "weaker" left arm to maintain the function of the right hand and arm, which is the "stronger" one in most individuals. In this respect, it is important to know whether the assailant and the victim are right or left handed.

There are a few special features regarding surviving victims of knife attacks: defense injuries are almost evenly distributed on the left and right arms, although the left half of the body—including the left upper arm—is again hit more frequently. Some victims surviving a knife attack show defense injuries, but no additional stab or cut wounds on other parts of their bodies. This may happen if the attacker uses the weapon primarily to threaten the victim or if he is severely handicapped in his ability to act, for example, due to the limited space available. In fact, it is to be assumed that the number of individuals injured in this way is rather high, but, as the experience in the courtroom shows, they are rarely examined by a forensic expert.

In rare cases, defense wounds are localized even on the legs; if the victim was in a lying position, he may have used his legs to ward off the knife or curled up to protect vital areas with his drawn-up extremities.

Stabbing actions do not necessarily result in actual stab wounds, but result in cuts if the blade contacts the curved surface of a limb tangentially (**Figure 3**). In transfixion stab wounds, the weapon passes through the soft tissues of an extremity and afterward possibly reenters another body region (**Figure 4**). Irregular, L-, Y-, or V-shaped stab wounds (**Figure 5**)

Figure 3   Multiple cuts of the left forearm and hand sustained when trying to ward off a knife attack against the neck.

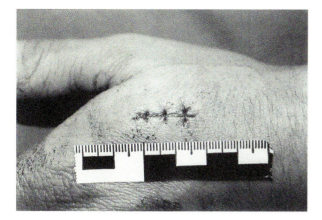

Figure 4   Transfixion stab wound of the left hand after surgical treatment. The victim tried to fend off an attack with a kitchen knife.

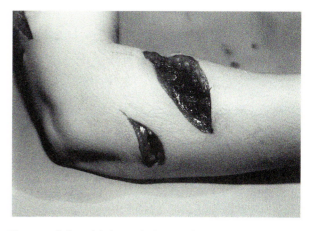

Figure 6   Defense injuries on the forearm of a victim who was killed by stab wounds to the chest and cut-throat wounds.

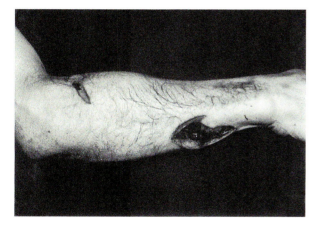

Figure 5   Irregular stab wounds on the dorsal and ulnar aspects of the right forearm: one of the stab wounds is extended by a superficial incision, and the other one is V-shaped due to twisting of the blade. The weapon used by the assailant was a survival knife.

Figure 7   Bruises on the dorsal face of the left hand of a female victim who tried to protect her head against fist blows. In addition, there is a shallow cut on the index finger (defense wound from a knife attack).

and wounds combining cutting and stabbing characteristics (**Figure 6**) may occur due to relative movements between the assailant and the victim. Defense injuries to the limbs covered by garments are usually accompanied by corresponding damages/cuts in the clothing.

Defense Wounds due to Blunt Force

Defense wounds of this kind are seen in blunt force attacks when the victim attempts to ward off kicks, blows of the fist, or blunt instruments. Their location is similar to defense wounds from knife attacks (hands, forearms, or, less frequently, the

legs). Injuries inflicted to the thighs possibly result from attempts to shield the genitals against blows or kicks aimed at the lower part of the body.

The injuries most often seen are abrasions and contusions (with concomitant bruising) on the back of the hands, wrists, and forearms (**Figure 7**). Though abrasions and bruises are the most common defense injuries due to blunt force, additional lacerations may occur in skin regions supported by bone (e.g., the metacarpal region and the knuckles). Lacerations from a blunt instrument possibly contain embedded foreign material indicative of the weapon used. Defense injuries inflicted together with wounds in the regions the victim wanted to protect with his hands and arms show the same stage of healing on later inspection.

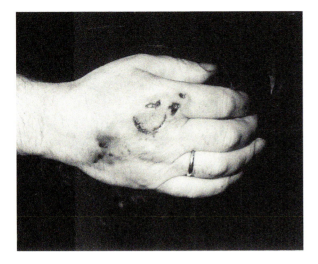

Figure 8 Defense injuries on the back of the right hand: excoriations, bruises, and a shallow laceration due to multiple blows with a pistol grip.

In rare cases, the victim may sustain fractures of the hand bones. Another classical fracture site is the ulnar shaft, which is exposed in victims parrying a blow or kick with their raised forearm. Depending on the site of the causal impact, these fractures usually occur at the transition from the proximal to the middle third or in the middle third of the ulna.

Defense wounds due to blunt trauma deserve special attention in suspected physical child abuse. In such cases, bruises or abrasions may reflect patterned details from the instrument delivering the blow (e.g., belt, stick, rod, heel of a shoe). In adults also, a great variety of blunt instruments can be used to inflict severe injuries, mainly to the head. If the hand is interposed in a protecting manner, it will primarily be hit by the weapon (**Figure 8**). By placing the hands on the top of the head, the victim tries to lessen the blows. Apart from typical blunt weapons as hammers, firm bottles, and wrenches, sometimes also (blank cartridge) pistols and revolvers are used for striking ("pistol whipping").

Defense Wounds from Other Weapons

Chop wounds are a special category of injuries due to sharp force by heavy instruments with a cutting edge such as axes, machetes, and meat cleavers. Such wounds are characterized by cuts of the skin in combination with sharp-edged notches or comminuted fractures of the underlying bone.

In a wider sense, even in firearm injuries, the upper limbs may reveal a special kind of defense wound when the victim raises an arm in an unsuccessful attempt to shield

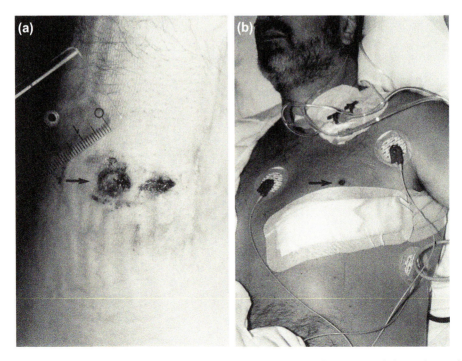

Figure 9 Entrance and exit wound of a caliber 0.32 bullet, which first passed through the right forearm (a) and afterward entered the chest (b). The victim had raised his arm when a burglar shot at him.

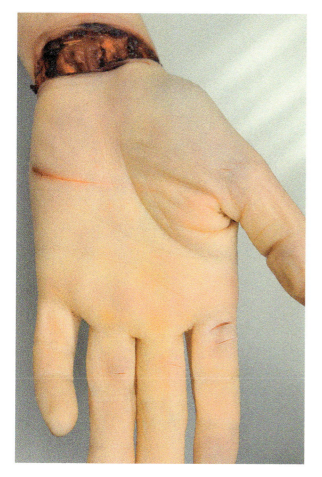

Figure 10 Left hand of a 48-year-old woman who killed herself by cutting both of her wrists and by ingestion of prescription drugs. Superficial cuts on the index, middle, and ring fingers, and on the palm.

vital areas of the body. Under such circumstances, the bullet first passes through the hand or the arm and afterward often enters the head or the thorax producing a reentry wound (**Figure 9**).

Misleading Findings Similar to Defense Wounds

Superficial cuts restricted to the skin are sometimes found on the fingers of suicides who used double-edged razor blades for cutting their wrists or who injured themselves when positioning and fixing the knife used by gripping its blade (**Figure 10**). Most of these cuts do not pass through all layers of the skin so that differentiation from real defense wounds should not be difficult.

If a perpetrator stabs his victim using a knife without a guard, his bloody hand may slip from the handle onto the blade producing cuts on the palm or the fingers, which at first sight give the impression of real defense wounds. As a consequence, blood stains of both the victim and the assailant might be detected on the blade.

Heavy blows with the fist sometimes result in injuries to the assailant's hand, for instance, bruises or wounds from the victim's incisors or even fractures of the metacarpal bones.

The features of self-inflicted injuries are dealt with in a separate chapter. Hands and arms may bear multiple incisions from a preliminary suicide attempt, mostly localized across the front of the wrists and on the flexor surface of the forearms. The typical appearance is characterized by multiple clustered wounds, mainly in a horizontal and parallel arrangement, some being very superficial tentative incisions ("hesitation cuts").

Apart from persons with a real suicidal tendency, numerous incisions are also seen among patients suffering from psychiatric disorders and in persons who want to draw attention to themselves ("sympathy cuts") particularly by making false accusation of assault.

See also: **Forensic Medicine/Causes of Death:** Sharp Trauma; **Forensic Medicine/Clinical:** Self-Inflicted Injury.

Further Reading

Buris, L., 1993. Forensic Medicine. Springer, Budapest, pp. 51, 59, 63, 71.

Crane, J., 1996. Injury. In: McLay, W.D.S. (Ed.), Clinical Forensic Medicine, second ed. Greenwich Medical Media, London, pp. 143–162.

DiMaio, D.J., DiMaio, V.J.M., 1989. Forensic Pathology. Elsevier, New York, pp. 102, 195–199.

Knight, B., 1991. Simpson's Forensic Medicine, tenth ed. Arnold, London, pp. 84–85.

Knight, B., 1996. Forensic Pathology, second ed. Arnold, London, pp. 162–163.

Kornberg, A.E., 1992. Skin and soft tissue injuries. In: Ludwig, S., Kornberg, A.E. (Eds.), Child Abuse, second ed. Churchill Livingstone, New York, pp. 91–104.

Mason, J.K., 1993. Forensic Medicine. An Illustrated Reference. Chapman & Hall, London, pp. 64, 128.

Metter, D., Benz, D., 1989. Defence injuries caused by sharp force in homicides. Zeitschrift für Rechtsmedizin 102, 277–291 (in German).

Prokop, O., Radam, G., 1992. Atlas der gerichtlichen Medizin, third ed. Ullstein Mosby (in German), Berlin. pp. 104, 240, 247, 249, 252, 275, 277, 328, 356.

Schmidt, U., 2010. Sharp force injuries in 'clinical' forensic medicine. Forensic Science International 195, 1–5.

Schmidt, U., Faller-Marquardt, M., Tatschner, T., Walter, K., Pollak, S., 2004. Cuts to the offender's own hand – unintentional self-infliction in the course of knife attacks. International Journal of Legal Medicine 118, 348–354.

Spitz, W.U., 1993. Sharp force injury. In: Spitz, W.U. (Ed.), Medicolegal Investigation of Death, third ed. CC Thomas, Springfield, pp. 252–310.

Spitz, W.U., Platt, M.S., 1993. The battered child and adolescent. In: Spitz, W.U. (Ed.), Medicolegal Investigation of Death, third ed. CC Thomas, Springfield, pp. 687–732.

Watson, A.A., 1993. Stabbing and other incisional wounds. In: Mason, J.K. (Ed.), The Pathology of Trauma, second ed. Arnold, London, pp. 97–108.

Self-Inflicted Injury

P Saukko, University of Turku, Turku, Finland
S Pollak, University of Freiburg, Freiburg, Germany

Glossary

Factitious dermatitis A disorder in which patients intentionally inflict skin lesions on themselves, mostly by scratching or using sharp instruments.
Malingering This term refers to fabricating or exaggerating the symptoms of mental or physical disorders.

Munchausen syndrome A psychiatric factitious disorder which is characterized by feigning disease, illness, or psychological trauma in order to draw attention or sympathy to oneself.

Introduction

The physical examination of persons with injuries that have been self-inflicted deliberately is a part of the routine work in clinical forensic medicine. The recognition of self-harm is of criminalistic importance when differentiating between assaults, accidents, suicidal, and other kinds of self-destructive behavior; the main categories are listed in **Table 1**. In cases of simulated offenses, early diagnosis prevents superfluous and inevitably unsuccessful investigations by the police and mystified worries by the public. In the context of this chapter, the chief stress is put on the medicolegal and criminalistic aspects of physical trau- matization by the victim himself or herself. Completed (fatal) suicides, nonaccidental poisonings, and self-induced bodily harm in psychiatric patients are dealt with in other chapters.

Simulation of Criminal Offenses

This group comprises self-inflicted injuries of individuals who claim to have been the victim of an assault. The bodily damage,

Table 1   Main categories of self-induced bodily harm

1. Simulation of a criminal offense:
   a. False rape allegation
   b. Feigned robbery or alleged attack for other fabricated reasons
2. Self-mutilation for the purpose of insurance fraud
3. Voluntary self-mutilation and/or malingering among soldiers and prisoners
4. Dermal artifacts, self-mutilation, and malingering in patients with personality disorders
5. Suicidal gestures, (attempted) suicide

therefore, is used as an alleged proof of a fictitious offense. The dramatic story told by the informant is often in obvious contrast to a uniform wound pattern (**Figure 1**) and a poor severity of the injuries so that the whole picture does not suggest a real struggle with the dynamics of a fight.

According to the literature, up to 20% of the sexual offenses reported to the police are fictitious. In false rape allegations, the informants frequently injure themselves in order to give support to their story. Women and girls, who falsely claim to have been raped, often live in a problematic situation or in conflict with their partners. The primary intention of the alleged victims is mostly to derive attention, or care and affection, but there are also some informants who accuse a definite person of having raped them for motives of hate or revenge.

Usually the self-inflicted injuries are caused with the help of pointed and/or cutting tools such as knives, razor blades, nail scissors, and broken glass. The resulting wounds are of a trivial nature, mostly consisting of superficial cuts or linear abrasions. The characteristics of a "classical" injury pattern are listed in **Table 2**. In typical cases, there is a multitude of equally shallow lesions, which are strikingly uniform in shape, often orientated in the same direction or in a crisscross manner. The cuts avoid especially sensitive areas like the eyes, lips, nipples, and geni- tals. They are mainly located on the frontal aspect of the trunk, on the face, the neck, the arms and hands, and sometimes on the lower limbs. Nevertheless, self-inflicted injuries may also be found on the back of the body as far as it is accessible for the alleged victim's hand or if the injuries have been caused with the assistance of another person (**Figure 2**). Often the relevant garments are either undamaged or the damage does not correspond to the skin lesions.

Some women who claim a fictitious sexual assault inflict blunt skin injuries on themselves: for instance, linear

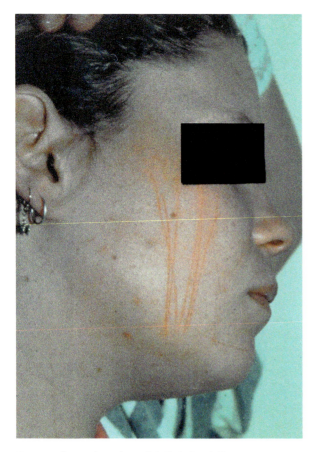

Figure 1   Group of mostly parallel skin lesions inflicted on the right cheek with nail scissors (a 23-year-old woman, who falsely claimed to have been the victim of a sexual assault; actually she wanted to arouse the attention of her unfaithful husband).

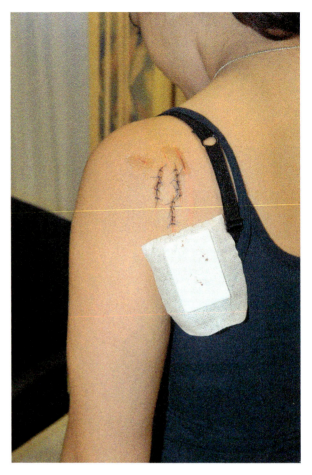

Figure 2   Unclothed left deltoid region of a 14-year-old girl who pretended to have been injured by an unknown aggressor on her way home from school. Note the presence of several mostly parallel, shallow cuts in a location easily reachable for the dominant right hand.

Table 2   Typical features of self-inflicted injuries fabricated to simulate a criminal offense

1. Infliction either by sharp/pointed instruments or by fingernails
2. Equally shallow, nonpenetrating cuts or fingernail abrasions (sometimes each of considerable length)
3. Multitude of individual lesions
4. Uniform shape, linear, or slightly curved course of the lesions
5. Grouped and/or parallel and/or crisscross arrangement
6. Symmetry or preference of the nondominant side of the body (usually the left)
7. Location in easily reachable body regions
8. Omission of especially sensitive body regions
9. No damage of the clothes or inconsistent damage
10. Lack of defense injuries
11. Additional presence of scars from former self-injurious behavior

excoriations produced by scratching with the person's own fingernails or by rubbing the skin against a rough surface. In rare cases, atypical findings such as contusions or singular cuts have been observed. As there are a few clinical reports on self-cutting after rape, the forensic expert has to be aware of uncommon self-destructive behavior, even in real victims with a posttraumatic stress disorder.

Apart from false rape allegations, there are some other categories of fictitious criminal offenses. Thus, an assault may be simulated and made credible by self-inflicted injuries in order to divert attention from the person's own theft or embezzlement. The authors have also seen several male "victims" who claimed to have been stabbed or cut by perpetrators because they wanted to arouse compassion and regain the affection of their wife or girlfriend (**Figure 3**). In the last 20 years, an increasing number of informants cut swastikas or

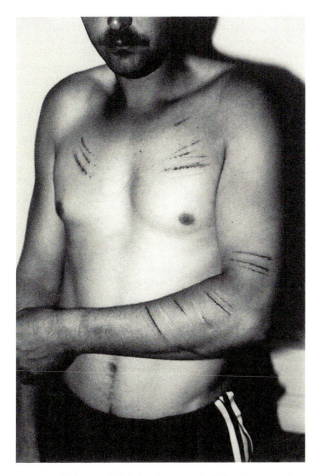

Figure 3 A 29-year-old right-handed man who inflicted cuts on his chest and left arm in order to gain the sympathy of his wife, who had engaged in an extramarital affair with her lover. Note the symmetric arrangement of the chest wounds, their parallelism, and uniformity. The whitish scars on the left forearm are due to former self-injurious episodes.

other Nazi symbols or words into their skin thus trying to gain sympathy as pretended victims of right-wing violence; if such incidents are covered in the media, they may be followed by an "endemic" series of copycat acts.

Another possible reason for claiming a feigned assault is dissimulation of an attempted, but not completed suicide (e.g., in cases of nonfatal wrist-cutting). Injuries from autoerotic manipulation may also be concealed by concocting a story of criminal victimization. False allegation of kidnapping in combination with self-injury has been made by young girls and boys in order to excuse absence without leave. From the criminalistic point of view, it has to be considered that perpetrators may inflict injuries on themselves in order to represent a homicide as permitted self-defense.

Self-Mutilation for the Purpose of Insurance Fraud

In this category of self-destructive behavior, an accident is simulated in a fraudulent attempt to obtain compensation from an insurance company. Usually the deliberate self-inflicted damage results in mutilation, that is, a substantial loss of a peripheral part of the body (mostly a finger or a hand). The instruments used for mutilation comprise sharp-edged tools such as axes, hatchets, meat cleavers and cutting machines, various kinds of motorized saws, and, less frequently, blunt objects such as presses or conveyor belts.

Voluntarily inflicted injuries from axe blows are mostly claimed to have been caused by a misplaced stroke of the axe when chopping wood. In typical cases, the thumb or index finger is cut off completely in a right angle to its axis resulting in an isolated proximal finger amputation. In contrast, an unintentional severance of the index finger is usually characterized

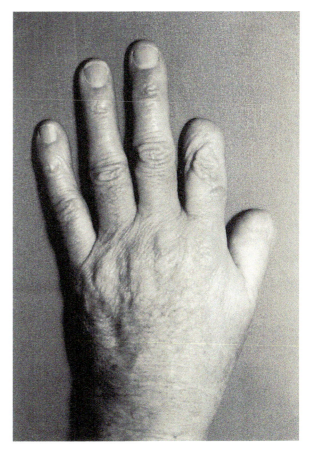

Figure 4 Left hand of a carpenter who injured himself accidentally when working with a milling machine. Note the oblique severance of the thumb and index finger. The distal phalanx of the middle finger was incompletely amputated and could be sewed on.

by accompanying injuries to the adjoining fingers. In authentic accidents, the amputation is often a distal and incomplete one, taking its course in an oblique angle to the finger's axis. The same is true for accidents with power saws or milling machines (**Figure 4**).

It has been justly stressed that in finger injuries from heavy axe blows, a complete amputation is to be expected only if the severed finger was lying on a solid base serving as a support. A proximal and complete amputation of the index finger without concomitant injuries of the neighboring fingers suggests a so-called "execution position," which is extremely suspect of intentional self-mutilation (**Figure 5**). In the recent past, a considerable number of physicians—the majority being males over 40 years of age who worked in the surgical field—have been convicted of defrauding insurance

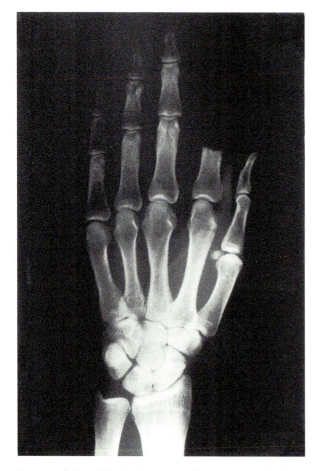

Figure 5 Self-mutilation for the purpose of insurance fraud. Radiograph of the left hand exhibiting a complete proximal amputation of the index finger at a right angle to its axis and without any injury to the adjoining fingers, allegedly caused by a misplaced stroke of the axe when chopping wood. Photograph by courtesy of Professor Barz.

companies by deliberately cutting off a finger, mostly the index finger of the nondominant left hand. Some reports have been published on cases in which members of medical professions applied a local anesthetic before injuring or mutilating themselves.

The proof of intentional self-infliction in cases of mutilation has been said to be one of the most difficult tasks in clinical forensic medicine. Apart from the medical aspects, some circumstantial indications may point to a possibly attempted insurance fraud: an insurance policy for inadequately high amounts taken out shortly before the injury occurs, a multiplicity of private accident insurance contracts, serious indebtedness of the policy holder, the absence of any witness, an inexplicable disappearance of the amputate, immediate tidying up of the scene, and removal of the biological traces. The presence of "tentative cuts" adjacent to the amputation cut can be a positive morphological indication of deliberate self-infliction. It is recommended that the expert's investigation should first focus on the medical findings concerning the injury (photographs, surgical report, radiographs, and physical examination) and on the course of the alleged accident as described and demonstrated by the mutilated victim. In addition, the external circumstances at the scene, the mechanical properties of the causative tool, the distribution of bloodstains, and other available pieces of evidence must be taken into consideration. Some experts have also carried out simulating experiments to reconstruct the alleged accident mechanism, which then turned out to be or not to be consistent with the injury in question.

Voluntary Self-Mutilation and/or Malingering among Prisoners and Soldiers

Autoaggressive behavior is a well-known problem in police custody and penal institutions. There may be different reasons for a prisoner to inflict injuries on himself: false allegations of having been physically maltreated by the police, the guard, or other inmates; the wish to be transferred to a hospital with less severe surveillance and increased chances of escape; as a correlate of a prisoner's low tolerance to stress. Common methods of self-harm under detention are cutting oneself with sharp instruments (for instance, a piece of glass, a razor blade, or a sheet iron), swallowing foreign bodies, and certain forms of malingering (voluntary provocation, aggravation, and protraction of disease by artificial means). Self-damage in prison covers a wide continuum ranging from amateurish tattooing and infliction of other skin lesions to life-threatening suicide attempts.

During war and sometimes even in peace time, soldiers may fabricate "accidental" injuries in order to avoid duty on the frontline or in the armed forces generally. The deliberately induced damage is intended to make the soldier unfit for military service (for example, because of traumatic amputation by shooting or cutting off fingers). Another kind of evading service aims at the pretense of sickness. By feigning a medical or psychiatric illness, the malingerer tries to get hospitalized or dismissed. Malingering comprises both the simulation of a nonexisting illness and the exaggeration/prolongation of an existing disease.

Artifacts in Patients with Psychic Disturbances or Mental Diseases

In neurotic patients, the main target of bodily harm is the skin, which may exhibit a great variety of lesions from scratching, pinching, squeezing, rubbing, and biting. The injuries are typically produced by the person's own fingernails, pointed/

edged instruments, or rough surfaces. If the skin damage extends to the corium, it will heal with scarring, and occasionally, pigmentation. The majority of neurotic excoriations are irregular in shape and located in easily reachable body regions, such as the chest and the lateral aspects of the face, arms, and thighs, often with preference of the nondominant side (**Figure 6**). The coexistence of fresh lesions and different stages of wound healing, including scars, hint at repeated episodes of self-injurious behavior.

If patients pretend to be unaware of the real origin of their skin artifacts, this phenomenon is called factitial dermatitis. The mysterious disease is intended to draw attention to the emotional suffering of the patient whose personality structure is characterized by strong intrapsychic tension, inhibited aggression, depressiveness, and low frustration tolerance. Psychological tests yield severe autoaggressive tendencies. The spectrum of skin lesions comprises scratches, ulcers, thermal and caustic burns (e.g., from cigarettes or acids) (**Figure 7**), hematomas, and many others. Self-manipulation should always be considered when symptoms persist for a very long time in spite of adequate therapy.

Munchausen syndrome is defined as a chronic factitious disorder with systemic malingering observed in adult patients who present themselves to physicians and hospitals with dramatic, but false stories of illness. In assuming the role of physically ill patients, they submit to unnecessary medical procedures including invasive, painful, and even dangerous treatment. The factitious diseases are made credible by complaining of symptoms such as abdominal pain, bleeding from body orifices, dermatological changes, and acute neurological manifestations. In contrast, Munchausen syndrome by proxy is a rare form of child abuse in which a parent or other carer,

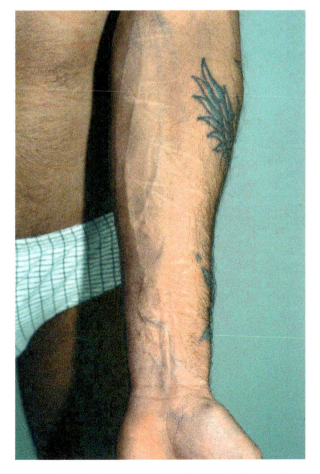

Figure 6 Multiple linear scars on the left forearm of a 31-year-old man with borderline personality disorder and many episodes of self-cutting.

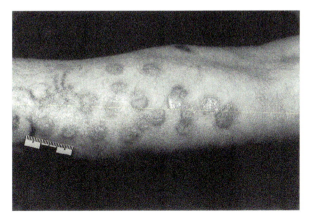

Figure 7 Multiple self-inflicted cigarette burns of equal age (1 day) on the left forearm of a 72-year-old psychiatric patient with paranoid ideas (main diagnosis: chronic alcoholism and cerebrovascular encephalopathy).

usually the mother, brings a child for medical assessment and care. The proxy either invents a false illness story or really induces an illness (e.g., by nonaccidental poisoning, smothering, or inflicting physical injuries on the child).

Some mentally retarded or disturbed children show special forms of self-destructive behavior such as lip biting, head bumping, and grinding of the teeth. Psychotic patients may be capable of mutilating themselves in a bizarre and painful manner so that the appearance of the injuries is often inconsistent with the outlined criteria of self-infliction. Thus, medicolegal literature reports on self-amputations (fingers, toes, scrotum, penis) and also on enucleation of an eye and severance of the tongue.

Attempted Suicide

An attempted suicide is an action performed with the stated intent of jeopardizing the person's own life. An individual, who in desperation gives the appearance of wishing to commit suicide, but lacks the real intention to do so, makes a "cry for help" or a "suicidal gesture." The methods of suicide attempts include the whole spectrum of intoxications and physical trauma: overdosed application of drugs, cutting and stabbing, jumping from heights or in front of a moving vehicle, gunshot injuries, electrocution, nonfatal asphyxia (**Figure 8**), burning, and jumping into water.

In the context of this chapter, only suicidal cutting and stabbing is discussed. Suicidal cuts are mostly inflicted by means of knives, razor blades, and other sharp-edged instruments. The flexor surfaces of the distal forearm, the cubital region, and the front of the neck are counted among the preferred "sites of election." The presence of linear scars may suggest previous attempts. Suicidal incisions are typically multiple, parallel, superficial, and arranged in groups. The shallow cuts, in particular, reflect the hesitant or tentative nature of the injuries (**Figure 9**).

In many suicide attempts, the individual abandons the method of cutting the wrists and/or throat after a few trial incisions and turns to another kind of self-destruction, which is expected to be more effective. In suicidal cuts of the wrists, the radial and ulnar arteries are severed only in rare cases. The left wrist is the most common target in right-handed persons, but about one-half of suicides cut both the left and the right wrist. In suicidal throat cuts, the incisions either pass obliquely across the front of the neck (for instance starting high on the left and ending at a lower level on the right) or the direction is rather a horizontal one. Again, numerous tentative cuts are regarded as a clue to self-infliction.

Suicidal stabbing is less frequent than cutting and usually confined to the precordial region and/or the neck. In both

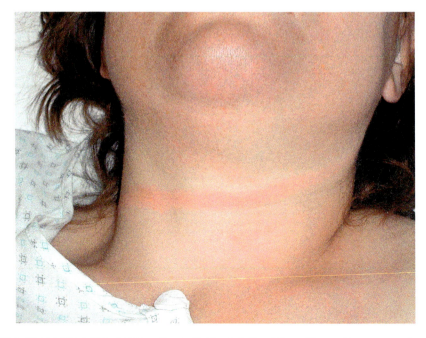

Figure 8   Survived attempt to commit suicide by hanging with an extension cord. The victim, a 39-year-old woman, was found with the buttocks supported on the floor. Due to incomplete suspension, only the weight of the upper part of the body contributed to the force exerted on the neck. Note the hyperemic hanging mark and the presence of multiple petechiae in the facial skin.

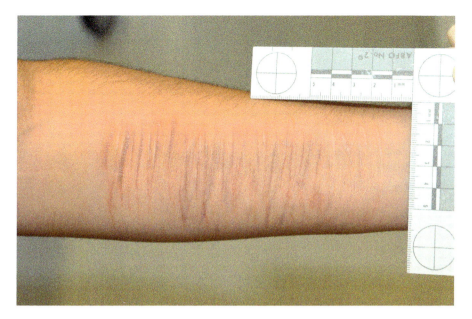

Figure 9 Left forearm of a young girl with dozens of linear scars from repeated self-cutting as suicidal gestures.

locations, the "classical" pattern is characterized by grouped stabs without concomitant damage of the covering clothes. The wound slits in the skin are often parallel with the pointed end (produced by the cutting edge of the blade) always being on the same side. Similar to suicidal cuts, the existence of multiple trial stabs is accepted as a hallmark of self-infliction.

See also: **Behavioral:** Forensic Psychiatry; **Forensic Medicine/ Causes of Death:** Sharp Trauma; **Forensic Medicine/Clinical:** Clinical Forensic Medicine—Overview.

Further Reading

Bonte, W., 2004. Versicherungsbetrug. In: Brinkmann, B., Madea, B. (Eds.), Handbuch gerichtliche Medizin, vol. 1. Springer, Berlin, pp. 1215–1230.

Crane, J., 2009. Injury. In: McLay, W.D.S. (Ed.), Clinical Forensic Medicine. Cambridge University Press, Cambridge, pp. 99–114.

Faller-Marquardt, M., Ropohl, D., Pollak, S., 1995. Excoriations and contusions of the skin as artefacts in fictitious sexual offences. Journal of Clinical Forensic Medicine 2, 129–135.

Faller-Marquardt, M., Pollak, S., 2006. Self-inflicted injuries with negative political overtones. Forensic Science International 159, 226–229.

Karger, B., DuChesne, A., Ortmann, C., Brinkmann, B., 1997. Unusual self-inflicted injuries simulating a criminal offence. International Journal of Legal Medicine 110, 267–272.

Mydlo, J.H., Macchia, R.J., Kanter, J.L., 1997. Munchausen's syndrome: a medico-legal dilemma. Medicine, Science, and the Law 37, 198–201.

Payne-James, J., 2003. Assault and injury in the living. In: Payne-James, J., Busuttil, A., Smock, W. (Eds.), Forensic Medicine: Clinical and Pathological Aspects. Greenwich Medical Media, London, pp. 543–563.

Payne-James, J., 2005. Deliberate self-harm, patterns. In: Payne-James, J., Byard, R.W., Corey, T.S., Henderson, C. (Eds.), Encyclopedia of Forensic and Legal Medicine, vol. 2. Elsevier, Oxford, pp. 153–158.

Pollak, S., 2004. Vortäuschung einer Straftat. In: Brinkmann, B., Madea, B. (Eds.), Handbuch gerichtliche Medizin, vol. 1. Springer, Berlin, pp. 1230–1238.

Pollak, S., Saukko, P.J., 2003. Atlas of Forensic Medicine. CD-ROM. Elsevier, Amsterdam (Chapter 19.3).

Pollak, S., Saukko, P.J., 2009. Wounds: sharp injury. In: Jamieson, A., Moenssens, A. (Eds.), Wiley Encyclopedia of Forensic Science. Wiley & Sons, Chichester, pp. 2646–2660.

Saukko, P., Knight, B., 2004. Knight's Forensic Pathology, third ed. Arnold, London, pp. 235–244.

Torture

H Vogel, University Hospital Eppendorf, Hamburg, Germany

Introduction

The definition of torture varies depending on the source of the definition and the political or social agenda of the organization that created the definition. Encyclopedias, governments, international organizations, and nongovernmental organizations (NGOs) commonly have different definitions for torture: for instance, the *Encyclopedia Britannica*, Wikipedia, the World Medical Association, Amnesty International (AI), and state governments may have strikingly different definitions of torture. In spite of the differences between these definitions, however, the existence of torture, and its coexistence with and dependence on violence are generally accepted facts. Torture is particularly dangerous because it is difficult to control: the application of physical or psychological violence for the purpose of torture often creates a dynamic of its own, causing the procedure to gain its own momentum and separating the torture from the original intent. In other words, the torture will be committed for its own sake, rather than for the sake of eliciting information. Furthermore, torture is typically inflicted by, at the instigation of, or with the consent or acquiescence of, a public official or other person in authority. Therefore, perpetrators of torture are often attached to government bodies or to others who exercise power, such as organized criminal groups or insurgents. The association of torture with persons of authority may decrease the likelihood that the victims receive appropriate medical care in the aftermath of the torture, particularly in the acute phase. Because torture often requires the services of health professionals and legal professionals, it raises (additional?) ethical conflicts.

Because intelligence is required to win wars, and torture is sometimes viewed as an acceptable and expeditious method for eliciting intelligence, torture may be practised by governments and opposition groups, such as terrorist and insurgent groups, in times of war. Governments may also use torture to obtain information about planned or committed crimes; for example, in an attempt to prevent a terrorist attack. Government officials may argue that torture is justified when:

- Regulated by law
- The laws governing torture have been established by democratically elected officials
- The laws governing torture are applied by democratically elected governments

Waterboarding is a recent example of government use of a practice that is widely believed to be a torture technique. Waterboarding was considered acceptable and used by the administration of US President George W. Bush for the purpose of interrogating suspected al-Qa'ida members following the 9/11 attacks. Use of waterboarding has been condemned by many NGOs, including AI.

Torture is an age-old activity that has become more sophisticated with the passage of time. It is usually carried out clandestinely, and there is often a deliberate attempt to reduce any physical evidence of its practice. Therefore, documentation of such abuse is usually difficult to find; in the absence of physical evidence at the time of examination, accounts of torture are often based solely on historical reports. Typically, most torture is carried out in the early stages of the victims' confinement. If the torture is not initially fatal, the physical signs of torture have typically healed by the time the victim is released.

Victims who survive torture have usually been less severely tortured than those who died. Victims who have escaped from torture and come to the attention of rehabilitation centers in Europe, America, and elsewhere are presumably less severely tortured than those victims who were unable to escape. Torture that results in mutilation increases the probability that the victim will die. Victims who have been stabbed in the trunk (wounds that are oftentimes followed by pleurisy and peritonitis) survive less often than those who have been wounded only in their extremities.

Documentation of torture employs similar procedures, techniques, and modalities as are employed in the investigation of other forms of abuse. These procedures, and the equipment necessary to properly implement them, are usually scarce in countries where torture is common. This is the case in times of peace or war.

These circumstances influence any description of torture and the possibilities as well as opportunities to prove that torture has occurred.

Forms

A majority of torture methods have been in practice for many years. It is common for aggressors to invent new names for old procedures in order to make the torture technique seem less harmful, so that the technique is more acceptable to the public. Variations on existing methods and new methods have been developed in order to make it impossible to prove torture through physical examinations.

If physical findings of torture are present, the differential diagnosis must include other forms of physical damage, such as that caused by the following:

- abuse/maltreatment
- accidents, self-inflicted injuries
- initiation rites
- diseases

Torture methods may be used on all parts of the body, including the hand and arm, foot and leg, trunk (including genital organs), and head and neck. Special torture procedures are used on fingers, hands, and arms. Torture procedures include the following:

- Postural torture
- Stabbing and cutting of any part of the body
- Finger, hand, and arm
- Toe, foot, and leg
- Compression injuries
- Petite guillotine
- Water torture
  - Submersion
  - Deprivation
  - Forced ingestion
- Electric torture
- Psychological torture methods
- Noise, music, light, cold, etc.

Combinations of the techniques listed above are frequent.

Fingers

Torture involving the fingers is quite common and may produce reversible or permanent anatomical alterations. The effects of a variety of techniques can be seen in rehabilitation centers for torture victims.

Foreign bodies: When fingers are injured with needles or other sharp instruments, foreign bodies (pieces of those instruments) may become permanently lodged in the fingers. The introduction of needles, wires, or wooden splinters beneath the fingernails is widespread. These foreign bodies are often directed to the distal interphalangeal joint or even beyond. When retracted, splinters or other fragments may remain and be radiographically detectable (**Figure 1(a)–(c)**).

Fingernails: In South America and elsewhere, the extraction of fingernails has been practised; this procedure, however, has reversible effects.

Loss of fingers and toes: Compression of digits by finger, thumb, and toe screws has been applied since medieval times. Bone damage may be minor (**Figure 3**) or major and lead to complete loss of a phalanx. Less severe mechanical compression injuries are inflicted by stomping or striking with rifle butts or other objects. Fingers can also be lost (**Figure 2(a) and (b)**) or severely damaged by direct violence or by neurovascular loss as a result of squeezing. Squeezing can be accomplished by placing a stick between the fingers and then compressing them against each other in order to damage nerves and vessels without leaving visible traces.

Petite guillotine: Using this device, the fingers, or parts of fingers, can be cut off in succession (**Figure 3**). The petite guillotine was developed in Iran during the times of the Shah and persists to present times.

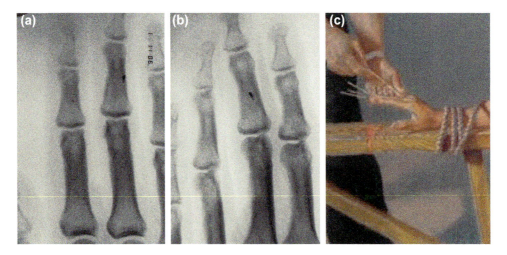

Figure 1   (a–c) Metallic foreign body left in soft tissues of the middle phalanx of the second and third fingers. During torture, needles or wires were introduced underneath the fingernails. Splinters remained after they were withdrawn.

(a)   **(b)**

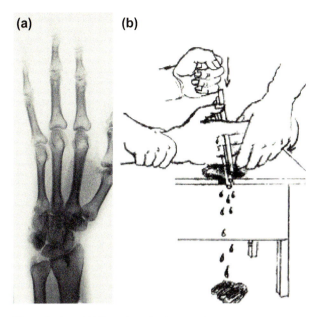

Figure 2   (a and b) Finger loss due to squeezing.

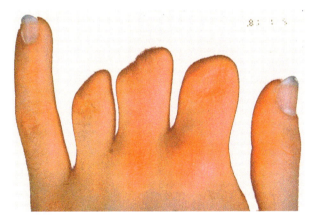

Figure 3   The guards of the Islamic Revolution imprisoned this 14-year-old girl. Parts of her fingers were cut off in the prison with the petite guillotine.

Suspension: Suspension on one or several fingers is reported from the Kurdish territories in the Arabic peninsula and in the neighboring countries. Suspension on fingers is an old method that has been in use since medieval times, for example, as punishment on sailing ships. It induces necrosis and loss of the finger. The thumb seems to be the preferred finger, perhaps for anatomical reasons (**Figure 4(a) and (b)**) and because of its major functional importance.

(a)   **(b)**

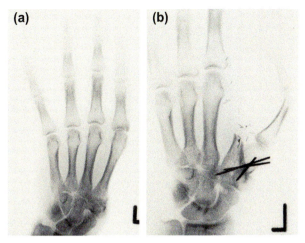

Figure 4   (a and b) Loss of thumb due to suspension (Kurd). This image from a hospital in Berlin shows how the fifth finger replaces the lost thumb.

Hands and Arms

Amputation: During the civil war in Sierra Leone, the hands of possible voters were cut off to prevent them from voting, as painting the fingers of individuals after they had voted controlled the national vote. Cutting off hands and feet of perpetrators of certain crimes is prescribed by Shari-ah, the law of the Koran. This punishment is applied in several Islamic countries where the Shari-ah is the official law.

Defensive fractures: The fracture of the forearm is a typical injury of defense. Persons instinctively or intentionally try to protect their head when under attack. A nightstick may fracture the ulna alone or the ulna together with the radius (**Figure 5**).

Mutilation: In Zaire, fractures of the hands and wrists are seen in journalists, writers, and artists (**Figure 6**). The aim is not only to hamper the victim's work, but also to cause functional injury by mutilating the part of the body that is the victim's main instrument of livelihood.

Fire: Scars from serious burns can cause contractures and deformation. Torture by fire has been reported in Africa.

Postural torture: This can be accomplished by requiring the victim to maintain a certain awkward (and even physiologic) posture for long periods of time, by binding the victim in various awkward and painful positions, or by suspension of the victim. Victims are sometimes suspended by the arms, which are bent backward with upward traction applied. Other forms bind the hands and feet together at the back (**Figure 7**).

Often, postural torture is applied with the intention to avoid evidence of the abuse. **Figure 8** depicts common forms of postural torture and suspension from South America.

Having been imprisoned in a cage less high than the prisoner's height is reported from Kurds, Chinese, and Chileans.

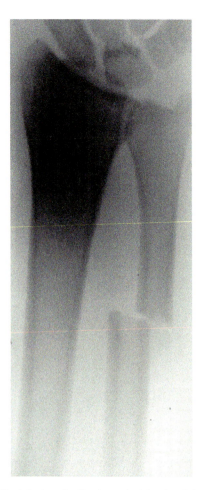

Figure 5 Fresh fracture (fending fracture) of the ulna. Defensive injuries sustained during beating.

"Uncomfortable" positions can be easily enforced. Torture methods used in the "Abu Ghreib" prison in Iraq forced prisoners to maintain similar or identical positions, according to photographic evidence.

Foot and Leg

Feet and legs are common targets of torture; some techniques are fairly specific to geographic regions. Imaging may show typical or even characteristic findings; examples are falaka and palmatoria.

Falaka: Falaka is a widespread form of torture, sometimes known as falanga and in Spanish-speaking areas as bastinado. Falaka means beating the foot, primarily (but not exclusively) on the sole of the foot. Falaka is perpetrated in the Middle East (especially in Turkey and Iraq), in the Far East, and in some

(a) **(b)**

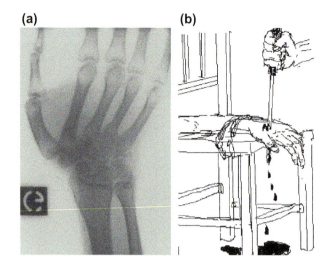

Figure 6 Crushed wrist of a journalist (Zaire).

(a) **(b)**

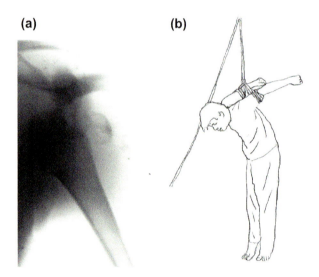

Figure 7 Dislocation of the glenohumeral joint: glenoid process of scapula, humeral head, Hill–Sachs lesion in proximal humerus. Suspension by the elbows, the arms bent backward. With such a suspension, dislocation of the shoulders is less common.

Spanish-speaking areas. Falaka produces edema; hematoma; fractures and injuries to the ligaments, tendons, fascia, and aponeurosis of the feet and ankle (**Figure 9(a)–(d)**). Shortly after torture, the clinical findings alone are usually diagnostic. Radiography can confirm or exclude fractures and allow estimation of the time interval since torture was applied.

In the author's experience, these beatings may fracture the toes, the metatarsals, the tarsals (especially the calcaneus), and occasionally the ankle. This is especially the case if the feet were

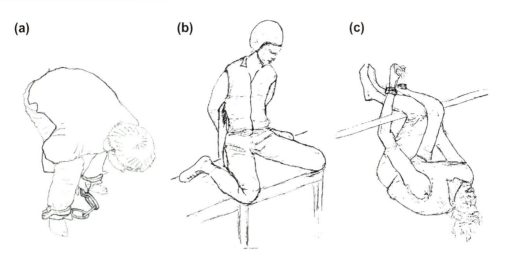

Figure 8   Common forms of postural torture, which hardly leave evidence, could be demonstrated by diagnostic imaging: "Il moto" (middle) and "la barra" on the right.

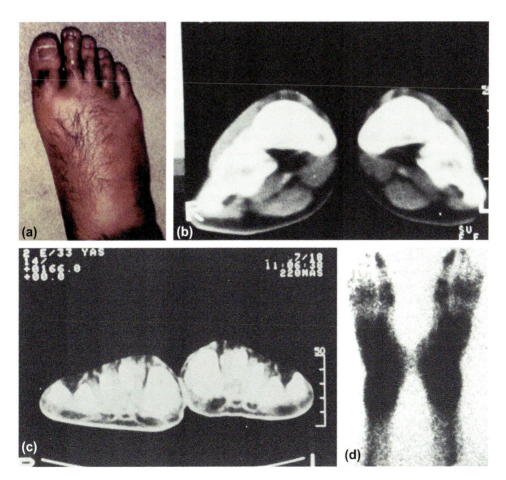

Figure 9   (a) Falaka. (b) Photograph of a foot after falaka. (c) CT, top: edema and hematoma, predominately plantar after falaka; below: chronic change after falaka, splay and flatfoot deformation due to relaxed ligaments and aponeurosis. (d) Scintigraphy: very high uptake in feet, several weeks after falaka.

fixed during the beating. Fractures of the lateral malleolus seem to be an exception; nevertheless, the lower leg near the ankle may be involved. Scintigraphy initially shows increased soft tissue activity after the beating (**Figure 9(d)**). Later, a generalized increased bony uptake with unusual degenerative changes may be found. When available, magnetic resonance imaging (MRI) is better than computed tomography (CT) in visualizing alterations of soft tissues including capsular thickening, atrophy, edema, and reparative changes. Later studies may prove earlier torture by demonstrating a thickened aponeurosis of the foot. MRI can also show bone bruises or edema.

Palmatoria: Palmatoria is an example of a method of localized torture that is virtually unique to a specific region——the small West African country of Guinea-Bissau. Palmatoria involves repetitive blows to the shin where the tibia lies closest to the skin. Radiographic examination may show periosteal reaction from subperiosteal hemorrhage and hematoma. Laminar or onionskin periostitis can persist for weeks or even years. Somewhat peculiar endosteal and medullary changes may be seen as well. Two case reports have shown that blows to this area of the tibia, using a rod, can produce a hidden endosteal fracture, which is likely to be undetected on plain films but obvious on CT. It is possible, and perhaps even likely, that some of the African cases would show similar findings, had more sophisticated imaging modality been applied.

Compression: Compression of digits by toe screws has been applied in Iran (**Figure 10(a) and (b)**). Bony damage can be of various degrees, and complete loss of a phalanx or an entire digit may occur. Mutilation is a possible consequence.

Foreign bodies: Corresponding to torture methods used on fingers and hands, foreign bodies are also introduced into the toes, often under the toenails (**Figure 1(a)–(c)**) and into the feet. Radiography might find remaining splinters.

Toenails: Like fingernails, toenails may be extracted.

Extreme cold: Exposure to low temperatures may result in frostbite or even frozen-off toes.

Kneecapping: Kneecapping is a term originally used to describe a gunshot wound in the knee, usually by a handgun, in order to permanently maim or cripple the victim. In America, it has been mostly associated with gang warfare. In recent years, it has been seen during the civil strife in Northern Ireland. It is not certain as to which country is the importer and which the exporter. Kneecapping is no longer limited to the knee; other joints, particularly the ankle and elbow, are also targeted. In one known extreme case, both knees, both ankles, and both elbows were shot. Occasionally, other parts of the leg are involved. Radiographs can easily document the extent of injury

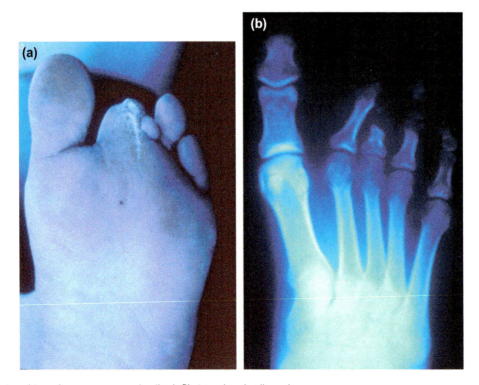

Figure 10   Destroyed toes after screw compression (Iran). Photograph and radiograph.

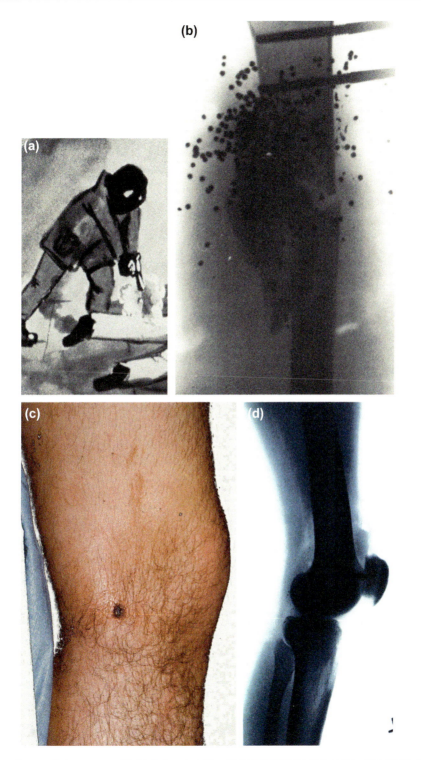

Figure 11   (a–d) Kneecapping, employing weapons. Shot into the upper leg with lead shot. Shot into the knee with a handgun. The projectile remains in the knee.

and frequently disclose the bullet path, trajectory of fire, and location of the bullet. Bullets are frequently found in situ, as low-velocity weapons are often employed. Arterial damage is not uncommon, and angiography is frequently employed (**Figure 11(a)–(d)**).

Fire: Another famous incident of torture happened to Cuauhtémoc, the last king of the Aztecs, whose feet were burnt to mutilation on October 15, 1521, by Hernàn Cortés.

Head

Torture applied to the head is often fatal, a consequence that is usually accepted or even intended by the torturers when they use such techniques.

Stabbing: Only a few cases of this typically lethal wound have been documented (**Figure 12(a) and (b)**).

Beating: Beating the head may fracture the bones and cause intracranial bleeding. Teeth are often broken or dislocated during beating. These may be extracted or drilled as a form of pain induction. These injuries, of course, can be demonstrated by direct inspection as well as by radiography. In Chad, an uncommon form of torture involves a prisoner being beaten in the face producing fractures of the facial bones that can be demonstrated radiologically. Opacification of the maxillary

sinuses is regularly seen due to bleeding, and subsequently sinusitis may develop.

Shaking: In the Middle East, the technique of violently shaking the suspect's upper torso is used. Occasionally, this may produce intracranial lesions much like those in the shaken baby syndrome. In Israel, the Supreme Court has outlawed this practice.

Neck

Strangulation: Strangulation as a special form of suffocation is employed worldwide, either for tormenting or for outright killing. Fracture of the larynx may be seen. Some European states have employed strangulation as one form of capital punishment. In Spain, the Garrotte was used for executions under Franco.

Trunk

Beating: Few specific injuries will be detected from generalized beating because, as pointed out, soft tissue and bony injury usually heal by the time the victim comes to sympathetic medical attention. Residual deformities of rib and spinal fractures may be present, as may be deformities due to ligamentous

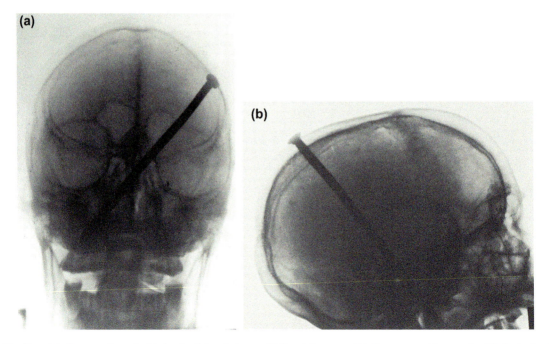

Figure 12   The original comment was "nail in head, witchcraft, deceased." The victim was said to be possessed by an evil spirit; the healer chose to liberate his patient from this evil by putting a nail into his head. The victim died after some days in hospital. Today, the author thinks this was a "medical killing" ("ritual murder") scheme, and that the killing was part of a magic procedure (Africa).

tears or ruptures. Scintigraphy (**Figure 13**) shows increased bone metabolism up to 2 years after the beating, and may indicate a pattern of the beating.

Stabbing: Stabbing in the trunk carries a high risk of injury to vital organs, with a consequent high probability of lethal infection. Therefore, this method is less seen and reported. In South Africa, gangs have been hunting young women to torture them by introducing bicycle spokes into the umbilicus. A variant of this was stabbing into the spine with the intent to produce paraplegia. When stabbing occurs, fragments of the weapon or foreign bodies may remain and can be documented by a radiological method (**Figure 14**).

Injection: In former East Germany, a young man on his way to a discotheque was attacked by a gang and rendered unconscious. Upon being brought to the hospital, it was discovered that mercury had been injected into his chest wall.

Fractures: Rib fractures are common. Scintigraphically, they may be especially helpful to show the pattern of beating. Less known is the fracture due to compressing of chest or the pelvis.

Anus and genitals: Violence is often directed at genital organs (**Figure 15**). Hours after the abuse, scintigraphy may show an

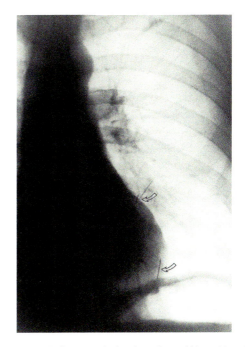

Figure 14 Needle fragments in the chest after stabbing with multiple needles.

increased activity at the site of the injury. Diagnostic imaging can document some of the consequences, for example, remaining foreign bodies after sexual torture. Some injuries associated with perforation will often provoke death before diagnostic imaging is done. Stabbing into the anus is sometimes performed to make the victim suffer before death and/or to hide the killing from the public.

Sexual abuse of women, including female circumcision, is well known; however, violation of men is reported less often. A famous case is that of Mugabe, current president of Zimbabwe, who was violated in his youth. In Abu Ghraib, male prisoners were forced to perform sex acts on each other.

Electric Torture

Electricity as an instrument of torture can be used in multiple ways. In the Middle East, it is common to place the electrode between the toes, on the tongue, on the teeth, or on the penis. The location between the toes and on the tongue is chosen in order to hide the place of entrance of the electric current. The placement on the penis is selected not only to inflict pain but also to humiliate. In Africa, electrodes are placed on the teeth. In the Middle East, large electrodes are used on wet skin, and collar-like electrodes are placed on the neck. Electric current induces muscle contractions, which may result in outright bone

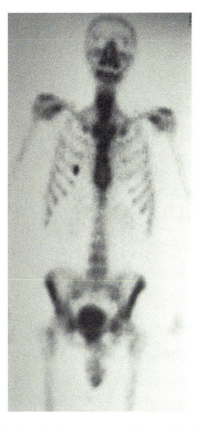

Figure 13 Beating. Scintigraphy. Increased bone metabolism in the anterior part of a rib on the right side of the victim due to beating.

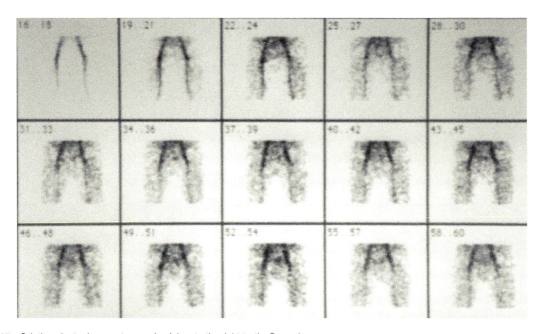

Figure 15   Scintigraphy to document squeezing injury to the right testis. Dynamic scan.

fractures and/or soft tissue injuries, with subsequent later degenerative bone or joint changes. Electroshock may produce compression fractures of the vertebrae. Grand mal seizures may cause high thoracic vertebral fractures. Moreover, teeth can be lost and jaws broken.

For proving electric torture, local incision and microscopic evaluation may show characteristic necrosis, which is accepted as evidence by judges in Turkey. If the victims were immediately available, torture by electricity could probably be confirmed by MRI, such as the findings of high signal alterations on MRI examination of the chest in (normal, not tortured) patients undergoing cardioversion have indicated.

Water submersion: In submersion, often called "submarine," the victim's head is forced underwater until near drowning. The water is often polluted with excrement. Aspiration is virtually inevitable and the subsequent radiography changes may vary from pulmonary edema to extensive pneumonia. The latter may result in residual pulmonary scarring and adhesions. The findings are nonspecific, however.

Water deprivation: Deprivation of water can be an effective, even deadly, form of torture.

Water ingestion: Victims from Chad, Africa, have reported that they were bound with their arms behind them, then forced to ingest several liters of water within a very short time. Thereafter, they were thrown, or caused to fall, from a height of several meters to land on their anterior chest and abdomen, with the aim of visceral rupture. One survivor was found to have a diaphragmatic hernia that might have been induced by this forced trauma.

Waterboarding: In this technique, a cloth or plastic wrap is placed over or in the person's mouth, and water is poured on to the person's head. In 2005, waterboarding was characterized as a "professional interrogation technique" by former CIA director Porter J. Goss; however, CIA officers who have subjected themselves to the technique lasted an average of 14 s before capitulating. There is a real risk of death from drowning, suffering a heart attack, or damage to the lungs from inhalation of water. Long-term effects include panic attacks, depression, and posttraumatic stress disorder.

Psychological Torture

Execution/Russian roulette/pretended execution: Victims of torture may be forced to assist in the execution and the torture of others. Not only do they see what they have to expect when it is their turn to be tortured, but they are often compelled to torture or kill a companion, friend, or relative. They may also be subjected to their own fake execution or forced to engage in Russian roulette.

Music/noise: Music may also be used for psychological torture. In nearly every German concentration camp, the SS forced victims to join orchestras that played military marches, folk songs, and popular songs, making the musicians feel as though they had joined forces with the SS; many of them committed suicide. Being exposed to loud or offensive music can break the victim's personality and give torturers absolute control.

Diagnosis and Differential Diagnosis

Torture can be classified as somatic, (bio)chemical (pharmacological), and psychological. However, multiple forms of somatic torture are designed and applied in a manner so as to avoid distinctive evidence by subsequent visual or radiologic inspection. Some techniques produce changes that can be depicted by imaging. In general, psychological and pharmacological torture does not lend itself to radiologic discovery; it seems possible, however, that, in the near future, functional MRI will be able to evidence findings which are characteristic for pharmacological torture and, in consequence will allow proving it. Diffusion tensor imaging (DTI) offers a promising approach: DTI can show damages of axons which are not visible on conventional MRI.

Physical and psychological examination is the basis of the investigation, and diagnostic imaging may contribute in certain cases. The findings have to be combined with the person's history and the cultural background of the case. There are regional differences in the design and infliction of torture and mistreatment throughout the world, and, unfortunately, new forms of torture are constantly being invented. The plausibility of the individual's history—specifically, the pattern of the inflicted physical and psychological violence—should be examined. These data are to be compared with what is known about the region, the time, and the forces/organizations which are said to have been involved in the torture. Diagnostic imaging sometimes allows visualizing a pattern and gives an approximation of the time passed. It is recommended to consider other causes of presumed torture trauma, such as accidents, crimes, local customs, and initiation rites, all of which may produce the same effects. Self-flagellation practiced by Shiites during the Ashura festival may serve as example: young men beat themselves on the back with multiple blades, resulting in bleeding, and the healing produces scars that should not be attributed to beating inflicted by others.

Ethics

Most medical organizations state that participating in torture is against medical ethics. However, physicians and other medical professions have been called upon to assist and/or supervise torture, provide expertise in rendering torture methods more effectively, help in covering up consequences of torture, or modify (falsify) a forensic certificate. A conflict is also apparent when a physician is called upon to provide medical care for a person who has been tortured, remains in custody, and will be tortured again. Leopara and Millum, both activists with Médecins sans Frontières, discuss this problem and conclude: "If a tortured patient demands medical care, the physician should accept some form and degree of complicity in torture in order to assist the tortured patient. Three main factors should guide a doctor's decision in such circumstances: the expected consequences of the doctor's actions, the wishes of the patient, and the extent of the doctor's complicity with wrongdoing."

Conclusion

While objectivity is required, one must also constantly bear in mind that the case is not merely theoretical, but actually concerns a real human being. Much of the evidence comes from worldwide centers of rehabilitation for torture victims. Imaging sometimes depicts lesions so characteristic that they can be considered legal proof of previous torture and verify a presumed victim's claims.

Criteria that support claims of torture are as follow:

- Correlation between the type of torture and the findings derived from imaging procedures
- Correlation between the date of torture and the imaging appearance of the lesion
- Specific alterations, such as the periosteal reactions from palmatoria
- Correlating findings in a particular situation, such as imprisonment and nutritional deficiencies or sequelae from denial of treatment or surgery
- Patterns of beatings (proven by imaging) typical for a particular geographic location and corresponding with the victim's story

> *See also:* **Forensic Medicine/Causes of Death:** Strangulation; **Forensic Medicine/Clinical:** Electrocution and Lightning Strike.

Further Reading

Aerzteblatt.de, 2011. Schädel-Hirn-trauma: Verbessertes MRT zeigt mehr Verletzungen. http://www.aerzteblatt.de/nachrichten/46118/ (retrieved 18 August 2011; 18:06).

Bauer, J., 2011. Musik im Konzentrationslager Sachsenhausen. http://www.gedenkstaettenforum.de/nc/gedenkstaetten-rundbrief/rundbrief/news/juliane_brauer_musik_im_konzentrationslager_sachsenhausen/ (retrieved 18 August 2011; 17:37).

Brogdon, B.G., 1998. Forensic Radiology. CRC Press, Boca Raton, FL (Chapter 17).

Brogdon, B.G., Crotty, J.M., 1999. The hidden divot: a new type of incomplete fracture? American Journal of Roentgenology 172, 789.

Bro-Rasmussen, F., Henriksen, O.B., Rasmussen, O., et al., 1982. Aseptic necrosis of bone following falanga torture. Ugeskrift for Laeger 144, 1165.

Falaka, 2012. Images. http://www.google.de/search?tbm=isch&hl=de&source=hp&biw=729&bih=1240&q=abu+ghraib&gbv=2&oq=Abu&aq=5&aqi=g10&aql=&gs_sm=c&gs_upl=4427l5074l0l9340l3l3l0l0l0l0l159l349l2. 1l3l0#hl=de&gbv=2&tbm=isch&sa=1&q=Falaka&pbx=1&oq=Falaka&aq=f&aqi=&aql=&gs_sm=e&gs_upl=267241l271063l0l273615l6l6l0l1l0l0l253l865l1.3.1l5l0&bav=on.2,or.r_gc.r_pw. &fp=bfe0aa86fbc4cb55&biw=729&bih=1240 (retrieved 17 August 2011; 14:24).

Forschergruppe: Musik, Konflikt und der Staat, 2011a. http://www.uni-goettingen.de/de/207622.html (retrieved 18 August 2011; 16:55).

Forschergruppe: Musik, Konflikt und der Staat, 2011b. Newsletter Nr. 8 vom 08.06.2011. http://www.uni-goettingen.de/de/217724.html (retrieved 18 August 2011; 17:10).

Gaessner, S., Gurris, N., Pross, C. (Eds.), 2001. At the Side of Torture Survivors. Johns Hopkins University Press, Baltimore, MD.

Genefke, I.K., 1986. Torturen I verden: Den angar os alle. Hans Reizels Forlag, Copenhagen, pp. 1–27.

Ghraib, 2012. Images. http://www.google.de/search?tbm=isch&hl=de&source=hp&biw=729 &bih=1240&q=abu+ghraib&gbv=2&oq=Abu&aq=5&aqi=g10 &aql=&gs_sm=c&gs_upl=4427l5074l0l9340l3l3l0l0l0l0l159l349l2.1l3l0 (retrieved 17 August 2011; 14:20).

Hayes, E., 1997. MRI illustrates history of torture. Diagnostic Imaging Europe 13, 17.

Hulverscheidt, M., 2011. Weibliche Genitalverstümmelung und ihre folgen. Konsequenzen für reisemedizinische Beratung. Flugmedizin ropenmedizin Reisemedizin 18 (4), 182–187.

Iacopino, V., Heiser, M., Pishever, S., Kirschner, R.H., 1996. Physician complicity in misrepresentation and omission of evidence of torture in postdetention medical examinations in Turkey. Journal of the American Medical Association 276, 396.

Jensen, T.S., Genefke, I.K., Hyldebrandt, N., Pedersen, H., Petersen, D., Weile, B., 1982. Cerebral atrophy in young torture victims. New England Journal of Medicine 307, 1334.

Leopara, C.H., Millum, J., 2011a. Should a Doctor Be Complicit with Torture. http://www.du.edu/korbel/news/2010/11/Chiara_Lepora_FSO.html (retrieved 11 August 2011; 12:40).

Leopara, C.H., Millum, J., 2011b. The tortured patient. A medical dilemma. Hastings Center Report 41 (3), 38–47. http://www.medscape.com/viewarticle/742725.

Lök, V., 1994. Oral communication. In: International Torture Meeting, Istanbul.

Lök, V., Tunca, M., Kumanlioglu, K., Kapkin, E., Dirik, G., 1991. Bone scintigraphy as clue to previous torture. Lancet 337, 846.

Moreno, A., Grodin, M.A., 2000. The not-so-silent marks of torture. Journal of the American Medical Association 284, 538.

Özkalipci, Ö., Sahin, Ü., Baykal, T., et al., 2007. Iskence Atlasi – Iskencenin tibbi olarak belgelendirilmesinde muayene ve tanisal inceleme sonuclarinin kullanilmasi. Türkiye insan Haklari Vakfi.

Petrow, P., Page, P., Vanel, D., 2001. The hidden divot fracture: Brogdon's fracture, a new type of incomplete fracture. American Journal of Roentgenology 177, 946.

Sidel, V.W., 1996. Commentary: the social responsibilities of health professionals: lessons from their role in Nazi Germany. Journal of the American Medical Association 276, 1679.

Skylv, G., 1997. Falanga: diagnosis and treatment of late sequellae. Torture (Suppl. 1994).

Sonteg, D., 1991. A Strike Against Brutality, Mobile Register, 9 Sept. 1.

Stem.de, 2011. Musik als Folter. Die 'Greatest Hits' von Guantanamo. http://www.stern.de/politik/ausland/musik-als-folter-die-greatest-hits-von-guantanamo-648547.html (retrieved 18 August 2011; 17:58).

Vogel, H., 2003. Torture. In: Brogdon, B.G., Vogel, H., McDowell, J.D. (Eds.), A Radiologic Atlas of Abuse, Torture, Terrorism, and Inflicted Trauma. CRC Press, Boca Raton, FL, pp. 105–124.

Wikipedia, 2011a. List of Methods of Torture. http://en.wikipedia.org/wiki/List_of_torture_methods_and_devices (retrieved 24 June 2011; 9:23h).

Wikipedia, 2011b. Female Genital Mutilation. http://en.wikipedia.org/wiki/Female_genital_mutilation.

Wikipedia, 2011c. Waterborarding. http://en.wikipedia.org/wiki/Waterboarding (retrieved 24 June 2011; 9:51h).

World Medical Association, 1994. The Declaration of Tokyo, 1975. Ethical Codes and Declarations Relevant to the Health Professions. Amnesty International, New York, p. 9.

Traffic Injuries and Deaths

M Graw and J Adamec, Institute of Legal Medicine, Munich, Germany

Road Traffic

Epidemiology

Traffic accidents are a very common cause of injury or even death (one of the leading causes of death in young adults) and as such are of high forensic relevance. The vast majority of deaths and injuries result from road traffic. In 2009, the number of accident victims and injured persons exceeded 33 000 and 2 200 000 in the United States; in the European Union, more than 35 000 persons died and 1 700 000 sustained nonfatal injuries in traffic accidents. WHO reports that approximately 1 300 000 people die each year worldwide and another 20–50 million are injured. According to the WHO statistics, low-income and middle-income countries have significantly higher road traffic fatality rates than high-income countries (the fatality rate in high-income countries is approximately 10 per 100 000 persons, in low-income countries twice as much).

Of the above-reported US fatalities, 72% were car occupants (52% drivers and 20% passengers), 13% motorcyclists, 12% pedestrian, and 2% cyclists; similar percentages have been reported in Europe. According to WHO estimates, the proportion of vulnerable road users among the fatalities is higher in low-income countries, so that globally almost half of those who die in road traffic crashes are pedestrians, cyclists, or riders—motorized two-wheelers. The numbers of fatalities are decreasing in most industrialized countries continuously. In most regions of the world, the epidemic of road traffic injuries is still increasing.

Relevant Injury Types

Accident investigation is a very complex interdisciplinary work aiming at the reconstruction of time history of parameters related to the movement and interactions of vehicles and persons immediately before and during an accident. Injuries constitute very important traces. The routine clinical documentation would typically be insufficient because some minor, and thus for the treatment irrelevant injuries, would potentially not be accounted for. For this reason, a thorough body inspection (in nonfatal injured) or an autopsy by a forensic pathologist is to be performed in order to assess the injuries and collect other traces (small parts from vehicle, etc.) from the body. Care must be taken regarding the anthropometric data—basic body measures as well as the exact locations of all injuries must be ascertained and documented. Apart from descriptions and photographs, computed tomographies, 3D-scans, and other methods can be employed for injury documentation. In accident investigation, the skin and bone injuries are the most important because they carry the most information about the interaction between the human body and its surroundings. Apart from injuries, an analysis of the clothing is to be performed (though not necessarily by the pathologist).

There are two types of information an injury analysis can offer—injuries enable inferences regarding the injury mechanism, that is, the art of loading, and regarding the amount of loading. Thus, based on injury analysis, the investigator can reason back as to the particular cause. The immediate injury cause is always the force acting in the injured tissue. However, there is not always a clear topographic relationship between the external force acting on the surface of the human body and the injury location; injuries might occur in distant body regions because of force transmission. An example—indirect rib fractures caused by thorax compression—is shown in **Figure 1**.

Skin injuries

Abrasions—superficial skin injuries resulting from tangentially inflicted force (scraping along the body surface). Its direction can be established based on the morphology (bevel descent at the beginning and a tag consisting of accumulated epidermis at the end). The shape of the injury gives clues about the size of the contacting object; sometimes a pattern can be found that reflects some of its morphology.

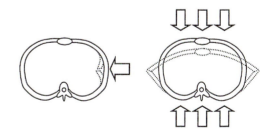

Figure 1 Direct (left) and indirect (right) rib fractures; the former as a result of an interaction with an object in the location of the fracture, the latter as a result of chest compression in the anterior–posterior direction (the ribs break on the side, i.e., not at the contact location).

Stretch injury—if the skin is stretched beyond its elasticity, injury occurs along the cleavage lines (defined by the natural orientation of collagen fibers). If the skin was stretched as a result of extensive movement of body segments, the injury shows in typical locations over protruding bony structures; such injuries give clues about the segmental movements during the accident. An example is shown in **Figure 2**.

Hematoma—soft tissue bleedings resulting from blood vessel damage. Depending on the size of the blood vessel and the surrounding soft tissue structure, even serious blood loss affecting the hemodynamics might occur. Hematoma shows on the skin typically only after a lag of several hours or days. Its resorption takes up to several weeks and is accompanied by color changes that might help an experienced investigator to narrow down its time of origin. Typically, its shape reflects initially the morphology of the contacting object, and in the course of time, it changes as the blood follows the cleavages in the soft tissue, the muscle fasciae, and so on. Tire profile might leave negative impression on the skin (see **Figure 3**).

Decollement—separation of the subcutis from the underlying fascia as a result of tangential blunt force imposed on the affected body part, accompanied by a formation of a wound cavity that might be filled with blood (see **Figure 4**). This injury type results typically from being ran over by a car tire or from a primary contact between a pedestrian and a car. The overlaying skin is frequently intact; sometimes tire marks can be observed.

Laceration—apart from incisions (cuts), open wounds can result from compression, shearing, and/or tensile force, that is, from blunt force. The edges of the wound might be ragged, bruised, or abraded and thus potentially giving hints as to the contacting object. Sometimes bridging strands (blood vessels, nerves, tissue strands) can be found especially in the deeper layers. The shape of the wound can help to identify the contacting object.

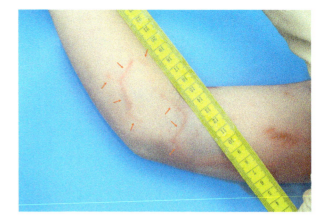

Figure 3 Tire profile marks on the skin of the right arm of an accident victim.

Head injuries

Traumatic brain injuries

Traumatic brain injuries (TBIs) are mechanical insults to the brain associated with temporary or permanent impairment of brain function. The distinguishing mark of TBI is an altered state of consciousness.

From a clinical point of view, TBIs are classified by using the Glasgow Coma Scale (GCS) of the patient shortly after the traumatic incident:

Mild TBI: $13 \leq GCS \leq 15$
Moderate TBI: $9 \leq GCS \leq 12$
Severe TBI: $GCS \leq 8$

The GCS quantifies the conscious state of a patient based on his/her eyes (eyes do not open—one point; eyes open in

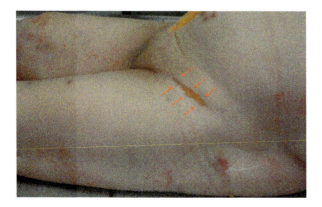

Figure 2 Typical stretch injury of the skin in the groin caused by extensive extension of the left hip (pedestrian accident victim).

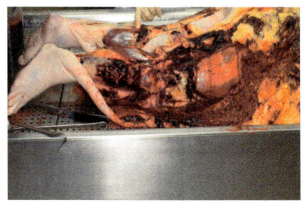

Figure 4 Wound cavity filled with blood developed as a result of direct blunt trauma (primary impact of a pedestrian hit by a passenger car).

response to pain—two points, eyes open in response to voice—three points, eyes open spontaneously—four points), verbal (no sound—one point, incomprehensible sound—two points, inappropriate words—three points, confused verbal statements—four points, normal conversation—five points), and motor (no movements—one point, extension in response to pain—two points, abnormal flexion in response to pain—three points, flexion/withdrawal in response to pain—four points, localization of pain—five points, obeying of commands—six points) responses.

The traditional and still widely used classification based on the morphology differentiates also three degrees:

1. Commotio cerebri (concussion)—a temporary and reversible impairment of brain function (diagnostic criteria: loss of consciousness, amnesia, nausea/vomit, headache)
2. Contusio cerebri (brain contusion)—a distinct injury of the brain tissue (cerebral contusion, intracranial bleeding)
3. Compressio cerebri (brain compression)—this grade is characterized by an increased intracranial pressure caused by brain swelling and/or intracranial bleeding; since the cranial cavity is not deformable, the only direction the brain can expand is toward the foramen magnum and that is where the brain can be clamped. Secondary bleedings especially in the pons area might follow leading to severe brain damage or even death

Intracranial hemorrhages

Intracranial hemorrhages are bleedings inside of the cranial cavity. According to their localization, they can be divided into following types:

Epidural hematoma—a bleeding between the skull bone and the dura mater. The bleedings are caused by damage to one of the meningeal arteries, typically as a result of skull fracture.

Subdural hematoma—a bleeding between the dura mater and the arachnoidea caused by damage to one or more of the bridging veins, typically in incidents with high head acceleration.

Subarachnoid hematoma—a bleeding between the arachnoidea and the pia mater, caused typically by damage to small brain arteries.

Intracerebral hematoma—bleeding within the brain tissue typically caused by damage to small blood vessels in the convolutions of the brain.

In head impacts with high linear acceleration of the head, focal brain injuries can occur not only directly underneath the impact site, but also on the opposite side of the brain (inertia of the brain and its interaction with the skull being the assumed cause). The hemorrhage areas on the impact side (coup, see **Figure 5**) are typically less pronounced than on the opposite side (contre-coup). High rotational accelerations typically lead to diffuse injuries of the brain tissue (DAI, diffuse axonal injuries).

A striking finding after head trauma are raccoon eyes (unilateral or bilateral)—a periorbital hematoma (bruising around the eyes). Its presence is strongly suggestive of skull base fracture (and not of blunt force acting in the eye region).

Thorax injuries

Heart contusion (contusio cordis)—occurs in blunt chest traumata and can lead to cardiac arrhythmia.

Lung contusion—because of contusions and bruises of lung tissue, the gas exchange might be impaired and/or blood might enter the respiratory tract leading potentially to death through suffocation.

Pneumothorax—if due to an open thorax injury air gets into the pleural cavity (between the lungs and the chest wall), the negative pressure is neutralized and one or both lungs might collapse. Sometimes a ventil mechanism forms that allows air to flow to the pleural cavity but prevents its escape (the so-called tension pneumothorax); the state of the injured might deteriorate rapidly and lead to death within a short period of time. Also an accumulation of blood in the pleural cavity (hemothorax) might lead to breathing and/or heart action impairment. A combination of both (air and blood in the chest cavity) is the hemopneumothorax.

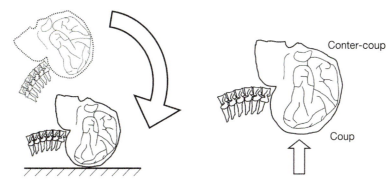

Figure 5 The coup and contre-coup injuries.

Flail chest—although simple rib fractures per se do not constitute a relevant danger, serial fractures in various locations can lead to a detachment of a part of the rib cage that moves (due to the pressure within the thorax) opposite to the rest of the chest (paradoxical breathing movement). This constitutes a life-threatening injury. Sharp rib fragments in displaced fractures might cause lung lacerations with (hemo) pneumothorax.

Aortic rupture—tears of the chest aorta are rarely the result of direct force (although sometimes seen in overrun accidents). Typically the aortic rupture is caused by high accelerations (e.g., an impact of a nonbelted driver on the steering wheel).

Diaphragm rupture—It can occur in car occupants as well as in pedestrian as a result of an impact. It is a relatively rare finding, but the fatality rate is high.

Pelvic injuries are of high clinical importance because they can be associated with severe bleeding. Fractures of the pelvic ring are typical for side collisions, whereas acetabulum fractures occur primarily due to femoral shaft axial loading, that is, due to force transfer from the knee/foot region in frontal collisions. This mechanism can also lead to posterior dislocations of the hip.

Abdominal injuries

Abdominal injuries result typically from blunt force and can be associated with very high danger to life. Perforations of the digestive system lead to infections and inflammations of the abdominal membrane (peritonitis).

Injuries to the extremities

Fractures of long bones

For accident reconstruction, fractures of long bones, especially of the legs, are of a great importance. Relevant are both the localization and the shape of the fracture. The latter enables to distinguish among torsion fractures, compression fractures due to axial loading of the bone, and bending fractures. All kinds of fractures can be observed in traffic accidents. In bending fractures, the direction of force can be reconstructed—if a bone is bent beyond its tolerance, it starts to fail on the tension side and the fracture lines typically form a wedge pointing in the direction of the acting force (see **Figure 6**). Complicated fracture patterns might be very difficult to interpret.

Car Occupants

Injuries of the car occupants are frequently the most important traces that enable to reconstruct their position in the car (driver vs passenger). Apart from injuries (among the most important are seat belt injuries—**Figure 7**; injuries caused by pedals, airbag injuries, and injuries from glass fragments—**Figure 8**), a thorough inspection of the car interior (contact locations, possibly with biological traces) must be performed. Since

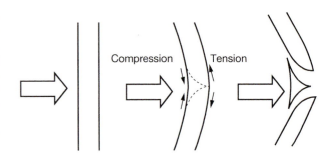

Figure 6 Wedge-shaped bending fracture of long bones, the apex of the wedge showing the direction of the acting force.

airbags deploy not until the crash, the existence of biological (DNA) traces is strong evidence regarding seating order. Another question that can be clarified by a thorough injury analysis (in combination with other methods) is the seat belt use. In multiphase accidents, the assignment of injuries to individual events (interactions) might be very tricky.

Frontal collisions

Seat belt injuries—occur as a result of the interaction between the restrained occupant and the (typically three-point) belt. In

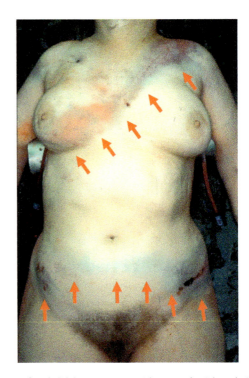

Figure 7 Seat belt injury, car occupant in severe frontal crash; the shoulder belt consistent with the driver position in the car (in left-hand drive vehicles).

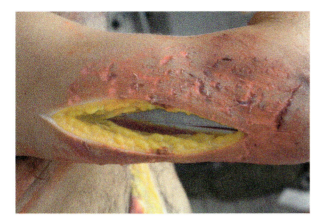

Figure 8 Superficial skin injury caused by shattered glass (right upper arm of a car occupant); the long and deep cut was made by a pathologist.

severe crashes, bony injury (ribs, clavicles, and sternum, fractures typically located along the belt contact site) can be found as well as abdominal wall disruptions and mesenteric tears. The typical seat belt sign—a skin abrasion running diagonally across the chest (shoulder belt) and/or across the lower abdomen (lap belt)—can show in an impressive way (see **Figure** 7) or not at all; sometimes, subcutaneous bleeding along the belt line can be found in the autopsy in spite of no visible trauma sign on the body surface. A missing seat belt injury does not necessarily imply that the belt was not used (e.g., the belt might have been rolled out because of precrash movements of the occupant). For the same reason, knee (and/or hip and/or pelvic) injuries as well as head injuries might occur in spite of seat belt use.

Airbag injuries—the interaction with the airbag can lead to face, skull and/or jaw fractures, teeth luxations, eye injuries, burns, or hearing damage. Depending on the hand location at impact, injuries of the hand and/or lower arm might occur (fractures, burns, etc.). Injuries might be caused by eyeglasses, pipes, and other objects between the face and the inflating bag.

Side collisions

With respect to a particular occupant, far-side and near-side (struck side) impact should be distinguished. An impact to the side of the vehicle, where the occupant sits, leads to direct loading via blunt force (the injuries result from cabin intrusion as well as its acceleration). Typically, the impact side of the head, the thorax, and the pelvis are affected. Seat belts are not effective in near-side impacts, and so seat belt injuries are not likely to occur. The injuries of occupants on the struck side are typically more severe than on the far side of the vehicle.

In far-side collisions, the torso of the occupants might slip out of the shoulder belt and severe head injuries can occur (interaction of the head with the dashboard, the near-side

occupant, or the intruding far-side cabin structures). The upper body of the occupant stays impinged by the belt and the excessive belt loading might lead to abdomen injuries including typical belt signs on the skin.

Rear-end collisions

Low-impact rear-end collisions are being frequently investigated because of whiplash-associated disorders (WADs). Severe crashes might lead to cervical spine injuries (fractures, dislocations) and/or head injuries.

Rollover collisions

The loading imposed on occupants in rollover crashes is variable. Isolated rollovers are rare and belted occupants frequently suffer only minor injuries in spite of extensive car damage. Severe injuries typically occur due to occupant ejection (possible in spite of belt usage if the seat collapses) or due car impact secondary to rollover; in the latter case, the injury patterns resemble those of frontal, side, or rear-end collisions depending on the impact direction. Severe blunt head traumata and/or compression cervical spine injuries occur as a result of roof crush.

Whiplash-Associated Disorders

Nonphysiological movements in the cervical spine region can cause significant disorders ranging from discomfort to neurological symptoms and/or injuries to the bones or ligaments. In Europe, more than one million car occupants report to suffer from WAD after a car crash, the costs are estimated to be between 5 and 10 billion euros. In the United States, more than one million people are affected every year and the costs are approximately 30 billion dollars. The WADs are typically classified according to the recommendation of the Quebec task force:

Grade 0	No symptoms
	No physical signs
Grade 1	Symptoms such as pain, stiffness, or tenderness
	No physical signs
Grade 2	Symptoms such as in Grade 1
	Musculoskeletal signs such as decreased range of movement and point tenderness
Grade 3	Symptoms such as in Grade 1
	Musculoskeletal signs such as in Grade 2
	Neurological sings such as decreased or absent deep tendon reflexes, muscle weakness, and sensory deficits
Grade 4	Symptoms such as in Grade 1
	Fracture or dislocation or spinal cord injury

The exact injury mechanism is not known; microlesions of soft tissue caused by combined translational and rotational movements of spine segments are frequently hypothesized. In traffic accidents, the torso is typically accelerated through the seat; as a result of inertia, a complex relative movement between the head and the torso including both traction and bending of the cervical spine follows. **Figure 9** shows typical spine kinematics during a rear-end collision—due to a force imposed by the seat back, the thoracic spine flattens and at the junction to the cervical segments, a vertical force component occurs (thoracic ramping); simultaneously, a retraction of the lower cervical spine can be observed. An extension of the cervical spine follows that is limited by the head restraint. Due to contact elasticity, the head as well as the torso typically rebound, which leads to protraction of the cervical spine. The forward movement of the torso is restrained by the seat belt so that a flexion of both upper thoracic and cervical spine follows. As a reference parameter for the amount of load imposed to the passengers, the collision-induced velocity change has been established. Because the collision duration lies typically in a tight range (0.1–0.15 s), the velocity change is proportional to the mean acceleration of the vehicle during the collision. Since the biomechanical tolerance limits were established based on the result of volunteer tests under controlled conditions, care must be taken that the value of the velocity change in the location of the person of interest is reconstructed (due to rotations, the velocity change in different locations of the car varies). The approximate reference values that result from various volunteer studies cannot be generalized as they refer to standardized (lab) situations. The assessment must always take into account the particular situation (especially deviations from the setup of the volunteer studies) and the individual parameters of the person. The most important factors influencing the injury outcome are the posture (especially of the head), the seat (and headrest) adjustment, degenerative or other preexisting alterations, or injuries of the cervical spine, and so on.

Pedestrian Collisions

The interaction between a pedestrian and a car have typically the form of an impact, that is, the pedestrian is hit in an upright position by the car front. Run-over collisions (without former impact) are much less common, but they may be of high forensic relevance (drunken pedestrian lying on the road vs camouflage of a homicide vs suicide). The injury outcome is dependent on the pedestrian kinematics, which can typically be divided into the following phases:

1. Primary impact—the contact between the pedestrian body and the car; typically, the lower legs are impacted by the bumper first and the hip and head impacts follow as the pedestrian body wraps around the car (the distance between the road surface and the head impact location measured along the car contour is called wrap around distance). In box-shaped cars (or in rear-end collision with station wagons, etc.), the impact of the leg, hip, thorax, and head regions can occur simultaneously.
2. Secondary impact—the contact of the pedestrian to the road (impact, sliding, and rolling). The distance between the point of collision and the end position of the pedestrian after the secondary impact is called throw distance; this parameter is frequently used for the collision speed estimation.
3. Tertiary impact—the contact between the pedestrian and the surrounding structures (another car, a tree, also a runover counts as tertiary impact).

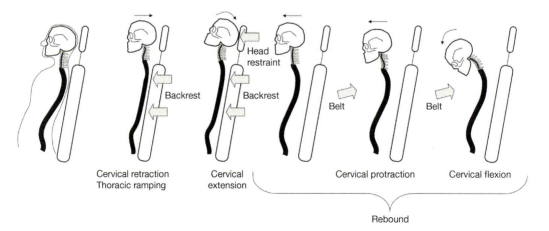

Figure 9   Typical spine kinematics during a rear-end collision. The wide arrows represent the external forces acting on the body, the fine arrows the movement direction.

The pedestrian kinematics and thus the injury pattern depend to a high degree on the relationship between his/her anthropometry and the geometry of the impacting car. Several different kinematics types can be discerned—wrap kinematics (the pedestrian upper body wraps around the front hood/windshield and after the head impact, he stays on the hood or slides off to the ground), forward projection (the pedestrian is projected forward, typical for box-shaped vehicles or children), fender vault (the pedestrian first wraps around the hood and than exits off the side of the vehicle front), roof vault (the pedestrian wraps around the hood and his legs rotate further upward so that he is lifted), and somersault kinematics (the pedestrian upper body wraps around the car front, after the head impact, the pedestrian is flipped into the air as he continues to rotate). Another collision type is a sideswipe, that is, a movement of a pedestrian along the side of a moving vehicle; in such cases, the pedestrian might twist (rotate about his longitudinal axis) and suffer leg injuries on one side and head injuries on the other side of the body, both resulting from contact to the car.

The most important are the injuries that are able to reconstruct the impact direction—apart from fractures of the long bones of the lower and/or upper leg, the soft tissue findings (contusions, wound caverns, etc.) are of high relevance. Sometimes ankle and/or knee injuries help to reason back as to the impact direction (supination vs pronation vs flexion vs extension in the joint due to impact, etc.). Only very rough estimation of collision speed based on the injuries is possible (and always to be performed also with the knowledge of the car damage); lower leg fractures can occur even in collisions with a speed of less than 10 km h^{-1}, multiple rib series fractures and/or severe TBIs require typically collision speeds of above 30 km h^{-1}, and amputations of body segments above 80 km h^{-1} (unless the body part gets stuck in a car structure). The assignment of the injuries to individual contacts during a multiphase accident might be very difficult due to overlapping of injury outcomes. Run-over leads sometimes to tire profile marks on the skin (that can appear as textile pattern due to clothing), massive soft tissue injuries with décollement is to be expected.

Two-Wheelers

Typically, the most serious injuries of riders are caused by the impacts—with the own vehicle (e.g., pelvic ring fractures due to impact on the tank), with other vehicles, road infrastructure (guard railing), and other objects (a tree, etc.). For the accident reconstruction, compression injuries of the hands/lower arms due to handlebar grip are important (e.g., to differentiate the driver and the passenger) as well as superficial injuries morphologically attributable to contacting objects (vehicle parts, etc.).

Helmet injuries—wearing of a helmet at the time of an accident can result in skin abrasions underneath the chin strap

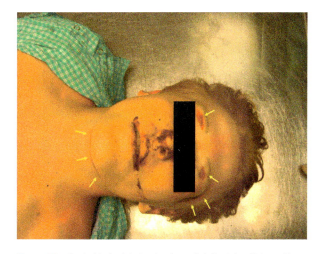

Figure 10 Typical helm injuries (motorcyclist, frontal collision with a passenger car); the helmet was found several meters away from the body, but its damage and the injuries prove it had been worn at the time of accident.

or impression mark of parts of the visor. An example of helm injuries is shown in **Figure 10**. In severe crashes, helmets cannot prevent skull fractures and/or brain damage.

In bicycle collisions, severe injuries to the head occur especially if the cyclist does not use helmet and a car is involved. For accident reconstruction, injuries in the upper leg/pelvis region due to the interaction with the bicycle seat might be important (e.g., to clarify whether the cyclist was riding or pushing the bicycle).

Severe or even lethal injuries result also from a collision between a cyclist and a pedestrian. Fatal injuries are rare and result typically from the secondary fall of the pedestrian with head impact on the road. For accident reconstruction, a characteristic wound on the lower leg of the pedestrian caused by the contact with the front wheel is the most important injury (though typically minor).

Railway

In 2009, 1391 people were killed and another 1350 were seriously injured in railway accidents in the European Union (European railway agency data). The total number of deaths is much higher, because the statistics do not include suicides (2719 in 2009, i.e., more than twice the number of accidental deaths). The number of deaths among railway passengers is very low; within the EU, only 196 persons died in the 3-year period (2007–2009). The US statistics reported 492 deaths and 5264 nonfatal injuries in 2011 (Federal Railroad Administration).

The most important factor determining injury severity in railway accidents is the huge mass of the vehicles. Injuries may be caused by an impact (pedestrian going/running/standing, car occupant), run over (pedestrian lying on the track, with or without contact to the wheels of the train), or dragging along by the train (a person or a whole car). In rare cases, persons fall out of a moving train, also known are deaths and serious injuries resulting from "train surfing" (riding on the outside of a moving train). The differentiation between a suicide and an accident (or a homicide) can be very difficult; in suicide cases, the person lies typically on the abdomen across the rail so that the head or the upper part of the torso are severed by the wheels.

Air Traffic

The number of air accident victims is low and shows irregularities because of the very few events that lead to fatalities—in 2008, there were 170 fatalities reported in the EU, 154 hereof caused by a single major crash. In the United States, there were 30 accidents reported that cost 757 lives in 2009 (Aviation safety network).

In plane crashes, fatal injuries typically result from severe impacts; carbon monoxide or cyanide intoxication is also possible. In crashes into the water, the ultimate cause of death might be drowning.

See also: **Anthropology/Odontology:** Biomechanics of Bone Trauma; **Engineering:** Forensic Engineering/Accident Reconstruction/Biomechanics of Injury/Philosophy, Basic Theory, and Fundamentals; **Forensic Medicine/Causes of Death:** Blunt Injury; **Forensic Medicine/Clinical:** Airplane Crashes and Other Mass Disasters.

Further Reading

Appel, H., Wanderer, S., Meißner, G., et al., 1984. Mechanik und Biomechanik des Unfalls. In: Wagner, H.J. (Ed.), Verkehrsmedizin. Springer, Berlin, p. 480.
Global status report on road safety, 2009. WHO. www.who.int/violence_injury_prevention (accessed October 2011.).
Goldsmith, W., Plunkett, J., 2004. A biomechanical analysis of the causes of traumatic brain injury in infants and children. The American Journal of Forensic Medicine and Pathology 25, 89–100.
Graw, M., König, H.G., 2002. Fatal pedestrian-bicycle collisions. Forensic Science International 126, 241–247.
Naci, H., Chisholm, D., Baker, T.D., 2009. Distribution of road traffic deaths by road user group: a global comparison. Injury Prevention 15, 55–59.
Nahum, A.M., Melvin, J.W. (Eds.), 2002. Accidental Injury: Biomechanics and Prevention. Springer, New York.
Schmitt, K.-U., Niederer, P.F., Walz, F., 2010. Trauma Biomechanics: Accidental Injury in Traffic und Sports. Springer, Heidelberg.
Spitzer, W.O., Skowron, M.L., Salmi, L.R., et al., 1995. Scientific monograph of the Quebec task force on whiplash associated disorders: redefining "whiplash" and its management. Spine 20 (Suppl. 8), 1–73.

Key Terms

Abdominal injuries, Abrasion, Abusive head trauma, Accident, Accidental injury, Acute respiratory distress syndrome (ARDS), Anus, Asphyxia, Asphyxial, Assault, Autopsy findings, Bite marks, Blood congestion, Blunt force, Blunt injury, Bruise, Burking, Burn shock, Burns, Capability of acting, Car, Carbon monoxide, Cardiogenic shock, Cause of death, Cerebral contusion, Child abuse, Child maltreatment, Chop wound, Circle of violence, Clinical forensic medicine, Close-range shot, Computed tomography, Congestion, Consumption by fire, Contact shot, Contusion, Criminal prosecution, Crush syndrome, Cut, Cyanide, Cyanosis, Death, Defense injury, Defense wound, Dermal artifacts, Diagnosis of vitality, Diatom test, Disseminated intravascular coagulation (DIC), Distant shot, Distributive shock, Domestic violence, Domestic violence and children, Drowning, Electricity, Epidural hematoma, Falaka, Finger torture, Forced position, Foreign bodies, Forensic documentation, Fractures, Fractures of the laryngeal cartilages, Hand injury, Hanging, Head, Head injuries, Hematoma, Hemorrhagic shock, Homicide, Hymen, Hyoid bone fracture, Hypovolemic shock, Imaging, Impact, Incised wound, Inflammatory mediator, Initiation, Injuries to the extremities, Injury, Institutional restraint, Insurance fraud, Intracranial hemorrhage, Knife attack, Lacerations, Lacerations of inner organs, Ligature strangulation, Malingering, Manual strangulation, Multiple organ dysfunction syndrome (MODS), Nail torture, Obstructive shock, Ollivier syndrome, Pattern of injury, Pedestrian, Penis, Perthes pressure congestion, Petechiae, Petechial bleedings, Physical abuse, Physical restraint, Posey restraint, Positional asphyxia, Postural asphyxia, Prone hogtie position, Public violence, Purtscher retinopathy, Radiographs, Rail, Rib fractures, Riot crush, Risk assessment, Scalds, Scintigraphy, Self defense, Self-inflicted injury, Self-infliction, Self-mutilation, Sepsis, Sexual violence, Sharp force, Sharp-force injury, Simulated offense, Site of drowning, Skin laceration, Skull fracture, Smothering, Stab wound, Stabbing, Strangulation, Stress response, Subdural hematoma, Suffocation, Suicidal gesture, Suicide, Systemic inflammatory response syndrome (SIRS), Thoracic trauma, Thorax, Torture, Traumatic asphyxia, Traumatic shock, Uncomfortable position, Water torture, Waterboarding, Whiplash.

Review Questions

1. What is blunt force trauma?
2. What is the difference between an abrasion and a contusion?
3. How are burns described?
4. What are the main types of asphyxia?
5. How does hanging kill someone?
6. What is a ligature mark?
7. What is traumatic asphyxia?
8. What is burking?
9. Why are deaths by immersion, such as drowning, difficult to diagnose?
10. What is the diatom test?
11. What is the common cause of death by sharp-force trauma?
12. How are firearm injuries classified?
13. What is stopping power?
14. What are the characteristics of gunshot entrance wounds? Exit wounds?
15. What are the typical injuries caused by domestic violence?
16. What are defense wounds? Where do they typically appear?
17. List three traits that might suggest that a wound is self-inflicted?
18. Who might wound themselves and why?
19. List three criteria that support claims of torture.
20. Which bones are most likely to be fractured in a traffic accident? Why?

Discussion Questions

1. How might a forensic pathologist distinguish self-inflicted wounds from those allegedly from torture?
2. How would a forensic pathologist determine whether blunt force trauma or sharp-force trauma was the cause of death if both are present? Why might this be necessary?
3. What are some of the ways that child abuse can be differentiated from normal childhood trauma?
4. Review the list of traumas in this section. Consider a traffic accident, broadly. Describe how each of these traumas might occur, individually or together, in a hypothetical accident.
5. Can a forensic pathologist say with certainty how long an object was that caused a stab wound? Why or why not?

Additional Readings

Pollanen, M.S., 2016. Fatal rhabdomyolysis after torture by reverse hanging. Forensic Science, Medicine, and Pathology 1–4.

Reber, S.L., Simmons, T., 2015. Interpreting injury mechanisms of blunt force trauma from butterfly fracture formation. Journal of Forensic Sciences 60 (6), 1401–1411.

Ubelaker, D.H. (Ed.), 2015. The Global Practice of Forensic Science. John Wiley & Sons.

Ubelaker, D.H., Smialek, J.E., 2015. The interface of forensic anthropology and forensic pathology in trauma interpretation. Hard Evidence: Case Studies in Forensic Anthropology 221.

Section 5. Causes of Death

Most laypeople confuse *cause* of death with *manner* of death: The former is the sequence of events that led to the cessation of life; the latter is the way in which those events came about. It is possible for a forensic pathologist to know the cause of death but remain undecided about the manner. Did the person fall or was he or she pushed? Did the husband shoot his wife intentionally or did she commit suicide? In this way, cause of death is more scientific and medical, while manner of death is more legal and cultural. Combined, these two designations form the core of the forensic pathologist's job.

Sudden Natural Death

A Thierauf and S Pollak, University of Freiburg, Freiburg, Germany

Glossary

Berry aneurysm The cerebral arteries, mainly those forming the circle of Willis on the basal surface of the brain, may show focal saccular outpouchings that are prone to rupture.

Coronary heart disease (CHD) This term describes the pathophysiological consequences of severe narrowing or blockage of coronary arteries, usually caused by atherosclerosis.

Esophageal varices This term means a pathological condition characterized by an extreme dilation of submucosal veins in the lower third of the esophagus, mostly as a consequence of portal hypertension in patients with liver cirrhosis.

Pulmonary embolism A blockage of the pulmonary artery and/or its branches, mostly caused by blood clots originating from the legs in the presence of deep vein thrombosis.

Definition

The term covers the following deaths from an internal (pathological) cause:

- *sudden* death without any previous symptoms ("in complete well-being"),
- *unexpected* death after a short period of complaints not regarded as threatening.

Some authors suggest a third category, namely, death following *rapid deterioration* of a known disorder not regarded as serious.

In practice, classification of these deaths may be difficult if the individual died alone with no history to suggest a cause of death. Quite often, a sudden and/or unexpected death can be diagnosed only on the basis of the circumstances under which the deceased has been found (e.g., at the wheel of a vehicle or his workplace). The fact that no medical treatment took place in the days preceding death can also be only a hint that death came unexpectedly.

Criminalistic Aspects

When an individual dies without having presented any previous symptoms (sudden death), the medical examiner can determine neither the manner (natural/unnatural) nor the cause of death. These cases have to be categorized as "manner of death undetermined" and can only be clarified by performing an autopsy and further examinations.

The circumstances under which death occurred, the situation at the scene, or the findings on the body may even be suggestive of the involvement of another person, such as:

- If an individual dies during an argument or in close temporal connection with an accident, a traumatic cause seems probable.
- Agonal falls or seizures sometimes cause suspicious injuries.
- Anticoagulant therapy or diseases associated with hemorrhagic diathesis may lead to multiple hematomas resembling blunt-force injuries from abuse.
- Massive external bleeding—especially if associated with extensive blood traces at the scene—is always suspicious.

In natural deaths, the following sources of bleeding are of major importance: bite marks of the tongue due to convulsions, esophageal varices, gastroduodenal ulcers, erosion of pulmonary vessels in the presence of tuberculosis or bronchial carcinoma, and spontaneous rupture of lower limb varices. Putrefactive changes and animal scavenging can be misinterpreted as vital injuries upon superficial inspection.

Sometimes, the antemortem symptoms may suggest an intoxication, for example, in spontaneous intracranial hemorrhages (ruptured berry aneurysm and nontraumatic intracerebral hemorrhage). Signs of increasing intracranial pressure, such as headache, nausea, vomiting, and coma, may be misinterpreted as symptoms of intoxication; conversely, a supposedly natural death may prove to be due to an intoxication at autopsy.

Special Categories

In *infancy*, the sudden infant death syndrome has to be differentiated from other natural and unnatural causes, such as smothering. Even in severe internal injuries, there may be no externally visible correlate. In any case, the forensic pathologist has to look for (sometimes inconspicuous) signs of mechanical suffocation. A potential intoxication and an electric shock also have to be considered.

Deaths at the *workplace* require particularly a thorough investigation to prove or exclude harmful external effects or influences such as occupational intoxications. Electrocution and lightning fatalities may also be overlooked at first. The electrothermal skin lesions and the corresponding damage in the clothing may be overlooked by the physician performing the external postmortem. In injuries due to a fall, the question arises whether death was due to the trauma or a preexisting disease suddenly becoming manifest and causing the individual to fall. A sudden loss of consciousness owing to an organic, vasomotor, or metabolic reason such as an epileptic seizure, aneurysmal bleeding, syncope, or hypoglycemic coma can result in a fatal industrial accident. Determination of the blood alcohol concentration is mandatory.

Sudden *death while operating a motor vehicle* is mostly seen in males in their sixth and seventh decade of life. Among the causes of death, coronary artery disease ranks first and accounts for over 80% of cases. The deceased are sometimes found in properly parked cars. After the onset of the premortal symptoms, the driver may still be able to stop the car, possibly with the assistance of the front-seat passenger. Serious accidents injuring or even killing other road users occasionally occur but are comparatively rare. If recent/acute pathological findings such as coronary thrombosis, acute myocardial infarction, aneurysmal rupture, or massive cerebral bleeding are detected, the fatality can easily be classified as a natural death at autopsy. Problems arise when exclusively chronic organ changes (stenosing sclerosis of the coronary arteries and scars from former myocardial infarction) and significant injuries from an additional car collision are found side by side. Unusual driving behavior, for which observers have no explanation, may in fact be due to a natural disease but can also be attributable to the influence of alcohol or drugs; if the driver approaches an obstacle without reducing speed, a suicidal act also has to be kept in mind. Deaths in motor vehicles should always induce the forensic pathologist to determine the CO-Hb concentration in the corpse blood. Exhaust gases emitted by motor vehicles contain carbon monoxide and can be inhaled either accidentally or with suicidal intent (accidents by running a car's engine in a closed garage and suicides by conducting exhaust gases into the interior of a car, especially in the absence of a catalytic converter).

If a person dies during sports activities, the first question to be answered is whether death was caused by a (accidental) trauma or a latent pathology. Depending on the external circumstances, a heat stroke also has to be taken into consideration. Natural deaths during sports activities predominantly occur in individuals with preexisting cardiovascular diseases, especially sclerosis of the coronary arteries and its sequelae, often in combination with cardiac hypertrophy. Males are far more frequently affected than females and the highest incidence is seen in the third to fifth decade of life. Preexisting chronic pathologies, such as coronary atherosclerosis, cardiac hypertrophy, and scars from myocardial infarction, lead to a propensity for arrhythmia and heart failure. Even in the absence of acute changes, such as fresh coronary thrombosis or myocardial infarction, the abnormal physical stress due to sports activities may trigger a fatal dysfunction of the structurally damaged heart. Sudden circulatory collapse can be the first manifestation of an undiagnosed heart disease. However, a seemingly "blank" medical history does not justify the conclusion that the underlying condition had really been without symptoms ("silent"). Many people do not talk about their stenocardiac complaints or misjudge and trivialize them. Physical fitness is no reliable indicator of a healthy cardiovascular system. Fitness and motivation do by no means rule out high-grade stenosing of the coronary arteries.

Sudden death during *sexual activity* often occurs under seemingly suspicious circumstances, such as when the deceased is found in a hotel room, car, or outdoors partially or completely undressed and sadomasochistically bound. Under criminalistic aspects, one then has to distinguish between natural death, autoerotic accident, and homicide. Males in their sixth and seventh decade of life are those most at risk of dying suddenly during sexual activities, sometimes after the use of sildenafil or other erectile dysfunction remedies. The most frequent cause of death is coronary heart disease.

Classification According to the Morphological Substrate

The following survey refers to adults and children older than 1 year.

Cardiovascular Diseases

In the statistics on sudden death, cardiovascular diseases were ranking at the top as early as the beginning of the twentieth century and now they account for about 70–80% according to more recent studies. Numbers vary dependent on the composition of the autopsy material and the nationally different classification criteria. The incidence in males continues to be significantly higher than in females, although it has dropped in the last few decades. In the male population, sudden death from a cardiovascular disease is relatively common in the fourth to sixth decades already, whereas in women a higher incidence is not observed before the seventh decade.

Coronary Heart Disease

Under nosological aspects, most deaths discussed here have to be attributed to coronary heart disease. The morphological correlate is "stenosing coronary atherosclerosis." Arteriosclerotic vascular changes may lead to acute coronary occlusion either due to edematous swelling of an atheromatous plaque or by bleeding in the intima or—most important—by thrombotic material adhering to the inner surface of the vascular wall (**Figure 1**). Sites of predilection are the great subepicardial vascular trunks (left coronary artery with its anterior interventricular and circumflex branch, right coronary artery), whereas embolic coronary occlusion is rare.

Stenosing coronary atherosclerosis can cause (relative) coronary insufficiency either alone or in combination with cardiac hypertrophy and is able to trigger a fatal arrhythmia (asystolia or ventricular fibrillation) at any time—that is, also without any exogenous stress. Nevertheless, these cases should only be classified as natural deaths after all other potential causes such as mechanical trauma, electric shock, and intoxication have been ruled out.

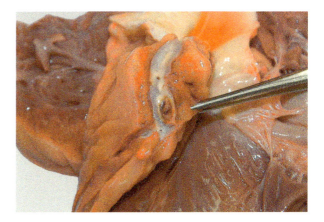

Figure 1   Coronary thrombosis.

Fresh myocardial necrosis (**Figure 2(a) and (b)**) need not always be discernible in acute coronary death. Sometimes, histological examination reveals only disseminated muscle fiber necrosis as evidence of a premortal coronary insufficiency. With the help of immunohistological staining, ischemic tissue lesions can be detected at an early stage already.

In 6–7% of sudden deaths from coronary heart disease, a rupture of the cardiac wall with consecutive hemopericardium is diagnosed at autopsy. The average age of these decedents is significantly higher than in the other groups of acute cardiac death; females are overrepresented in this subgroup.

In the forensic autopsy material, infarction scars (**Figure 3(a) and (b)**) are seen more often than fresh myocardial necroses. If the inner layer of the ventricular wall is affected, parietal thrombi may form on the endocardium and break away (risk of embolic complications). When the outer myocardial layer is involved, epistenocardiac pericarditis and sometimes also adhesion between the parietal and visceral layers of the pericardium (concretio cordis) develop. Transmural necroses may result in chronic aneurysms of the cardiac wall (**Figure 3(a) and (b)**).

Nonischemic Heart Disease

From a statistical point of view, cardiac diseases without sclerotic changes of the coronary arteries play a smaller role in sudden deaths from a natural cause.

Severe hypertrophy of the myocardium always involves the risk of acute cardiac death, especially if the critical heart weight (500 g) has been surpassed. Even if the overstrain is limited to the right ventricle (cor pulmonale), unexpected and sudden death may occur.

The large group of cardiomyopathies (CMs) comprises noninflammatory myocardial diseases not associated with coronary stenosis, any organic heart defect, or hypertension in

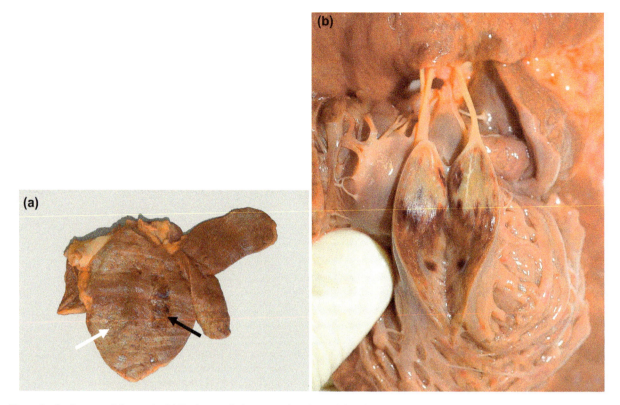

Figure 2 Fresh myocardial necrosis. (a) Fresh necrosis (*white arrow*) and granulation tissue (*black arrow*) in the wall of the left ventricle. (b) Fresh necrosis in a papillary muscle.

the systemic and pulmonary circulation. They are of forensic relevance because an acute arrhythmia or forward heart failure may trigger sudden cardiac death.

In primary congestive CM, the strong dilatation of all cardiac cavities is the major morphological feature. Idiopathic hypertrophic subaortic stenosis is characterized by "asymmetrical" thickening of the ventricular septum. Alcoholic CM manifests itself in eccentric hypertrophy with a varying degree of fibrosis.

Among the inflammatory heart diseases, the different forms of myocarditis (bacterial, viral, infectious toxic, rheumatic, idiopathic, etc.) have to be emphasized. Macroscopically, the heart is mostly flaccid and dilated and its cut surface occasionally shows small pale areas; in chronic forms, the myocardium may be interspersed with small scars. Microscopically, the picture is characterized by inflammatory processes in the interstitium and degenerative changes of the muscle cells. For histological investigation, tissue samples should be taken from both atria and ventricles (including the conduction system).

Congenital and acquired heart defects as well as vascular malformations (aortic isthmus stenosis, anomalies of the coronary arteries, etc.) also have to be borne in mind as causes of sudden cardiac death. As is generally known, aortic valve stenosis with compensatory left ventricular hypertrophy involves a high risk of acute cardiac failure.

Aortic Rupture

Spontaneous aortic ruptures account for about 1.4% of sudden deaths. At autopsy, aortic ruptures often present as a spontaneous laceration or a dissection of the vascular wall. Major risk factors are systemic hypertension or a congenital weakness of the aortic wall as seen in Marfan's syndrome (cystic degeneration of the middle layer). The most common primary rupture site is in the ascending aorta or the aortic arch, and less often the thoracic or abdominal segment of the aorta. The direct cause of death is typically a cardiac tamponade due to a secondary rupture into the pericardial sac (**Figure 4(a)–(c)**). Less often, the rupture is followed by acute bleeding into one of the thoracic cavities.

Arteriosclerotic aortic aneurysms (**Figure 5**) mostly rupture—corresponding to the infrarenal site of predilection—into the retroperitoneal space or the abdominal cavity or, if located in

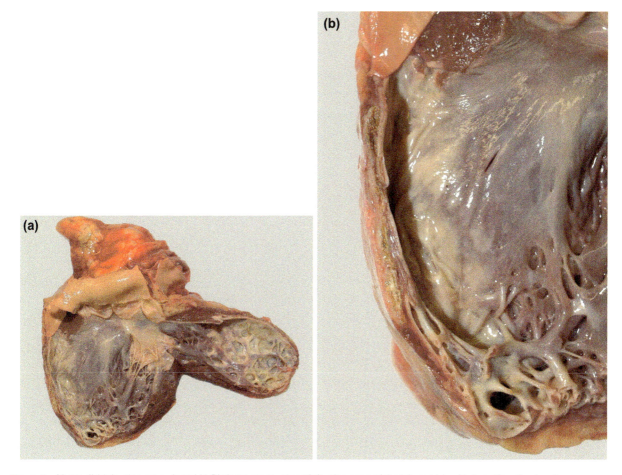

Figure 3   Myocardial infarction scars. (a and b) Distinct transmural postinfarction scars of the left ventricle with formation of a chronic aneurysm.

the thorax, into the mediastinum and one of the pleural cavities.

The incidence of luetic aneurysms has strongly declined in the past few decades.

Pulmonary Embolism

The significance of pulmonary embolism (**Figure 6(a)**) as a cause of sudden death is assessed differently. In clinical pathology, postoperative pulmonary artery embolism and embolism associated with clinically manifest leg and/or pelvic deep vein thrombosis (**Figure 6(b)**) are predominant. Forensic pathologists see acute fatalities from pulmonary embolism also without any previous symptoms of thrombosis in seemingly healthy persons who die during routine activities such as climbing stairs.

This type of "spontaneous" thromboembolism is observed especially in older women; in premenopausal women,

a potential relation with hormonal contraception has to be kept in mind. Usually, the deep veins of one or both legs still contain residual thrombi; the pelvic veins alone are rarely the origin of acutely lethal pulmonary embolism.

Posttraumatic pulmonary embolism is a sequel of the preceding injury. It should therefore not be classified as a natural death.

Diseases of the Respiratory Tract

Apart from cardiovascular diseases, the various forms of pneumonia are the most common cause of unexpected death. This may come as a surprise, as pneumonia is usually associated with impressive symptoms. However, sometimes there is a striking discrepancy between the subjective feeling and the objective findings.

A considerable part of untreated pneumonias ending in sudden death concerns persons from marginal social groups

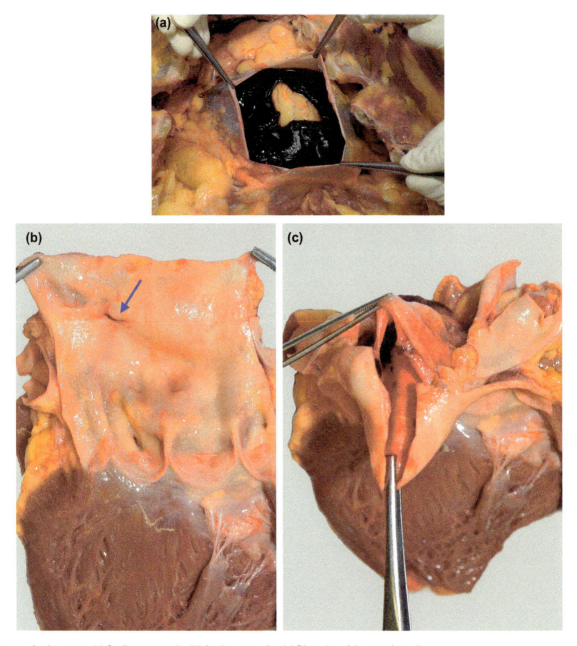

Figure 4 Aortic rupture. (a) Cardiac tamponade. (b) Aortic rupture site. (c) Dissection of the vascular wall.

(homeless people and alcoholics). In persons living alone and found dead in their flat, it is hardly possible to find out in retrospect whether, and if so, how long they had suffered from manifest symptoms.

Focal pneumonia (bronchopneumonia) diagnosed only at autopsy may occur as a consequence of a preceding intoxication (alcohol, psychotropic drugs, narcotics, and carbon monoxide); toxicological analyses should therefore be mandatory, especially in aspiration pneumonia.

Most focal pneumonias originate from the initially affected bronchi, often due to a bacterial superinfection following a viral infection. Since the 1970s, the spectrum of microorganisms causing bacterial pneumonia has been extended by *Legionella pneumophila*.

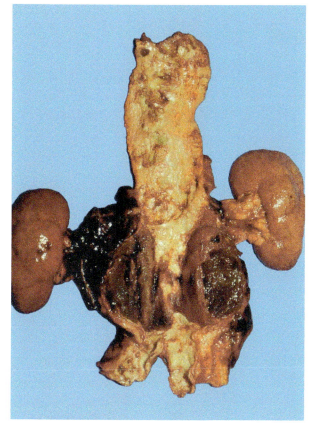

Figure 5   Arteriosclerotic aortic aneurysm.

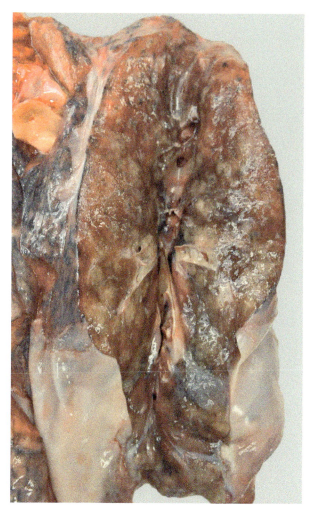

Figure 7   Lobar pneumonia.

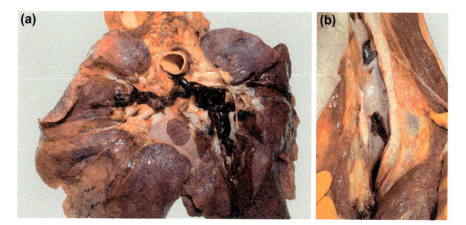

Figure 6   Pulmonary embolism. (a) Embolized thrombi in the central pulmonary arteries. (b) Deep vein thrombosis.

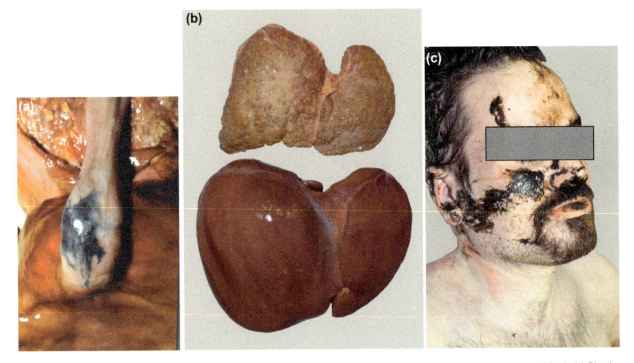

Figure 8   Bleeding of the esophageal varices. (a) Esophageal varices. (b) Liver cirrhosis (cirrhotic liver in comparison to a normal liver). (c) Blood around the mouth from terminal hematemesis.

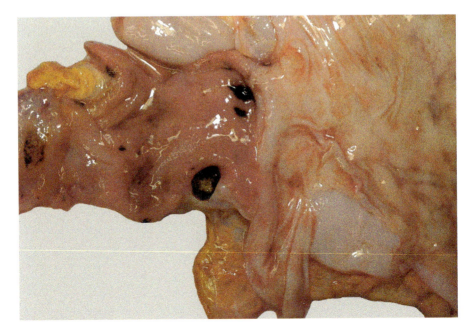

Figure 9   Peptic ulcer of the duodenum.

In the forensic autopsy material, lobar pneumonia accounts for a surprisingly high percentage of inflammatory pulmonary diseases (**Figure 7**). Individuals whose immune system is impaired (e.g., after chronic alcohol abuse or exposure to cold) are particularly at risk.

Tuberculosis is now less common in developed countries. However, although its morbidity and mortality have dropped, deaths from untreated tuberculosis are still observed. By detecting unknown sources of infection, forensic pathologists help to further eliminate tuberculosis as an endemic infectious disease.

Pulmonary tuberculosis manifests itself in exsudative and/or productive changes; the additional presence of fibrous or calcified residues suggests that an old tuberculous focus was reactivated due to reduced resistance. In cavernous forms of pulmonary tuberculosis, massive hemoptysis (hematorrhea) occasionally leads to rapid death.

In influenza infections, primary hemorrhagic pneumonia may result in peracute death. Apart from pulmonary changes such as focal hemorrhages and hemorrhagic edema, the dark red discoloration of the tracheal and bronchial mucosa is a characteristic finding.

Among the noninfectious pulmonary diseases, bronchial asthma has to be mentioned as a potential cause of unexpected death. At autopsy, obstructive pulmonary emphysema and copious, viscous mucus in the deep respiratory tract are found. Histologically, characteristic signs are mucous obstruction of the bronchi, Curschmann's spirals and Charcot–Leyden crystals, an increased number of beaker cells, infiltration of the tunica propria with eosinophil granulocytes, and thickening of the basal membrane.

Patients with central bronchial carcinoma may die unexpectedly due to erosion of a pulmonary vessel with subsequent hemoptysis and blood aspiration.

Gastrointestinal Diseases

Most esophageal varices (**Figure 8(a)**) develop due to portal hypertension, with liver cirrhosis (**Figure 8(b)**) being the best-known and most important cause.

The subepithelial veins at the lower end of the esophagus are most prone to rupture. The risk of a fatal hemorrhage is especially high in patients with cirrhosis because they often have also a coagulation defect. As a result of the terminal hematemesis, blood will be found around the mouth (**Figure 8(c)**) and at the scene.

Sparse postmortem lividity may suggest blood loss already before autopsy. The organs are strikingly pale; stomach and gastrointestinal tract contain blood looking like coffee grounds or tar. At autopsy, it is advisable to leave the esophagus connected to the stomach so that vascular lesions located near the cardia can also be identified. In the Mallory–Weiss syndrome, severe vomiting or retching may be followed by tears at the junction of the stomach and esophagus. Such lacerations are mainly seen in alcoholics and are a major cause of gastrointestinal bleeding.

In peptic ulcers of the stomach and duodenum (**Figure 9**), hemorrhage from arterial erosion is a potentially fatal complication. In these cases, hematemesis can also produce suspicious evidence at the scene.

Further diseases which can also cause unexpected death will only be mentioned briefly here: hemorrhagic necrotizing pancreatitis, various forms of mechanical ileus (obstruction by tumors, adhesions, hernia, volvulus, invagination, etc.), and paralytic ileus (subsequent to a perforated ulcer, occlusion of a mesenterial vessel, etc.). Most of these individuals die unobserved without prior medical treatment.

Diseases of the Central Nervous System

Massive cerebral hemorrhage (**Figure 10**) is a dreaded complication of arterial hypertension. Apart from high blood

Figure 10 Massive cerebral hemorrhage.

pressure, which is regarded as the most important etiological factor, the following causes of bleeding have to be mentioned: aneurysms, leukosis, hemorrhagic diathesis, angiomas, and tumors. When classifying massive hemorrhages according to their localization, the region of the basal ganglia is the most frequently affected part, but the pons and the cerebellum are also involved relatively often.

Aneurysms of the basal cerebral arteries not caused by trauma are attributed to congenital, atherosclerotic, or inflammatory vascular changes. Sites of predilection are the bifurcations of the circulus arteriosus Willisii (**Figure 11(a)**). Accordingly, subarachnoidal hemorrhages, which tend to be most pronounced in the region of the basal cisterns, are often found after ruptured berry aneurysms (**Figure 11(b)**).

Deaths of epileptics often have an unnatural cause such as craniocerebral trauma due to a fall or drowning in the bathtub. Fresh tongue bites may suggest that seizure and death occurred in quick succession; moreover, attention should be paid to soiling by stool and urine. The examination of the brain focuses on the identification of primary focal lesions (in symptomatic epilepsy) and secondary long-term damage such as cell loss and gliosis in the hippocampus. At autopsy, some deaths in people with epilepsy do not reveal any abnormalities. The term "sudden unexpected death in epilepsy" describes a fatality from unexplained respiratory failure or cardiac arrest.

Unexpected death is occasionally seen in inflammatory diseases of the brain and its meninges. A generally known clinical picture, which occurs primarily in children, is per-acute meningococcal sepsis with hemorrhages of the adrenal glands (Waterhouse Friderichsen syndrome). Pneumococcal meningitis can also take a fulminating course.

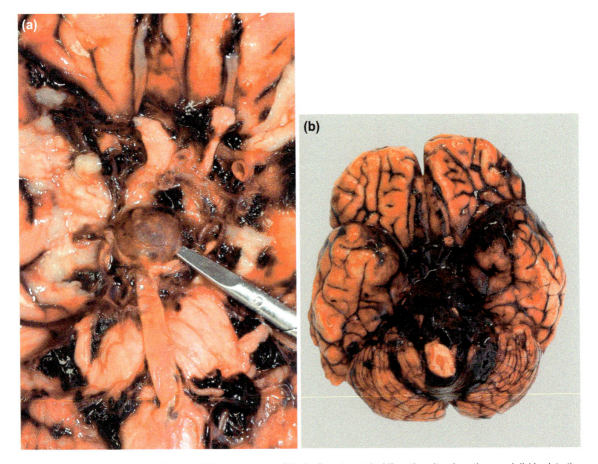

Figure 11   Aneurysm of a basal cerebral artery. (a) Berry aneurysm of the basilar artery at its bifurcation site where the vessel divides into the posterior cerebral arteries. (b) Subarachnoidal hemorrhage.

Other Causes of Sudden Death

Among the metabolic diseases, diabetes mellitus is of special forensic relevance (death in hypo- or hyperglycemic coma).

In the presence of an (isthmic) tubal pregnancy, rupture of the fallopian tube may lead to internal exsanguination within a very short time. Eclampsia and amniotic fluid embolism are also associated with a high maternal mortality.

If a bacterial or parasitic infection is misdiagnosed as a "trivial" disease, a fatal outcome not expected by the environment may occur (e.g., streptococcal sepsis after trivial injuries and malaria tropica after staying in an endemic territory).

See also: **Forensic Medicine/Causes of Death:** Sudden Infant Death Syndrome (SIDS); **Forensic Medicine/Pathology:** Autopsy; Forensic Pathology—Principles and Overview; **Methods:** Analytical Light Microscopy; Microscopy (Electron).

Further Reading

Byard, R.W., 2003. Unexpected infant and childhood death. In: Payne-James, J., Busuttil, A., Smock, W. (Eds.), Forensic Medicine: Clinical and Pathological Aspects. Greenwich Medical Media Ltd., London, pp. 231–246.

Christiansen, L.R., Collins, K.A., 2007. Natural death in the forensic setting: a study and approach to the autopsy. American Journal of Forensic Medicine and Pathology 28, 20–23.

Chugh, S.S., Reinier, K., Teodorescu, C., et al., 2008. Epidemiology of sudden cardiac death: clinical and research implications. Progress in Cardiovascular Diseases 51, 213–228.

Di Maio, D., Di Maio, V.J.M., 2001. Forensic Pathology, second ed. CRC Press, Boca Raton, FL, pp. 43–91.

Dowling, G., 2005. Sudden natural death. In: Matshes, E.W., Lew, E.O., Dolinak, D. (Eds.), Forensic Pathology: Principles and Practice. Elsevier Academic Press, Amsterdam, pp. 71–120.

Fabre, A., Sheppard, M.N., 2006. Sudden adult death syndrome and other non-ischaemic causes of sudden cardiac death. Heart 92, 316–320.

Fineschi, V., Pomara, C., 2004. A forensic pathological approach to sudden cardiac death. In: Tsokos, M. (Ed.), Forensic Pathology Reviews, vol. 1. Humana Press, Totowa, NJ, pp. 139–168.

Hirsch, C.S., Adams, V.I., 2006. Sudden and unexpected death from natural causes in adults. In: Spitz, W.U., Spitz, D.J., Fisher, R.S. (Eds.), Spitz and Fisher's Medicolegal Investigation of Death: Guidelines for (NOT for T) the Application of Pathology to Crime Investigation, fourth ed. Charles C. Thomas, Springfield, IL, pp. 137–174.

Karch, S.B., Fineschi, V., Riezzo, I., 2009. Cardiac and natural causes of sudden death. In: Jamieson, A., Moenssens, A. (Eds.), Wiley Encyclopedia of Forensic Science, vol. 2. Wiley, Chichester.

Kleemann, W.J., Bajanowski, T., 2004. Plötzlicher Tod im Säuglings-und Kindesalter. In: Brinkmann, B., Madea, B. (Eds.), Handbuch Gerichtliche Medizin, vol. 1. Springer-Verlag, Berlin, Heidelberg, pp. 1071–1128.

Langlois, N.E., 2009. Sudden adult death. Forensic Science, Medicine, and Pathology 5, 210–232.

Pollak, S., Saukko, P., 2003. Atlas of Forensic Medicine. CD-ROM. Elsevier, Amsterdam (Chapter 4).

Püschel, K., 2004. Plötzlicher Tod im Erwachsenenalter. In: Brinkmann, B., Madea, B. (Eds.), Handbuch Gerichtliche Medizin, vol. 1. Springer-Verlag, Berlin, Heidelberg, pp. 965–1069.

Saukko, P., Knight, B., 2004. The pathology of sudden death. In: Saukko, P., Knight, B. (Eds.), Knight's Forensic Medicine, third ed. Arnold, London, pp. 492–526.

Sudden Infant Death Syndrome (SIDS)

T Bajanowski, University of Duisburg-Essen, Essen, Germany
M Vennemann, University of Münster, Münster, Germany

Introduction

Despite a considerable decline in its incidence, sudden infant death syndrome (SIDS) is still the leading cause of death among infants between 8 and 365 days of age in industrialized countries. In the United States, more than 4500 infants die suddenly every year for no obvious cause. According to the CDC, half of these cases are due to SIDS. The incidence of this in the United States in 2005 was 0.54 per 1000 live births.

In addition to these SIDS cases, there are deaths of undetermined cause, and death due to accidental suffocation and strangulation in the bed or crib/cot, representing a further 0.38 per 1000 live births. The combined number of SIDS cases plus undetermined deaths and deaths due to suffocation and strangulation is 0.93 per 1000 live births. In Europe, the numbers are slightly lower. In Germany, the SIDS incidence for 2009 was 0.29, whereas in England and Wales, it was 0.38 per 1000 live births. The highest incidence is still found in New Zealand with a rate of 0.8 in 2005 and the lowest are in the Netherlands with 0.06 and Japan with 0.13 in 2007 (**Figure 1**).

However, the number of sudden unexplained deaths (SUDI) in the first and second years of life has not changed substantially in the last 10 years. Similar statistics have been reported by many industrialized countries.

Reduction in SIDS rates is mirrored by the commensurate reduction in postneonatal mortality. This is largely attributable to the decline in prone sleeping following studies by de Jonge and Engelberts in the Netherlands and Fleming in the United Kingdom, which found that the prone sleeping position was a major risk factor in sudden infant deaths. However, despite worldwide research, the cause or causes of sudden deaths in infancy have not yet been found.

Forensic significance of these deaths arises from the relatively high SIDS frequency, the necessity to differentiate SIDS from nonnatural causes of death in each single case (**Table 1**), and in particular, the fact that infants and younger children constitute a special group of victims. The intensity of violence causing injury may be smaller compared to adults. Certain types of violence can be observed (e.g., shaken baby syndrome), and infants also display certain types of injury (e.g., greenstick fracture).

Definition

The term sudden and unexpected death in infancy refers to the proportion of infant deaths occurring more or less suddenly and unexpectedly. SUDI was defined by Huber in 1992. The postmortem examination, which should ideally include a history of gestation, delivery and postnatal development, a death scene investigation, a psychosocial family history, a complete autopsy, and a confidential case conference may:

- reveal changes that alone—or in combination—sufficiently constitute the cause of death (non-SIDS);
- reveal changes that even when clearly present are not sufficient to explain the death ("borderline" SIDS); and
- fail to demonstrate any abnormalities (SIDS).

This means that SUDI is the most heterogeneous group, as it includes all categories of sudden and unexpected infant deaths.

In comparison, the term SIDS describes deaths that occur within the first year of life during sleep or in association with sleep. The first definition was introduced by Beckwith in 1969

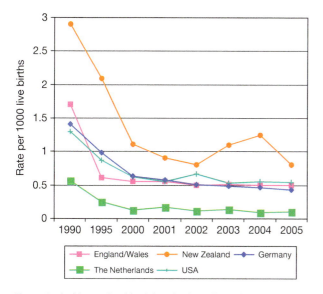

Figure 1 Incidence of sudden infant death syndrome in selected countries between 1990 and 2005.

Table 1   Causes of sudden unexpected death in infancy

Natural causes of death	Unnatural death
SIDS	Suffocation by
Infection	● Soft covering
● Various types of pneumonia	● Occlusion of mouth and nose
● Meningoencephalitis	● Chest compression
● Gastroenteritis	● Aspiration of stomach contents
● Myocarditis	
● Septicemia	Shaken baby syndrome
	Poisoning
Metabolic diseases	Other types (masked) of blunt
● Disturbances of fatty acid	trauma
oxidation	Munchhausen syndrome by proxy
● Pyruvate dehydrogenase	Neglect
deficiency	Hyperthermia of external causes
● Biotinidase deficiency	
● Hyperinsulinism	
● Disturbances of thiamine	
metabolism	
Malformation	
● Blood vessels	
● Cardiac malformation	
● Fibroelastosis of the myocardium	
● Pierre Robin sequence	
Reye syndrome	
Hyperthermia from natural causes	
Dysplasia of lungs	

who combined this typical phenomenology with the autopsy results: "the sudden death of any infant or young child, which is unexpected by history, and in which a thorough postmortem examination fails to demonstrate an adequate cause of death." Since that time, the definition has been the subject of controversy and the application of the definition has shown wide variation from country to country and from researcher to researcher, leading to an inconsistent use on death certificates and for research. In 1989, the Seattle definition was introduced by a panel of experts (NICHD definition), and the term "thorough postmortem examination" was defined more precisely. Furthermore, "the examination of the death scene, complete autopsy, and review of the clinical history" were introduced. In the 1990s, various authors proposed and used different subclassifications of SIDS for scientific investigations. As a result of Beckwith's call for reexamination of the definition, an expert group proposed a new definition in 2004 (San Diego definition). A more general definition was agreed upon, to be used for certification purposes and in general epidemiological studies, together with a subclassification based on specific epidemiological features and the amount of information available from other sources.

According to the San Diego definition of SIDS, this diagnosis can be made only if "an infant under one year of age has died suddenly and unexpectedly, the onset of the fatal episode

was apparently associated with sleep, and a thorough investigation of the case, including performance of a complete autopsy and review of the circumstances of death and the clinical history does not provide an explanation for the death." If these criteria are not fulfilled, the cases should be termed "unclassified infant death" or "sudden unexpected death in infancy".

The stratified section of the San Diego definition may be applied in scientific investigations of SIDS cases. There are three subtypes of SIDS, which rely on 30 different pieces of information from specific investigations, such as the autopsy findings (including additional investigations), death scene investigation, and clinical history (**Table 2**).

Epidemiology and Risk Factors

SIDS is a rare event in the first month of life. Most SIDS victims die between the second and fifth months of life and 60% are male.

Since the epidemiological studies in the late 1980s and early 1990s, a number of important risk factors for SIDS have been identified. The most widely recognized risk factor is the prone sleeping position. Since then, many countries have begun encouraging parents to avoid this sleeping position and to place infants on their back. The prevalence of infants sleeping prone has since decreased by 50–90% in most countries and the rate of SIDS has decreased proportionally by 50–90%. The side sleeping position is also discouraged, as it is unstable and infants placed on their side will subsequently roll to a prone position.

There used to be a peak of deaths in the winter months, due to the prevalence of upper respiratory tract infections. But since the decline in prone sleeping this winter, that peak has disappeared. In all epidemiological studies, maternal smoking during pregnancy emerged as an important risk factor in SIDS. Although postnatal smoking is also a risk factor, it is difficult to isolate this from prenatal smoking. If all smoke exposure could be eliminated, it is highly likely that one-third of SIDS cases could be prevented.

Since the decrease in prone sleeping, other risk factors have become apparent, such as an unsafe sleeping environment. Soft or loose bedding, pillows, quilts, and sheepskins have been identified as risk factors in SIDS. Additional risk factors are warmer room temperatures or multiple layers of clothing. Quilts and loose bedding increase not only the risk of smothering, but also overheating.

Sharing the parental bed with an infant facilitates breastfeeding and promotes parent–infant bonding. However, epidemiological studies have shown that bed sharing constitutes an increased risk mainly when the parents are smokers or the infant is very young (under the age of 12 weeks). Bed sharing on a sofa is always dangerous and should always be avoided.

Table 2   Criteria used in the San Diego definition of SIDS

	Previous history	Circumstances of death	Autopsy findings
General definition	• Sudden and unexpected death • Under 1 year of age • Lethal episode during sleep • Death unexplained by CH	• Unexplained after review of the circumstances	• Unexplained after complete autopsy
Specific definition			
Category Ia SIDS	1. Older than 21 days, under 9 months 2. Normal CH 3. Full-term pregnancy (≥37 weeks) 4. Normal growth and development 5. No similar deaths in siblings/relatives	• Scene investigation performed and gave no explanation • Safe sleep environment • No evidence for an accident	1. No lethal pathological findings 2. No unexplained trauma, abuse, neglect, or unintentional injury 3. No substantial thymic stress 4. Toxicology, microbiology, radiology, vitreous chemistry, and metabolic screening negative
Category Ib SIDS	1–5 (criteria for category Ia SIDS)	Scene investigation was not undertaken	1–4 and 5. One or more of the following analyses were not performed: Toxicology, microbiology radiology, vitreous chemistry, and metabolic screening
Category II SIDS	Differences to category I criteria: 6. Age range (0–21 days, 270–365 days) 7. Neonatal/perinatal conditions that have resolved by the time of death 8. Similar deaths in siblings, near relatives	Mechanical asphyxia or suffocation by overlaying not determined with certainty	1–5 and 6. Abnormal growth and development not thought to have contributed to death 7. More marked inflammatory changes or abnormalities not sufficient to cause the death
USID	• Criteria for cat. I or II SIDS are not fulfilled	• Alternative diagnoses of natural or unnatural death are equivocal	• Autopsy has not been performed

USID, unclassified sudden infant death; *CH*, clinical history; *SIDS*, sudden infant death syndrome.

Case–control studies have shown that using a dummy reduces the risk of SIDS, and a recent meta-analysis has shown a strong protective effect. Results from many studies, including a recent meta-analysis, have demonstrated the protective effect of breast-feeding against SIDS. Immunizations in infancy are often seen by lay people as a risk factor. A couple of studies have confirmed the protective effect of immunizations in infancy (**Table 3**).

Results of Autopsy

Investigation of cases of sudden and unexpected deaths in all age groups is one of the major fields of forensic medicine. The investigation of infant deaths requires the application of special diagnostic methods and includes forensic pathology as well as other fields of forensic medicine and medicine in general, for example, radiology, toxicology, microbiology, virology, neuropathology, pediatric pathology, pediatrics, clinical chemistry, physiology, epidemiology, and genetics. An autopsy seeks to achieve five main aims:

1. Determining the manner of death (natural/unnatural)
2. Diagnosing the cause of death

3. Deducing whether or not the death would have been preventable
4. Informing parents on the risk of further deaths (SIDS) in the family
5. Amending the death certificate

It is recommended that a standardized protocol should be used for all postmortem investigations. In 2007, an international and interdisciplinary group published such an extended protocol in Forensic Science International. This protocol includes a recommendation for additional investigations as well as a detailed sampling scheme.

Typical Macroscopic Findings

In SIDS cases, unspecific but typical findings can be seen. Most of the infants are properly developed in accordance with their age and well nourished. In about 35% of cases, signs of sweating have been determined before death: the hair, clothing, and sometimes the bedclothes are found to be wet. Lips and nail beds are cyanotic. Livores are often found on the front side because of the frequent use of the prone sleeping position. Livores are absent around the mouth and nose in cases of a face-down position, which may be indicative of the occlusion of both.

Table 3   Risk factors for sudden infant death syndrome

Modifiable risk factors	OR (95% CI)
Prone sleeping position	6.08 (3.33–11.08)
Side sleeping position	2.01 (1.38–2.93)
Smoking of the mother in pregnancy	3.43 (1.39–8.46)
Smoking in the presence of the baby	3.41 (1.98–5.88)
Soft sleeping surface	3.0 (1.1–8.7)
Quilts, duvets, and sheepskin in the baby bed	2.20 (1.21–4.00)
Bed sharing in the parental bed	2.73 (1.34–5.55)
Sofa sharing	21.77 (3.79–125.00)
Overheating (hot room temperature and/or many layers of clothing and/or thick duvet)	3.52 (1.74–7.11)
Other risk factors	
Young mother (<20 years)	18.71 (6.00–58.32)
Low socioeconomic status	3.00 (1.35–6.69)
Protective factors	
Breast-feeding	0.48 (0.28–0.82)
Use of pacifier	0.39 (0.25–0.59)
Timely immunizations	0.54 (0.39–0.76)

Odds ratios and 95% confidence intervals from the CESDI study and the German GeSID study.
Source: Blair, P.S., Sidebotham, P., Evason-Coombe, C., Edmonds, M., Heckstall-Smith, E.M., Fleming, P., 2009. Hazardous cosleeping environments and risk factors amenable to change: case–control study of SIDS in south west England. British Medical Journal 339, b3666; Fleming, P.J., Gilbert, R., Azaz, Y., et al., 1990. Interaction between bedding and sleeping position in the sudden infant death syndrome: a population based case–control study. British Medical Journal 301 (6743), 85–89; Fleming, P.J., Blair, P.S., Bacon, C., et al., 1996. Environment of infants during sleep and risk of the sudden infant death syndrome: results of 1993–5 case–control study for confidential inquiry into stillbirths and deaths in infancy. Confidential Enquiry into Stillbirths and Deaths Regional Coordinators and Researchers. British Medical Journal 313 (7051), 191–195; Vennemann, M.M., Findeisen, M., Butterfass-Bahloul, T., et al., 2005. Modifiable risk factors for SIDS in Germany: results of GeSID. Acta Paediatrics 94 (6), 655–660.

In about 40–60% of victims, a white, sometimes hemorrhagic foam is localized in and sometimes around the mouth, indicating the development of lung edemas. In more than 90% of all victims, petechial hemorrhages are found subpleurally, subepicardially, and in the thymus.

- Generally normally developed infants
- Heavy sweating before death (around 35% of all cases)
- Signs of vomiting and terminal aspiration of stomach contents (**Figure 2**)
- Cyanosis of nail beds and lips
- Often typical livores at the front (due to prone sleeping position)
- Bloody foam in front of nose and mouth
- Often a hemorrhagic lung edema
- Dystelectatic lungs
- Subpleural and subepicardial petechia (**Figure 3**)
- Petechia in the thymus (**Figure 4**)
- Empty bladder
- Mild brain edema

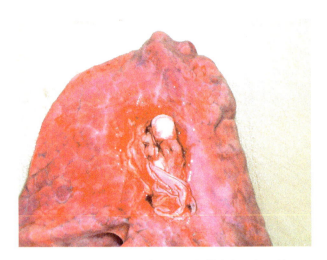

Figure 2   Aspiration of stomach contents (milk) in large bronchi.

Histological Changes

A histological investigation is mandatory in pediatric pathology. Histology is necessary to describe the quantity and quality of preexisting diseases, hypoxic changes, and other findings indicating unnatural causes of death. It is therefore necessary to take samples of all organs and tissues during autopsy. If possible, the central nervous system should be investigated by a neuropathologist experienced in infant death. Findings such as mild edema, congestion, and some foci of gliosis are common in SIDS. Meningoencephalitis, aplasia, or severe dysplasia of important nuclei or signs of acute or repeated hypoxemia also have to be considered as causes of death.

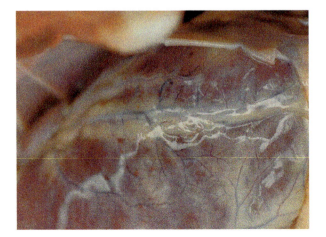

Figure 3   Petechial hemorrhages subepicardial.

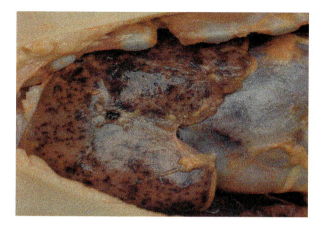

Figure 4 Hemorrhages in thymus.

In the lungs, hemorrhagic alveolar edema, dystelectatic regions, congestion, and bronchus-associated lymphatic tissue in the lung periphery are common findings in SIDS, as are intraalveolar macrophages. Mild respiratory tract infections—often caused by various types of viruses—can be observed in up to 60% of cases, but these are usually not sufficient to explain the death. Only in cases showing severe infection (interstitial pneumonia showing bacterial superinfection, bronchopneumonia, and severe bronchiolitis) with septicemia/viremia, it is possible to consider infection as a cause of death.

In a small number of cases, histological investigations of the myocardium show findings typical for myocarditis, structural anomalies, or disturbances of the cardiac conductive system. In case of inflammation, immunohistochemistry can assist in characterizing the cell types involved.

The histological investigation of the intestinum can show malformations (congenital aganglionic megacolon), infections, and other disturbances, which sometimes cannot be diagnosed macroscopically. Gastroenteritis can be of relevance to the cause of death if the disease is accompanied by significant dehydration or if it is caused by bacteria, which are able to excrete toxins.

The investigation of lymphatic tissue is helpful in diagnosing stress before death and in detecting a systemic reaction as a symptom of local inflammation. Until now, it has not been possible to show pathological immunoreactions as a cause of SIDS.

Postmortem Investigation

According to the SIDS definition, the circumstances of death and the place of event should be investigated by an experienced medical specialist, forensic scientist, pediatric pathologist, or pediatrician in collaboration with the police. In some countries, this is carried out by forensic nurses. The autopsy should be performed as early as possible to avoid significant postmortal changes of the body. The autopsy may also need to incorporate additional investigations regarding histology, toxicology, bacteriology, virology, neuropathology, and clinical chemistry. Finally, the infant's development should be analyzed, taking into account all the medical documents that are available.

Death Scene

This investigation should be performed as early as possible. In some cases, the death scene investigation can give important hints to explain the situation leading to death as well as the cause of death (rebreathing of CO_2 or hyperthermia). Furthermore, the investigator has the opportunity to ask the parents directly for details of the clinical history before autopsy. The investigation includes an initial external examination of the body, the measurement of the body temperature, an investigation of the room conditions (size, temperature, heating system, air exchange rate, and bed covering), and of the sleeping environment, and necessitates equipment (thermometer, scales, and camera, **Table 4**).

Autopsy

An autopsy is a mandatory part of any investigation into sudden and unexpected infant deaths as the external investigation alone is not sufficient for rendering diagnosis with regard to the cause and manner of death. The autopsy should be done by a pathologist with experience in pediatric and forensic pathology. Some standardized autopsy protocols (Sheffield Protocol, Nord SIDS Protocol, International

Table 4 Death scene investigation

External conditions	Surrounding	Situation found dead	External examination of the corpse
Size of room	Type of bed	Body position	Sings of death
Size of windows	Type of blanket	Clothing	Time of death
Heating	Size and weight of blanket	Covering	Resuscitation
Air exchange rate	Type of mattress	Sweating	Signs of violence
Room temperature	Toys in bed	Vomiting	Body temperature
Temperature outside		Fixation used	

standardized autopsy protocol) have been developed and published. Before autopsy, an X-ray investigation should be done to detect fresh and old fractures and bone anomalies. Then, material can be taken for microbiology (swabs from the mouth and nose, and fluid from the spinal canal). The next stage involves an external examination of the corpse, followed by an internal investigation, including all body cavities. Body fluids and specimens for microbiology and virology should be taken using sterile instruments. The most common findings are *Staphylococcus aureus* in the nose and CMV or RSV in lungs. Further material has to be taken for toxicological and histological investigations. Different staining methods are useful to investigate the tissue specimens (**Table 5**).

Clinical History

An analysis of the pregnancy (complications), delivery (position of infant, duration, complications, APGAR score, percentile), the infants' development (height and weight, previous diseases, hospital treatment, food, vaccination state), and the situation immediately before death (signs of infection, crying, feeding problems) is recommended. To evaluate autopsy findings, it is important to know if resuscitation attempts were done and by whom (parents and/or emergency doctor).

Cause of Death

In accordance with the investigation described, approximately 3–6% of cases can be classified as unnatural deaths. Up to 25–30% can be diagnosed as natural deaths due to defined causes (**Table 1**). The remaining 60% plus can be attributed to SIDS. The diagnosis is made by exclusion. Of these, a small percentage can be diagnosed as SIDS Ia (San Diego definition), whereas the majority displays minor pathological changes compatible with the diagnosis of SIDS Ib or SIDS II.

Table 5   Routine staining methods for tissue specimens

Staining method	Tissue
Hematoxylin–eosin	All specimens
Fat	Myocardium, liver, muscle
Alcianblue-PAS	Lungs
Berlin blue	Lungs, spleen
PAS	Kidney
Giemsa	Ribs
Van Gieson	Brain

PAS, periodic acid–Schiff.

Hypotheses of Possible Causes of SIDS

A number of theories on possible causes of SIDS have been proposed in the past, but only a few have been clearly proven, mostly in individual cases. The earliest recorded death is that of an infant reported in the Old Testament, which was attributed to suffocation caused by overlaying (I Kings, 3:19). In 1830 Paltauff, supposed that such death could be due to suffocation by an enlarged thymus gland, which compressed the trachea (Status thymolymphaticus). After the Second World War, suffocation by a soft blanket on the mouth and nose was the favored theory. About 40 years ago, Naeye published his observations of SIDS cases, suggesting that seven different findings could be suitable as tissue markers indicating hypoxia. By measuring the biochemical marker of acute hypoxia, hypoxanthine in vitreous humor, Rognum et al. showed in 1988 that a large proportion of SIDS victims had had significant periods of hypoxia before death. In 1972, Steinschneider introduced his sleep apnea theory, which became the theoretical basis for the monitoring of infants showing "atypical" breathing patterns. He investigated five infants who showed prolonged periods of apnea during sleep. However, it was later found that two of these infants had died due to homicide. In parallel, it was discussed whether or not infections could influence or trigger the sudden death. Blackwell et al. hypothesized that an overwhelmingly proinflammatory response to bacterial toxins (as an inflammatory response to sepsis) may cause physiological changes leading to death. In the late 1980s and 1990s, SIDS research became more and more interdisciplinary, and typical risk factors for SIDS were identified by a number of epidemiological studies in different countries and regions. In the second half of the 1990s, molecular genetic studies were performed to investigate the genetic basis of functional disturbances. Possible cardiovascular causes of SIDS, for example, include abnormalities of the cardiac conduction system. In addition, ventricular tachycardia or fibrillation, often found without evidence of structural heart disease (so-called primary electrical disorders), may be associated with sudden cardiac death in neonates. One such disorder is long-QT syndrome (LQTS), which is characterized by increased sensitivity of the myocardium, with an increased propensity to developing ventricular fibrillation. Several studies have investigated a potential association of prolonged QT interval and SIDS and found that 1–10% of SIDS victims showed mutations in genes associated with LQTS. Other study groups investigated the serotonin transporter gene because of a reported decreased serotonergic receptor binding in brain stems of SIDS victims, but with inconcordant results. Further studies focused on genes that are involved in the early embryology of the autonomic nervous system, genes of nicotine metabolism, and genes regulating inflammation, energy production, hypoglycemia, other metabolic disturbances, and thermal regulation. Rognum investigated the significance of mtDNA changes, complement component C4 polymorphisms, and polymorphisms of the interleukin 10 gene. Schneider first demonstrated the link between signs of infection before death in SIDS and partial deletions of the C4 gene.

Nevertheless, the main result of these studies is that SIDS victims show different gene variants for some of the investigated genes compared to controls. However, only in a small percentage of SIDS cases can the death be explained by such changes.

As early as 1972, Wedgewood introduced a "three-hit model" for SIDS suggesting that sudden and unexpected death may occur if three conditions are fulfilled simultaneously:

1. An infant is at a vulnerable developmental stage.
2. A predisposing endogenous factor(s) is present.
3. An exogenous trigger initiates the lethal process.

This hypothesis was later taken up and modified by Rognum and Saugstad, Filiano and Kinney, and Kahn. In particular, Rognum et al. included "genetic risk factors" or "genetic makeup" as predisposing factors The main advantages of these "three-hit theories" (in contrast to others) are that most of the information from pathology, neuropathology, microbiology, physiology, epidemiology, and pediatrics can be included in one of the three main areas, and that these models enable integration of new knowledge.

Currently it is very difficult to maintain an overview of the multiple investigations being conducted in the various fields of SIDS research, that is, a search of PubMed for the term "SIDS" finds nearly 10 000 publications—including 1300 from the years 2005–2010. The results reported are sometimes not directly comparable as some authors have used their own definitions for cases and controls, and the diagnosis of SIDS has not always been confirmed by autopsy and additional investigations, and is therefore not in accordance with standard definitions.

See also: **Forensic Medicine/Pathology:** Autopsy; Histopathology; **Investigations:** Crime Scene Analysis and Reconstruction.

Further Reading

Bajanowski, T., Vennemann, M., Bohnert, M., Rauch, E., Brinkmann, B., Mitchell, E.A., 2005. Un-natural causes of sudden unexpected deaths initially thought to be sudden infant death syndrome. International Journal of Legal Medicine 119, 213–216.

Bajanowski, T., Vege, A., Byard, R.W., et al., 2007. Sudden infant death syndrome (SIDS) – standardised investigations and classification: Recommendations. Forensic Science International 165, 129–143.

Blackwell, C.C., Moscovis, S.M., Gordon, A.E., et al., 2005. Cytokine responses and sudden infant death syndrome: genetic, developmental, and environmental risk factors. Journal of Leukocyte Biology 78, 1242–1254.

Blair, P.S., Sidebotham, P., Berry, P.J., Evans, M., Fleming, P.J., 2006. Major epidemiological changes in sudden infant death syndrome: a 20-year population-based study in the UK. Lancet 367 (9507), 314–319.

Blair, P.S., Sidebotham, P., Evason-Coombe, C., Edmonds, M., Heckstall-Smith, E.M., Fleming, P., 2009. Hazardous cosleeping environments and risk factors amenable to change: case–control study of SIDS in south west England. British Medical Journal 339, b3666.

Byard, R.W., Krous, H.F., 2001. Sudden Infant Death Syndrome – Problems, Progress and Possibilities. Arnold, London.

Carpenter, R.G., Irgens, L.M., Blair, P.S., et al., 2004. Sudden unexplained infant death in 20 regions in Europe: case control study. Lancet 363, 185–191.

Fracasso, T., Vennemann, M., Klöcker, M., Bajanowski, T., Brinkmann, B., Pfeiffer, H., 2010. Petechial bleedings in sudden infant death. International Journal of Legal Medicine 125, 205–210.

Guntheroth, W.G., Spiers, P.S., 2002. The triple risk hypothesis in sudden infant death syndrome. Pediatrics 110 (e64), 1–70.

Kinney, H.C., Richerson, G.B., Dymecki, S.M., Darnall, R.A., Nattie, E.E., 2009. The brainstem and serotonin in the sudden infant death syndrome. Annual Review of Pathology 4, 517–550.

Krous, H.F., Beckwith, J.B., Byard, R.W., et al., 2004. Sudden infant death syndrome (SIDS) and unclassified sudden infant deaths (USID): a definitional and diagnostic approach. Pediatrics 114, 234–238.

Mitchell, E.A., 2009. What is the mechanism of SIDS? Clues from epidemiology. Developmental Psychobiology 51, 215–222.

Mitchell, E.A., Milerad, J., 2006. Smoking and the sudden infant death syndrome. Reviews on Environmental Health 21, 81–103.

Mitchell, E.A., Thompson, J.M.D., Becroft, D.M.O., et al., 2008. Head covering and the risk of SIDS: findings from the New Zealand and German SIDS case control studies. Pediatrics 121, e1478–e1483.

Moon, R.Y., Horne, R.S., Hauck, F.R., 2007. Sudden infant death syndrome. Lancet 370, 1578–1587.

Opdal, S.H., Rognum, T.O., 2011. Gene variants predisposing to SIDS: current knowledge. Forensic Science, Medicine, and Pathology 7, 26–36.

Vennemann, M.M.T., Höffgen, M., Bajanowski, T., Hense, H.W., Mitchell, E.A., 2007. Do immunisations reduce the risk for SIDS? A meta-analysis. Vaccine 25, 4875–4879.

Vennemann, M., Bajanowski, T., Brinkmann, B., Jorch, G., Sauerland, C., Mitchell, E.A., 2009. Sleep environment risk factors for SIDS: the German SIDS Study. Pediatrics 123, 1162–1170.

Hyperthermia and Hypothermia

T Ishikawa and H Maeda, Osaka City University Medical School, Osaka, Japan

Glossary

Acclimatization Physiological accustomization to a new climate or new conditions, especially to a change in environmental temperature or geographic elevation.

Chilblain A painful, itching swelling with erythema on the skin, occasionally accompanied by blisters or ulcers, in the peripheries including the hands, feet, ears, and nose, caused by impaired microcirculation, as a consequence of persistent or intermittent cold exposure, usually in combination with high moisture.

Dehydration A state of body water loss sufficient to cause intravascular volume deficits, with or without loss of electrolytes.

Drug adverse effect An unintended result of therapeutic use of a drug, usually with an undesirable harmful effect.

Frostbite A severe local skin lesion caused by freezing cold, usually on the hands, feet, ears, and nose, as a consequence of stagnant blood flow and edema due to paralytic vasodilatation in combination with inflammation and necrosis.

Heat cramp Usually nonfatal, painful muscle spasms with headache, thirst, and hypotension, but without hyperpyrexia, induced by exertion in a hot environment, typically related to salt deficiency.

Heat exhaustion A continuum with heatstroke, mainly resulting from hypotonic dehydration due to excessive sweating (hyperhidrotic heat exhaustion), marked by prostration, weakness, fainting, and vascular collapse, usually with nearly normal body temperature; otherwise, a thermal disorder accompanied by failure of sweating (anhidrotic heat exhaustion), possibly due to dysfunction of the sweat mechanism.

Heat-shock protein A ubiquitous protein group, which is induced by various stressors, including heat and cold, and functions to reduce the harmful consequences.

Heatstroke A severe potentially fatal illness involving thermoregulatory disorder due to extremely high environmental temperature, characterized by hot and dry skin, and cerebral dysfunction involving confusion, accompanied by an elevated body temperature (often over 40°C), resulting in vascular collapse and coma.

Heat wave A prolonged period of unusually hot weather as a climatic cause of accidental heatstroke.

Hide and die A peculiar aspect of some cases of fatal hypothermia, where the victim is found hiding away from sight, often undressing (paradoxical undressing), indicating hypothermic brain dysfunction.

Hyperpyrexia Excessive unusual elevation of the core body temperature over 40.0–41.5 °C (104.0–106.7 °F), or extremely high fever, caused by various exogenous and endogenous factors, including an extremely hot environment, drugs, toxins, and fibril diseases.

Hyperthermia A pathological condition with an elevated core body temperature, usually over 40 °C (104 °F), caused by high environmental temperature or induced by drugs or other chemicals: synonym of hyperpyrexia.

Hypothermia A pathological condition with a decreased core body temperature, usually below 35 °C (95 °F), caused by low environmental temperature (cold exposure), or induced by drugs, or artificial cooling for therapeutic purposes.

Malignant hyperthermia A rare life-threatening condition involving an extreme rise of core body temperature (hyperthermia), triggered by exposure to specific drugs used for anesthesia in patients with a genetic defect: synonym of malignant hyperpyrexia.

Malignant syndrome A potentially life-threatening neurological disorder involving an extreme rise of core body temperature (hyperthermia) and rhabdomyolysis, induced by drugs, mainly narcotics, psychotropics, and analgesics.

Multiple organ dysfunction syndrome (MODS) A clinical condition defined as the presence of altered organ function, usually involving two or more organ systems, in an acutely ill patient such that homeostasis cannot be maintained without intervention, describing the process as a continuum of physiological derangement (dysfunction) that changes over time, instead of earlier terminology such as multiple organ failure and multisystem organ failure.

Paradoxical undressing A peculiar aspect of some cases of fatal hypothermia, where the victim is found partly or even totally naked in a cold environment, aggravating heat loss, possibly as a consequence of hypothermic brain dysfunction.

Rhabdomyolysis Diffuse skeletal muscle injury involving myogloninemia and myoglobinuria, caused by various factors, including injury, ischemia or hypoxia, alcohol, drugs, and other chemicals, resulting in renal dysfunction.

Serotonin syndrome A potentially life-threatening neurological disorder involving an extreme rise of core body temperature (hyperthermia) and rhabdomyolysis, as a drug adverse effect of selective serotonin reuptake inhibitor (SSRI, antidepressant).

Social deprivation Living conditions lacking adequate social care or support.

Sunstroke A form of heatstroke caused by excessive exposure to the sun's rays, presenting with hypotension, tachycardia, and cold sweat due to vascular collapse, often without hyperpyrexia.

Suspended animation A temporary state simulating death, where vital signs cannot be detected clinically.

Systemic inflammatory response syndrome (SIRS) A clinical concept that implies a systemic inflammatory process arising from a variety of severe insults, including infection and noninfectious causes. The systemic response is termed "sepsis" when it is the result of a confirmed infectious process.

Thermoregulation The physiological regulation of body temperature, which is maintained by a balance between heat load and loss; heat is produced in the oxidative metabolic process and acquired from the environment, and is lost by conduction, radiation, and evaporation involving sweating and insensible heat loss (mainly, moisture loss from the skin and lungs). The thermoregulatory center is located in the preoptic anterior hypothalamus.

Wischnewsky spot Multiple dark-brownish punctate gastric hemorrhages or erosions as a sign of disturbed microcirculation in fatal hypothermia.

Introduction

The normal human core body temperature is approximately 37 °C, maintained by a balance between heat load and loss; heat is produced in the oxidative metabolic process and acquired from the environment, and is lost by conduction, radiation, and evaporation involving sweating and insensible heat loss (mainly, moisture loss from the skin and lungs). The thermoregulatory center, located in the preoptic anterior hypothalamus, is affected in systemic hyperthermia and hypothermia. These systemic thermal disorders usually occur in unusual environments accidentally; however, fatalities may occur with abuse or neglect, which is of forensic concern, whereas those of deprived people, and at work and during sports are of social concern. The victims mostly include children and elderly people, who are susceptible to extreme temperatures. These fatalities may also involve predisposing health conditions and individual susceptibility, including inadequate nutrition, alcohol or drug abuse, trauma, and mental or physical disability. Adverse or toxic effects of drugs and other chemicals can also induce systemic thermal disorders.

Hyperthermia

Social and Forensic Issues

Systemic hyperthermia occurs in a hot environment (exogenous hyperthermia) or by a rise in body temperature due to excess heat generation (endogenous hyperthermia). A typical condition that causes exogenous hyperthermia is extreme exertion in an inadequate environment involving high temperature and humidity (exertional hyperthermia); however, the contribution of predisposing health conditions and individual susceptibility should be considered as usually only some people are affected under the same conditions; these include preexisting disease (e.g., cardiac and cerebral disorders, and dermatitis), obesity, physical weakness, inadequate nutrition, alcoholism, and use of diuretic, neurotropic, and anticholinergic drugs, as well as heavy clothing.

Apart from incidental hyperthermia due to intolerably hot ambient temperature during summer heat waves, exogenous fatal hyperthermia can occur under various situations involved in abuse or neglect, and social issues related to health care, work, and sports or recreation. Child abuse and neglect are major issues of forensic interest, for example, confined in a small compartment, or left in a room or automobile unattended in summer. In winter, however, inadequate use of heating can cause infantile casualties. Elderly fatalities during prolonged heat waves occur frequently with a lower socioeconomic status or social deprivation; however, fatalities of healthy young adults (e.g., athletes, laborers, and military recruits) are not rare; deliberate or even torturous exposure to extreme conditions is a forensic issue.

Malignant hyperthermia induced by anesthetics, associated with a genetic predisposition, is regarded as a form of endogenous heat generation. A similar disorder is involved in the toxicity of drugs and other chemicals, especially illicit drugs, and the adverse effect of a spectrum of therapeutic drugs. These raise clinical and medicolegal issues.

Pathophysiology and Clinical Manifestations

Heatstroke and related syndromes

The human body is more susceptible to an elevated body temperature than to a decrease; both exogenous and endogenous hyperthermia is life-threatening. Hyperthermia involves water and salt depletion due to perspiration, presenting with various clinical manifestations, which may be classified into four classic forms: (1) Heatstroke: a fatally severe condition involving thermoregulatory disorder, characterized by hot and dry skin, and cerebral dysfunction involving confusion, as well as tachycardia and hyperventilation, accompanied by hyperpyrexia (often over 40 °C), resulting in vascular collapse, coma, rhabdomyolysis, and multiple organ dysfunction syndrome (MODS) ultimately. (2) Sunstroke: a form of heatstroke caused by excessive exposure to the sun's rays, presenting with hypotension, tachycardia, and cold sweat due to vascular collapse, often without hyperpyrexia. (3) Heat exhaustion: a form having a continuum with heatstroke, mainly resulting from hypotonic dehydration due to excessive sweating (hyperhidrotic heat exhaustion), marked by prostration, weakness, fainting, and vascular collapse, usually with nearly normal body temperature; otherwise, a thermal disorder accompanied by failure of sweating (anhidrotic heat exhaustion), possibly due to dysfunction of the sweat mechanism. (4) Heat cramps: usually nonfatal, painful muscle spasms with headache, thirst, and hypotension, but without hyperpyrexia, induced by exertion in a hot environment, typically related to salt deficiency, partly including possible exertional rhabdomyolysis, and sometimes associated with hyperventilation, alcohol abuse, or ill health.

The human body can be fairly well adapted to a hot environment (acclimatization); however, an extreme environment in combination with predisposing factors and individual susceptibility ultimately impairs thermoregulation, and the body temperature rises precipitously in association with a failure to sweat. High humidity interferes with the dissipation of heat from the skin. Obesity is a risk factor due to increased load on the heart, increased metabolic heat, reduced heat loss because of the large volume-to-area ratio, and extra insulation by fat. A rise in the body temperature results in generalized vasodilatation, reducing circulatory blood volume. Lowered peripheral resistance enhances venous return and increases cardiac output, leading to elevated venous pressure that induces high-output cardiac failure and circulatory collapse, and can ultimately extinguish sweating. A rise in body temperature increases the metabolic rate (around 10%/1 °C), subsequently increasing tissue oxygen consumption; however, alkalosis and increased blood flow impair oxygen supply to the tissues from blood, resulting in decreased arterial and increased venous oxygen saturation. Thus the main pathophysiology of heatstroke consists of hyperpyrexia involving impaired thermoregulation, accompanied by dehydration due to extreme sweating, and profound systemic hypoxia. An individual who survives the acute phase develops further complications of pneumonia secondary to pulmonary edema, renal tubular necrosis, adrenal hemorrhage, hepatic necrosis, myocardial necrosis, rhabdomyolysis, systemic inflammatory response syndrome (SIRS), disseminated intravascular coagulation (DIC), and MODS ultimately.

Children and elderly people are apparently more susceptible. A child's small body with a large area-to-volume ratio is easily affected by ambient temperature, and physical immaturity is predisposed to thermoregulatory disturbance because of lower sweating capacity and a high metabolic rate, which is aggravated by excessive self-exertion involving crying and struggling. The elderly can develop heatstroke without substantial exertion due to physical, mental, and social predispositions, including diminished physical compensatory capacity, debilitation, physical and mental disability, and inadequate nutrition, as well as a low socioeconomic situation and social deprivation. Sedentary (nonexertional) hyperthermia of the elderly during heat waves usually occurs around the end of the first week as a result of gradual deterioration of the heat-adaptive function.

Drug-related hyperthermia

Malignant hyperthermia is a rare life-threatening condition, caused by specific drugs used for anesthesia, including a halogenated volatile anesthetic and succinylcholine (neuromuscular blocking agent). The patient has an autosomal dominant genetic defect causing disruption of intracellular calcium homeostasis involved in excitation–contraction coupling in skeletal muscles. Exposure to a trigger drug causes and sustains an unusually high myoplasm calcium level and persistent skeletal muscle contraction, resulting in a marked increase in oxidative metabolism, leading to a serious condition with a rapid rise in body temperature, including tachycardia, skeletal muscle rigidity, arterial hypoxemia, metabolic and respiratory acidosis, electrolyte disturbance involving hyperkalemia, profound hyperthermia, circulatory collapse, and death if not treated promptly. In addition, some illicit drugs (e.g., amphetamines) can cause severe hyperthermia, accompanied by rhabdomyolysis (drug-induced hyperthermia). A spectrum of other drugs, mainly including narcotics, psychotropics, and analgesics, can induce rhabdomyolysis with hyperthermia, which is called "malignant syndrome." "Serotonin syndrome" is a similar drug adverse effect of selective serotonin reuptake inhibitor (antidepressant).

Autopsy Findings

Macropathology
External findings

There is no specific pathology of fatal hyperthermia; however, it is important to note findings related to predisposition (e.g., general condition, skin disease, and drug abuse) and physical abuse or neglect as well as those needed to differentiate other insults. Intradermal multiple petechial hemorrhages in the chest and extremities can be a sign of prolonged death involving DIC and MODS. An extraordinarily high rectal temperature in the early postmortem period, with reference to rigor and lividity, may suggest death involving hyperpyrexia, although other fibril diseases and traumas should be excluded.

Internal findings

The aim of pathology in the context of a diagnosis of fatal heatstroke is the first to exclude other insults, and the second to detect findings compatible with heatstroke, although they are not specific. These include punctate hemorrhages in the intrathoracic (pleural, pericardial, and epicardial) serosa, cerebral periventricular petechiae, and pulmonary and/or cerebral edema in short survival case, and cloudy swelling of the skeletal muscle and other viscera with edema, and overall serosal and mucosal multiple hemorrhages, suggesting DIC and MODS in prolonged deaths. Dark red or brown urine suggests myoglobinuria. Postmortem CT morphology of the lungs presents findings similar to congestive heart failure.

Histopathology and immunohistochemistry

Histology demonstrates the findings of MODS compatible with fatal heatstroke, including pulmonary edema with/without secondary pneumonia, renal tubular necrosis, adrenal hemorrhage, hepatic centrilobular necrosis, acute pancreatitis, myocardial necrosis, rhabdomyolysis, cerebral edema with diffuse neuronal injury involving Purkinje cell necrosis, DIC, and SIRS. Myofiber hypercontraction necrosis and plaque-like signs of decomposition are characteristic of drug-induced malignant hyperthermia.

Possible immunohistochemical markers include heat-shock proteins (HSPs), ubiquitin, catecholamines, and chromogranin A to detect a systemic response to thermal stress, and myoglobin to detect rhabdomyolysis. Low dopamine and chromogranin A positivity in the hypothalamus, and high noradrenaline and dopamine positivity in the adrenal medulla are possible indicators of a prolonged systemic response to prolonged hyperthermia. Patchy myoglobin loss in skeletal muscles with deposition in the kidneys indicates rhabdomyolysis.

Toxicology

Toxicological screening is important to evaluate the contribution of alcohol and drugs to predispose accidental hyperthermia, and to detect drugs and other chemicals that can induce systemic hyperthermia and rhabdomyolysis: malignant hyperthermia, malignant syndrome, and serotonin syndrome.

Biochemistry

Clinical findings: Biochemical findings are crucial for a clinical diagnosis of heatstroke. Serum electrolyte changes vary by case, but hyperkalemia is a sign of poor prognosis. Hepatic damage is evident, for example, as indicated by elevated serum aspartate aminotransferase (SGOT) and lactate dehydrogenase levels. Elevated serum creatine phosphokinase level, myoglobinemia, myoglobinuria, and hypocalcemia indicate rhabdomyolysis. Hyperventilation causes alkalosis, but acidosis can result from lactic acidosis and/or renal failure involved in MODS. Elevated blood urea nitrogen and creatinine indicate combined influences of dehydration, skeletal muscle damage, and renal failure. Other findings indicative of SIRS, DIC, and MODS are signs of poor prognosis. Elevated serum procalcitonin and growth hormone levels were reported in heatstroke survivors.

Postmortem findings: Biochemistry is also important in postmortem investigations; findings that indicate dehydration, electrolyte disturbance, systemic skeletal muscle damage, SIRS, and MODS involving renal, hepatic, cardiac, and pulmonary damage can be detected. In early death without MODS, elevated creatinine levels in blood and body fluids indicate skeletal muscle damage; however, infantile and elderly subjects only present with signs of dehydration, as indicated by an elevated urea nitrogen level and electrolyte disturbance. Catecholamines, serotonin, and chromogranin A in blood and body fluids are possible indicators of stress responses to prolonged thermal stress.

Molecular Pathology

Hyperthermia along with an increased metabolic rate leads to protein denaturation in viscera, involving damage to membrane integrity, the cytoskeleton and nucleus, and ultimate cellular death. These processes involve systemic activation of biomarkers related to self-protection, inflammation, and repair, which include cytokines, chemokines, antiapoptotic factors, and cell components.

Key Points of Diagnosis

Clinical diagnosis of heatstroke and related syndromes is usually not difficult, considering hyperpyrexia and laboratory findings, and excluding other causes of hyperpyrexia, but early diagnosis and management is needed to improve prognosis; however, postmortem diagnosis is obstructed by a lack of specific findings. The diagnosis should be established by collecting pathological findings compatible with heatstroke, related to the predisposition, drug abuse, and physical abuse or neglect, and for differentiating other insults, in combination with toxicology and biochemistry. Circumstantial evidence may also be considered when available.

Hypothermia

Social and Medicolegal Issues

Systemic hypothermia occurs due to cold exposure, or is induced by drugs, or artificial cooling for therapeutic purposes. Hypothermia in a cold environment is usually accidental, predominantly due to a cold climate (environmental hypothermia), but is often associated with alcohol or drug abuse, or illness, including debilitation, inadequate nutrition, and metabolic or endocrinological disorders. The contribution of individual susceptibility should also be considered. Cold exposure may induce a cardio- or cerebrovascular accident.

Most victims of environmental hypothermia are children and elderly people, involving abuse or neglect or health-care problems. In particular, abuse and neglect are major issues for children, and elderly fatalities in the cold season are frequent with a lower socioeconomic status or social deprivation; however, fatalities in healthy young adults (e.g., athletes, laborers, and military recruits) can occur in inadequate or accidental conditions, even during recreation (e.g., hiking and skiing), often accompanied by exhaustion, raising social and legal issues. Another situation is immersion hypothermia in cold water, for example, in shipwrecks and/or falling into ice-cold water. Fatalities in therapeutic hypothermia involve medicolegal issues.

Pathophysiology and Clinical Manifestations

The human body can be poorly adapted to a cold environment, and systemic hypothermia occurs due to uncontrollable lowering of the core body temperature (usually below 35 °C); this involves enhanced loss and reduced production of body heat under the influence of various factors: (1) environmental factors, including low temperature (not necessary below 0 °C), wind/air movement, contact heat loss from the body, and wet clothes/body; (2) physical factors, including poor body fat mass, children and elderly people, and alcohol intake; (3) reduced heat production, for example, due to inadequate nutrition, debilitation, and metabolic or endocrinological disorders (e.g., hypothyroidism and hypopituitarism); (4) impaired thermoregulation, for example, due to exhaustion, alcohol or drug intoxication, aging, and cerebrovascular disease or head injury. In addition, various factors interfere with escape: (1) disturbed consciousness, for example, due to cerebrovascular disease, head injury, alcohol or drug intoxication, metabolic coma, and mental disorder; (2) physical or mental disability, for example, due to exhaustion, disease, and trauma; (3) low socioeconomical status; (4) disaster and physical abuse or neglect.

In a cold environment, the human body conserves heat by vasoconstriction in the skin and muscles, and compensates for heat by shivering and an increased cellular metabolic rate, initially accompanied by elevated blood pressure (so-called "excitation phase"). The subcutaneous fat layer serves as an insulator. Thus the body temperature is maintained (compensation phase). Cold diuresis, induced by depressed renal reabsorption and relatively increased central blood flow, decreases body fluid, causing hemoconcentration, which is aggravated by leakage of plasma into the extracellular space (cold edema). The body temperature falls below 35 °C in extreme cold, causing mental and physical disorders with maximum respiratory stimulation but without hypotension (decompensation phase; mild hypothermia).

Compensatory heat production can function to about 32 °C, below which body temperature rapidly decreases, shivering ceases, and metabolic processes and the cardiopulmonary status deteriorate (paralysis phase; moderate hypothermia). Thus respiration becomes less frequent and shallower, and the pulse rate decreases with hypotension. Below about 28–30 °C, cerebral dysfunction is apparent, presenting with analgesia, consciousness disturbance, hallucinations, often involving "paradoxical undressing" or "hide and die," and diminished reflexes; the thermoregulatory center loses its function, and narcosis appears, finally resulting in loss of reflex (collapse phase; severe hypothermia). Cardiac function is also depressed, showing bradycardia, arrhythmia, prolonged PQ, widened QRS, and flattened/inverted T waves on an electrocardiogram. Atrial fibrillation often appears at 30 °C, below which vital signs diminish progressively with significant hypotension and possible development of pulmonary edema. Ventricular fibrillation occurs finally at 22–28 °C. Electrolyte disturbance and metabolic acidosis also affect cardiorespiratory function. Below about 20 °C, vital signs are hardly detectable with a flat electroencephalogram and bradycardia progressing to asystole (profound hypothermia). The lowest body temperature in accidental hypothermia survival was reported as approximately 14 °C.

Victims often have localized skin lesions: Chilblains are mild lesions usually in the peripheries, including the hands, feet, ears, and nose, and also on the elbows and knees, presenting with erythema, bluish or pale areas on the skin with edema, occasionally accompanied by blisters or ulcers. These lesions are a consequence of persistent or intermittent cold exposure (not necessary below 0 °C), usually in combination with high moisture, caused by impaired microcirculation, involving peripheral vasoconstriction, blood sludge due to cold agglutinins, endothelial damage, and edema, partially depending on individual predisposition. Frostbite is a more severe form, involving local skin tissue destruction, usually on the hands, feet, ears, and nose, directly caused by freezing cold, as a consequence of stagnant blood flow and edema due to paralytic vasodilatation in combination with inflammation and necrosis. The severity of this lesion is classified into four degrees: (1) erythema, (2) superficial vesiculation, (3) hemorrhagic blisters involving microvasculature, and (4) damage to deeper tissues; these depend on the temperature and duration of cold exposure and individual factors.

Survival time in dry cold can vary widely, depending on multiple factors other than temperature (e.g., wind velocity, humidity, and flooring material), but usually not shorter than hours. Immersion in cold water causes more rapid loss of heat. Previous reports described that survival time in immersion hypothermia was about 2 h in water for shipwreck victims, half an hour in water at 0 °C, and was possibly nonfatal in water at >20 °C; however, immersion in ice-cold water may result in fatal neurogenic shock.

Alcohol intake is a well-known risk factor because of vascular dilatation in the skin predisposed to heat loss, suppressed shivering due to skeletal muscle relaxation, and interference with physical and mental activity. Ethanol also antagonizes ketonemia induced by hypothermia, and impairs metabolic heat generation using ketones; however, opposite observations involving alcoholic survivors who recovered from profound hypothermia have been reported. These are attributed to the protective effect of alcohol against cardiac fibrillation or on the brain by increased blood perfusion and reduced oxygen consumption.

Infants are much more susceptible to hypothermia than adults because of their small body with a larger surface area to body mass ratio and a thin subcutaneous fat layer, which enhances heat loss per body mass. Poor muscle volume allows less compensatory increase of heat production, which contributes to chemical thermogenesis by shivering. Newborn infants for a few weeks after birth need special care to avoid hypothermia because of immature thermoregulatory function; mortality is quite high when neglected. Susceptibility of the elderly is apparent when deteriorated physical and mental abilities as well as frequent complications of debilitating diseases are considered; these conditions are readily aggravated by inadequate nutrition, low socioeconomic status, social deprivation, or neglect.

The status of "suspended animation" is a special medicolegal issue in systemic hypothermia. Advanced hypothermia involves an extremely lowered metabolism; an individual can survive with very low oxygen in the body under a condition in which vital signs cannot be detected clinically, ready for recovery without significant mental or physical deficit by adequate medical management. Such examples often include children, despite their susceptibility to hypothermia. The combined effect of narcotic intoxication or a state of subnutrition, which decreases the metabolic status, may also be considered.

Autopsy Findings

Macropathology

External findings: Classic signs of prolonged cold exposure should be noted, although these are not always present or are not specific. These include cherry-red postmortem lividity, which reflects increased blood oxyhemoglobin, and erythema (chilblains and frostbite) as local signs of cold exposure (**Figure 1**). It is also important to note pathologies related to the predisposition (e.g., general condition, head trauma, and drug abuse) and physical abuse or neglect as well as those for excluding other insults. An extraordinarily low rectal temperature in the early postmortem period, with reference to rigor and lividity, and "paradoxical undressing" may suggest death involving hypothermia.

Internal findings: The pathology of viscera is not uniform, largely depending on the death process and survival time, which are related to the severity of cold exposure (environmental factors) and the tolerance of victims; however, classic signs of fatal hypothermia are frequently detected: cherry-red

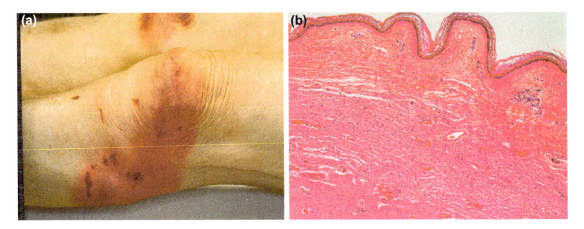

Figure 1   Erythema at the knee joint (a) and the histology (b), showing hyperemia and edema (HE, 40×).

Figure 2 Marbling of bilateral heart blood in the pericardial sac after removing the heart.

lungs with mild edema, suggesting cold air inhalation, a striking difference between bilateral heart blood colors (bright red in the left and dark red in the right) depending on their blood oxyhemoglobin saturation (**Figure 2**), clotting of cadaveric blood after preservation (retained coagulability), multiple dark-brownish punctate gastric hemorrhages or erosions (Wischnewsky spots) as a sign of disturbed microcirculation (**Figure 3**), and relatively intact other viscera with mild edema; however, complications of pneumonia and predisposing diseases are not rare. Hemorrhages in large muscles (especially the iliopsoas) have been reported. Postmortem CT

demonstrates diffuse alveolar inflation (hyperaeration) of the lungs with mild edema, hematoma in the iliopsoas, and urine retention in the bladder.

Histopathology and immunohistochemistry

The histology of chilblains involves dermal edema and congestion, occasionally accompanied by inflammatory cell infiltrates, different from subcutaneous hemorrhages. Internal viscera often do not show evident morphological signs of cellular damage; however, precise histology detects vacuolization of cardiomyocytes; hepatocytes; and adrenal, pancreatic, and renal tubular cells. Vacuoles in the anterior pituitary gland cells are indicative of prolonged hypothermic death, often detected in adrenocorticotropic hormone cells, followed by gonadotrophs, but infrequently in thyroid-stimulating hormone cells. Erythrocyte sludge may be seen in small blood vessels, accompanied by microinfarcts of the viscera.

The histology of Wischnewsky spots is focal pigmentation with hemoglobin immunopositivity in the gastric epithelia, often without erosions. With regard to stress responses to cold, previous immunohistochemical studies demonstrated increased expressions of HSP-70 and ubiquitin in the kidney, liver, lungs, and pancreas. Renal ubiquitin immunopositivity is increased. Chromogranin A immunopositivity is low in the hypothalamus neurons, suggesting a prolonged stress response to cold.

Toxicology

Toxicological screening is important to evaluate the contribution of alcohol and drugs to the predisposition to accidental hypothermia, and to discriminate intoxication.

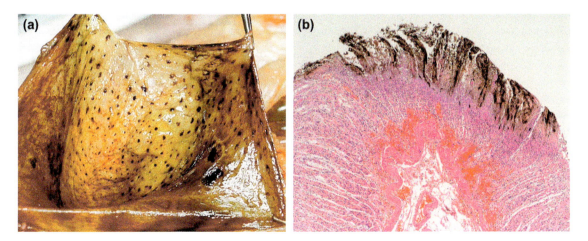

Figure 3 Whischnewsky spots (a) and the histology (b), showing focal necrosis and pigmentation (HE, 40×).

Biochemistry

Clinical findings: Systemic hypothermia involves dehydration, accompanied by increased concentrations of various blood constituents (e.g., erythrocytes, serum proteins, and urea nitrogen). Serum glucose is elevated due to glycolysis in the initial phase. In advanced hypothermia, however, hypoglycemia and elevated serum amylase are common. Increased ketone bodies suggest enhanced fat metabolism.

Postmortem findings: Typical findings include respective high and low oxygen saturations of left and right heart blood, azotemia (increased urea nitrogen) without significant elevation of creatinine and C-reactive protein (CRP), and ketosis (acetonemia); however, ketosis may not be evident in cases involving alcohol intake, but serum CRP may be elevated due to complications of pneumonia. Signs of myocardial and brain damage are usually mild, and even blood catecholamine levels are lower than in other fatalities; however, urinary catecholamine levels are increased. Chromogranin A is low in the blood, but high in the cerebrospinal fluid, suggesting prolonged cold stress. Pericardial brain natriuretic peptide is often increased, suggesting heart failure before death. In most cases, elevation of the serum amylase level is milder than in other fatalities, mostly including salivary fractions.

Molecular Pathology

Hypothermia may trigger systemic macrophage tumor necrosis factor (TNF)-α production and further neural preconditioning stimuli dependent on TNF-α. Postmortem investigation of humans demonstrated damage to the interstitial matrix and mild activation of cytokines in the lung, and intact pulmonary surfactants.

Key Points of Diagnosis

Clinical diagnosis of hypothermia is usually not difficult when an extremely low body temperature and laboratory findings are considered, excluding other causes of hypothermia, especially narcotic drug intoxication, and metabolic disorders or endocrinopathies; however, the status of "suspended animation" should be carefully considered in determining death.

In contrast, poor specific pathology may obstruct a postmortem diagnosis of hypothermia as the cause of death. The diagnosis should be established by collecting pathological findings characteristic of hypothermia, those related to the predisposition, drug abuse, and physical abuse or neglect, as well as for differentiating other insults, in combination with toxicology and biochemistry. A cold-induced cardiac or cerebrovascular accident should be excluded. Circumstantial evidence may also be considered when available.

See also: **Biology/DNA:** Forensic Laboratory Efficiency and Funding; **Forensic Medicine/Clinical:** Child Abuse; Domestic Violence; Elder Abuse; **Forensic Medicine/Pathology:** Autopsy; Forensic Pathology—Principles and Overview; Histopathology; Postmortem Imaging; Vital Reactions and Wound Healing.

Further Reading

Fauci, A.S., Braunwald, E., Kasper, D.L., Hauser, S.L., et al. (Eds.), 2008, Harrison's Principles of Internal Medicine, seventeenth ed., vol. 1. McGraw Hill, New York, pp. 117–139.
Maeda, H., Zhu, B.L., Ishikawa, T., Michiue, T., 2010. Forensic molecular pathology of violent deaths. Forensic Science International 203, 83–92.
Maeda, H., Ishikawa, T., Michiue, T., 2011. Forensic biochemistry for functional investigation of death: concept and practical application. Legal Medicine (Tokyo) 13, 55–67.
Marx, J.A., Hockberger, R.S., Walls, R.M., Adams, J.G., et al. (Eds.), 2010. Rosen's Emergency Medicine, Concepts and Clinical Practice, seventh ed. Elsevier, Philadelphia, pp. 1868–1892.
Saukko, P., Knight, B., 2004. Knight's Forensic Pathology, third ed. Arnold, London.

Electrocution and Lightning Strike

S Pollak, University of Freiburg, Freiburg, Germany
P Saukko, University of Turku, Turku, Finland

Glossary

Amperage Amperage, also called current, is the amount of electric charge passing a point in an electric circuit. The SI unit of electric current is the ampere (A) named after the French physicist André-Marie Ampère.

Electrical resistance The electrical resistance of an object (e.g., human tissue) is defined as the ratio of voltage across it to current through it. This proportionality is called Ohm's law.

Joule heating Passage of an electric current through conductive material (e.g., human tissue) releases heat which is proportional to the square of the current multiplied by the electrical resistance of the conductor. The conversion from electrical to thermal energy results in

a local rise of temperature possibly causing burns, for instance, electric marks on the skin.

Ventricular fibrillation Ventricular fibrillation (VF) is a life-threatening cardiac arrhythmia in which there is uncoordinated contraction of the heart ventricles so that they fail to pump blood into the arteries. The underlying condition is characterized by disorganized electrical activity. If VF continues, it mostly will be followed by cardiac arrest and brain damage due to cerebral hypoxia. Defibrillation (electric discharge of direct current from a defibrillator) may reverse VF.

Voltage Voltage (electrical tension) means the difference in electric potential energy between two points; it is measured in volts (V).

Introduction

In spite of the increasing use of electrical energy, statistics show that the number of accidents caused by electricity is declining. This tendency is apparent for fatal and nonfatal accidents and can be observed both in industrial and domestic surroundings. As electrocution is relatively rare, at least in developed countries, deaths due to the passage of electric current are not always recognized in the external postmortem examination. If the situation at the scene and the findings on the body do not provide unambiguous evidence suggesting electrocution, this cause of death may remain undetected.

In the low-voltage range (<1000 V), electrical accidents occur mostly when touching a live electroconductive object or surface. If the electrical current does not cause any biological damage, this is called an inconsequential flow of electricity through the body. Accidents caused by electricity play a special role within the field of traumatology because of their high lethality.

Low-Voltage Effects

Electricity can harm the human organism in two ways:

- By triggering *excitation processes* in muscles and nerves ("physiological effects") and
- By transformation to *heat energy* resulting in thermal tissue damage (Joule burn).

Low voltage is mainly dangerous because of its effect on the myocardium: When electric current passes through a body, it may cause fatal *ventricular fibrillation*. The risk of fatal cardiac arrhythmias depends on numerous external and internal factors including the following:

- The type of current (AC = alternating current, DC = direct current): AC is more likely to generate cardiac arrhythmias and to prevent a person from releasing an electrical source due to tetanic spasm of the muscles. In AC, the number of cycles per second (Hertz) usually is 50 (household current in Europe) or 60 (in the United States).

- The time of the electric shock in relation to the vulnerable period of the heartbeat, which corresponds to the relative refractory period and the ascending leg of the T-wave in the ECG.
- Duration of current exposure (contact times of <100 ms are usually not dangerous; if the current continues to flow through the body for an extended time, the amperage threshold triggering ventricular fibrillation may decrease to about 50 mA).
- Route of the current through the body (if the electric current passes from hand to hand, a smaller part flows through the heart than if it flows from hand to foot).
- Age: With increasing age, the lethality of electrical accidents rises probably because of the higher prevalence of preexisting heart conditions.
- Amperage A as a function of the given voltage V (usually ranging from 110 to 400 V in households and industrial plants) and resistance R (total of body and contact resistance). The amount of current flow is directly related to the voltage and inversely related to the resistance according to Ohm's law ($A = V{:}R$).

The effects of current on the human body mainly depend on the amperage, the exposure time, and (in the case of alternating current) also on the frequency. A current of approximately 15 mA ranging clearly below the fibrillation threshold may cause persistent contraction of the affected muscles preventing release of the electric line ("hold-on effect").

The probability of *thermal tissue damage* rises with increasing current density. As a consequence, a local skin burn is more likely when the contact area is small. Further parameters are the specific resistance of the tissue passed and the duration of the contact. In the low-voltage range, the thermal effects of electricity are mostly confined to the skin. In the case of electrocution, the initial high resistance of the skin rapidly decreases due to the structural damage of the epidermis. If the victim does not succeed in breaking away from the conductor, the skin will become cratered and charred thus largely losing its protective function.

Electric current has been called an "anonymous threat": Humans do not realize electromagnetic fields surrounding charged conductors. The well-known fact that very short contacts with an electric source can be survived without damage induces people to underestimate the risk of fatal ventricular fibrillation, especially in electrocution from alternating current. If the frequency is very high, the current will primarily cause thermal damage at the interface with the electrode (e.g., in surgical high-frequency cauterization).

In most electrical accidents, the victim's body acts as a link between a live conductor and the point of grounding. The current flowing through the body is limited by the total resistance composed of the insulation from ground on the one hand and the body resistance on the other hand. If the current passes to earth, the contact resistance depends on the clothing (especially the soles of the shoes) and the insulating effect of the surface underneath. Body resistance is mainly determined by the skin, namely its properties at the contact sites; internal resistance is comparatively low.

With increasing thickness of the horny layer, skin resistance rises. When the skin is damp (e.g., from sweating, soap suds, or bathwater), skin resistance drops sharply. Sweating is particularly strong under physical stress and at high ambient temperatures; in the presence of high humidity (damp rooms), sweat cannot evaporate, which makes contact with a charged electrical source more dangerous.

Electric burns are due to the local effect of Joule heating. Thermal skin damage is intensified by high amperage, a small area of contact, and long exposure to the current. However, even fatal electrocution does not necessarily leave any electric marks if the contact area is large and skin resistance is small (e.g., in a water-filled bathtub). It is estimated that in about 30% of all low-voltage fatalities no electric marks are discernible on the body surface, whereas surviving victims may show distinct electric marks in the form of second- and third-degree burns.

In the residential voltage range, faulty insulation of electrical devices, power points, connectors, adapters, and extension cords is a particularly frequent cause of *accidents*. Very often these occur in damp rooms (e.g., bathrooms) where even an intact appliance (with charged parts protected against touch) may become the origin of currents, for instance, if a hair dryer drops into a grounded bathtub (accidentally, in suicides, or homicides). A ground-fault circuit interrupter generally prevents fatal electrocution by disconnecting the circuit in a split second.

Apart from the already mentioned method of committing suicide in a bathtub filled with water, *suicides* using electricity are rare in spite of the general availability of power sources. In the remaining cases, conductors such as bare wires are attached to various parts of the body (wrists, ankle joints, fingers, toes, trunk, neck, or head), sometimes in combination with timers to start the current flow (**Figure 1**). Suicidal electrocution is predominantly committed by persons who are familiar with electrotechnical matters ("occupation-related suicide").

In cases in which the electrodes are fixed in the genital and/or anal region and/or to the nipples, the possibility of an accident in the context of *autoerotic practices* must also be taken into account. In such deaths from "electrophilia," usually pornographic material is found at the scene.

To recognize lethal low-voltage accidents, a careful external *postmortem examination* is essential. If a body is found under circumstances suggesting a premortal effect of electric power, an autopsy is indispensable. Apart from any electric burns, the *premortal symptoms* and the conditions under which death occurred may also point to electrocution: tetanic muscle

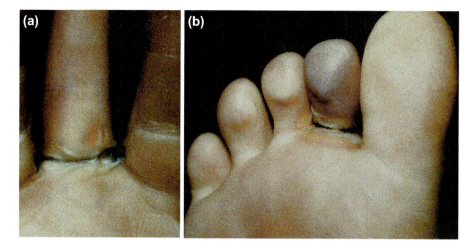

Figure 1 Suicide by electrocution: Circular electric burns from contact with naked wires originally wound around the left middle finger (a) and the right second toe (b).

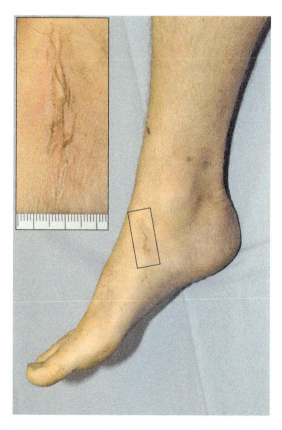

Figure 2 Medial side of the right foot, which touched a bare wire (230 V) while unclothed. Linear electric burn above the arch with wrinkled detachment of the epidermis.

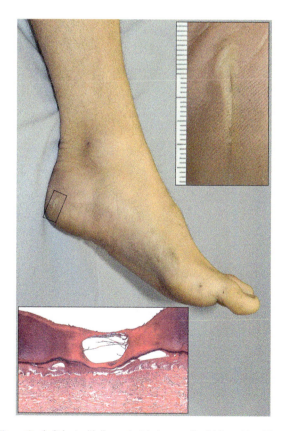

Figure 3 Left foot with linear electric burn on the friction skin of the heel. Grayish white electric burn with slightly raised margins. The box in the left lower corner shows the histological view with a large gas bubble in the stratum corneum and elongation of the basal epidermal cells.

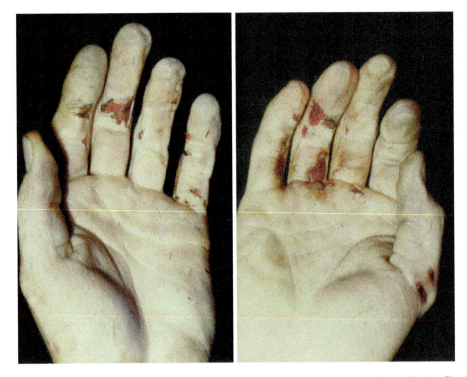

Figure 4 Accidental electrocution with multiple skin burns on both hands, to some extent in combination with metallization. The detached epidermis partly peeled off as it stuck to the surface of the conductor.

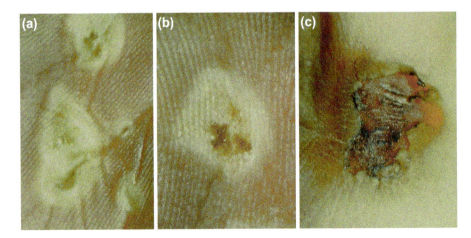

Figure 5 Close-up views of low-voltage burns on friction skin (a and b) and nonfriction skin (c).

contractions, grasping an electrical wire, sudden screaming with subsequent loss of consciousness and absence of pulse, sudden fall while near a charged source.

By identifying electrocution as the real cause of death, the investigator helps to protect other persons being exposed to the same source of danger. The evaluation of deaths in a bathtub is

particularly difficult and challenging. In the absence of any electric marks, the diagnosis of electrocution can sometimes be made only *per exclusionem* and on the basis of the electro-technical findings. Under criminalistic aspects, it has to be clarified whether the electrocution in the bathtub is to be interpreted as an accident, suicide, or homicide.

Electric Burn

The most important sign of electrocution is the electric mark. Its appearance resembles a local second- to fourth-degree burn which is caused by Joule heating. The *morphology* of an electric mark depends on numerous modifying influences: shape and surface structure of the conductor, amperage and current density, duration of contact, and skin resistance (dependent on the thickness of the horny layer and dampness). Under special circumstances, the size and shape of the conductor may be reflected by a congruent ("patterned") electric burn (**Figures 2 and 3**). Such marks are localized at the contact sites of the charged conductor and/or at the point of grounding. Most often, the hands are affected (**Figure 4**).

On the friction skin with its thick horny layer (digits, palms, and soles; **Figure 5(a) and (b)**), electric marks are macroscopically discernible as blisterlike skin lesions with elevated grayish margins, whereas the center often shows yellowish-brown discoloration or charring with tiny perforation holes and fused nodules of keratin; surviving victims may develop fluid-filled burn blisters within a short time. In body regions covered with thin-layered skin, the electrothermal lesions are rather uncharacteristic and all that may be seen are parched brown areas (**Figure 5(c)**).

On *histological examination* (**Figure 6**), the electric marks typically reveal stretching of the basal epidermal cells and their nuclei producing a palisade-type appearance in combination with "honeycombing" (vacuoles/micro-blisters formed by vaporized tissue fluid and located especially in the corneal layer). Differentiation from burns not caused by electricity can be difficult; one characteristic feature of electric burns is their inhomogeneity (dependent on the structurally different resistance behavior: for example, good conductivity along the sweat ducts). Metal traces from the conductor deposited at the site of contact ("metallization") can be proved by histochemical reactions or atomic absorption spectrometry. In principle, electric burns can also be of postmortem origin and are therefore no reliable proof that the electric shock occurred before death, unless the survival time was long enough for an inflammatory response of the affected tissue or for the development of fluid-filled burn blisters.

The *internal findings* seen in electrical fatalities are usually unspecific. Because of the diagnostic problems outlined above, careful examination of the death scene with regard to potential power sources is essential in every case in which electrocution is suspected.

High-Voltage Effects

In contrast to low voltage, the effects of high-voltage electricity may also cause delayed deaths, although 4/5th of the victims still die at the site of the accident, mostly from cardiac arrhythmia (ventricular fibrillation). The survival time of the remaining one-fifth varies depending on the degree and extension of the burns suffered.

Some textbook authors state that deaths caused by high voltage are always easy to recognize. However, as electric marks are very variable in shape and appearance, even high-voltage electrocutions may remain undetected (**Figure 7**). In cases of a firm and only short contact, the electric marks may resemble low-voltage lesions. Nevertheless, most high-voltage effects on skin differ from the "standard" appearance of electric marks as they are known from exposure to domestic voltage (blisters showing pale raised margins). Local thermal damage includes craterlike lesions, deep charring, and severed tissues.

In about half of all high-voltage accidents with a fatal outcome, extensive *burns* are seen. These are mostly due to

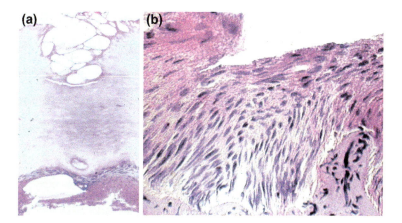

Figure 6 Histological sections of an electric burn showing microblisters within the detached horny layer (a) and "streaming of the nuclei" in the basal layers (b).

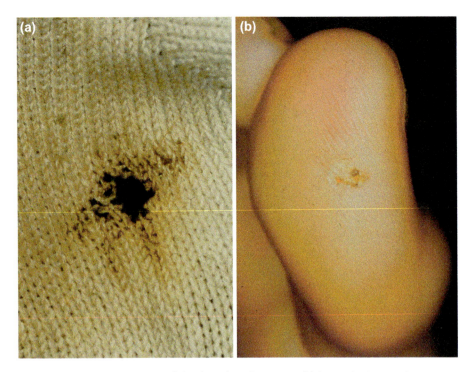

Figure 7 Burn hole in a sock (a) corresponding to a small electric mark on the great toe (b) from arcing to ground.

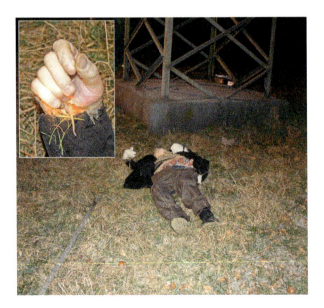

Figure 8 Suicide by high-voltage electricity. The victim used a long aluminum pole (left foreground) to touch a conductor rope of a high-voltage line. Extensive electric mark with deep tissue transection on the right hypothenar (close-up view).

arcing from the conductor to the body of the victim. If a person comes near a high-voltage electric conductor, an electric arc forms between the conductor and the body. The temperature in the center of such an electric arc may reach several thousand degrees Celsius. The arc marks on skin and clothing are characterized by a multitude of scattered individual or confluent burns producing a "crocodile skin" effect. On shoes, the leather uppers and sometimes even the soles show punctured perforation holes with scorched margins. Flash burns from arcing or flame burns from ignited clothing may cause extensive heat damage involving nearly the whole body surface. Apart from mostly third-degree skin burns, singeing of the head, beard, and body hair can be seen; eyebrows and eyelashes may be affected in the same way. Electric arcing sometimes causes grayish-black deposits of material from the conductor ("metallization") on exposed body parts and clothes.

It is self-evident that additional *blunt traumatization* is particularly frequent in high-voltage accidents. Other than with domestic voltage, contact is essentially limited to power lines, overhead cables, transformers, and electric power substations. Consequently, the electric shock often occurs several meters above the surrounding level and a subsequent fall from a height may cause serious secondary injuries sometimes constituting the real cause of death. As electric marks can be minimal after a short contact with the conductor, fatal occupational accidents should always arouse suspicion of a previous electric shock.

In the face, burns and metallization effects from electric arcing can be spared along the skin folds resembling "crow's feet." In the past, crow's feet were interpreted as a vital sign caused by squinting the mimic muscles. Nowadays, an electrically induced contraction of the muscles and thus a potentially supravital origin is assumed. Sometimes, petechial hemorrhages are found in the conjunctivae, the facial skin, and the mucosa of the upper respiratory tract after high- or low-voltage electrocution, occasionally in combination with subepicardial and subpleural blood extravasations. Some authors have interpreted these findings as signs of "electrical asphyxia." As a potential explanation, tetanic contraction of the respiratory muscles with subsequent increase in intrathoracic pressure is discussed.

After *prolonged exposure* to the current, direct and indirect burn sequelae are the dominant effects. The manifestations include extensive charring, a cooked appearance of the muscles, and even bursting of joints. In contact with high-voltage power lines, electrothermal transections of body parts have been observed. If cortical bone is affected, whitish osseous pearls can be present due to local melting and secondary resolidification of bone mineral.

High-voltage fatalities are usually *accidents*, and the victims are mostly men dying while doing occupation-related work near overhead cables (e.g., operating cranes and other high-construction machinery) or in electric power substations. Accidental contact with a high-tension grid transmission cable while using a long metal object (e.g., when harvesting fruits in high trees) is also possible.

Sometimes persons climb parked railway carriages or high-voltage pylons out of carelessness or to prove their courage. Very rarely *suicides* are committed by climbing a high-voltage mast or intentionally approaching power lines (**Figure 8**). Another method is to throw a bag attached to a wire over a power line or an overhead cable (**Figures 9 and 10**).

Lightning Strikes

Lightning is a natural phenomenon of "atmospheric electricity" based on a sudden environmental discharge of static electricity between a cloud and the ground resulting in a high-voltage direct current of extremely short duration. Correspondingly,

Figure 9 Suicide by high-voltage electricity: A bare wire was attached to the handles of a bag filled with stones and thrown over the overhead line of the railway. The victim was found lying flat on his back.

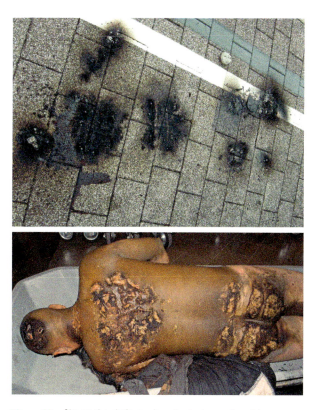

Figure 10 Site on the platform where the body was found (upper photograph). The charred deposits correspond with the fourth-degree burns on the back of the body (lower photograph).

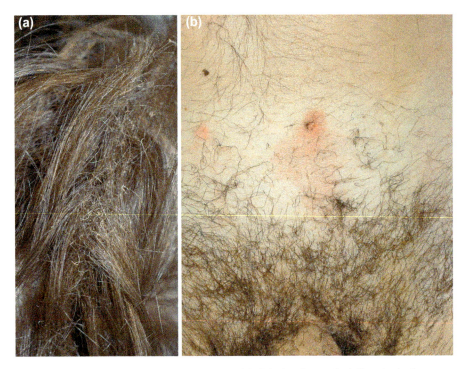

Figure 11   Singed head hair (a) and pubic hair (b) of a man who was struck by lightning, but survived. Note the tiny burn surrounded by a zone of reddening above the pubic hair (from contact with a metal buckle).

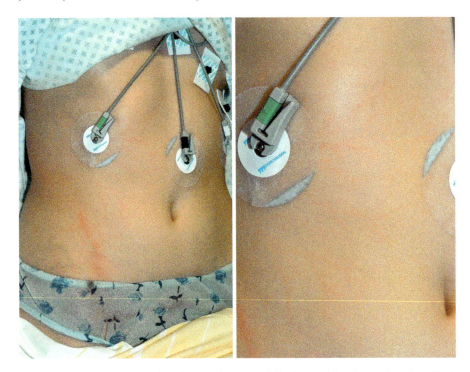

Figure 12   Abdominal wall of a woman who was struck by lightning, but survived. Fernlike reddish pattern on the skin, which is already fading some hours after the lightning strike.

the amperage along the path is so high that the thermal radiation causes an explosion-like extension of the air. In damp materials such as trees, the water evaporates along the lightning path forming high-pressure steam which causes mechanical damage.

If the flash of lightning strikes the ground next to a standing or walking person, a "stride (step) potential" forms between the feet so that a current flows through the body. Lightning accidents may also be due to a direct strike, a contact voltage (the victim carries a (metal) object struck by lightning), a side splash (after a primary strike to an object the lightning discharges to a victim standing nearby), as well as a wire-mediated strike (e.g., via the telephone line).

The lethality of lightning accidents is estimated at about 30%. Surviving victims often present with thermal lesions and blunt trauma (the latter mostly caused by the blast force) as well as transient neurological sequelae such as paralyses, aphasia, vertigo, and sensibility disturbances, and also cataract or rupture of the tympanic membrane. In fatal cases, the question arises which of the vital functions was the first to fail. On the one hand, death can result from central respiratory paralysis followed by hypoxia-induced secondary circulation failure. On the other hand, electric cardioversion may cause primary cardiac arrest.

The criminalistic significance of lightning injuries is underlined by the numerous possibilities of potential misinterpretation. For example, the absence of conspicuous burns may wrongly suggest death from a natural cause or blunt trauma. Sometimes, the situation at the scene seemingly points to homicide (torn clothing and blown off shoes due to water vaporization, concomitant mechanical injuries).

Findings on the *clothing* may include a broad spectrum of mechanical and thermal changes. Holes densely arranged in groups are a typical effect of lightning strikes (comparable with lesions from shotgun pellets). On metallic elements of the victim's clothing (buckles, snap-fasteners, etc.) as well as on watches and pieces of jewelry, small molten beads may be found. Shoes often show tiny holes or circumscribed tears in the sole or the adjacent upper leather. On textiles made from synthetic fibers, uncharacteristic tears can be seen as well as heat changes with local hardening and rolled-in margins with microscopically detectable melting effects (club-shaped fiber ends).

In fatal strikes, the lightning current usually enters in the parietal region singeing the head hair ("fox-red" discoloration, frizzy appearance, and clublike ends of the hairs). Extensive burns on the body surface are sometimes present, but are by no means a constant finding. The lightning current predominantly passes over the surface of the (mostly wet) skin so that only a small proportion of the current flows through the victim's body. This phenomenon is called "flashover." The route of electricity is indicated by multiple first-to third-degree burns and singeing of head hair, eyebrows, eyelashes, body, and pubic hair (**Figure 11**).

At the exit sites toward ground, the skin burns may resemble typical electric marks. Metal objects such as a necklace, a watch, or a belt buckle are heated by the lightning current so that they may leave congruent contact burns which are often accompanied by metallization extending also to the intact skin adjacent to the burn.

The best-known morphological finding in victims struck by lightning is the so-called Lichtenberg figure, a reddish, fernlike ("arboresque") skin pattern resulting from transient hyperemia (not from intra- or subcutaneous extravasation of blood!), which blanches or disappears after several hours (**Figure 12**). Histologically, Lichtenberg figures consist of small dilated vessels in the corium, sometimes combined with elongation and palisading of the basal epidermal cells.

See also: **Forensic Medicine/Causes of Death:** Burns and Scalds; **Forensic Medicine/Pathology:** External Postmortem Examination.

Further Reading

Di Maio, V.J., Di Maio, D., 2001. Forensic Pathology, second ed. CRC Press, Boca Raton, FL, pp. 410–421.

Donoghue, E.R., Lifschultz, B.D., 2006. Electrical and lightning injuries. In: Spitz, W.U., Spitz, D. (Eds.), Spitz and Fisher's Medicolegal Investigation of Death, fourth ed. Charles C. Thomas, Springfield, IL, pp. 882–902.

Marc, B., 2005. Electric shocks and electrocution, clinical effects and pathology. In: Payne-James, J., Byard, R.W., Corey, T.S., Henderson, C. (Eds.), Encyclopedia of Forensic and Legal Medicine, vol. 2. Elsevier, Oxford, pp. 259–263.

Pollak, S., 1980. Pathomorphological constellation in death resulting from high voltage electricity. Archiv für Kriminologie 165, 1–16 (in German).

Pollak, S., Saukko, P., 2003. Atlas of Forensic Medicine. CD-ROM. Elsevier, Amsterdam (Chapter 10).

Saukko, P., Knight, B., 2004. Knight's Forensic Medicine, third ed. Arnold, London, pp. 326–338.

Schmidt, P.H., Padosch, S.A., Madea, B., 2005. Occupation-related suicides. In: Tsokos, M. (Ed.), Forensic Pathology Reviews, vol. II. Humana Press, Totowa, NJ, pp. 145–165.

Seidl, S., 2004. Accidental autoerotic death. In: Tsokos, M. (Ed.), Forensic Pathology Reviews, vol. I. Humana Press, Totowa, NJ, pp. 235–262.

Seidl, S., 2006. Pathological features of death from lightning strike. In: Tsokos, M. (Ed.), Forensic Pathology Reviews, vol. IV. Humana Press, Totowa, NJ, pp. 3–23.

Wick, R., Byard, R.W., 2008. Electrocution and the autopsy. In: Tsokos, M. (Ed.), Forensic Pathology Reviews, vol. V. Humana Press, Totowa, NJ, pp. 53–66.

Deaths Associated with Medical Procedures

G Lau and M Wang, Health Sciences Authority, Singapore, Republic of Singapore

Glossary

Anastomosis A surgical connection between two structures.

Atelectasis Collapse of part or all of a lung.

Bariatric surgery A variety of surgical procedures performed on severely obese patients for the purpose of losing weight.

Bioprostheses A device containing biological material used to replace missing body parts.

Cholecystectomy Surgical removal of the gallbladder.

Coronary artery bypass graft surgery A surgical procedure in which one or more blocked coronary arteries are bypassed by a blood vessel graft to restore normal blood flow to the heart.

Disseminated intravascular coagulation A pathological activation of coagulation mechanisms in response to a variety of diseases.

Embolization The blocking of a blood vessel supplying an organ that may, on occasion, be undertaken as a therapeutic procedure.

Endocarditis Inflammation of the inner layer of the heart, often involving the heart valves, usually, but not always, due to an infection.

Endoscopic retrograde cholangiopancreatography (ERCP) A procedure that uses an endoscope to visualize the bile ducts and pancreatic ducts.

Hemangioma A type of blood vessel malformation.

Hemoperitoneum A collection of blood in the abdominal cavity.

Hemostasis A process that causes bleeding to stop.

Hemothorax A collection of blood in the chest cavity.

Hysterectomy Surgical removal of the uterus.

Iatrogenic An adverse condition in a patient resulting from the activity of physicians.

Mastectomy Surgical removal of one or both breasts.

Necrotizing enterocolitis A condition commonly seen in premature infants, where portions of the bowels undergo tissue death.

Necrotizing fasciitis A life-threatening bacterial infection that destroys skin fat and tissue covering muscles.

Nephrectomy Surgical removal of a kidney.

Osteomyelitis Infection of the bone.

Percutaneous coronary intervention (PCI) Also known as coronary angioplasty. A nonsurgical method to open narrowed or blocked coronary arteries.

Percutaneous endoscopic gastrostomy (PEG) An endoscopic procedure whereby a tube is passed into the patient's stomach through the abdominal wall to facilitate feeding.

Percutaneous transhepatic cholangiography (PTC) A radiographic technique employed in the visualization of the biliary tracts, involving a transhepatic insertion of a needle into a bile duct.

Peritonitis Inflammation of the inner lining of the abdominal cavity, resulting in a collection of fluid within the abdominal cavity.

Thrombosis The process by which a blood clot is formed inside a blood vessel.

Thromboprophylaxis The practice of giving calibrated amounts of anticoagulation drugs to individuals at increased risk of thrombosis, in order to reduce this risk.

Introduction

When referring a patient to hospital, should a doctor say, "I must warn you that the simple fact of being admitted to hospital means that you have something above a 1:10 chance of suffering an adverse event and a 1:100 chance of dying?" Richard Smith, Formerly Editor, BMJ.

An Emerging Challenge

The forensic evaluation of deaths occurring during, or following, various forms of medical and surgical intervention often presents a formidable challenge to practicing forensic pathologists who are required, perhaps with increasing frequency, to conduct medicolegal autopsies on patients who are suspected of having died from iatrogenic causes.

An iatrogenic illness is, literally, a disorder induced by, or resulting from, the activities of the attending physician. From a forensic perspective, it might be more useful to consider iatrogenic injury to be attributable to the adverse effects (including mishaps) arising from medical treatment, including various diagnostic and invasive procedures to which a patient has been subjected and which may result in serious morbidity or death. Such unfortunate deaths usually constitute the adverse outcomes of any number of procedures undertaken with diagnostic or therapeutic intent, or often both, as in the case of gastrointestinal endoscopy, coronary angiography (often coupled with percutaneous coronary intervention (PCI)), exploratory laparotomy, or interventional radiology.

Indeed, the concept of iatrogenesis may extend considerably beyond the mere confines of the medical profession to include the actual and potential complications of various forms of therapy administered by the ever-expanding ranks of health-care professionals allied to medicine, as well as complementary and traditional health-care practitioners.

Under the prevailing circumstances, at least in some jurisdictions, forensic pathologists may well be required to contend with the iatrogenic potential of a bewildering array of conventional, innovative, quasi-experimental, and traditional diagnostic and therapeutic modalities (including robotic surgery, which appears to be gaining ascendency in some areas at one extreme and moxibustion at the other). Clearly, familiarity with the complications of all, or even most, of these procedures is impossible and it, thus, behooves the forensic practitioner to be receptive to acquiring the requisite knowledge and experience required to rise to this challenge, particularly when these matters fall outside the traditional boundaries of forensic pathology.

Caveat

It is of the utmost importance to note that not all periprocedural deaths are necessarily iatrogenic in nature. Accordingly, the attending pathologist should, at the very least, be aware of the following possibilities:

1. Death was due, primarily, to a preexisting natural disease process, or traumatic injury, for which the procedure(s) was (were) performed (e.g., a patient who dies from the very ischemic heart disease for which coronary artery bypass surgery was performed).
2. Death was due, primarily, to an underlying natural disease process (which may have been undiagnosed, clinically), other than that for which the procedure(s) was (were) performed (e.g., a patient who dies from chronic obstructive pulmonary disease or an acute myocardial infarct following a hemicolectomy for colonic carcinoma).
3. Death was due, substantively, to an underlying natural disease process, with a secondary contribution from an

iatrogenic injury attributable to a procedural complication (e.g., an elderly patient with multiple, severe comorbidity comprising various potentially lethal conditions, who suffers from relatively minor perioperative hemorrhage, or develops severe postoperative nosocomial sepsis).
4. Death was due, substantively, to a therapeutic/procedural complication, which may include surgical and/or anesthetic mishaps, with a secondary contribution from an underlying natural disease process (e.g., a patient with some significant comorbidity, who suffers major perioperative hemorrhage, which may or may not have been lethal by itself).
5. Death was, to a variable extent, associated with, or related to, patient-specific events (e.g., postoperative self-extubation or the self-removal of a large-bore vascular catheter).

It must be emphasized, of course, that the preceding list of possible scenarios is by no means exhaustive and that one should also be cognizant of the existence of any plausible preprocedural conditions which may have placed a patient at an increased risk of periprocedural death, such as extensive comorbidity aggravated by a drug-induced predisposition to perioperative hemorrhage (e.g., an elderly patient with a history of stroke and/or ischemic heart disease, who had been prescribed antiplatelet agents as secondary cardiovascular prophylaxis).

Accordingly, an open mind is, perhaps, the most important prerequisite which a forensic pathologist attending to a periprocedural death should possess, in order to avoid prejudging the true nature of the case at hand.

An Overview of Procedural Complications Commonly Encountered in Forensic Practice

The most common forms of periprocedural iatrogenic complications comprise hemorrhage and sepsis.

Hemorrhage

Primary hemorrhage may occur intra- or postoperatively as a consequence of slipped hemostatic ligatures, dehiscence of vascular anastomoses, or direct vascular or organ trauma.

Hemopericardium

A hemopericardium may, occasionally, complicate coronary artery bypass graft surgery, due to bleeding from defects in the vascular anastomoses (between a saphenous vein or internal mammary artery graft and the corresponding native coronary artery), which would require immediate surgical reexploration. In addition, mediastinal hemorrhage may occur in patients who have bleeding tendencies or are subjected to protracted periods of cardiopulmonary bypass. Conversely, off-pump coronary surgery, when indicated, apparently reduces the need for blood transfusion and inotropic support, as well as the occurrence of atrial fibrillation and infection.

PCI, a common form of interventional cardiology comprising coronary transluminal coronary angioplasty (PTCA), often combined with the insertion of either bare metal, or increasingly, drug (e.g., placitaxel, sirolimus) eluting stents (BMS, DES) to relieve severe coronary stenosis and for acute coronary events, may be complicated by intrapericardial hemorrhage due to coronary artery dissection (**Figure 1**) and perforation. The concomitant use of an anticoagulant (e.g., heparin) and antiplatelet agents (e.g., a glycoprotein IIb/IIIa inhibitor such as abciximab, tirofiban, or eptifibatide) may further increase the risk of hemorrhage. Interestingly, in some jurisdictions, emergency PCI is not infrequently used as a last resort in patients with massive acute myocardial infarction associated with cardiogenic shock.

Occasionally, one might encounter a completely unanticipated complication, such as an iatrogenic hemopericardium resulting from relatively simple procedure, such as the puncture of a coronary artery during fine needle aspiration of a breast lesion and perforation of the right atrium during catheter angiography.

Hemothorax

The insertion of a chest drainage tube (a common bedside procedure) may, especially if a trocar is used, result in an inadvertent pulmonary puncture. Indeed, the puncture of an exceptionally enlarged or dilated heart in a patient with severe or terminal cardiac failure may occasionally occur if the tube is inserted through the left lateral chest wall.

Similarly, a central venous catheter inserted into an internal jugular or subclavian vein may deviate from its intended course (to terminate in the superior vena cava or at its confluence with the right atrium) and, instead, perforate, say, a brachiocephalic vein (**Figure 2**), resulting in a massive hemothorax or pneumohemothorax. Occasionally, fluids and even blood may have been infused or transfused through these misaligned central lines, with possibly disastrous consequences.

Hemoperitoneum and retroperitoneal hemorrhage

Somewhat tragically, a chest drainage tube inserted through the lower part of the right lateral chest wall, such as the seventh or eighth intercostal space, may traverse the right hemidiaphragm and puncture the right hepatic lobe, sometimes to depths of 6–8 cm, culminating in a fatal, massive hemoperitoneum (possibly accompanied by a corresponding hemothorax) which is only discovered at autopsy (**Figures 3 and 4**).

More commonly, intraperitoneal hemorrhage may complicate partial gastrectomy; colonic resection; iliofemoral arterial dissection caused by intra-aortic balloon pump insertion (for cardiogenic shock); percutaneous liver and renal biopsies (even when radiologically guided), computer/computerized tomography(CT)-guided drainage of a liver abscess, percutaneous transhepatic cholangiography and biliary drainage, laparoscopic procedures (e.g., laparoscopic cholecystectomy, nephrectomy, hysterectomy, or bariatric surgery), which are attended by the potential for trocar-induced injuries and the slippage or misapplication of hemostatic clips (**Figure 5**); and laser vaporization of intraperitoneal lesions, such as endometriotic cysts. In fact, massive retroperitoneal hemorrhage may, reportedly, arise as an unusual complication of percutaneous endoscopic gastrostomy (PEG), should an

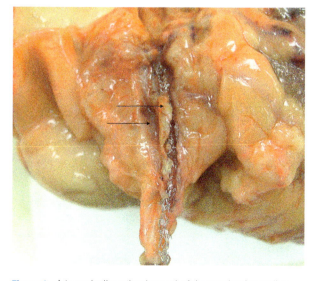

Figure 1 Iatrogenic dissection (arrows) of the anterior descending branch of the left coronary artery, induced by percutaneous coronary intervention.

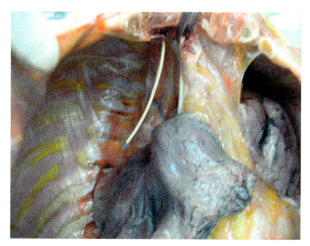

Figure 2 A central venous catheter entering the right pleural cavity through a perforation in the right brachiocephalic vein.

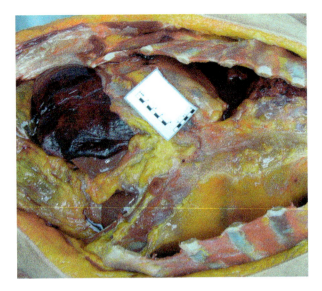

Figure 3 An iatrogenic hemoperitoneum (with a hemothorax) caused by chest drainage tube insertion.

initial, unsuccessful, attempt at an endoscopically guided needle puncture of the stomach result in the iatrogenic perforation or laceration of the splenic and mesenteric veins.

Indeed, in forensic terms, the introduction of any needle, trocar, endoscope, thoracoscope, or endoscope into any region of the body, may be likened to the infliction of a "stab wound," albeit with explicit therapeutic (rather than malicious) intent and usually with due regard for the relevant precautions. Nevertheless, such procedures are inherently invasive and, it may be argued, carry a variable potential for inadvertently causing organ and vascular damage that is similar to that of stab wounds commonly encountered in forensic practice.

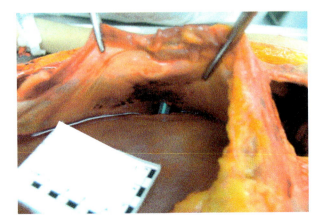

Figure 4 Penetration of the right hepatic lobe by the chest drainage tube, as described in **Figure 3**.

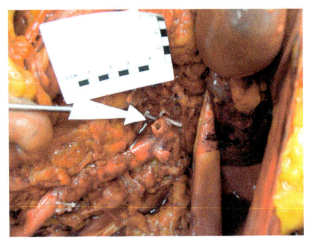

Figure 5 Apparent slippage or misapplication of two hemostatic clips which were supposed to have been applied to the stump of a renal artery in the course of a laparoscopic nephrectomy.

Other forms of periprocedural hemorrhage

Vascular injury (e.g., carotid artery "blow out") attending radical neck dissection (often accompanied by partial mandibulectomy and/or glossectomy) for advanced oral, esophageal, pharyngeal, and laryngeal malignancies (e.g., squamous cell carcinoma, neuroendocrine tumors), or even thyroid carcinomas, may result in intractable and lethal hemorrhage.

It should be noted that any form of periprocedural coagulopathy, such as disseminated intravascular coagulation (DIC), such as that induced by corrective surgery for complex congenital heart disease, the repair of an abdominal aortic aneurysm, a Whipple's operation for pancreatic carcinoma, extensive bowel resection for intestinal ischemia or infarction, and reconstructive surgery for major congenital craniofacial anomalies and necrotizing enterocolitis in premature neonates, is likely to be a predisposition for serious intra- or postoperative hemorrhage which may prove to be lethal.

Preexisting comorbidity, particularly if extensive, may also pose a similar risk. Thus, preoperative sepsis, malignancy, obstetric complications, impaired liver function, chronic or end-stage renal failure (such as that complicating diabetic nephropathy or chronic glomerulonephritis), as well as thrombocytopenia and other bleeding diatheses are frequently associated with a serious risk of perioperative hemorrhage. Also, due consideration should be given to the hemorrhagic risks associated with preoperative anticoagulation (e.g., warfarin, heparin, enoxaparin, or fraxiparine (low-molecular-weight heparins) for thromboprophylaxis); antiplatelet agents (e.g., aspirin or thienopyridines, such as ticlopidine, clopidogrel, and prasugrel, and adenosine diphosphate (ADP) P2Y12 receptor inhibitors, such as ticagrelor and cangrelor) following a myocardial infarction or cerebrovascular accident.

Sepsis

It has been said that methicillin-resistant *Staphylococcus aureus* (MRSA), a surrogate marker for hospital-acquired infections, may be responsible for up to nearly 70% of all cases of *S. aureus* bacteremia and surgical wound infection, respectively. Nursing staff dressing wounds with MRSA may have an 80% risk of carrying the organism on their hands for up to 3 h while possibly 40% of patient–nurse interactions in intensive care may result in the transmission of *Klebsiella* and *Clostridium difficile*. Both MRSA and *Pseudomonas aeruginosa* are often implicated in postoperative respiratory infections. Indeed, multidrug resistant and newly emergent strains of pathogenic bacteria (e.g., Vancomycin-resistant *Enterococi*, *Burkholderia cepacia*, *Stenotrophomonas maltophilia*, and extended spectrum beta-lactamase-producing coliforms, such as *Escherichia coli* and *Klebsiella*) and fungi (e.g., *Candida*, *Cryptococcus*) are commonplace in intensive care units. Even organisms such as *Acinetobacter baumannii*, once considered to be merely an opportunistic pathogen, now often falls into the same category.

Pulmonary and urological infections

Fatal postsurgical infections commonly include broncho-pneumonia and urinary tract infection, with resultant septicemia from protracted immobilization. Prolonged dependency on mechanical ventilation may also predispose to pulmonary infection, as might underlying diabetes mellitus and any form of immunosuppression resulting from the use of steroids or cytotoxic agents, or immunocompromise. Indeed, highly drug-resistant strains of tuberculosis have been known to be transmitted by contaminated bronchoscopes to cancer patients. Conversely, it is important to bear in mind that, in some instances, these infections may be developed before the operations in question, but worsened subsequently.

Peritonitis

Not infrequently, acute peritonitis from anastomotic dehiscence may complicate partial gastrectomy, entero-enterostomy, and colonic or colorectal resection (in which case, the peritoneal fluid may be feculent).

Endoscopically induced perforations may cause large bowel perforation during colonoscopy, while endoscopic retrograde cholangiopancreatography (ERCP), for the removal of biliary calculi, could result in the perforation of the duodenum (possibly retroperitoneally). Biliary tract injuries, with resultant biliary leakage, peritonitis, and septicemia may complicate laparoscopic cholecystectomy (**Figure 6**) with fatal consequences.

Chronic leakage around a PEG tube, a consequence of the intra-abdominal migration of the intragastric bumper, may cause localized cellulitis of the skin around the stoma and, occasionally, lead to lethal peritonitis and necrotizing fasciitis.

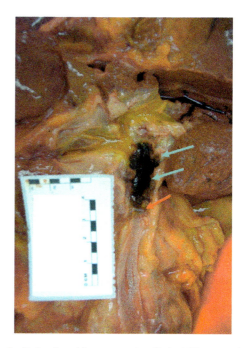

Figure 6   Perforation of the common hepatic duct (blue arrows) following inadvertent application of surgical clips (red arrow) to the extrahepatic biliary tract during laparoscopic cholecystectomy.

Other postsurgical infections

These would include spinal sepsis (e.g., bacterial leptomeningitis and epidural abscesses) following laminectomy and decompression; vertebral osteomyelitis following surgical stabilization of cervical dislocation; and acute suppurative meningitis following neurosurgery (e.g., trans-sphenoidal resection of a pituitary adenoma and open resection of a meningioma).

Life-threatening pelvic retroperitoneal sepsis, caused by *Bacteroides fragilis* and *Clostridium* species, may complicate stapled hemorrhoidectomy, presumably due to the entry of these gas-producing organisms from the rectal lumen into the pararectal space during the firing of the stapler.

Cardiac valvular replacement operations, which may involve the excision of more than one valve at a time (e.g., both the mitral and aortic valves) and the insertion of the corresponding mechanical or bioprostheses, may occasionally be complicated by postoperative infective endocarditis. At autopsy, the infected prostheses may bear friable vegetations, possibly accompanied by thrombosis and para-valvular dehiscence (which may also occur in the absence of an infection).

Also, the infection of indwelling vascular catheters may result in what is colloquially referred to as "line sepsis," although this would have to be distinguished from mere microbial "colonization" (possibly in consultation with a clinical microbiologist or infectious diseases physician). Ultimately, whether this was the source of a lethal infection would have to be decided by way of a thorough clinico-pathological correlation in any given case.

Mention should also be made of rather mundane, yet potentially devastating consequences of assisted enteral feeding through a nasogastric tube erroneously inserted into the trachea or a main bronchus, resulting in fatal aspiration pneumonia, particularly in elderly patients suffering from neurological dysphagia.

It might be added that, not infrequently, repeated antemortem (i.e., clinical) microbial cultures conducted on blood and other body fluids may have persistently yielded negative results and the same outcome may be observed with postmortem blood cultures in certain cases of severe sepsis, including those where it is deemed to be lethal. This may be due to prior administration of broad spectrum antibiotics. In such instances, recourse to elevated serum procalcitonin levels (a largely reliable indicator of bacterial sepsis) may prove to be useful.

Periprocedural Trauma

Various invasive procedures carry the attendant risks of direct visceral trauma, which may prove to be lethal. In this respect, it might be argued that, at least from a forensic perspective, most medical procedures are, to a greater or lesser degree, inherently traumatic in nature. Thus, they may be said to represent instances of "therapeutic trauma" or, more precisely, controlled trauma inflicted with (largely beneficent) therapeutic intent, presumably (although not invariably) with the expressed consent of the patients concerned.

Endoscopy
Colonoscopic perforation of the large bowel could result in sudden and unexpected death, presumably from reflex cardiac inhibition, even in the absence of any significant peritoneal soiling. It appears that a possible sequence of such perforations commences with the muscularis propria, followed by the serosa and, finally, the mucosa, although serosal tears without mucosal damage have been known to occur. Similarly, iatrogenic tracheo-bronchial ruptures may, occasionally, be caused by bronchoscopy, particularly if a rigid bronchoscope had been used, or even in the course of intubation.

The potential for ERCP to cause iatrogenic acute (hemorrhagic) pancreatitis is well documented, while the insertion of a PEG may be complicated by gastric necrosis and hemorrhage (attributed to excess tension between the intragastric bumper and the skin attachments of the tube), gastric wall dissection, acute gastric dilatation, tension pneumoperitoneum, and bowel obstruction. Iatrogenic gastric rupture associated with the balloon tamponade (through the agency of a Sengstaken–Blakemore or Linton–Nachlas tube) for esophageal varices complicating hepatic cirrhosis have also been reported.

Aorto-esophageal fistula
The occurrence of an aorto-esophageal fistula usually results in massive gastrointestinal hemorrhage, classically preceded by an initial episode of relatively mild, "sentinel" hemorrhage. Its iatrogenic causes include thoracic irradiation, the occasional use of a rigid esophagoscope, prolonged nasogastric tube placement, and anastomotic dehiscence after a prosthetic graft repair of an aortic aneurysm.

Obstetric procedures
Forceps-assisted delivery may sometimes be complicated by cervical or uterovaginal ruptures. Conversely, fatal perinatal subgaleal hemorrhage may, occasionally, confound instrumental (vacuum- and forceps-assisted) delivery. Indeed vacuum extraction itself may, rarely, cause iatrogenic neonatal intracranial (mostly subdural) hemorrhage arising from tentorial laceration and rupture of the dural venous sinuses.

Resuscitative injuries
A wide range of resuscitative injuries may be observed at autopsy. On the whole, these tend to be artifactual in nature and are usually attributable to vigorous cardiopulmonary resuscitation. Accordingly, they are mostly concentrated in the thoracic region (e.g., electric defibrillator pad markings, bruising of the subcutaneous tissues of the anterior chest wall and the pectoral muscles, sternal and rib fractures, hemothoraces, mediastinal bruising, cardiac rupture, pulmonary laceration, and damage to the upper and lower airways), although intra-abdominal structures may be involved (e.g., esophageal, gastric, and intestinal/mesenteric ruptures and lacerations of the liver and/or spleen). Even subarachnoid hemorrhage is not unknown. The list is endless and that almost any form of blunt-force-type injury could complicate vigorous and protracted resuscitative efforts, including thoracic vertebral fracture dislocation in the elderly.

Ironically, it is in rare instances when an erstwhile moribund patient is "successfully" resuscitated (in the sense that his/her circulation is briefly restored for several hours, albeit at the cost of considerable inotropic and, indeed, advanced life support) that substantial and even potentially lethal hemorrhage may emanate from the damaged organs, thereby confounding the subsequent forensic evaluation of the case.

Perioperative Embolic Phenomena

Pulmonary thromboembolism
Deep vein thrombosis often develops insidiously and massive pulmonary thromboembolism may supervene with unexpected suddenness, as early as the first postoperative week. Apart from prolonged, complete, or relative immobility, the

other classical risk factors include trauma, obesity, sepsis, malignancy, and pregnancy. In a minority of patients, it may present as a manifestation of thrombophilia (either hereditary, or induced by autoantibodies). In any event, the perplexing medical dilemma which prevails in respect of venous thromboembolism is that even the institution of appropriate forms of thromboprophylaxis is attended by the ever-present risk of lethal intracranial or retroperitoneal (and occasionally pulmonary) hemorrhage. Either outcome may, in turn, carry rather unpleasant medicolegal consequences which may ensue in their aftermath.

Fat and bone marrow embolism

Fat embolism may complicate surgical operations on fatty tissues (e.g., mastectomy), steroid injections, spinal and orthopedic surgery (e.g., vertebroplasty for osteoporotic vertebral collapse, total joint replacement operations), and tumescent liposuction. In contrast to fat embolism, which may be pulmonary or systemic in distribution, concomitant bone marrow embolism tends to be restricted to the pulmonary circulation. Notably, mild pulmonary fat and bone marrow embolism may represent artifacts of resuscitation.

Pulmonary cartilage embolism

Iatrogenic pulmonary cartilage embolism may present as a rare complication of orthopedic surgery (e.g., humeral fracture followed by open reduction and internal fixation), but may also be a consequence or artifact of cardiopulmonary resuscitation. Its occurrence should be distinguished from the potentially lethal condition of fibrocartilaginous embolism resulting in spinal cord infarction or acute myelopathy.

Air embolism

Air embolism may complicate head and neck operations (e.g., neuro- and thyroid surgery), where a breach in the internal jugular and, possibly other, veins in the neck may result in the entry or suction of air into the venous drainage and, ultimately, the cardiac chambers. Procedures involving central venous access (e.g., the infusion of total parenteral nutrition or hemodialysis through the subclavian or internal jugular veins) may also be attended by a similar risk.

Cholesterol embolism

Cholesterol embolism (causing acute renal failure and, possibly, multiorgan involvement, accompanied by marked eosinophilia) may occur in patients with generalized atherosclerosis, hypertension, diabetes, and aortic aneurysm, undergoing angiography, anticoagulation, thrombolysis, and any form of vascular surgery (e.g., coronary artery bypass grafting, repair of an abdominal aortic aneurysm).

Iatrogenic foreign body embolism

Examples of this category of rare phenomena include suture embolism to the left anterior descending coronary artery, following mitral valve replacement surgery, occlusion of the left coronary artery by a fragment of a femoral artery during PTCA, systemic "meat and vegetable" embolization to the heart, kidneys, and brain arising from an esophageal–atrial fistula caused by a nasogastric tube, and intracardiac embolism of a distal fragment of an indwelling central venous catheter to the right ventricle and pulmonary trunk, presumably culminating in a fatal cardiac arrhythmia.

Occasionally, neuroradiological procedures, such as the therapeutic embolization of extra- and intracranial vascular lesions, such as a large facial hemangioma, by way of the introduction of polyvinyl alcohol particles and gelfoam suspended in radiocontrast media through the right external carotid artery and facial arteries, may be complicated by fatal cerebral infarction. In such an instance, it is thought that some of these particles may have entered the cerebral circulation through naturally occurring anastomoses between the external and internal carotid arteries (**Figure 7**).

Complications Associated with Solid Organ Transplantations

A detailed description of the various long- and short-term complications arising from solid organ transplantation as well as allograft rejection issues is beyond the scope of this chapter. Only a brief summary of the common anatomical complications which might be encountered in the course of a forensic autopsy on a deceased patient who had undergone liver, renal, and heart transplants (which are among the most

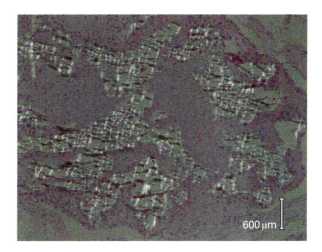

Figure 7   Birefringent foreign body emboli in the cerebral microvasculature: a complication of therapeutic embolization of a facial hemangioma (H&E, polarized ×400).

common form of organ transplant operations) are presented here. In all of these instances, it is hardly surprising that the most common cause for sudden cardiovascular collapse in the early postoperative period is hemorrhage, either consequent to hemostatic failure due to issues concerning the application of surgical staples or sutures, or due to existing DIC.

Liver transplants

In liver transplantations, the postoperative mechanical complications relating to the hepatic artery include acute thrombosis, luminal stenosis, pseudoaneurysm, and arteriovenous fistula. Disruption of the hepatic artery flow results in biliary ischemia, with subsequent biliary strictures, bile leaks, biloma, infected bilomas, and frank intrahepatic abscesses. Hepatic infarction, fulminant hepatic failure, and bacteremia may also occur. Causes of hepatic artery thrombosis include allograft rejection, hepatic artery kinking due to vascular redundancy, and technical problems at anastomosis. Hepatic artery stenosis can be caused by clamp injury, intimal injury due to perfusion catheters, anastomotic ischemia due to a disrupted vasa vasorum, and rejection. Hepatic artery pseudoaneurysm can occur at the extrahepatic portion, usually at the donor–recipient arterial anastomosis. They are usually caused by infection or technical failure and carry the potential for rupture and life-threatening hemorrhage.

Early bile duct strictures at the anastomosis may result from technical difficulties or by fibrosis and scarring associated with bile leaks. They can also be related to marginal blood supply of the cut ends of the donor and recipient ducts. These can give rise to rapid onset of allograft dysfunction and sepsis. Portal vein stenosis and thrombosis, usually at the anastomotic site and extrahepatic segment, can result in graft dysfunction and portal hypertension. The usual causes include surgical difficulties, excessive vessel redundancy, and hypercoagulability. The development of posttransplantation inferior vena cava stenosis or thrombosis is uncommon. Causes include technical problems, inferior vena cava compression due to fluid collection or a hematoma, and a mass effect from hepatic regeneration. This can lead to the development of the Budd–Chiari syndrome comprising pleural effusion, hepatic enlargement, ascites, and lower limb edema.

Renal transplants

Early postrenal transplantation complications that the forensic pathologist may encounter include thrombosis or stenosis of the renal vessels and urine leak or obstruction at the ureteric anastomotic site.

Renal artery thrombosis generally is an early complication of the immediate posttransplant period, though it may present later. It is caused by a low perfusion from hypotension or vascular kinking due to technical difficulties. This may present as sudden cessation of urine output, and the likely outcome is graft loss. Renal vein thrombosis is also typically an early

complication manifesting as graft tenderness and edema, with the patient experiencing dark hematuria and diminished urine volume.

Urine may leak from the anastomotic connection of the ureter to the graft, resulting in a perigraft fluid collection which may be infected and/or give rise to graft dysfunction. On the other hand, late posttransplant ureteric obstruction may be consequent to hematuria or chronic fibrotic changes at the anastomosis site or due to extrinsic compression from urinoma, hematoma, or lymphocele. The graft becomes distended and edematous with ensuing hydronephrosis.

Cardiac transplants

The surgery of cardiac transplantation has many complications similar to those of other open heart procedures. These include hemorrhage from suture lines at the vascular cannulation sites for cardiopulmonary bypass or the various anastomotic sites between donor and recipient vessels and atrial walls, cerebral infarction, and acute donor heart infarction due to prolonged perioperative ischemia.

Anesthetic Complications

Anesthesia with mechanical ventilation may be attended by impairment of gaseous exchange, leading to decreased blood oxygenation. Indeed, atelectasis is said to occur in 85–95% of patients, often immediately after induction of general anesthesia, affecting some 20–25% of basal lung tissues.

However, significant anesthetic mishaps seem to occur at a much lower frequency than primarily operative complications, but often carry devastating consequences. Accordingly, while anesthesia might contribute to death in 1:1700 operations, probably not more than 1:10 000 patients die exclusively from an anesthetic complication. It might be added that surgeons and anesthetists/intensive care specialists may differ quite sharply on the surgical mortality risk presented by a patient, especially one who is severely ill or is erstwhile stable, but has extensive, severe comorbidity.

The following events may be encountered in forensic practice:

1. Oxygen deficiency culminating in hypoxic–ischemic encephalopathy (e.g., failed intubation, dislodgement of the endotracheal tube, faulty connections, and prolonged reversal).
2. Intraluminal airway obstruction by blood, mucus, or a foreign body (e.g., a piece of gauze).
3. Extrinsic airway obstruction by mediastinal mass lesions (e.g., thymoma, thymic carcinoid, and germ cell tumors; large B-cell, lymphoblastic and Hodgkin's lymphomas), where life-threatening or lethal tracheo-bronchial compression supervenes, with resultant respiratory distress during intubation and induction of anesthesia, or even

after extubation, with the combination of muscle paralysis and the supine position conspiring to impede respiratory movements of the thoracic cage (**Figure 8**).

4. Aspiration of regurgitated gastric contents or contrast medium.

5. Prolonged or excessive neuromuscular blockade. Thiopentone, which is used in induction, may cause cardiorespiratory failure, while trichloroethylene and premedication with atropine may result in sudden circulatory failure.

6. Malignant hyperthermia, a rare, autosomal dominant condition (with an estimated incidence of 1:5000–1:70 000), which predisposes the patient to sudden uncoupling of oxidative phosphorylation, with the resultant massive overheating, induced by exposure to certain muscle relaxants (e.g., suxamethonium) and halothane.

7. Halothane hypersensitivity (at an estimated incidence of 1:6000–1:600 000), with halothane-induced hepatitis, or even resultant massive hepatocellular necrosis, usually after repeated exposure to the agent. There is evidence that it is mediated by the immune sensitization of susceptible individuals (carrying CYP2E1) to trifluoroacetylated liver protein neoantigen formation resulting from oxidative halothane metabolism.

8. Isoflurane has also been reported to cause fatal massive hepatocellular necrosis after a second exposure to this supposedly nonhepatotoxic alternative to halothane in a woman with a history of alcohol use and mild obesity. Instances of enflurane-induced hepatotoxicity have also been reported (167).

9. Propofol, a sedative-hypnotic agent used for the induction of anesthesia and for sedating mechanically ventilated patients in intensive care units, has been associated with fatal cardiac failure, both in children and in adult head-injured patients. In fact, the constellation of myocardial failure, metabolic acidosis, and rhabdomyolysis in children receiving propofol infusions for >48 h has been termed the propofol-infusion syndrome. In addition, propofol has been known to induce hypertriglyceridemia which may, in turn, predispose a patient to necrotizing pancreatitis.

10. Iatrogenic cervical dislocation has been reported in children undergoing lymph node biopsy under general anesthesia. Rotation of the head and neck during the procedure is believed to have caused atlanto-axial rotary dislocation, requiring neurosurgical intervention (open reduction). From a forensic perspective, it is not at all difficult to appreciate that this is a potentially life-threatening complication.

11. In some instances, intraoperative hypothermia may supervene. It has been demonstrated that maintaining perioperative normothermia could reduce the risk of hemorrhage, wound infection, and acute cardiac events this being particularly emphasized for patients with cardiac risk factors. It is conceivable that there might be occasions when such factors might have to be taken into account when conducting a perioperative autopsy.

12. It has been suggested that common foods, such as potatoes, tomatoes, and aubergines, may contain naturally occurring solanaceous glycoalkaloids (which are naturally occurring insecticides that remain in the body for several days after ingestion) that, even in small quantities, may inhibit butyryl cholinesterase and acetylcholinesterase, resulting in the persistence of anesthetic agents and muscle relaxants in the body and, thus, a longer recovery time of as much as 5–10 h. The potentially lethal consequence of this largely unanticipated, if rare, complication is self-evident.

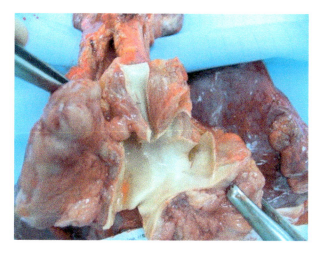

Figure 8 A clinically undiagnosed mediastinal tumor (diffuse B-cell lymphoma) encasing the aortic arch and the associated major arteries, contributing to postanesthetic death.

Nonanesthetic Causes of Iatrogenic Hypoxia

Iatrogenically induced hypoxia may occur in settings which are not related to anesthesia. Profound hypovolemic, septicemic, cardiogenic, or neurogenic shock, as well as cardiac arrhythmias may lead to protracted cardiorespiratory arrest and resultant hypoxic–ischemic encephalopathy.

Indeed, oxygen desaturation is known to occur even in less-dramatic situations, as for instance, during upper gastrointestinal endoscopy (e.g., esophago-gastroscopy, ERCP) performed under sedation, at an incidence estimated at 55–91% and associated with a mortality risk of ~1 in 2000 procedures.

Even common and usually mild therapeutic complications may have lethal consequences when the latter present with exceptional severity. In one instance, extensive postextraction hemorrhage into the floor of the mouth, larynx, and cervical muscles, following upon the extraction of an impacted mandibular molar, caused fatal mechanical asphyxia.

Similarly, Ludwig's angina, a life-threatening, diffuse infection of the submandibular and sublingual spaces, caused by various Gram-negative organisms, as well as *Streptococcus viridans*, *S. aureus*, and *Staphylococcus epidermidis*, may spread inferiorly to cause mediastinitis, empyema, pericarditis, and pericardial tamponade. Apart from sepsis, it can also cause critical airway obstruction requiring tracheostomy. While dental abscesses, intravenous drug abuse, and pharyngotonsillitis are the usual etiological factors, it may occasionally complicate dental extraction.

The Forensic Evaluation of Periprocedural Deaths

The Postmortem Examination

The undertaking of an impartial and meaningful forensic evaluation of a periprocedural death would, quite naturally, be centered on the findings of a thorough postmortem examination. In this respect, the attending forensic pathologist may wish to take note of the following matters:

1. Comprehensive clinicopathological correlation is usually indispensable to the process, as it enables the autopsy findings to be interpreted in the appropriate clinical context. In forensic terms, this may be regarded as being analogous to a correlative analysis of the autopsy findings relative to the scene and circumstances of death in any other form of medicolegal death investigation.
2. An awareness of the corresponding medicolegal implications of the case in question is essential. The mere occurrence of an iatrogenic injury, even if patently demonstrable at autopsy, does not, in and of itself, necessarily signify negligence on the part of the attending clinician(s) or operator(s).
3. The inestimable importance of preautopsy review of the relevant medical records pertaining to the case at hand cannot be overemphasized, as this would enable the attending pathologist to identify the key clinicopathological and medicolegal issues of concern that would largely determine the manner in which the autopsy proper is to be conducted. In this context, it must be said that performing a periprocedural autopsy without the benefit of being guided by the clinical records is a most unwise venture which is likely to result in a woeful misinterpretation of the autopsy findings. Indeed, the unwary pathologist may very well encounter preventable technical difficulties in the course of the autopsy should he decide to proceed "blind."
4. Both pre- and postautopsy consultations with clinical colleagues in the relevant specialities or subspecialities, who are unconnected with the case at hand, may very well be in

order, particularly when one is faced with a complex periprocedural death following a series of operations, or an unusual procedure. At the very least, this would afford the attending pathologist with a reasonable understanding of the indications and complications of these procedures and their associated risks of mortality.

Conduct of the Autopsy

The purpose of a periprocedural autopsy obviously consists of ascertaining the medical cause of death with particular reference to the following issues:

1. Whether an iatrogenic injury had occurred and is demonstrable at autopsy, or by means of the relevant ancillary investigations.
2. Whether an iatrogenic injury, if present, is likely to have been the primary or substantive cause of death.
3. Whether an iatrogenic injury, if present, is likely to have been a contributory, rather than the substantive, cause of death.
4. Whether an iatrogenic injury, if present, had a negligible contribution to the causation of death.

It should be noted that the answers to these questions are by no means easily elicited, in view of the fact that the altered anatomy resulting from various and, not infrequently, multiple, surgical, and other invasive procedures could confound the autopsy itself. Indeed, an iatrogenic injury (e.g., a surgically induced intestinal perforation) which might have been documented in the clinical records could have healed, or perhaps no longer demonstrable as the affected organ, or part thereof, had been resected or excised prior to the patient's demise. Consequently, it might be advantageous to the attending pathologist to secure the attendance of the principal operators (particularly surgeons, endoscopists and interventional cardiologists and radiologists) at periprocedural autopsies.

Moreover, irrespective of whether morphological evidence of such a therapeutic complication is discernible at autopsy, one is often obliged to address the critical question of whether it actually played a significant role in causing the patient's death. This issue may be extremely perplexing especially in instances where the patient had, with the aid of intensive care, advanced life support (including mechanical ventilation and the administration of inotropic agents), as well as repeated surgery, interventional radiology, and other means, managed to withstand the deleterious effects of various iatrogenic complications for protracted periods of time, possibly in the order of many weeks, months, or even in excess of a year, before succumbing to other complications, such as sepsis, venous thromboembolism, and multiorgan failure. Under such circumstances (which is by no means uncommon in some jurisdictions), the increasing temporal remoteness between the occurrence of an iatrogenic injury, however life-threatening or potentially lethal it may have been, and the eventual demise of the patient would have very considerably weakened the putative causal relation between both events.

In conducting a periprocedural autopsy, the attending pathologist would be well served to note and document the following features and processes, which should be clearly reflected in the corresponding autopsy report:

1. The location, dimensions, and condition of the marks of recent and previous operations (e.g., surgical incisions and scars, injection and puncture marks, as well as evidence of healing, dehiscence, or infection at these sites). Where possible, it is good practice to avoid incising along, or across, existing surgical incisions, so that they can be examined in their original state. It may also be necessary to examine, in situ, various organs and anatomical structures which had been subjected to surgical alteration, prior to their evisceration.

2. The placement of various medical devices, tubes, catheters, and drains (e.g., esophageal as opposed to proper endotracheal intubation (**Figure 9**), proper cannulation of a central venous catheter as opposed to misplacement (**Figure 10**) or venous perforation and proper placement of a chest drainage tube as opposed to the iatrogenic perforation of a lung).

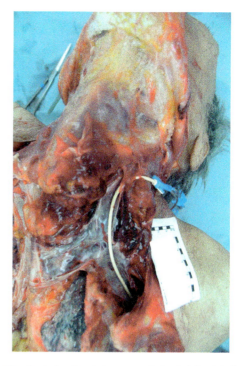

Figure 10   A misplaced central venous catheter deviating into the left subclavian vein.

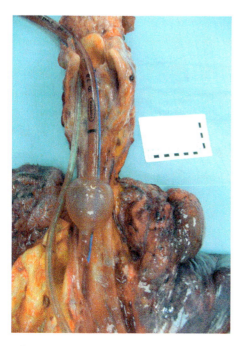

Figure 9   Esophageal intubation.

3. Performing an in situ examination of the anatomical structures in and around the operative site(s), to detect or exclude the presence of suspected dehiscence of vascular, gastrointestinal, biliary, or other surgical anastomoses (e.g., following a repair of an aortic aneurysm, a hemicolectomy with an ileo-colic anastomosis, or a hepatico/choledocho-jejunostomy created in the course of a Whipple's operation or liver transplant). Similarly, where appropriate, in situ examination of the stumps of surgically divided blood vessels should also be undertaken in order to ascertain the integrity of hemostatic ligatures and, increasingly, clips which had been applied to them, in the course of the operation (e.g., apparent slippage of a hemostatic clip from a renal artery following a nephrectomy). Obviously, this part of the examination should be undertaken prior to the evisceration of the internal organs, in order to prevent artifactual damage to delicate and, possibly friable, surgically altered anatomical structures and any dislodgement hemostatic devices (or subsequent allegations thereof, as the ensuing legal proceedings in these cases may be extremely contentious, indeed).

4. The sampling of the relevant tissue and body fluid samples for the relevant ancillary investigations, including postmortem histology (which may be crucial in establishing a clinicopathological correlation (**Figure 11**), or, in some

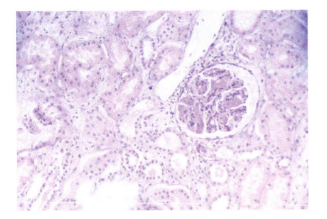

Figure 11 Disseminated intravascular coagulation: fibrin thromboemboli in the glomerular capillaries (H&E ×200).

instances, ascertaining the proximate cause of death from acute myocarditis, massive hepatocellular necrosis, or tubulointerstitial nephritis); toxicology (to confirm to exclude periprocedural medication errors, which may require the analysis of antemortem blood samples, particularly if death had occurred after a lapse of some days or weeks); postmortem serology, microbiological examination and molecular analysis, where indicated, to detect the presence of various bacterial, fungal, and viral pathogens believed to have been responsible for causing lethal postoperative sepsis; occasionally, postmortem angiography to evaluate the possibility of air or gas embolism, or to assess the integrity and patency of vascular (coronary or peripheral arterial) bypass grafts, as well as that of their respective anastomoses, and the localization of endovascular stents.

In addition, photographic documentation of the relevant pathology and iatrogenic injuries may serve to provide a permanent, visual record of the various significant features detected in the course of the autopsy. This may be particularly useful in instances where the sheer complexity of these features may, occasionally, defy precise and comprehensive description, although it behooves the attending pathologist to endeavor to do so in all circumstances.

Postautopsy Evaluation

The autopsy report may be regarded as being, primarily, a precise and appropriately comprehensive statement of fact, describing the findings of the postmortem examination in full. Here, it is held that, where possible, it should also provide a neutrally worded interpretation of all the postmortem findings, including those derived from the relevant ancillary investigations.

Certainly, a forensic pathologist should refrain from expressing opinions on matters pertaining to the propriety of the patient's clinical management, simply because the former is not a clinician and also in view of the highly subspecialized nature of contemporary medical practice. Nevertheless, it may be argued that he has a professional obligation to identify and raise issues of medicolegal concern to the proper authorities under whose direction the postmortem investigations were undertaken. Indeed, these matters, which may have to be addressed by the relevant clinical specialists, either in an appropriate judicial setting (e.g., a coroner's inquest), or a medical forum (e.g., departmental morbidity and mortality discussions), may contribute substantially to medical audit and patient safety. Naturally, there are limitations to what a postmortem examination, however thorough, may accomplish and it must be acknowledged that electrolyte disturbances and coagulation and platelet defects are best assessed by having recourse to the clinical data.

Indeed, situations may arise where it would be advantageous, if not essential, to have recourse to external expertise to conduct technical evaluations of various medical devices, such as anesthetic machines, laparoscopes, surgical lasers, robotic surgical appliances, and hemostatic devices, in order to determine if equipment failure might have caused or contributed to the occurrence of a fatal iatrogenic complication.

Classification

At the conclusion of what is often a rather protracted and, one might add, tedious evaluative process, any particular periprocedural death which warrants a detailed medicolegal or forensic investigation may expediently fall into one of the following categories:

Category A: Deaths in which the postmortem examination reveals an unequivocal morphological cause of death, quite independently of the patient's clinical history. These cases, it may be said, are increasingly rare. An example would be sepsis or organ perforation resulting from the inadvertent retention of surgical devices (e.g., sponges, gauze, and towels, which may give rise to *gossypibomas*—essentially masses within a patient's body comprising a cotton matrix encapsulated by foreign body granulomata; scalpels, artery forceps, and so on), which must be distinguished from those which were intended to be left in situ for a variable period. Other eminent examples would be fatal hemorrhage from the open stump of a blood vessel arising from hemostatic failure, or the insertion of a chest drainage tube into a lung or through the right diaphragmatic dome into the liver.

Category B: Deaths wherein plausible morphological causes of death were discernible at autopsy, but where comprehensive reviews of the relevant clinical records were essential for a proper evaluation of the temporal and causal relations between the procedural interventions undertaken and the associated pathology. Examples include postoperative hemorrhage or suppurative meningitis following upon the trans-sphenoidal resection of a pituitary tumor, sepsis, DIC, and multiorgan failure supervening after bowel infarction and perforation after colonoscopy, or even the more mundane instance of massive pulmonary thromboembolism complicating deep vein thrombosis (which may have been undiagnosed, clinically) after practically any form of surgery, where multiple risk factors including some form of preexisting thrombophilia (e.g., Factor V Leiden) may have predisposed the patient to its development. Notably patients, whose deaths fall within this category, tend to have extensive and serious or life-threatening comorbidity, including chronic organ failure.

Category C: Cases which would inevitably require detailed clinicopathological correlation to formulate the causes of death, in the absence of unequivocal, or demonstrable, morphological causes of death. Prime examples of such cases comprise situations where the anatomical structures which had sustained various forms of iatrogenic injury (e.g., a segment of the small or large bowel which was inadvertently perforated in the course of adhesiolysis, or a previously dehiscent ileo-colic anastomosis of gastro-jejunostomy) had been resected or removed during further exploratory or corrective surgery. Recourse to the antemortem histopathology (anatomical pathology) reports on the resected surgical specimens may be useful in the postmortem evaluation of these cases. The forensic evaluation of these cases also tends to be confounded by the coexistence of extensive and serious comorbidity.

In all probability, a majority of cases (possibly $\geq 50\%$) would be placed in the last category, thus emphasizing the importance of clinicopathological correlation in the forensic evaluation of periprocedural deaths.

In some jurisdictions where periprocedural autopsies are conducted routinely, forensic pathologists with a philosophical bent may marvel at the fact that major surgery—sometimes a series of extensive operations requiring general anesthesia—is actually conducted on some severely and chronically ill, elderly patients, each with myriad comorbidity involving almost every major organ system. In such instances, the apparent value of the autopsy would be to demonstrate, morphologically, that any of these conditions would have been sufficient in the ordinary course of nature to cause death, but that the perioperative complications which (inevitably) supervened, arguably constituted a *novus actus interveniens* which abruptly converted what would otherwise have been death from natural causes to an iatrogenic one.

Conclusion

There can be no doubt that the postmortem examination and forensic evaluation of a periprocedural death, with all its inherent clinicopathological and medicolegal complexities, is often onerous and may well stretch the attending pathologist to the very limit of his or her professional capacity, endurance, and patience. Moreover, as the preceding overview of periprocedural complications clearly illustrates, the iatrogenic potential of a medical procedure is not merely limited by its invasiveness, but is often heightened by a variety of adverse drug reactions associated with them.

Nevertheless, in embracing this vast and fascinating subject—which is, essentially, boundless in its manifestations—forensic pathologists may help to bring about some measure of closure to these perplexing events and make a significant contribution to medical audit and, ultimately, patient safety. This may be regarded, as it were, as a natural extension of the more traditional role of enhancing occupational, transportation, and general public safety that forensic pathology has played in the past and, indeed, continues to fulfill (albeit often unacknowledged).

At the very least, forensic pathologists who have the privilege of engaging in this aspect of medicolegal death investigation, should be immensely grateful to their clinical colleagues for supplying them (intermittently or endlessly, as the case may be) with the intellectual stimulation which, it may be said, is so very vital to their continuing professional development.

Perhaps a fitting conclusion to this section on deaths associated with medical procedures would be the following quotation from the *Father of Morbid Anatomy*, the late *Giovanni Battista Morgagni (1682–1771)*:

> Those who have dissected or inspected many bodies have at least learned to doubt, while those who are ignorant of anatomy and do not take the trouble to attend to it, are in no doubt at all.

See also: **Forensic Medicine/Pathology:** Autopsy; External Postmortem Examination; Histopathology; **Legal:** Expert Witness Qualifications and Testimony; **Methods:** Spectroscopic Techniques; **Toxicology:** Pharmacology and Mechanism of Action of Drugs.

Further Reading

Delbridge, M.S., Raffery, A.T., 2007. Renal transplantation. Medicine 35, 479–482.

Eufrásio, P., Parada, B., Moreira, P., et al., 2011. Surgical complications in 2000 renal transplants. Transplantation Proceedings 43, 142–144.

Gill, J.R., Goldfeder, L.B., Hirsch, C.S., 2006. Use of 'therapeutic complication' as a manner of death. Journal of Forensic Sciences 51, 1127–1133.

Grocott, M.P.W., Ingram, S., 2003. Perioperative deaths. In: Payne-James, J., Busuttil, A., Smock, W. (Eds.), Forensic Medicine: Clinical and Pathological Aspects. Greenwich Medical Media Ltd, London, pp. 201–212.

Lau, G., 1994a. A case of sudden maternal death associated with resuscitative liver injury. Forensic Science International 67, 127–132.

Lau, G., 1994b. Fatal haemorrhage following intra-aortic balloon counterpulsation: a case report and a brief review of its clinico-pathological and medico-legal aspects. Medicine, Science, and the Law 34, 111–116.

Lau, G., 1996. Perioperative deaths – a comparative study of coroner's autopsies between the periods 1989–1991 and 1992–1994. Annals of the Academy of Medicine, Singapore 25, 509–515.

Lau, G., 2000. A further comparative review of perioperative deaths, with particular reference to the occurrence of fatal iatrogenic injury. Annals of the Academy of Medicine, Singapore 29, 486–497.

Lau, G., 2003. Death may have its benefits: the role of forensic pathology in medical audit. In: Paper Presented at the International Conference on Risk Management for Preventive Medicine. Tokyo. http://www.urmpm.org.

Lau, G., 2005. Iatrogenic injury: a forensic perspective. In: Tsokos, M. (Ed.), Forensic Pathology Reviews, vol. 3. The Humana Press Inc., New Jersey, pp. 351–442.

Lau, G., 2007. Post-anaesthetic maternal death in a patient with mediastinal large B-cell lymphoma – a case report. Medicine, Science, and the Law 47, 74–78.

Lau, G., 2008. Fatal cerebral infarction complicating therapeutic embolisation of a facial cavernous haemangioma: a case report. Medicine, Science, and the Law 48, 256–260.

Lau, G., Lai, S.H., 2001. Fatal retroperitoneal haemorrhage: an unusual complication of percutaneous endoscopic gastrostomy. Forensic Science International 116, 69–75.

Lau, G., Lai, S.H., 2008. Forensic histopathology. In: Tsokos, M. (Ed.), Forensic Pathology Reviews, vol. 5. The Humana Press Inc., New Jersey, pp. 239–265 (Springer Science).

Lau, G., Thamboo, T., Lai, S.H., 2003. Fatal pulmonary thromboembolism in Singapore: has anything changed? Medicine, Science, and the Law 43, 307–314.

Lee, E.H., Lau, G., Paul, G., et al., 2008. Coroner's Practice in Medical Cases. Singapore Academy of Law. Academy Publishing, Singapore.

Meyer, C.G., Penn, I., James, L., 2000. Liver transplantation for cholangiocarcinoma: results in 207 patients. Transplantation 69, 1633–1637.

Saukko, P., Knight, B., 2004. Deaths associated with surgical procedures. In: Saukko, P., Knight, B. (Eds.), Knight's Forensic Pathology, third ed. Arnold, London, pp. 480–487.

Tsokos, M., 2007. Post-mortem diagnosis of sepsis. Forensic Science International 165, 155–164.

Wang, M., Lau, G., 2012. When is a periprocedural death iatrogenic in nature? Forensic Science, Medicine, and Pathology 8, 23–33.

Relevant Websites

http://www.asahq.org/—Physical Status Classification System. American Society of Anesthesiologists.

http://www.ncepod.org.uk/—National Confidential Enquiry into Patient Outcome and Death (NCEPOD).

http://www.sasm.org.uk/—Scottish Audit of Surgical Mortality (SASM).

Neonaticide

NEI Langlois and RW Byard, Forensic Science SA, Adelaide, SA, Australia
C Winskog, University of Adelaide, Adelaide, SA, Australia

Introduction

Infanticide is a general term for the murder of a child aged less than 1 year, and filicide is used when the perpetrator is the parent, but neonaticide is used to refer to deliberate killing of a child up to 24 h of age by his or her parent.

Nonhuman primates have been observed to kill their offspring, and the act of neonaticide in human cultures dates back to before historical records were kept. In the past, in some cultures, it was not necessarily a crime; a father's right to murder his children was recognized in Roman law under *patria potestas*, and infanticide was not uncommon in China up to the nineteenth century. Infanticide in Britain in early times was largely a matter for the church but became better recognized as a crime in the Middle Ages.

Incidence

Neonaticide would appear to be uncommon, but it is likely official statistics are an underestimate of the true incidence. A review of cases in France revealed that a variety of factors (including miscoding) resulted in the official published rate (0.39 per 100 000 live births) being lower than the rate disclosed by a retrospective review (2.1 per 100 000)—the higher rate being in accord with an American study. Furthermore, it is probable that a number of cases remain hidden and are not detected.

Males rarely perform the act of neonaticide. Women who commit neonaticide are often young, poorly educated, and unmarried or single. Frequently, they have concealed or denied their pregnancy and have made no plans for caring for their child. However, a married mother who had received some antenatal care was encountered in around 21% of cases in one study. It may not be their first pregnancy, and they may have other children. Thus, it must be recognized that offenders may be of any (reproductive) age, status, educational level, and marital status. Although mental illness may be a feature in some, it is not a common feature and it is more likely in older offenders.

Male and female newborn infants have been regarded as equal victims of neonaticide, although a higher rate of males are suggested in certain communities, which may be a consequence of a higher male than female birth rate. There is no predisposition toward those with congenital abnormalities. The majority of cases are found in the mother's place of residence, such as in the toilet or an associated structure (such as a shed); frequently, the bodies are placed in a rubbish receptacle, but bodies may also be recovered outdoors and from lockers.

Methods

Neonates are small and have no ability to defend themselves. In one case series, strangulation was the most common method of homicide (12 cases), followed by drowning (7 cases) and hypothermia (4 cases). Blunt head trauma was rare (2 cases) as was stabbing (1 case). Other case series agree that strangling, smothering, or suffocation by other means are the most common means of homicide, with less common methods including blunt force and sharp force. Strangulation is easily accomplished by the mother's own hands, whereas drowning may be performed in the toilet. Death may also be effected by inaction, such as abandonment leading to exposure. Some rarer methods include use of opium on the nipples and insertion of a needle into the cranium through the fontanel or via the orbit.

Assessment

When a dead newborn is found and neonaticide is considered, the pathologist has two questions to answer: did the child have an independent existence and if so, what was the cause of death. It is a requirement to prove a child was born live and had an independent existence in order to form the charge of neonaticide (deliberate killing of a newborn in the first day of life). Live birth and separate existence are not clearly defined but can be regarded as maintenance of a circulation and respiration when the child has been completely delivered of its mother, which may be extended to require division of the umbilical cord. If the case can be shown to be that of a stillbirth (death before extraction/expulsion independent of duration of pregnancy) then it will most likely be outside of medicolegal jurisdiction.

A first step toward determining if a newborn may have been born alive requires assessment for signs of maceration, which

Figure 1   Macerated fetus from case of intrauterine death displaying redness of the skin with peeling of the epidermis.

manifest as redness of the skin with peeling of the epidermis and flaccidity of the body with laxness of the joints (**Figure 1**). Maceration is a sign of death *in utero*, but the changes take several days to develop and the absence of maceration cannot be used to indicate a live birth. A further guide to the likelihood of live birth may be obtained by forming an assessment of gestational age (i.e., if born full term at 40 weeks or premature) as live birth becomes unlikely at under 20 weeks of gestation. Methods to estimate gestational age include assessment of ossification centers, odontological appraisal of development of the teeth buds, and histological examination of tissues with referral to standard texts. A third consideration is for the examination of abnormalities that would be considered likely to result in stillbirth, such as severe malformations (including chromosomal and other genetic syndromes); attention should be paid to the placenta, which should be sought for examination.

If it is determined that live birth was possible, the next step is to assess for signs of a separate existence. Tests that have been proposed for proving vitality include the lung flotation test, assessment of stomach content, and examination of the umbilical cord.

The lung floatation test is based on the assumption that an infant who has not breathed will have airless lungs that will sink in water, whereas if breathing has occurred after birth, the

lungs will be buoyant in water. However, artificial respiration can aerate the lungs and gaseous accumulation can occur in advanced decomposition, which may invalidate the test. Pneumonia, atelectasis (due to a deficiency of surfactant), and early decomposition can cause the lungs to sink. Histological observation of pulmonary interstitial emphysema has been proposed as a more specific marker of live birth; however, equivocal changes may occur as an artifact and an absence of pulmonary interstitial emphysema does not exclude live birth.

Examination of stomach contents may provide evidence of an independent existence if milk is found as it indicates the newborn has been able to ingest food, which can be regarded as proof of a period of survival sufficiently long to feed. The presence of air may indicate that gulping had occurred with swallowing of air, but this can be invalidated by resuscitation, which can force air into the stomach. Similarly, the presence of air in the middle ear has been proposed as an indicator of life, but it must be presumed that air could be present due to decomposition or resuscitation.

The infant end of the umbilical cord should show evidence of an inflammatory reaction if there has been a survival of some hours after birth, which would be good evidence for a period of survival following birth. However, this may be discounted if there is a funisitis of the cord and an absence of inflammation does not exclude live birth.

The pathological findings may not be contributory to the question of whether the child had been born live. The investigator should also consider any witness accounts from the scene, such as any reports of the sounds of a child crying. The determination of an independent existence may be impossible if the remains are decomposed or skeletonized.

If it is possible a live birth had occurred, the pathologist will need to examine the infant to determine the cause of death. In such cases, the assistance of a suitably qualified pediatric pathologist may be sought. The cause of death may be natural but is likely that ancillary tests (including histological and microbiological) that will necessitate expert interpretation will be required. Furthermore, the brain will be markedly softened due to the low level of myelination, such that fixation followed by expert neuropathological assessment should be performed as this would be expected to increase the documentation of pathological lesions. Radiology, including use of CT (computed tomography) and/or MRI (magnetic resonance imaging) may assist in the assessment.

As noted above, the most common means of neonaticide are strangulation and suffocation. Strangulation may be performed by the mother's own hands or by ligature. Suffocation may be achieved by inserting material into the mouth (e.g., a piece of wadding) or by using an object such as a pillow. The pathologist will need to bear the possibilities in mind while performing the external examination and internal dissection. The use of CT may disclose a mass obstructing the airway even when there has been a significant postmortem interval. However, due to the innate weakness of the neonate, there is usually no evidence of defensive action or a struggle and there may be minimal signs; fractures of the hyoid or larynx are unlikely due to the elasticity of the structures. Death caused by smothering from a pillow would be particularly difficult to detect. However, the pathologist should extend the external examination to search for deposited fibers (on the neck or within the oropharynx). The use of histology including modified Poley's acid fuchsin-methyl green has been suggested to visualize microscopic appearance of a neck compression and immunohistochemical staining may reveal changes. The proposed signs of asphyxiation, congestion of the organs, petechial hemorrhages, cyanosis, fluid blood, and dilation of the heart, have been dismissed as an obsolescent quintet. Care must be taken not to misinterpret neck trauma resulting from the mother's efforts to deliver the child or from the cord having been wrapped around the neck during birth. Determination of death by drowning (e.g., by delivery into or by directly pacing into a toilet bowl) may be not distinguishable from stillbirth as both will show a lack of aeration of the lungs with or without fluid in the airway. However, a search should be made in the airways and stomach for aspiration of any material that is also represented in the water of the possible site of drowning.

The newborn may be abandoned resulting in death from exposure by inaction of the mother. It is unclear if signs of hypothermic death develop in the neonate. Blunt head trauma may be difficult to differentiate from birth trauma and expert neuropathological assessment should be sought; the possibility that a mother has accidentally dropped a newborn would also have to be considered. Other accidental trauma may occur as part of the delivery process. Death due to exsanguination from an umbilical cord that has not been properly clamped or tied should be prevented by natural hemostatic processes, but it has been recorded. The determination of the cause of death may be prevented by postmortem changes of decomposition.

The pathologist may assist with confirming the identity of the mother by taking of samples for DNA comparison with the putative parents. Any items, such as wrappings, with the child should be examined as these may also provide clues to the identity of an unknown mother.

A visit to the scene by a pathologist may provide vital information and should be performed whenever possible. Assessment of the scene may provide valuable information: the use of luminol (or other chemiluminescent agent for hemoglobin) may disclose a trail from a site of delivery to the site of the body. In addition, the mother's medical records (including birth and any psychiatric history) should be obtained from hospitals and medical centers. Questioning of friends and family may provide useful information, particularly, any person who was present around the likely scene of birth. The

mother may need medical assistance and should be examined for signs of birth. As soon as possible, she should provide a statement. Wherever possible, the placenta should be retrieved and examined.

Illustrative Case

Some of the findings associated with neonaticide are illustrated by the following case. A newborn child was found partially hidden in the snow behind a fence close to a small sawmill. Blood was spread over a large area (**Figure 2**). The scene examination revealed the presence of a placenta as well as the umbilical cord. The dead child was examined at the scene and signs of blunt force trauma were identified with a palpable skull fracture. Due to the low temperature, the body was well preserved with minimal decomposition. Examination in the mortuary revealed superficial lacerations resembling nail marks from grabbing (**Figures 3 and 4**) and patterned injuries in the shape of a sole of a shoe (**Figure 5**)—it was later established that the mark matched the heel of the shoe the mother wore at the time of the delivery. Autopsy findings included extensive skull fractures with subarachnoid and subdural hemorrhages together with intracerebral and brain stem hemorrhages. It was also established that there was air in the gastrointestinal tract. A national alarm was issued and a vehicle that was suspected to contain the parents was intercepted at the border before it could leave the country. The mother of the child was taken into custody and revealed what had taken place. She claimed that she had been unaware of the pregnancy (it was her second child) and that she had walked off behind the fence to urinate. She gave birth and left the scene shocked and in disbelief of what had occurred. She hid bloody clothing and joined her

Figure 2 The scene of discovery of the body in the snow (see *arrows*). Blood has been spread by birds predating the placenta and cord.

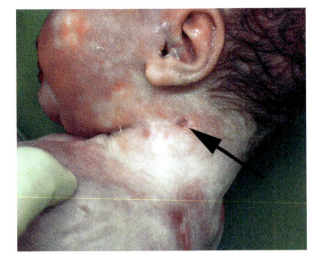

Figure 3   Abrasion on side of neck (*arrow*) from fingernail of mother inflicted while grabbing child during birth.

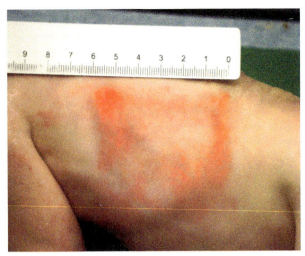

Figure 5   Patterned injury from sole of mother's shoe.

Conclusion

The investigation of possible cases of neonaticide may involve many issues. The pathologist should consider utilizing assistance from other disciplines, including pediatric pathologists. In the case example above, it was possible to establish that the child had been born alive and to determine that the mother had caused the death. However, in many cases, it will not to be possible to determine with certainty if the child was born alive, or if live birth is determined the cause of death may remain elusive.

> *See also:* **Behavioral:** Criminal Profiling; Detection of Deception; Investigative Psychology; **Biology/DNA:** Parentage Testing and Kinship Analysis; **Forensic Medicine/Causes of Death:** Strangulation; Immersion Deaths; Sudden Infant Death Syndrome (SIDS); Asphyctic Deaths—Overview and Pathophysiology; **Forensic Medicine/Clinical:** Child Abuse; Forensic Age Estimation; Identification.

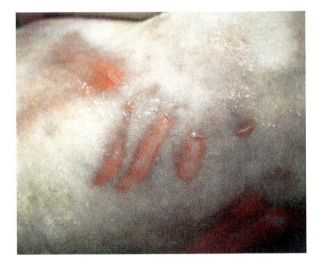

Figure 4   Abrasions caused by mother while grabbing newborn.

husband (father of their first child and the newborn) as they began their journey home. When apprehended the father had no knowledge of what had occurred. Death was attributed to blunt head trauma, but hypothermia in combination with obstructed airways (due to the position of the newborn when found) together with blood loss from the torn umbilical cord was mentioned in the final report as possible contributory factors. Following a trial, the mother was found to have caused the death, but it was also established by the court that she suffered from a psychiatric illness at the time of the act and so she was sentenced to psychiatric care.

Further Reading

Bowen, D.A.L., 1989. Concealment of birth, child destruction and infanticide. In: Masson, J.K. (Ed.), Paediatric Forensic Medicine and Pathology. Chapman and Hall, London.

Byard, R.W., 2010. Sudden Death in the Young. Cambridge University Press, Cambridge.

Craig, M., 2004. Perinatal risk factors for neonaticide and infant homicide: can we identify those at risk? Journal of the Royal Society of Medicine 97, 57–61.

Friedman, S.H., Resnik, P.J., 2009. Neonaticide: phenomenology and considerations for prevention. International Journal of Law and Psychiatry 32, 43–47.

Herman-Giddens, M.E., Smith, J.B., Mittal, M., Carlson, M., Butts, J.D., 2003. Newborns killed or left to die by a parent. A population-based study. Journal of the American Medical Association 289, 1425–1429.

Keeling, J.W., Yee, K.T., 2007. Fetal and Neonatal Pathology. Springer, London.

Kellet, R.J., 1992. Infanticide and child destruction – the historical, legal and pathological aspects. Forensic Science International 53, 1–28.

Lavezzi, W.A., McKenna, B.J., Wolf, B.C., 2004. The significance of pulmonary interstitial emphysema in live birth determination. Journal of Forensic Sciences 49, 546–552.

Porter, T., Gavin, H., 2010. Infanticide and neonaticide: a review of 40 years of research literature on incidence and causes. Trauma, Violence & Abuse 11, 99–112.

Resnick, P.J., 1970. Murder of the newborn: a psychiatric review of neonaticide. The American Journal of Psychiatry 126, 1414–1420.

Shelton, J.L., Corey, T., Donaldson, W.H., Hemberger, E., Dennison, E.H., 2011. Neonaticide: a comprehensive review of investigative and pathologic aspects of 55 cases. Journal of Family Violence 26, 263–276.

Tursz, A., Cook, J.M., 2010. A population-based survey of neonaticides using judicial data. Archives of Disease in Childhood. Fetal and Neonatal Edition 96, F259–F263.

Key Terms

Accidental electrocution, Alcohol abuse, Asphyxia, Autopsy, Autopsy findings, Cardiovascular diseases, Causes of death, Cerebral bleeding, Child abuse, Clinical history, Cold exposure, Coronary heart disease, Criminal act, Death scene investigation, Definition, Diabetes, Drowning, Drug abuse, Drug adverse effect, Electric burn, Electric mark, Electric shock, Electrocution, Electrophilia, Epidemiology, Epilepsy, Forensic evaluation, Heat cramp, Heat exhaustion, Heat stroke, Heat wave, Histology, Homicide, Hyperthermia, Hypothermia, Hypotheses, Iatrogenic injury, Incidence, Infanticide, Lichtenberg figure, Lightning strike, Low-voltage electrocution, Natural death, Neglect, Neonaticide, Peptic ulcer, Periprocedural deaths, Pneumonia, Pulmonary embolism, Rhabdomyolysis, Risk factors, Smothering, Social deprivation, Standardized autopsy protocol, Strangulation, Sudden infant death syndrome, Suicidal electrocution, Thermoregulation, Ventricular fibrillation.

Review Questions

1. What is the difference between sudden death and unexpected death?
2. How do males in their 60s or 70s are most likely to die?
3. What factors may mislead an investigator away from considering sudden death in an adult?
4. What is SIDS?
5. What factors seem to contribute to SIDS?
6. What are some of the hypotheses about what causes SIDS?
7. Who are most susceptible to death by hyperthermia or hypothermia?
8. What is heatstroke?
9. What is the specific pathology that diagnoses hyperthermia?
10. Who is likely to succumb to hypothermia? Give at least five examples.
11. What are the two ways that electricity can harm a person?
12. What factors increase the trauma from electricity?
13. Is trauma from electricity (low or high voltage) always easy to diagnose? Why or why not?
14. What is a periprocedural death? What does iatrogenic mean?
15. What are the possibilities that a forensic pathologist must consider when investigating a potential death from medical procedure?
16. What is gossypibomas?
17. What is neonaticide?
18. Has neonaticide always been against the law?
19. Who most often commits neonaticide, women or men?
20. What are the two questions a forensic pathologist must answer when faced with a dead newborn?

Discussion Questions

1. Why is SIDS such a contentious diagnosis? What factors beyond the scientific or medical could contribute to this continuing argument?
2. How would a forensic pathologist potentially distinguish between a death from hyperthermia and sudden death? Is there a difference?

3. How would a forensic pathologist potentially distinguish between a death from hyperthermia and death from electrical trauma?
4. Given that medical errors are the third leading cause of death, why are not more autopsies carried out on these cases?
5. If a forensic pathologist is asked to investigate a potential death due to a medical procedure, what information, data, documents, and other evidence would they want to review prior to viewing the body or conducting the autopsy?

Additional Readings

Alunni, V., Crenesse, D., Pierccechi-Marti, M.D., Gaillard, Y., Quatrehomme, G., 2015. Fatal heat stroke in a child entrapped in a confined space. Journal of Forensic and Legal Medicine 34, 139–144.

Heinemann, A., Vogel, H., Heller, M., Tzikas, A., Püschel, K., 2015. Investigation of medical intervention with fatal outcome: the impact of post-mortem CT and CT angiography. La Radiologia Medica 120 (9), 835–845.

Huchzermeier, C., Heinzen, H., 2015. A young woman who killed 5 of her own babies: a case of multiple neonaticide. Journal of Forensic and Legal Medicine 35, 15–18.

Hunt, C.E., Darnall, R.A., McEntire, B.L., Hyma, B.A., 2015. Assigning cause for sudden unexpected infant death. Forensic Science, Medicine, and Pathology 11 (2), 283–288.

McGuire, A.R., DeJoseph, M.E., Gill, J.R., 2016. An approach to iatrogenic deaths. Forensic Science, Medicine, and Pathology 12 (1), 68–80.

Reed, R.C., February 2015. Iatrogenic injury and unexpected hospital death in the newborn. In: Seminars in Perinatology, vol. 39 (1). WB Saunders, pp. 64–69.

Wennergren, G., Nordstrand, K., Alm, B., Möllborg, P., Öhman, A., Berlin, A., Katz-Salamon, M., Lagercrantz, H., 2015. Updated Swedish advice on reducing the risk of sudden infant death syndrome. Acta Paediatrica 104 (5), 444–448.

Section 6. Identification

How someone died is second only to who that person was. Identifying the dead is centrally important for many legal and social reasons, such as criminal charges, insurance, inheritance, public health, and many others. In some ways, a forensic pathologist has it easy compared to a forensic scientist. At a crime scene where the perpetrator has fled, the scientist may only have a fingerprint or a drop of blood to identify the person. If that method fails, they may not be able to use another. A forensic pathologist, however, has the entire body (or what is left of it) to work with, ideally providing multiple chances to identify who it is. This is not always the case, however, as burned, dismembered, or badly decomposed remains pose their own specific challenges.

Identification

C Cattaneo and **D Gibelli,** Università degli Studi di Milano, Milano, Italy

Introduction

Personal identification is one of the most relevant issues in forensic pathology. In all countries with a structured legal system, cadavers must be formally identified. The reasons behind such obligations are certainly moral and also concern aspects of criminal and civil procedures: in fact, without knowing who the victim of a crime is, it is very difficult to begin investigating and without appropriate identification of the deceased, civil matters such as insurance policies and questions concerning inheritance cannot be concluded. As to what each specific legal system implies as reliable identification, this is another matter. If the body is well preserved, it is frequently sufficient to have family or acquaintances formally, and responsibly, identify the body. But in the case of decomposed cadavers or remains, this cannot or must not be the case, although some judges would like to conclude identification issues (saving on expenses is usually the issue) relying on personal belongings, clothing, or other nonbiological evidence. It is clear that this is incorrect and that biological identification, when possible, should always be sought in order to avoid serious mistakes: Interpol protocols, for one, stress this point.

How to identify a cadaver or human remains is another issue. In this age of DNA, usually, identification is relatively, quickly, and cheaply achieved by genetic testing. Nonetheless, particularly in the case of severely decomposed human remains, many other methods can be as reliable but quicker and cheaper, such as odontology. In many cases, as will be discussed later, particularly in cases of vagrants or when neither antemortem DNA or relatives nor clinical dental or medical data are available, judges and pathologists should be aware that other methods exist.

A final preliminary comment that must be made concerns the degree of confidence and reliability of a specific identification method or rationale. Many different schools exist as to how to classify levels of identification: the two extremes are exclusion and positive (certain) identification. In between, there are a series of nuances that can be summed up as different degrees of compatibility, for example, no elements allowing for exclusion but concordant characters are very general, or several and specific characters with a high identification potential but not sufficient to reach positive identification. The question is how much is enough for positive identification? Unfortunately, there is no real answer. Some methods, such as DNA and fingerprinting, have managed to quantify the degree of correspondence of two biological samples (e.g., the cadaver and the toothbrush of the person whom the cadaver was thought to "belong to" in life). In other words, a statistical analysis of the frequency of discrete characters (alleles, minutiae) can lead the expert to express the probability of these two samples belonging to the same person as a number (e.g., 98%). Obviously, any method of this sort will be very popular among judges as it has a known error and neatly complies with Daubert and Kumho rules. Other methods, particularly those based on the comparison of morphology (e.g., odontological and radiological/osteological ones), have more difficulty in quantifying their response. For example, how can an odontologist say what the probability of two different persons sharing the same asset of dental features is? Dental assets change in time and discrete characters are difficult to standardize and study worldwide (although some authors have approached this issue). Or, more simply, what is the probability that two individuals share the same two scars and three tattoos? The answer depends on the types of scars and tattoos, of course, and also on a large deal of subjectivity. Nonetheless, most pathologists will (correctly) continue to identify with morphological and clinical features; one should, however, bear in mind the limits and issues that can be raised with such methods.

The following is a brief survey of identification approaches. The authors wish to stress, however, how the world of identification concerns not only positive identification, that is, matching antemortem with postmortem data (when there already is a possible match), but also cases where there is no clue as to who the body belongs to. This is a frequently underestimated issue, and in these cases, the pathologist must use as many disciplines as necessary to build a biological profile of the cadaver or human remains that should be automatically matched with missing persons databases (when these exist, and hoping the person has been reported missing by someone) and give maximum circulation of the biological profile on newspapers, television, and so on. Thus, this chapter is divided into two parts: the first dealing with unidentified cadavers and the second with positive identification.

Part I. Unidentified Cadavers

The issue of unidentified decedents is a large and underestimated one, also because of the lack of knowledge concerning the frequency of unknown decedents in different geographical contexts. Very few countries have a database for the comparison of missing persons and unidentified decedents, which is surprising, given the increase in legal and illegal immigration and a society with looser family and social ties and obligations. Hanzlick et al. published epidemiological data from Fulton County (Georgia) and created one of the first Web sites with information and demographical data on unidentified decedents.

Very few indications are available in Europe, and in different countries, the precise number of unknown decedents is not recorded or still partially known; a recent study from Italy (a high immigration rate country) reported that at least 800 individuals are recorded as unidentified in medicolegal institutes. Similar orders of magnitude have been given for France by the press but official numbers do not exist. However, the real frequency of unknown decedents is likely to be higher than reported, due to the occurrence of unrecorded immigrants and the lack of precise information on unidentified bodies in different institutes of legal medicine and morgues.

Identification in every case requires a comparison between antemortem information from the "suspect" (the person who the remains may belong to) and postmortem data from the corpse; however, this comparison can be performed between profiles only if a possible match has been reached. And the possible match(es) is selected because it shows compatible characters, for example, such as sex, race, age, and stature, with those of the cadaver. Building up general data from remains is called "general identification," and the biological data extrapolated from the cadaver or human remains is the so-called "biological profile."

The biological profile consists of general characteristics of sex, age, race, and height of the individual and all individual markers that can be useful for identification (tattoos, scars, bone calluses, dental work, etc.). When the cadaver is in good condition, the pathologist can be independent in extrapolating all relevant information (although a toxicologist may be useful for detecting the presence of helpful (identification-wise) substances or medication in the blood or tissues). If the remains are badly preserved or skeletonized, then an anthropologist and odontologist may be useful. Most of the steps and diagnoses in these disciplines, particularly anthropology, go through are discussed in the relevant chapters. Briefly, when genitalia are not recognizable, sex can be easily defined by the analysis of the pelvis, and especially of the pubis, whereas cranial characteristics are less reliable; an accurate diagnosis can exceed 98% with the pelvis. In addition, the cranial features may suffer important modifications with time, as shown by masculinization usually reported in the crania of old females. On the other hand, osteological diagnosis of sex is difficult or even impossible to reach in case of subadults, where DNA must come in.

On the contrary, age estimation is easier in subadults than in adults, where it can be performed from the analysis of skeletal and dental development. The error of age estimation increases with age. In adults, age estimation can be linked only to degeneration processes. The main methods are Suchey–Brook's method on the pubic symphysis, Iscan's method on the fourth rib's osteochondral surface, and Lovejoy's method on the auricular surface of the ilium. Most commonly applied dental methods are Lamendin's and Kvaal–Solheim's methods. Ancestry determination in decomposed corpses can rely on the histological analysis of residual skin and hair, which show decisive differences between the main races. In skeletonized remains, the diagnosis of ancestry may be reached by morphological and metrical assessments of the cranium and postcranial bones. In addition, race determination may be performed by Fordisc software®, based on different cranial and postcranial measurements taken in American samples from different ancestries, although its adherence to the main racial groups is questionable. Stature is related to the length of long bones and can be determined also from fragmented bones by specific formulae, but in this case, the inaccuracy is high. A complete X-ray analysis is obligatory in order to verify the presence of bone traits (e.g., Harris lines, calluses), as well as dental traits (e.g., restorations), which can be useful. Finally, facial reconstruction should be performed provided investigators have the final "identikit" circulate with the appropriate precautions: facial reproductions may remind observers of a person who has been missing, but it may not necessarily bear a close resemblance.

Once the biological profile is complete, the obtained identikit should be compared with missing persons and/or circulate as much as possible in the hope that someone (investigators or the general public) may come up with a possible match for identity.

Part II. Personal Identification: Comparison between Antemortem and Postmortem Data

Once circumstantial evidence, comparison with missing persons or other investigative activities, have led to a suspicion of identity, personal identification is then based on the analysis of the specific and individualizing characteristics observed in the unknown decedent and their comparison with similar data from the matching "suspect": every type of identification requires a comparison that must be founded on biological features. Positive identification may be reached by different methods. The first and most immediate for well-preserved cadavers is visual recognition of facial characteristics (e.g., with a photograph). The comparison may also be performed through fingerprints or genetic comparison if an adequate antemortem reference sample is available. In addition, since dental and skeletal features are unique, odontological and radiological methods may be applied with success if consistent antemortem material from the identity suspect can be obtained. Finally, superimposition methods (craniofacial and dental superimpositions) can be used when other procedures cannot be applied, although the significance of results is questionable and their importance is limited to specific cases.

Individual Markers

Specific descriptors such as tattoos, prostheses, nevi, and scars may be useful for identification and, therefore, should be described and photographed. For this reason, with decomposed and burnt remains, specific care must be taken to clean the skin surface, at times by scraping off the initial epidermal layer, in order to visualize scars, moles, and tattoos that may be hidden underneath soot and superficially burnt skin.

As for most morphological methods of comparison between antemortem and postmortem material, there is no consensus concerning how many descriptors are needed in order to reach a positive identification; literature recently has attempted at standardizing the frequency of specific human descriptors among the general population. This may give the first impulse for statistical evaluation of bodily markers. However, one should consider that every descriptor from a morphological point of view is unique, although it may be found in other individuals. For example, a surgical scar is likely to be useful for personal identification; however, other persons may have a similar marker in the same bodily area. Most of markers are highly individualizing, since their morphology is unique; for example, a thoracotomy follows a standard procedure, but the profile of the cut mark, the sutures, and manner of bone remodeling leads to a unique profile of the marker, which is different among individuals.

The following is a list of more specialized identification procedures that go beyond the pathologist's competence.

Facial Identification

In different countries, the main identification procedure consists of showing the corpse to the relatives or acquaintances who are requested to give a positive identification, although visual recognition is often influenced by the emotional status of the observers, who are perhaps often more prone to identify the corpse by clothes and personal belongings. At times, however, even though the cadaver is easily identifiable visually, no acquaintances seem to exist or can be contacted. At this point, comparison of facial traits with identity papers such as drivers' licenses can be requested.

Indeed, facial features may be of some help for personal identification through a scientific process, although their reliability still needs to be verified. How can two faces (antemortem photograph and the cadaver) be proven as belonging to the same person? In cases of personal identification of the living from video surveillance systems, for example, comparison and superimposition of facial features is commonly used. In these cases, the morphological features of two facial profiles are compared in order to point out possible differences that may lead to an exclusion or similarities that may justify an identification. However, many limits still affect such procedures, particularly the lack of a standardized manner of comparison between two images. Therefore, at the moment, the comparison of facial features may be useful only for an exclusion of identity, if gross and otherwise inexplicable discordances between the two facial profiles are found. In addition, one should consider that these methods have been tested for personal identification in the living, whereas at the moment there are no experimental studies concerning this topic in case of unknown decedents (**Figure 1**). A similar rationale can be used for other parts of the body, for example, venous and mole patterns, with the limitations stated above.

Figure 1　Example of superimposition between a 3D scan of the cadaver (in yellow) and the 2D image of the antemortem photograph.

Fingerprint Analysis

Fingerprints are among the most individualizing features, since they are also different in homozygous twins and are usually recorded by qualified police personnel: in addition, literature shows that even in corpses radically compromised by decomposition or charring processes, they can be recorded and used for identification, provided antemortem prints are available. In many counties, however, this is limited to individuals who have a criminal record. Databases such as AFIS (automated fingerprint identification system) have proven to be efficient for this purpose worldwide. The problem concerning the pathologist or forensic expert in general may be in extracting prints from dead bodies that have already undergone decomposition.

According to the specific alterations, fingerprints can be recovered by different procedures and treatments: when hands are mummified or charred, which implies a loss of liquids, fingerprints have to be softened and reinflated, for example, by alternate incubation in alcohol and sodium hydroxide solutions. Once the fingerprints are softened, they may be inflated by injection of saline solution. In case of carbonized hands, the fists are often clenched and, therefore, are better preserved from the heat; in this case, they should be accurately preserved and cleaned avoiding any further damage; then, the application of specific types of latex can be useful in recovering a print (**Figure 2**).

In case of putrefaction, the first procedure consists of stopping any further modification, which can be reached by hardening the skin in ethanol for a time between a few minutes and 1–2 h. Saponification causes flattening of the papillary crests, so before inking the fingerprints should be reinflated.

Several methods have been published for recovering prints from decomposed human remains. It is important to realize that even in a cadaver that seems badly preserved and beyond fingerprinting, these methods can give useful fingerprints.

DNA Testing

Genetic analysis is usually considered the main method of identification in the cases of unknown decedents and is undoubtedly the most popular one. In countries with DNA databases, this may be, indeed, the best way to a quick and reliable identification. Comparison of the DNA postmortem asset from the cadaver or human remains with the antemortem asset of a "suspect" implies obtaining biological material that certainly contains DNA of that specific person from, for example, a toothbrush, a razor, or other personal belongings. It must be certain that they are not contaminated. DNA from close relatives can also be useful and easily obtained with a mouth swab.

Nonetheless, sometimes the recovery of antemortem material may not be possible, for example, in cases where relatives are not present (this may occur for mass graves where the bodies are discovered decades after the massacre or in cases of vagrants or illegal immigrants). On the other hand, some postmortem substrates such as calcined tissues or dry bone may still be challenging for the geneticist since DNA extraction may not be banale. Furthermore, sometimes DNA testing may be longer and more expensive than other methods, for example, dental comparison.

Odontological Methods

Teeth are highly individualizing markers, thanks to anatomical uniqueness and modifications that may derive from therapeutical and pathological variables; these factors contribute to creating a unique profile, different from one individual to the other. In addition, teeth are resistant to many taphonomical agents and carbonization and can be easily analyzed for personal identification.

Antemortem data usually comes from the dentist who treated the person in life and may provide descriptions, casts and orthopantomographs, and other dental radiographs (**Figure 3**). In collecting antemortem material, one should

Figure 2   Phases of fingerprint reproduction from a mummified finger by application of a latex layer.

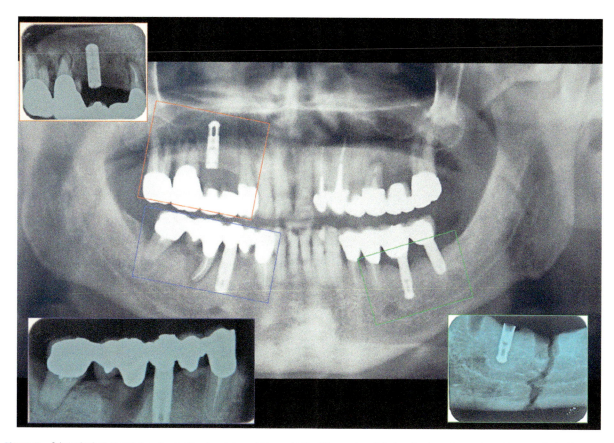

Figure 3   Odontological comparison by postmortem intraoral X-rays (defined by a colored line) and antemortem orthopantomography in the background.

always keep in mind that the dental asset may vary with time; therefore, clinical data sometimes may not be reliable, according to time lapse and treatment between when the data was created and death. This explains the difficulties encountered in cases of personal identification of subadults, which often undergo to frequent odontological treatments and are affected by growth, with consequent progressive modification of the odontological profile.

Teeth individualizing markers are not only in the oral cavity but also in the palatal rugae. Palatal rugae are irregular ridges of connective tissue across the front portion of the palate and are highly variable and stable with time, regardless of odontological treatment. Recent articles also show that radical modifications of the palate caused, for example, by rapid maxillary expansion do not appreciably modify the profile, which can still be used for identification. In addition, comparison of the palatal profile does not require specific skills, since the results do not seem to vary between observers with and without odontological experience. The only condition for applying this method is the availability of an antemortem cast of the upper arch, which is usually taken before many odontological treatments.

Radiological Methods: Comparison of Bone Profiles

The morphology of bones can also be extremely useful, usually from antemortem radiological analyses; in addition, some radiological examinations are frequently performed on the general population, for example, chest X-rays, and the bones visible on these exams can be useful for identification. However, this osteological approach is based on the morphological assessment of bone structures; this means that the results will not be easily quantifiable, with clear limits in expressing the probability of positive identification. In fact, while most physiological, surgical, and pathological bone features seem to be quite common as proven by the first studies concerning the analysis of frequencies of specific markers within the general population, the morphology of every bone is unique although difficult to fit in a numerical perspective. At the moment, very few bone districts have reached an adequate standardization from a statistical point of view and precise algorithms by which to identify; the comparison of frontal sinuses is the most reliable method of identification, since they are different even in homozygous twins, and their applicability is limited only by the low frequency of this cranial radiograph in the general population (**Figure 4**). Other attempts at the standardization of the comparison of other districts such as the thoracic vertebral margin are still experimental and need further studies.

Some authors have attempted at determining a minimum criteria for identification, which are stated in one to four unique analogous features without discrepancies, but a general agreement concerning this topic actually does not exist. There is no univocal and valid definition for the term "unique"; therefore, the main difficulty consists of determining which feature may be considered unique and how many features are needed to reach an identification. In addition, since the comparison is based on a morphological evaluation, the matches and mismatches between the two profiles are often subjective and left to the personal opinion of the observer.

Superimposition Methods

When none of the previously cited methods can be used, a last possibility lies in the superimposition of photos from the identity suspect and images of the cranium of the unknown decedent. This procedure, called craniofacial superimposition, cannot be used alone to reach a positive identification because of its low reliability. The main reasons consist of the difference between the two compared profiles (soft tissues and hard tissues); in addition, the results and success of this method of identification are highly variable according to different authors. At the moment, the only reliable use consists of excluding identity if gross incompatibilities are observed (**Figure 5**).

A similar procedure can be applied to dental profiles: if antemortem photos of the missing individual when smiling and showing his or her front teeth are available, a comparison can be performed by a superimposition of the dental elements visible in the photograph and those visible in a photograph of the cadaver or of a dental cast of the remains. In this case, the identification potential is greater because the method compares the same structures (teeth): one should only pay extreme caution to obtaining the same orientation and verifying that gross alterations of the teeth did not occur after the picture was taken.

Conclusions

An unidentified body may come in different conditions, ranging from well preserved to skeletonized or burnt. For this reason, the expert should be familiar with most methods of identification in order to choose the most reliable, cheapest, and fastest one for that specific case.

This survey is concluded with an outline summarizing, at present, possible solutions for performing positive identification of human remains by comparing antemortem and postmortem data, with the relative advantages and disadvantages.

Well-Preserved Body

It should be stressed that it may be more difficult to compare a dead face with the picture of a living face in the attempt to declare that it is the same person. This is confirmed by the difficulties encountered by anthropologists dealing with the

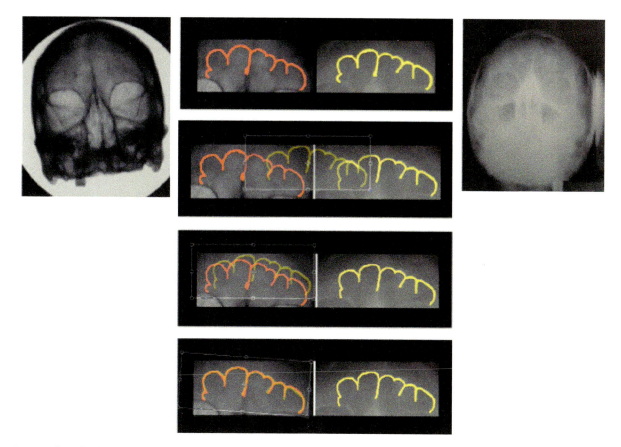

Figure 4 Example of superimposition of frontal sinuses between antemortem X-rays from the identity suspect (on the right) and the unknown decedent (on the left); frontal sinuses in the antemortem are in yellow and the postmortem in red; the results of the superimposition in orange.

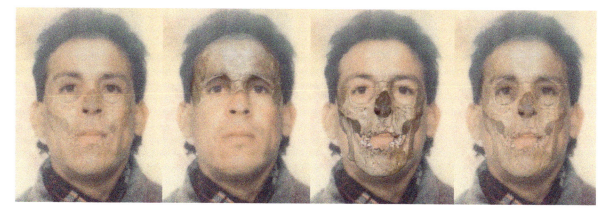

Figure 5 Example of craniofacial superimposition.

identification of living individuals on photographic material (e.g., on video surveillance recordings of bank robberies, etc.). In these cases, it is necessary to compare the physiognomic traits of the person represented on tape or on a photograph with the face of the suspected thief or assailant. While this appears to be a banale and intuitively simple activity, it is anything but simple. Comparing the morphological and metric traits of two images for the purpose of arriving at a definite identification of the subject is still complex: this is due to the differences in orientation of the two images and to the lack of standardization of such procedures. In the same manner, in the case of a well-preserved cadaver to be compared with a photograph of a living person, serious problems in determining the traits that may be crucial for identification can turn up. It is for this reason that it is important to support a mere resemblance with specific descriptors such as scars, tattoos, moles, and so on.

Identification can obviously be performed by the methods suggested below.

Putrefied, Burnt, Partly, or Completely Skeletonized Human Remains

For this type of material, depending on which districts are better preserved, the following methods should be applied.

Significant descriptors: This is the case of putrefied bodies presenting countermarks (or features) so singular as that they may be used for identification purposes. Examples of these identification instruments are residues of tattoos, scars, bone prostheses or anomalies, unusual mutilations, and surgical operations.

Fingerprinting (dactyloscopy): It is always worth while trying to restore the papillary crests in order to be able to obtain sufficient dactyloscopic data for the comparison of fingerprints. This, however, presumes that the subject's prints were taken during his lifetime and that antemortem fingerprints of the subject are available.

Odontology: If a detailed antemortem dental chart, dental radiographs, or other clinical dental data exist, they can be used for comparison with the dentition of the human remains. Such data, however, must be available and the dentition of the remains fairly well preserved. The advantages of this method are its rapidity and low costs. One disadvantage, compared to DNA analysis, could be the nonquantifiability of the result. For example, it is almost impossible to provide a judge with the numerical probability that two different individuals may share the same dentition. Many odontologists, however, feel that quantification of the result would be useless and that morphological methods are based on the operator's experience and common sense.

DNA: This is the most popular method and most expensive. It is necessary, nevertheless, to be able to extract the DNA from the remains, and in the case of dry bone, this can be difficult for the presence of polymerase chain reaction (PCR) inhibitors and degradation. Furthermore, there may exist no adequate relatives for DNA comparison or objects such as toothbrushes and combs from which to extract the individual's antemortem DNA may not be retrievable, as in the case of vagrants and illegal immigrants. The advantages of this method consist in being able to supply a quantitative result, owing to the studies on the distribution of the alleles of specific loci within a certain population, which makes it possible to provide the probability that another person shares the same genetic asset. Other possible setbacks may be that it is more expensive and requires more time.

Anthropology–osteology: image superimposition: These methods are used when the above described methods are not applicable. Superimposition can be dental or craniofacial. As already mentioned, dental superimposition requires the existence of a decent-quality photograph of the living subject, smiling, in order to be able to compare his or her dental profile with that of the human remains. Craniofacial superimposition, where craniometric points of the soft tissues are compared with craniometric points of the remains, is less reliable. These investigations require good quality photographs. In the case of dental superimposition, the methodology, although incapable of quantifying the error, at least compares the same structures.

Radiological comparison of frontal sinus shape or the morphological correspondence between the shape of any bone (e.g., vertebra) can be a valid method of identification, although one must be very cautious in matching the orientation of the antemortem and postmortem radiographs and in looking for sufficient corresponding traits.

In conclusion, results always need to be carefully examined by an experienced observer. Personal identification has to be carried out with a set of data, after having carefully evaluated the limits and the possible sources of error of each method.

See also: **Anthropology/Odontology:** Aging the Dead and the Living; Ancestry; Facial Approximation; Odontology; Personal Identification in Forensic Anthropology; Sexing; Stature and Build.

Further Reading

Besana, J.L., Rogers, T.L., 2010. Personal identification using the frontal sinus. Journal of Forensic Sciences 55 (3), 584–589.

Brooks, S.T., 1955. Skeletal age at death: the reliability of cranial and pubic age indicators. American Journal of Physical Anthropology 13, 567–597.

Brooks, S.T., Suchey, J.M., 1990. Skeletal age determination based on the os pubis: a comparison of the Acsadi-Nemeskèri and Suchey-Brooks methods. Human Evolution 5, 227–238.

Cattaneo, C., Ritz-Timme, S., Schutz, H.W., et al., 2000. Unidentified cadavers and human remains in the EU: an unknown issue. International Journal of Legal Medicine 113 (3), N1–N3.

Cattaneo, C., Porta, D., De Angelis, D., Gibelli, D., Poppa, P., Grandi, M., 2010. Unidentified bodies and human remains: an Italian glimpse through a European problem. Forensic Science International 195, 167 e1–e6.

Christensen, A.M., 2005. Testing the reliability of frontal sinuses in positive identification. Journal of Forensic Sciences 50, 18–22.

Ciaffi, R., Gibelli, D., Cattaneo, C., 2011. Forensic radiology and personal identification of unidentified bodies: a review. La Radiologia Medica 116, 960–968.

Daubert v. Merrell Dow Pharmaceuticals, 1993. 509 U.S. 579, 92–102.

De Angelis, D., Riboli, F., Gibelli, D., Cappella, A., Cattaneo, C., 2012. Palatal rugae as an individualising marker: reliability for forensic odontology and personal identification. Science and Justice 52 (3), 181–184.

Fenton, T.W., Heard, A.N., Sauer, N.J., 2008. Skull-photo superimposition and border deaths: identification through exclusion and the failure to exclude. Journal of Forensic Sciences 53 (1), 34–40.

Fischman, S.L., 1985. The use of medical and dental radiographs in identification. International Dental Journal 35, 301–306.

Ghosh, A.K., Sinha, P., 2001. An economised craniofacial identification system. Forensic Science International 117, 109–119.

Giles, E., Elliot, O., 1963. Sex determination by discriminant function analysis of crania. American Journal of Physical Anthropology 21, 53–68.

Grivas, C.R., Komar, D.A., 2008. Kumho, Daubert, and the nature of scientific inquiry: implications for forensic anthropology. Journal of Forensic Sciences 53 (4), 771–776.

Hanzlick, R., 2006. Identification of unidentified deceased and locating next of kin. The American Journal of Forensic Medicine and Pathology 27, 126–128.

Hanzlick, R., Clark, S., 2008. The unidentified decedent reporting system – a model national website registry for the unidentified deceased. The American Journal of Forensic Medicine and Pathology 29, 106–113.

Hanzlick, R., Smith, G.P., 2006. Identification of unidentified deceased – turnaround times, methods and demographics in Fulton County, Georgia. The American Journal of Forensic Medicine and Pathology 27, 79–84.

Iscan, M.Y., Loth, S.R., Wright, R.K., 1984. Age estimation from the rib by phase analysis: white males. Journal of Forensic Sciences 29, 1094–1104.

Iscan, M.Y., Loth, S.R., Wright, R.K., 1985. Age estimation from the rib by phase analysis: white females. Journal of Forensic Sciences 30, 853–863.

Ishii, M., Yayama, K., Motani, H., et al., 2011. Application of superimposition-based personal identification using skull computed tomography images. Journal of Forensic Sciences 56 (4), 960–966.

Italian Department of the Interior, June 2010. Extraordinary Commissioner for Missing People, V Semestral Report.

Kahana, Y., Grande, A., Tancredi, D.M., Penalver, J., Hiss, J., 2001. Fingerprinting the deceased: traditional and new techniques. Journal of Forensic Sciences 46, 908–912.

Kahana, T., Goldin, L., Hiss, J., 2002. Personal identification based on radiographic vertebral features. The American Journal of Forensic Medicine and Pathology 23 (1), 36–41.

Kumho Tire Co. v. Carmichael, 1999. 526 U.S. 137.

Kvaal, S.I., Kolltveit, K.M., Thomsen, I.O., Solheim, T., 1995. Age estimation of adults from dental radiographs. Forensic Science International 74 (3), 175–185.

Lamendin, H., Baccino, E., Humbert, J.F., Tavernier, J.C., Nossintchouk, R.M., Zerillia, A., 1992. A simple technique for age estimation in adult corpses: the two criteria dental method. Journal of Forensic Sciences 37, 1373–1379.

Lovejoy, C.O., Meindle, R.S., Mensforth, R.P., Barton, T.J., 1985. Multifactorial determination of skeletal age at death: a method and blind tests of its accuracy. American Journal of Physical Anthropology 68, 1–14.

Meindl, R.S., Lovejoy, C.O., Mensforth, R.P., Don Carlos, L., 1985. Accuracy and direction of error in the sexing of the skeleton implications for paleodemography. American Journal of Physical Anthropology 68, 79–85.

Muthusubramanian, M., Limson, K.S., Julian, R., 2005. Analysis of rugae in burn victims and cadavers to simulate rugae identification in cases of incineration and decomposition. The Journal of Forensic Odonto-Stomatology 23, 26–29.

Ohtani, M., Nishida, N., Chiba, T., Fukuda, M., Miyamoto, Y., Yoshioka, N., 2008. Indication and limitations of using palatal rugae for personal identification in edentuolous cases. Forensic Science International 176, 178–182.

Ousley, S.D., Jantz, R.L., 1996. Fordisc 2.0: Personal Computer Forensic Discriminant Function. The University of Tennessee, Knoxville.

Page, M., Taylor, J., Blenkin, M., 2011. Forensic identification science evidence since Daubert: part I – a quantitative analysis of the exclusion of forensic identification science evidence. Journal of Forensic Sciences 56 (5), 1180–1184.

Paulozzi, J., Cox, C.S., Williams, D.D., Nolte, K.B., 2008. John and Jane Doe: the epidemiology of unidentified decedents. Journal of Forensic Sciences 53 (4), 1–6.

Phenice, T.W., 1969. A newly developed visual method of sexing os pubis. American Journal of Physical Anthropology 30, 297–302.

Prince, D.A., Ubelaker, D., 2002. Application of Lamendin's adult dental aging technique to a diverse skeletal sample. Journal of Forensic Sciences 47, 107–116.

Quatrehomme, G., Fronty, P., Sapanet, M., Grevin, G., Bailet, P., Ollier, A., 1996. Identification by frontal sinus pattern in forensic anthropology. Forensic Science International 83, 147–153.

Ramenzoni, L.L., Line, S.R.P., 2006. Automated biometrics-based personal identification of the Hunter-Schreger bands of dental enamel. Proceedings of the Royal Society B 273, 1155–1158.

Saukko, P., Knight, B., 2005. Forensic Pathology, third ed. Arnold Ed, London.

Scheuer, L., Black, S., 2000. Developmental Juvenile Osteology. Academic Press, New York.

Schmitt, A., Cunha, E., Pinheiro, J., 2006. Forensic Anthropology and Medicine – Complementary Sciences from Recovery to Cause of Death. Humana Press, Totowa, NJ.

Shepherd, K.L., Wlash-Haney, H., Coburn, M.U., 2010. Surgical sutures as a means of identifying human remains. Journal of Forensic Sciences 55 (1), 237–240.

Smith, V.A., Christensen, A.M., Myers, S.W., 2010. The reliability of visually comparing small frontal sinuses. Journal of Forensic Sciences 55 (6), 1413–1415.

Stephan, C.N., Winburn, A.P., Christensen, A.F., Tyrrell, A.J., 2011. Skeletal identification by radiographic comparison: blind tests of a morphoscopic method using antemortem chest radiographs. Journal of Forensic Sciences 56 (2), 320–332.

Trotter, M., Gleser, G., 1952. Estimation of stature from long bones of American Whites and Negroes. American Journal of Physical Anthropology 10, 463–514.

Trotter, M., Gleser, G., 1958. A re-evaluation of estimation of stature based on measurements of stature taken during life and of long bones after death. American Journal of Physical Anthropology 8, 79–123.

Ubelaker, D.H., 1999. Human Skeletal Remains: Excavation, Analysis, Interpretation, third ed. Taraxacum, Washington, DC.

Watamaniuk, L., Rogers, T., 2010. Positive personal identification of human remains based on thoracic vertebral margin morphology. Journal of Forensic Sciences 55 (5), 1162–1170.

Williams, B.A., Rogers, T.L., 2006. Evaluating the accuracy and precision of cranial morphological traits for sex determination. Journal of Forensic Sciences 51 (4), 729–735.

Wilson, R.J., Bethard, J.D., DiGangi, E.A., 2011. The use of orthopaedic surgical devices for forensic identification. Journal of Forensic Sciences 56 (2), 460–469.

Yoshino, M., Miyasaka, S., Sato, H., Seta, S., 1998. Classification system of frontal sinus patterns. Journal of the Canadian Society of Forensic Science 22, 135–146.

Forensic Age Estimation

A Schmeling, Institute of Legal Medicine, Münster, Germany

Introduction

Despite the alleged use of the eruption of second molars by the ancient Romans to evaluate readiness for military service, age diagnostics in living individuals is a relatively young branch of applied research within the forensic sciences. However, in recent years, its value and importance as an assessment tool has risen exponentially as the requirements for an informed opinion on the age of an individual have assumed increasing importance for the assessment of both legal and social categorization.

There are many areas in which the evaluation of age in the living have gained significant importance in recent years but the most prevalent concern issues are pertaining to refugee and asylum seekers, suspects and delinquents, human trafficking, and child pornography. Age evaluation is also required for adoptive children from countries without birth registration. A further category which is on the rise is age evaluation in competitive sports to ensure that athletes are competing within an age-appropriate banding both for the sake of fairness and health protection. Parents have also been known to falsify the ages of their children, particularly of their sons, to obtain preferential educational opportunities. While it is undeniable that the majority of issues raised concerning age evaluation are predominantly within the juvenile aspect of the human age range, there are issues of legality in relation to the elderly, which tend to relate to matters of eligibility for state pension support or retirement law.

The first transregional scientific analysis of forensic age diagnostics in living individuals was conducted on the occasion of the 10th Lübeck Meeting of German Forensic Physicians in December 1999. At this meeting, it was suggested that a study group be set up, which would include forensic pathologists, dentists, radiologists, and anthropologists. They were tasked with producing recommendations for the issuing of expert opinions in order to standardize the hitherto common and partly varying procedure and to achieve quality assurance for expert opinions.

The international and interdisciplinary "Study Group on Forensic Age Diagnostics" was established in Berlin, Germany, on March 10, 2000. This study group has given recommendations for forensic age estimation in living individuals in criminal proceedings, in civil and asylum procedures, as well as in pension procedures. As an external quality control measure, the Study Group on Forensic Age Diagnostics annually organizes proficiency tests in which participants receive the X-rays and physical examination results for a set of subjects and asked to estimate their ages.

Because of the explosive growth in knowledge over recent years, only qualified specialists in the field of forensic age diagnostics are capable of supplying expert opinions based on the current state of the sciences. A member list of the Study Group on Forensic Age Diagnostics can be downloaded from the Study Group's home page. Successful participants in the Study Group's proficiency tests are also published on this home page.

Outlined below are the methodological principles of forensic age diagnostics as applied to adolescents and young adults, child victims in child pornographic picture documents as well as to older adults for the purposes of clarifying pension entitlements.

Age Estimation in Adolescents and Young Adults

General Remarks

The persons to whom forensic examination is to be applied are foreigners without valid identity documents who are suspected of making false statements about their age and whose genuine age needs to be ascertained in the course of criminal, civil, or asylum proceedings. In many countries, the legally relevant age thresholds lie between 14 and 22 years of age.

According to the recommendations of the Study Group on Forensic Age Diagnostics, for an age estimate, the following examinations should be performed in combination:

- Physical examination with determination of anthropometric measures (body height and weight, constitutional type), inspection of signs of sexual maturation, as well as identification of any age-relevant developmental disorders
- X-ray examination of the left hand
- Dental examination with determination of the dental status and X-ray examination of the dentition
- If the skeletal development of the hand is complete, an additional examination of the clavicles should be carried out, preferably by means of a conventional X-ray examination and/or a computed tomography (CT) scan.

Guidelines for the use of ionizing radiation vary from country to country. When utilizing X-rays, the local regulations, statutes, or professional guidelines should be observed. As X-ray examinations for forensic age diagnostics take place without medical indications, the question should first be pursued as to whether the effective radiation doses given during the procedures could be detrimental to the health of the persons examined.

Radiation Exposure in X-ray Examinations for the Purpose of Age Estimation

The effective dose from an X-ray examination of the hand is 0.1 microsievert (µSv), from an orthopantomogram (OPG) 26 µSv, from a conventional X-ray examination of the clavicles 220 µSv, and from a CT scan of the clavicles 600 µSv. According to the relatively high effective dose of the X-ray and CT examinations of the clavicles, their use should be restricted to individuals with completed hand ossification.

In order to assess the potential health risk of these X-ray examinations, the amounts of naturally occurring and civilizing radiation exposure are compared to amounts of radiation exposure from radiological procedures. The effective dose from naturally occurring radiation exposure in Germany is 2.1 millisievert (mSv) on average per year. Apart from the direct cosmic radiation of 0.3 mSv and the direct terrestrial radiation of 0.4 mSv, the ingestion of naturally occurring radioactive substances in the food contributes 0.3 mSv to the radiation exposure. For the inhalation of radon and its disintegration products, 1.1 mSv must be added. Compared to naturally occurring radiation exposure, one-hand X-ray equals the naturally occurring radiation exposure of 25 min, one OPG is equivalent to 4.5 days, one X-ray of the clavicles is equal to 38 days, and one CT of the clavicles equals 104 days.

The radiation exposure from an intercontinental flight at an altitude of 12 000 m is 0.008 mSv h^{-1}. It follows that the dose for a flight from Frankfurt to New York is 0.05 mSv. This means that the radiation exposure from two OPGs is equivalent to the radiation exposure from an intercontinental flight.

On the basis of this comparison, a relevant health risk as a result of X-ray examinations for forensic age estimations can be denied.

Concerning a possible health risk, the biological effect of X-rays needs to be discussed as well. In this case, a distinction between stochastic and nonstochastic radiation effects has to be made. Nonstochastic effects appear above 100 mSv and are therefore irrelevant to radiological diagnostics. DNA damage leading to mutations of the genotype and malign diseases is one of the stochastic effects. On the assumption that there is a linear dose–effect relation without a threshold between the risk of radiation exposure and the delivered radiation dose and thus that even X-rays in the low-dose region can cause a malign disease, cancer mortality risks can be calculated for adults and children. It has to be pointed out that the risk for children is twice the risk for adults. The German radiation biologist Jung compared the mortality risk of X-ray examinations for age estimations with the mortality risk resulting from the participation in traffic. He came to the conclusion that the mortality risk of an OPG is comparable to the participation in traffic for 2.5 h. Thus the radiation risk of the X-ray examinations is as high as the risk the examined individual is exposed to on the way to the examination or the trial date. If the risk of an appointment for age estimation seemed acceptable, this should also apply to the radiation risk of the X-ray examination.

It can be concluded that compared to other life risks, a relevant health risk of X-rays for the purpose of age estimation can be denied as well.

However, as long as the discussion about the biological radiation effect in the low-dose region is undecided, the so-called minimizing order remains valid without restrictions. It demands that any necessary examination is carried out with the minimum amount of radiation and without unnecessary exposure. Thus, no X-rays should be made beyond the examination range specified in scientific recommendations.

Physical Examination

The physical examination includes anthropometric measures such as body height, weight, and constitutional type, as well as visible signs of sexual maturity. In boys, these are penile and testicular development, pubic hair, axillary hair, beard growth, and laryngeal prominence; in girls, these are breast development, pubic hair, axillary hair, and shape of the hip.

Tanner's staging for sexual maturation is commonly used to determine the status of genital development, breast development, and pubic hair growth. Axillary hair growth, beard growth, and laryngeal development may be assessed using the four-stage classification of Neyzi et al.

Of the forensic methods recommended for age estimation, evaluating sexual maturity shows the largest range of variation and therefore should be used for age diagnostics only in conjunction with an evaluation of skeletal maturity and tooth development. However, the physical examination is indispensable to rule out any visible signs of age-related illness and to cross-check whether skeletal age and tooth age correspond to overall physical development.

Most diseases delay development and are thus conducive to underestimation of age. Such underestimation of age would not disadvantage the person concerned in terms of criminal prosecution. By contrast, overestimating age due to a disease that accelerates development should be avoided at all costs. Such diseases occur very rarely and include, above all, endocrinal disorders, which may affect not only the attainment of height and sexual development, but also skeletal development. Endocrinal diseases that may accelerate skeletal development include precocious puberty, adrenogenital syndrome, and hyperthyroidism.

The physical examination should look for symptoms of hormonal acceleration of development, such as gigantism, acromegaly, microplasia, virilization of girls, dissociated virilism of boys, goiter, or exophthalmos. If no abnormality is detected, it may be assumed that the probability of such a disease occurring is well below one per thousand. Another indication for a possible hormonal disease is a discrepancy between skeletal age and dental age, as dental development normally remains unaffected by endocrinal disorders.

X-ray Examination of the Hand

Within the area of forensic age estimations in adolescents, skeletal maturation is a vital diagnostic pillar. In this connection, the hand skeleton is particularly suitable until the developmental processes are completed at the age of about 17–18 years. The maturity status of the hand may be considered to be representative for the entire skeletal system.

As agreed, an X-ray of the left hand is taken as, in all populations, the number of right-handers is higher, and, as a result, the right hand is more often exposed to traumata which can impair the skeletal development. However, there are no reported significant differences in the ossification rate of right and left hands.

Criteria for evaluating hand radiographs include the form and size of bone elements and the degree of epiphyseal ossification. To this effect, either a given X-ray image is compared with standard images of the relevant age and sex (radiographic atlas), or the degree of maturity or bone age is determined for selected bones (single bone method).

Various studies have demonstrated that although the single bone method requires more time, it does not necessarily yield more accurate results. Therefore, the two atlas methods developed by Greulich and Pyle as well as by Thiemann et al. seem to be appropriate for forensic age diagnostics.

Dental Examination

The main criteria for dental age estimation in adolescents and young adults are eruption and mineralization of the third molars.

Tooth eruption is a parameter of developmental morphology which, unlike tooth mineralization, can be determined in two ways: by clinical examination and by evaluation of dental X-rays. While "eruption" incorporates the entire journey of the tooth from its formation in the alveolar crypts to full occlusion, "emergence" is restricted to the time when any part of the tooth finally clears the gingival margin and becomes visible in the mouth until the stage when the tooth finally comes into occlusion with its partner tooth from the opposing jaw. Olze et al. defined a stage classification of third molar eruption based on evidence from conventional OPGs (**Figure 1**):

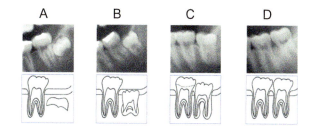

Figure 1 Stages of third molar eruption.

Stage (A) Occlusal plane covered with alveolar bone.
Stage (B) Alveolar emergence; complete resorption of alveolar bone over occlusal plane.
Stage (C) Gingival emergence; penetration of gingiva by at least one dental cusp.
Stage (D) Complete emergence in occlusal plane.

Various classifications have been devised for evaluating tooth mineralization. They differ with regard to the number of stages, the definition of each stage, and the presentation. To assess tooth mineralization, the classification of stages made by Demirjian et al (**Figure 2**) is the most suitable as the stages are defined by changes in form, independent of speculative estimates of length:

Stage (A) Cusp tips are mineralized but have not yet coalesced.
Stage (B) Mineralized cusps are united so the mature coronal morphology is well defined.
Stage (C) The crown is about half formed; the pulp chamber is evident and dentinal deposition is occurring.
Stage (D) Crown formation is complete to the dentinoenamel junction. The pulp chamber has a trapezoidal form.

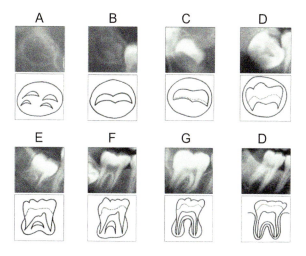

Figure 2 Demirjian's stages of third molar mineralization.

Stage (E) Formation of the interradicular bifurcation has begun. Root length is less than the crown length.
Stage (F) Root length is at least as great as crown length. Roots have funnel-shaped endings.
Stage (G) Root walls are parallel, but apices remain open.
Stage (H) Apical ends of the roots are completely closed, and the periodontal membrane has a uniform width around the root.

Both the eruption and the mineralization of third molars can be complete before the conclusion of the 18th year of life. Proof of completion of the 18th year of life may be provided by complete mineralization of the roots of impacted third molars as well as the lack of radiographic visibility of the root pulp or the periodontal ligament of the third molars.

Radiological Examination of the Clavicles

If the skeletal development of the hand is completed, an additional evaluation of the ossification status of the medial epiphysis of the clavicle should be performed because all other examined developmental systems may already have completed their growth by that age.

Radiological methods to examine the medial clavicular epiphysis in living individuals are conventional radiography (CR), CT, as well as new approaches using magnet resonance imaging and ultrasound sonography.

While traditional classification systems differentiate between four stages of clavicle ossification (stage 1: ossification center not ossified; stage 2: ossification center ossified, epiphyseal plate not ossified; stage 3: epiphyseal plate partly ossified; stage 4: epiphyseal plate fully ossified), Schmeling et al. divided the stage of total epiphyseal fusion into two additional stages (stage 4: epiphyseal plate fully ossified, epiphyseal scar visible; stage 5: epiphyseal plate fully ossified, epiphyseal scar no longer visible). **Figure 3** shows the stages of clavicular ossification for CR and CT.

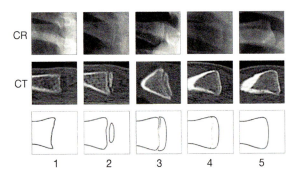

Figure 3 Stages of clavicular ossification (CR, conventional radiography; CT, computed tomography).

There is only one study referring to CR that meets the requirements of a reference study as stated by the Study Group on Forensic Age Diagnostics. In this study, the earliest age at which stage 3 was detected in either sex was 16 years. Stage 4 was first observed in women at 20 years and in men at 21 years. Stage 5 was first achieved by both sexes at age 26. It was concluded that plain chest radiographs can essentially provide a basis for assessing clavicular ossification. If overlap in posterior–anterior views impedes evaluation, additional oblique images should be taken to facilitate age estimation.

As the potential to assess CT images is dependent on slice thickness, a maximum of 1 mm slice thicknesses should be in the practice of age estimation.

Recently, Kellinghaus et al. published data from a thin-slice CT study. In this study, stage 3 was first achieved by male individuals at age of 17 years and in females at age of 16 years. The occurrence of stage 4 was first found in both sexes at the age of 21 years. In either sex, the earliest observation of stage 5 was at age of 26 years.

A further improvement of age diagnostics based on clavicular ossification was the subdivision of stages 2 and 3 by Kellinghaus et al. Stage 3c first appeared at the age of 19 years in both sexes. If stage 3c is found, it is therefore possible to substantiate that an individual has already reached the legally important age threshold of 18 years.

Comparative examinations showed that conventional X-rays and CT scans of the same clavicle can result in different ossification stages contingent on the method used. For the purposes of age estimation, this leads to the requirement to employ modality-specific reference studies.

Summarizing Age Diagnosis

The results of the physical examination, the radiographic examination of the hand, the dental examination, and the radiographic examination of the clavicles, as the case may be, should be compiled by the expert in charge of coordinating all contributions in a summarizing age diagnosis. The summarizing age estimate should include a discussion of the age-relevant variations resulting from application of the reference studies in an individual case, such as different ethnicity, different socioeconomic status, and their potential effect on the developmental status, or diseases that may affect the development of the individual examined, including their effect on the estimated age. If possible, a quantitative assessment of any such effect should be given.

The individual's most likely age is estimated on the basis of all partial diagnoses and a critical discussion of the individual case. If independent features are examined as part of an age diagnosis that combines several methods, it may be assumed that the margin of error for the combined age diagnosis is smaller than that for each individual feature. Combining methods makes it possible to identify statistical outliers, which should also reduce the scale of variation of the overall diagnosis to a certain nonquantifiable extent.

On the basis of the verification of age estimations carried out at the Berlin Institute of Legal Medicine (Charité), it may be assumed that the range of scatter of the summarizing age diagnosis lies at around ±12 months. Once development of the systems of characteristics examined is complete, only minimum age can be specified.

Influence of Ethnicity on the Development Systems Examined

As no forensically applicable reference studies are, as a rule, available for the regions of origin of the persons under examination, the question arises whether there are serious differences in development in diverse ethnic groups, which would prohibit the application of relevant age standards to members of ethnic groups other than the reference population.

Extensive studies of the relevant literature has demonstrated that defined stages of ossification, tooth development, and sexual maturation in the main ethnic groups relevant to forensic age estimation will proceed in the same fixed sequence so that the relevant reference studies can, in principle, be applied to other ethnic groups.

In the relevant age group, ethnicity evidently has no appreciable influence on skeletal maturation. The rate of ossification is primarily dependent on the socioeconomic status of a population. Comparatively, low socioeconomic status leads to a delay in development and thus to an underestimation of age. The application of the relevant reference studies to members of socioeconomically less-developed populations has no detrimental consequences for those affected as far as criminal proceedings are concerned, on the contrary.

With regard to the eruption and mineralization of the third molars, it has been ascertained that black Africans display an accelerated development in comparison with Europeans; by contrast, a relative retardation can be recorded in the case of Asians. For this reason, population-specific reference studies should be used to assess development of third molars in the practice of age estimation.

Methodology in Cases Where Legitimization of X-ray Examinations Is Lacking

For age estimations without legitimization of X-ray examinations, the Study Group on Forensic Age Diagnostics recommends a physical examination covering anthropometric measurements, signs of sexual maturation, and potential age-related developmental disorders, as well as a dental examination with dental charting.

For legal reasons, findings from a radiological examination of the teeth or the hand skeleton, or other radiological characteristics of individual maturation may only be called upon if images with verified identity and known time of origin already exist.

It is to be expected that a considerable improvement in the reliability of such age estimations will be achieved in the near future by using radiation-free imaging techniques (ultrasound and magnetic resonance imaging).

Age Diagnostics in Child Victims in Child Pornographic Image Documents

In principle, age estimations in children in image documents too are made by evaluating outwardly visible growth and development processes. An evaluation of signs of sexual maturity, odontogenesis, and general proportions of the body and the face come into question.

In the evaluation of sexual maturation, the stagings commonly used in age estimations in living persons are applied. However, because of the wide variability of sexual maturation, it is only possible in exceptional cases to determine with the necessary probability that the individual portrayed is a child in the legal sense.

An assessment of dental development is a classic method of age diagnostics in children. When evaluating pictorial material, however, the examiner is reliant on sufficiently good visibility of the front teeth and on high picture quality. However, in exceptional cases where the milk teeth are well recognizable, important information on age can be gained.

Body proportions change in a characteristic way in the course of the individual development of infants into adults. Typical shifts in proportions are the result of different speeds of growth of the different regions of the body during certain phases of development. In particular, the proportional ratios between the trunk and the extremities and/or the trunk and the head, as well as the breadth and length ratios of each of the body segments can be used in age estimation. Although the assessment of body proportions alone only yields a rough age classification, it should always be included in the overall assessment.

The development of a child's face too is characterized by certain growth principles resulting in age-related facial proportions. In general, in the course of development from an infant to an adolescent and an adult, the neurocranium, which is very prominent in childhood, recedes with increasing age compared to the viscerocranium. The face itself undergoes ongoing extension, the mandible is emphasized, and as a whole, growth in height and depth as opposed to growth in breadth predominates in development. In a current pilot study, various measurements were surveyed on standardized facial photos of 373 persons in the age groups of 6, 10, 14, and 18 years. Using discriminant analysis, it was ascertained that it was possible to classify 60.3% of cases in the correct age group. Moreover, software is at present being developed within the scope of an EU project for automated age estimation on the basis of facial morphology.

Age Diagnostics in Older Adults for Clarification of Pension Entitlements

Age diagnostics in living persons for clarification of old-age pension entitlements must be carried out almost without exception on older adults (mostly from the fourth decade of life and upward). In this age range, age estimations using morphological procedures do not, as a rule, provide adequate exactitude. However, if radiological examinations of the teeth or appropriate sections of the skeleton were carried out in childhood, adolescence, or early adulthood for medical reasons and the relevant records are still available, these can be checked for suitability for morphological age estimation. In this process, it must be ensured that the records submitted really do come from the person in question. If the issue cannot be adequately resolved by means of this approach, biochemical age estimation on the basis of the degree of racemization of aspartic acid in the dentine can be discussed. In adulthood, determining the degree of racemization of aspartic acid in the dentine leads to significantly more accurate results than morphological methods.

To determine the degree of racemization of aspartic acid in the dentine, a tooth is necessary. The extraction of a tooth is, in principle, a bodily injury which is only justified in the event of appropriate medical indications and with the informed consent of the patient. In an identity assurance protocol to be signed by the dentist and the applicant, the identity of the applicant has to be determined as well as the fact that the tooth originated from the applicant. The examinations must be carried out in a competent laboratory with an adequate quality assurance system.

Conclusions

Forensic age diagnostics in living individuals has gained considerably in significance over recent years.

For the purposes of age estimation in adolescents and young adults, the Study Group on Forensic Age Diagnostics recommends a combination of a physical examination, an X-ray examination of the hand, a dental examination providing an OPG, as well as an additional radiological examination of the clavicles in cases where the hand skeleton is fully developed.

Where there is no legitimation for X-ray examinations, the range of methods is limited to a physical examination and dental charting. By using radiation-free imaging techniques, a significant improvement of the reliability of age estimations without legitimation of X-ray examinations may be expected.

The influence of ethnicity and socioeconomic status on the age characteristics examined must be taken into account in compiling a report.

Age estimation in child victims shown in child pornographic image documents is possible by means of assessment of signs of sexual maturity, dental development, general body proportions, and facial proportions. However, owing to wide variations in the characteristics available until now, it is only possible in individual cases to ascertain with the necessary probability that the legally relevant age limits have not been reached.

Age estimations in pension proceedings can be made on the basis of radiological records dating from childhood and adolescence insofar as identity is proven. If such records are not available, an ascertainment of the degree of racemization of aspartic acid in the dentine may be considered. The extraction of the tooth required for this method is only legitimized in the presence of a medical indication and with the informed consent of the person affected.

> *See also:* **Digital Evidence:** Child Pornography; **Forensic Medicine/Clinical:** Identification.

Further Reading

Black, S., Aggrawal, A., Payne-James, J. (Eds.), 2010. Age Estimation in the Living: The Practitioner's Guide. Wiley-Blackwell, Hoboken.

Cattaneo, C., Obertová, Z., Ratnayake, M., et al., 2012. Can facial proportions taken from images be of use for ageing in cases of suspected child pornography? A pilot study. International Journal of Legal Medicine 126, 139–144.

Gabriel, P., Obertová, Z., Ratnayake, M., et al., 2011. Schätzung des Lebensalters kindlicher Opfer auf Bilddokumenten. Rechtliche Implikationen und Bedeutung im Ermittlungsverfahren. Rechtsmedizin 21, 7–11.

Greulich, W.W., Pyle, S.I., 1959. Radiographic Atlas of Skeletal Development of the Hand and Wrist. Stanford University Press, Stanford.

Kellinghaus, M., Schulz, R., Vieth, V., Schmidt, S., Pfeiffer, H., Schmeling, A., 2010a. Enhanced possibilities to make statements on the ossification status of the medial clavicular epiphysis using an amplified staging scheme in evaluating thin-slice CT scans. International Journal of Legal Medicine 124, 321–325.

Kellinghaus, M., Schulz, R., Vieth, V., Schmidt, S., Schmeling, A., 2010b. Forensic age estimation in living subjects based on the ossification status of the medial clavicular epiphysis as revealed by thin-slice multidetector computed tomography. International Journal of Legal Medicine 124, 149–154.

Lockemann, U., Fuhrmann, A., Püschel, K., Schmeling, A., Geserick, G., 2004. Empfehlungen für die Altersdiagnostik bei Jugendlichen und jungen Erwachsenen außerhalb des Strafverfahrens. Rechtsmedizin 14, 123–125.

Olze, A., Schmeling, A., Taniguchi, M., et al., 2004. Forensic age estimation in living subjects: the ethnic factor in wisdom tooth mineralization. International Journal of Legal Medicine 118, 170–173.

Olze, A., van Niekerk, P., Ishikawa, T., et al., 2007. Comparative study on the effect of ethnicity on wisdom tooth eruption. International Journal of Legal Medicine 121, 445–448.

Ritz-Timme, S., Kaatsch, H.-J., Marré, B., et al., 2002. Empfehlungen für die Altersdiagnostik bei Lebenden im Rentenverfahren. Rechtsmedizin 12, 193–194.

Schmeling, A., Schulz, R., Reisinger, W., Mühler, M., Wernecke, K.-D., Geserick, G., 2004. Studies on the time frame for ossification of medial clavicular epiphyseal cartilage in conventional radiography. International Journal of Legal Medicine 118, 5–8.

Schmeling, A., Schulz, R., Danner, B., Rösing, F.W., 2006. The impact of economic progress and modernization in medicine on the ossification of hand and wrist. International Journal of Legal Medicine 120, 121–126.

Schmeling, A., Grundmann, C., Fuhrmann, A., et al., 2008. Criteria for age estimation in living individuals. International Journal of Legal Medicine 122, 457–460.

Tanner, J.M., 1962. Growth at Adolescence. Blackwell, Oxford.

Thiemann, H.-H., Nitz, I., Schmeling, A. (Eds.), 2006. Röntgenatlas der normalen Hand im Kindesalter. Thieme, Stuttgart.

Personal Identification in Forensic Anthropology

CV Hurst, Michigan State University, East Lansing, MI, USA
A Soler, Pima County Office of the Medical Examiner, Tucson, AZ, USA
TW Fenton, Michigan State University, East Lansing, MI, USA

Glossary

Antemortem Events, materials, or records occurring or collected before death.

Comparative radiography The direct, point-by-point comparison of antemortem radiographs (X-rays) of a missing person with those obtained from the remains.

Decedent The deceased person.

Exclusion A conclusion based on sufficient evidence to determine that the known identity and the decedent are not the same individual.

Failure to exclude A conclusion based on sufficient evidence to determine that the known identity and the decedent may be the same individual but lacking information to make a personal identification.

Insufficient evidence A conclusion that the available evidence is lacking to the degree that no determination of inclusion or exclusion can be made.

Lot number A number assigned to identify a particular group, shipment, or lot of material from a manufacturer.

Morphology The overall shape or structure of the bone.

Multiple corresponding factors The matching of a number of nonscientific physical characteristics and contextual evidence between a known individual and a set of remains.

Personal identification The matching of a set of remains to a known individual.

Positive identification See scientific identification.

Postmortem Events, materials, or records occurring or collected after death.

Scientific identification The matching of antemortem and postmortem records to sufficient detail in a scientific systematic point-by-point comparison to conclude that they are from one individual to the exclusion of all other reasonable matches.

Serial number A unique set of numbers assigned for the identification of a specific item.

Tentative identification A potential match of a known person to the decedent.

Trabecular bone Also known as cancellous bone or spongy bone, the light and porous bony structure that is found at the end of long bones and within vertebrae.

Visual recognition The identification of a known person by a family member or friend who views the remains of the decedent.

Introduction

Identification of human remains is one of the foremost goals in a medicolegal death investigation. An expedient and accurate identification is imperative to serve both the family of the decedent and the medicolegal system. A personal identification can provide a sense of closure to the bereaved, allows for the release of the body, and is necessary to file an accurate death certificate for the distribution of benefits and to initiate an investigation in cases of homicide or suspicious deaths. Medicolegal death investigation is the responsibility of the medical examiner or coroner, and it is ultimately these medicolegal authorities that must decide whether there is sufficient evidence to establish a personal identification and authorize a death certificate. Therefore, the degree to which a forensic anthropologist is involved in a case is at the discretion of the medical examiner or coroner. As such, it is the duty of the forensic anthropologist to utilize his or her expertise to fulfill these requests.

Personal Identification

Personal identification is the matching of a set of remains to a known individual and it is the ultimate goal in a forensic investigation. Positive identification is a term that has long been used in medicolegal investigations to indicate an identification based on the scientific methods of fingerprint analysis, comparative dental or medical radiography, and nuclear DNA assessments. However, this terminology is problematic because it implies that a legal personal identification based on methods not considered "positive" is a weaker form of identification. Thus, in this work, the term "scientific identification" is utilized to describe an identification that is accomplished through the matching of antemortem and postmortem records to sufficient detail in a scientific point-by-point comparison to conclude that one individual is represented to the exclusion of all other reasonable matches. However, a personal identification can be established via a variety of different processes, including scientific identification, visual recognition of a cadaver, and multiple corresponding factors where there is a preponderance of evidence that matches between the decedent and the missing person. Each of these techniques represents a different level of identification; however, all are considered personal identification and ultimately lead to the release of the remains from the medical examiner's office.

In a majority of cases, someone who knew the decedent can identify the person through visual recognition of the face. This type of identification is a common process in many medical examiners' offices, especially in cases of recent deaths. Either people who knew the decedent are asked to view the physical remains or driver's license photographs are consulted to visually confirm the identification. This form of personal identification is outside the purview of forensic osteology, however, and is not discussed in detail in this chapter. In cases where visual recognition is not possible, including those with severe trauma, burning, decomposition, or skeletonization, medical examiners or coroners may consult with a forensic anthropologist to aid in the identification process. Forensic anthropologists can assist in either establishing a scientific identification or contributing to an identification with information from skeletal analyses to limit potential matches to the decedent. Before the discussion of forensic anthropological methods, levels of personal identification must first be defined and addressed.

Types of Personal Identification

Scientific Identification

Scientific identification is a classification that systematically compares known antemortem information of a missing person with postmortem information of the deceased to ensure that they represent one and the same individual. A scientific identification is accomplished when biological antemortem and postmortem information match, with no unexplainable differences, and in sufficient detail to conclude that they represent the same individual to the exclusion of all other individuals. Examples of scientific identification methods include comparisons of nuclear DNA, fingerprints, and dental and medical radiography. Each of these techniques has demonstrated utility in scientifically identifying individuals by focusing on unique aspects of the human body.

A common question from medicolegal investigators, judges, and juries is, "How many points of similarity are necessary to reach a scientific identification?" Currently, no minimum number of consistent morphologies required for a scientific identification has been established. What this means is that a single point of consistency can represent a scientific identification if considered individualizing. However, practitioners of comparative radiographic methods strive to use multiple morphologies in their analyses.

Although a scientific identification can be considered an optimal method for identifying human remains, it is not always possible or practical. A major impediment to scientific identifications is access to the appropriate resources—the absence of either finances or properly trained forensic experts. A medical examiner or coroner may not have access to forensic professionals trained in methods suitable for scientific identifications. In other cases, financial constraints may prevent medical examiners/coroners from utilizing such consultants or laboratory analyses. Lack of time to process such cases may also preclude a scientific identification. Both families and funeral homes can apply significant pressure to medicolegal investigators for the release of the decedent, and many scientific identification techniques can take time to complete.

A final limitation that may prohibit a scientific identification is lack of appropriate or adequate antemortem records. Although dental and medical radiographs seem commonplace, there remains a large segment of the population that has never had a radiograph taken. In other cases, the antemortem radiographs may be difficult or impossible to locate or the quality of radiographs may be too poor to be useful. As a result of these potential barriers, many medical examiner's or coroner's offices rely on more expedient and cost-effective methods to personally identify human remains.

Multiple Corresponding Factors

In cases where there is no scientific antemortem information available for comparison between the missing person and decedent, medical examiners or coroners may rely on multiple corresponding factors to support a potential identification. This approach utilizes contextual evidence in conjunction with a number of physical features to arrive at an identification. Contextual evidence may refer to the location where the decedent was found and personal effects associated with the remains, whereas physical features may include the biological profile, tattoos, piercings, dental characteristics, surgical alterations, and mitochondrial DNA. These identifications are made by a preponderance of matching nonscientific or nonunique characteristics and vary in strength depending on the number and the quality of factors contributing to the identification. Furthermore, it is the combination of distinctive physical features and contextual evidence that makes an identification via multiple corresponding factors a personal identification. For instance, if the remains of an edentulous female in her mid-

80s with a hysterectomy and evidence of a healing hip fracture were found in the secured home of an elderly woman of that same description, there would be multiple physical and contextual characteristics to indicate that the decedent and the woman who lived in the home were the same person. This identification by multiple corresponding factors is much stronger than an identification of a young woman found in a public location and identified through visual comparison to a driver's license or passport found with the remains.

Methods of Scientific Identification

Personal identifications, as outlined above, can be made at several levels of confidence, with a scientific identification being the gold standard. Although there are a number of methods that forensic anthropologists can utilize to contribute to the identification process, comparative medical and dental radiography are the only scientific techniques that can establish a scientific identification.

Comparative Radiography

Comparative radiography is the point-by-point comparison of antemortem radiographs of a missing person with the corresponding postmortem films of the decedent. To control for differences caused by radiographic imaging, it is essential that

the postmortem radiographs simulate the antemortem films as closely as possible in both scope and angulation, making sure to highlight the same skeletal features. This can be particularly challenging in cases where remains are in a state of decomposition or skeletonization that make them more difficult to appropriately position. This may require the anthropologist to take many sets of postmortem films, but without such efforts a radiographic comparison is not possible.

Dental radiographic comparisons

Radiographic comparisons fall into two broad categories—dental and medical. With annual dental examinations becoming the standard of care, the likelihood of an individual having antemortem dental radiographs is quite high. Additionally, the mineral composition of teeth makes them extremely resilient to postmortem damage, decomposition, temperature extremes, and fire destruction. Thus, both antemortem and postmortem dental information are likely to be available for comparison. Furthermore, the variety of dental structures and dental treatments provides numerous features that, when taken in combination, can offer an individualizing suite of characteristics. Features of dental radiographs that can be used in forensic identifications include crown and root morphology, tooth angulation, bone trabecular patterns, maxillary sinus morphology, the location and morphology of dental restorations, cavities or other dental pathologies, and missing teeth (**Figure 1**). Beyond the tooth structures visible in

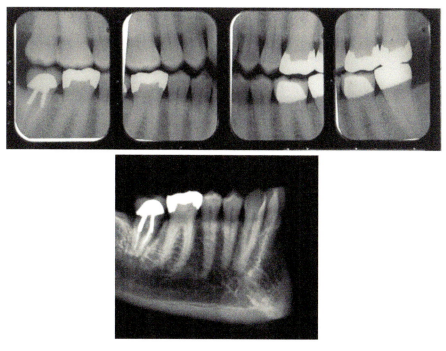

Figure 1 The postmortem (bottom) dental radiographs highlight the same dental restorations and simulate the antemortem (top) radiographs for a scientific identification.

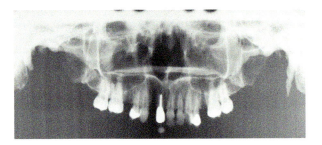

Figure 2 A panoramic radiograph showing maxillary dentition, nasal aperture, septum, conchae, and eye orbits.

dental radiographs, other anatomical landmarks are also used to corroborate an identification. The increasing use of panoramic radiographs provides even more features for comparison, including the nasal aperture, the nasal septum, nasal conchae, inferior and lateral borders of the eye orbits, and mandibular morphology (**Figure 2**).

Medical radiographic comparisons

Although dentition is the most common feature used for positive identification, any area of the body documented in antemortem radiographs could potentially be employed for such purposes. In medical radiographic images, overall morphology of the bone, anatomical landmarks, trabecular patterns, orientation, placement of foreign materials including bullets or shrapnel and surgical implements, skeletal anomalies, pathological conditions, and evidence of traumatic injury can be used. Relatively common areas for radiographs to be taken during life include the head, chest, and limbs.

An antemortem radiograph of the head can be extremely helpful for a forensic anthropologist attempting to make an identification. Beyond the potential of using the dental information contained within such a radiograph, it has been demonstrated that the frontal sinus is a structure that has a unique morphology in all individuals (**Figure 3**). Located above the eye orbits in a person's forehead, the bilateral frontal sinus is a hollow air cavity that is commonly asymmetrical and highly variable between individuals. Thus, it is an ideal structure to be used in a scientific identification. In the case of young individuals, however, the frontal sinus may not be fully developed and may not be available for comparison.

The chest is another common anatomical region for comparative radiography. While antemortem radiographs are often taken to visualize the lungs or other organs, skeletal features may be visible and useful for comparative purposes. Studies have shown that features of the vertebral column are individualizing and can be used for scientific identifications. Similar to dental comparisons, it is the suite of features of the vertebral column that makes it personalizing (**Figure 4**). Areas that are visible on radiographs and can be used in a point-by-point comparison include the shape of the vertebral bodies, the

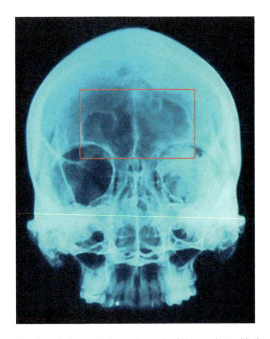

Figure 3 An anterior–posterior radiograph of the cranium with the unique morphology of the frontal sinus highlighted in the red box.

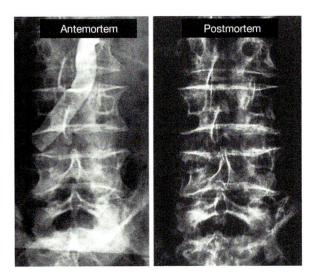

Figure 4 Antemortem and postmortem radiographs demonstrating consistency in shape and location of spinous processes, pedicles, and centra.

spinous processes, the transverse processes, the pedicles, intervertebral disc space, and any arthritic lipping or other degenerative changes. Studies have shown that features of the vertebral column outlined above are consistent in radiographs that have been taken decades apart and prove the utility of such radiographs for use in scientific identifications.

An interesting application for the use of anterior–posterior chest radiographs is the identification of missing American soldiers from past military operations at the Joint POW/MIA Accounting Command Central Identification Laboratory (JPAC-CIL). Owing to tuberculosis concerns, chest radiographs became a routine procedure across the United States Armed Forces in 1942, unknowingly creating an archive of antemortem radiographs for American soldiers. Thus, forensic anthropologists are utilizing these archives to help identify the remains of soldiers that went missing during the Korean War.

In many skeletal radiographs, the details of the trabecular bone can be seen and used in the comparison. As bone is a living tissue that is constantly remodeling, the consistency of such structures through the passage of time may be considered a concern. If the trabecular bone structure changes over time, an individual could be wrongfully excluded. However, studies of trabecular patterns have shown that the morphology is maintained over time and through subsequent remodeling events. It has now been demonstrated that even with age-related bone loss, trabecular bone patterns can provide individualizing information to aid in identification.

The role of experience

While forensic anthropologists can provide important contributions to personal identifications using comparative radiography, it is of utmost importance that the individual has been trained in comparative radiographic comparisons and is aware of the limitations of the method and their experience in making identifications. A number of studies have demonstrated that the interpreter's experience level directly affects his or her ability to make a correct identification. To the untrained eye, standard anatomical landmarks may be identified as consistencies between antemortem and postmortem radiographs. In reality, however, these features are relatively consistent between most individuals and are not always individualizing. Forensic anthropologists with training and experience are able to differentiate the distinctive skeletal features that will be useful for a personal identification from those that are commonplace. This underscores the importance of appropriate forensic training and experience for practitioners to accurately make scientific identifications.

Validation studies

Historically, scientific identifications have been admissible in the court of law; however, new standards for expert testimony have encouraged the publication of validation studies for various types of dental and medical radiographs for scientific identification purposes. Therefore, many validation studies have either been published or are forthcoming. To test the utility of various skeletal structures, researchers investigate its uniqueness within a sample population or practitioners' ability to utilize the structure to match simulated antemortem and postmortem radiographs. By establishing known error rates and statistical probabilities of the antemortem and postmortem radiographs originating from a single person, forensic anthropologists can confidently report on the accuracy of their methods in the court of law.

Possible Conclusions in a Scientific Identification

In every scientific identification consultation, the forensic anthropologist may reach one of three possible conclusions—a personal identification, an exclusion, or an insufficiency of evidence for determination.

Identification

To establish a scientific identification, a forensic anthropologist must perform a systematic detailed comparison with the goal of finding consistency in the overall skeletal morphology and in unique or identifying features. If a significant amount of time has passed since the antemortem radiograph was taken, there may be noticeable differences between the two sets of radiographs. Such time discrepancies must be taken into account. Alternatively, any noticeable differences between radiographs must be explainable by the passage of time or slight differences in angulation of the image. If one of these explanations cannot be used to describe a discrepancy between sets of radiographs, the antemortem and postmortem records are likely not from the same individual, and the potential match may be excluded.

Exclusion

In the case of an exclusion, sufficient evidence is available from the antemortem records to conclude that the presumptive individual and the decedent could not possibly represent the same individual. This results when disparities between antemortem and postmortem records cannot be explained by the passage of time, by differences in radiographic angulation, or for any other reasonable cause. The exclusion of a missing person means they are eliminated from the list of potential matches and it is necessary for new potential matches to be located and tested. Although the exclusion of a potential identification may send medicolegal investigators back to the field to gather more information, it is an important contribution toward the proper identification of the deceased, as it narrows down the list of possible matches.

Insufficient Evidence

At times, antemortem records are unavailable, too generalized, of poor quality, or too far removed in time to be useful. In such cases, a forensic anthropologist is unable to determine whether the antemortem and postmortem records originated from the same individual. This includes situations where the available antemortem information is consistent with the postmortem evidence from the decedent; however, the consistent features are not individualizing to the extent required to make a personal identification. Essentially, the forensic anthropologist is unable to exclude the owner of the antemortem records from the list of possible identities of the decedent but cannot definitively make a match. As an example, if no antemortem medical or dental records are available, the forensic anthropologist may only be able to comment on whether the biological profile of the skeletal remains is consistent with those of the potential decedent.

In cases where the antemortem data simply do not exist, or are of poor quality, the forensic anthropologist may be unable to either support or reject the hypothesis that the decedent and the remains represent the same individual. At this point in an analysis, a forensic anthropologist cannot contribute any further until investigative work is able to locate more complete or better quality antemortem records that may be used to retest the hypothesis that the missing person and the decedent represent the same individual.

Methods Contributing to Identification

While comparative radiographic techniques are the only anthropological methods that can directly identify a decedent, there are a number of analytical techniques a forensic anthropologist can employ to contribute to the identification process. These efforts generally help by limiting the list of potential matches to the decedent, moving the investigation closer to a personal identification.

Biological Profile

Acquiring antemortem records is a critical first step toward making an identification; however, this requires some idea of the identity of the deceased. This would be a person or a list of reported missing persons that are potential matches to the decedent. Therefore, the forensic anthropologist may be consulted to assess the biological profile of the remains to narrow the list of potential matches. Once a short list of possible matches has been compiled, antemortem records and other identifying information may be gathered for these individuals. A biological profile consists of the sex, age, ancestry, and living stature of an individual. In cases where soft tissue is unavailable for visual determination of these characteristics, a forensic anthropologist can assess particular skeletal morphologies to estimate each feature of the biological profile. A report of the biological profile and any unique skeletal features of the individual may help investigators identify potential missing person matches to the decedent. Once a possible identity is ascertained, a forensic anthropologist may be asked to employ the techniques outlined above to obtain a personal identification.

Skeletal Pathologies and Anomalies

In cases where antemortem radiographs are not available, photos or descriptions of individualizing features may lead to an identification through multiple corresponding factors. Similar to comparative radiography, this requires a possible missing person match and cooperation with those that knew the decedent to obtain information on potentially identifying features. Although medical records may not contain radiographs for comparison, they can still be used for information on dental procedures, such as extractions and root canals, or medical intervention, including fracture stabilization or surgeries that may be reflected in the skeletal remains. Additionally, skeletal anomalies, such as a cleft palate or scoliosis, can also be used as identifying features. If soft tissue is still present on the decedent, distinctive freckles, birthmarks, or tattoos may also be used to corroborate a potential identity. If one of these features is particularly rare or unique, it may serve as strong evidence of a decedent's identity. In most cases, however, a forensic anthropologist must be cautious in relying on such characteristics for identifications because any single characteristic may not be unique in isolation.

Surgical Implants

Beyond biological features of an individual, identifications may result from the analyses of objects found within a person. As previously discussed, dental restorations in the form of fillings, root canals, and crowns can display a unique morphology useful in comparative radiography. Other foreign objects within the body can serve a similar purpose. The

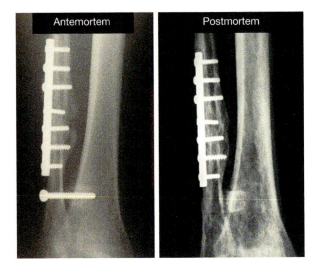

Figure 5 The antemortem (left) and postmortem (right) radiographs of a surgical plate and screws used to stabilize a fibula after injury.

placement of metal plates, screws, or rods for bone stability after traumatic injury or the persistence of a bullet or shrapnel can help individualize a decedent (**Figure 5**). Sternotomy wires used to suture the sternum after open-heart surgery are especially useful. Unlike other surgical implants that have a particular shape and often standardized placement within the body, sternotomy wires are pliable and are hand-twisted making a series of wires entirely unique (**Figure 6**). If antemortem medical radiographs exist of such structures, a radiographic comparison may be possible leading to a scientific identification.

An additional benefit to surgical implants is the potential for obtaining individualizing information to reach a tentative identification. Many surgical implants are etched with the company's logo in addition to a serial or lot number (**Figure 7**). In some cases, these serial numbers are unique and can be traced to the individual in which the implement was placed. In

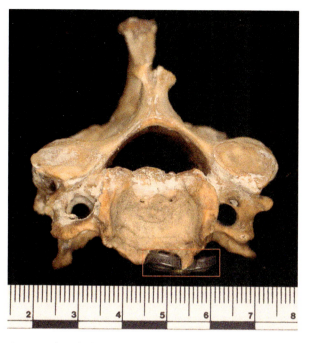

Figure 7 A cervical vertebra with a surgical plate displaying a lot number.

cases where only a lot number is present, it may be possible to track that number to a batch of implants, time period, and the hospitals to which they were sent. Through collaborative efforts by the forensic anthropologist, surgical supply companies, and hospitals, it may be possible to produce a list of potential patients that received the medical implant in question. The forensic anthropologist is often responsible for the careful removal of the surgical implement to minimize damage to both the bone and the implant, and to retrieve the important information.

Photographic Imaging Techniques

Although they are not often considered a form of identification, techniques that utilize photographic images can be used to either exclude a possible identification or support its continued inclusion in a list of potential matches. Skull–photo superimposition is a method in which an electronic mixer is used to superimpose the photo of a known individual onto the skeletal remains of the decedent (**Figure 8**). These two images are expertly manipulated and scaled to align relevant physical features and assess facial proportionality (**Figure 9**). Features that can be aligned between the fleshed face and the skeletonized cranium include the teeth, the outer edge of the eye orbits, the bottom margin of the nasal aperture, the midpoint of the chin, and the openings for the ear canals. If these points

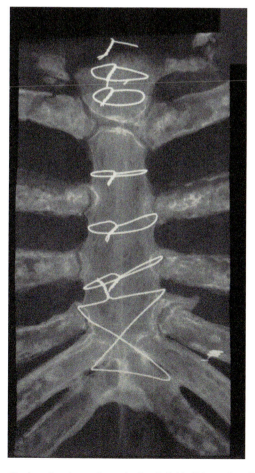

Figure 6 A postmortem radiograph of an individualizing series of sternotomy wires.

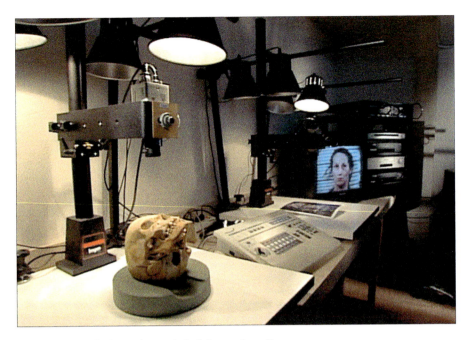

Figure 8   The laboratory equipment utilized to perform a skull–photo superimposition.

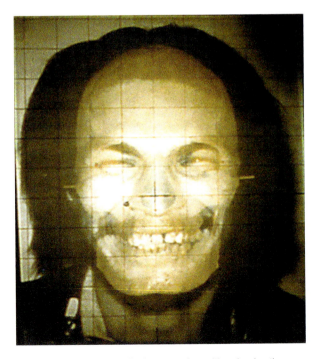

Figure 9   A successful skull–photo superimposition showing the matching of skeletal structures to facial features, including the missing left central maxillary incisor.

can all be brought into alignment, effectively superimposing the photograph onto the cranium, the two remain a potential match. Alternatively, if the features cannot be aligned, the presumptive identification may either be excluded or a conclusion of insufficient evidence made if the images lack clarity.

The use of photographic superimposition may also be applied to cases of living individuals. Specially trained forensic anthropologists use photo–photo or photo–video superimpositions to compare images of a perpetrator and a suspect to determine if they could represent the same person. A methodology similar to skull–photo superimposition is employed, where the two images are aligned to compare facial proportions; eye shape and spacing; nose size and shape; ear location, size, and shape; lip morphology; and any additional unique features such as freckles, moles, or scars.

Conclusion

Medical examiners and coroners are charged with the important responsibility of legally identifying a deceased individual. This may require consultation with forensic specialists in other fields of study who have expertise in various methods of personal identification. As specialists in skeletal biology and human variation, forensic anthropologists are experts in the assessment of a biological profile and are proficient in distinguishing atypical or unique skeletal features that can be used in an identification. Furthermore, those experts with additional training in comparative dental and medical radiography can utilize scientific methods to affect a scientific identification. In every case, a forensic anthropologist should employ all of their education and experience to ensure that a proper personal identification is made. This also means that forensic anthropologists must know the boundaries of their own knowledge and the limitations of the methods they are employing. As personal identification legally confirms a person's death and is necessary for the execution of a death certificate and the resulting distribution of benefits, a nonidentification is always superior to a misidentification. Thus, it is of great importance that forensic anthropologists pursue thoughtful and thorough consideration in every case.

> *See also:* **Anthropology/Odontology:** Aging the Dead and the Living; Ancestry; Identification of the Living; Odontology; Sexing; Stature and Build; **Biology/DNA:** Disaster Victim Identification; The National Missing and Unidentified Persons System (NamUs); **Forensic Medicine/Clinical:** Forensic Age Estimation; Identification; **Legal:** Expert Witness Qualifications and Testimony.

Further Reading

Anderson, B.E., 2008. Identifying the dead: methods utilized by the Pima County (Arizona) office of the medical examiner for undocumented border crossers: 2001–2006. Journal of Forensic Sciences 53 (1), 8–15.

Brogden, B.G., 1998. Radiological identification of individual remains. In: Brogden, B.G. (Ed.), Forensic Radiology. CRC Press, New York, pp. 149–187.

Christensen, A.M., 2005. Testing the reliability of frontal sinuses in positive identification. Journal of Forensic Sciences 50 (1), 8–22.

Dix, J., Graham, M., 2000. Time of Death, Decomposition, and Identification: An Atlas. CRC Press, Boca Raton, FL.

Fenton, T.W., Heard, A.N., Sauer, N.J., 2008. Skull-photo superimposition and border deaths: identification through exclusion and the failure to exclude. Journal of Forensic Sciences 53 (1), 34–40.

Fierro, M.F., 1993. Identification of human remains. In: Fisher, W.U. (Ed.), Medicolegal Investigation of Death. Charles C. Thomas, Springfield, IL, pp. 71–117.

Hogge, J.P., Messmer, J.M., Doan, Q.N., 1994. Radiographic identification of unknown human remains and interpreter experience level. Journal of Forensic Sciences 39 (2), 373–377.

Jablonski, N.G., Shum, B.S., 1989. Identification of unknown human remains by comparison of antemortem and postmortem radiographs. Forensic Science International 42 (3), 221–230.

Kahana, T., Hiss, J., Smith, P., 1998. Quantitative assessment of trabecular bone pattern identification. Journal of Forensic Sciences 43 (6), 1144–1147.

Koot, M.G., Sauer, N.J., Fenton, T.W., 2005. Radiographic human identification using bones of the hand. Journal of Forensic Sciences 50 (2), 263–268.

Kuehn, C.M., Taylor, K.M., Mann, F.A., Wilson, A.J., Harruff, R.C., 2002. Validation of chest x-ray comparisons for unknown decedent identification. Journal of Forensic Sciences 47 (4), 1–5.

Lundy, J.K., 1986. Physical anthropology in forensic medicine. Anthropology Today 2 (5), 14–17.

Maclean, D.F., Kogon, S.L., Stitt, L.W., 1994. Validation of dental radiographs for human identification. Journal of Forensic Sciences 39 (5), 1195–1200.

Mann, R.W., 1998. Use of bone trabeculae to establish positive identification. Forensic Science International 98 (1–2), 91–99.

Messman, J.M., 1986. Radiographic identification. In: Fierro, M.F. (Ed.), CAP Handbook for Postmortem Examination of Unidentified Remains: Developing Identifications of Well-preserved, Decomposed, Burned, and Skeletonized Remains. College of American Pathologists, Skokie, IL.

Rathbun, T.A., Buikstra, J.E. (Eds.), 1998. Human Identification: Case Studies in Forensic Anthropology. Charles C. Thomas, Springfield, IL.

Richmond, R., Pretty, I.A., 2010. Identification of the edentulous individual: an investigation into the accuracy of radiographic identifications. Journal of Forensic Sciences 55 (4), 984–987.

Rogers, T.L., Allard, T.T., 2004. Expert testimony and positive identification of human remains through cranial suture patterns. Journal of Forensic Sciences 49 (2), 1–5.

Sauer, N.J., Brantley, R.E., Barondess, D.A., 1988. The effects of aging on the comparability of antemortem and postmortem radiographs. Journal of Forensic Sciences 33 (5), 1223–1230.

Scientific Working Group for Forensic Anthropology (SWGANTH), 2010. Personal Identification Issue Date: 6/30/2010. Revision: 0. [online]. Available at: www.swganth.org.

Sholl, S.A., Moody, G.H., 2001. Evaluation of dental radiographic identification: an experimental study. Forensic Science International 115, 165–169.

Soomer, H., Lincoln, M.J., Ranta, H., Penttila, A., Leibur, E., 2003. Dentists' qualifications affect the accuracy of radiographic identification. Journal of Forensic Sciences 48 (5), 1–6.

Steadman, D.W., Konigsberg, L.W., 2003. Multiple points of similarity. In: Steadman, D.W. (Ed.), Hard Evidence: Case Studies in Forensic Anthropology. Prentice Hall, Upper Saddle River, NJ.

Stephan, C.N., Winburn, A.P., Christensen, A.F., Tyrrell, A.J., 2011. Skeletal identification by radiographic comparison: blind tests of a morphoscopic method using antemortem chest radiographs. Journal of Forensic Sciences 56 (2), 320–332.

Ubelaker, D.H., Jacobs, C.H., 1995. Identification of orthopedic device manufacturers. Journal of Forensic Sciences 40 (2), 168–170.

Valenzuela, A., 1997. Radiographic comparison of the lumbar spine for positive identification of human remains. The American Journal of Forensic Medicine and Pathology 18 (1), 40–44.

Wilson, R.J., Bethard, J.D., DiGangi, E.A., 2011. The use of orthopedic surgical devices for forensic identification. Journal of Forensic Sciences 56 (2), 460–469.

Relevant Websites

http://www.swgdvi.org/—The Scientific Working Group for Disaster Victim Identification.

www.swganth.org—The Scientific Working Group for Forensic Anthropology.

http://www.theiai.org/—The International Association for Identification.

Identification of the Living

P Gabriel and W Huckenbeck, University Clinic Düsseldorf, Düsseldorf, Germany

Abbreviations

Alare (al)	The most lateral point on each alar contour
Cheilion (ch)	The point located at each labial commissure
Endocanthion (en)	The point at the inner commissure of the eye fissure. The soft endocanthion is located lateral to the bony landmark that is used in cephalometry
Exocanthion (ex)	The point at the outer commissure of the eye fissure. The soft exocanthion is slightly medial to the bony exocanthion
Gnathion (gn)	The lowest median landmark on the lower border of the mandible. It is identified by palpation and is identical to the bony gnathion
Gonion (go)	The most lateral point of the jawline at the mandibular angle
Postaureale (pa)	The most posterior point on the free margin of the ear
Preaureale (pra)	The most anterior point of the ear, located just in front of the helix attachment to the head
Pronasale (prn)	The furthest protruding point of the apex nasi, identified in a lateral view of the head in the rest position
Pupil (p)	Determined when the head is in the rest position and the eye is looking straight ahead
Sellion (se)	The deepest landmark located at the bottom of the nasofrontal angle
Stomion (sto)	The point at the intersection of the mid-sagittal plane (MSP) with the horizontal labial fissure between gently closed lips, with teeth shut in the natural position
Subaureale (sba)	The lowest point on the free margin of the earlobe
Subnasale (sn)	The midpoint of the angle at the columellar base where the lower border of the nasal septum and the surface of the upper lip meet
Superaureale (sa)	The highest point on the free margin of the auricle
Tragion (t)	The notch on the upper margin of the tragus
Trichion (tr)	The point on the hairline (if present) in the MSP
Zygion (zy)	The most lateral point of the cheek region

Glossary

Comparison analysis Comparison of the features of a person shown on a reference image with the features of a suspect shown on a comparison image.

Comparison photo Photo showing a suspect in the same perspective as the perpetrator on surveillance material.

Feature analysis Analysis and description of individual features of a person shown on a reference image.

Reference photo or video Photo or video recorded by a surveillance camera showing the perpetrator.

Introduction

The study of recognition and identification processes probably has to do more with the cognitive sciences; however, in the forensic scenario, it is frequently necessary to identify people according to their somatic traits. In theory, each person can be distinguished from all others according to appearance. For this, the features must be closely examined. In daily life, one is sometimes mistaken by confusing a person with somebody else, but the actual existence of a real "look-alike" who displays the exact combination of features has not been scientifically proven. In fact, differences in certain features that are not noticed with a fleeting glance or when the person is not really well known to us (celebrity doubles) can always be found. Even identical (monozygotic) twins display differences in features that enable them to be differentiated.

In forensic practice, the degree of individualization is highly dependent on the quality of the images (photos and videos) and the frequency of the identifiable features/traits. Due to the hereditability of some features, close kinship can make the distinction of persons more difficult. Overall, a positive identification is very difficult to achieve and every feature has to be analyzed critically.

Established methods in forensic anthropology and classical criminology are used for the determination of individuality on the basis of facial and body appearances.

Despite the rapid advancement and increased practical application of DNA technology, the criminological importance of image analysis has not diminished, especially due to the fact that more and more areas of daily life are under video surveillance and can, in principle, be controlled. The increasing anonymization of business life (ATMs) and increasing mobility (forged identity documents) create further potential applications.

The general aspect of a person is important; nonetheless, initially, the study of single traits can be very useful, before proceeding to a unified comparison of the entire physiognomy. As a result, the general appearance of a person on a speed-camera image, surveillance photo, or video can initially be separated into traits or features.

As in all morphological contexts of identification, for a high level of confidence, a large number of corresponding and/or unique features are required. If, for example, extremely rare features (skin lesions such as scars, warts, tattoos, or birthmarks) are present on the reference photograph, a lower number of features may be sufficient. Exclusion of identity, on the other hand, can be reached by the difference in one trait, if its evaluation was objective and if the discordance cannot be explained by other reasons, for example, surgery, and weight gain. On the other hand, in the case of a slight feature dissimilarity, the possibility of the dissimilarity being explained through lighting, image quality, contrast, masking, artifacts, etc., should be investigated.

The scientific methods of image identification were initially described in the German-speaking countries; this discipline has, however, gained, in the past decades, a widespread diffusion in international literature, and actually represents a relevant field of application of forensic anthropology.

Facial Assessment

Checking for Suitability of Images

Initially, the examiner must view the available evidence material. In the case of video recordings, it is vital that he or she analyzes the material and produces suitable still images. Photo material should—whenever possible—be requested in digital form. After a successful digitalization of the evidence material, an attempt at an improvement in quality can be made. This must be limited to brightness, tone, and contrast; must be understandable; and must on no account lead to feature alterations. At this point, the assessor should decide whether the reference photograph/image material is suitable for an assessment or the maximum level of confidence that can be achieved in an identification. One should keep in mind that there is always the risk of image deformation, especially in digital images. A transformation of the image format can lead to a modification of image proportions. These deformations can sometimes only be corrected by specialists (e.g., engineers). Even image compression techniques that are very common in the storing of digital images can lead to feature alterations. For that reason, one should be very careful with images that show a high compression rate.

Feature Analysis: The Preliminary Step

It is recommended that the reference photograph/image be carefully analyzed. The individual areas of the head (head shape; face shape; facial proportions; hairline; forehead-, eye-, nasal-, mouth-, chin-, lower jaw-, cheek-, ear region; and neck) can be analyzed, described, and classified usually according to specific references, such as Interpol atlases or more modern and complete ones such as the Department of Motor Vehicles (DMV) one (see Appendix). As far as the quality of the image material allows, an attempt is made in determining fine structures. Each feature complex is subdivided into numerous individual features. For instance, in the eye region, these can be eyebrows, upper eyelid, distance between the eyes, eyelid axis, and lower eyelid.

Optical properties of the surveillance camera must be taken into account. In the case of surveillance cameras in ATMs, strong wide-angle lenses are often used to enable the capture of a wide area. Such "fish eye" lenses lead to image distortions: whereas the central portions appear squashed, the structures in the edge areas appear bent or stretched. Once again, specialists in such cases should be consulted in order to correct, if possible, dangerous image distortions.

Comparison Image

For the assessment, a comparison image whose perspective matches that of the reference photograph should be available. Ideally, the comparison image should be prepared by the examiner himself. Only then can a safe, detailed, and reliable feature comparison be performed. Recordings from police identification records are standardized for their requirements and therefore often of limited use for an assessment. In addition, the dates when the reference and the comparison recordings were made must be taken into account, because alterations in the manifestations of features due to aging can have an effect to varying extents. Chronic illnesses can also change the appearance, whereby a relatively short time span between source and comparison photograph is required. Alterable features typically include hair style and beard style, and increase and decrease in weight. The possibility of previous surgery having taken place, as previously mentioned, must also be considered. In some cases, it may be necessary to record the comparison image with the same camera setup with which the evidence/reference photograph was made. In case an estimate of the height of the perpetrator is required, a reconstruction at the crime scene is required. The comparative images can also come from a 3D scan of the suspect, which would allow the examiner to virtually orient the 3D head and find the best-matching orientation subsequently on a computer. Feature analysis and classification can then be performed as mentioned for the reference photograph.

Comparison Analysis

After completion of the feature analysis of the reference photograph and of a suitable photograph of the suspect, a comparison can be performed. All the described features on the reference photograph are compared with all evaluated features and fine structures on the suspect's image. The similarities and dissimilarities are described and discussed according to set standards (e.g., DMV atlas). As far as single traits are concerned, the examiner can verify the existence of discordant traits or that of similar ones. This step therefore will give an idea of consistency of the two faces, that is, of how similar they are. Positive identification should not, however, be attempted at this point (and especially not on frequency and distribution of single traits among different populations).

Positive identification should be achieved once a global comparison of all traits and other more general features is performed. Different approaches exist. Some experts also use the superimposition of lines and general patterns on the images and verify the match. Another possibility is super-imposing the face in toto. However, this is extremely laborious and requires a lot of equipment. In addition, overlapping techniques may have a suggestive effect. Any examiner using such a method must be aware of this. The use of 3D techniques is becoming more and more important: 3D-comparison images of the suspect can be much more easily adjusted to the perpetrator's face on a reference image and the geometric comparison may be more objective. The influence of the focal length and the distortion of the objective lens can be eliminated by using 3D laser scanning and optical surface digitalization. On the other hand, 3D scans are much more time-consuming than conventional photography. However, in many practical cases, only a combination of different techniques will lead to reliable results.

At what point, however, can one say to have reached identification, or how should the expert express his or her judgment? Unlike geneticists, the morphologist cannot respond in a quantified manner for obvious reasons. Forensic experts who deal with facial identification often are reluctant to define from a numerical point of view the strength of their results. However, many courts and judges often require some understanding of the strength of their conclusions; in 2003, the Forensic Imagery Analysis Group (FIAG), born within BAHID (British Association for Human Identification), established a common procedure for describing the level of ascertainment of personal identification according to the degree of support (provided exclusion has not been achieved):

Level 0 Lends no support.
Level 1 Lends limited support.
Level 2 Lends moderate support.
Level 3 Lends support.
Level 4 Lends strong support.
Level 5 Lends powerful support.

Many other "classifications" exist. The problem still remains, however, just like with the anthropological or odontological identification of human remains, of what is enough for a positive identification beyond reasonable doubt.

Other Body Traits

Determining the height of the perpetrator

It has been mentioned above that the comparison of the stature of the perpetrator with that of the suspect can take place at the crime scene provided metric references exist on the reference photograph. Significant problems may arise concerning body posture, clothing, heels, etc., which must be taken into account. The procedure is, however, rather imprecise and therefore contains a large margin for error. For a negative identification in the case of an unusual height of the perpetrator, the procedure can be regarded as sufficiently secure. The most recent studies concerning this topic have highlighted that the reliability of height estimation in personal identification depends on the rarity of the estimated perpetrator's height and its closeness to the suspect's height. As in the preparation of comparison photographs, the question as to whether there has been any change in the camera equipment in the meantime must be investigated beforehand.

Another method for height estimation consists of using a virtual telecamera with the same characteristics of the video surveillance system with which the images were taken. The experimental data showed an average difference between estimated and real height of about 10 mm, together with a standard deviation of 10 mm. This procedure obviously requires that the individual be represented in his entire figure from the feet to the head.

Gait analysis

In video recordings, gait is recorded alongside the body size. In the case of an unusual gait, this can lead to a narrowing down of the number of suspects or in the ideal case, to a positive identification of the perpetrator. The expert must, however, bear in mind that in a recreation of the sequence of events of the crime, the gait of the accused can intentionally be falsified. To prevent this, it has proven useful to film suspects when they believe that they are not being observed.

In addition, being systems based on the periodical nature of gait, they face clear limits when the subject is moving at a nonconstant speed and on a route which is nonlinear. Finally, these systems presuppose the analyses of sequences of gait, which usually cannot be defined by the few useful photograms of persons, taken during a generic walking phase. In addition, the entire methodology of gait analysis has not been standardized. Moreover, although gait can be considered an individualizing marker, the same individual can express different manners of walking according to different conditions (speed, mood, and environmental conditions). At the moment, gait analysis is a promising field of application, but still has to be standardized and thoroughly tested.

Age

The manifestation of facial features is, within certain limits, age dependent, although the modifications of facial features at different ages still need to be verified. During the growth phase, the main changes are in facial proportions from a child's to an adult's face; in addition, some measurements such as the ear length go on increasing after 18 years of age also. This may be used in the future to estimate the age of children and young people. In the last few years, increased attention has been given to the measurements of facial surfaces and volumes by the application of 3D image acquisition systems, which may be useful for the development of an age estimation method. However, further research is needed. Individual variability must, however, be taken into account. In adults, as the growth processes come to an end, facial modifications are due to natural aging, which, however, is less predictable, and therefore less applicable to a possible age estimation method.

Further Features on the Skin, Hands, and Genitals

Occasionally, no facial features are visible on images but additional features that could lead to an identification are visible. In general, only features that are unusual should be described. These could, for instance, be scars on a part of the body, anatomical anomalies, anomalies after accidents or illnesses, tattoos, piercings, etc. The pattern of skin veins, for instance on the back of the hand, has also been shown to be highly individual.

In conclusion, in order to identify persons on the basis of features, these must be visible and should not be affected by strong environmental influences or rapid age changes. A prerequisite for objectivity in identification is the clear definition of the features and the description of the different manifestations of features. A general limitation of the examiner's evaluation lies in the quality of the reference photograph. Often, very individual features such as scars, birthmarks, warts, etc. cannot be evaluated due to graininess, lack of contrast, reflections, unsuitable perspective of the image, or artificial masking. The examiner must decide whether the number of features and their manifestation are sufficient for a positive or negative identification. **Figure 1** shows surveillance photos of the same driver (senior author). The number of facial features and therefore the reliability of a feature comparison vary widely from photo to photo.

Appendix Morphological Assessment of Facial Features: The DMV Atlas

The following section shows the different areas of the human face, and deals briefly with the manifestations of the main features, included in the DMV atlas, one of the most recent amplifications of the traditional Interpol standards. Listing all fine structures is beyond the scope of this chapter. Nevertheless, this limited list shows that the subfeatures of the main areas—face shape, hairline, forehead, eye region, nose, mouth area, cheek area, chin, and ear—can be divided into different feature manifestations. The following sections therefore describe the manifestation of some main and subfeatures of the human face, which are included in the atlas for the evaluation of facial features. The atlas describes a total of 46 facial features that have been scientifically studied and the frequency of different manifestations determined. Special emphasis is placed on user-friendliness. Take as an example the face shape: In the atlas only six face shapes are examined, which are well distinguishable from one another. More than 20 different face shapes are found

(a)   **(b)**

(c)   **(d)**   **(e)**

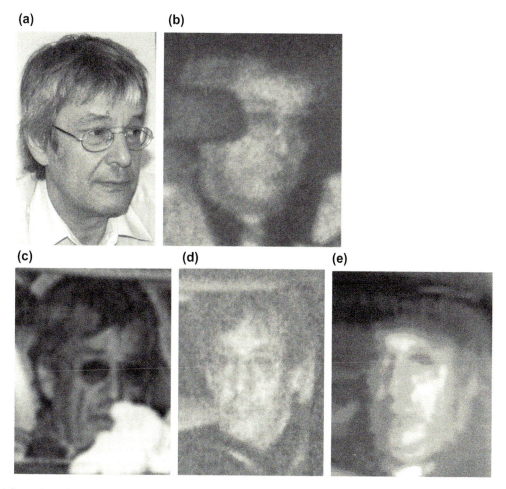

Figure 1   (a) Comparison photograph. (b–e) Traffic surveillance pictures.

in older anthropological literature, some of which even experts find hard to distinguish between.

Face Shape

Face shapes are classified as rectangular, oval, round, pentagonal with pronounced mandible, wedge-shaped, and pentagonal with pronounced cheekbones. Examples are shown in **Figure 2**.

Forehead

The height of the forehead is classified relative to the height of the entire head (trichion–sellion). The breadth of the forehead is expressed in terms of the complete head. Possible

descriptions for the frontal height are shown in **Figure 3**. Seen from the side, the forehead bias can be described.

Frontal Hairline

The shape of the hairline in frontal view can be described as shown in **Figure 4**.

Eye Region

The human eye region contains many features. Eyebrow height, eyebrow density, which can be medial or laterally pointed, and eyebrow shape can be described. There may be a monobrow which is shown in **Figure 5**. The distance of upper eyelid–eyebrow in comparison to the complete face can be described

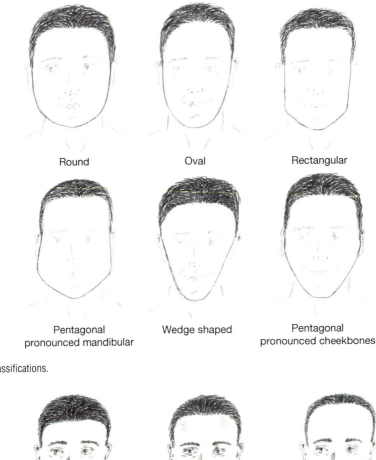

Round   Oval   Rectangular

Pentagonal
pronounced mandibular   Wedge shaped   Pentagonal
pronounced cheekbones

Figure 2   Face shape classifications.

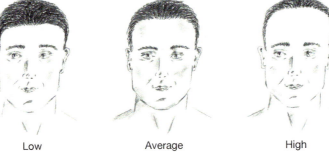

Low   Average   High

Figure 3   Forehead classifications.

as well as the lid axis, the size of the visible eye, and the distance between the eyes.

Nasal Region

The nasal region contains numerous subfeatures that can provide important information for positive or negative identification in the case of good-quality images.

The nose bridge length is defined as the distance between nasal root and nasal tip (sellion–pronasale) in comparison to the complete face. The breadth of the nasal bridge is described in comparison to the complete nose in frontal view. Nose bridge process describes the run of the nasal bridge in frontal view. The nose profile must be estimated from a lateral view. The orientation of the nose tip is defined as the location from pronasale to subnasale in lateral/frontal view. In frontal view, the nose tip shape can be specified. In lateral view, the nose protrusion (in comparison to the complete face) can be described (**Figure 6**). In frontal view, the nasal breadth is expressed as the degree of puffing of the alar wings (al–al). The length of the skinny alar wings in comparison to the complete nose in lateral view is

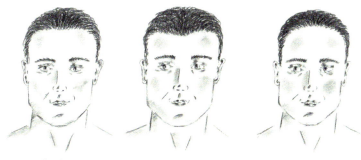

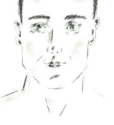

Straight   Convex   Concave

With medial tip   Medially rounded, sides back

Figure 4   Frontal hairline classification.

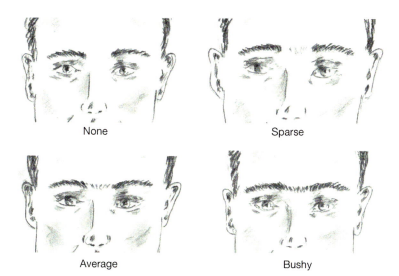

None   Sparse

Average   Bushy

Figure 5   Monobrow classifications.

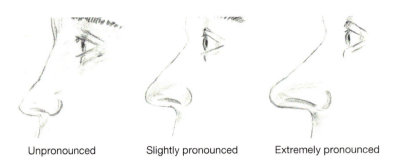

Unpronounced   Slightly pronounced   Extremely pronounced

Figure 6 Nose protrusion in lateral view.

called alar wing length. In lateral view, the nostrils can be specified.

Oral Region

The distance between upper vermillion and the nasal baseline (labiale superius–subnasale) is called the philtrum height (**Figure 7**). The degree of impression between lips and nose is called philtrum depth. Labial breadth is expressed as the distance between the corners of the mouth (cheilion–cheilion) in comparison to the complete face in frontal view. The shape of the upper rim of the vermillion (upper lip notch) can be described as well as the angle of the outer ends of the mouth slit.

Chin Shape

The form of the chin contour can be evaluated. The degree of transition from chin to the basis of the mandible can be described. In lateral view, the chin protrusion can be specified (**Figure 8**). Some individuals show a dimple in the chin. The height of the chin may also be differentiated.

Ear Region

In addition to the main features such as pinna and earlobe, the human ear contains a wide range of highly differentiated fine features, which can be very typical for an individual.

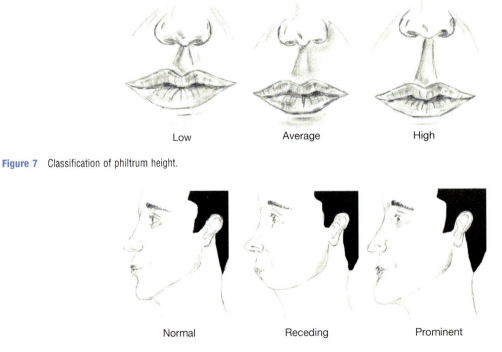

Low   Average   High

Figure 7 Classification of philtrum height.

Normal   Receding   Prominent

Figure 8 Protrusion of the chin.

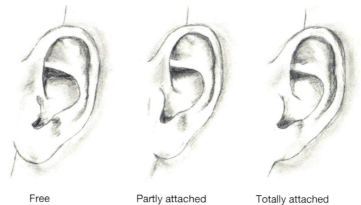

Free   Partly attached   Totally attached

Figure 9 Attachment of the earlobe.

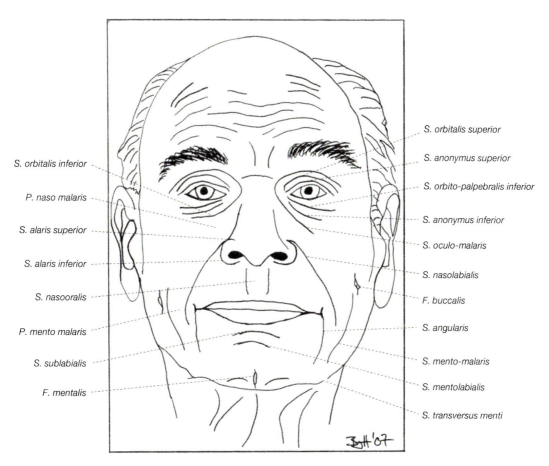

S. orbitalis superior
S. anonymus superior
S. orbito-palpebralis inferior
S. anonymus inferior
S. oculo-malaris
S. nasolabialis
F. buccalis
S. angularis
S. mento-malaris
S. mentolabialis
S. transversus menti

S. orbitalis inferior
P. naso malaris
S. alaris superior
S. alaris inferior
S. nasooralis
P. mento malaris
S. sublabialis
F. mentalis

Figure 10 Wrinkles and dimples.

Unfortunately, in practice, the quality of the reference photographs usually only allows an evaluation of the gross structures.

The distance from the highest to the lowest point of the ear in lateral view (superaureale–subaureale) in comparison to the complete head is called ear height. The distance from the most anterior to the most posterior point of the ear (preaureale–postaureale) can be described. The size of the earlobe is evaluated in comparison to the complete ear. The degree of attachment of the earlobe is shown in **Figure 9**. In frontal view, the degree to which the ears stick out (ear protrusion) can be judged.

Cheek and Throat Area

Depending on the subcutaneous fat tissue and bone structure, the cheek and throat area can be differently manifested. The cheek region can be extremely sunken (gaunt) or extensively to roundly padded. Flat depressions or "fleshy pockets" may be present. In the chin–throat area, a double or triple chin may be present. A depression below the cheekbones in frontal view may be visible.

Wrinkles and Dimples

As **Figure 10** shows, wrinkles and dimples can give the human face very individual, sometimes individual typical, traits. Precise definitions are required to describe these features, and these are also provided in **Figure 10**.

> *See also:* **Anthropology/Odontology:** Aging the Dead and the Living; Facial Approximation; History of Forensic Anthropology; Personal Identification in Forensic Anthropology; **Digital Evidence:** Child Pornography; Digital Imaging: Enhancement and Authentication; **Forensic Medicine/Clinical:** Forensic Age Estimation; Identification; **Foundations:** Overview and Meaning of Identification/Individualization.

Further Reading

Bertillon, A., 1896. Signaletic Instructions Including the Theory and Practice of Anthropometrical Identification. National Library of Medicine, Chicago.

Brinker, H., 1985. Identifizieren und Wiedererkennen. Bemerkungen zum Unterschied und zur Beweisqualität. Archiv fur Kriminologie 176, 142–145.

Buck, U., Naether, S., Kreutz, K., Thali, M., 2011. Geometric facial comparison in speed-check photographs. International Journal of Legal Medicine 125, 785–790.

Cattaneo, C., Ritz-Timme, S., Gabriel, P., et al., 2009. The difficult issue of age assessment on pedo-pornographic material. Forensic Science International 183, 21–24.

Cattaneo, C., Cantatore, A., Ciaffi, R., et al., 2011. Personal identification by the comparison of facial profiles: testing the reliability of a high-resolution 3D–2D comparison model. Journal of Forensic Sciences 57, 182–187 (Epub ahead of print). http://dx.doi.org/10.1111/j.1556-4029.2011.01944.x.

Cavanagh, D., Steyn, M., 2011. Facial reconstruction: soft tissue thickness values for South African black females. Forensic Science International 206 (1–3), 215.e1–215.e7.

De Angelis, D., Sala, R., Cantatore, A., et al., 2007. New method for height estimation of subjects represented in photograms taken from video surveillance systems. International Journal of Legal Medicine 121 (6), 489–492.

De Angelis, D., Sala, R., Cantatore, A., Grandi, M., Cattaneo, C., 2009. A new computer-assisted technique to aid personal identification. International Journal of Legal Medicine 123 (4), 351–356.

De Greef, S., Claes, P., Vandermeulen, D., Mollemans, W., Suetens, P., Willems, G., 1996. Morphological classification of facial features in adult Caucasian males based on an assessment of photographs of 50 subjects. Forensic Science 41 (5), 786–791.

Edler, R., Agarwal, P., Wertheim, D., Greenhill, D., 2006. The use of anthropometric proportion indices in the measurement of facial attractiveness. European Journal of Orthodontics 28 (3), 274–281.

Farkas, L.G., Katic, M.J., Forrest, C.R., 2007. Comparison of craniofacial measurements of young adult African-American and North American white males and females. Annals of Plastic Surgery 59, 692–775.

Ferrario, V.F., Sforza, C., Schmitz, J.H., Miani Jr., A., Taroni, G., 1995. Fourier-analyses of human soft tissue facial shape: sex differences in normal adults. Journal of Anatomy 187, 593–602.

Gabriel, P., Obertová, Z., Ratnayake, M., et al., 2010. Schätzung des Lebensalters kindlicher Opfer auf Bilddokumenten. Rechtsmedizin 21, 7–11.

Goos, M.I.M., Alberink, I.B., Ruifrok, A.C.C., 2005. 2D/3D image (facial) comparison using camera matching. Forensic Science International 163 (1–2), 10–17.

Hajnis, K., Farkas, L.G., Ngim, R.C.K., Lee, S.T., Venkatadri, G., 1994. Racial and ethnic morphometric differences in the craniofacial complex. In: Farkas, L.G. (Ed.), Anthropometry of the Head and Face, second ed. Raven Press, New York, pp. 201–217.

Halberstein, R.A., 2001. The application of anthropometric indices in forensic photography: three case studies. Journal of Forensic Sciences 46 (6), 1438–1441.

Heathcote, J., 1995. Why do old men have big ears? British Medical Journal 311, 1668.

Hirthammer, B.J., 2007. Die physiognomische Alterung des Menschen. Quantifizierung mittels 3DLaserscanners (Master thesis). University of Ulm, Germany.

Iscan, M.Y., 1993. The introduction of techniques for photographic comparison: potential and problems. In: Iscan, M.Y., Helmer, R.P. (Eds.), Forensic Analyses of the Scull: Craniofacial Analyses, Reconstruction and Identification. Wiley-Liss, New York, pp. 57–70.

Kleinberg, K.F., Vanezis, P., 2007. Variation in proportion indices and angles between selected facial landmarks with rotation in the Frankfort plane. Medicine, Science, and the Law 47 (2), 107–116.

Kleinberg, K.F., Vanezis, P., Burton, A.M., 2007. Failure of anthropometry as a facial identification technique using high-quality photographs. Journal of Forensic Sciences 52 (4), 779–783.

Knussmann, R., 1983. Die vergleichende morphologische analyse als Identitätsnachweis. Strafverteidiger 3, 127–129.

Knussmann, R., 1988. Lehrbuch Anthropologie, vol. I/1. G. Fischer-Verlag, Stuttgart.

Knussmann, R., 1991. Zur Wahrscheinlichkeitsaussage im morphologischen Identitätsgutachten. NStZ 11 (4), 175–177.

Lynnerup, N., Andersen, M., Lauritsen, H.P., 2003. Facial image identification using Photomodeler. Legal Medicine 5, 156–160.

Macho, G.A., 1986. Cephalometric and craniometric age changes in adult humans. Annals of Human Biology 13 (1), 49–61.

Martin, R., Saller, K., 1957. Lehrbuch der Anthropologie in Systematischer Darstellung mit Besonderer Berücksichtigung der Anthropologischen Methoden. Gustav-Fischer-Verlag, Stuttgart.

Ohlrogge, S., Nohrden, D., Schmitt, R., Drabik, A., Gabriel, P., Ritz-Timme, S., 2008. Anthropologischer Atlas Männlicher Gesichtsmerkmale – Anthropological Atlas of Male Facial Features. Verlag der Polizeiwissenschaften, Frankfurt/Main.

Ohlrogge, S., Arent, T., Huckenbeck, W., Gabriel, P., Ritz-Timme, S., 2009. Anthropologischer Atlas Weiblicher Gesichtsmerkmale – Anthropological Atlas of Female Facial Features. Verlag der Polizeiwissenschaften, Frankfurt/Main.

Porter, G., Doran, G., 2000. An anatomical and photographic technique for forensic facial identification. Forensic Science International 114 (2), 97–105.

Ritz-Timme, S., Gabriel, P., Tutkuviene, J., et al., 2011a. Metric and morphological assessment of facial features: a study on three European populations. Forensic Science International 207, 239.e1–239.e8.

Ritz-Timme, S., Gabriel, P., Obertova, Z., et al., 2011b. A new atlas for the evaluation of facial features: advantages, limits, and applicability. International Journal of Legal Medicine 125, 301–306.

Roelofse, M.M., Steyn, M., Becker, P.J., 2008. Photo identification: facial metrical and morphological features in South African males. Forensic Science International 177 (2–3), 168–175.

Rösing, F.W., 2008. Morphologische identifikation von Personen. In: Buck, J., Krumbholz, H. (Eds.), Sachverständigenbeweis im Verkehrsrecht. Nomos-Verlag, Baden-Baden, pp. 201–219.

Shaner, D.J., Bamforth, S., Peterson, A.E., Beattie, O.B., 1998. Technical note: different techniques, different results – a comparison of photogrammetric and caliper-derived measurements. American Journal of Physical Anthropology 106, 547–552.

Thompson, T., Black, S., 2007. Forensic Human Identification – an Introduction. CRC Press, Boca Raton, FL.

Vanezis, P., Lu, D., Cockburn, J., et al., 1996. Morphological classification of facial features in adult Caucasian males based on an assessment of photographs of 50 subjects. Journal of Forensic Sciences 41, 786–791.

Ventura, F., Zacheo, A., Ventura, A., Pala, A., 2004. Computerized anthropomorphometric analyses of images: case report. Forensic Science International 146, 211–213.

Yoshino, M., Matsuda, H., Kubota, S., Imaizumi, K., Miyasaka, S., 2000. Computer-assisted facial image identification system using a 3-D physiognomic range finder. Forensic Science International 109, 225–237.

The National Missing and Unidentified Persons System (NamUs)

MM Houck, Consolidated Forensic Laboratory, Washington, DC, USA

Introduction

It has been estimated that there are approximately 40 000 unidentified human remains in the offices of the nation's medical examiners and coroners or were buried or cremated before being identified. In June 2007, OJP's Bureau of Justice Statistics (BJS) confirmed that, in a typical year, medical examiners and coroners handle approximately 4400 unidentified human decedent cases, 1000 of which remain unidentified after a year. BJS further identified the need to improve record-retention policies. As of 2004, more than half (51%) of the nation's medical examiners' offices had no policy for retaining records—such as X-rays, DNA, or fingerprints—on unidentified human decedents. BJS also noted, however, that more than 90% of offices servicing large jurisdictions did have such a policy. Cases of missing persons of age 18 years and below must be reported, but reporting adult missing persons is voluntary. Only a few states have laws that require law enforcement agencies to prepare missing person reports on adults. Overall, there is a low rate of reporting these cases through NCIC.

The National Missing and Unidentified Persons System (NamUs) is a national centralized repository and resource center for missing persons and unidentified decedent records. NamUs is a free online system that can be searched by medical examiners, coroners, law enforcement officials, and the general public from all over the country in the hope of resolving these cases. The Missing Persons Database contains information about missing persons, which can be entered by anyone; however, before it appears as a case on NamUs, the information is verified. NamUs provides a user with a variety of resources, including the ability to print missing persons' posters and receive free biometric collection and testing assistance. Other resources include links to state clearinghouses, medical examiners and coroners' offices, law enforcement agencies, victim assistance groups, and pertinent legislation.

The Unidentified Persons Database contains information entered by medical examiners and coroners. Unidentified persons are people who have died and whose bodies have not been identified. Anyone can search this database using characteristics such as sex, race, distinct body features, and even dental information.

The newly added UnClaimed Persons database (UCP) contains information about deceased persons who have been identified by name but for whom no next of kin or family member has been identified or located to claim the body for burial or other disposition. Only medical examiners and coroners may enter cases in the UCP database. However, the database is searchable by the public, using a missing person's name and year of birth.

When a new missing person or unidentified decedent case is entered into NamUs, the system automatically performs cross-matching comparisons between the databases, searching for matches or similarities between cases. NamUs provides free DNA testing and other forensic services, such as anthropology and odontology assistance. NamUs' Missing Persons Database and Unidentified Persons Database are now available in Spanish.

Acknowledgment

Material provided by OJP from Web site http://www.namus.gov.

See also: **Biology/DNA:** DNA Databases; **Investigations:** Fingerprints; **Pattern Evidence/Fingerprints (Dactyloscopy):** Identification and Classification.

Further Reading

Ritter, N., 2007. Missing persons and unidentified remains: the nation's silent mass disaster. NIJ Journal 256, 2–7. http://www.nij.gov.

Disaster Victim Identification

WH Goodwin and T Simmons, University of Central Lancashire, Preston, UK

Abbreviations

AM	Antemortem	PM	Postmortem
DVI	Disaster victim identification	STR	Short tandem repeat
ICRC	International Committee of the Red Cross	VNTR	Variable number tandem repeat

Introduction

In every disaster or conflict, the need to recover and identify the deceased is a matter of urgency, foremost on behalf of the psychological needs of relatives of those missing; the right to know the fate of one's missing relatives is a fundamental right and should be respected and enacted—this principle holds regardless of the circumstances that have led to the death. Alongside humanitarian needs, disaster victim identification (DVI) also addresses legal concerns regarding everything from civil suits concerning liability in an aviation, train, or ferry disaster, the need to provide death certificates for purposes of inheritance and remarriage, through to the prosecution of perpetrators of war crimes.

The scope of DVI operations has evolved significantly since the mid-1990s, when most instances centered on transport accidents involving up to a few hundred victims. Advances have been driven in part technically by developments, particularly in DNA analysis, that have increased the circumstances in which identification of human remains is possible. Politically, the response to several events of international importance in the late twentieth and early twenty-first centuries, such as conflicts in the Balkans 1991–1999, the World Trade Center attack 2001, and the pan-Asian Tsunamis 2004, focused a large amount of resource to the identification of the victims. This led to logistical and technical advances in DVI and also to higher expectations for forensic science to be used for human identification following disasters and conflicts, even when there are thousands of victims.

Disaster Classification

A disaster can be defined as an unexpected event causing death or injury to many people. Traditional considerations for activating a DVI response related to "mass disasters," where external assistance was required following a catastrophic event that overwhelmed the resources of an affected community and rendered it unable to respond adequately acting alone. There are many different types of disaster that can necessitate DVI including traffic accidents, natural disasters, technical/industrial accidents, terrorist attacks, and events that occur during conflict, both within and between countries.

In addition to the type of disaster, an important aspect when considering DVI is whether it is open or closed. Closed disasters, such as aircraft crashes, are those in which the identities of the victims are known through crew and passenger manifests (although these may not be entirely accurate in all cases); in such instances, the task of the DVI team is largely to match the identity of the remains to individuals known to be missing. In many of these cases, access to relevant antemortem (AM) information necessary for matching is also facilitated by the relative ease of locating kin, medical and dental records, and DNA samples. Open disasters are those in which the identity and even the number of the victims are unknown. Establishing who was indeed a victim can be quite complicated even in a thoroughly modern society where it may take several days or weeks, even years to resolve in a situation of limited fatalities; in the case of a natural disaster involving multiple countries or locations within a country and thousands to tens of thousands of victims of multiple nationalities, it can take years to resolve. For victims of conflict, where the number and identity of victims are unknown, individuals disappeared over several years (or decades), the location of graves has been obscured, AM records are scant or lacking in their entirety and political will and monetary resources are slim, identification, when possible, can take decades. It should also be noted that it is possible to have a classification of combined, for example, when a plane crashes on a populated area killing people of the ground as well as those in the plane.

Management of DVI

Interpol recommends that each member state should establish a permanent DVI team, with preplanning and training for disasters. In planning for and following a disaster, multiple facets of the DVI operation have to be considered, for example: initial assessment of the scope of the disaster, mapping and searching of the affected area, estimating the number of victims and degree of fragmentation, methodology to recover and transport the corpses, methodology to be used for identification, and identifying the individuals/medicolegal institutes that are to be involved in the identification process. The criteria that must be met before identifications are made must also be agreed upon prior to bodies being released to families—this becomes increasingly important with increasing numbers of victims as this augments the probability of incorrect identifications.

Another important decision is the scope of the identification process, that is, with fragmented remains what will the operation aim to identify—whole bodies only, recognizable body parts, body parts of a specific size? In cases of extreme fragmentation (e.g., plane crashes) or disruption of primary burials into secondary and even tertiary mass burials (e.g., Bosnia), it is also necessary to have a policy in place regarding how relatives of the missing will be informed when a portion of their missing person has been identified. Through this policy, relatives of the missing may, for example, elect to be notified when (1) the entire identification process has been completed and all the remains identified of the individual are collected and returned at a single time; (2) the first body part has been identified; or (3) every time a body part has been identified. This allows the relatives of the missing to assert some control over their relationship to the identification process and also decide at which point they wish to hold memorial and/or funeral services.

Principles of Identification

Identification of individuals killed in mass disasters and conflicts should be held to the same standards as identification of individuals killed (or found dead) under any other circumstance. The processes used in identifying individuals must be robust and the families of the missing must have confidence in the identification process. Decisions regarding the methods of identification to be employed are influenced by the condition of the victims, personnel involved in the identification, resources, and technology, as well as by the availability of AM comparatives. There are four widely recognized means of positive identification, whereby a single method alone can be used to make an identification; all others must be regarded as a means of presumptive identification, which can be used to support identification or generate further leads to

identity, but may not in themselves "make" an identification. Fingerprints, dental/medical records (including radiographs), nuclear DNA, and unique medical identifiers are all means of primary positive identification. Visual recognition (of tattoos, facial features, birth marks, scars, etc.), a matching biological profile generated by forensic anthropologists (age, sex, race, stature, and AM trauma/pathology), matching medical conditions identified by pathologists, facial superimposition, matching personal effects and clothing, matching identification documents, exclusion (when, for example, there is only one child among the victims) and/or matching mitochondrial DNA (mtDNA) profiles are secondary means of identification, ideally for use in support of the primary methods (**Figure 1**).

Methods of Identification

Objective Methods

Objective methods, sometimes referred to as scientific methods, if applied appropriately, can give unambiguous identifications.

Fingerprints

Identification of individuals through fingerprints is a well-established scientific method and is routinely used worldwide. In humans, the palms and fingers are covered in skin that is thickened with ridges that help to grip surfaces (friction ridge skin); the soles of the feet and toes are also covered with friction ridge skin. Friction ridge skin is considered to be unique and over the last 100 years of application, with millions of fingerprints used for forensic identification, only a handful of issues of misidentification have been reported, making fingerprints a powerful means of identification; importantly fingerprints remain unchanged throughout life, other than through scarring.

Several systems have been developed to classify fingerprints, all of which are based on categorization of the overall pattern that is loops, arches, and whorls, and then identification of distinct combinations of features within the pattern, such as bifurcations, lakes, and ridge endings. Its utility to DVI identification varies from case to case. The remains have to be fleshed and in a state of preservation that allows for prints to be taken—this may be possible even with partially decomposed and even burned remains, as fingers curl inward when exposed to fire, thus preserving the ridge details.

As with all other forms of identification, AM records also need to exist for comparison. Whether extensive AM records are available varies depending on the country or countries involved; many countries collect fingerprints from all of its citizens once they reach adulthood and this information is typically held in a national computer, which allows rapid searching—in other countries legislation may prevent the storage of fingerprints, or restrict it to those arrested in

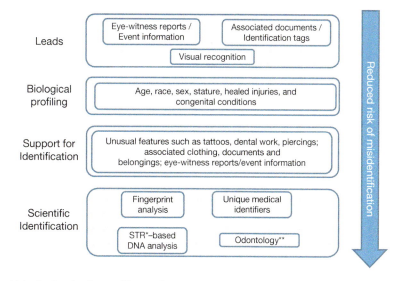

Leads
- Eye-witness reports / Event information
- Associated documents / Identification tags
- Visual recognition

Biological profiling
- Age, race, sex, stature, healed injuries, and congenital conditions

Support for Identification
- Unusual features such as tattoos, dental work, piercings; associated clothing, documents and belongings; eye-witness reports/event information

Scientific Identification
- Fingerprint analysis
- Unique medical identifiers
- STR*–based DNA analysis
- Odontology**

Reduced risk of misidentification

Figure 1 Identifications obtained using visual recognition or other customary means are, where possible, supported by comparing antemortem and postmortem data to allow biological profiling and collection of additional evidence to support the identification. Ideally, identifications should be supported by at least one form of scientific identification, which greatly reduces the possibility of misidentification. *, SNP-based DNA analysis could also provide scientific identification but is not widely used; **, scientific identification using odontology would normally require comparison of dental radiographs or other features that would be considered to be unique. STR, short tandem repeat.

connection to a criminal offense. If no AM records are available, it may be possible to recover AM prints from the personal possessions of the missing person(s), assuming there is reliable information on who is actually missing. With a computer-based search using an automated fingerprint identification system (AFIS), a list of candidate matches can be produced in seconds; however, the algorithms are not sufficiently refined to produce exact matches, and computer-generated matches have to be examined manually by an expert to establish a confirmed match.

Dental radiographs

The identification of individuals based on a comparison of AM and postmortem (PM) radiographs is, arguably, a somewhat subjective process, but one which is nonetheless recognized as a scientific means by which a positive identification may be made. While in the past, radiographic equipment may not have been available in situ and radiographers were forced to ship bulky equipment and improvise darkrooms in which to develop the films, this is no longer an obstacle. Portable digital radiographic equipment—some even handheld— is widely available, and rapidly becoming cost-effective. If not available in the country in which the disaster or conflict has occurred, this equipment is so portable that it can be carried as hand luggage in the passenger compartment of aircraft deploying individuals to the scene.

The AM–PM matching of radiographs for identification is more widely accepted in forensic dentistry than in forensic anthropology, where the former is most often based on radiographic images of dental restorations and/or implants, which evince the unique characteristics of both the morphology of the lesion and that of the dentist's individual technique and thus afford multiple surfaces for examination (**Figure 2**), the latter relies upon matching frontal sinus, cranial

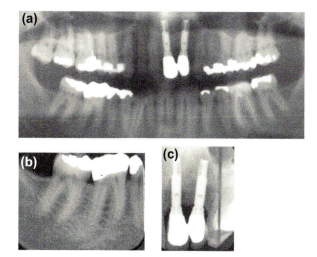

Figure 2 (a) Antemortem orthopantogram, (b) postmortem mandibular, and (c) maxillary radiographs from the same individual (Radiographs courtesy of Dr John Robson).

sutures, vertebral morphology, and even bone trabecular patterns, not just the orthopedic equivalent of implants, fixators, pins, plates, screws, and artificial joints. Although the angle at which an AM radiograph is taken may cause distortion, elongation, and superimposition of features in a dental radiograph, the problem is often compounded in an orthopedic image by additional factors such as age-related changes in joint surfaces and trabecular realignment caused by the application of differing stresses due to activity level and type with age. In all radiographic comparisons, the years elapsed between when the AM image was made and the individual's death must be taken into consideration. Superimposition of the AM–PM images of restorations is a frequently used technique in conjunction with the correspondence of measurements. Again, there is somewhat better correspondence within dental images than even within internal fixators used in fracture repair, as remodeling of bone due to weightbearing contributes to the movement of implanted devices over time. Dental records themselves (e.g., notations of teeth treated, condition of teeth, etc.) are not definitive in DVI as both omissions and mistakes in recording do occur, however, such records are potentially useful when comparing large numbers of AM and PM records to establish possible matches and in providing additional support for an identification; in some contexts dental records are used when radiographs are not available.

The utility of dental radiographs tends to be limited to developed countries where individuals typically visit the dentist, and radiography is commonly used as part of routine examinations or following any major dental work. The dentist normally keeps either the developed radiographs themselves, microfilm of those radiographs, or stores digital radiographic images in the patient's electronic file. When disaster victims have not been subjected to trauma that has resulted in disruption of the dentition and AM records are available, forensic odontology is a powerful means of achieving identifications.

Nuclear DNA

Since its introduction into forensic science in 1985, DNA profiling has become commonplace in forensic laboratories worldwide. Its primary forensic use is for the identification material recovered from scenes of crimes; however, it is also widely used in the identification of human remains, particularly following on from transport disasters, such as plane crashes.

By the early to mid-1990s, the analysis of short tandem repeats (STRs) had replaced variable number tandem repeat-based analysis. STRs had several advantages: they could be analyzed using polymerase chain reaction (PCR)-based methods, which made them much more sensitive; the alleles of STR loci are also much shorter, making the analysis of degraded material easier; several STR loci could be analyzed in one reaction and analyzed together using capillary electrophoresis, which greatly reduced the time taken to carry out the analysis; and the profiles could be broken down into a series of numbers corresponding to the number of core repeats present in each allele, which allows comparisons to be made between DNA profiles generated within a laboratory and also to compare profiles generated in different laboratories.

STRs are found throughout the genome and they are composed of short blocks of sequence that are repeated in tandem—the STRs commonly used for forensic analysis have blocks of sequence that are 4- or 5-bp long (**Figure 3**). While there are numerous STR loci in the human genome that could be used as forensic markers, around 20–25 are commonly used. These have been selected for being highly discriminating (typically having a large number of variants (alleles) that differ in the number of core repeats) and for being easy to analyze using PCR-based technology. Using current methodology DNA profiles can, in principle, be generated within a few hours and produce a profile that is extremely rare, if not unique (**Figure 4**).

Because of the limited discrimination capacity of the early profiling systems, it was not until 1991 that DNA profiling was successfully employed in the identification of human remains—in this case, a murder victim in the UK. It has since been successfully applied to cases that range from the identification of individual bodies to more complex scenarios with multiple victims following, for example, air crashes, fires and explosions, terrorist attacks, natural disasters, and conflicts. A distinct advantage of DNA analysis in DVI is that all tissues contain DNA, and therefore the method will work on highly fragmented remains and enable fragments of bodies to be reassociated.

As with the other forms of identification, the use of DNA analysis in DVI will vary from context to context. Whether DNA can be recovered from the human remains depends on the degree of environmental insult, for example, if the remains have been subjected to high temperatures in excess of 200 °C or there has been a long delay in locating and recovering the

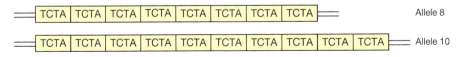

Figure 3   The structure of a short tandem repeat. This example shows the structure of two alleles from the locus D8S1179. The DNA either side of the core repeats is called flanking DNA. The alleles are named according to the number of repeats that they contain—hence alleles 8 and 10.

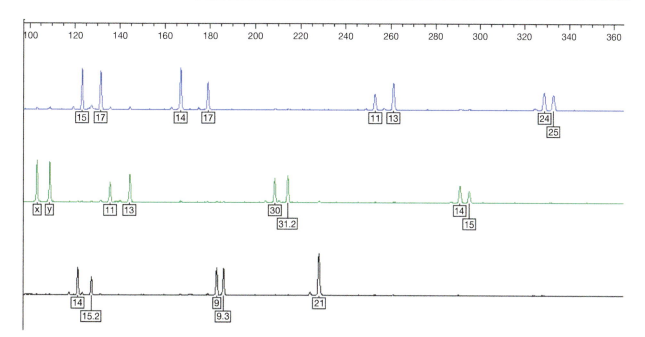

Figure 4 A DNA profile is represented by a series of peaks that can be broken down into a numerical code—the numbers correspond to the number of core repeats in each short tandem repeat (STR) allele. The profile above contains the information on 10 STR loci and the amelogenin locus, which differentiates between the X and Y chromosomes—in this profile, labeled X and Y (showing that this DNA sample is from a male).

remains the DNA can be highly degraded, and it may not be possible to generate a profile. AM data are required for comparison: this can be in the form of a direct comparison if a biological sample from the missing person is available, or more commonly by comparison to biological relatives of the missing person.

Unique medical identifiers

On occasions, PM analysis of human remains may happen upon a medical implant; typical examples are artificial joints and pacemakers. These medical devices come with a unique serial number and can allow for unambiguous identification as long as the relevant information can be located. Needless to say, identifications through this method are not common.

Data Collection

Data collection, both PM and AM, is a critical component of the DVI operation. Several agencies, both national and international, have developed forms that facilitate the systematic collection of data that can be used in the identification process. The most commonly employed system for DVI work uses the Interpol forms—these have been specifically developed for DVI work. The International Committee of the Red Cross (ICRC) has also developed AM and PM forms, which have been designed for use in postconflict scenarios (**Figure 5**). Both these

systems can be computerized with the data entered into a relational database, allowing AM and PM data to be cross-searched. National authorities have also developed their own systems, for example, in the United States, the Disaster Mortuary Operational Response Team (DMORT) has its own set of recording forms and database recording similar information. Obviously, the more victims and the greater the fragmentation of those individuals, the more imperative it is to computerize PM and AM records. Searching by hand through records for matches, especially when the personnel who originally recorded PM details are no longer available and memory is lacking, is a frustrating exercise.

Postmortem

The cooperation and teamwork of experts, sharing of information, and agreement concerning and adherence to criteria by which an identification will be made, are critical to the management and effective performance of any DVI team. The work flow in the morgue, and hence floor plan, should be arranged to facilitate the processing of remains as well as the communication among the various teams of experts. The technical experts involved in the collection of data will vary depending on the state of the human remains; typically teams will comprise some or all of a pathologist, who will undertake a PM examination; an anthropologist to examine skeletal material; an odontologist to take radiographs and examine the

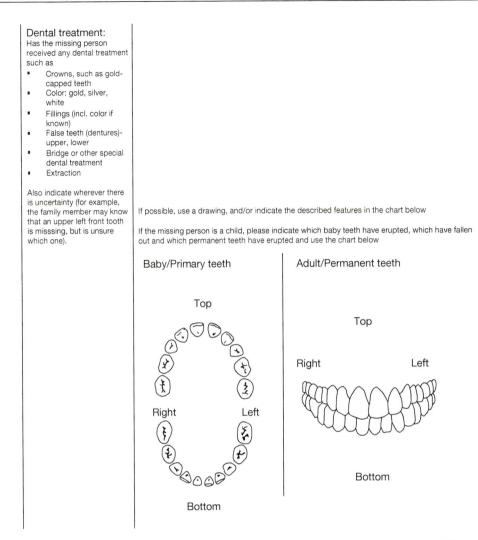

Dental treatment:
Has the missing person
received any dental treatment
such as
- Crowns, such as gold-capped teeth
- Color: gold, silver, white
- Fillings (incl. color if known)
- False teeth (dentures)-upper, lower
- Bridge or other special dental treatment
- Extraction

Also indicate wherever there
is uncertainty (for example,
the family member may know
that an upper left front tooth
is misssing, but is unsure
which one).

If possible, use a drawing, and/or indicate the described features in the chart below

If the missing person is a child, please indicate which baby teeth have erupted, which have fallen
out and which permanent teeth have erupted and use the chart below

Baby/Primary teeth

Top

Right   Left

Bottom

Adult/Permanent teeth

Top

Right   Left

Bottom

Figure 5   A section of the antemortem data collection form developed by the International Committee of the Red Cross (ICRC).

teeth; a radiographer to take whole body X-rays; a fingerprint expert; and a biologist to take samples for DNA analysis. Other individuals, for example, police officers and crime scene investigators, will also be involved carrying out tasks such as documenting personal belongings, clothing, taking photographs, and ensuring chain of custody for any evidential items.

Antemortem

A prerequisite to the application of any of these methods is the existence of relevant, reliable AM data. Following a mass disaster, an AM data collection interview is typically conducted with relatives of the missing. The collection of AM data is as much a specialized process as conducting a PM examination, and interviews of relatives of the missing should be performed only by trained personnel. Interviews are best performed by

native speakers of the language, so in-country training of personnel should be planned. During the interview, information concerning the individual's physical description, a description of the clothing the individual was wearing, and any personal effects that were with the individual are recorded on an AM data form—this form should be compatible with the PM form to allow searching of comparable fields of information. A photograph of the missing person is collected, and the existence and whereabouts of medical and dental records for that individual are noted so that these can be requested from doctors and dentists at a later date. Photographs of the victim's smiling can be also useful as the teeth may have distinguishing morphology or features such as spots caused by hypoplasia. During this interview, if possible, DNA samples are taken and latent fingerprints are enhanced and collected from the home of the missing person. DNA samples may be direct reference samples (e.g., from the missing person's toothbrush or hairbrush) or indirect reference samples, preferably from their immediate kin (father, mother, children).

The above methods work very well in developed countries, and the process above describes the situation in a country with well-developed infrastructure. However, the infrastructure of many less developed countries does not facilitate the collection, maintenance, and storage of such relevant records that drive the DVI process for the citizenry of developed countries. In postconflict situations, even where such records may have existed at one time, they may have been destroyed during the conflict or its aftermath or have become unavailable due to political and boundary shifts. In natural or other mass disasters in less developed countries, the same may be true regarding destruction of extant records or the lack of relevant records. Furthermore, subsequent to mass disasters and conflicts, many individuals are frequently displaced internally or have become refugees in neighboring countries. This makes locating relevant kin of the missing difficult, and organizing and conducting AM interviews challenging. Whenever possible, it is recommended to avoid retraumatizing the relatives of the missing by repeated visits and questions, as these doubtless reopen wounds, doubts, and raise anxiety.

Selection of Methods for Identification

In any mass disaster, the method that can be employed successfully will be dictated according to the condition of the remains, the composition of experts in the DVI team, the technical and financial resources available, and the choices made by the team's leadership during the course of its operational mandate.

Prior to DNA analysis, comparison of dental records was the most widely used method to achieve identifications. Analysis of five disasters in the UK between 1985 and 1989 which comprised three air disasters, a capsized ferry, and a fire on an oil platform, identified that dental records had been used to identify, on average, over 80% of the recovered bodies. In more recent large-scale disasters, for example, in the World Trade Center investigations, DNA was the first choice for identification and generated the majority of identifications by a single modality (86%), dental and fingerprints combined only yielding an additional 10% of identifications. Similarly, since the inception of the International Commission for Missing Person's (ICMP) DNA laboratory in Tuzla (Bosnia), identifications from the 1992 to 1995 Bosnian conflict have been DNA-led, with secondary means of identification used, where possible, to support the DNA-based identification— as of mid-2011, over 13 000 individuals in Bosnia and Herzegovina had been identified and returned to their families. In contrast, although DNA was initially a method of first choice in the Asian tsunami identifications in Thailand, 11 months after the

tsunami, 80% of foreign victims had been identified using dental comparisons—dental analysis with local victims identified 55% of Thai victims, lower than with foreign victims due to the lack of AM records in many cases. Overall, in the 15 months following the disaster, identifications had been made using: dental alone, 1105; dental plus others, 1451; fingerprints alone, 670; fingerprints plus others, 927; DNA alone, 27; DNA plus others, 459.

There are reasons for the success ratios of the identification methods in each of the above examples. In the World Trade Center, victim fragmentation was extreme, and the goal was set to identify every piece of tissue greater than or equal to 5 cm^3, thus necessitating the use of DNA. In Bosnia, lack of AM medical and dental records, commingling in secondary mass graves and time elapsed since the deaths of the victims are but a few of the factors that dictated the reliance on DNA rather than other primary identifiers. In Thailand, important factors included that dental-based identifications could be made for many of the foreign victims relatively rapidly; many bodies were not fragmented, removing the requirement for DNA-based reassociation; fingerprint analysis was successful with many Thai victims; limited in-country facilities were capable of handling the volume of DNA samples from the disaster; and decomposition of tissue was rapid in the tropical environment, making DNA analysis difficult.

Evaluation of Identification Data

The exact procedures used in the identification process vary from country to country and from scenario to scenario. Typically, identifications are made through an organization that acts as an identification commission or board; this would typically include an expert from the main disciplines involved in making identifications— investigators/crime scene investigators, fingerprint examiners, odontologists, pathologists, anthropologists, and DNA analysts— and should be presided over by the legal authority charged with issuing death certificates. In this manner, all the evidence contributing to the identification of an individual in a mass disaster is reviewed a final time by everyone who has contributed to that process, and a legal decision concerning the establishment of positive identity and repatriation of the remains to kin can be completed.

Evaluating the identification is a complex task, especially as the number of victims increases—this heightens the possibility of coincidental matches, which, if not detected, can lead to misidentifications. An often cited example where this occurred is the identification of a fire officer recovered from the World Trade Center following 9/11, who was misidentified on the basis of his clothing that identified him as a fire officer from a particular unit coupled with a rare congenital anomaly in spinal vertebra. The identification was not confirmed by any of the recognized objective methods of identification, and DNA analysis later exposed the misidentification but only after the remains had been returned to the wrong family—the rare medical condition had been shared by one of his colleagues in his unit. Such seemingly remote coincidences become more likely as the number of victims increases.

Conclusions

The requirement for governments and indeed the international community to be able to mount an effective DVI response following disasters and conflicts is widely accepted. Recent technological advances in terms of DNA analysis, portable radiographic equipment, and sophisticated computer databases that allow comparison of AM and PM data have increased the number of cases where the identification of human remains is possible. There will always be limitations as to what is possible; for example, following the World Trade Center identifications, even with an enormous effort expended, no identification could be made for over 40% of the victims, which should not distract from the success in identifying over 1500 victims. With continued improvements in technology, preparedness, and infrastructure to deal with a large number of samples in a timely fashion, there is the potential to have a greater proportion of victims identified and returned to their families following future disasters and conflicts.

See also: **Anthropology/Odontology:** History of Forensic Anthropology; Odontology; Personal Identification in Forensic Anthropology; **Biology/DNA:** DNA Extraction and Quantification; MiniSTRs; Mitochondrial DNA; Short Tandem Repeats; Single-Nucleotide Polymorphisms; The National Missing and Unidentified Persons System (NamUs); **Forensic Medicine/Clinical:** Airplane Crashes and Other Mass Disasters; **Forensic Medicine/Pathology:** Autopsy.

Further Reading

Ballantyne, J., 1997. Mass disaster genetics. Nature Genetics 15, 329–331.

Biesecker, L.G., Bailey-Wilson, J.E., Ballantyne, J., et al., 2005. Epidemiology – DNA identifications after the 9/11 World Trade Center attack. Science 310, 1122–1123.

Bowers, C.M., 2004. Forensic Dental Evidence: An Investigator's Handbook. Elsevier, Amsterdam.

Brenner, C.H., 2006. Some mathematical problems in the DNA identification of victims in the 2004 tsunami and similar mass fatalities. Forensic Science International 157, 172–180.

Dolan, S.M., Saraiya, D.S., Donkervoort, S., Rogel, K., Lieber, C., Sozer, A., 2009. The emerging role of genetics professionals in forensic kinship DNA identification after a mass fatality: lessons learned from Hurricane Katrina volunteers. Genetics in Medicine 11, 414–417.

Donkervoort, S., Dolan, S.M., Beckwith, M., Northrup, T.P., Sozer, A., 2008. Enhancing accurate data collection in mass fatality kinship identifications: lessons learned from Hurricane Katrina. Forensic Science International. Genetics 2, 354–362.

Huffine, E., Crews, J., Kennedy, B., Bomberger, K., Zinbo, A., 2001. Mass identification of persons missing from the break-up of the former Yugoslavia: structure, function, and role of the International Commission on Missing Persons. Croatian Medical Journal 42, 271–275.

International Committee of the Red Cross, 2004. The Missing and Their Families – Documents of Reference. ICRC, Geneva.

International Committee of the Red Cross, 2009. Missing People, DNA Analysis and Identification of Human Remains. ICRC, Geneva.

Interpol, 2009. Disaster Victim Identification Guide. Interpol, Lyon.

Keough, M.E., Simmons, T., Samuels, M., 2004. Missing persons in post-conflict settings: best practices for integrating psychosocial and scientific approaches. The Journal of the Royal Society for the Promotion of Health 124, 271–275.

Morgan, O.W., Sribanditmongkol, P., Perera, C., Sulasmi, Y., Van Alphen, D., Sondorp, E., 2006. Mass fatality management following the South Asian tsunami disaster: case studies in Thailand, Indonesia, and Sri Lanka. PLoS Medicine 3, e195.

National Institute of Justice, 2005. Lessons Learned from 9/11: DNA Identification in Mass Fatality Incidents. US Department of Justice, Washington, DC.

Prinz, M., Carracedo, A., Mayr, W.R., et al., 2007. DNA Commission of the International Society for Forensic Genetics (ISFG): recommendations regarding the role of forensic genetics for disaster victim identification (DVI). Forensic Science International. Genetics 1, 3–12.

Schuller-Gotzburg, P., Suchanek, J., 2007. Forensic odontologists successfully identify tsunami victims in Phuket, Thailand. Forensic Science International 171, 204–207.

Ubelaker, D.H., Jacobs, C., 1995. Identification of orthopedic device manufacturer. Journal of Forensic Sciences 40, 168–170.

Airplane Crashes and Other Mass Disasters

O Peschel, Institut für Rechtsmedizin, München, Germany
W Eisenmenger

Glossary

Identification Process of assigning a preexisting individual's identity and name of a corpse by different means of forensic sciences.

Mass disaster Man-made or natural incident with more fatalities than the local resources can handle; some sources declare incidents involving more than 100 victims as a mass disaster.

Definition

Generally, a mass fatality is described as a man-made or natural incident with more fatalities than the local resources can handle. As important infrastructures such as rescue and treatment services may be damaged, a certain dependency on the character and locality of the incident is obvious. Events of the last decade show the great variety of scenarios influencing the possibilities and requirements for forensic pathology:

- 2000 Cable car disaster—Kaprun, Austria—155 victims
- 2001 World Trade Center—USA—3000 victims
- 2002 Refugee—Ferry Le Joola—Gambia—1863 victims
- 2003 Gas mine explosion—Chuandongbei—191 victims
- 2004 Tsunami—Thailand and Indonesia—230 000 victims estimated
- 2005 Train crash—Amagasaki, Japan—107 victims
- 2006 Car ferry—Dhiba, Saudi Arabia—1026 victims
- 2007 Bomb attack—Bhutto's parade, Pakistan—135 victims
- 2008 Plane crash-Spanair—Madrid, Spain—154 victims
- 2009 Air France Flight 447—Rio de Janeiro to Paris, Brazil—228 victims
- 2010 Earthquake—Haiti—200 000 victims estimated
- 2011 Tsunami and reactor disaster—Fukushima, Japan—20 000 victims

The identification of the victims is the main objective of forensic efforts related to mass disasters. Criminalistic reconstruction is very important too, but the consequences of missing identifications seem to be greater for the bereaved than the lack of information concerning the reason of the incident. Knight describes some reasons for identification efforts:

- Ethical and humanitarian need to know which individual has died, especially for the information of surviving relatives.
- To establish the fact of death with respect to particular individuals for official, statistical, and legal purposes.

- To record their identity for administrative and ceremonial purposes with respect to burial or cremation.
- To discharge legal claims and obligations in relation to property, estate, and debts.
- To prove claims for life insurance contracts, survivor's pensions, and other financial matters.
- To allow legal investigations, inquests, and other tribunals, such as those held by coroners, procurators fiscal, medical examiners, judges, and accident inquiries to proceed with accurate information about the identity of the decedent.
- To facilitate police inquiries into overtly criminal or suspicious deaths, as the identity of the deceased person could be a vital factor for investigations.

Comparable to the great variability of the different scenarios listed earlier, there are great differences in the ways of handling identification problems. Information concerning all forensic efforts are not regularly published in the forensic literature or in political statements. Full autopsies were performed in the Kaprun cable car disaster (156 victims) (**Figures 1 and 2**) but not in the Eschede train disaster in 1998 that claimed 101 victims. Identification in these incidents was mainly based on molecular genetic investigations. The tsunami in Thailand in 2004 resulted in ~230 000 victims. Only a very small part of the fatalities was handled according to the Interpol identification recommendations (predominantly European victims in the main tourist areas). The major part of the German victims was identified by forensic odontology. Due to severe decomposition of the dead bodies, molecular genetic methods played a secondary role. A completely different situation was encountered in the World Trade Center terrorist attack in which identification without DNA-based methods was inconceivable. The airplane accident involving the Air France Flight in 2007 resulted in a majority of missing person cases with a few victims recovered some years

Figure 1   Obsequies, Kaprun disaster, Austria, 2000. Prof. Dr E. Tutsch-Bauer, Department of Forensic Medicine, Salzburg University.

Figure 2   Scene before recovery of the bodies, Kaprun disaster, Austria, 2000. Prof. Dr E. Tutsch-Bauer, Department of Forensic Medicine, Salzburg University.

later. As for the Haiti earthquake in 2010, which claimed ~200 000 lives, no information regarding a global identification effort has been reported. The identification procedures after the Fukushima disaster have also been awkward to handle, published forensic measures being very scarce.

In general, it can be ascertained that a high number of victims in a less developed area results in a lack of forensic identification activities. Contrary to this, a smaller number of victims (particularly from regions in Europe, the United States, or other highly industrialized states) in an incident happening in a highly developed area, leads to intensive forensic procedures executed over a long period of time (more than 1 year in the Thailand tsunami tourist areas).

Usually, forensic pathologists are embedded in disaster victim identification (DVI) teams, which have been constituted in most countries and which consist of a number of different specialists to cover the majority of possible situations. DVI teams have been established following different problems in the identification of mass disaster victims in the 1960s and 1970s. They are mostly governmental organizations, but recently, private companies have also begun to offer comparable services.

After an incident, the initial chaotic phase is usually followed by organization and acquisition of responsibilities by the different departments in charge. Typically, the police is the leading authority, but cooperation with experts in different fields is also sought. Incident management implies the establishment of command structures, emergency systems, law enforcement operations, family assistance, media operations, and logistical support, as well as financial and administrative support. A competent incident management requires experience and authority. The forensic pathologist can be a valuable advisor concerning all decisions belonging to the recovery and identification procedures.

The complexity and character of the operations depend necessarily on the specific situation and mainly on the estimated number of fatalities and the condition of the bodies. Also, responder protection has to be considered according to the individual nature of the incident.

Airplane crashes and major fires may be the most frequently emerging problems for the forensic pathologist in this field. In crashes involving light planes, the number of bodies is small and the identification procedure is that much easier. In crashes involving big commercial aircraft, especially in collisions occurring at a flying altitude of more than 30 000 ft (9000 m), grave problems can be expected with the number of dismembered bodies being high. DNA analysis will play a decisive role in these incidents.

In all kinds of accidents involving means of transportation, investigations concerning evidence of explosion should be carried out.

In all kinds of accidents involving means of transportation, investigations concerning evidence for explosion should be made. Nowadays, the first question is the differentiation between an accident due to a technical defect (possibly resulting in civil action) and a terrorist attack. Also, the examination of victims, for example, for evidence of fire or bomb residue, may prove helpful.

Besides the passengers, there is a special interest concerning the pilot or the train driver. These victims require a full autopsy with a screening for diseases, signs of intoxication, or trauma not related to death. All cases in which a mistake on the part of the personnel is discussed as the reason for the crash, a detailed

knowledge of any impairment of health is essential for all further deliberations. Prior to this, of course, is the identification of the pilot or other staff members from individual criteria and personal effects (dress code). Also, special injury patterns such as severe hand or foot injuries in a pilot may be helpful for identification; however, with the modern technology in airplanes, this kind of injury-dependent identification has lost its relevance in most cases.

Very important are all kinds of natural disease which may lead to an individual mistake as a reason for an accident: predominantly all kinds of heart disease, especially typical coronary atherosclerosis leading to a myocardial infarction, but also neuromuscular diseases or hypoxic changes in the central nervous system leading possibly to unconsciousness are to be discussed. Another aspect may be an impairment of a pilot due to alcohol consumption or intoxication with legal or illegal drugs. For this reason, analysis of blood alcohol concentration and toxicology are indispensable in all investigations concerning airplane crashes or train accidents.

Eisenmenger reported one case of a helicopter crash, in which the pilot was found intoxicated with a blood alcohol content of 2.3 g%. There were also reports on airplane crashes where the pilot was found with a lethal gunshot injury or a stab wound, obviously having been killed by one of the passengers in the context of a homicide–suicide event.

Tasks

The main tasks involving activities of forensic pathologists are the following:

- Recovery of the bodies at the scene.
- DVI.
- Assistance in criminalistic incident reconstruction.

Recovery of the Bodies at the Scene

In the scenario of a mass disaster, the forensic pathologist is an auxiliary force working in line with the police after rescue operations have been terminated. The recovery of the bodies from the scene is an important step in successful catastrophe management. Not only in airplane crashes but also in other mass incidents, severe fragmentation of the bodies may be one of the main problems. The forensic pathologist's opinion and an anatomic classification of the body fragments, as well as the differentiation between human and animal tissue, will be helpful. This applies accordingly to exhumations from mass graves and major fire accidents. A compartmentation of the scene in different sectors with the establishment of a grid system is usually a police exercise. The same applies to the documentation of bodies or body fragments, concerning the place of discovery and personal effects.

Tags should be applied to the bodies or body bags to ensure a continuous flow of the case file. The body has to pass through the different morgue stations (see below), and all the data have to be documented and compared afterward. Up to the final report and the release of the body, the case file and the identification form have to be signed by the leading police officer, the authorized forensic pathologist, and dentist.

Disaster Victim Identification

Identification is the main task of the forensic pathologist. The necessity for identification results from different laws. Inheritance is usually connected to the declaration of death of a person. The same applies to the payment from insurance companies, the possibility of a new marriage, and so on. Identification may result from different measures and is basically a duty of the police. One possibility often used in countries without a functioning forensic system is the ascertainment of identity by inspection of human remains by means of visual recognition. Also, a comparison with photographs is sometimes used for identification. In case of severe traumatic damage or decomposition of the bodies, this procedure is not feasible. However, even in cases with well-preserved bodies, erroneous identification has been reported, obviously very difficult situation for relatives or loved ones. For this reason, other methods for identification must be preferred.

Personal effects

Personal effects are items from victims' pockets, clothing, ID papers, or jewelry. The value for identification usually is limited to single items with an outstanding individual character. A certain commingling of all these items may happen due to events prior to the incident as well as by the catastrophe itself. However, important is also the return of personal items to the relatives and families of the victims. Special police units usually arrange for recovery, processing, and handing over of personal effects. In the Kosovo Identification Project, individual clothing was the main factor for identification success.

Fingerprinting

Fingerprints are very useful for identification as well as footprints and palm prints. Fingerprint experts are a part of all DVI teams. If possible, all opportunities should be taken to get fingerprint evidence processed by forensic experts belonging to the police. Finger, foot, and palm prints can be compared with prints taken from the assumed person's home or objects, which can be assigned to a certain person. Sometimes, this can be difficult and the assignment may be doubtful. Comparative prints may be missing (e.g., in a plane crash in a residential zone; after destruction of the accommodations, it will usually be impossible to get comparative prints). In some countries, fingerprints are part of identity papers. Sometimes, a police investigation with a documentation of fingerprints years ago

can be helpful. Nowadays, computer processing of all the evidence is possible, facilitating comparison in cases with large numbers of individuals.

Fingerprinting becomes less important in cases of severe fragmentation of the bodies or in major fires. Amputation of fingers or hands for fingerprint or palm processing at the fingerprint station as was commonly recommended in the past should be avoided because commingling is possible afterward and control of the results becomes more difficult.

Autopsy

Depending on the local factors, setting up of a temporary morgue might be necessary. Additional resources (staff, equipment, etc.) are required to perform autopsies, but the results of a forensic autopsy are essential for a complete identification procedure and for control purposes. The autopsy may be limited to special findings or procedures according to the condition of the bodies and the needs of identification. The main findings are related to gender, age estimation, body height, race, and individual markers such as tattoos, scars, results of a medical treatment, or malformations.

Gender determination: Depending on the condition of the bodies, primary or secondary sex organs may be detectable; body hair may be shaved; for skeletonized individuals, molecular genetics is an option.

Age estimation: Will cover only the biological age, not the actual age. Degenerative changes in the ankles or the spine may help as well as the degree of atherosclerosis and abrasion in the dental state.

Race: Determination of race will be impossible in cases of major fire and severe decomposition. Comparable effects occurred after the Southeast Asian tsunami in 2004 within a few days so that a differentiation between the local Asian people and Caucasian tourists was not possible any more.

Body constitution and nutritional status: May be difficult or impossible to assess in cases of fragmentation, burn injuries, and decomposition.

The report of the forensic pathologist should (if possible or determinable) contain the following information: body number, condition of the body, weight of the remains, missing body parts, gender, height, diagram of injury pattern, foreign bodies, hair color and length, eye color, scars and tattoos, birthmarks or other typical features, operations and prostheses, diseases, and X-rays or photographs of important findings.

The value of the findings depends on the condition of the body and the number of individuals who have to be identified. In cases of severe decomposition, fragmentation, or mass grave exhumation, the help of a forensic anthropologist is necessary. If the victims are skeletonized, special discriminant analyses can be helpful even if they are very complex. Prostheses and implants, as well as artificial lenses, radiological seeds, or pacemakers may offer a quick, simple, and safe means of identification of single individuals. An autopsy also offer the possibility to retain body fluids for further investigations (DNA, alcohol, toxicology) and to find some evidence concerning the cause of death or items such as projectiles, bomb fragments, or other injuries important for the criminalistic reconstruction. Interpol forms for antemortem and post-mortem investigations offer the possibility for an exhaustive data collection and a safe comparison of the findings even when supported by computer technology. However, in a number of mass disasters, only a small portion of the individual parameters can be collected as the Interpol forms require. In this situation, priorities have to be established.

In general, two possible ways can be discussed for identification: The first one is a systematic comparison between all antemortem and postmortem data, after all the operations have been completed. The second one is the selective identification and release of single bodies in a good condition with characteristic identity features and a stepwise narrowing of the group of unknown individuals. Additionally, a classification in different age groups or concerning gender may be helpful. In incidents involving a large number of victims and cooperation between DVI teams of different nationalities, a systematic approach is mandatory.

Forensic odontology

DVI requires support of experienced forensic odontologists. Teeth are very resistant concerning physical influences. Especially in cases of severe decomposition or major fire, pathological findings or DNA may be difficult, even impossible, to assess. In a large number of cases, therefore, forensic odontology has been a key to successful identification. However, with the growing number of individuals and the higher quality of dental care, the number of individuals without individualizing findings will become the norm. Finally, in children, a precise estimation of age will be possible by evaluating the dental state; however, typical findings for individualization such as inlays with different materials, crowns, or prostheses will be missing. Perhaps signs of an orthodontic treatment may be helpful.

In conclusion, DVI without forensic odontology is hardly conceivable. Odontology exclusively in scenarios with a high number of victims will miss a lot of important findings.

Radiology

The comparison of radiographs can be a very effective means for identification. However, a quick acquisition of X-rays for comparisons may be difficult. Also, the path of rays has to be comparable in standard pictures. The application of CT technology is possible, but very expensive and not feasible in all conditions. Interpretation of CT scans for identification purposes need an expert in forensic radiology and cannot be done by a clinical radiologist. X-rays of the skull (frontal sinus), fractures, prostheses, and malformations are applicable for comparisons. Dental radiography has a special relevance in identification.

Molecular genetics

DNA fingerprinting is the most important development in forensics during the last 25 years. The benefit of DNA technologies for identification is very high since international agreements made investigations and results comparable. Advantages are the high degree of safety concerning distinction between different individuals and the possibility to identify even very small portions of tissue in cases of extreme fragmentation of bodies. Familial relationships can be detected and complete families can be assigned (however, sometimes, a familial relationship is assumed before the incident, which is, in actual fact, missing—problem of the cuckoo's child). The disadvantages are that it is a time-consuming process compared with forensic odontology and involves the impairment of the results by decomposition and degradation of DNA. Also, for DNA analysis, the comparison samples may be difficult to attend. Furthermore, the DNA analysis usually cannot be carried out in the morgue and needs special laboratories. The success of DNA techniques is not always guaranteed as experiences in the Thailand tsunami disaster demonstrated. However in DNA results, computer technology makes the data processing easier.

Forensic anthropology

The forensic anthropologist can be helpful in distinguishing human remains from nonhuman remains and in determining the gender, age, race of the victims, and the number of fatalities. Also an experienced anthropologist can easily detect certain abnormalities or individualizing traits in skeletal elements. Sometimes, additional X-ray investigations may be necessary.

Criminalistic Reconstruction

Cause and time of death investigation may belong to the data needed for a criminalistic reconstruction as well as miscellaneous findings like foreign bodies with evidence for an explosion or toxicological analysis. Carbon monoxide may give evidence that a person was alive when a fire was set. In incidents resulting from toxic agents, special analysis may be helpful in the therapy of survivors if there is a lack of information concerning the toxic substance or even a specific misinformation, as was reported in the Bhopal incident in 1984—an estimation of between 4000 and 25 000 victims.

In conclusion, victim identification after a mass disaster is an important task for police forces and all forensic, medical, and biological experts and normally a basic necessity from the ethical point of view. Cooperation between the different forensic disciplines with varying focuses concerning the type of incident will be the base of success.

See also: **Biology/DNA:** Disaster Victim Identification; **Forensic Medicine/Clinical:** Traffic Injuries and Deaths.

Further Reading

Blau, S., Robertson, S., Johnstone, M., 2008. Disaster victim identification: new applications for postmortem computed tomography. Journal of Forensic Sciences 53 (4), 956–961.

Brkic, H., Strinov, D., Kubat, M., Petrovecki, V., 2000. Odontological identification of human remains from mass graves in Croatia. International Journal of Legal Medicine 114, 19–22.

Budimlijy, Z.M., Prinz, M.K., Zelson-Mundorff, A., et al., 2003. World Trade Center human identification project: experiences with individual body identification cases. Croatian Medical Journal 44, 259–263.

Budowle, B., Bieber, F.R., Eisenberg, A.J., 2005. Forensic aspects of mass disasters: strategic considerations for DNA-based human identification. Legal Medicine 7, 230–243.

Dedouit, F., Temon, N., Costagiola, R., et al., 2007. New identification possibilities with postmortem multislice computed tomography. International Journal of Legal Medicine 121, 507–510.

DiMaio, V.J., DiMajo, D., 2001. Forensic Pathology, second ed. CRC Press, Boca Raton/London/New York/Washington.

Eisenmenger, W., 2004. Massenkatastrophen. In: Brinkmann, B., Madea, B. (Eds.), Handbuch Rechtsmedizin. Springer-Verlag, Berlin/Heidelberg/New York.

Fullerton, C.S., Ursano, R.J., Wang, L., 2004. Acute stress disorder, posttraumatic stress disorder and depression in disaster or rescue workers. American Journal of Psychiatry 161 (8), 1370–1376.

Jensen, R.A., 2000. Mass Fatality and Casualty Incidents: A Field Guide. CRC Press, Boca Raton, FL.

Knight, B., 1996. Forensic Pathology, second ed. Arnold, London/Sydney/Auckland.

Leclair, B., Shaler, R., Carmody, G.R., et al., 2007. Bioinformatics and human identification in mass fatality incidents: the world trade center disaster. Journal of Forensic Sciences 52, 806–819.

Meyer, H.J., 2003. The Kaprun cable car fire disaster – aspects of forensic organisation following a mass fatality with 155 victims. Forensic Science International 138 (1), 1–7.

Meyer, H.J., Chansue, N., Monticelli, F., 2006. Implantation of radio frequency identification device (RFID) microchip in disaster victim identification (DVI). Forensic Science International 157, 168–171.

Moody, G.H., Busuttil, A., 1994. Identification in the Lockerbie air disaster. American Journal of Forensic Medicine and Pathology 15 (1), 63–69.

Peschel, O., Eisenmenger, W., 2010. Rechtsmedizinische Aspekte bei Großschadensereignissen. In: Schutzkommission beim Bundesministerium des Inneren. Katastrophenmedizin, Bonn.

Peschel, O., Lessig, R., Grundmann, C., Peter, J., Tsokos, M., 2005. Tsunami 2004. Rechtsmedizinische Erfahrungen aus dem Einsatz der Identifizierungskommission in den ersten Tagen in Thailand. Rechtsmedizin 15, 430–437.

Peschel, O., Müller, E., 2003. Beweissicherung und Identifizierung. Bericht über den Einsatz von Rechtsmedizinern im Kosovo 1999. Rechtsmedizin 13, 194–200.

Prinz, M., Carracedo, A., Mayr, W.R., et al., 2007. DNA Commission of the International Society for Forensic Genetics (ISFG): recommendations regarding the role of forensic genetics for disaster victim identification (DVI). Forensic Science International: Genetics 1, 3–12.

Rutty, G., Robinson, C., Morgan, B., Black, S., Adams, C., Webster, P., 2009. Fimag: the United Kingdom disaster victim/forensic identification imaging system. Journal of Forensic Sciences 54 (6), 1438–1442.

Schuller-Götzburg, P., Suchanek, J., 2007. Forensic odontologists successfully identify tsunami victims in Phuket, Thailand. Forensic Science International 171, 204–207.

Soomer, H., Ranta, H., Penttila, A., 2001. Identification of victims from the M/S Estonia. International Journal of Legal Medicine 114, 259–262.

Stevens, P.J., 1970. Fatal Civil Aircraft Accidents. Wright, Bristol.

Tsokos, M., Lessig, R., Grundmann, C., Benthaus, S., Peschel, O., 2006. Experiences in tsunami victim identification. International Journal of Legal Medicine 120, 185–187.

Key Terms

3D techniques, Adolescent, Adult, Age, Age estimation, Airplane crash, Biological profile, Body-height determination, Child, Comparative radiography, Comparison analysis, Comparison photo, Criminalistic reconstruction, Disaster victim identification, DNA, Estimate, Facial features, Feature analysis, Fingerprint analysis, Fingerprints, Forensic anthropology, Forensic dentistry, Forensic odontology, Forensic pathology, Forensic radiology, Gait analysis, Identification, Identity, Mass disaster, Medicolegal investigation, Missing persons, Multiple corresponding factors, Personal identification, Positive identification, Probability of identification, Radiography, Recovery of bodies, Reference photo, Scientific identification, Short tandem repeats, Skull–photo superimposition, Surgical implants, Surveillance photo, Surveillance video, X-ray.

Review Questions

1. Why is personal identity such an important issue for forensic pathology?
2. How accurate does a personal identity need to be? Why?
3. Why is the real frequency of unidentified decedents likely to be higher than what is reported?
4. Why is estimating a decedent's age of importance?
5. What is the most accurate method for age estimation?
6. Which areas of the body are best for estimating the age of a child?
7. How many points of similarity are necessary to reach a conclusion of identification?
8. Why are decomposed remains difficult to radiograph for comparison purposes?
9. What kind of radiographs are used for identification?
10. What are the three conclusions that can be drawn when attempting an identification?
11. How does identification of the living differ from identification of the dead?
12. What kinds of characteristics are used to identify the living?
13. What is feature analysis?

14. What is the estimate of unidentified human remains in the United States?
15. What percentage of US medical examiners have *no* policy on handling unidentified remains?
16. What is NamUs?
17. What does DVI stand for?
18. Why is time of the essence when identifying remains from a mass disaster?
19. What policies must be in place before starting the process of DVI?
20. What is the preferred order of methods for identifying mass disaster victims? Is there a single approach?

Discussion Questions

1. What is the best way to identify a body? Think about the logistical, cultural, and legal implications before you answer—it could be an airplane crash on a remote mountainside, a bombing in a large city, or a single person found in a field.
2. Given the implications of child exploitation (abuse, pornography), why is estimating a child's age so important? How can one be sure of the age of a child in a photo? Of a deceased child? How can a forensic pathologist assist in these matters?
3. Is a forensic pathologist an appropriate expert to make a determination of identity? If so, in what contexts?
4. How does context—location and scene circumstances—affect the modes and confidence of identification?
5. Why would NamUs be publicly searchable? If anyone could search for one of your missing relatives or friends, doesn't this violate the Health Insurance Portability and Accountability Act (HIPPA, www.hhs.gov/hipaa/)? Explain why it does or does not.

Additional Readings

Kaneko, Y., Ohira, H., Tsuda, Y., Yamada, Y., 2015. Comparison of hard tissues that are useful for DNA analysis in forensic autopsy. Legal Medicine 17 (6), 547–552.

Sharma, G., Nagpal, A., 2015. Mass disaster: will dental records be effectively useful in developing nations? Journal of Forensic Science and Medicine 1 (1), 72.

Wright, K., Mundorff, A., Chaseling, J., Forrest, A., Maguire, C., Crane, D.I., 2015. A new disaster victim identification management strategy targeting "near identification-threshold" cases: experiences from the Boxing Day tsunami. Forensic Science International 250, 91–97.

Section 7. Professional Issues

Forensic pathology has been a recognized profession perhaps longer than any other forensic discipline. Anchored in the medical profession, forensic pathology relies not only on the ethics and codes of conduct for that area of expertise but must also adhere to professional expectations in the criminal justice arena, like for expert testimony. The health and safety concerns for forensic pathologists and technicians are also rooted in the nonforensic medical arena but have additional considerations revolving around working with the dead and decomposing. As a "watcher of watchers," the forensic pathologist must also be concerned with important criminal justice issues, like deaths in custody, and social phenomena, like suicide, both of which are fundamental concerns for a society based on a rule of law.

Crime Scene to Court

K Ramsey and E Burton, Greater Manchester Police Forensic Services Branch, Manchester, United Kingdom

Glossary

CBRN Chemical, biological, radiation, and nuclear incidents.
CCTV Closed circuit television (evidence from cameras).
CPD Continuous Professional Development.
CPS Crown Prosecution Service (UK).
HTCU Hi-tech crime unit (examination of hardware/software/data/images from any system or device).
L2 Level 2 investigations, specific skills required for, e.g., covert operations, deployment and substitution of items, forensic markers.
LCH Local clearing house (firearms).
NaBIS National Ballistic Intelligence Service (UK).

NCA National Crime Agency (UK).
NOS National Occupational Standards.
T1/2/3 CSI Skill tiers defined for crime scene investigation officers, with 1 being the most basic level of training (usually volume crime offenses only); 2 being the range of volume, serious and major crime investigations; and 3 being trained in crime scene management/the coordination of complex investigations.
VSC/ESDA Video spectral comparison—the analysis of inks, primarily in fraudulent documents; electro static detection analysis—the examination of (writing) indentations on paper.

Introduction

A multitude of disciplines evolved within forensic science during the twentieth century, resulting in highly specialized fields of evidential opportunities to support criminal investigations. Many of the more traditional disciplines, for example, footwear analysis and blood pattern interpretation, now have well-established principles and methodologies that have been proven in a criminal justice context; developments in these areas are largely confined to technical support systems and information sharing through databases. The very rapid rate of development of DNA profiling techniques during the 1980s and 1990s led to the emergence of national and international DNA databases; however, the pace of change has now significantly reduced. Conversely, the end of the twentieth century and the early part of the twenty-first century have seen an explosion of new forensic evidence types that are less established in court—disciplines such as CCTV, mobile phone, computer analysis, and the use of digital images and social media are collectively referred to as e-forensics.

Owing to the highly specialized nature of each forensic discipline and the varied rate of evolution, forensic science effectively represents a composite of interrelated, and often distinct, opportunities to support criminal investigations.

Most current models of forensic service delivery, especially where part of a wider organization, for example, police forces and enforcement agencies, have arisen over time by bolting on additional elements and clustering together within related fields. If the current capability of forensic science were to be designed from scratch as an effective entity, it is certain that a more integrated, and hence effective, structure would be proposed.

In addition, there has been a professionalization of forensic science in the workplace and increasing requirements for regulation; as recently as the 1980s, crime scene investigation, for example, was widely undertaken by police officers and was largely restricted to recording/recovering visible evidence; this was used in a limited capacity to support that particular investigation without scope for wider intelligence development. Now, crime scene investigation is predominantly undertaken by specialist staff employed to exclusively undertake these duties.

To practise in a forensic discipline, specialized training, qualifications, and competency levels are required. The range of evidence types that have potential to support investigations has widened considerably. Some disciplines lend themselves to cross-skilling.

Public expectations of what forensic science can deliver have been heightened by highly popular mainstream television programs, both documentary and fictional. Often, the expectation of what can be delivered exceeds what is either possible or financially sensible. This leads to a requirement on service providers and users to make informed (evidential and financial) decisions regarding the best use of forensic evidence in support of investigations.

This chapter considers options to optimize the use of forensic evidence types recovered from crime scenes in the context of the different models available to criminal justice systems; the concept of integrated case management is outlined and discussed.

Task

To bring together all potential forensic evidential opportunities, holistically review their significance to the investigation, prioritize the progression of work, deliver the best evidence to the court for testing (complying with all continuity, integrity, and quality requirements), and ensure the best value for money when determining spend on forensic evidence.

Internationally, there are variable constraints and opportunities due both to the different criminal justice models and the commercial market situation at state/regional and country levels.

Models

1. All forensic evidence sourced within a law enforcement agency, for example, a police laboratory.
2. All forensic evidence provided by external specialists contracted to a law enforcement agency.
3. Composite of (1) and (2).

Forensic Strategies

The recovery of evidence from the crime scene is only the start of the forensic process. Once the evidence has been collected, packaged, and preserved, it needs to be analyzed in order to provide meaningful information to the investigation and subsequently the courts.

Forensic examinations are carried out in order to implicate or eliminate individuals and also in order to establish what has occurred during the commission of an offense or incident.

Deciding what analysis is required can be a complex process. Some of the issues for consideration include the following:

- Is it necessary to examine all the evidence that is recovered?
- Should every possible test be carried out?

In an ideal world, it would be preferable to carry out every possible analysis; however, in reality, it is likely that this will be neither practicable nor financially viable. In addition, carrying out every possible analysis would overload forensic laboratories.

When making decisions about what forensic analysis should be carried out, it is vitally important that consideration is given to both the potential prosecution and defense cases. An impartial approach must be taken to assessing examination requirements. It is often not necessary to carry out an examination of every item of evidence recovered, but examinations should be directed to where value could potentially be added to an investigation.

A forensic strategy should be developed around every case where forensic evidence plays a part, and may relate to an overall case or to an individual item of evidence. A forensic strategy should be developed in a holistic manner taking into account all potential evidence types and should direct and coordinate the forensic examinations/analyses that are required.

Forensic strategies can be developed in different ways by one or more of the following:

- Investigating officer
- Crime scene investigator (CSI) or crime scene manager
- Forensic scientist/forensic specialist
- Forensic submissions officer (forensic submissions officer is a role that can be variably named; this role relates to an informed individual within a police force or law enforcement agency who uses knowledge and expertise to advise on forensic analysis and who has decision-making authority

and control of the budgetary spend. May also be known as forensic advisor, scientific support manager, etc.)
● Legal representative
● Pathologist

Forensic strategies are generally initially developed and applied by individuals involved in the prosecution aspects of a crime. Although this is the case, it is vitally important that a balanced and unbiased approach is taken to the development of a strategy and consideration given to information that may support the defense case as well as the prosecution case. Examinations that are likely to add value or provide information to an investigation (irrespective of whether it will support or weaken the prosecution case) should be carried out and all results must be disclosed to the defense team. Defense should also be given the opportunity to carry out any review of strategies, examination processes, and/or results that they require and be provided with access to any items of evidence that they want to examine themselves in order to build the defense case.

In order to develop the forensic strategy and make appropriate decisions about which forensic examinations will be of value to the investigation, the following are necessary:

● To be able to gather as much information as possible about the circumstances of the case
  ● circumstances of evidence recovery
  ● accounts given by victim(s), witnesses, suspect(s), etc.
● To have an understanding and knowledge of forensic science and its application to investigations

A forensic strategy meeting is a useful way of ensuring that all relevant parties are aware of the full circumstances of the case and enables a "multiagency" discussion about the processing of all exhibits to optimize evidential potential in a comprehensive and coordinated manner.

It can often be the case that police officers do not have a full understanding or knowledge of forensic science, likewise forensic scientists historically have had a relatively poor understanding of police and investigative processes; this can lead to miscommunication and confusion in relation to the application of forensic science to meet investigative needs. A joint approach to the development of forensic strategies helps to improve the communication and understanding on a case-by-case basis.

A formal forensic strategy meeting is often required only in more serious cases; however, the general approach can be applied to any investigation. Even in the most simple of cases, it is often beneficial for discussions to take place between the investigating officer, the CSI, the forensic advisor/budget holder/decision maker, and the prosecutor. Alternatively, generic strategies can be implemented, for example, for a particular crime type or *modus operandi*.

When making an assessment regarding the potential examination of a particular item and the development of a forensic strategy, the requirements of the investigation are the primary concern and consideration should be given to the following issues:

● The type and nature of the item/exhibit
● The context of the item
  ● Exactly where and when it was recovered
  ● Condition of the item, that is, wet, damaged, etc.
● The integrity of the item
  ● Has it been appropriately recovered, handled, packaged, and preserved?
  ● Is the security and continuity of the item intact?
● The potential evidence that may be obtained from the item, for example, DNA, fingerprints, fibers, footwear marks
● The information these evidence types may provide to the investigation
● Whether this potential information is likely to add value to the investigation
  ● Is it possible that new information will be provided?
  ● Is it possible that an account given by a witness, victim, or suspect will be supported or refuted?
  ● Will the information help to establish what has occurred?
● Whether there is a conflict between potential evidence types, and if so, which evidence type will be of most value under the circumstances
  ● For example, swabbing/taping for DNA may damage fingerprints, but where the DNA is likely to be at low levels and requires specialized low-template DNA analysis, the presence of DNA may not necessarily prove contact with an item, whereas fingerprints will always prove that contact has occurred
● The chances of success, that is, obtaining a result/information of value to the investigation (this may be inclusive or exclusive)

Much work has historically been completed in relation to developing and understanding the success rates relating to DNA profiling; however, relatively little work has been undertaken to fully understand the success rates associated with other forensic evidence. This is largely due to the fact that other evidence types, such as fibers, gunshot residue, footwear marks, etc. are generally more complex to interpret than DNA. In relation to DNA profiling, success rates are generally based on the chances of obtaining a DNA profile; however, with the other evidence types, the value of the outcome is very much dependent on the circumstances of the investigation. For example, when searching an item of clothing taken from a suspect for glass, the absence of glass or the presence of glass could both be of value to the investigation depending on the circumstances. The presence of glass on the clothing that matches control sample(s) from the crime scene is only of value if its presence cannot be accounted for in any legitimate way; conversely, the absence of glass on the item of clothing may lead to a conclusion that the suspect was not involved in the offense, depending on the circumstances of the offense and arrest.

In addition to being able to understand and evaluate the chances of being able to obtain a meaningful result, it is also vital that the value of the overall contribution to the entire case is understood. This involves being able to understand the value and contribution of the forensic examination to the detection of the offense as well as the outcome of the court process. This is an even more difficult issue to evaluate and understand than the chances of being able to obtain a forensic test result.

Because the value of forensic evidence is so dependent on the individual case circumstances, decisions about examinations must be made on an individual case basis. There have been recent developments in some agencies/forces to better understand the chances of success of different types of forensic evidence and the value to investigations; this will help to better

inform decisions about evidential potential and examination viability as well as assisting to achieve value for money. This approach is best described as *forensic effectiveness*.

The forensic strategy should also take into account the timescales associated with the investigative process and the criminal justice system, and it should be ensured that forensic analysis can meet the requirements of the criminal justice process, including court dates and any requirements to disclose appropriate information to the defense team(s).

Each police force/law enforcement agency will have its own approach to the submission of exhibits for forensic examination/analysis; irrespective of whether the analysis is carried out in an internal police laboratory, external commercial company, or government owned laboratory, these approaches can be applied to all examinations and all evidence types.

These approaches help to ensure that decisions are made based on scientific knowledge, viability, and evidential value

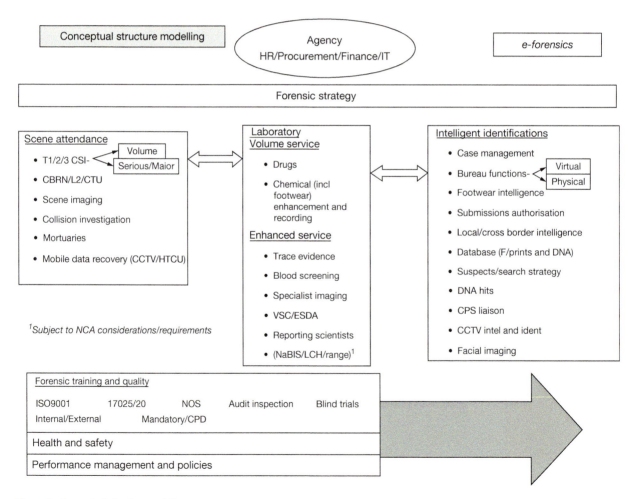

Figure 1 Conceptual structure modeling.

taking into account all aspects of the investigation. They will help to ensure that the best evidence is obtained while considering value for money and that it can be applied to any investigation irrespective of the seriousness of the offense or the scale of the investigation.

Integrated Case Management

The concept and use of forensic strategies in directing investigations is not new, but is often limited by the evolved structure of forensic disciplines within investigative agencies. Classically, DNA and fingerprint evidence from volume crimes will be independently submitted at the same time by different routes, and this often results in wasted effort/spends and duplicated results. The development and use of forensic intelligence has been variable. Emerging thinking includes organizational redesign of forensics to better integrate with related functions such as intelligence collection, targeted deployment of resources, and prioritized forensic submissions.

The concept of integrated case management draws together informed operational deployment (e.g., of crime scene investigators) followed by a more holistic approach to submissions for testing. The strategy takes greater account of supporting intelligence and desired outcomes. Regular reviews and trigger points are included for the staged submission of potential evidence, and communication with investigators is enhanced so allowing for a more responsive and directed investigation.

Ultimately, the production of *intelligent identifications* can be better achieved by having an integrated process that links the enforcement priorities, available resources, potential forensic evidence, intelligence, and prosecutor requirements; this model provides flexibility to respond to changing demands and gives an increased likelihood of efficient and effective spend on forensic support to investigations. There is no single way to achieve this, but an illustration of how to rethink some of the traditional silo-based forensic disciplines is provided in **Figure 1**.

Summary

The single biggest challenge to the forensic science community during the twenty-first century is to modernize delivery of integrated services in support of investigations. This must:

- build on the previous development of each discipline;
- accommodate the new and emerging technological disciplines;
- meet the regulatory requirements;
- reflect the changing workforce and skills;
- deliver the best evidence to courts in support of investigations.

> *See also:* **Foundations:** Forensic Intelligence; History of Forensic Sciences; Principles of Forensic Science.

Further Reading

Faigman, et al., 2006. Modern Scientific Evidence: The Law and Science of Expert Testimony.

Fisher, B.A.J., Fisher, D.R., 2012. Techniques of Crime Scene Investigation, eighth ed. CRC, Boca Raton, FL.

Houck, M., Crispino, F., McAdam, T., 2013. The Science of Crime Scenes. Elsevier.

Innocence Project, 2011. http://www.innocenceproject.org/Content/Facts_on_PostConviction_DNA_Exonerations.php (accessed 10.03.11.).

Kirk, P.L., 1974. In: Thornton, J.L. (Ed.), Crime Investigation, second ed. Wiley, New York. (1985 reprint edn. Krieger Publishing Company, Malabar, FL).

NAS, 2009. Strengthening Forensic Science in the United States: A Path Forward. NAS Report: Committee on Identifying the Needs of the Forensic Sciences Community. National Academies Press, Washington, DC.

White, P., 2010. Crime Scene to Court: The Essentials of Forensic Science. Royal Society of Chemistry, Cambridge, ISBN 978-1-84755-882-4.

Expert Witness Qualifications and Testimony

C Henderson, Stetson University College of Law, Gulfport, FL, USA
KW Lenz, Saint Petersburg, FL, USA

Introduction

The field of scientific interpretation of evidence and its portrayal in popular media has progressed to the point that expert testimony at trial is not only commonly accepted by judge and jury, but also expected. This chapter addresses the factors that influence the selection of an expert, including the importance of investigating the expert's credentials and making an informed assessment of the credibility that the expert's qualifications will project to a judge and jurors.

Although this chapter is written from a US perspective, many of the issues discussed here are applicable to expert witness testimony worldwide. This chapter will not, however, address the legal standards for the admissibility of expert testimony or attorneys' ethics in dealing with experts.

Selecting an Expert

Many variables should be considered in selecting an expert witness, including the expert's availability, cost, experience, and reputation. When an expert serves as a consultant or in the pretrial phases of litigation, the criteria for selecting that expert may be limited to the expert's competency in the field. As a trial witness, however, the expert's integrity, charisma, and overall effectiveness as a witness must also be considered.

Thus, consideration should be given not only to the expert's formal training but also to the expert's personality, demeanor, and capacity to organize, express, and interpret complex concepts for the jury. The weight accorded to the expert's opinion by the judge or jury will be determined in large part by the expert's perceived character, objectivity, and impartiality.

Of course, the quality of the expert's credentials remains an important factor to consider as well. A thorough evaluation of an expert should take into account matters such as (1) the membership requirements of the associations to which the expert belongs, (2) how the expert's credentials compare to those of the opposing expert, (3) whether the journals in which the expert's articles appear are held in high regard in the field, and (4) whether the conclusions in those articles were subject to peer review. Studies of jurors' perceptions of experts can be particularly helpful in guiding this evaluation.

Care should always be taken to verify the credentials of one's own expert, as well as those of an adversary's expert, for although it is unlikely that an expert has faked credentials, it has occurred. Indeed, experts have come under increased scrutiny in recent years for fabricating or inflating their qualifications.

Qualifications

The court must determine whether a proffered witness is qualified to testify as an expert, and that determination will not be overturned except for an abuse of discretion (*Kumho Tire Co. Ltd. v. Carmichael*); but see, for example, *Radlein v. Holiday Inns, Inc.* (holding that the trial court's decision will not be reversed unless there is a clear showing of error). Federal Rule of Evidence 702 states that a witness may qualify as an expert on the basis of knowledge, skill, training, experience, or education. An expert witness must possess only one of these traits for the judge to find the expert qualified to give an opinion. In making this evaluation, the judge may consider the expert's educational background, work experience, publications, awards, teaching, speaking, or other professional engagements, prior expert-witness testimony, and membership in professional associations.

Often, the expert may have to educate the attorney proffering the expert regarding the significance of particular experience, achievements, and certifications to ensure that they are appropriately presented to the judge. An expert must be prepared to explain board certification and licensure requirements to the judge in detail.

Experience as an Expert Witness

Experience and training are often more significant than academic background and are accorded more weight by jurors, according to at least one study evaluating juror perceptions of fingerprint experts. However, experience as an expert witness, standing alone, does not qualify someone as an expert in later cases. One court rejected the opinion of a witness who had testified as an expert 126 times (*Bogosian v. Mercedes-Benz of North America Inc.*). Another court noted that, "it would be absurd to conclude that one can become an expert by accumulating experience in testifying" (*Thomas J. Kline, Inc. v. Lonillard, Inc.*). Conversely, a lack of previous experience as an expert witness does not disqualify one from testifying as an expert, because "even the most qualified expert must have his first day in court" (*US v. Locascio*).

Education and Training

An expert may be qualified on the basis of academic credentials, including the expert's undergraduate, graduate, and postgraduate work. An expert's academic credentials should only be issued by accredited educational institutions and programs, because the proliferation of the Internet, while laudable for so many reasons, has also rekindled the old-fashioned diploma mill. One such business, Diplomas 4U, once provided bachelor's, master's, MBA, or PhD degrees in its customers' field of choice; advertisements assured that no one would be turned down and that there would be no bothersome tests, classes, books, or interviews. After studying this issue, the National Academy of Sciences has concluded that it is crucially important to improve undergraduate and graduate forensic science programs with, among other things, attractive scholarship and fellowship offerings and funding for research programs to attract research universities and students in fields relevant to forensic science.

An expert should continuously perform research and publish in the expert's field, preferably in peer-reviewed publications. Teaching experience is another of the qualifications that judges will evaluate: all forms of teaching—regular, specialty, guest lecturing, visiting professorships, continuing education, and short courses—weigh in as credentials. An expert should also be up to date with developments in his or her field of expertise by reading the current literature, enrolling in continuing education seminars, joining professional societies, and attending professional meetings.

Membership in Professional Associations

A study published by the US Department of Justice in 1987 found that jurors perceived those fingerprint experts who belonged to professional associations to be more credible than other experts, and presumed experts would belong to such groups (Illsley, *supra*). It is therefore important for an expert to remain active and participate in professional societies; the expert's credibility is diminished if the expert has not recently attended a professional meeting. Professional associations that only require annual payments to become a member are not as prestigious as associations that are joined by special invitation only, by approval of special referees, or by passing an examination.

Thus, an expert should be selective about which professional associations to join. The U.S. National Academies of Science (NAS) Report calls for standardized accreditation and/or certification, as well as a uniform code of ethics:

> Although some areas of the forensic science disciplines have made notable efforts to achieve standardization and best practices, most disciplines still lack any consistent structure for the enforcement of "better practices," operating standards, and certification and accreditation programs …. Accreditation is required in only three states … [and] [i]n other states, accreditation is voluntary, as is individual certification…. NAS Report at 213.

Thus, the NAS Report calls for the creation of a federal agency to develop tools to advance reliability in forensic science; to ensure standards that reflect best practices and serve as accreditation tools for laboratories; and as guides for the education, training, and certification of professionals (NAS Report at 214).

Increased Scrutiny of Experts

Experts have come under increased scrutiny for either fabricating or inflating their qualifications. In Florida, in 1998, a person who had been testifying as an expert in toxicology for 3 years for both the prosecution and defense in criminal cases was prosecuted for perjury for testifying with fraudulent credentials. The expert claimed to possess master's and doctorate degrees from Florida Atlantic University, but when a prosecutor sought to confirm the claims, he discovered that the registrar's office had no record of the expert attending or receiving a degree from the university.

In another case, a Harvard medical professor was sued for trademark infringement for falsely claiming to be board-certified by the American Board of Psychiatry and Neurology (ABPN) in five trials (*ABPN v. Johnson-Powell*). The board sought to seize the expert's witness fees and treble damages, but the court denied that relief because it believed the expert was unlikely to infringe in the future.

In 2007, a court granted the plaintiff a new trial in her product liability action when it was discovered that the pharmaceutical company's cardiology expert had misrepresented his credentials by testifying that he was board-certified in internal medicine and cardiovascular disease when in fact those certifications had expired (*In re Vioxx Products*).

In addition to perjury prosecutions for false qualifications, some jurisdictions also prosecute for academic fraud. For example, in Florida, a person who misrepresents association with, or academic standing at, a postsecondary educational institution is guilty of a first-degree misdemeanor (Fla. Stat. § 817.566).

Courts have also overturned convictions where the experts testified outside their field of expertise. Instances include a medical examiner testifying to shoe-pattern analysis and an evidence technician with no ballistics expertise giving testimony about bullet trajectory (see *Gilliam v. State*; *Kelvin v. State*).

There is evidence to suggest that, since the Supreme Court's decisions in *Daubert v. Merrell Dow Pharmaceuticals, Inc.*, and Kuhmo Tire Co., courts have been more willing to exclude expert testimony. The Federal Judicial Center compared a 1998 survey of 303 federal judges with a 1991 survey. In 1998, 41% of the judges claimed to have excluded expert testimony, whereas only 25% of the judges did so in 1991. A 2001 RAND study similarly concluded that judges were becoming more vigilant gatekeepers; for example, in the US Third Circuit Court of Appeals, the exclusion rate in products liability cases rose from 53% to 70%. This contradicts most of the reported case law following *Daubert*, which seems to indicate that the exclusion of expert testimony remains the exception, not the rule (see Fed. R. Evid. 702).

Weight of the Evidence

Once a judge decides that an expert may testify, the jury must then decide the weight to accord the expert's opinion. Jurors have become familiar with the role of the expert witness at trial through the coverage of high-profile cases in the popular media and fictional television depictions such as "CSI." Studies have shown that jurors have increased expectations for scientific evidence, and that in cases based on circumstantial evidence, jurors are more likely to acquit a defendant if the government did not provide some form of scientific evidence. Expert witnesses and attorneys should be aware of studies regarding jurors' perceptions of expert witnesses and how those perceptions have evolved over time.

For example, a 1994 study revealed that the characteristics of experts that were most important to jurors in determining the experts' credibility were (1) the expert's willingness to draw firm conclusions and (2) the expert's ability to convey technical information in plain language that a layperson could understand. Another study concluded that an expert's believability is linked to the expert's qualifications, familiarity with the facts of the case, good reasoning, and perceived impartiality. Jurors were also influenced by independent research that corresponded with the expert's opinion.

A 1998 study exposed jurors as a more skeptical, cynical group. Among the findings, the study concluded that 50% of those surveyed thought that expert witnesses say only what they are paid to say; 33% did not believe police testimony; and 75% said they would set aside what a judge says the law requires and reach a verdict the jurors felt was right. Yet another study concluded that using expert testimony to counter the prosecution's expert in criminal cases caused jurors to be skeptical of all expert testimony, rather than simply sensitizing them to flaws in the prosecution expert's testimony. In fact, jurors rendered more guilty verdicts when they heard defense expert testimony than when they did not. This study throws into question the Supreme Court's assumption in *Daubert* that opposing expert testimony effectively safeguards against "junk" science in the courtroom.

Increasing awareness of errant experts and exonerations of the wrongly accused has influenced how jurors perceive scientific evidence. For example, background beliefs about the possibility of laboratory errors and intentional tampering affect the weight jurors afford to a DNA report, and jurors with such beliefs gave probability estimates less weight. A separate poll regarding forensic fraud and its impact on potential jurors found that 32% think wrongful convictions happen frequently and 23% said that wrongful convictions are rarely an accident.

Experts must understand that effective communication with jurors requires organized content, and the effective use of visual presentation techniques including, whenever possible, demonstrative exhibits that incorporate large, user-friendly data presentation monitors and systems for use both by the court and by individual jurors, as well as interactive electronic timelines and e-documents that allow jurors to feel they are in control of and have access to all information regarding the facts of the trial. Data also suggest that when testifying to jurors, experts should attempt to associate themselves with a more collaborative, personalized role such as a teacher, rather than a more hierarchal and impersonal profession such as a scientist. Surveys confirm these conclusions distinguish jurors from generations X and Y from past generations. For example, while 64% of jurors overall believe that the police tell the truth when they testify, only 51% of jurors aged 18–24 years old share that belief; 60% overall and 72% of those aged 18–25 viewed presentations using videos, simulations, and computers positively.

Conclusion

Expert testimony will continue to play an important role in the future. Expert witnesses have been facing increased scrutiny in the United States and worldwide. For more effective expert testimony, lawyers and experts must be aware of the factors that the courts will evaluate in order to determine whether an expert is qualified or not, as well as jurors' changing perceptions of experts.

Further Reading

ABPN v. Johnson-Powell, 129F.3d 1 (1st Cir. 1997).

Aronson, P., November 2, 1998. Jurors: a biased, independent lot. National Law Journal A1.

Bogosian v. Mercedes-Benz of North America Inc., 104F.3d 472, 477 (1st Cir. 1997).

Committee on Identifying the Needs of the Forensic Sciences Community, National Research Council, August 2009. Strengthening Forensic Science in the United States: A Path Forward. The "NAS Report". National Academy of Sciences, pp. 238–239.

Daubert v. Merrell Dow Pharmaceuticals, Inc., 509 U.S. 579 (1993).

Dixon, L., Gill, B., 2001. Changes in the standards in admitting expert evidence in federal civil cases since Daubert decision. RAND Monograph.

Fed R. Evid. 702, Adv. Cmte. Note to the 2000 Amendment (2000).

Fitzgerald Jr., H., December 1, 1998. Phony "expert" Jailed for 3 Years. Ft. Lauderdale Sun-Sentinel 3D.

Fla. Stat. } 817.566 (2004).

Gilliam v. State, 514 So. 2d 1098 (Fla. 1987); Kelvin V. State, 610 So. 2d 1359 (Fla. App. 1 Dist. 1992).

Godfrey, E., May 27, 2001. Poll shows Oklahomans distrust system. The Daily Oklahoman A1.

Hamlin, S., 2000. Who are today's jurors and how do you reach them? Litigation 9 (Spring).

Illsley, C., July 1987. Juries, fingerprints, and the expert fingerprint witness. Presentation at the International Symposium on Latent Prints at the FBI Academy.

In re Vioxx Products, 489F. Supp. 2d 587 (E.D. La. 2007).

Kim, Y.S., Barak, G., Shelton, D.E., 2009. Examining the 'CSI-effect' in the cases of circumstantial evidence and eyewitness testimony: multivariate and path analyses. Journal of Criminal Justice 37, 452.

Kumho Tire Co. Ltd. v. Carmichael, 526 U.S. 137, 143 (1999).

Levett, L.M., Kovera, M.B., 2007. The effectiveness of opposing expert witnesses for educating jurors about unreliable expert evidence. Law and Human Behavior. Published online October 17, 2007.

National Clearinghouse for Science, Technology and the Law at Stetson University College of Law. Bibliography of Resources Related to the CSI Effect. http://www.ncstl.org/education/CSI%20Effect%20Bibliography (accessed 24.07.11.).

Radlein v. Holiday Inns, Inc., 971 So.2d 1200 (La. App. 4 Cir. 2007).

Schklar, J., Seidman, S., 1999. Juror reactions to DNA evidence: errors and expectancies. Law and Human Behavior 23, 159.

Shelton, D.E., Kim, Y.S., Barak, G., 2009. An indirect-effects model of mediated adjudication: the CSI myth, the tech effect, and metropolitan jurors' expectations for scientific evidence. Vanderbilt Journal of Entertainment and Technology Law 12, 1.

Shuman, D.W., et al., 1994. An empirical examination of the use of expert witnesses in the courts – part II: a three city study. Jurimetrics 35, 193.

Shuman, D.W., et al., 1996. Assessing the believability of expert witnesses: science in the jurybox. Jurimetrics 37, 23.

The Technical Working Group on Education and Training in Forensic Science, June 2004. Education and training in forensic science: a guide for forensic science laboratories, educational institutions and students. National Institutes of Justice Special Report.

Thomas J. Kline, Inc. v. Lonillard, Inc., 878F.2d 791, 800 (4th Cir. 1989), cert. denied, 493 U.S. 1073 (1990).

U.S. v. Locascio, 6F.3d 924, 937 (2d Cir. 1993) "Even the most qualified expert must have his first day in court," cert. denied, 511 U.S. 1070 (1994).

Voris, B.V., October 23, 2000. Jurors to lawyers: dare to be dull. The National Law Journal A1.

Health and Safety

N Scudder and B Saw, Australian Federal Police, Canberra, ACT, Australia

Glossary

Clandestine laboratory ("Clan labs") Setting up of equipment or supplies for the manufacture of illegal compounds such as drugs or explosives.

Confined space An enclosed or partially enclosed space that is not intended or designed primarily for human occupancy, within which there is a risk of one or more of the following: (1) An oxygen concentration outside the safe oxygen range. (2) A concentration of airborne contaminant that may cause impairment, loss of consciousness, or asphyxiation. (3) A concentration of flammable airborne contaminant that may cause injury from fire or explosion. (4) Engulfment in a stored free-flowing solid or a rising level of liquid that may cause suffocation or drowning.

Dynamic risk management The continuous assessment of risk in the rapidly changing circumstances of an operational incident, in order to implement the control measures necessary to ensure an acceptable level of safety.

Hazard The potential for a substance to cause adverse effects.

Hierarchy of control measures Ranking of measures taken to prevent or reduce hazard exposure according to effectiveness, from the most effective measures that eliminate hazards to the least effective that achieve only limited protection.

OHS policy A policy document indicating an organization's commitment to OHS, its intentions, objectives, and priorities, and identifying roles and responsibilities.

Risk The likelihood of injury or illness arising from exposure to any hazard(s) and the magnitude of the adverse effect.

Occupational Health and Safety Policy

The legislation in many countries places the onus of responsibility on employers to provide a healthy and safe working environment under occupational health and safety (OHS) legislation and common law. Employers should ensure that all managers, supervisors, and staff are aware of their OHS responsibilities. Management leadership can positively influence OHS outcomes for an organization.

Workplace health and safety is an ongoing process. Subject to the legislative requirements of each jurisdiction, in most instances a documented OHS policy is required. The development of such a policy requires the commitment of both staff and management. Once commitment has been achieved, the OHS policy should be developed with involvement from all stakeholders and promulgated.

The OHS policy should include the following:

- articulate the organization's commitment to OHS;
- indicate that sufficient resources (both financial and personnel) will be provided to promote and maintain OHS standards and meet OHS requirements;
- outline the organization's intentions, objectives, and priorities OHS;
- describe in broad terms the means by which the objectives will be met;
- identify the roles and responsibilities of management, supervisors, and staff in meeting OHS requirements; and
- be signed off by the most senior manager of the organization, reflecting the importance of the policy.

The OHS policy should be reviewed periodically to ensure its currency.

The OHS policy is, however, only one part of an appropriate OHS strategy for a forensic organization. It must be underpinned by risk assessments and incident/accident reports that enable the organization to assess its OHS exposure, to meet legislative requirements such as reporting obligations, and to respond to risks appropriately.

An organization can develop a list of the main hazards that its staff are likely to be exposed to in the course of their duties, utilizing OHS reports, incident/accident reports, and previous risk assessments. Prioritizing the main health and safety issues allows the organization to develop appropriate action plans to meet the objectives of its OHS policy.

Forensic organizations may consider integration of some OHS requirements with their quality assurance system. Many laboratories effectively use their quality system to embed OHS requirements in their documented procedures, to review OHS hazards as part of a periodic audit program, or to manage elements of their OHS action plans through their corrective action system. OHS, like quality, can then be viewed as an important yet integrated component of an effective management system.

Risk Assessments

Once potential OHS hazards have been identified, forensic organizations should evaluate the likelihood of injury from the interaction to the hazard and the magnitude of the adverse effect. The process of risk assessment will be very useful for managing potential OHS hazards within the facility and the expected external work environment. The purpose of the risk assessment process is to ensure that all workplace hazards have been identified, recorded, assessed, controlled, and reviewed. The desired outcome of this process is to eliminate, as far as practicable, the risk of injury or illness to personnel, damage to property, and damage to the environment. The process of developing risk assessment is often better suited to the known work environment. An OHS assessment of an office or laboratory can quickly identify specific hazards that may require attention. Obviously, this works well for the office and laboratory environment within one's control; however, each external scene will be different.

It is important that the range of potential hazards in external crime scenes and work environments is considered. While some risks can be grouped and managed collectively, the specific hazard and risk mitigation and control will vary from scene to scene given the circumstances. Given this, forensic practitioners should have an ability to undertake dynamic risk assessments, or "risk on the run" as it is known in some jurisdictions.

Dynamic Risk Management

Dynamic risk assessments are conducted by a forensic practitioner as a part of the attendance and examination process. In some instances, such as attendance at a clan lab, a person may be designated as the Site Safety Officer and have carriage of this as well as health and safety for all personnel at the site. Practitioners should be trained to assess the risk given the circumstances at the time, considering the actual hazards present at a crime scene.

A designated forensic practitioner or Site Safety Officer should undertake a quick reconnaissance of the crime scene to ensure the safety of forensic practitioners and others working at the scene. A review of the scene should be repeated whenever the situation at the scene changes. This could involve a visual inspection without entering the crime scene, and asking a number of questions such as the following:

- Does the crime scene involve structures that are now unstable?
- Has confirmation been obtained from the fire brigade or other emergency responders that power, gas, and water to the site have been turned off?
- Is there adequate shelter so that practitioners can rest without succumbing to environmental stressors such as heat, cold, wind, or rain?

It is important to close the loop, and incorporate any strategic elements of each dynamic risk assessment in OHS policy and planning. After each incident, any relevant information obtained during the dynamic risk assessment should be recorded and collated for strategic analysis.

Hierarchy of Control Measures

Within OHS, there is a "hierarchy of control" designed to mitigate or resolve a risk deemed unacceptably high.

The hierarchy of control is a sequence of options which offer a number of ways to approach the hazard control process. Various control options may be available. It is important to choose the control that most effectively eliminates the hazard or minimizes the risk in the circumstances. This may involve a single control measure or a combination of different controls that together provide the highest level of protection that is reasonably practicable.

1. Eliminate the hazard. If this is not practical, then:
2. Substitute the hazard with a lesser risk. If this is not practical, then:
3. Isolate the hazard. If this is not practical, then:
4. Use engineering controls. If this is not practical, then:
5. Use administrative controls, such as safe work practices, instruction, and training. If this is not practical, then:
6. Use personal protective equipment (PPE), such as gloves, eye protection, boots, and respirators.

It is important that management and staff discuss and consult, where possible, during all phases of the hazard identification, risk assessment, and risk control process.

Examples

1. If an organization is considering purchasing a piece of analytical equipment, and two products have the same capabilities but substantially different noise levels during operation, the organization may consider the noise level of the equipment during procurement, and opt for the quieter system. This example demonstrates the principle of eliminating the hazard at source, which is the most effective

control measure, when compared to training and provision of PPE such as hearing protection.

2. In the case of a fire scene of a building, applying a hierarchy of control approach, it is first necessary to consider the elimination or substitution of hazards. In a fire scene, this is not possible. It is, however, possible to isolate the scene to prevent danger to the public and to maintain the integrity of the scene. Power, water, and gas to the building should be disconnected prior to entering the site. A structural engineer's opinion may be necessary prior to entry to the building. Safe entry and exit to the site can be established. Other administrative controls, such as briefing practitioners and maintaining records of the entry and exit of personnel, may be applied. Finally, practitioners can be prevented from entering the fire scene unless utilizing the appropriate PPE.

Specific Laboratory Hazards

The likely hazards within a laboratory environment include the following sections.

Chemicals

Chemical exposure may occur through inhalation, skin absorption, or direct ingestion and, once absorbed, are either stored in a particular organ or tissue, metabolized, or excreted. The effect of a chemical on a person is dependent on a number of factors such as duration and frequency of exposure, concentration of the chemical, and an individual's metabolism. A synergistic effect may occur when the undesirable effects of one substance are intensified if exposure has occurred to another substance.

Some nanomaterials exhibit different chemical properties compared to what they exhibit on a macroscale. As this is a relatively new field, there is insufficient knowledge regarding the hazards posed by nanomaterials. The potential hazards associated with nanomaterials may include increased reactivity because of their increased surface area to volume ratio, the ability to cross some of the body's protective mechanism, and the lack of the body's immunity against such small particles. Because of this lack of knowledge, the suggested control strategy to be used when working with nanomaterials should be "as low as reasonably achievable" approach to reduce exposure.

The effects of chemicals on the body may be categorized as follows:

- poisonous or toxic chemicals are absorbed into the body and exert either an acute or short-term effect, such as headache, nausea, or loss of consciousness, or a long-term effect such as liver or kidney damage, cancer, or chronic lung disease;

- corrosive chemicals burn the skin, eyes, or respiratory tract;
- irritants can inflame the skin or lungs, causing conditions such as dermatitis or bronchitis;
- sensitizers may exert long-term effects, especially to the skin (such as contact dermatitis) and to the respiratory tract (such as occupational asthma) by inducing an allergic reaction; and
- explosive or flammable substances pose immediate danger of fire and explosion, causing damage to the body through direct burning, or through inhalation of toxic fumes emitted during combustion.

Safety data sheets (SDS), also known as material safety data sheets, are designed to provide relevant information regarding the identity, physical characteristics, safe storage, use, disposal, first-aid treatment, and spill management of substances that are handled in the workplace. The information includes whether the substance is deemed to be a hazardous and/or a dangerous goods item. At a minimum, the SDS should be consulted before the first use of a chemical or other substance within a laboratory, or if practitioners are unfamiliar with the product. Copies of SDS should be retained according to legislative requirements. In some jurisdictions, electronic SDS management systems can allow an efficient way of accessing up-to-date SDS information.

Sharps

Sharps are objects that have sharp edges or points, which have the potential to cut, scratch, or puncture the skin. Sharps can cause physical injury and have the potential to introduce infectious and toxic agents through the wounds created in the skin. Examples include hypodermic syringes and needles, knives, or broken glassware.

All forensic practitioners have a responsibility to handle and package sharps safely. Particular care should be given to ensure that sharps are appropriately labeled when packaged. Sharps such as knives could, for example, be packaged in clear plastic tubes, making it easier for a person opening the item to identify the contents and the direction the sharp items is facing. Forensic labs should be encouraged to develop policies that encourage forensic practitioners and others that submit items to develop safe-packaging procedures.

Biological Material

Examples of "biological material" commonly encountered in forensic examinations include body tissue, blood, and body fluids (urine, saliva, vomit, pus, seminal fluid, vaginal fluid, and feces). Biological material is potentially hazardous as it may contain infectious agents such as viruses, bacteria, fungi, and parasites that cause a variety of communicable diseases.

Hair, fur, and items of clothing that have been in close contact with humans or animals may also harbor parasites such as fleas or nits.

When examining plant material such as cannabis, consideration should be given to the presence of *Aspergillus* sp. mold. If the *Aspergillus* spores are inhaled into the lungs, a serious, chronic respiratory or sinus infection can result. If mold is visible, the cannabis should be treated as a biological and respiratory hazard.

It is impossible to determine the prevalence of infectious or communicable diseases in the environment in which forensic practitioners work. Consequently, practitioners should adhere to recommended procedures for handling biological material and adopt an approach known as the "standard precautions." This approach requires practitioners to assume that all biological material is a potential source of infection, independent of diagnosis or perceived level of underlying risk.

Vaccinations should be offered for practitioners. The types of vaccinations given may depend on whether work is confined to the laboratory or whether work is performed in the field, as well as whether forensic practitioners are likely to be deployed overseas where other diseases may be more prevalent.

Firearms

Forensic practitioners may retrieve firearms from crime scenes. All personnel who may be required to handle firearms, either in the field, in the laboratory, or in support roles such as property or exhibit stores should be trained in how to render a firearm safe. As with the "standard precautions," it is important to consider all firearms as potentially loaded, and adopt the practice of never pointing a firearm in the direction of another person, even after it has been rendered safe.

Firearms examiners, who undertake firearms investigations including test firing and bullet recovery, will be exposed to hazards such as noise and lead. They should have their hearing and blood lead levels monitored on a regular basis, to ensure that hearing protection is being worn and is functioning correctly, and any exposure to lead from the firearms is quickly identified and addressed.

Computer Forensics Laboratory

Computer forensic examiners specialize in obtaining, analyzing, and reporting on electronic evidence stored on computers and other electronic devices. Crimes involving a computer can range across the spectrum of criminal activity, from child pornography to theft of personal data to destruction of intellectual property. Potential hazards involve static postures, occupational overuse, and stress from viewing graphic images.

Some suggestions to minimize the stress from viewing graphic images are as follows:

- psychological assessment before and after viewing graphic material, and also periodically;
- exposure to only one medium, for example, visual material only, rather than examining both sound and visual material simultaneously;
- specifying limits as to the amount of time spent examining explicit material in a day; and
- ceasing any examination of explicit material at the end of their shift, to allow themselves some time to refocus attention away from this stressor.

Electrical/Machinery

Forensic laboratories use a wide range of electrical equipment and machinery. Practitioners need to ensure that any inherent risk from electric shock is mitigated. The use of residual current devices (safety switches) is an appropriate strategy, as is visual inspection and periodic testing and tagging of power cords, to detect obvious damage, wear and other conditions which might render it unsafe by a person qualified to do so under the legislation in effect in the jurisdiction.

Fume Cupboards

Fume cupboards are integral to minimizing the risk of exposure to chemical and biological hazards. Not all fume cupboards are suitable for all hazards. Fume cupboards should be maintained and inspected periodically. During maintenance, attention should be given to the following:

- The fume cupboard itself, including flow rates and replacement of absorbents or filters.
- In the case of externally vented fume cupboards, the ductwork, and location of external vents. This is particularly important during any building maintenance or refurbishment.
- Fume cupboards must be used for all operations that have the potential to release hazardous fumes, mists, or dusts.
- Before commencement of work, ensure that the fume cupboard is clean and free from contamination.
- Ensure minimum equipment is stored in the fume cupboard and is placed toward the back of the cupboard to reduce disturbance to the air flowing into the fume cupboard.
- Lower the sash as far as practicable during use to improve fume containment.

Recirculating fume cabinets rely on filtration or absorption to remove airborne contaminants released in the fume cabinet before the exhaust air is discharged back into the laboratory. They are suitable for light to moderate use with a known range of substances. The range of substances for which each cabinet can be used is limited by the need for compatibility with the chemicals in use as well as with the particular type of absorbent or filter fitted to the cabinet.

Robotics

The introduction of automated robotic platforms has significantly enhanced the efficiency of forensic analysis. The use of robotics is becoming more common and is very useful for a range of repetitive laboratory tasks. Besides saving time, robotics overcomes the need for repetitive work involved in pipetting, eliminating musculoskeletal injuries.

Hazards associated with robotics include the risk of exposure to the chemicals used in the work, electrocution, and cutting, stabbing, or shearing from the moveable parts of the robot. The interlocks on the robots should not be bypassed.

X-rays

X-rays are used in analytical and imaging instrumentation. Potential exposure to X-rays is generally localized to specific parts of the body, usually the hands or fingers. Depending on the X-ray energies delivered, effects may range from erythema (redness) at point of exposure, blood changes, cancer through to death. Depending on the legislative requirement in each country, practitioners working with X-ray equipment may be required to use dosimeters to assess radiation dose.

Lasers

Lasers span the visible and nonvisible electromagnetic spectrum and have many applications in forensic science, including Raman spectroscopy. Lasers are generally classified according to the level of risk they represent. Damage from laser beams can be thermal or photochemical. The primary sites of damage are the eyes and skin. Hazards associated with laser work may include the following:

- fire,
- explosion,
- electrocution, and
- inhalation of contaminants from laser interactions.

Precautions for use of lasers include the following:

- Display the class of laser in use.
- Appropriate protective eye wear with side protection and appropriate attenuation for the wavelength(s) in use must be worn.
- Interlocks on the laser should not be bypassed.
- Keep the laser beam path away from eye level whether one is seated or standing.

High-Intensity Light Sources

High-intensity light sources such as the Polilight® provide a range of colored light bands and white light for forensic work.

- Care should be taken that high-intensity white light is not directed onto any object at short distances from the end of the light guide, as this can cause severe heat damage to the object and may result in a fire.
- The light beam should never be directed at eyes as the light can cause permanent damage.

Manual Handling

Manual handling refers to any activity that involves lifting, lowering, carrying, pushing, pulling, holding, restraining, or the application of force. Only a very small number of manual handling injuries are caused by the lifting of heavy weights alone. Actions such as reaching, twisting, bending, or maintaining static postures contribute to injury affecting the muscle or skeletal systems of the body. These musculoskeletal injuries predominantly involve the neck, back, or shoulder or arm muscle, tendon, ligament, or joints.

Injuries may be caused from activities such as maintaining static postures while working at fume cupboards, repetitive keyboard and mouse work, pipetting, prolonged use of comparison microscopes.

Some preventative strategies include the following:

- Seeking further assistance to have the activities assessed to minimize the manual handling risks inherent in the activity.
- Planning tasks so that rest breaks are scheduled.
- Choosing the best tools for the tasks.
- Alternate hands while using a mouse, if possible.

There is a move to make instruments smaller and more portable for use at crime scenes. While this has significant benefits, including potentially reducing the number of exhibits collected, moving equipment can also raise manual-handling concerns.

General Laboratory Management

Housekeeping is important in laboratories. It is important to maintain clear passageways, have proper labeling of chemicals, clean and uncluttered work areas and appropriate storage. The handling of powders is a potentially hazardous operation and good housekeeping can help minimize airborne contamination from spilled materials. Having a planned preventative maintenance program and regular inspections of the workplace, plant, and equipment are essential for the smooth running of the laboratory.

Handling of Exhibits in Court

Each evidential item must be appropriately packaged and sealed, if this is not already the case, before it is exhibited in court. Items such as clothing which are normally stored in paper may need to be repackaged in clear plastic allowing the item to remain sealed, and minimizing the risk of cross contamination when handled in court. Caution should be exercised against opening exhibits in court, in case any hazards such as mold or irritant fumes are released.

Hazards in the Field

Forensic practitioners are often required to work or train in the field. Consideration should be given to managing hazards which may affect practitioners, including the following:

- environmental hazards such as heat, cold, humidity or wet weather, the terrain, and fauna or flora at the scene;
- the type of operation, for example, working in a clandestine laboratory often involves quite specific hazards;
- the possible presence of offenders or other security risks such as booby traps at a scene; and
- the availability of first aid and emergency response domestically and overseas.

The risks from these hazards should be considered within the scope of the exercise or operation. Some possible responses to hazards, which may be considered in a dynamic risk assessment, include the following:

- Designating a location for emergency equipment, such as a crime scene vehicle, and ensuring that disinfectants, antiseptics, and a first-aid kit are easily accessible;
- Planning an emergency exit from the scene and ensuring that this is communicated to all personnel present;
- Establishing a decontamination point if there is exposure to chemical or biological material;
- The use of appropriate PPE including sunglasses, sunscreen, and hats when working outdoors;
- Depending on the external temperature, work activity, duration, and PPE worn, practitioners should have access to shade for rest and adequate fluids if required during hot weather to prevent heat stress. The wearing of PPE including chemical suits and respirators requires longer and more frequent periods of rest break for recovery in hot temperatures and humid environment;
- In cold weather, provision should be made to have adequate warm clothing and a sheltered area;
- The risk of animal or dog bites while attending a crime scene should not be discounted. If practitioners are searching in vegetated areas, the risk of snake or tick bites should be

considered, along with possible exposure to plants such as poison ivy or stinging nettles.

Confined Spaces

Forensic practitioners may have to enter confined spaces. Due to the high risks associated with entering the confined space, many jurisdictions mandate that entry into a confined space must not be made until a confined-space permit has been issued. Practitioners must receive specific training before work or entry into confined spaces.

Chemical, Biological, and Radiological and Nuclear Incidents

Forensic practitioners may be required to attend a chemical, biological, and radiological and nuclear (CBRN) incident. CBRN incidents where forensic practitioners may attend and conduct examinations include the following:

- chemical (warfare agent, toxic industrial chemical);
- biological (weaponized agent, natural disease);
- radiological (discrete or wide area contamination); and
- nuclear.

Depending on the response agency protocol in place, forensic practitioners may be working closely with the fire brigade and other emergency first responders. Entry must not be made into the "warm" or "hot" zone of the scene without consultation with the other emergency first responders.

Clan Labs

Clan labs pose a significant threat to the health and safety of police officers, forensic practitioners, the general public, and the environment. There are many hazards associated with clan labs including the following:

- flammable materials and/or explosive atmosphere;
- acutely toxic atmospheres;
- leaking or damaged compressed gas cylinders; and
- traps and hazards deliberately set to cause injury or death to police and other responders.

As a result of the frequency at which clan labs are encountered and the severe and variable risks associated with the investigation, many jurisdictions have developed specific policies and procedures concerning clan lab investigations.

For forensic practitioners to deal with clan labs requires a high level of fitness as well as technical expertise. Practitioners have to understand the following:

- illicit drug chemistry;
- how to neutralize the risks of explosions, fires, chemical burns, and toxic fumes;

- how to handle, store, and dispose of hazardous materials; and
- how to treat medical conditions caused by exposure.

Practitioners must also wear full protective equipment including respirators and may be required to move equipment at the clan lab in the process of collecting evidence. The storage and handling of unknown chemicals from clandestine laboratories or seizures should also be considered. Preliminary identification should take place before its storage or disposal.

When unknowns such as "white powders," chemicals (in liquid, solid, or gas state), or biological materials are encountered in the field, it is prudent to be cautious and obtain up-to-date intelligence to shed more light on what is at the scene. It may be an explosive material or contain anthrax spores or ricin or something as innocuous as talc.

Some precautions include the following:

- wearing the appropriate level of protective clothing/equipment for the activity;
- avoiding direct contact with the substance, even if only in small quantities;
- not smelling or tasting anything from the scene;
- noting physical characteristics such as color, form, and consistency;
- where it is safe to do so, looking for hazard symbols on packaging or labels if available; and
- seeking specialist advice if unable to identify the substance.

Potential Hazards during an Overseas Deployment

Forensic practitioners can be required to work overseas to assist with large-scale disasters. An example was the Thailand Tsunami Victim Identification process involving forensic practitioners from 30 countries working to recover and identify bodies. Forensic practitioners need to be mindful of hazards likely to be encountered during an overseas deployment depending on the location, magnitude of the operation, and how many practitioners are deployed. Some hazards to be considered include the following:

- climatic demands;
- remote and sometimes dangerous terrain;
- different cultural sensitivities;
- security requirements;
- different levels of infrastructure support at the locality;
- logistics, including the transport of large quantities of equipment, manual handling, setting up, and packing up;
- different hygiene levels;
- diseases that can be transmitted by insect and or animal vectors;
- the possibility of infectious diseases; and
- asbestos and other hazards in buildings.

Work-Related Stress

Practitioners at work may experience work-related stress. There are some specific stressors unique within forensic work. Forensic practitioners may experience workplace-related stress due to their attendances at morgues, violent crime scenes, disaster victim identification, or from requirements to view explicit or graphic material or images.

Indicators of stress include changes in eating habits, tiredness due to changes in sleep patterns, frequent absences from work, reduced productivity, concentration, motivation, and morale. Physical symptoms may include headaches, abdominal pains, diarrhea, constipation, high blood pressure, insomnia, anxiety state, and depression.

Many organizations offer programs to provide assistance to employees, including counseling to help practitioners to deal with work-related stress or resilience training to manage work–life balance.

See also: **Management/Quality in Forensic Science:** Principles of Quality Assurance; Risk Management; Principles of Laboratory Organization.

Further Reading

Clancy, D., Billinghurst, A., Cater, H., 2009. Hazard identification and risk assessment – understanding the transition from the documented plan to assessing dynamic risk in bio security emergencies. In: World Conference on Disaster Management, Sydney, Australia. http://www.humansafety.com.au/getattachment/da338cb7-29b0-4d3a-8a06-d7dc0b569a87/C20.aspx.

Furr, K., 2000. Handbook of Laboratory Safety, fifth ed. CRC Press, Florida.

Green-McKenzie, J., Watkins, M., 2005. Occupational hazards: law enforcement officers are at risk of body fluid exposure. Here's what to expect if it happens to you. Law Enforcement Magazine 29 (9), 52–54, 56, 58.

Hanson, D., 2007. Hazardous duty training officers to tackle hazmat emergencies. Law Enforcement Technology 34 (4), 80–85.

Haski, R., Cardilini, G., Bartolo, W., 2011. Laboratory Safety Manual. CCH Australia Ltd., Sydney.

Horswell, J., 2000. The Practice of Crime Scene Investigation. CRC Press, Florida.

Jackel, G., 2004. The high cost of stress. AUSPOL: The Official Publication of the Australian Federal Police Association and ALAJA 1, 4–37.

Mayhew, C., 2001a. Occupational health and safety risks faced by police officers. Australian Institute of Criminology. Trends and Issues in Crime and Criminal Justice 196, 1–6.

Mayhew, C., 2001b. Protecting the occupational health and safety of police officers. Australian Institute of Criminology. Trends and Issues in Crime and Criminal Justice 197, 1–6.

Rothernbaum, D., 2010. Exposed: an officer's story. Clan Lab Safety Alert 7 (2), 1–2.

Smith, D., 2005. Psychosocial occupational health issues in contemporary police work: a review of research evidence. Journal of Occupational Health and Safety, Australia and New Zealand 21 (3), 217–228.

Tillman, C., 2007. Principles of Occupational Health and Hygiene: An Introduction. Allen & Unwin. Crows Nest.

Whitman, M., Smith, C., 2005. The culture of safety: no one gets hurt today. Police Chief LXXII (11), 20–24, 26, 27.

Winder, C., 2011. Hazard Alert: Managing Workplace Hazardous Substances. CCH Australia Ltd., Sydney.

Witter, R., Martyny, J., Mueller, K., Gottschall, B., Newman, L., 2007. Symptoms experienced by law enforcement personnel during methamphetamine lab investigation. Journal of Occupational and Environmental Hygiene 4, 895–902.

Relevant Websites

http://www.ccohs.ca/oshanswers/occup_workplace/labtech.html—Canadian Centre for Occupational Health and Safety (CCOHS).

http://www.ccohs.ca/oshanswers/occup_workplace/police.html—What do Police do?

http://www.cdc.gov/niosh/—Centers for Disease Control and Prevention (CDC).

http://www.forensic.gov.uk/html/company/foi/publication-scheme/health-and-safety/—Forensic Science Service, Health and Safety.

http://www.hse.gov.uk/services/police/index.htm—Health and Safety Executive (HSE).

http://www.londonhealthandsafetygroup.org/archive.html—London Health and Safety Group.

http://www.osha.gov/—Occupational Safety & Health Administration.

http://www.police.qld.gov.au/Resources/Internet/rti/policies/documents/QPSForensicServicesHealth_SafetyManual.pdf—Health and Safety Manual, Police Forensic Services, Queensland Police.

Deaths in Custody

S Heide, University of Halle-Wittenberg, Halle, Germany

Introduction

The deaths of persons in police custody pose a particular challenge to postmortem and forensic assessments. These deaths typically generate substantial public and media interest, with law enforcement officers often blamed for the deaths. The media often cite a lack of medical independence in the assessment of the decedents' fitness for custody, as well as inadequate medical care while the decedents were in police custody. Reports of ill treatment by law enforcement officers, sometimes including torture, are not infrequent. Torture in police custody, sometimes with a fatal outcome, has been reported in Egypt, China, Nepal, Zimbabwe, South Africa, Bangladesh, Iran, Peru, Syria, Turkey, and Uganda.

The circumstances in which the death occurred and the range of possible causes of the death must be known in order to develop an objective expert assessment of deaths in police custody and to develop preventive strategies. For this purpose, the authors have completed systemic and significant studies of deaths in police custody from cases that occurred in North America, Australia, and Europe.

Frequency of Death in Police Custody

Throughout the world, there is a high risk of serious health hazards or death in police custody because arrested individuals are often intoxicated or were involved in physical conflicts just prior to arrest. Although determining the incidence of deaths in police custody requires a reference to the total number of police arrests, such figures are not available. Therefore, this study will relate the number of deaths to the population figure. Literature gives the frequency of such deaths as at least 0.1 per 100 000 citizens; however, the exact death rate varies considerably. A German study on death in police custody showed, at 0.14 per 100 000 citizens, that Germany has a relatively low death rate compared to similar countries. Significantly higher mortality rates in police custody were shown, for instance, for Finland (2.02 per 100 000 citizens), Canada (0.87 per 100 000 citizens), and Australia (0.89 per 100 000 citizens).

Distribution of Age and Gender

The majority of studies on death in police custody state that 90% of the persons who die in police custody are males. The low percentage of female deaths is due, primarily, to the fact that women are comparatively taken into custody less often. In Halle and Bremen, two large German towns, 90.5% of the 3669 persons in police custody were males.

Contrasting age distribution of persons who die in police custody and the range of causes of death in police custody shows considerable differences between North American and European deaths in custody. Because of the different structures of prisons and custody (such as the length of time that a person may be held in police custody) in these regions, however, the studies are not fully comparable. National differences in the police and justice systems mean that, in Europe, deaths in police custody are not always distinguished from deaths in prisons. In a German study of 60 in-custody deaths that were followed by a postmortem, age distribution was widely spread, the mean age being 41.1 years (**Figure 1**). In contrast, deaths in custody in Denmark, Great Britain, Canada, and the Netherlands occurred in much younger persons. Men in Florida (the United States) died mainly in their 40s or 50s. An awareness of these age distributions is of considerable importance for the medical assessment of a person's fitness for custody. The process of finding a person fit for custody must be the same for every person, even if the arrested person is of younger age.

Manner and Cause of Death

In the North American region, the proportion of natural deaths in police custody is significantly higher than in Europe. More than half of the 229 deaths in Florida (the United States) had natural causes. In stark contrast, natural causes of death in Europe are only 20%. In European countries, causes of unnatural death are predominately intoxication and trauma. The German study found that alcoholic intoxication and cerebrocranial trauma were prevalent (**Figure 2**).

Other European countries show a similar pattern. In Finland and Denmark, the most frequent cause of death was acute alcoholic intoxication; in the Netherlands, the most common cause of death was intoxication by a variety of substances. In England and Wales (Great Britain), intoxication induced by alcohol or medical and illegal drugs was responsible for one-third of all deaths. The number of deaths caused by trauma was smaller: the proportion of deaths caused by craniocerebral injuries in Europe, for instance, was largely between 10% and 20%.

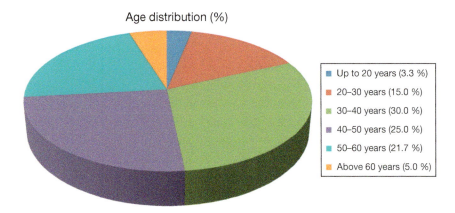

Age distribution (%)

- Up to 20 years (3.3 %)
- 20–30 years (15.0 %)
- 30–40 years (30.0 %)
- 40–50 years (25.0 %)
- 50–60 years (21.7 %)
- Above 60 years (5.0 %)

Figure 1   Age distribution of 60 deaths in German police custody.

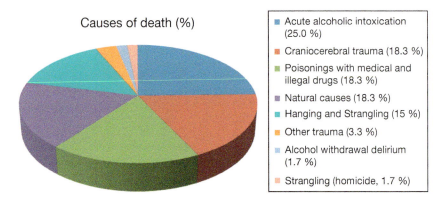

Causes of death (%)

- Acute alcoholic intoxication (25.0 %)
- Craniocerebral trauma (18.3 %)
- Poisonings with medical and illegal drugs (18.3 %)
- Natural causes (18.3 %)
- Hanging and Strangling (15 %)
- Other trauma (3.3 %)
- Alcohol withdrawal delirium (1.7 %)
- Strangling (homicide, 1.7 %)

Figure 2   Causes of death for the 60 deaths in German police custody.

In North American studies, the distribution of the cause of death differs significantly. In Florida (the United States), for instance, heart and lung diseases, secondary diseases of alcohol consumption, and suicides were prevalent. The Florida data therefore rather corresponds to the causes of death observed in persons in the custody of European prisons, which are predominated by cardiovascular diseases and suicides by hanging.

An international comparison reveals that, compared to European countries, death of excited persons during police restraining and transport measures can be found more frequently in North America. This may be due to a greater frequency of drug intoxication (such as excited deliria influenced by cocaine) and different restraining techniques.

Error Analysis for Deaths in Police Custody

Only few publications provide detailed information on the assessment of medical fitness for custody of persons who died

shortly after being taken into custody. In Germany, the proportion of cases where the person had been assessed by a physician prior to his or her death was 38%; in the Netherlands 42%; and in Denmark 46%. The Dutch study found that, although medical examinations are conducted relatively frequently, the physicians' recommendations are not implemented. This failure is caused primarily because of the following: doctors underestimate the arrestees' degree of intoxication, doctors overlook arrestees' injuries, and police and doctors have difficulty communicating. For the 60 fatalities in Germany, the study identified an exact error analysis which also included the applicable legal basis (**Table 1**).

In medical assessment, diagnostic errors and the failure to admit arrestees' to the hospital were most frequent. In many cases, unconscious persons and persons with obviously serious head injuries, for instance, were left in custody after having been medically assessed. Considerable deficiencies in medical documentation or in monitoring recommendations were also

Table 1 Error analysis of the 60 fatalities in Germany

Area	Error frequency (%)	Typical errors
Medical assessment of fitness for custody	65	• Diagnostic error or failure to admit to hospital • Deficient orders to police officers • Deficient documentation
Police responsibility	55	• Failure to seek medical attention • Deficient qualitative mode of monitoring • Failure to observe monitoring intervals • Physician was given insufficient information on case history
Organizational deficiencies	17	• Admittance to hospital denied by paramedics or nurses

quite frequent. Even in cases where the person was unresponsive, for instance, physicians gave no monitoring recommendations whatsoever.

The police sometimes failed to consult physicians in cases where they were legally required to do so. Law enforcement also failed to conduct sufficient searches: in one case, the person placed in custody was insufficiently searched, enabling an arrestee to take a lethal dose of methadone. Deficiencies in the quantitative and qualitative mode of monitoring also occurred. The person's case history was sometimes insufficiently conveyed to the attending physician. For instance, police officers may fail to inform the doctor of an intake of numerous tablets, which witnesses had observed, or of a known case of binge drinking.

In 27% of the cases, however, retrospective analysis showed that death was very probably unavoidable even if the necessary diligence would have been applied. These include deaths caused by myocarditis, peritonitis, or coronary thrombosis where the persons did not express any typical complaints, neither before nor during their detention. There were also some suicides by hanging inside the cell although no one had noticed any psychological peculiarities before.

Forensic Assessment

In the assessment of whether officers of the police or a physician had violated their duty of due diligence, the estimation of the time of death is often of decisive importance. This is why in

cases of death in police custody, the corpse should, as a principle, always be forensically inspected in situ. This, unfortunately, is rarely the case.

When inspecting the corpse, the decedent's clothing and the cell must first be searched for packages of medication or drug utensils. Close attention should also be paid to potential conspicuous odors, the contents of the oral cavity (to identify, e.g., tablet residues, aspirated stomach contents, foreign bodies), or injection marks in atypical locations. In addition, the hairy and hairless scalp should be examined for injuries (swellings, abrasions, ecchymosis, or lacerated–contused wounds).

In cases of death in police custody, officers or physicians are often blamed after the fact. An objective assessment of such allegations requires the identification of the cause of death by a medicolegal autopsy. The result of a multinational survey, however, shows that this approach is not a matter of course. Although Germany claimed to be a role model in these matters—leading one to believe that all deaths in custody are subject to a postmortem examination—the German study on death in police custody found that, due to different legal regulations in individual German lands and a need to reduce costs, these postmortem examinations did not always occur. By a visual inspection of the corpse alone, lethal intoxications of alcohol, drugs, or medical drugs—which account for 40–50% of all deaths in custody in Europe—cannot be diagnosed.

The forensic assessment of potential due diligence violations requires, besides the postmortem examination result, an identification of blood alcohol content, a chemical–toxicological analysis, current medical findings (if available), and information provided by witnesses on the person's condition before and during his or her detention. The assessment must also take applicable legal provisions on the treatment of persons in police custody into account. In Germany alone, the differences between the lands' custody ordinances and policing laws are considerable: for instance, rules for how an arrestee should be monitored by police personnel, or the procedure to be applied if a person is unfit for custody.

Criminal Prosecution in Cases of Death in Custody

Although many deaths in police custody could probably be avoided, the physicians and police officers involved rarely face criminal prosecution. Their risk to become subject to potential civil litigation, however, is somewhat larger.

An analysis of the criminal consequences of deaths in police custody in Germany showed that the sentences imposed were very moderate, because of the high requirements German law places on evidence. The analysis looked at 21 preliminary investigations against doctors, officers of the police, and paramedics. Three-quarters of the investigations were stopped because of insufficient suspicion, because the evidence did not prove with the required certainty that death had been caused by wrong conduct. In a case of lethal alcohol intoxication (BAC: 0.51%), the prosecution dropped the matter without asking for an expert report. According to them, the quantity of alcohol the person had drunk had not been noticeable to the doctor despite the fact that the man had already been unresponsive when examined for fitness for custody 4 h before.

There were only a few cases in which the prosecution took a stricter approach. In two of them, proceedings were dropped on conditions and, due to low culpability, both doctors had to pay a fine. In the first of these two cases, the physician had found a man fit for custody who had died of cerebrocranial trauma shortly afterward. Witnesses, however, had observed that the man had at first been unresponsive and had later complained of a headache. In the other case, involving lethal intoxication with alcohol and medical drugs, the physician had affirmed fitness for custody despite the fact that the person displayed strong symptoms of intoxication when he was examined.

The only noted conviction concerned a physician who was fined for having caused bodily injury by passive negligence. The physician declared fitness for a man who had to be carried into the cell and had a bruise on his head. The postmortem revealed that death had been caused by subdural hematoma, and the forensic expert report stated that surgical intervention would very probably have saved the man's life.

A Case History

A 38-year-old man was found helpless and unresponsive on the pavement by pedestrians. At the police station, he was shown to a physician in order to assess his fitness for custody. The doctor did not note any neurological symptoms but described, among others, facial abrasions. He declared the man fit for custody and recommended hourly checks. An officer of the police described that the man's speech had been slurred during the examination and that he had been unable to get up on his own. Thereafter, the officers conducted only sporadic checks. Although the man's mind clouded increasingly, the officers abstained from consulting a physician again. The man died 14 h after having been brought to the station. The postmortem examination revealed that death had been caused by cerebrocranial trauma with fracture of the skull and epidural hemorrhage. The torso showed several hematomas up to a size of 15 × 6 cm and fractures of the fifth, sixth, seventh, and eighth left ribs. The blood alcohol content was 0.03%, meaning that the man had been clearly intoxicated at the time he was taken into custody. The chemical–toxicological analysis was negative.

The arresting officers were investigated for involuntary manslaughter or failure to lend assistance. The forensic expert report emphasized that the monitoring of the arrestee's mental state had been objectively inappropriate, both in terms of frequency and the monitoring measures applied. Nevertheless, the prosecution dropped the case. It was not possible to prove involuntary manslaughter because they were unable to prove with the certainty required by criminal law that medical intervention would have prevented death. The prosecution also regarded the evidence for failure to lend assistance as insufficient since the officers had believed that the man was sleeping it off.

The physician was also investigated, but the investigation was dropped because his description of the person's condition at the time of his assessment differed considerably from the account given by the officers. Thus, it was a case of his word against theirs and the principle of "in dubio pro reo" had to be applied.

Prevention of Death in Custody

Medical care for persons in police custody is often seen as critical, not only by the general public but also in the specialized literature. Possible deficiencies are caused by unregulated medical responsibilities, a lack of assessment standards, and confusing legal provisions. The factors would be a good starting point to facilitate the prevention of death or of relevant health hazards in police custody.

The assessment for fitness for custody, which is an area of enormous responsibility, should be carried out by experienced and trained physicians. The range of physicians who assess fitness for custody is, however, on an international level, extremely heterogeneous. Depending on the legal bases and regional conditions, the aim should be to assign medical responsibility clearly. In Sweden, for instance, such assessments are given by specialists in forensic medicine; in the Netherlands, by medical officers of health. The lack of clear assignation in Germany, for instance, means that physicians often refuse to conduct such examinations. In these cases, the ministries and police authorities concerned have to try to enter into service agreements with individual physicians or institutions, which can be problematic.

International standards or national guidelines for the examination of fitness for custody are currently widely missing. Opinions on requirements for these examinations vary from a short assessment or symptom-oriented statement over a standardized process, to an examination of the whole body. Written documentation of these examinations and the decision on fitness for custody is not always compulsory. Here, the aim should be to reach at least a national consensus. This would offer the chance to improve medical care in police custody and to formulate preventative strategies.

Examinations for the assessment of fitness for custody are often carried out in unfavorable conditions. Diagnostic means are commonly limited, and the examinees are often not particularly cooperative. However, even in such circumstances, physicians must exhibit due diligence. This requires calling an interpreter if the examinee speaks a different language, knowledge of legally prescribed monitoring modes, and written documentation of the arrestee's condition. Especially in problematic cases, a person should only be found fit on conditions (e.g., requirements and instructions on monitoring, instructions on intake of food and medical drugs, consultation of a specialist) in order to limit the extent of medical responsibility. Traumatized or clearly intoxicated persons in particular require checkups on their wakeability to spot a potential clouding of consciousness; these checkups must be defined by a physician if there are no respective legal provisions. Unconscious persons or persons whose consciousness is clearly clouded must be classified as medical emergencies and do not belong in the custody of the police.

In revising legal bases or formulating national guidelines, sufficient examination conditions and certain requirements for cells should also be stipulated. The assessment of fitness for custody has to be conducted in a sufficiently heated and lit room that provides the possibility to examine the person in a horizontal position. Bunks must be designed in a way that prevents dangerous falls. Cells should not contain any structures that would provide inmates with the opportunity to affix ropelike instruments for suicide attempts. Especially in cases of the arrest of a large number of persons, it will not always be possible to avoid multiple occupancy of a cell. But by introducing general video surveillance, potential conflicts between the occupants can be faster detected and addressed.

The high proportion of intoxications and trauma contributing or causing death in custody shows that persons with head injuries or clear alcohol- or drug-induced loss of functions must be seen by a physician. Literature, however, frequently reports that it is not always easy for police officers to get medical assistance when required. Nevertheless, medical examination must not be dispensed with, especially in problematic cases. Local police stations must have the opportunity to consult a doctor speedily even at night or on weekends.

Police officers must provide the attending physician with comprehensive information on details and history of the case. Observations, particularly on the intake of drugs, tablets, or binge drinking, must be passed on. Police monitoring of persons in custody must strictly comply with the legally prescribed monitoring mode or the one recommended by the doctor. Police officers should be trained on what they have to pay attention to when making these checkups.

Central custody suits offer a good possibility for the optimization of monitoring and adequate response to potential health deterioration. In contrast to detention at a station, the staff working in these central facilities is not involved in any other duty and can therefore focus on the required checks and any consequent measures.

In approximately 10% of all arrests, the person is judged unfit for custody. The responsibility for the life and well-being of these persons, however, cannot be placed on medical laypersons (e.g., police officers). Here, appropriate regional solutions such as central, medically monitored custody suites or agreements with hospitals must be provided.

Even if the utmost care is applied, not every death in custody can be avoided. But by taking suitable preventative measures, it will be possible to reduce the number of deaths and injuries in police custody considerably. The German study also showed that in a quarter of all cases, death was likely unavoidable even if due diligence had been applied. Other countries have had similar experiences.

The systematic analysis of death in police custody can provide concrete indications for preventative measures. The Netherlands has a special analyses structure, designed for use by the police; however, this structure is probably not feasible for every country. It is, however, absolutely necessary to subject all persons who die in police custody to postmortem examination, because only an objective postmortem result will allow dealing with allegations of blame and developing preventive strategies.

See also: **Forensic Medicine/Clinical:** Self-Inflicted Injury; Suicide.

Further Reading

Anon, 1993. Three-faced practice: doctors and police custody [editorial]. Lancet 341, 1245–1247.

Blaauw, E., Vermunt, R., Kerkhof, A., 1997. Death and medical attention in police custody. Medicine and Law 16, 593–606.

Chan, T.C., 2006. Medical overview of sudden in-custody deaths. In: Ross, D.L., Chan, T.C. (Eds.), Sudden Deaths in Custody. Humana Press, Totowa, NJ, pp. 9–14.

Chariot, P., Martel, P., Penneau, M., Debout, M., 2008. Guidelines for doctors attending detainees in police custody: a consensus conference in France. International Journal of Legal Medicine 122, 73–76.

Copeland, A.R., 1984. Deaths in custody revisited. The American Journal of Forensic Medicine and Pathology 5, 121–124.

Frost, R., Hanzlick, R., 1988. Deaths in custody. The American Journal of Forensic Medicine and Pathology 9, 207–211.

Heide, S., Kleiber, M., Hanke, S., Stiller, D., 2009. Deaths in German police custody. European Journal of Public Health 19, 597–601.

Heide, S., Stiller, D., Lessig, R., Lautenschläger, C., Birkholz, M., Früchtnicht, W., 2012. Medical examination of fitness for police custody in two large German towns. International Journal of Legal Medicine 126 (1), 27–35. http://dx.doi.org/10.1007/s00414-011-0557-6.

Johnson, H.R.M., 1982. Deaths in custody in England and Wales. Forensic Science International 19, 231–236.

McDonald, D., Thomson, N.J., 1993. Australian deaths in custody, 1980–1989. The Medical Journal of Australia 159, 581–585.

Norfolk, G.A., 1998. Death in police custody during 1994: a retrospective analysis. Journal of Clinical Forensic Medicine 5, 49–54.

Payne-James, J.J., 2000. History and development. In: Stark, M.M. (Ed.), A Physician's Guide to Clinical Forensic Medicine. Humana Press, Totowa, NJ, pp. 1–14.

Segest, E., 1987. Police custody: death and medical attention. Journal of Forensic Sciences 32, 1694–1703.

Tiainen, E., Penttila, A., 1986. Sudden and unexpected deaths in police custody. Acta Medicinae Legalis et Socialis 36, 281–292.

Wobeser, W.L., Datema, J., Bechard, B., Ford, P., 2002. Causes of death among people in custody in Ontario, 1990–1999. Canadian Medical Association Journal 167, 1109–1113.

Relevant Website

http://www.cpt.coe.int—Council of Europe. European Committee for the Prevention of Torture and Inhuman or Degrading Treatment or Punishment.

Suicide*

M Große Perdekamp, S Pollak, and A Thierauf, University of Freiburg, Freiburg, Germany

Glossary

Copycat act Imitating the act of another person.
Dissimulation Hiding one's intention under a feigned appearance.

Murder–suicide Killing another person before committing suicide.

Introduction

The term "suicide" refers to the intentional taking of one's own life. A suicidal act can either be uncompleted (attempted suicide) or can result in death (completed suicide). Although there are no reliable statistical data on the incidence of suicide attempts, it is assumed that their number is several times that of completed suicides. Nonfatal suicide attempts are predominantly committed by females. Even if some of these acts suggest that they are rather suicidal gestures or cries for help and that death is not really intended, such acts also have to be taken seriously—last but not least because the attempt may be repeated with the risk of an uncalculated fatal outcome. In fact, evidence of previous suicide attempts (e.g., scars from wrist cuts) is often found on persons who took their own lives.

Epidemiology

All around the world, suicide is a frequent manner of death. According to the WHO, every year almost one million people die by suicide. The global incidence indicated for 1 year is 16 per 100 000 people. Furthermore, the WHO reports that in the last 45 years, suicide rates have increased by 60%.

In different regions of the world, there is a wide range of methods of suicide. In mainly agricultural areas, particularly in developing countries, intoxications by pesticides are among the leading ways of suicide. Worldwide, approximately one-third of all suicides are caused by pesticide self-poisoning. Up to

40% of all suicides on the Indian subcontinent and the Middle East are committed by self-immolation. Easy access to firearms facilitates their use also for suicides. For instance, they account for about 60% of suicides in the United States. In Central and Western Europe, the most common methods are hanging (**Figure 1**), death by firearms, falls from height, intoxication, drowning, and collisions with rail vehicles (**Figure 2**).

Suicide is one of the alternatives of "unnatural death." According to medicolegal definition, the manner of death is classified as unnatural if a fatality was brought about by suicide, accident, criminal action, or some other external effect.

In view of the wide range of the subject, only some forensic aspects can be addressed here. Therefore, this chapter concentrates on the diagnosis of completed suicide and its differentiation from homicide.

Fundamentals and Definitions

Possible Reasons and Dispositions

"Balance-sheet suicide" is defined as taking one's own life after thoroughly considering one's personal situation and perspectives. In practice, it often remains doubtful whether suicides were really committed voluntarily, that is, after making a calculated, rational decision, or whether external reasons (e.g., a personal crisis), or psychopathological dispositions may have led to the development of suicidal thoughts and impulses.

High-risk groups are patients suffering from depression and schizophrenia, drug and alcohol addicts, lonely and uprooted persons, as well as individuals with suicidal crises or suicide attempts in their history. There are also cases in which individuals unexpectedly kill themselves in a mental blackout (e.g., after a seemingly trivial dispute or because their driving license was withdrawn).

---

* Parts of this chapter were published as a scientific article in Forensic Science, Medicine and Pathology (Medicolegal evaluation of suicidal deaths exemplified by the situation in Germany, Forensic Science, Medicine, and Pathology, 2010, Volume 6, Number 1, pages 58–70, Markus Große Perdekamp, Stefan Pollak, and Annette Thierauf). The material is used with kind permission of Springer Science+Business Media.

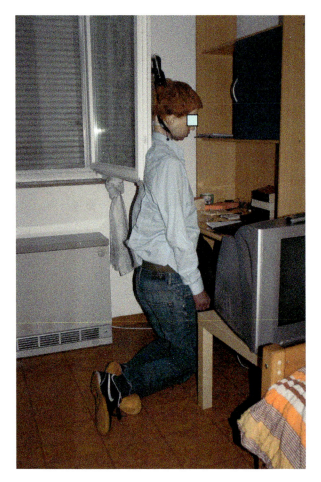

Figure 2 Frontal aspect of a train after collision with a 63-year-old woman who remained standing between the rails in an upright position in spite of warning signals. The back was penetrated by a hook so that the body was carried along until the train came to a standstill. Death was caused by blunt cranial trauma with exenteration of the brain.

Figure 1 Suicidal hanging of a young man with the knees bent and the feet touching the floor. The hanging device was a belt forming an open noose fixed to the handle of a window. The blinds had been pulled down to prevent early detection of the victim. A suicide note was found on the desk.

Complex Suicides

The criminalistic and medicolegal evaluation of suicides can be difficult if two or more suicide methods were applied simultaneously or rapidly one after the other within one and the same act. Such cases are called "complex suicides" and can be divided into primary (planned) or secondary (unplanned, improvised) forms. For "secondary complex suicide," it was also suggested to use the term "protracted suicide."

In primary (planned) complex suicides, the fatal outcome is to be guaranteed by deliberately using two or more mutually accelerating methods (such as infliction of a gunshot injury together with hanging, see **Figure 3**). A secondary (unplanned) complex suicide is defined as one in which the first method fails, turns out to be unexpectedly painful, or does not cause death quickly enough, so that the individual spontaneously

switches to a different method (e.g., superficial wrist cuts in the first phase followed by hanging to complete the act). Recently, the existence of still another subgroup has been demonstrated. These cases are characterized by a failure of the chosen suicide method so that the victim would normally survive. Owing to special circumstances at the scene, an unintentional secondary trauma (e.g., fall from a height after breaking of a noose) causes the victim's death. This constellation was defined as a separate entity called complicated suicide.

Suicide Pacts

The term "dyadic suicide" (double suicide or suicide pact) refers to cases in which two or more individuals mutually agree to die together and either kill themselves or agree to be killed by their partner. This type of suicide has some common characteristics:

- Simultaneous or directly consecutive suicide/homicide acts
- Application of the same suicide method
- Act committed at the same place (typically in the apartment)
- Intimate (mostly heterosexual) relationship between the persons involved
- Serious physical illness as the predominant motive for committing suicide

Murder–Suicide

The term "murder–suicide" (homicide–suicide) refers to the case of an individual intending to commit suicide, which

place or near to it. Perpetrators with pseudo-altruistic motives may show "undoing" behavior (e.g., "posing" of the victim, decoration of the scene with flowers, pictures, and candles).

Occupation-Related Suicide

Often forensic experts are confronted with occupation-related suicides. It is quite understandable that persons with special vocational skills, experiences, or knowledge will also apply these when committing suicide. In addition, in some fields of activity, potential suicidal tools not available to others are readily accessible. Well-known examples are suicides using firearms by persons allowed to carry guns (police officers, soldiers, hunters, sports marksmen), the use of livestock stunners by butchers, slaughterhouse workers, and farmers, as well as the suicidal use of explosives by blasters.

A pilot may take his life by willfully crashing the aircraft. Physicians and other health-care professionals mostly commit suicide by taking drugs orally or parenterally; another occupation-related mode is the painless infliction of cut wounds with a scalpel after applying a local anesthetic. The method used can also be related to the special anatomical/postoperative situation of a patient (e.g., transection of a shunt placed for hemodialysis).

Lethal cyanide poisoning is particularly often seen in chemists, jewelers, and metal workers. In farmers and horticulturists, toxic pesticides may be used for committing suicide by poisoning, which is sometimes indicated by a characteristic smell or warning dye (**Figure 4**). Electricians sometimes construct special devices with timers to electrocute themselves while they are asleep.

Dissimulation

Both attempted and completed suicides can be subsequently disguised. The motives for covering up the true facts are manifold. In the past, religious reasons and the wish for a church burial may have been of importance. Even today, the surviving partner may sometimes be afraid of being held responsible by the suicide's family, especially if the relationship was full of conflict. There are even cases in which a suicide victim stages an act similar to a homicide so that the survivors will receive the full amount of his or her life insurance.

Suicidal gunshot injuries are sometimes inflicted such that they resemble an accident (shot allegedly triggered unintentionally during the hunt or while cleaning the firearm). The same applies to self-killings in road traffic, which are difficult or impossible to distinguish from genuine accidents without special circumstances (e.g., previous announcement of suicide, additional self-inflicted injuries within the definition of a complex suicide). After incomplete suicidal acts, the suicide sometimes pretends to have become the victim of a criminal offense.

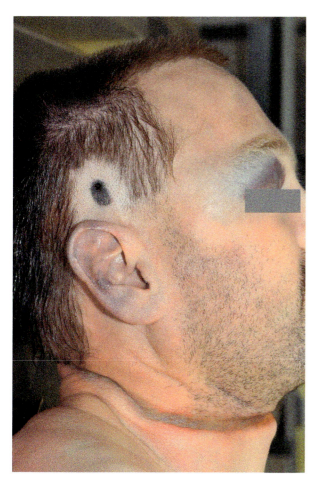

Figure 3 Complex suicide by an angled contact shot to the right temple and consecutive hanging. The weapon used was a small caliber rifle (0.22 lr). The noose was fixed to a water pipe mounted on the ceiling of a cellar room. The periorbital hematoma was caused by gunshot fractures of the anterior cranial fossa. The man had suffered from depression and insomnia.

includes at least one person into the killing act without the latter's agreement or against the latter's will; in most cases, there is a close relationship between the persons involved (family members, sexual partner). As mentioned above, this group does not include dyadic suicide in which the partner has agreed to be killed. The same applies to suicides committed after a homicide—so to speak as a reaction to it—and essentially determined by feelings of remorse, guilt, and fear of punishment. An important factor of homicide–suicide is the rapid chronological order of homicide and suicide. Most male perpetrators kill with the help of firearms, less often by means of manual/ligature strangulation or sharp force; preferential methods for the subsequent suicide are shooting and hanging. In most cases, homicide and suicide are committed at the same

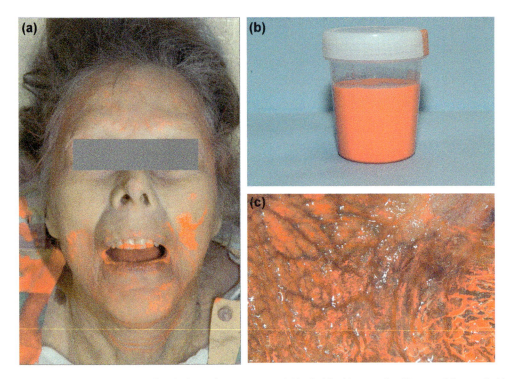

Figure 4 Poisoning with methiocarb (mercaptodimethur), a carbamate-type pesticide. Red liquid covers the skin around the mouth (a). It also discolored the stomach contents (b). and the gastric mucosa (c). The suicide victim was an 80-year-old woman who had suffered from dyspnea and severe pain due to osteoporosis.

Examples for (attempted) dissimulation of a suicide by family members are removal of a hanging device and application of a chin strap before calling the doctor for the postmortem examination; change of the situation at the scene, for example, by removing evidence pointing to suicide such as a suicide note, empty drug packages, or a drinking glass; removal of a plastic bag pulled over the head. This has to be distinguished from wrong postmortem diagnoses made by the examiner without being consciously or intentionally misled.

Of particular medicolegal relevance are cases disguised as a suicide in order to cover up a homicide. In the literature, it has been pointed out again and again that a firearm found in the victim's hand may have been placed there to simulate suicide. However, the number of homicides covered up in this way is very small. On the other hand, there are many proven suicides in which the weapon was found in the suicide's hand after firing the shot. In homicides, superficial cuts on the forearms or neck may create the impression of tentative or hesitation cuts thus simulating a suicide—independent of whether this was intended by the perpetrator or not. When a severely traumatized body is found near railway tracks, homicide (e.g., by shooting) with subsequent simulation of a railway accident or suicide has to be taken into consideration.

A particularly important category, which is not sufficiently discussed in the Anglo-American literature, comprises alleged suicides by hanging, which are actually homicides. Basically, two procedures have to be distinguished:

1. The victim is killed by hanging or
2. Subsequent hanging of the victim injured or killed before by some other method (e.g., blows, manual, or ligature strangulation)

Copycat Acts

Already Goethe's novel *The Sorrows of Young Werther* showed that suicidal acts reported by the media can prompt copycat acts in emotionally labile persons. Serious journalists therefore take care to avoid excessive detail about the method used in their reports. A well-known example that press reports can actually prompt copycat acts is the massive increase of suicidal self-suffocations by means of plastic bags pulled over the head, after the publication of the book, *Final Exit: The Practicalities of Self-Deliverance and Assisted Suicide for the Dying* by Derek Humphry (New York). In medicolegal practice, copycat acts are seen not only in connection with suicides and homicides but also in fictitious criminal offenses.

Criminalistically Relevant Phenomena and Suicide Scenes

The incidence of different suicide methods depends on temporal, cultural, and regional influences. Societal change is also reflected in the availability of certain means of suicide, for which carbon monoxide poisoning is an excellent example: Town gas, which played a major role as a source of poisoning in the twentieth century, has long been replaced by natural gas, which does not contain carbon monoxide. Until the 1990s, nonaccidental carbon monoxide intoxications were mostly brought about by conducting exhaust fumes into the interior of a car, but nowadays this method has lost its former importance due to the common use of catalytic converters in automobiles. At present, an increasing number of suicidal carbon monoxide poisonings is due to charcoal fires in closed spaces.

A similar change can also be observed with other poisons formerly used for committing suicide: arsenic poisoning verified by autopsy has drastically declined just as intoxications by caustic and topically irritating agents such as acids, lyes, certain metal salts, phenol and its derivatives, which were frequently seen before the Second World War. In the 1950s and 1960s, E 605 (parathione), an insecticide belonging to the substance class of phosphorous acid esters, was so commonly used for committing suicide or poison murders that there was really an "E 605 fashion." Even the spectrum of drug intoxications has changed in the more recent past (decrease of barbiturate intoxications, increased use of tricyclic antidepressants, neuroleptics (**Figure 5**), and parenterally administered insulin preparations as a means to commit suicide). Nowadays, suggestions for "new" suicide methods are often obtained from the Internet, such as suffocation by breathing a helium-enriched atmosphere.

A suicide locality that has become increasingly popular for about three decades is the bathtub. Apart from traditional forms (cuts to the wrists or the neck, stab wounds to the heart), the number of suicides combining an overdose of drugs or alcohol with subsequent drowning in the bath water is increasing. Electrocution in the bathtub, a method of suicide mostly chosen by women, presents significant diagnostic problems, as very often there are no electrothermal skin lesions. Deaths due to electric shock in the bathroom always raise the possibility of an accident or a homicide.

Regional differences in the frequency distribution of the methods of suicide are partially attributable to special construction features and means of transportation: Thus, suicides in the underground railway can occur only in metropolitan areas; suicides by falls from height are seen not only in cities with multiple-storey houses, but also in places with high stand-alone buildings such as viaducts, high bridges, viewing towers, or at deep precipices (cliffs, steep rock walls). Near natural bodies of water such as rivers, ponds, or lakes, drowning is a preferred method of suicide, which can even be reflected in local expressions used for announcing a suicide ("to

Figure 5 Suicide by ingestion of psychotropic drugs (antidepressants and neuroleptics). About 70 tablets had been mixed with some water (a). At autopsy, the stomach still contained a large amount of the pastelike material (b). The victim was a 55-year-old woman who suffered from depression and had made several suicide attempts before.

go into the water"). In rural areas, where hunting weapons are common, it goes without saying that these are also often used for suicide ("to put a bullet through one's head").

Suicide Under the Influence of Alcohol and/or Drugs

A high percentage of suicides are committed under the influence of alcohol. The largest number of intoxicated victims is found in the third-to-fifth decade of life. In connection with suicidal acts, a moderate amount of alcohol consumption is also called a courage dose.

Consumers of illicit drugs may kill themselves out of despair over their personal circumstances or under the influence of withdrawal symptoms. It is difficult or even impossible to distinguish overdoses with an unintended fatal outcome from intentional suicidal acts, unless the external circumstances (announcement, suicide note, etc.) provide hints in this respect. As in suicides by an overdose of medicine, one has to bear in mind that suspicious utensils may have been removed by flatmates or family members before the postmortem examiner sees the deceased. Quite often, drug victims are taken to another place and dumped there to hide their actual place of death and make police investigations in the drug scene more difficult.

Certain illicit drugs with psychedelic effects such as LSD, mescaline, and psilocybin intensify emotional experiences and sensory perceptions; cause illusions and hallucinations; or change the orientation as to place, time, and person; occasionally, they may cause feelings of omnipotence followed by fatal trauma (e.g., by jumping from a height under the impression of being able to fly).

Suicide in Road Traffic

As most cars are now equipped with catalytic converters, the number of suicides by conducting exhaust fumes into the interior of the car or in a closed garage with the engine running has decreased. Another method is that the suicide intentionally causes a fatal pseudo accident. It is estimated that at least 1% of the traumatic deaths occurring in road traffic (without pedestrians) have a suicidal background. Certainly, there are a considerable number of undetected cases, as in single-vehicle accidents, often no autopsy is performed and no technical opinion is obtained.

Suicide in road traffic always has to be suspected if a vehicle is driven at high speed against a solid object, into an oncoming truck, deep water, or a precipice for no apparent external reason and without a reaction of the driver. Clues pointing to suicide may be a suicide note, announcements of suicide, economic and personal problems, and the absence of braking or skid marks. The forensic literature contains numerous reports on very unusual forms of killing oneself with the help of a motor vehicle (for instance, a suicidal gunshot to the head while driving a car). Under differential diagnostic aspects, suicides committed in or with motor vehicles have to be differentiated not only from genuine traffic accidents, but also from natural deaths at the steering wheel and homicides (with attempted disguise by staging a pseudo traffic accident).

Suicide in Hospitals, Police Custody, or Prisons

It is estimated that about 3% of all suicides are committed by hospital patients. About half of these are inmates of psychiatric institutions (mainly patients suffering from schizophrenic psychoses or endogenous depression). Among nonpsychiatric patients, those with malignancies play a major role. Preferred methods of suicide are jumping from a height (e.g., from an upper floor window or balcony, see **Figure 6**) or hanging.

Suicides in police custody, pretrial detention, and prison constitute a special category. The peak age of this group—composed almost exclusively of males—is reached in the third decade of life. Several studies arrived at the conclusion that suicides are particularly frequent during pretrial detention and at the beginning of the prison term. Hanging is the preferred method with objects available in the cell such as bed sheets or clothes being used as ligatures. The noose is fixed, for example, at the bolt of the window, a bar of the window grill or a heating pipe. Less often, suicidal intoxications or completed suicides due to sharp force are observed. Every death in prison or police custody requires an autopsy in which not only suicides, accident-related traumata (sub- or epidural hematomas), and injuries inflicted by another party, but also natural causes of death (such as ischemic heart disease, myocarditis) are detected.

Suicide by Drowning

Genuine or alleged suicides in the water are a challenge for the examiner, even when excluding the abovementioned deaths in the bathtub. Suicides in the bathtub and in natural bodies of water are predominantly committed by women. Especially after a prolonged postmortem interval, it is difficult to distinguish between suicide, accident, homicide, and death from a natural cause. Tying is seen both in suicides and homicides; the same applies to weights (stones, dumbbells, etc.), which are used to make a body heavier and prevent it from surfacing. Sometimes the presence of tentative cuts or stabs suggests a (secondary complex) suicide. Concomitant injuries sustained by falling into the water, hitting obstacles, or drifting along a stream of flowing water can make it even more difficult to differentiate between suicide, homicide, and accident. Most suicide victims drowning themselves in the open air are fully clothed. Many of them are significantly intoxicated.

Self-cremation

Compared to former centuries, the number of suicidal self-cremations has increased. While in the 1960s and 1970s self-incineration was a means of political protest and prompted copycat acts, most suicidal acts nowadays do not seem to have a political or religious background, at least in the Western countries. The number of psychotic patients is particularly high. In the majority of cases, a fire accelerant (petrol, spirit, turpentine, etc.) is used. The victims have often attempted suicide before. Burns are typically more pronounced on the upper-half of the body than on the lower extremities. This seems attributable to an initially upright posture. The COHb concentration can be very low even with clearly vital burns; COHb values above 30% are rare. Self-incineration can be combined with other suicide methods such as stab or cut wounds, jumping from a height, gunshot injuries, or hanging.

Figure 6 Scene of suicide. The victim was a 57-year-old psychiatric inpatient who had left her ward unnoticed and jumped from an outside stair-case of the hospital (height about 20 m).

Medicolegally, differentiation between accident-related burns, self-cremation, fire homicides, and homicidal fire deaths is of prime importance. Homicides by burning ("fire homicides") are either committed by directly setting the victim on fire or by setting fire to a building/vehicle with the intent to kill. This must be distinguished from "homicidal fire deaths," which refers to premeditated murder with the subsequent attempt to cover up the traces of the crime and to eliminate the victim as far as possible by starting a fire.

Strangulation

Death by hanging is often too readily associated with suicide. Although accidental self-hanging (e.g., of children or in connection with autoerotic practices) is known among experts, it can be overlooked by postmortem examiners, particularly if the situation at the scene is not obvious, or was subsequently changed.

The opinion that hanging by another person is possible only if there is a significant disproportion between the strength of the perpetrator and the victim or if the victim is impaired in his/her ability to act (e.g., by alcohol or drugs), is not absolutely true. Clues pointing to homicide are, for example, injuries on the neck (additional ligature mark, fingernail abrasions, bruising), traumatization of other body regions not related to the hanging, signs of a fight or drag marks, suspicious situation at the scene (free suspension without something to step on, distance between the neck and the suspension point too short, grooves caused by pulling up the body).

Differentiation between suicidal and homicidal ligature strangulation may also involve significant diagnostic problems. In addition to general medicolegal aspects (no evidence of forced entry, a suicide note, no evidence of a struggle), the following findings may suggest self-strangulation: no other neck injuries away from the ligature mark, no evidence of previous physical overpowering, no defense injuries, ligature positioned tightly around the neck. Several ligatures and/or complex knots or the use of a gag do not exclude self-strangulation; the same applies to hairs or jewelry caught between the neck and the noose. The additional presence of tentative incisions supports the assumption of (secondary complex) suicide. Signs of congestion are particularly pronounced in self-strangulation (facial congestion, cyanosis, petechial hemorrhages above the strangulation level). On the other hand, the skin mark discernible after removing the ligature can be very inconspicuous. Fractures of the laryngeal structures are very rare in self-strangulation.

Sharp Force

Sharp force injuries are much more frequent in suicide attempts than in completed suicides. Suicidal stab wounds are predominantly localized in the precordial region (**Figure 7**). The number of wounds can vary greatly (from a singular stab wound to the chest up to more than 100 individual wounds). Often further injuries by sharp force (wrist and/or neck cuts) are found. Typical morphological criteria for self-inflicted are as follows: localization in the cardiac region, lesions largely parallel and arranged in groups, presence of shallow hesitation cuts, combination with tentative cuts, and absence of defense injuries.

While some older textbooks describe perforation of the clothing as a clear sign of injury inflicted by another person, it is now generally accepted that the "rule" of exposing the chest before suicide has many exceptions. Especially in psychotic patients, perforation of the clothes is by no means rare. The tool used is not only found near the corpse, but can also be lodged in the body or—provided that the ability to act was maintained long enough—may even have been removed by the suicide victim himself/herself. Occasionally, suicidal stabs are also located in the cervical area (**Figure 8**), the upper abdomen, the inguinal region, or the arms. Highly atypical suicidal acts (e.g., stab to the nape of the neck) may be difficult to differentiate from homicides.

The above criteria also apply to the differentiation between suicide and homicide in victims with cut wounds. Sites of predilection for suicidal cuts are the front of the distal forearms and the neck (**Figure 9**). Apart from "classical" constellations of findings with a multitude of equally shallow tentative cuts arranged in parallel, there are also exceptional suicides with only one deep cut severing the tissue. Here, several extensions in the corner of the wound may indicate that the blade was repeatedly moved backward and forward. Both on the forearms and the neck, cuts may run either in a transverse or a diagonal direction. Some suicide victims even inflict cuts along the longitudinal axis of the arm. In about half of all suicides with wrist cuts, these are localized on both forearms. In other cases, they are typically located on the side opposite to the dominant hand (i.e., mostly on the left). In suicidal cuts to the neck, the clothing usually remains undamaged.

Firearm Injuries

Experience has shown that the medical evaluation of gunshot injuries is particularly prone to misinterpretation—last but not least because of the great variability and complexity of gunshot findings, which even experts sometimes find difficult to interpret. In view of the large variety of suicidal gunshot wounds, the criteria described in the following can only be an approximate guide.

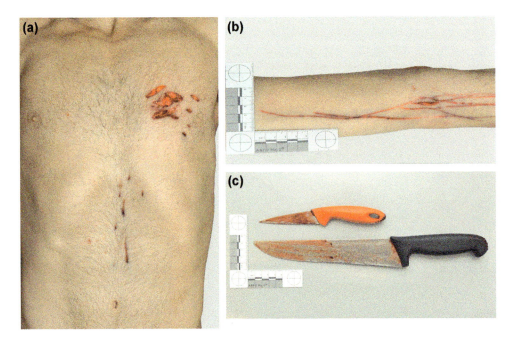

Figure 7   Suicide by sharp force (42-year-old man addicted to alcohol and illicit drugs). Multiple stabs to the cardiac region and tentative lesions in the precordial and upper abdominal region (a). Superficial cuts on both arms running parallel to the longitudinal axis (b). At the scene, two kitchen knives with blood-stained blades were found (c).

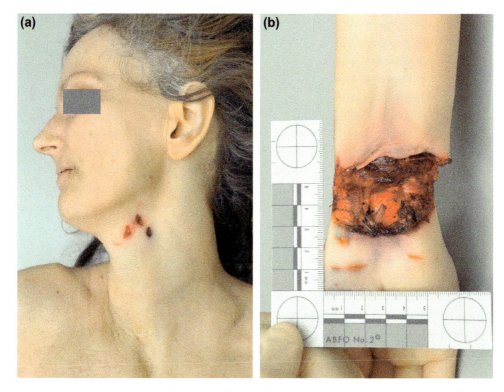

Figure 8 Complex suicide by sharp force and ingestion of drugs (48-year-old woman who had suffered from depression). Three superficial stabs to the left side of the neck (a). One deep and several shallow cuts to the right wrist (b). The victim was found in the open air and a suicide note was detected in her car parked near the scene.

Localization of the gunshot entrance wound

Regions considered typical of suicide are the temple (more often on the right than on the left, no strict correlation with the dominant hand), the mouth (intraoral shot), the cardiac region (in four of five suicidal shots to the chest the area is not bared), the forehead, and the submental region ("shots to the floor of the mouth"). If long guns are used, shots to the temple are less common and shots to the chest are more frequent than with handguns. Livestock stunners are mostly applied to the forehead—as with animals to be slaughtered. Wounds in the upper abdominal region are mostly regarded as "misdirected shots to the heart."

Atypical suicidal gunshot entrance sites are the occiput, the nape of the neck, and the parietal region; although in suicides committed with a slaughterer's gun, the latter is often chosen as the preferred site. Occasionally, gunshots into the ear or eye are observed.

Firing distance

Suicidal shots are usually fired with the muzzle pressed against the skin. For this reason, they normally show the characteristics of a contact shot (powder cavity, muzzle mark, and sometimes stellate skin laceration) unless they are intraoral shots.

Interposed textiles may modify the findings, especially in shots to the chest, and cause external soot soiling around the entrance wound in spite of the close contact between the muzzle and the body. External soot deposits are also possible in near/loose or incomplete contact shots or angled contact (e.g., **Figure 3**). Suicidal shots from a longer distance are possible when special devices are used (e.g., fixation of the weapon in a vice, triggering the shot with a string).

Number of hits and bullet track direction

In questionable suicides with more than one gunshot wound, it must be decided whether after the primary injury the suicide victim could have retained or regained the ability to act. If this is so, suicide victims with two or more gunshot wounds to the chest (or the adjacent abdominal region), to the head, or to the chest and the head are possible. Continued ability to act after a gunshot wound to the brain may occur if low-energy ammunition has been used and/or the bullet track avoided the "targets of immediate incapacitation"; in most of these cases, the projectile hits either only the frontal lobe or one of the temporal lobes. Further causes of suicidal multiple gunshot injuries are initial self-infliction of graze shots or shots to the limbs, use of automatic weapons, simultaneous firing of two weapons or two barrels, the

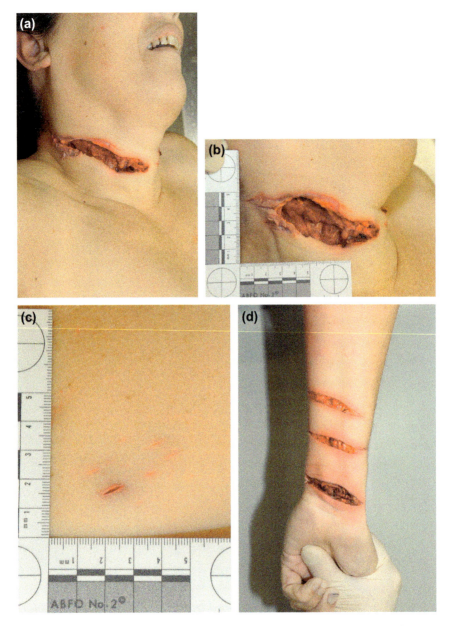

Figure 9 Suicide of a 53-year-old woman who inflicted cuts to both sides of her neck and to the flexor sides of her forearms. As only minor vessels had been severed, the victim survived for a prolonged time and finally died from hypothermia due to the low outside temperature. The cuts were inflicted with a scalpel found close to the body. The rear end of the incision on the right side of the neck (a and b) showed some shallow notches indicating that the blade had been moved back and forth several times. The skin of the precordial region displayed superficial tentative lesions (c). Another three cuts were located on the flexor side of left forearm (d). The woman had a history of paranoid psychosis and several suicide attempts.

occurrence of tandem projectiles (a bullet stuck in the barrel is expelled by the next one), and unintended double shots due to a technical defect of the disconnector.

The question as to whether a bullet track is compatible with a self-inflicted gunshot wound cannot be generally answered, but depends on the weapon used (long gun or handgun), the way in which the weapon was held, the position of the body, and the way in which the trigger was pulled.

Findings on the hands

Quite often suicides use both hands: the firing hand proper (with the index finger or thumb at the trigger) and the supporting hand, with which the barrel is positioned and held (mostly by grasping it around the barrel end). In any case, careful preservation and documentation of all findings on the firing hand is of utmost importance. As to the technical methods for performing this kind of examinations and the interpretation of the results, reference must be made to the relevant special literature. Traces of blood droplets and tissue particles flung backward ("backspatter") may be found on the firing hand of a suicide. Lesions due to the slide moving back are a rarity.

See also: **Forensic Medicine/Causes of Death:** Asphyctic Deaths—Overview and Pathophysiology; Gunshot Wounds; Immersion Deaths; Sharp Trauma; Strangulation; **Forensic Medicine/Clinical:** Deaths in Custody; Electrocution and Lightning Strike; Self-Inflicted Injury; Traffic Injuries and Deaths; **Forensic Medicine/Pathology:** Autopsy; External Postmortem Examination.

Further Reading

Aggrawal, A., 2006. Agrochemical poisoning. In: Tsokos, M. (Ed.), Forensic Pathology Reviews, vol. 4. Humana, Totowa, NJ, pp. 261–327.

Auwärter, V., Große Perdekamp, M., Kempf, J., Schmidt, U., Weinmann, W., Pollak, S., 2007. Toxicological analysis after asphyxial suicide with helium and a plastic bag. Forensic Science International 170, 139–141.

Bilban, M., Skibin, L., 2005. Presence of alcohol in suicide victims. Forensic Science International 147, 9–12.

Bohnert, M., 2005. Complex suicides. In: Tsokos, M. (Ed.), Forensic Pathology Reviews, vol. 2. Humana, Totowa, NJ, pp. 127–143.

Bohnert, M., Rothschild, M.A., 2003. Complex suicides by self-incineration. Forensic Science International 131, 197–201.

Byard, R.W., 2005. Murder–suicide: an overview. In: Tsokos, M. (Ed.), Forensic Pathology Reviews, vol. 3. Humana, Totowa, NJ, pp. 337–347.

Chan, P., Duflou, J., 2008. Suicidal electrocution in Sydney: a 10-year case review. Journal of Forensic Sciences 53, 455–459.

Große Perdekamp, M., Nadjem, H., Weinmann, W., Pollak, S., 2001. Plastic bag as the method in suicide and homicide. Archiv für Kriminologie 207, 33–41.

Hartwig, S., Tsokos, M., 2008. Suicidal and accidental carbon monoxide poisonings due to charcoal fires in closed spaces. Archiv für Kriminologie 222, 1–13.

Henderson, J.P., Mellin, C., Patel, F., 2005. Suicide – a statistical analysis by age, sex and method. Journal of Clinical Forensic Medicine 12, 305–309.

Jensen, L.L., Gilbert, J.D., Byard, R.W., 2009. Coincident deaths: double suicide or murder-suicide? Medicine, Science, and the Law 49, 27–32.

Karger, B., Billeb, E., Koops, E., Brinkmann, B., 2002. Autopsy features relevant for discrimination between suicidal and homicidal gunshot injuries. International Journal of Legal Medicine 116, 273–278.

Kõlves, K., Värnik, A., Tooding, L.M., Wasserman, D., 2006. The role of alcohol in suicide: a case-control psychological autopsy study. Psychological Medicine 36, 923–930.

McGirr, A., Tousignant, M., Routhier, D., et al., 2006. Risk factors for completed suicide in schizophrenia and other chronic psychotic disorders: a case-control study. Schizophrenia Research 84, 132–143.

Pollak, S., Missliwetz, J., 1979. Suicides in hospitals of Vienna. Zeitschrift für Rechtsmedizin 83, 233–244.

Pollak, S., Saukko, P., 2003. Atlas of Forensic Medicine. CD-ROM. Elsevier, Amsterdam.

Rothschild, M.A., Raatschen, H.J., Schneider, V., 2002. Suicide by self-immolation in Berlin from 1990 to 2000. Forensic Science International 124, 163–166.

Saukko, P., Knight, B., 2004. Knight's Forensic Pathology, third ed. Arnold, London, pp. 379–394.

Schmidt, P., Freudenstein, P., Bonte, W., 1991. Suicide in prison and police custody. Rechtsmedizin 2, 16–19.

Schmidt, P.H., Padosch, S.A., Madea, B., 2005. Occupation-related suicides. In: Tsokos, M. (Ed.), Forensic Pathology Reviews, vol. 2. Humana, Totowa, NJ, pp. 145–165.

Schröer, J., Püschel, K., 2006. Special aspects of crime scene interpretation and behavioural analysis – the phenomenon of 'undoing'. In: Tsokos, M. (Ed.), Forensic Pathology Reviews, vol. 4. Humana, Totowa, NJ, pp. 193–202.

Shields, L.B.E., Hunsaker, D.M., Hunsaker, J.C., 2005. Trends of suicide in the United States during the 20th century. In: Tsokos, M. (Ed.), Forensic Pathology Reviews, vol. 3. Humana, Totowa, NJ, pp. 305–335.

Thierauf, A., Strehler, M., Schmidt, P., Madea, B., 2007. Suicide by self-immolation. Archiv für Kriminologie 220, 103–114.

Thierauf, A., Gnann, H., Bohnert, M., Vennemann, B., Auwärter, V., Weinmann, W., 2009. Suicidal poisoning with mercaptodimethur – morphological findings and toxicological analysis. International Journal of Legal Medicine 123, 327–331.

Törö, K., Pollak, S., 2009. Complex suicide versus complicated suicide. Forensic Science International 184, 6–9.

Travis, A.R., Johnson, L.J., Milroy, C.M., 2007. Homicide-suicide (dyadic death), homicide, and firearm use in England and Wales. The American Journal of Forensic Medicine and Pathology 28, 314–318.

Türk, E.E., 2008. Fatal falls from height. In: Tsokos, M. (Ed.), Forensic Pathology Reviews, vol. 5. Humana, Totowa, NJ, pp. 25–38.

National Association of Medical Examiners (NAME)

MM Houck, Consolidated Forensic Laboratory, Washington, DC, USA

Introduction

The National Association of Medical Examiners (NAME) is the national professional organization of physician medical examiners, medical death investigators, and death investigation system administrators who perform the official duties of the medicolegal investigation of deaths of public interest in the United States. NAME was founded in 1966 with the dual purposes of fostering the professional growth of physician death investigators and disseminating the professional and technical information vital to the continuing improvement of the medical investigation of violent, suspicious, and unusual deaths. NAME has expanded its scope to include physician medical examiners and coroners, medical death investigators, and medicolegal system administrators from throughout the United States and other countries.

NAME members provide the expertise to medicolegal death investigation that is essential to the effective functioning of the civil and criminal justice systems. NAME is now the national forum for the interchange of professional and technical information in this important segment of public administration. NAME seeks to promote excellence in the day-to-day investigation of individual cases as well as to improve the interaction of death investigation systems with other agencies and political entities that interface with death investigation in each jurisdiction in this country.

The evolution of excellence in the medicolegal investigation of death in the United States has been slow and arduous. In many jurisdictions the medical aspects of death investigation remain relegated to personnel without medical training, or are performed by persons with little or no education in death investigation. NAME serves as a resource to individuals and jurisdictions seeking to improve medicolegal death investigation by continually working to develop and upgrade national standards for death investigation. The published NAME standards for a Modern Medicolegal Investigative System provide a model for jurisdictions seeking to improve death investigation. NAME aims to involve competent professional medicolegal death investigators in every jurisdiction in the United States.

NAME, as an association and through its members, maintains active cooperative relationships with the College of American Pathologists, American Society of Clinical Pathologists, and other professional organizations. NAME representatives participate and serve in an advisory capacity to federal, public, and private organizations on projects of mutual interest. As the official specialty association of physician medical examiners, the NAME promotes its vision of competent national death investigation from a seat in the House of Delegates of the American Medical Association. The educational functions of NAME are simultaneously directed toward the development and improvement of administratively efficient, cost-effective death investigation systems. The Association serves as the national forum for medical death investigators and system administrators for the discussion and dissemination of such information. NAME further encourages members to participate in the training of law enforcement officers, allied health professionals, paramedical personnel, and others who interface with death cases.

The work of the Association is carried out under the direction of its Officers and a Board of Directors elected by the membership. An executive committee is responsible for the fiscal affairs and management of the Association. Standing committees deal with issues of membership and credentials, education, program and publications, ethics, standards, inspection and accreditation, and finance, among others. All members are encouraged to participate in the committee activities. A permanent Executive Director and part time Executive Vice-President, headquartered in Atlanta, provide yearlong administrative support.

As part of its mission to improve the quality of death investigation nationally and to recognize excellence in death investigation systems, the NAME offers a voluntary inspection and accreditation program for medicolegal death investigative offices. This program is designed to offer expert evaluation and offer recommendations for the improvement of functioning offices. Accreditation by NAME is an honor and significant achievement for an office. It signifies to the public that the office is performing at a high level of competence and public service. NAME also offers consultative services for jurisdictions seeking to establish medicolegal death investigation systems and for political entities wishing to evaluate death investigation systems under their administrative purview.

Membership in the NAME is open to all physicians, investigators, and administrators who are active in medicolegal death investigation.

Membership is comprised of Fellows, Members, Affiliate Members, and Emeritus Members. Fellows are physician medicolegal death investigators who are either (1) certified in forensic pathology by the American Board of Pathology or its international equivalent as determined by the Board of Directors or (2) prior to 2008 have completed a training program in forensic pathology that is accredited by the Accreditation Council on Graduate Medical Education or have been officially "qualified for examination" in forensic pathology by the American Board of Pathology. Members are physician medicolegal death investigators other than those meeting the criteria designated in the definition of Fellow. The Member category includes pathologists, forensic pathology fellows, physician medical examiners, and physician coroners at the time of their application. Resident members are pathology residents who are involved in pursuing a career in any field that allows Association membership as delineated above. Affiliate members are those who assist Fellows or Members at the time of their application for membership, members of military commands who conduct death investigations, administrators within an official death investigation system, persons having expertise utilized by or affiliated with Fellows or Members in the official investigation of deaths, nonconsultant support personnel who assist Fellows, Members, other Affiliates or others in performing death investigation or other forensic duties, and Trainee Affiliates who are students beyond high school graduation who are involved in pursuing a career in any field that allows Association membership. Emeritus Members are those members in any of the categories described above who have had specified years of NAME membership and are fully retired from the practice of forensic science.

Acknowledgment

Material provided by NAME Web site www.namus.gov.

> *See also:* **Forensic Medicine/Pathology:** Autopsy; Forensic Pathology—Principles and Overview.

Further Reading

Hanzlick, R., Combs, D., 1998. Medical examiner and coroner systems history and trends. Journal of the American Medical Association 279 (11), 870–874.
Hickman, M., Strom, K., Hughes, K., Ropero-Miller, J., 2004. Medical Examiners and Coroners' Offices, 2004. US Department of Justice, Bureau of Justice Statistics, Washington, DC.

Key Terms

Admissible, Autopsy, Best evidence, Complex suicide, Daubert, Death investigation, Deaths, Evidence, Expert, Fitness for custody, Forensic, Frye, Hazard, Health, Holistic approach, Homicide–suicide, Improvement of medical care, Inspection of the scene, Integrated case management, Investigations, Juror, Kuhmo, Legal assessment, Medical decision, Medical negligence, Methods of suicide, Occupational health and safety (OHS), Pathology, Police custody, Preliminary investigation, Prevention, Professional organizations, Responsibility for medical assessment, Risk, Safety, Strategy, Submissions, Suicide, Witness.

Review Questions

1. What is "Brady material"?
2. What is "OHS"? What should this policy articulate?
3. What is a risk, in OHS terms? How is it prevented or mitigated? What is the hierarchy of control measures?
4. List some specific laboratory hazards. What are their risks, how are they managed?
5. Why is good housekeeping important in a forensic facility?
6. What specific risks and hazards are there in a medical examiner's facility as opposed to a regular forensic laboratory?
7. Why is stress a health and safety issue? What types of analysis are particularly prone to mental or stress issues?
8. Why is experience alone not enough to qualify one as an expert witness?
9. What is NAME? Who can join?
10. Why is being in police custody so risky?
11. Of the people who die in police custody, what percentage are males?
12. How do the causes of death in police custody vary by geography?
13. How does intoxication or being under the influence affect the risk of being in police custody?
14. The majority of nonfatal suicide attempts are committed predominately by whom?
15. How many people commit suicide worldwide each year?
16. What is balance sheet suicide?
17. What is a dyadic suicide?

18. What is dissimulation in regards to suicide?
19. What indications might a forensic pathologist use to distinguish between a suicide and a homicide? A suicide and an accidental death (for example, by gunshot)?
20. Is tying of the hands or feet in a drowning case necessarily reason to think it might be a homicide?

Discussion Questions

1. What legal, cultural, social, and political issues does a forensic pathologist face when investigating a death of a person in police custody? Why?
2. How do methods of suicide vary by geography and culture? Why do you think this is?
3. Does good general laboratory practice hold true for a medical examiner's facility or are there reasons to go above and beyond those precautions?
4. How does one provide quality and safety when operating in the field, say, at the site of an aircraft crash in the middle of a wooded area?
5. Should color photographs from an autopsy be used as demonstrative evidence in court? Are they prejudicial because of the blood and other vivid colors? Could they be black and white? Should there be photographs at all? Remember, family and friends could be in the gallery or the trial might even be televised.

Acknowledgment

Material provided by NAME Web site www.namus.gov.

Additional Readings

Aasebø, W., Orskaug, G., Erikssen, J., 2016. Can deaths in police cells be prevented? Experience from Norway and death rates in other countries. Journal of Forensic and Legal Medicine 37, 61–65.

Dias, M.S., Boehmer, S., Johnston-Walsh, L., Levi, B.H., 2015. Defining 'reasonable medical certainty' in court: what does it mean to medical experts in child abuse cases? Child Abuse & Neglect 50, 218–227.

Drake, S.A., Cron, S.G., Giardino, A., Trevino, V., Nolte, K.B., 2015. Comparative analysis of the public health role of two types of death investigation systems in Texas: application of essential services. Journal of Forensic Sciences 60 (4), 914–918.

Mangin, P., Bonbled, F., Väli, M., Luna, A., Bajanowski, T., Hougen, H.P., Ludes, B., Ferrara, D., Cusack, D., Keller, E., Vieira, N., 2015. European Council of Legal Medicine (ECLM) accreditation of forensic pathology services in Europe. International Journal of Legal Medicine 129 (2), 395–403.

Rockett, I.R., Hobbs, G.R., Wu, D., Jia, H., Nolte, K.B., Smith, G.S., Putnam, S.L., Caine, E.D., 2015. Variable classification of drug-intoxication suicides across US states: a partial artifact of forensics? PLoS One 10 (8), e0135296.

Tøllefsen, I.M., Helweg-Larsen, K., Thiblin, I., Hem, E., Kastrup, M.C., Nyberg, U., Rogde, S., Zahl, P.H., Østevold, G., Ekeberg, Ø., 2015. Are suicide deaths under-reported? Nationwide re-evaluations of 1800 deaths in Scandinavia. BMJ Open 5 (11), e009120.

INDEX

Note: Page numbers followed by "f" indicate figures and "t" indicate tables.

A

Abdominal injuries, 124, 124f, 240
Abdominal stab wound, 165f
Abduction, 2
ABPN. *See* American Board of Psychiatry and Neurology (ABPN)
Abrasions, 115–116, 116f
  collar, 185–186
Abusive head trauma (AHT), 206
Accident injuries, 169–170
Accidental traumatic asphyxia, 149–150
Acclimatization, 269
Accreditation, 32, 397
Acid fuchsin, 93
Acinetobacter baumannii (*A. baumannii*), 289
"Active" defense wounds, 211
Acute kidney injury (AKI), 176–177
Acute lung injury (ALI), 173, 179
Acute respiratory distress syndrome (ARDS), 176–177, 179
  postmortem findings, 179
Adenosine diphosphate (ADP), 288
Adenosine triphosphate (ATP), 43
Adipocere, 37–38
Adolescents, age estimation in, 315–319
ADP. *See* Adenosine diphosphate (ADP)
AEIOU rule, 75, 75t
AFIS. *See* Automated fingerprint identification system (AFIS)
Age diagnostics
  in child victims in child pornographic image documents, 319
  in older adults for clarification of pension entitlements, 320
Age estimation, 334
  in adolescents, 315–319
  dental examination, 317–318, 317f

ethnicity on development systems, 319
forensic examination, 315
physical examination, 316–317
radiological examination of clavicles, 318, 318f
summarizing age diagnosis, 318–319
x-ray examinations
  of hand, 317
  legitimization of, 319
  radiation exposure in, 316
Aging bruises, 205
AHT. *See* Abusive head trauma (AHT)
AI. *See* Amnesty International (AI)
Air embolism, 291
Air traffic injuries, 244
Airplane crashes
  DVI, 355
  German victims, 353–354
  Kaprun disaster, 354f
  mass fatality, 353
  tasks, 355–357
Airway obstruction visualizing, PMI, 104
AKI. *See* Acute kidney injury (AKI)
Alcohol, 23
  abuse, 269
  intake, 272
Algor mortis, 44–47
ALI. *See* Acute lung injury (ALI)
AM. *See* Antemortem (AM)
American Board of Psychiatry and Neurology (ABPN), 368
American Osteopathic Board of Pathology, 89
Amnesty International (AI), 225
Amperage, 276, 281–283
Anal findings in girls and boys, 208–209

Analogous trait, 14
Analogy, 13, 15−16
Anastomosis, 292
Anesthetic complications, 292−293, 293f
Animal and cultural indicators, 36
Animal predation, 52
Anomalies, 326
Anonymous threat, 276
Antemortem (AM), 321−322, 326f, 345, 347f
   data collection, 350−351, 350f
   data comparison with postmortem, 307−310
Anthropology, 312, 343
Aortic rupture, 250−251
Aorto-esophageal fistula, 290
Apparent death, 75
ARDS. *See* Acute respiratory distress syndrome (ARDS)
Arm torture, 227−228
Arthropods, 35−36
Asphyctic deaths. *See also* Immersion deaths
   burking, 135−136
   chemical asphyxiants, 136
   choking, 134
   choking game, 136
   compression of neck, 134−135
   drowning, 136
   smothering, 134
   suffocation, 134
Asphyxia, 133, 139
   autoerotic sexual, 136
   mechanisms, 134
   plastic bag, 134
   positional, 136
   restraint, 136
   signs, 133
   traumatic, 135
Asphyxial, 133
   deaths, 133, 135−136
   signs, 134
Asphyxiation, 300−301
Aspiration, 99, 104
Assault, 211, 215
Atelectasis, 292
ATP. *See* Adenosine triphosphate (ATP)
Attempted suicide, 222−223
Autoaggressive behavior, 220
Autoerotic practices, 276
Autolysis, 48
Automated fingerprint identification system (AFIS),
   346−347
Autopsy, 25, 79, 83, 86−88, 131, 135, 263−264, 264t
   accreditation, 86
   anatomical dissection, 83
   clinical, 84, 84f−85f, 86

   conduct of, 294−296, 295f−296f
   evidentiary material at, 27
   findings, 142−143, 143f, 157−158, 260, 264, 301−302,
      356−357
      histopathology, 270, 273
      immunohistochemistry, 270, 273
      macropathology, 269−270, 272−273, 273f
   histopathology, 89−91, 90f
   medicolegal, 83−86, 84f
   rate, 84−86
   report, 88
   results of, 261

B

Bacillariophycae, 159
"Backspatter", 395
Bacterial infection, 177
Bacterial translocation, 178
Bacteroides fragilis (*B. fragilis*), 289
BAHID. *See* British Association for Human Identification
   (BAHID)
"Balance-sheet suicide", 385
Bariatric surgery, 287−288
Barnacle, 36
Base fracture, 118−119
Bertillon, Alphonse, 30
Best evidence, 362
Bilateral frontal sinus, 324
Biochemistry
   hyperthermia, 270
   hypothermia, 274
Biological material hazards, 373−374
Biological profile, 306, 326
Bioprostheses, 289
BJS. *See* Bureau of Justice Statistics (BJS)
Blank cartridge pistol, 214
Blood congestion, 142
Blunt injury
   abdominal injuries, 124, 124f
   head injuries, 118−122
   injuries of chest, 122−124, 123f
   injuries to extremities, 124−125
   to integument, 115−118
Blunt trauma, 102f, 104, 115
Blunt traumatization, 123−124, 280
Blunt-force injuries, 123−124, 213−214, 238, 241
Body cooling, 56−58
Body traits
   age, 334
   gait analysis, 334
   height of perpetrator, 333−334
Bog bodies, 52−53

Bones, 36–37
    comparison of bone profiles, 310
    impressions, 120
    marrow embolism, 291
Botany, 36
Brain, 99, 139
    death, 76
    temperature time of death nomogram, 58
British Association for Human Identification (BAHID), 333
Bronchopneumonia, 252
Bruises. *See* Contusions
Brush abrasions, 115–116
Bullet wipe-off, 186
Bureau of Justice Statistics (BJS), 343
Burking, 135–136, 154
Burns, 127
    "burn shock", 175
        pathophysiology and clinical manifestation, 176
        postmortem findings, 176
    diagnosis of vitality, 129–130, 130t
    external findings, 127–128, 131
        consumption by fire, 128
        shrinkage of tissue, 127–128
    internal findings, 128–129, 131
        bones, 128–129
        cranial cavity and brain, 129
        gastrointestinal tract, 128
        respiratory tract, 128
        vessels, 128

C

C-reactive protein (CRP), 176, 274
Cadavers, preservation processes in, 52–53
Calcination, 129
Calcitonin, immunohistochemical detection, 63–64
"Canuto's ends", 166–167
Car occupants, 240–241
    frontal collisions, 240–241
    rear-end collisions, 241
    rollover collisions, 241
    side collisions, 241
Carbon monoxide hemo-globin (CO-Hb), 129
Carbon monoxide poisoning, 136, 389
Cardiogenic shock, 173, 176
Cardiomyopathies (CMs), 249–250
Cardiovascular disease, 249
Casper's law, 50–51
Cause of death, 26, 92, 264
    determination, 130
    investigation system, 83
    by WHO, 86b

CBRN incidents. *See* Chemical, biological, and radiological and nuclear incidents (CBRN incidents)
Cell proliferation, 68
Central nervous system diseases, 255–256
Cerebral
    bleeding, 248
    contusions, 121–122
    edema, 122
    injuries, 121–122, 121f–122f
Cerebrospinal fluid (CSF), 59
Chelation, 37
Chemical, biological, and radiological and nuclear incidents (CBRN incidents), 376
Chemical asphyxiants, 136
Chemical hazards, 373
Chilblains, 271–272
Child abuse, 109–112, 110f–111f, 205, 268
    findings in possible cases, 209
    interpretation of findings, 209
    interpretation of medical findings, 208–209
    physical abuse, 205–206
    physician or child care professional, 205
    sexual abuse, 205–206
Child maltreatment, 203
Choking game, 136
Cholecystectomy, 287–288
Cholesterol embolism, 291
Chop wounds, 166, 166f, 214
Circle of violence, 197, 198f, 199–200
Clandestine laboratory (Clan labs), 376–377
Clinical autopsy, 84, 84f–85f, 86
Clinical forensic medicine, 19, 20t
    clinical examination of living victims, 19–21
    external findings in physically injured victims of criminal assaults, 21t
    injuries of surviving victims and of assailants, 21–23
    medical hazards in police custody, 23
    neck of rape victim, 22f
    torture, 24
Close-range shots, 189–191
Closed disasters, 345
CMs. *See* Cardiomyopathies (CMs)
CN. *See* Cyanide (CN)
CO-Hb. *See* Carbon monoxide hemo-globin (CO-Hb)
Cocconeis placenta (*C. placenta*), 160f
Cocconeis placentula (*C. placentula*), 160f
Cold exposure, 271–272
Collagens, 69
Collateral harm, 201
Comparative method
    analogy, 13
    analogy and comparison within forensic process, 15–16

Comparative method (*continued*)
  biology, 14
  within forensic science, 16–17
  French naturalist, 13
  hammers, 15f
  skeletal structures of birds and humans, 14f
Comparative method, 30, 32
Comparative radiography, 323–325
  dental radiographic comparisons, 323–324, 324f
  experience, 325
  medical radiographic comparisons, 324–325, 324f
  validation studies, 325
Comparison
  analysis, 333
  image, 333
  photograph, 325–326, 333
Compartment syndrome, 175
Complex suicides, 386, 387f, 393f
Complex type of death, 77, 78f
Compound method, 58–59
Compression trauma, 102f, 104
Computed tomography (CT), 27, 228–230, 315
Computer forensics laboratory hazards, 374
Concussion of brain, 121
Confined spaces, 376
Congestion, 133, 135
  of brain, 152
Constrictor snakes, 154
Contact shots, 188–189
Contusions, 116–117, 116f–117f, 205
Conventional radiography (CR), 318
Converging type of death, 77, 78f
Cooling dummy, 58
Copycat Acts, 388
Coronary artery bypass graft surgery, 285
Coronary heart disease, 249
Corpses, destruction of, 49–50
Corrective factors, 57–58, 57t
Council of Europe, 85
Courage dose, 389
CR. *See* Conventional radiography (CR)
Cranial cavity and brain, 129
Crime, 7, 10–11
  forensic pathologist at, 27–28
  integrating chart for casework at scene, 60f–61f
Crime scene investigator (CSI), 362
Crime scene to court. *See also* Evidence; Expert witness
  conceptual structure modeling, 364f
  forensic science, 361
  forensic service delivery, 362
  forensic strategies, 362–365
  integrated case management, 365
  models, 362
  task, 362

Criminal
  anthropometry, 30–31
  criminal prosecution, 199, 201–202
    in cases of death in police custody, 381–382
  offenses, 217–219
Criminalistic(s), 29
  aspects, 184, 247–248
  reconstruction, 357
  relevant phenomena and suicide scenes, 389
CRP. *See* C-reactive protein (CRP)
Crush asphyxia. *See* Traumatic asphyxia
Crush syndrome, 175
Crushing abrasion, 116
CSF. *See* Cerebrospinal fluid (CSF)
CSI. *See* Crime scene investigator (CSI)
CT. *See* Computed tomography (CT)
Cut wounds, 164, 164f–165f
Cutis anserina, 157
Cyanide (CN), 129, 136
Cyanosis, 133, 140, 146f
Cyclotella stelligera (*C. stelligera*), 160f
Cymatopleura solea (*C. solea*), 161f
Cymbella helvetica (*C. helvetica*), 160f
Cytokine storm, 177
Cytokines, 173, 177

D

Dactyloscopy, 312
DAI. *See* Diffuse axonal injury (DAI)
Data collection, 349–351
  antemortem, 350–351, 350f
  postmortem, 349–350
Daubert, 369
Death(s)
  associated with medical procedures
    caveat, 286
    emerging challenge, 285–286
    forensic evaluation of periprocedural deaths, 294–297
    procedural complications encountered in forensic practice, 286–294
  cause determining, 76–79, 77f, 79t, 80f
  complex type, 77, 78f
  converging type, 77, 78f
  death certification, external postmortem examination before, 73–74, 74t
  determination, 73
  diagnosis on death certificate and autopsy, 79
  investigation, 25, 397–398
  manner of, 26, 79–81, 193–194
  in police custody, 379
    case history, 382
    criminal prosecution in cases, 381–382
    distribution of age and gender, 379, 380f

error analysis, 380–381, 381t
  forensic assessment, 381
  frequency, 379
  manner and cause, 379–380, 380f
  prevention, 382–383
  scene investigation, 263, 263t
Decay, 47
  gas, 99
Decedent The deceased person, 321
Deceleration trauma, 102f, 104, 120
Decollement, 238
Decomposition, 35–37, 50
  body in grave–saponification, 52
  preservation of decomposing bodies, 49–52
Deduction, 2–3
Defense wounds, 211. *See also* Gunshot wounds
  due to blunt force, 213–214
  from knife attacks, 211–213
  misleading findings similar to, 215
  from other weapons, 214–215
Defensive fractures, 227
Dehydration, 269
Dental
  examination, 317–318, 317f
  radiographic comparisons, 323–324, 324f
  radiographs, 347–348
Deoxyribonucleic acid (DNA), 31, 312, 343
  analysis, 345
  DNA-based methods, 353–354
  fingerprinting, 357
  profiling, 31, 349f, 361, 363–364
  testing, 308
Depressed fractures, 120
Dermal artifacts, 217t
Diabetes mellitus, 257
Diagnosticity, 16
Diastatic fractures, 118
Diatom test, 159–161
DIC. *See* Disseminated intravascular coagulation (DIC)
Diffuse axonal injury (DAI), 122
Diffusion tensor imaging (DTI), 235
Digital evidence, 31–32
Disaster Mortuary Operational Response Team (DMORT), 349
Disaster victim identification (DVI), 345, 355–357. *See also* Airplane crashes
  data collection, 349–351
  disaster classification, 345
  evaluation of identification data, 351–352
  management, 346
  objective methods, 346–349
  principles of identification, 346
  selection of methods, 351

Disseminated intravascular coagulation (DIC), 176–179, 269, 288
  postmortem findings, 179
Dissimulation, 387–388
Distant-range shots, 191
Distributive shock, 176
Diverging type of death, 77, 78f
DMORT. *See* Disaster Mortuary Operational Response Team (DMORT)
DMV atlas, 333–340
  cheek and throat area, 340
  chin shape, 338, 338f
  ear region, 338–340, 339f
  eye region, 335–336, 337f
  face shape, 335, 336f
  forehead, 335, 336f
  frontal hairline, 335, 337f
  nasal region, 336–338, 338f
  oral region, 338, 338f
  wrinkles and dimples, 339f, 340
DNA. *See* Deoxyribonucleic acid (DNA)
Domestic violence (DV), 197, 199–200, 200t
  children and, 203
  circle of violence, 197
  diagnosis, 200–201
  epidemiology, 198–200
  risk factors for, 199
  sexual violence and, 202–203
  violence against women, 197
Donor–recipient arterial anastomosis, 292
Double suicide. *See* Suicide pacts
Drowning, 104, 136, 158, 299
Drug abuse, 268
Drug adverse effect, 269
Drug-related hyperthermia, 269
DTI. *See* Diffusion tensor imaging (DTI)
Duluth model, 197
DV. *See* Domestic violence (DV)
DVI. *See* Disaster victim identification (DVI)
Dyadic suicide. *See* Suicide pacts
Dynamic risk management, 372

E

"E 605 fashion", 389
E-forensics, 361
ECG. *See* Electrocardiogram (ECG)
ECLM. *See* European Council of Legal Medicine (ECLM)
ED. *See* Emergency department (ED)
Edema, 129, 152
Education and training, 368
Ek. *See* Kinetic energy (Ek)

Electric
  burn, 277f–278f, 279
  marks, 276, 279
  shock, 276, 280
  torture, 233–234
Electrical excitability of facial muscles, 58
Electrical resistance, 275
Electrical/machinery hazards, 374
Electricity as instrument of torture, 233–234
Electrocardiogram (ECG), 74
Electrocution, 275
  electric burn, 277f–278f, 279
  high-voltage effects, 279–281, 280f–281f
  low-voltage effects, 275–278
Electrophilia, 276
Embolization, 291
Emergency department (ED), 200
Emphysema aquosum, 158
End Violence Against Women Coalition (EVAW Coalition),
    198
Endocarditis, 289
Endoscopic retrograde cholangiopancreatography (ERCP),
    289
Endoscopy, 290
Endosteal fracture, 230
ENFSI. See European Network of Forensic Sciences (ENFSI)
Entomology, 35–36
Entrance wounds, 184–187
  abrasion collar, 185–186
  bullet wipe-off, 186
  characteristics, 184
  classification, 187–191
  entrance hole, 184
Enzyme histochemistry, 70
Epidemiology, 260–261
Epidural hematoma, 120, 122, 239
Epidural hemorrhages, 120
Epigastrium, 163
Epilepsy, 256
Epiphyseal fractures, 206
ERCP. See Endoscopic retrograde cholangiopancreatography
    (ERCP)
Error analysis for deaths in police custody, 380–381
Erythema, 272, 272f
European Council of Legal Medicine (ECLM), 85
European Network of Forensic Sciences (ENFSI), 32
EVAW Coalition. See End Violence Against Women Coalition
    (EVAW Coalition)
Evidence, 7. See also Crime scene to court; Expert witness
  class level information, 9
  forensic approaches to classification, 8
  manufactured evidence, 8
  relationships and context, 10–11

set theory, 7
taxonomy, 7–8
uniqueness and individualization, 9–10
Evidentiary material at autopsy, 27
Excitation processes, 275
Excited delirium, 153
Exclusion, 321–322, 325
Exenteration shots, 181
Exit wounds, 184–187
Expert witness, 20t. See also Crime scene to court
  education and training, 368
  experience as, 367–368
  increased scrutiny of experts, 368–369
  membership in professional associations, 368
  qualifications, 367
  selecting expert, 367
  weight of evidence, 369
Explosion, 101–102, 102f
Exsanguinating hemorrhage, 168
External examination, 26, 87
External postmortem examination, 73
  apparent death, 75
  brain death, 76
  death certificate and autopsy, 79
  before death certification, 73–74, 74t
  determination of death/death and dying, 74
  determining cause of death, 76–79, 77f, 79t, 80f
  functions and importance, 74t
  manner of death, 79–81
  problem areas, 81
  time since death, 76, 76t
Extradural hemorrhages. See Epidural hemorrhages

F

Facial assessment, 335f
  body traits, 333–334
  checking for suitability of images, 332
  comparison
    analysis, 333
    image, 333
  feature analysis, 332
  skin, hands, and genitals, 334
Facial features, 326–327
Facial identification, 307, 308f
Fact witness, 19
Factitial dermatitis, 221
Failure to exclude, 321
Falaka, 228
Fat embolism, 291
FGFs. See Fibroblast growth factors (FGFs)
FIAG. See Forensic Imagery Analysis Group (FIAG)
Fibrin, 163

Fibroblast growth factors (FGFs), 67
Fibroblasts, 68–69
Field studies, 58
Finger torture, 226–227
Fingernails torture, 226
Fingerprints, 312, 343, 346–347, 356
    analysis, 308, 309f
Fire
    consumption by, 128
    homicides, 391
Firearm injuries, 181, 392–395
    findings on hands, 395
    firing distance, 393
    of hits and bullet track direction, 393–395
    localization of gunshot entrance wound, 393
Firearms, 373–374
Firing distance, 393
Fitness for custody, 379–380, 382–383
Fixation method, 92
Flash suppressors, 189–190
Fluid displacement, 99
Fluid-filled organs, 181
Foam organs–organs, 48–49
Foot torture, 228–232
Foreign bodies, 226–228
Forensic Imagery Analysis Group (FIAG), 333
Forensic pathology–principles, 25
    additional investigations, 27
    cause of death, 26
    evidentiary material at autopsy, 27
    external examination, 26
    forensic pathologist, 25
        at scene of crime/death, 27–28
    internal examination, 27
    manner of death, 26
    medicolegal autopsy, 25–26
    medicolegal systems and investigation of deaths, 25
Forensic practice, procedural complications in, 286–294
    anesthetic complications, 292–293, 293f
    complications associated with solid organ transplantations, 291–292
    hemorrhage, 286–288
    nonanesthetic causes of iatrogenic hypoxia, 293–294
    perioperative embolic phenomena, 290–291
    periprocedural trauma, 290
    sepsis, 289–290
Forensic science, 1–2, 29, 361
    accreditation, 32
    "barbers–physicians", 29
    comparative method within, 16–17
    DNA profiling, 31
    native principles, 3–4
    nonnative principles, 4–5

scientific methods, 32
trace as basic unit, 2–3
in United States, 30
Forensic Science International, 261
Forensic(s), 2, 25
    anthropology, 357
    assessment of death in police custody, 381
    autopsy, 89–90
    dentistry, 347–348
    effectiveness, 364
    evaluation of periprocedural deaths
        conduct of autopsy, 294–296, 295f–296f
        postautopsy evaluation, 296–297
        postmortem examination, 294
    forensic evidence, histological findings as, 94, 94f
    forensic medicine, 25
        documentation, 202
    histopathology, 91
    intelligence, 2
    investigation of deaths, 127
    medical examiner, 19
    odontology, 348, 357
    pathologist, 25
        at scene of crime/death, 27–28
    radiology, 202
    strategies, 362–365
    submissions officer, 362–363
Fractures, 206, 228–230, 232–233
    of hyoid bone, 145
    of laryngeal cartilages, 140
Frostbite, 271–272
Fume cupboards, 374–375

G

Gait analysis, 334
Garroting, 135
Gas, 97–99, 98f
    case report, 99
Gastric contents, 62
Gastrointestinal diseases, 255
Gastrointestinal tract, 128
GCS. See Glasgow Coma Scale (GCS)
General laboratory management, 375
Genitals, facial assessment, 334
Ghon method, 27
Glasgow Coma Scale (GCS), 238
Glomus caroticum, 140
Grave–saponification, 52
Grayish-black soot, 189
"Grease ring", 186
GSR. See Gunshot residues (GSR)

Gunshot, 100–101, 100f
    entrance wound localization, 393
    injury, 182
Gunshot residues (GSR), 189
Gunshot wounds, 181. *See also* Defense wounds
    classification of entrance wounds, 187–191
    criminalistic aspects, 184
    death manner, 193–194
    entrance and exit wounds, 184–187
    forensic examination and documentation, 193
    injuries caused by explosives, 194–195
    internal findings, 191–193
    shotgun injuries, 191
    wound ballistics, 181–184
Gunsmoke, 187

H

Hand injury, 211–212
Hand torture, 227–228
Handling of exhibits in court, 376
Hands, facial assessment, 334
Hanging, 134–135, 140–142, 390–391
    autopsy findings, 142, 143f
    external findings, 142
    mark, 141–142, 141f
    mechanism, 140
    methods, 141
Hazards
    in field, 376–377
    during overseas deployment, 377
    specific laboratory, 373–376
Head injuries, 118–122, 200–201
    cerebral injuries, 121–122, 121f–122f
    intracranial hemorrhages, 120–121, 120f, 239
    skull fractures, 118–120, 119f
    TBI, 238–239
Head torture, 232
Heat exhaustion, 269
Heat shock proteins (HSPs), 270
Heat waves, 268–269
Heatstroke, 269
Hemangioma, 291
Hematoma, 153–154, 238
Hematoxylin-basic fuchsin-picric acid stain, 93
Hemopericardium, 176, 286–287, 287f
Hemoperitoneum, 287–288, 288f
Hemorrhage, 286–288
    hemopericardium, 286–287, 287f
    hemoperitoneum, 287–288, 288f
    hemorrhagic pneumonia, 255
    hemorrhagic shock
        pathophysiology and clinical manifestation, 175
        postmortem findings, 175

hemothorax, 287, 287f
    periprocedural, 288
    retroperitoneal, 287–288
Hemostasis, 285
    hemostatic clips, 287–288, 288f
    hemostatic processes, 301
Hemothorax, 287, 287f
"Heterolytic" alkaline colliquative process, 48
Heuristic process, 2–3
"Hide and die", 271
Hierarchy of control measures, 372–373
High-intensity light sources, 375
High-voltage effects, electrocution, 279–281, 280f–281f
Hinge fracture, 118
Histology, 129
    examination, 279, 279f
    investigation, 262–263
Histopathology, 89, 270, 273
    autopsy, 89–91, 90f
    diagnosis, 93–94
    fixation, 92
    forensic, 91
    guidelines, 91–92
    histological findings as forensic evidence, 94, 94f
    histopathological diagnosis, 93–94
    pathology as medical specialty, 89
    problem areas, 94–95
    quality, 91
    sampling, 92
    staining, 92–93
HIV. *See* Human immunodeficiency virus (HIV)
Hogtied prone position, 153
Holistic approach, 365
Holistic process, 2
Homicide, 182f, 192f, 193, 299
    injuries, 169–170
Hormonal disease, 317
Housekeeping, 375
HSPs. *See* Heat shock proteins (HSPs)
Human bite marks, 205
Human immunodeficiency virus (HIV), 48
Hydrogen sulfide, 136
Hymen, 207–208
Hymenal injuries, 208
Hypercapnia, 139
Hyperemia, 129
Hyperpyrexia, 269
Hyperthermia
    autopsy findings, 269–270
    biochemistry, 270
    key points of diagnosis, 270
    molecular pathology, 270

pathophysiology and clinical manifestations
   drug-related hyperthermia, 269
   heatstroke and related syndromes, 269
  social and forensic issues, 268
  toxicology, 270
Hypothermia, 299, 301–302
  autopsy findings, 272–273
  biochemistry, 274
  key points of diagnosis, 274
  molecular pathology, 274
  pathophysiology and clinical manifestations, 271–272
  social and medicolegal issues, 271
  toxicology, 273
Hypovolemic shock, 175
Hypoxia, 140, 157
Hysterectomy, 287–288

I

Iatrogenic foreign body embolism, 291, 291f
Iatrogenic hypoxia, nonanesthetic causes of, 293–294
Iatrogenic injury, 286, 294
ICAM. *See* Interstitial cell adhesion molecule (ICAM)
ICMP. *See* International Commission for Missing Person (ICMP)
ICRC. *See* International Committee of Red Cross (ICRC)
Identification, 325. *See also* Personal Identification
  assurance protocol, 320
  documents, 315
  of living
    DMV atlas, 334–340
    facial assessment, 332–334, 335f
  methods contributing to, 326–328
  putrefied, burnt, partly, 312
  unidentified cadavers, 306–307
  well-preserved body, 310–312
IHD. *See* Ischemic heart disease (IHD)
IL. *See* Interleukin (IL)
Illicit drugs, 390
Imaging, 228, 235
Immediate cause of death, 76
Immersion deaths, 157. *See also* Asphyctic deaths
  autopsy findings, 157–158
  biochemical markers, 158–159
  diatom test, 159–161
  histology, 158
  physiopathology, 157
Immunohistochemistry, 27, 70, 92, 270, 273
  advances, 93
  detection of insulin, thyroglobulin, and calcitonin, 63–64
In situ hybridization, 93
Incaprettamento, 154
Incised wounds, 164, 165f

Indicators of stress, 377
Individualization, 9–10
Induction, 2
Infancy, 248
Infanticide, 109–112, 110f–111f, 299
Inflammatory mediator, 173
Infliction, 163
Influenza B-virus in an inflammatory round cell, 93f
Initiation rites, 226, 235
Injury
  caused by explosives, 194–195
  to extremities, 124–125
  to extremities, 240
  from glass, 166–167, 167f
  types, 237–240
Institutional restraint, mechanical asphyxia during, 154
Insufficient evidence, 325–326
Insulin, immunohistochemical detection, 63–64
Insurance fraud, self-mutilation for, 219–220
Integrated case management, 365
Integument, blunt injury to
  abrasions, 115–116, 116f
  contusions, 116–117, 116f–117f
  lacerations, 117–118, 117f–118f
Intelligent identifications, 365
Interleukin (IL), 177
Intermediate-range shots, 189–191
Internal examination, 27, 87–88
International Code of Medical Ethics, 91
International Commission for Missing Person (ICMP), 351
International Committee of Red Cross (ICRC), 349
Interpretation method. *See* Comparative method
Interstitial cell adhesion molecule (ICAM), 67
Intracranial hematomas, 120
Intracranial hemorrhages, 120–121, 120f, 239
Intradermal bruises, 116
Invasive medicine and care, 109
Iris, pharmacological excitability of, 42–44
Ischemic heart disease (IHD), 94
Isoflurane, 293

J

Joint POW/MIA Accounting Command Central Identification Laboratory (JPAC-CIL), 325
Joule heating, 276, 279
Juror, 367–369

K

Kinetic energy (Ek), 181
Kirk's principle, 4
Kneecapping, 230–232

Knife attacks, 211—213
Known source (Ks), 16
Kuhmo, 369

L

Laceration(s), 117—118, 117f—118f, 207—209, 213, 238
Ladder-rung tears, 123—124
Laryngeal spasm, 157
Lasers, 375
Latent interval, 120
Leg torture, 228—232
Legitimization of x-ray examinations, 319
Lethal cyanide poisoning, 387
Lethal gunshot injuries, 183
Letulle method, 27
Leukocyte function-associated antigen-1 (LFA-1), 67
Leukocytes, 67
LFA-1. See Leukocyte function-associated antigen-1 (LFA-1)
Lichtenberg figure, 283
Ligature strangulation, 21—23, 135, 142—143, 146f
    autopsy findings, 143
    mark, 143, 144f—145f
    mechanism, 142
Lightning strikes, 281—283, 282f
"Line sepsis", 289—290
Linear fractures, 118
Linear type of death, 77, 77f
Linkage blindness, 2
Linnaean method, 7—8
Lipophages, 68f
Liver transplants, 292
Living victims, clinical examination of, 19—21
Local vitality, 174—175
Localization, 100
Locard's principle, 3—4
Long-QT syndrome (LQTS), 264—265
Longitudinal fractures, 118
Lot number, 327
Low-voltage effects, electrocution, 275—278, 278f
LQTS. See Long-QT syndrome (LQTS)
Lucid, 120
Lung, fluid displacement in, 99

M

Macaque, 7—8
Maceration, 299—300, 300f
Macropathology, 272—273, 273f
    external findings, 269—270
    internal findings, 270
Macrophages, 68
Magnetic resonance imaging (MRI), 27, 228—230

Magnetic resonance spectroscopy (MRS), 62
Malignant brain tumor, 95f
Malignant hyperthermia, 268—269
Malignant syndrome, 269
Malingering, 220—221
Manner of death, 26, 79—81, 193—194
Manual handling, 375
Manual strangulation, 21—23, 135, 143—146, 146f. See also
        Strangulation
    autopsy findings, 145—146
    mechanism, 143—145
    skin marks from, 145
Manufactured evidence, 8
Mass disasters, 353, 355, 357
Mass fatality, 353
Mastectomy, 291
Material safety data sheets. See Safety data sheets (SDS)
Mechanical asphyxia. See also Postural asphyxia;
        Traumatic—asphyxia
    cases, 154
    during institutional restraint, 154
Medical care for persons in police custody, 382
Medical Examiner and Coroner system, 25
Medical findings, interpretation of
    anal findings in girls and boys, 208—209
    genital findings
        in boys, 208
        in girls, 208
Medical hazards in police custody, 23
Medical radiographic comparisons, 324—325, 324f
Medicolegal autopsy, 25—26, 83—86, 84f, 89—91
Medicolegal investigations, 321—322
Medicolegal systems, 25
Membership in NAME, 397—398
Mental diseases, artifacts in patients with, 221—222
Mercury, 37
Met-Hb. See Methemoglobin (Met-Hb)
Metaphyseal fractures, 206
Methemoglobin (Met-Hb), 129
Methicillin-resistant Staphylococcus aureus (MRSA), 289
Microorganisms, 93
Microscopy, 89, 91
Microsievert (μSv), 316
Millisievert (mSv), 316
"Mini-STR" approach, 31
Minimal intensity projection (MinIP), 100
mitochondrial DNA (mtDNA), 346
MODS. See Multiple organ dysfunction syndrome (MODS)
Moisture, 37—38
Molecular genetics, 357
Molecular pathology
    hyperthermia, 270
    hypothermia, 274

Morphological substrate, 249–257
    aortic rupture, 250–251
    cardiovascular disease, 249
    central nervous system diseases, 255–256
    coronary heart disease, 249
    diseases of respiratory tract, 251–255
    gastrointestinal diseases, 255
    nonischemic heart disease, 249–250
    other causes of sudden death, 257
    pulmonary embolism, 251
Morphology, 279, 323–325
Mortality statistics, 84–85
MRI. *See* Magnetic resonance imaging (MRI)
MRS. *See* Magnetic resonance spectroscopy (MRS)
MRSA. *See* Methicillin-resistant *Staphylococcus aureus* (MRSA)
MSCT. *See* Multislice CT (MSCT)
mSv. *See* Millisievert (mSv)
mtDNA. *See* mitochondrial DNA (mtDNA)
Multiple corresponding factors, 321–323
Multiple organ dysfunction syndrome (MODS), 174,
        177–178, 269
    altered organ function, 177
    pathophysiology and clinical manifestation, 177–178
    postmortem findings, 178
Multislice CT (MSCT), 97, 100
Mummification, 37, 52
Munchausen syndrome, 221–222
Murder–suicide, 386–387
Muscle, mechanical excitability of, 41
Mutilation, 227, 230
"Muzzle abrasion", 189
Mycobacterium tuberculosis (*M. tuberculosis*), 93
Myofibroblasts, 69

N

NAME. *See* National Association of Medical Examiners
        (NAME)
NamUs. *See* National Missing and Unidentified Persons
        System (NamUs)
National Association of Medical Examiners (NAME),
        397–398
National Missing and Unidentified Persons System (NamUs),
        343
Native principles, 3–4
Navicula protracta (*N. protracta*), 159f
Navicula radiosa (*N. radiosa*), 160f
Neck torture, 232
Necropsy, 25, 83
Necrotizing enterocolitis, 288
Necrotizing fasciitis, 289

Neonaticide, 109–112, 110f–111f, 299
    incidence, 299
    methods, 299–302
Nephrectomy, 287–288
Neurogenic shock, 176
Newton's law, 45
Newton's rule of cooling, 56
NF-kB. *See* Nuclear factor-kB (NF-kB)
NGOs. *See* Nongovernmental organizations (NGOs)
Nitzschia recta (*N. recta*), 160f
Nomogram
    brain temperature time of death, 58
    method, 56, 58
    rectal temperature time of death, 56–58
Nonaccidental injury, 205
Nonaccidental skull fractures, 206
Nonalignable differences, 16–17
Nonanesthetic causes of iatrogenic hypoxia,
        293–294
Nonfatal suicide, 385
Nongovernmental organizations (NGOs), 225
Nonischemic heart disease, 249–250
Nonnative principles, 4–5
Nuclear DNA, 348–349
Nuclear factor-kB (NF-kB), 177
Nysten's rule, 43

O

Obesity, 269
Objective methods, 346–349
    dental radiographs, 347–348
    fingerprints, 346–347
    nuclear DNA, 348–349
    unique medical identifiers, 349
Obstetric procedures, 290
Obstructive shock, 174
Occupation-related Suicide, 387
Occupational health and safety (OHS), 371
    dynamic risk management, 372
    hazards in field, 376–377
    hierarchy of control measures, 372–373
    policy, 371–373
    risk assessments, 372
    specific laboratory hazards, 373–376
Odontology, 308–310, 309f, 312, 343
OHS. *See* Occupational health and safety (OHS)
Ollivier syndrome, 150t
Ontario Forensic Pathology Service, 92
Open disasters, 345
Orthopantomogram (OPG), 316

Osteomyelitis, 289
Overarm stabbing, 168
Oxidant, 174

P

Palmar strangulation, 135
Palmatoria, 230
Paradigm, 3
Paradoxical undressing, 271–272
Parallel connectivity, 16
Paranasal sinuses, 99
"Passive" wound, 211
Pathology, 25, 89
Pathomechanisms, 143–145
Pathophysiological mechanism, 130
Pattern of injuries, 200–201
PCI. *See* Percutaneous coronary intervention (PCI)
PCR. *See* Polymerase chain reaction (PCR)
Pedestrian collisions, 242–243
PEG. *See* Percutaneous endoscopic gastrostomy (PEG)
Pelvic injury, 240
Penis, 208
Peptic ulcers, 254f, 255
Percutaneous coronary intervention (PCI), 286
Percutaneous endoscopic gastrostomy (PEG), 287–288
Percutaneous transhepatic cholangiography (PTC), 287–288
Perioperative embolic phenomena
    air embolism, 291
    cholesterol embolism, 291
    fat and bone marrow embolism, 291
    iatrogenic foreign body embolism, 291, 291f
    pulmonary cartilage embolism, 291
    pulmonary thromboembolism, 290–291
Periprocedural deaths, forensic evaluation of, 294–297
Periprocedural hemorrhage, 288
Periprocedural trauma, 290
    aorto-esophageal fistula, 290
    endoscopy, 290
    obstetric procedures, 290
    resuscitative injuries, 290
Peritonitis, 289, 289f
Permafrost bodies, 52
Personal effects, 353–354
Personal identification, 305, 307–310. *See also* Scientific identification
    DNA testing, 308
    facial identification, 307, 308f
    fingerprint analysis, 308, 309f
    in forensic anthropology, 321–322
        methods contributing to identification, 326–328
        multiple corresponding factors, 322–323
        scientific identification, 322–325

individual markers, 307
    odontological methods, 308–310, 309f
    radiological methods, 310
    superimposition methods, 310, 311f
Perthes pressure congestion, 150t
Petechia in thymus, 262, 263f
Petechiae, 133, 135, 140
Petechial hemorrhages, 146
Petite guillotine, 226
PFT. *See* Pulmonary function testing (PFT)
Pharmacological excitability of iris, 42–44
Photographic imaging techniques, 327–328, 328f
Physical abuse, 205–206
Physical examination, 316–317
Physical restraint, 149, 153–154. *See also* Institutional restraint
Physiopathology, 157
Pinnularia viridis (*P. viridis*), 161f
Pistol whipping, 214
Pleura sign, 131
PM. *See* Postmortem (PM)
PMCT. *See* Postmortem computed tomography (PMCT)
PMI. *See* Postmortem imaging (PMI); Postmortem interval (PMI)
PMN cells. *See* Poly-morphonuclear cells (PMN cells)
Pneumonia, 251
Pneumothorax, 110, 123, 239
Police custody
    death in, 379
    forensic assessment of death in, 381
    manner and cause of death, 379–380, 380f
    medical hazards in, 23
Poly-morphonuclear cells (PMN cells), 67
Polymerase chain reaction (PCR), 31, 312, 348
Posey restraint, 154
Positional asphyxia. *See* Postural asphyxia
Positive identification, 305–307, 310, 321–322, 324
Postautopsy evaluation, 296–297
Postmortem (PM), 263, 322–323, 323f, 327f, 347, 347f
    biochemistry, 27, 174–175
    body cooling, 44–47
    chemistry, 27
    cutaneous lividity, 42
    data collection, 349–350
    data comparison with antemortem, 307–310
    early and late changes, 47–49
        algor mortis, 44–47
        development cycle of fly, 50f
        dying and death, 41
        electrical excitability of skeletal muscle, 41–42
        mechanical excitability of muscle, 41
        pharmacological excitability of iris, 42–44
        postmortem body cooling, 44–47

preservation of decomposing bodies, 49–52
preservation processes in cadavers, 52–53
supravitality, 41
temperature–time of death nomogram for ambient temperatures, 46f
examination, 25, 83, 276–278, 294
lividity, 42
magnetic resonance imaging, 87–88
Postmortem computed tomography (PMCT), 97, 101, 105–106
gas filling of vertebral vessels, 99
integration of 3D data, 101
localization, 100
multislice, 106–107
radiographs and, 100–101, 107
in shaken baby syndrome, 109
tool for quality control, 109
visualizing malformations of the skeleton, 110
Postmortem imaging (PMI), 97, 100–102, 107
child abuse, 109–112, 110f–111f
deceleration trauma, compression, blunt trauma, and blows, 102f, 104
explosion, 101–102, 102f
fluid, 99–100
gas, 97–99, 98f
gunshot, 100–101, 100f
identification, 105f, 106–107
infanticide, 109–112, 110f–111f
invasive medicine and care, 109
neonaticide, 109–112, 110f–111f
reanimation, 107–109
sharp trauma, 102
stillbirth, 109–112, 110f–111f
strangulation, 101f, 104
sudden death, 103f–104f, 104–106
suffocation, 101f, 104
water-logged corpse, drowning, and aspiration, 104
Postmortem interval (PMI), 35, 55. See also Time since death
adipocere, 37–38
animal and cultural indicators, 36
botany, 36
chemical approaches, 38
entomology, 35–36
mummification, 37
radiocarbon analysis, 38–39
tissue morphology, 36–37
Postsurgical infections, 289–290
Postural asphyxia, 150–153, 151f. See also Traumatic—asphyxia
diagnostic criteria, 151t
positional asphyxia, 151f–152f
Postural torture, 227
"Powder cavity", 188–189

Preservation processes
in cadavers, 52–53
of decomposing bodies, 49–52
Pressure abrasion, 116
Prevention of death in police custody, 382–383
Proinflammatory
cytokines, 178
mediators, 179
Prostate carcinoma, 77
Pseudomonas aeruginosa (P. aeruginosa), 289
Psychological torture, 234
PTC. See Percutaneous transhepatic cholangiography (PTC)
Ptomaines, 48
Pulmonary
cartilage embolism, 291
embolism, 251
infections, 289
thromboembolism, 290–291
tuberculosis, 255
Pulmonary function testing (PFT), 153
Puppe's rule, 118
Puppet organs, 128
Purtscher retinopathy, 150
Putrefaction, 48–50, 62–63, 158

Q

Qualitative analysis, 159
Quality control, 91, 109
Questioned source (Qs), 16

R

Radiation exposure in x-ray examinations for age estimation, 316
Radiocarbon analysis, 38–39
Radiographs, 100–101, 230–232
Radiology, 357
radiological examination of clavicles, 318, 318f
radiological techniques, 27, 310
Railway traffic injuries, 243–244
Range of fire, 187, 189–191, 193
rDNA. See ribosomal RNA (rDNA)
Reanimation, 107–109
circulation, 108, 108f
medication, 108–109, 109f
respiration, 107
Recidivism, 29
Reconstruction of events, 27–28
Recovery of bodies at scene, 355–356
Rectal temperature time of death nomogram, 56–58
"Red flags", 205, 206t
Reference photograph, 332–334

Renal transplants, 292
Respiratory tract, 128
Restraint asphyxia, 153–154. *See also* Postural asphyxia;
    Traumatic—asphyxia
Resuscitation period, 41
Resuscitative injuries, 290
Retroperitoneal hemorrhage, 287–288
Retrospective analyses of death certificates, 79–80
Rhabdomyolysis, 269
Rib fractures, 122–123, 206, 233
ribosomal RNA (rDNA), 158–159
Rigor mortis, 42–44
Ring fracture, 120
"Ring of dirt", 186
Riot crush, 149–150
Risk assessments, 199–200, 372
Risk factor, 259–261, 262t
Road traffic injuries
    car occupants, 240–241
    epidemiology, 237
    injury types, 237–240
    pedestrian collisions, 242–243
    two-wheelers, 243
    WADs, 241–242
Robotics, 375
Rokitansky method, 27

S

Safety data sheets (SDS), 373
Sampling
    method, 92
    rate, 93–94
    technique, 87
Scalds, 127, 130–131
Scientific identification, 321–325. *See also* Personal
    identification
    comparative radiography, 323–325
    exclusion, 325
    identification, 325
    insufficient evidence, 325–326
Scientific methods. *See* Objective methods
Scintigraphy, 228–230, 233, 233f–234f
SDS. *See* Safety data sheets (SDS)
Self-cremation, 390–391
Self-defense, 198, 201
Self-digestion. *See* Autolysis
Self-incineration, 390
Self-inflicted injury, 217. *See also* Traffic injuries and deaths
    artifacts in patients with psychic disturbances,
        221–222
    attempted suicide, 222–223
    criminal offenses, 217–219

self-mutilation for insurance fraud, 219–220
    self-mutilation/malingering, 220–221
Self-mutilation, 219–221
Sepsis, 177, 289–290
    pathophysiology and clinical manifestation, 177
    peritonitis, 289, 289f
    postmortem findings, 177
    postsurgical infections, 289–290
    pulmonary and urological infections, 289
    systemic inflammatory process, 177
Serial numbers, 327
"Serotonin syndrome", 269
Serum aspartate aminotransferase (SGOT), 270
Set(s), 7
    theory, 7
Sexual abuse, 205–208
Sexual violence, 202–203
SGOT. *See* Serum aspartate aminotransferase (SGOT)
"Shaken baby syndrome", 206
Sharp force, 163, 211, 392, 392f–393f
Sharp trauma, 102
    capability of acting, 170–171
    chop wounds, 166
    epidemiology, 163–164
    homicide, suicide, and accident injuries, 169–170
    incised wounds, 164
    injuries from glass, 166–167
    level of force, 163
    physics and dynamics of stabbing, 167–168, 168f
    sequelae and causes of death, 168–169
    sharp-force injuries, 163
    stab wounds, 164–166
    wound morphology and biomechanics, 164
Sharp-force injuries, 163
Sharps, 373
Shock, 175–176
    burn shock, 176
    cellular oxygenation, 175
    hemorrhagic shock, 175
    to isolated trauma, 176
    traumatic shock, 175
Short tandem repeats (STRs), 31, 348, 348f
Shotgun
    injuries, 191
    slugs, 191
SIDS. *See* Sudden infant death syndrome (SIDS)
Single set, 7
Singleton set. *See* Single set
SIRS. *See* Systemic inflammatory response syndrome (SIRS)
Site of drowning, 161
Skeletal muscle, electrical excitability of, 41–42
Skeletal pathologies, 326
Skeleton, 36–37

Skeletonization, 36–37, 50–51
Skeletonized human remains, 312
Skin
  burns, 127
  facial assessment, 334
  injury, 237–238
  maceration, 157
  wound healing
    cellular reactions, 67–68
    early vascular phase, 67
    lipophages, 68f
    physiology, 67–69
    proliferative changes, 68–69
Skull fractures, 118–120, 119f, 206
Skull–photo superimposition, 327–328, 328f
Slashes wounds, 164
Sleep apnea theory, 264–265
Smothering, 134, 299–301
Social deprivation, 268–269
Solid organ transplantations, complications associated with,
    291–292
  cardiac transplants, 292
  liver transplants, 292
  renal transplants, 292
"Sparing effects", 206
Specific laboratory hazards, 373–376
Specimen handling, 92
Sphagnum, 37
Sphygmomanometer, 133
Stab wounds, 164–166, 165f–166f
Stabbing, 167–168, 168f, 232–233
Staining method, 92–93
Standard precautions, 374
Standardized autopsy protocols, 263–264
Staphylococcus aureus (S. aureus), 263–264
Statistical analysis, 10
Stephanodiscus neostraea (S. neostraea), 161f
Stillbirth, 109–112, 110f–111f
Stopping power, 183–184
Strangulation, 21–23, 101f, 104, 139, 143–146, 201–202,
    232, 299–301, 391. See also Manual strangulation
  airway occlusion, 139
  autopsy findings, 140
  compression of cervical arteries, 139
  hanging, 140–142
  by ligature, 142–143
  occlusion of neck veins, 139–140, 140f
  reflex mechanisms, 140
Stress cardiomyopathy, 153
Stress response, 174
Stress ulcers, 179
Stretch injury, 238
Strontium levels in blood, 158

STRs. See Short tandem repeats (STRs)
Structurally consistent alignment, 16
Subarachnoid hematoma, 239
Subcutaneous bruises, 116
Subdural hematomas, 121, 239
Sudden death in epilepsy (SUDEP), 92, 95f
Sudden infant death syndrome (SIDS), 259–260, 259f
  autopsy, 263–264, 264t
  cause of death, 264
  causes of sudden unexpected death in infancy, 260t
  clinical history, 264
  death scene, 263, 263t
  epidemiology and risk factors, 260–261
  histological changes, 262–263
  hypotheses of possible causes, 264–265
  postmortem investigation, 263
  results of autopsy, 261
  San Diego definition, 261t
  typical macroscopic findings, 261–262, 262f
Sudden natural death
  classification of death, 247
  criminalistic aspects, 247–248
  internal cause, 247
  morphological substrate, 249–257
  special categories, 248–249
Sudden unexplained infant deaths (SUDI), 259
SUDEP. See Sudden death in epilepsy (SUDEP)
SUDI. See Sudden unexplained infant deaths (SUDI)
Suffocation, 101f, 104, 134
Suicide(s), 215, 385
  complex suicides, 386, 387f, 393f
  copycat acts, 388
  criminalistically relevant phenomena and suicide scenes, 389
  dissimulation, 387–388
  by drowning, 390
  epidemiology, 385
  firearm injuries, 392–395
  in hospitals, police custody, or prisons, 390
  under influence of alcohol and/or drugs, 389–390
  injuries, 169–170
  murder–suicide, 386–387
  occupation-related suicide, 387
  pacts, 386
  possible reasons and dispositions, 385
  in road traffic, 390
  self-cremation, 390–391
  sharp force, 392, 392f–393f
  strangulation, 391
  suicidal electrocution, 276, 277f
  suicidal gesture, 222
  suicidal gunshot injuries, 387
  suicide pacts, 386
Sunstroke, 269

Superimposition methods, 310, 311f
Superior vena cava (SVC), 97–98
Superposition, 4
Supravitality, 41
Surgical implants, 326–327, 327f
Survival period, 41
Suspended animation, 272
Suspension on fingers, 227
SVC. *See* Superior vena cava (SVC)
Systematics, 8
Systemic inflammatory response syndrome (SIRS), 174, 177, 269
    pathophysiology and clinical manifestation, 177
    postmortem findings, 177
    systemic inflammatory process, 177

T

Tangential abrasions, 115–116
Taxon, 7–8
Taxonomy, 7–8, 13–14
TBI. *See* Traumatic brain injuries (TBI)
Temperature of corpses, 55–56
Tentative identification, 327
Thermal tissue damage, 276
Thermoregulation, 269, 271
Thiopentone, 293
3D image acquisition systems, 334
3D techniques, 333
Thorax injury, 239–240
Thromboprophylaxis, 288, 290–291
Thrombosis, 289, 292
Throttling. *See* Manual strangulation
Thyroglobulin, immunohistochemical detection, 63–64
Time since death
    brain temperature time of death nomogram, 58
    compound method, 58–59
    cooling dummy, 58
    corrective factors for body weight, 57t
    estimation, 55
    field studies, 58
    gastric contents and, 62
    immunohistochemical detection, 63–64
    integrating chart for casework at scene of crime, 60f–61f
    minimal time interval of immersion, 64t
    PMI, 55
    putrefaction, 62–63
    rectal temperature time of death nomogram, 56–58
    on supravital reactions and postmortem changes, 59t
    temperature of corpses, 55–56
    vitreous potassium, 58–59
Tissue morphology, 36–37
Tissue specimens, 92

TNF. *See* Tumor necrosis factor (TNF)
Tooth eruption, 317
Torture, 24, 225
    diagnosis and differential diagnosis, 235
    electric torture, 233–234
    ethics, 235
    fingers, 226–227
    foot and leg, 228–232
    forms, 225–226
    hands and arms, 227–228
    head, 232
    neck, 232
    psychological torture, 234
    trunk, 232–233
Toxicology, 129
    hyperthermia, 270
    hypothermia, 273
    toxicological analysis, 153–154
Trabecular bone, 325
Trace as unit of forensic science, 2–3
Traffic accidents, 237
Traffic injuries and deaths. *See also* Self-inflicted injury
    air traffic, 244
    railway, 243–244
    road traffic, 237–243
Transmission electron microscopy, 92
Trauma, 174
    in acute phase, 175–176
    delayed complications, 179
    in early phase, 176–179
    pathophysiology and clinical manifestation, 174
    postmortem findings, 174–175
Traumatic
    aortic ruptures, 123–124
    asphyxia, 149–150, 152. *See also* Postural asphyxia
        external findings in, 150t
        internal and microscopic findings in, 150t
    shock, 175
        pathophysiology and clinical manifestation, 175
        postmortem findings, 175
    subarachnoid bleeding, 121
Traumatic brain injuries (TBI), 238–239
Trunk torture, 232–233
Tuberculosis, 255
Tumor necrosis factor (TNF), 176
    TNF-α, 274
Two-exponential model, 58
Two-wheelers, road traffic injuries, 243

U

Uncertain signs of death, 75, 75t
UnClaimed Persons database (UCP), 343

"Uncomfortable" positions, 227–228
Urological infections, 289

V

Vaccinations, 374
Validation studies, 325
Valsalva maneuver, 136
Variable number tandem repeats (VNTRs), 31
Vascular cell adhesion molecules (VCAMs), 67
Ventilation, 139
Ventricular fibrillation (VF), 275–276
Verbal autopsy, 83
Very late activation antigen 4 (VLA-4), 67
VF. See Ventricular fibrillation (VF)
VH. See Vitreous humor (VH)
Videocolposcopy, 207
Violence Against Women Act, 197
Virchow method, 27
Visual recognition, 321–322
Vita minima, 75, 75t
Vita reducta, 75, 75t
Vital fibrin reactions, 67
Vitality
    diagnosis, 129–130, 130t
    of human skin wounds, 70t
    and wound age estimation, 27
Vitreous humor (VH), 59
Vitreous potassium, 58–59
VLA-4. See Very late activation antigen 4 (VLA-4)
VNTRs. See Variable number tandem repeats (VNTRs)
Volatile fatty acids, 38
Voltage, 276
Voluntarily inflicted injuries, 219–220

W

WADs. See Whiplash-associated disorders (WADs)
Water
    boarding, 225, 234
    deprivation, 234
    ingestion, 234
    putrefaction in, 63
    submersion, 234
Water-logged corpse, 104
Whiplash-associated disorders (WADs), 241–242
WHO. See World Health Organization (WHO)
Wick principle, 127
Wischnewsky spots, 272–273, 273f
Work-related stress, 377
Workplace health and safety, 371
World Health Organization (WHO), 77, 86
Wound age estimation, 69–71
Wound ballistics, 181–184
    ability to act, 183
    delayed effects, 184
    embolism of projectiles, 184
    intermediate targets, deflection of projectile, 182–183
    lethal gunshot injuries, 183
    stopping power, 183–184
    wound track, 182
    wounding capacity, 181–182
Wound healing, 171
    principles of forensic wound age estimation, 69–71
    skin wound healing physiology, 67–69
Wound morphology and biomechanics, 164
Wound pattern analysis, 27–28
Wrist cutting, 23

X

X-ray(s), 375
    examination, 315
    of hand, 317
    legitimization, 319
    radiation exposure for age estimation, 316

Y

Young adults, age estimation in, 315–319

Z

Zygomatic bone, 168